# WCS
## Woodstock Country School

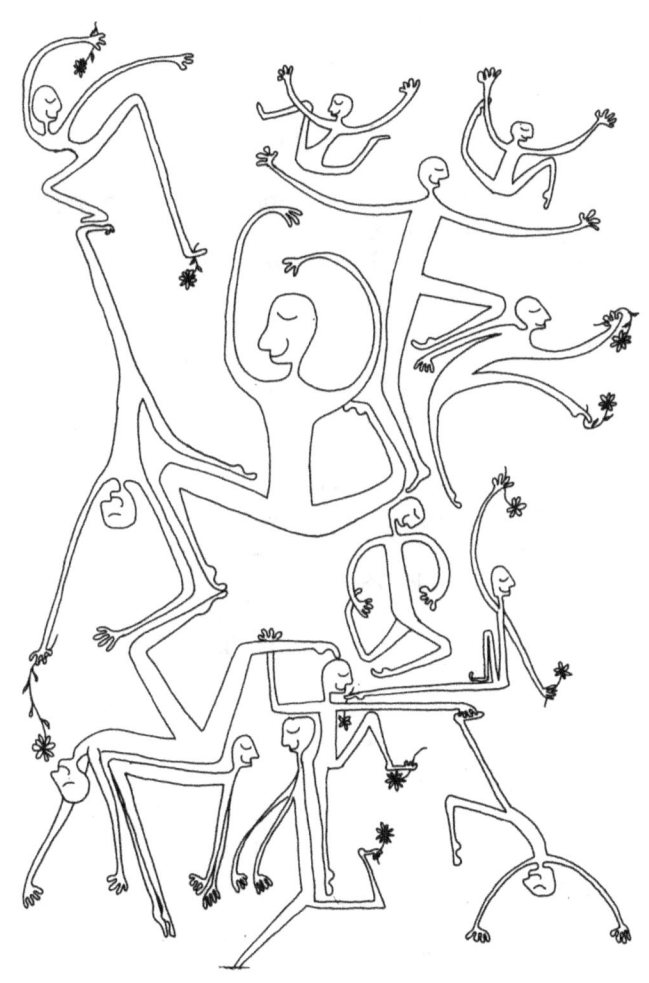

Revised Edition

Copyright © 2018 by William Boardman

All rights reserved. No part of this publication may be reproduced,
stored in a retrieval system, or transmitted, in any form or by any means, electronic,
mechanical, photocopying, recording, or otherwise, without the written prior
permission of the publisher.

Published by
Yorkland Publishing
12 Tepee Court
Toronto, Ontario M2J 3A9
Canada
www.yorklandpublishing.com

ISBN: 978-0-9697127-7-0

Book Design by SpicaBookDesign

Printed in Canada by Island Blue Book Printing, Victoria, B.C.

# WCS
## Woodstock Country School

A History of Institutional Denial

*Revised Edition*

# William Boardman

YORKLAND PUBLISHING

## FOR REBECCA

WCS French teacher (1970-76), E. Rebecca Silliman Boardman, 66, on October 3, 2014, holding her granddaughter Carter Belle Boardman, 78 days

**Rebecca notes of 10.3.14, discovered 6.16.16**

*Be present. Make love. Make tea. Avoid small talk. Embrace conversation.*
*Buy a plant, water it. Make your bed. Make someone else's bed.*
*Have a smart mouth and quick wit. Run. Make art. Create. Swim in the ocean.*
*Swim in the rain. Take chances. Ask questions.*
*Make mistakes. Learn. Know your worth. Love fiercely. Forgive quickly.*
*Let go of what doesn't make you happy. Grow*

# Table of Contents

**Introduction** .................................................. **xiii**
*Touches on the magic, community, denial and other strands that run through the book and ran through the school. The author makes two brief appearances.*

1   **Before WCS Opens** .......................................... 1
*Woodstock takes shape slowly with some academic seriousness, which disguises the fundamental denial on which the Woodstock Country School was founded: Elizabeth Johnson's insistence that such an ill-suited match as Ken Webb and David Bailey should somehow manage the marriage necessary to be co-headmasters.*

2   **Fall 1945 – Spring 1948** .................................. 21
*Although the school opens and runs successfully, Ken and David do not blend and their separation turns on David's and the community's denial that smoking is bad for you. Ken leaves with remarkable grace.*

3   **Summer 1948 – Summer 1951** ............................... 57
*With David in complete command, the school survives some intense crises and approaches its tenth anniversary with some uncertainty.*

4   **Fall 1951 – Fall 1955** .................................... 89
*Woodstock's main classroom building burns down creating a crisis to which the school community rises splendidly and which David uses to re-invent the school on the former estate of a gentleman farmer.*

5   **Fall 1955 – Spring 1962** .................................. 127
*Woodstock thrives in its new location, but David Bailey develops emphysema. The disease slowly weakens him, undermining his effectiveness, which he denies. Inside the tight community, the denial spreads with an etiology of its own.*

6   **Fall 1963 – Summer 1965** .................................. 177
*Even as David's illness becomes undeniable, his mostly handpicked school trustees have a hard time making good decisions for the preservation of the school out of concern for his feelings.*

7   **Spring 1965 – Spring 1967** . . . . . . . . . . . . . . . . . . . . . . . . . 237
    *David finally faces his health reality and announces he will resign after
    a sabbatical year. Trustees are divided over whether supporting David or
    preserving the school is their higher priority.*

8   **Fall 1967 – Summer 1968** . . . . . . . . . . . . . . . . . . . . . . . . . . 293
    *John Holden, interim headmaster during David's sabbatical, has a quiet
    year. David's supporters can't say enough bad things about him.*

9   **Summer 1968 – Summer 1970** . . . . . . . . . . . . . . . . . . . . . 329
    *Trustees choose David's successor, Tawny Kilborne: a Yale graduate
    with years of experience as a teacher at the Fort Worth Country Day
    School. He has never been at a boarding school, he has never been a
    headmaster and he lasts less than two years at Woodstock.*

10  **Summer 1970 – Fall 1973** . . . . . . . . . . . . . . . . . . . . . . . . . . 389
    *In the crisis left by Tawny's departure, Phil Hansen becomes acting
    headmaster almost by default, then permanent headmaster. He never
    wanted to be headmaster, but he manages to stabilize the school for a
    while, until it wears him down and out.*

11  **Fall 1973 – Summer 1980** . . . . . . . . . . . . . . . . . . . . . . . . . . 441
    *Once again, the trustees choose a headmaster, Walter Hill, an architect
    with years of experience in administration at St. Paul's School. He has
    never been a headmaster and he quits under pressure after little more
    than a year and a half, with the school in desperate condition. Trustees
    are set to close the school, but through a curious series of events, Robin
    Leaver becomes the next headmaster and manages to keep the school
    going until he, too, is overwhelmed.*

**End Note #1** . . . . . . . . . . . . . . . . . . . . . . . . . . . . . . . . . . . . . . . . . . 481
**End Note #1A** . . . . . . . . . . . . . . . . . . . . . . . . . . . . . . . . . . . . . . . . 491
**End Note #2** . . . . . . . . . . . . . . . . . . . . . . . . . . . . . . . . . . . . . . . . . 493
**End Note #3** . . . . . . . . . . . . . . . . . . . . . . . . . . . . . . . . . . . . . . . . . 501
**End Note #4** . . . . . . . . . . . . . . . . . . . . . . . . . . . . . . . . . . . . . . . . . 504
**End Note #5** . . . . . . . . . . . . . . . . . . . . . . . . . . . . . . . . . . . . . . . . . 505

**Acknowledgements** . . . . . . . . . . . . . . . . . . . . . . . . . . . . . . . . . . . 517
**About the Author** . . . . . . . . . . . . . . . . . . . . . . . . . . . . . . . . . . . . 521

Commencement 1947 (l. to r.): June O'Hara, Lillian Russell, Phoebe Gay, Pauline Lubitsch, Molly Blake, Mary Lois Doggett.

Smoking Room 1971 (l. to r.): Ira Chaplain, Martin Ship, Jerome Berryhill, Nash Brittingham, Andy Gordon.

*There is no formula for education. No system will serve all times and individuals. There is no such thing as 'new' education. We can only take what we have learned about the subject and apply it in such a way that it is suited to our time.*

*Our education at Woodstock depends on three main ingredients. These are flexibility, atmosphere, and good teachers. We are convinced that our teaching staff is second to none – that its members are not only effective in the classroom, but are also people of warmth and understanding, who are interested in the children as people rather than just as pupils. It is difficult to have a poor school with excellent teachers. But to make these teachers most effective we believe they should be allowed to live and teach in a climate of friendliness, of freedom, and of informality. The students also do their best learning and growing in an atmosphere of trust and group responsibility.*

*Our flexibility is maintained so that we may be receptive to new ideas, and able to shift our methods to suit new demands and individual needs.*

*David W. Bailey, 1912-1981*
*WCS Headmaster 1945-1967*

*Some teachers teach their subjects instead of the students.... In order to have the freedom to be a really good teacher, one has to be just a little bit mad. ~ David Bailey*

### WCS – WOODSTOCK COUNTRY SCHOOL, A HISTORY OF INSTITUTIONAL DENIAL

# Introduction

**I**

This is the only history of WCS ever written. Another is unlikely. Why is there even one? Among the reasons: that the school profoundly mattered to many of us who experienced it. Like the school itself as we knew it, this book is partly a labor of love: love for the people in it, love for its settings, most of all love for the ineffable magic the school managed to create powerfully for so many of us, in so many combinations, from beginning to end. Through most of its existence, even as it seemed to change radically, Woodstock could be a wonderful place for an adolescent to go to high school. Even as it ended, with pale resemblance to its most vital incarnations, the Country School could still radiate lives. No book can recreate the living mystery of such a shared experience, but I have tried here to give the knowledgeable reader, the reader who experienced Woodstock or a school like Woodstock, at least a frisson of recognition of what was once real for him or her. This book has always been intended for a general audience as well, although non-WCS people may find it something of a Rorschach text in which reflections of the adolescence of others may set off echoes of your own.

Woodstock was all about adolescence, and about teachers who enjoyed adolescents. The school allowed adolescents great freedom to experiment with adult behaviors of all sorts, without significant restriction or confinement except at the extremes; with positive reinforcement and expectations, personally and academically; but without confusing the students with actual adults. As I talked to hundreds of alumni and others from all periods of the school, I was surprised that, no matter when they went to Woodstock, the ones for whom the school worked well described an essentially similar experience at schools that seemed superficially very different. One 17-year-old girl who came to Woodstock for her senior year was typically unhappy with her present, rigid, suffocating prep school and her pressured home life where she was expected to enjoy all the unpleasantries of a pre-debutante social life. Even though headmaster David Bailey had accepted her immediately during the admissions interview, she didn't realize it until she later asked if she'd gotten in. This was her first time away from home and she was frightened:

> *I was very anxious to be accepted and David was very accepting.... I thought, well, gee, here's someone who likes me. I was miserable – desperate, miserable, anxiety ridden. The idea that David could like me was very thrilling to me.... He really helped me. There he was, a person in authority, an attractive person with all the right kind of background and everything, who actually thought the way I was was all right, and that was earth-shaking.... All that year I just felt like I was walking on air.... I had more freedom to learn at Woodstock than I ever had at any other educational institution.... It was a dream, it was like being in love – only we never got married, so even I know it couldn't have been like that – but it was like being in love, the school just seemed perfect.*

Twenty years later, Susan Cheever '62 still believed the Country School had changed her life. She went from WCS to Brown, "which I hated, as you can imagine." She taught at the Colorado Rocky Mountain School precisely because it was like Woodstock, led by another charismatic founding headmaster, and "because I felt so strongly that that was the only way to educate kids – and I still feel that way."

The Woodstock Country School (1945-1980) was never as well known as some of its alumni – such as Larry Hagman, Severn Darden, Mike Seeger, Jon Nordheimer, Ellen Sheehan, David Whitney, Sigrid McRae, Sandy Bull, Susan Cheever, Thomas Edsall, Kathy Cronkite, Jameson Parker, Amy Ephron, Deborah Eisenberg, Margaret Diehl, Lori Bloustein, Amy Wallace, Jim Hagedorn, Lahly Poore, Bill Dwight, John Beerman, Sarah Van Arsdale, Chris Benson, David Luers, Paul Joffe, Nicole Bass, Blair Breard, Erica Essner, or Allyson Downey. If you don't recognize all those names, that's part of the point. Woodstock was less about celebrity than about trying to be a whole and decent person. In the world of education, for most of its life, Woodstock was a reasonably well known and respected American institution, one of the best alternative, coeducational boarding schools in the country, with a challenging academic curriculum and good college acceptance for its graduates.

The school was always small, intimate, personal. Students, faculty, and staff all knew each other, many knew each other quite well, and a few perhaps too well. The full campus community rarely numbered as much as 150 people, only a third of whom were technically adults. In a setting as intimate and sealed-off as Woodstock, it was always possible to know a lot of secrets about a lot of people. It was also possible to pretend not to know people's more challenging

## INTRODUCTION

secrets, and to evade confronting them, sometimes, it was argued, for their own good, or for the good of the school.

Denial is a familiar human trait. Less frequently is denial thought of as an institutional trait, even when we have lived for years under governments riddled with denial. This book, subtitled "A History of Institutional Denial," tries to show how a thriving, dynamic, productive institution manages slowly to destroy itself by trying to operate ever more deeply in denial. An institution's denial of an early power struggle for control of that institution is not inherently unhealthy, because the denial should end with the end of the power struggle. At Woodstock, the denial continued with the winner denying that there ever was a power struggle. When that charismatic central figure in the closed community of a small school later denied that his debilitating illness was eroding his ability to run the institution, others in the institution had to act in time if the institution was to be saved. When WCS faced that choice in the mid-1960s, none of those in a position to make a difference, especially the Trustees, was willing, or perhaps able, to confront the charismatic central figure with a firm enough, timely enough response to maintain institutional integrity. Instead they institutionalized the denial to the degree that when it came time for them to choose successors for the charismatic leader, they made absurd, institutionally destructive choices. All this played out slowly, sometimes invisibly over the 35-year life of the school (and even after it closed).

"WCS – Woodstock Country School, a History of Institutional Denial" describes how the school was created, flourished, and gradually failed. The book uses a mixed technique of collage and narrative, letting participants and documents speak for themselves about the quality and life of the school while the narrative focuses more on what the people who were supposedly running the place told themselves they were doing, when often they were doing something else. As a story of multi-layered denial, the book has a Rashomon quality in which each character has a relatively believable version of events, but no one is truly credible. Unlike *Rashomon*, in which the victim gets to speak for herself, the school has no voice but this.

## II

In 1952, when I was 14, I was sent to the Country School mainly because I didn't care where I went, if anywhere, and Woodstock would accept me with few questions asked, perhaps considering whatever problems I might be having as a suitable challenge for the school. I came from fours years as a boarder at the Harvey School, a strict, all boys, English-style boarding school that I had hated. At Harvey I had been in chronic disciplinary difficulty and I was always academically first in my class. Harvey was not about human or humane interaction, Harvey was more of a holding cell for troubled children who were thought to need discipline more than anything else. In my class of thirteen, twelve of us came from broken families of one sort or another. The one exception was the headmaster's only child, but he had his issues as well. My father had died of pancreatitis when I was four, my mother died of Hodgkins when I was seven, and I had gone to live with my mother's sister's dysfunctional, hostile, broken family. When I was ten, my divorced aunt Rhoda sent me to boarding school, against my will. She moved to Woodstock, Vermont, where her former mother-in-law provided a house. I had no voice in any of it. I didn't really understand what was happening to me, I just knew that I hated it, and was furious at being unable to escape. I had no one to turn to for protection, not even to people I trusted, since there were none. The Harvey School headmaster, who had taken some kind fatherly interest in me, was a distant authoritarian figure who understood nothing real about my life and ended up, in a bizarre misapprehension, falsely accusing me of doing things that others were doing to me. The Harvey headmaster suggested I go to the Woodstock Country School, skipping ninth grade. He also suggested I live at home, so that Rhoda could work with me. She was incapable of any beneficial attention. Eventually her slapping my face for standing up for myself turned out to be a helpfully clarifying moment for a bewildered 14-year-old.

So I entered Woodstock as an immature, socially unprepared, intimidated and withdrawn tenth grader. Slowly Woodstock would become the first place I'd known in more that seven years where I felt safe, the first place I knew where I wasn't beaten up, the first place where I didn't have to live in constant fear and wariness. After so many years of grown-ups lying to me, at WCS I would find some who sometimes told the truth – that was stunning, and liberating. At first I knew no one at the school and I knew nothing about the school except that my foster family spoke mockingly of it and of their cousins, the McDills, who worked hard to support it (and who had always treated me kindly). If there was any orientation for new day students, I don't remember it. Rhoda would drive me to school in the morning, almost always late, and I would walk the mile or so back to her house at the end of the day. As the school year progressed, as I became more a part of the school, that walk was later and later at night. At first I was the quiet, guarded day student who wore pants with creases and cuffs at a school where casual blue jeans were the norm. During the summer my upper front four teeth had been pulled and I wore a partial denture (regular dental care was not part of Rhoda's foster parenting). A year earlier, at Harvey, I had wanted to play soccer but the school made me play football (quarterback). In the first game I was tackled for a loss and my foot was broken (which at least allowed me to watch the World Series of 1951 when Monte Irvin stole home). My state of mind by the fall of 1952 was such that I asked the Woodstock headmaster for permission not to play soccer (there was no football), using my new false teeth as a reason. David Bailey treated it casually, letting me do what I wanted, not even pointing out that I didn't need to ask his permission. That was part of what made the school so wonderful – not that so much was allowed, which was good, but that so little was insisted on, which was better.

Slowly, unsurely, I became a part of the school. I overcame the embarrassment of realizing that the boy I had been chatting with was actually a girl (as far as I know she didn't know I didn't know). She was the daughter of a famous author and we became friends (even though I'd never heard of her father). Gradually I realized that I wasn't the only wounded bird in the school. It was an aviary. I might have been the only student to wear pants with cuffs, but David Bailey also wore pants with cuffs. I was fascinated by his habit of collecting his cigarette ash in his cuff. Slowly I came to accept this new, unusual reality in which people were kind, and tolerant of difference, and patient, and even interested in who you might be – totally unlike my foster family prison. By the spring I was almost happy, I played basketball in the winter, baseball in the spring, and I was in love for the first time. I was beginning to understand that the school, for all its limitations, was the closest I would come to having something like a home again until I was in my thirties. At Woodstock I was able to begin the lifelong process of healing. That life is part of what I bring to this book, as well as a twist or two where my personal plot meets the later story of the school.

Woodstock was very much David Bailey's school for the four years I was a student. He was the undisputed, mostly honored center of our little universe. Since he managed mostly by mystique and suggestion, the school felt free and open, rarely oppressive (although there were moments). David was like the weather and the landscape, always changeable and always there, more or less predictable but with surprises. His authority was absolute, sometimes arbitrary (or so it seemed), but rarely questioned and almost never challenged. Mostly he exercised his power subtly, preferring indirection to find directions out. He referred to himself as a benign dictator. He wanted students (he called them "the children") to be as free as possible to grow up to be their best selves. He nudged us on with the casual remark, the apparently impulsive gesture, the genuine interest, the casual discussion, or the impromptu game of chess or bridge. He engaged with people constantly. His office seemed to be largely in his head and he spent as much time as he could out and about in the school, whether teaching English or geography or even Spanish, coaching soccer and baseball, playing games in the common room, or just hanging out. Among students he was known as "the bird" (never to be uttered in his presence) and was assumed to be everywhere, watching everything. According to legend, the nickname derived from his habit of saying, when asking students about their suspected behavior, "a little bird told me." As one alumna recalled, "David always looked at you as if he knew all about what you'd been doing last night, so the sensible thing was to confess." Some students confessed, some didn't. Sometimes David knew, sometimes he didn't. One result of this psychological hide-and-seek was that students often felt the need to prove themselves to David – either the real David or the David in their heads – and that need sometimes lasted much of the rest of their lives.

David Bailey expected his faculty to be as engaged with students as he was, but in their own ways. Peter Sauer taught English at the school in the early 1960s and was a dorm parent in French House. He was married with two young children, but still managed to engage well with students. He was good enough at it that, for awhile, he was thought a likely successor to David (who seemed to harbor that thought himself). Years later, Peter described David's school this way:

> *I know David was frustrated by teachers who were unable to understand that their individual relationships with the kids were equally as important as the subject matter they were teaching.… The afternoon was really David's time and he would spend time with the baseball team, he came to tea, at least in the first years I was there he came to tea almost every afternoon. I remember remarking on several occasions as a teacher there, that the school felt like it was David's canvas and we were the tubes of paint, not the paint itself, but the tubes that held the paint and David was the one who wielded the brush.*

### III

When David Bailey and Ken Webb started the Country School in 1945, Ken put much of his energy into writing the school's philosophy, catalogue, and curriculum. He wanted a Quaker school clearly defined for all to understand. David did not interfere with Ken's effort, nor did he much participate in it. After Ken left the school in 1948, Woodstock went without a catalogue or other defining documents for almost two decades. Woodstock never understood itself to be a Quaker school. David wanted the school understood for itself, intuitively and flexibly, without need for precise explanation. What David wanted for the Country School was a strong sense of community, almost a sense of family. He wanted the kinds of bonds that begin to dissolve as soon as you try to formalize them in writing. Students and faculty during David's era mostly understood this, referring in their reminiscences to the school's close-knit community or extended-family qualities. This was Woodstock's core value, the core value within which a good school could thrive. People inevitably came and went, changing the school slightly with each arrival or departure, but the ideal of the WCS community was a constant, always aspirational and dynamic, and an inherent function of the school's small size. Because the school was small, isolated, relentlessly introspective, it created a level of intimacy and intensity that few people would experience in their later lives, and which some people never experience at all (and some even scoff at its possibility). But it was real, almost palpable, evanescent, and it permeated every level of the school from academic to social, from romantic to solitary. Not everyone gets Woodstock, even those who were there. But no matter when they were there, the people who get Woodstock perceive essentially the same amazing possibilities at variations of Woodstock that seem radically different in time, place, and make-up. At Woodstock, each person was supposed to matter. As Peter Sauer put it: "David believed we should remake the school every time a new student walked in."

An extravagant example of the school's flexibility at its most open-ended came in the early 1960s. Woodstock initiated courses in Arabic. Few if any other schools in the country then taught Arabic, nor did many colleges or universities (but teaching Arabic was an active project of the Nation of Islam). Woodstock sought support for its Arabic courses by applying for a grant from the Central Intelligence Agency. If the CIA responded, that response has disappeared, and there is no record of any government funding. The courses continued, at least for awhile.

In an odd way, the lack of interest in Woodstock's Arabic courses reinforced a perspective that David expressed in a letter published in the New York Times of March 13, 1955, in which he argued for greater philanthropic support for secondary education, not just colleges. But he also argued a deeper point:

> *The problem [with American education] stems from a combination of factors which our complex, dynamic civilization has produced. The pressures and tensions of modern society, the influences of the "gang" mentality, of the automaton-like conformity to local mores and standards, are depriving the children of individuality and initiative. They have no standards by which to make decisions; they distrust the adult world; they lack motivation and direction.... We are an immature nation and people, and we are perpetuating our immaturities.*

A more mature nation and people would have been more open to learning Arabic, not to mention a few other languages. A more mature nation and people would have learned about Arab and other cultures, and understood their locations as more than just bomb targets.

## IV

In 1971, I came back to the Country School as a teacher, teaching a single summer drama class. My first marriage had ended badly, I moved to Vermont on February 29, and set about trying to learn to live alone comfortably. Grateful for the token opportunity to teach, I welcomed the familiar shelter of the school, even though I was well aware that it wasn't at all the same familiar shelter I had known in 1952. The school had gone through considerable upheaval by 1971, and I had even quixotically applied to be its headmaster during the turmoil of the previous year. Now, at 33, I became one of the older faculty members. Eventually I would teach drama, English, and US History courses (such as "Watergate" and "Newspeak"), and I would be the "Director of Publication," responsible for weekly news releases, annual catalogue and brochures, quarterly alumni magazine, and other miscellany.

My first drama class that summer was stressful, only two students showed up and they came late. My second class made clear just how different the school had become since my day. There were four women enrolled in the class and six showed up. We all sat on the grass in the amphitheatre. It seemed clear to me that I was new talent being assessed and that I had better decide quickly whether or not I would sleep with students, since my consent was apparently the only barrier. With some regret, I decided not to accept the unspoken offers. Besides, there was a friendly 22-year-old French teacher, Rebecca Silliman, who would turn out to be the love of my life, the mother of two of my children, and my adored companion for the next 43 years. (The drama class turned out OK, too, as we put on a staged reading of "The Killing of Sister George.")

Rebecca had started at Woodstock a year earlier, when she was 21 and hired to be a dorm head in a boys dorm. We worked at the school together until the summer of 1976, just before WCS almost closed. The years 1971-1976 were increasingly tense and unstable for the school for many reasons. The faculty was bitterly divided and remarkably selfish. The Trustees were feckless and remarkably obtuse. The student Trustees and other students tried without much success to get the grown-ups to understand how they were destroying the school. I was never in a position to influence critical decisions. I was a deeply engaged participant in the life of the school and an inveterate note taker, all of which informs this book.

Once I realized in 1975 that I wouldn't send my adolescent son to the school I was working at, I wondered why I was there. I didn't see any way headmaster Walter Hill would figure out the school that he didn't seem to know he didn't understand (and the Trustees and senior faculty didn't show much awareness of their own misunderstandings either). I gave a school year's notice. My plan, to join with some friends to buy and run the local TV station, never worked out (and the TV station is long gone). Instead I eventually went to work as a local reporter and covered WCS on occasion, including the bizarre final graduation ceremony.

## V

As you read this book, I hope you'll come to understand that there was no good reason for the school to die, and many good reasons it should have survived. In my view, those who failed the school, failed most profoundly to understand the difference between the school itself and its personalities. Any healthy institution will enjoy interplay among its personalities and its institutional values, with the institutional values usually winning, even while changing. An unhealthy institution is run by its personalities, without necessary regard to its institutional values (sound like any country you're familiar with?). Woodstock was small enough that its best institutional values might have been securely established and maintained, had it had conscious, conscientious leadership.

Student smoking was at the center of one of the earliest struggles of the school define itself. One of Woodstock's co-founders, Ken Webb, was a non-smoker and wanted no smoking at all. The other co-founder, David Bailey, was a heavy smoker with a tolerance for others' smoking. The students mostly wanted to smoke. The nation had been in denial about smoking for decades. Even in the 1940s, if people actually believed cigarettes were harmless, why did they call them "coffin nails" for half a century before mass advertising? In 1941, George Seldes published his first cigarette story, detailing a Johns Hopkins medical study showing that smoking shortened people's lives (a study largely ignored by the mainstream media of the day, dependent as they were on tobacco advertising). One could know about smoking if one wanted to know, and one could pursue willful ignorance. Perversely, Woodstock decided (Chapter 2) to make smoking a privilege, rooting denial in a medical oxymoron. This denial led directly to the deeper, more destructive collective denial, that David Bailey's relentless emphysema wasn't choking the life out of the school. It's all such a waste, as I hope you'll come to see.

## VI

Talk of an oral history of WCS turned briefly into action in the early 1970s, when Liz Stevens in the Development Office (while it lasted) taped some of David Bailey's reminiscences. Then the Trustees did not act on a more formal proposal in 1973 to buy a tape recorder and tapes (at an estimated cost of $200) and make a more systematic approach to a WCS oral history. As the school was winding down in 1980, a number of Trustees (Gerry Freund '48, Russ Mead, Buffy Dunker, Anita McClellan '64, Peter Sauer and others) again discussed an oral history or a more formal history of Woodstock. This led, almost two years later, to my signing a contract to write an institutional history with a strong oral history component, which I did. I finished a second draft of the history by the July 1987 deadline. Then it got controversial, the Trustees broke the contract, and the manuscript went unattended until more propitious conditions came along (this is covered in more, perhaps boring detail in an End Note #2). That, in a nutshell, is why it took longer to publish a history of the Woodstock Country School than the school's actual history lasted.

The manuscript and its support materials sat in my house, my basement, and my barn for almost thirty years, accessed only occasionally in response to some inquiry (such as the film production house that wanted Larry Hagman materials for a documentary – there wasn't much). Occasionally Country School people would ask about the book and some even suggested I publish, but no one actually put up the money. Then at the Country School reunion of 2015, someone I'd known since about 1957 talked me into re-visiting the book. Ed Shiller '60, with his typical brash enthusiasm, persuaded me we could publish it ourselves. His pitch was something like: you do all the work revising the manuscript and I'll get it published. He had self-published before. A year later, responding to an early draft of this intro, Peter Dembski '71 wrote: "I would guess that it must be a careful balancing act to try to catch the highly personal spirit and intimate nature of the school while also keeping an accurate account. But as you mentioned, it inevitably will be a Rorschach test – as I suppose it should be. Some dry account of the place would not live up to its *reason d'etre* and atmosphere to which everyone seemed so attached." So here we are, in late 2016 as I write, and what I find to be an intriguing story is almost ready to meet its fate.

But first this nostalgic bit of shameless self-promotion: in the spring of 1976, my last term as a Country School teacher, Jan Poore and I co-directed an elaborate, semi-documentary revue titled "The Buy Sentimental Apple Pie #1," in mock-honor of America's bicentennial silliness. Jan Poore, twenty years my senior, taught dance and drama at WCS for more than a decade. She had danced professionally with Martha Graham. With her agreement, when I took over the drama department, I did it only on the condition that she and I collaborate directing the school's major productions. Jan had danced with Martha Graham back in the day and brought a dancer's discipline to her dance classes. She brought an exuberant personality to everything she did, whether teaching, creating costumes, being a

## INTRODUCTION

dorm head, or a parent (three of her children, Robert, Lahly, and James also enlivened WCS). Working with Jan was one of the great joys of my time at the school. After the last performance of "Buy Sentimental," and as a total and wonderful surprise – I'm still moved – the cast gave each of us a "mock diploma" (a Woodstock Plan tradition for each term's graduates). Mine was headed "Honors Citation" (another school tradition) and it read, in its entirety:

> *We the students of your Drama class, past and present, cite you for honors for your outstanding direction of the Drama Department for the past five years. Your time, effort, and personal involvement in every production and workshop enriched the experience for all students participating, and gave us a taste of true dedication. We thank you for your interest, your sympathy, and your patience; but moreover we thank you for your impatience, so aptly applied. Tongue in cheek, we say goodbye. Keep 'em rockin' on their heels....*
> *The All of Us*

It seems like more than a coincidence that the Woodstock Country School closed just as the country was about to elect President Reagan. So what? That was what one alumna '62 and longtime Trustee asked, in effect, during her interview for this book. She had doted on David but slowly lost interest in the school after he retired. Instead she put her energy into Amnesty International and its worldwide efforts to stop torture. *That*, she told me, is something immediate and real, it means something if you keep someone from being tortured – compared to that, what does it matter if a little privileged school in New England runs out of breath? Despite her long, intimate contact with Woodstock, she seemed not to have absorbed the universal importance of a school that educated people for whom torture is not acceptable in the first place.

That was ingrained in the spirit of the place, the spirit that gave the school whatever importance it deserves, the spirit that was so meaningful, so vital in the lives of so many of its students and teachers. The spirit of the place kept it going long after it had ceased to be a school in any meaningful sense (though it remained a place where people could learn). The spirit of the place goes on, part of the larger contrarian, independent, quirky tradition that again and again keeps the dominant American conformity from making life completely rigid and hopeless. The spirit of the Country School survives in all the spontaneous, cheerful, idiosyncratic, caring gestures of its scattered population.

Greenhithe

# WCS
## Woodstock Country School

A History of Institutional Denial

*Revised Edition*

## William Boardman

YORKLAND PUBLISHING

WCS co-founders, Ken and Susan Webb (above) and David and Peggy Bailey (below), circa 1946

Greenhithe, circa 1946

CHAPTER ONE

# Before WCS Opens

**I**

### Ken Webb, WCS prospectus (Second Edition), March 1945

*A Proposal for the Establishment of a Coeducational Progressive Farm and Day School in Woodstock.*

OBJECTIVES

**A.** *INTELLECTUAL. Woodstock Country School will strive to stimulate in manifold ways intellectual curiosity, mental alertness, and pride in sound scholarship. The organization of classes, the type of men and women who will constitute the faculty, the close contact with real life thru (sic) work experience around the School itself and its farm, the weekend campus experiences made possible by the facilities of*

Camp Timberlake, participation in the community life of the town of Woodstock – all these will serve to provide an environment broad and richly stimulating to a growing mind.

**B.** RELIGIOUS. The School will endeavor to emphasize a simple, genuine type of religion, first of all thru a faculty, which, while naturally differing widely as to individual point of view on religion, will share the conviction as to its validity and importance in their own lives and the lives of their students. Brief daily chapel services will be supplemented by frequent weekend visits of inspiring men and women from outside, and by participation in (not merely attendance at) church life in the town.

**C.** PHYSICAL. The Greek idea of developing one's body to its maximum health strength, agility and beauty is a goal too frequently lost sight of in the pressure of interscholastic sports competition. Woodstock Country School may eventually develop teams and take part in games with other schools, but this type of activity, fine as it is in its place, will not be allowed to overshadow other reasons for athletics rugged health and physical fitness, skill in games and in athletic activities, which may become hobbies later in life.

**D.** SOCIAL. Among the precious intangibles which a school may give its students is that spirit of gay and generous cooperation which can come from living together, sharing common tasks, with kindly humor and Christian forbearance helping one another to grow in strength and breadth of character. Places like Pendle Hill, the Quaker graduate school near Philadelphia, Black Mountain College, Putney School, Bedales in England, and other fine institutions suited to the modern age, show that this can be done. The Nation needs more such places.

The education of boys and girls together, a feature of Friends education from the first, is more and more coming to be recognized as a most salutary and valuable experience. To know members of the other sex not only as the glamorous partners of the dance floor but in everyday situations, working and playing together, striving together for common objectives, is not only a wholesome experience but the best preparation for a sympathetic understanding of the other sex on which so much of later happiness is based.

BEFORE WCS OPENS

## Ken Webb report to Harvard 25th class reunion, 1949

*A number of years ago, we joined the Religious Society of Friends and have been most happily in it ever since.*

*But this still left us dissatisfied with American schools, so in 1945, finding some interest in Woodstock, Vermont, in financing a school, we founded, with the aid of many friends generous with time and money, the Woodstock Country School, a coeducational college preparatory boarding school for seventy students. It sent students out into the highways and byways imbued with a social concern that gives them no rest.*

• • •

In the fall of 1944, after years of dreaming and planning, Ken Webb took the first practical steps toward opening his own school for the following school year. He found a good site. He started writing a prospectus for students, teachers and backers. And he put out his first, discreet feelers for local support. Ken's hope was "to have one more fine Quaker school with the values and outstanding education those schools provided," Susan Webb recalled years later. While Ken succeeded in raising the necessary support to open the school, he would eventually pay an unanticipated price for his success: a position of compromised authority he would come to regret a few years later.

Kenneth Webb was born in 1902, in Springfield, Mass. He attended the public primary and secondary schools there before attending Harvard College, where he graduated with honors in Greek and English literature in 1924. Nine years later, he earned a Harvard M.A. in comparative literature. He started teaching in 1925 at the Storm King School, later moving on to the American University in Beirut, the Peddie School (where he was head of the Latin Department), Vermont Academy and the Baltimore Friends School (again heading the Latin Department), among others.

A short, vigorous man of intense and serious demeanor, Ken believed deeply in the values which he wanted his school to embody. He expected Woodstock to be no less demanding of its students than he was of himself. Left with a limp by a childhood brush with polio, Ken pushed his body constantly to its limits, hiking, splitting wood, clearing brush or working out at home with barbells. His diaries show him pushing his mind and spirit just as hard. A convinced Friend, he regularly exhorted himself to do more and to be a better person doing it.

His wife Susan was born Susan Howard in 1908 in Burlington, Vermont. Her mother, Dr. Susan E. Howard, was a suffragist and Burlington's first woman doctor, whom the male medical establishment barred from the local hospital. Oliver Otis Howard, the younger Susan's paternal grandfather, had served as commissioner of the Freedman's Bureau following the Civil War, and had founded Howard University in Washington, D.C. Growing up in a strong Quaker family with powerful traditions of independent thought and social responsibility, Susan developed a quiet drive that would carry her, in "retirement" in the 1970s, into an eight-year career as a Vermont state legislator. She attended local public schools as a girl and then graduated from the University of Vermont in 1930.

A slim, vigorous, forthright young woman determined to make a useful contribution to the world, she met Ken Webb the following year, as she was at Radcliffe College completing work for her M.A. in classics. Years later, Susan recalled her and Ken's instant rapport – both classicists, both teachers, both socially concerned: "We talked all the first evening that we met, and we never stopped talking for fifty-two years."

Ken and Susan Webb married in 1932 and for the rest of their lives together, theirs was a relationship based on equality, partnership and mutual respect. At first, they pursued joint teaching careers, but always with the thought that they would some day start their own, progressive school when they could raise the money. Meanwhile, they did what they could afford. In 1939, they started an all-boys Camp Merlicht ("more light" in German) – soon changed to Timberlake – in Plymouth, Vermont, about 15 miles west of Woodstock. Ken was the director of the first camp, but two years later they added Indian Brook Camp for girls that Susan directed until she and Ken retired in 1973. They kept adding camps over the years eventually creating the complex known as Farm and Wilderness Camps that was still going strong more than 75 years later. Based on a philosophy of cooperation and equality, all the camps had relatively rugged regimens designed to foster both individual and group self-reliance. At the same time, the camps, while non-sectarian, were deeply influenced by the Webbs' Quaker beliefs and global concerns.

By the fall of 1944, when Ken started writing his school prospectus, he and Susan had moved to Woodstock with their three small children. They had given up their teaching positions to devote all their energies to establishing Farm and Wilderness Camps on a solid base. Now Ken felt secure enough to turn to a new enterprise. He was 42 then, he had been thinking about and planning his own school for more than a decade, he was confident of his own abilities, he had a successful record of educational achievement. With Susan committed first to their children and still a partner in the Farm and Wilderness enterprise, Ken felt he needed an assistant – but he was not looking for another partner. And he certainly wasn't looking for a 32-year-old stranger like David Bailey, even if David was a fellow teacher who believed in progressive education. During the summer of 1943, David had suddenly started talking to family and friends about starting his own school in Woodstock, which he considered his hometown. Ken knew only that David had an unimpressive academic record, a spotty teaching career and a reputation for impracticality. None of this was enough to persuade him to join David in a mutual venture.

But Elizabeth Forrest Johnson was.

## Elizabeth F. Johnson, Baccalaureate Sermon at Baldwin School, June 1937

*We must seek clarity of definition, precision of thinking, we are not helpless, nor are we without power. Every time we ally ourselves with activities impelled by understanding altruism, we find that the sails of our craft are full of wind and that we can steer in the direction to which we would go... I say "understanding altruism," for the head and the heart must work together. We despair equally of the well-meaning fool and the selfish intellectual.*

*Leadership in our confused world situation we must have. The fundamental difference between leadership and dictatorship should not escape us. The real leader knows that strength and power and true worth come from the group rather than from himself. He can call out these powers because he understands and loves the group, and from this generous attitude of his, the power of the group grows. He is not in a hurry. He knows that it is this growth of group thinking, planning and doing that counts.*

*In such group living there is a sense of mutual give and take. In a family that so lives the parents derive strength from the children as well as give it. In a school there is the same mutual strengthening between teachers and students. No one is thinking of himself more highly than he ought to think. The atmosphere is of group joys, group responsibilities. I am sure that only in such an atmosphere can we attain sound progress in our present complicated civilization.*

*It is a revolution to which you go out. Gone is the pioneer America of the '70s, gone the confident America of the '90s, gone the smug*

*America of the post-war period. There are things in the new America finer and fairer than in any of the earlier Americas. For such a group as you, this new America will be a very special challenge, for it will be an America in which there will be a less favored place for you and the families and friends whom you represent. Where will be the center of gravity of your lives? In yourself or in others? I come to be increasingly sure that only the generous and the sensitive can grow and be happy and indeed live fully under the impact of modern life. The selfish and the hard are doomed to sorrow and defeat.*

## Peggy Bailey interview, June 21, 1982

*[Elizabeth Johnson] was an extraordinary person... She never married. She was a very strong, indeed intelligent, active woman. She had a house on Mountain Avenue [in Woodstock] and a lovely garden and at one time I think she ran for selectman and didn't win because in those days you didn't have women, and personally she was just too much of a fireball for the selectmen... She was a very wise person, and surprisingly, considering that she had run a girl's school and that she had never married, she was surprisingly broadminded, about certain things. She was also extremely intelligent and good at figures and so she became the treasurer of the school for at least the first two years I think, she did it entirely for love and she ran the school on a very tight schedule. That is, whenever a bill came in, she sat down and wrote a check for it. She never let things pile up. She was a trustee, but she was also treasurer, and also active in the day-to-day management... She was really in some ways, I suppose a new woman.*

• • •

When Elizabeth Forrest Johnson retired to Vermont in 1941, still vital and active, she immediately immersed herself in local affairs. Having summered in Woodstock since 1933, she was familiar with the community and eager to contribute to it in a myriad of ways. Years later, after more than two decades of Miss Johnson's community work, her close friends in Woodstock wrote in her obituary, "One could say that over the years practically no good purpose of importance was carried out without her participation."

Born in Frederick, Maryland, in 1881, Miss Johnson graduated Phi Beta Kappa in mathematics from Vassar College in 1902 and took her M.A. there the following year. At 22, she accepted a position at the Baldwin School for girls in Bryn Mawr, Pennsylvania, where "I had a corridor, I taught mathematics and current events, I was assistant secretary, I did odd jobs of all sorts." She earned $3,000 a year, on which she supported herself and her parents, who lived with her in a tiny cottage off campus.

Miss Johnson remained at Baldwin for 38 years, first becoming Assistant to the Head, and then Headmistress in 1915. Under her leadership for the next 26 years, the school more than doubled the size of its faculty and student body, while achieving institutional security on its own property, which it had previously only rented. During these years, Miss Johnson also ran a girls' camp on Lake Winnipesaukee in New Hampshire and served as a Vassar trustee. A stocky, plain woman of great energy and intelligence, Miss Johnson was a formidable presence in any company. And a contradictory one, as well, for she was both forward-looking in fostering personal independence, as well as accustomed to having people obey her mere suggestions.

In her Woodstock retirement, Miss Johnson worked with the town's selectmen and the village's trustees on budget analysis and planning. She took an active role in creating local institutions, including a recreation center, a health center and a nursing home, in addition to the Woodstock Country School. At the St. James Episcopal Church, she served as a member of the vestry, as treasurer, as president of the Women's Auxiliary and in the Sunday school. And she sustained her interest in world affairs through the Woodstock Community Forum, where concerned citizens considered such issues as "the Negro question," "Zionists in Palestine" and "national sovereignty and a durable peace." Miss Johnson herself spoke on the problems of Japanese Americans, who were then still incarcerated in internment camps. The Community Forum, a small, somewhat isolated group in a reflexively unquestioning Republican town and state, comprised most of Woodstock's progressive thinkers, including Ken Webb and Ruth Bailey, who was David's mother and Miss Johnson's good friend.

During the fall of 1944, Miss Johnson took increasing interest in Ken Webb's emerging plans for a local school and gradually became his mentor in the project. In late October, Ken noted in his diary that his plans for a school were progressing nicely. He described going to inspect the suitable site he had found on Church Hill, a large old house called Greenhithe, a former inn with 19 rooms and a nearby tight barn, which could probably serve as a boys' dorm and classroom building. The buildings were set on forty acres of fields and woods above the village, but still within the village line, just a few minutes walk to "down street."

Greenhithe itself was wonderful, a three-story Victorian structure set on the brow of the hill. Wrapped on three sides by a wide porch that was welcoming in summer and sheltering in winter, Greenhithe's various rooms and corridors surrounded the wide central staircase, which led in three graceful stages from the front hall to the comfortable floors above. Everything about the place was on a human scale – homey, lived-in, warm, cozy and spacious all at once. (David Bailey also approved of Greenhithe: "As a child I grew up right across the mowing... I skied in the moguls and gentle slopes there... Mrs. Moore who owned it was in deep trouble financially – and there was a driveway lined on both sides with nice maples, and she couldn't pay her taxes, so she'd been cutting down, every so often, every other maple to sell them – and so we got the place for something like $11,000.") Greenhithe would become the new school's central building and the only such comfortable, welcoming central building the school would ever have.

After Ken Webb first visited Greenhithe in October 1944, he wrote in his diary, he went "Then to see Miss Johnson by invitation, to talk about the School. She says the Giles, Mr. Moon – and Mrs. Moon – the McDills might be interested, that it should be incorporated at low-interest bearing bonds, deferred retirement. David Bailey much beloved in town, not so impractical as [he] was. Wants to found a school which will have the spirit of Black Mountain College."

Typically brief and oblique, the diary entry says no more. But the gist of the meeting seems clear: Miss Johnson will help Ken start his school – on her terms. The promised help was basic: money. Miss Johnson was experienced at grooming the wealthy to contribute to her causes – the three families Ken mentioned, with fortunes derived primarily from ink, newspapers and railroads respectively, would soon become some of the school's most important benefactors. Miss Johnson's *quid pro quo* for this help was that Ken make room for David Bailey in the enterprise.

Ken's diary does not make this bargain explicit, but Susan Webb remembers Miss Johnson insisting that David be part of the school. Ken's own recollection is that, despite David's loyal following in Woodstock, no one, including Miss Johnson, quite trusted him to start a school on his own; that he needed someone with Ken's experience, ability and steadiness to make it work. Ken would have had to do most of the groundwork in any event, since David was then a housemaster and teacher at the Lawrenceville School in New Jersey. Whatever the precise nature of Ken's understanding with Miss Johnson, he promptly obeyed her suggestion. He wrote David the very next day, outlining the new school's brochure and seeking David's counsel.

For her part, within a week of their formal interview, Miss Johnson arranged for Ken to meet with Owen D. Moon, Jr., at his home at Upwey Farms in South Woodstock. A Pennsylvania Quaker, Owen Moon had graduated from Swarthmore College in 1894 and later married the daughter of the president of the Scott Paper Company, a position in the family business he assumed himself in 1927. In the mean time, he had built a fortune of his own through such enterprises as a suburban trolley line, several newspapers and a pioneering radio station. In 1910, he bought the first piece of what was to become his 2,000-acre Upwey Farms, named after the home of his wife's English ancestors. Over the years, with the help of professional farm management, Upwey became an internationally known horse and dairy cow showplace, on which the gentleman farmer also built terraced, formal gardens and a replica of a Greek amphitheater enclosed by cypress trees. During his later years, the multi-millionaire grew less entrepreneurial and more philanthropic in his interests. In 1942, he sponsored the Woodstock Associates, a non-profit organization for local improvement, of which Elizabeth Johnson was a trustee.

In preparation for his meeting with Owen Moon, Ken Webb spent most of the next week polishing his school proposal and preparing a financial plan based on enrolment of 25 boarders and 15 day students for the first year. Ken's long-term goal then was to have a school of 50 boarders and 50 day students, though he also thought perhaps 100 boarders would be possible after some building. Miss Johnson reviewed and approved these plans as they developed and Owen Moon found them worthy of his support. On Halloween, he signed the papers pledging to put up $10,000 to secure Greenhithe and its 40 acres for the school. Ken next approached another of Woodstock's great benefactors, and Miss Johnson's Mountain Avenue neighbor, Mrs. Marianne G. Faulkner, who had inherited her husband's $3 million fortune derived from importing fine fabrics. She, too, supported the Woodstock Associates and would later provide most of that organization's endowment.

Ken had met Mrs. Faulkner some time earlier, shortly after he came to the area. He tutored her informally in French and become her friend. She gave him $5,000 for his school. Owen Moon's South Woodstock neighbors, Howard and Evelyn Carter Giles, of the Carter ink family, promised another $1,000. And still another $1,000 came from Julia McDill, a member of the Billings family, whose Northern Pacific Railroad fortune had been reshaping Woodstock since the late 19th century. There were several lesser donors as well, including Ken's friend, Gerald Cabot, who put up $600 to cover current expenses. According to Ken's diary, "Gerald says the School sounds pretty nearly sure-fire, much better than the camp. He thinks we have got something there."

Two days after meeting with Owen Moon, Ken was in Lawrenceville to confer with David for the first time face to face. No record of that meeting exists beyond Ken's sparse diary entry, which also notes that he had supper at the Baileys' house and spoke at one of David's Bible classes the next morning. David was not a diary-keeper, but rather kept his own counsel so closely that his wife often did not know what he truly thought. In later years, neither man would ever explain the reasons for their collaboration either clearly or convincingly.

Throughout November and into December, Ken put most of his energies into the school – raising more than $20,000, developing the articles of association and by-laws, publishing the first brochure, working with contractors to modify Greenhithe, lining up teachers, visiting other schools and laying the groundwork for getting students by the following September. He spent a day at the Putney School, where he consulted with Carmelita Hinton, one of the legends of the progressive education movement. Later, after he visited the more traditional Vermont Academy in Saxtons River, Ken observed in his diary, "Went to the evening meeting and saw the 101 boys. What a contrast after the sensitive, alert faces at Putney." In another of his prospecting visits, Ken talked to a friend who was a chemist turned screenwriter, who offered an observation Ken took to heart – and one that David Bailey would repeat many times over the years: "In a faculty of a secondary school we want personalities, men and women who want to teach children rather than subjects." This was a guiding principle of the Country School for most of its life.

Recalling this period 37 years later, David Bailey was sparing in his acknowledgement of Ken's part in starting the school: "Ken Webb and I were brought together by a mutual friend, who became the most important trustee of the school, and we got together and found some ideas in common. The most important idea perhaps was that the school should be located in Woodstock... we were in general agreement philosophically about high schooling. We agreed obviously about co-education and we agreed on having a relaxed, socially informal school, with disciplined, academic standing." On an earlier occasion, but also well after he had retired, David responded to questions about the school's beginnings by telling the 1973 faculty that "it wasn't very interesting, really... We mostly disagreed, Ken and I, but we agreed on coeducation, which was awfully daring for those days."

Ken's retrospective view of the partnership was more nuanced: "We grew up in the era of progressive education, before progressive education had a very unfortunate interpretation and meaning. Both David Bailey and I subscribed to the best tenets of progressive education. We wanted to see them implemented.

But aside from that similarity, there was nothing to draw us together. We looked at everything differently... For him, progressive education meant a great deal of permissiveness. And I don't go along with that at all. So we should have explored each other's thinking more before we hooked up, just as some people wouldn't get married who went into the characteristics of each before taking the jump."

In reality, a careful exploration of each other's philosophy was not a practical option in late 1944, not only because time was short until the next September, but moreso because Miss Johnson was eagerly pushing ahead without such "clarity of definition, precision of thinking." By the end of November, Ken and Miss Johnson agreed they had progressed so far that, before pushing on, they should wait for David Bailey to come home for his Christmas vacation, so that he could play a more active role in the planning. Ken "got off a four-page letter to David, which capitulates [sic] all progress to date."

When David returned to Woodstock in mid-December, the school was largely defined along lines Miss Johnson had suggested, but consistent with Ken's original plans. David had contributed little to that definition and he and Ken still hardly knew each other. They had their first formal meeting about the school three days after David's return. They were an unexpected match at best, David, 32 years old and tall, Ken, 42 years old and shorter. Both were thin. David was languorous and poetic, something of an afghan to Ken's terrier directness and persistence. Ken was constantly exercising, pushing his body to its limits, while David's natural poses were leaning and lounging. And David smoked, almost chain-smoked, while Ken abstained. Nor was there ever any great warmth between them that anyone recalls. They had little in common and they didn't really like each other. But they were on their best behavior then, for Miss Johnson's sake, for without her, each feared there would be no school. And so Ken would write optimistically of their discussion: "Historic day. David and I talked from nine thirty to three thirty, eating a sandwich lunch up stairs... I feel that David and I have gone along quite far with this affair now; we still see eye to eye. Worked on discussion of the first items of budget, then stopped to talk over teachers, then classes. Planned the whole curriculum, working out the classes and the day's schedule, idea of ten lectures during the winter on subjects which wouldn't be taken up at other times: understanding human personality, Chinese literature or history, Egyptian history or archeology, archeology everywhere, popular astronomy etc."

This was largely wishful thinking on Ken's part and testimony to Miss Johnson's authority in shaping the school. When she died in 1963 David wrote that she "was as responsible as anyone for the foundation of the school and the preservation of it in its first years. As former Trustee and Treasurer and as general educational godmother, she was of invaluable assistance to the school." At the same time, the trustees, making a formal contribution to the town in her memory, recognized "that her service to the community of Woodstock was outstanding both in its generosity and its sagacity. Her integrity, her concern for her fellow man, her noble practicality, her strong adherence to the highest ethical standards combined with a deep understanding of human frailties have served as an inspiration and example to us all." A brief biography of Miss Johnson, prepared by the Baldwin School in 1963, reported with lighter touch and ironic inexactitude: "When Miss Johnson retired in 1941, she bought a small cottage in Woodstock, VT., and of course almost immediately amused herself by giving – whatever the female form of avuncular advice is – to a young couple who were just starting a new progressive school there. As a mathematician, I believe she taught them a bit about how to keep their financial records in a realistic form."

### Elizabeth Forrest Johnson, Baccalaureate Sermon to the Baldwin School, June 1938

*"Where and how will you find the strength to meet the challenge of your lives, of our common American life, of the common world life of which you are a part? You cannot fail to be puzzled and anxious. You see wrong triumphant in too high places. You see stupidity and fear in the saddle, riding headlong. Outside of America you see the apparent history of points of view which all Americans abhor; inside America you see a bitterness of struggle between irreconcilable forces, all claiming to be the true and right American way... Somehow you must find experiences that will integrate these contradictions. So only can you live purposefully and effectively. To achieve this integration is the real challenge of adulthood. I want to suggest to you – and I hope that I can do so in a way that will seem usable to you, that the faith which leads us to live our lives as in the presence of God is that unifying experience. One real difficulty in making this seem real and significant to you is that you are still to some extent under the sway of the eighteenth-century conviction that Christianity is a safe, easy, and respectable way to live. In actual fact – and I mean this literally – Christianity is revolutionary and in every period of history when it has been vital and moving, and in every human life where it is dominant, there is revolution."*

BEFORE WCS OPENS

## Ken Webb, press release in the Vermont Standard newspaper, Woodstock, March 8, 1945

*Enrolment of students at the Country School already has begun, it has been announced by Kenneth B. Webb, co-director of the new day and boarding school which is scheduled to begin this coming fall.*

*The catalog, recently published by the Elm Tree Press, gives information about the school, lists the curriculum, gives organization of the school day and other pertinent facts. As stated in the catalog, the aim of the institution will be to provide a high standard of scholarship and effective instruction in various arts and crafts.*

*Students will do most of maintenance plus learning to care for livestock and do other farm activities. The 400-acre Timberlake Camp in Plymouth will be used for additional farming activities and for weekend camps...*

*David W. Bailey, now at the Lawrenceville School for Boys in New Jersey, will act as co-director and will teach classes in English and social studies. Mr. Webb, co-director, will teach general language, Latin and Greek...*

*Two women teachers and several part-time assistants will be announced later.*

● ● ●

The Woodstock Country School, Inc., came into legal existence on the winter solstice of 1944 with the signing of its articles of association and first by-laws by the incorporators: Ken, David, Owen Moon, Julia Lee McDill and Elizabeth F. Johnson. The simply stated purpose of the corporation was to establish and maintain "a school for the education and training of boys and girls, with power and authority... to do any lawful act which is necessary or proper to accomplish its purposes." At this time, the school became a profit-making capital corporation (like the Webbs' camps), which planned an initial capitalization of $50,000 through a stock offering of 500 shares at a par value of $100 per share.

As 1945 began, Ken Webb looked ahead optimistically: "The beginning of what should be an even finer year than the previous. The first six months, then the two of camp, will be perfect. Then the School with all its promise, all its unknown challenges. The greatest satisfaction of the moment is the fact of finding remunerative work right here which makes possible my staying in town the rest of the season and also doing something which will be pleasant, even thrilling."

Several weeks later, Ken added with his usual shorthand spelling, "Looked back the other day thru some 1940 diaries, and found how surprisingly fertile my ideas were then. Most every page had a treatise on something. Now I scarcely have time to write in this diary. Not a decline in fertility, but I am putting into action, creating, so many of the things I could only dream about. And my thots now and visions are so much more clear, feasible, and detailed. Experience has helped, and I must not forget the part that prayer has played, nor let it play less; rather much more."

Much of Ken's time and energy during that winter went into organizing the camps in Plymouth for the following summer. Still, he managed to remain attentive to Susan and their three small children, he taught Sunday school, he continued fund raising for the school, he took recruiting trips, he shoveled snow off the roof at Greenhithe ("stripped to the waist and enjoyed it greatly"), and led an active social life, including serving on the steering committee of the Woodstock Community Forum, which sponsored a March program on the question, "Are we doing too much for our youth?" Ken reported: "Good discussion, with half a dozen boys present from the group who are going to start the youth center. I spoke informally on the therapeutic value of work. Think we must give more attention to this, which is really central in our philosophy. The joy of creative work, the kinesthetic pleasure of work etc."

All during the winter, Ken was also writing and rewriting the first Woodstock Country School catalog, with such help as David could provide through the mail. The first edition (referred to in Ken's press release above) has not survived. But the second edition, revised in the spring, is the clearest, fullest statement of what Ken had in mind for his and David's school. The catalog begins with a statement of the school's goals (quoted above), and then continues on the following four tightly typed, single-spaced pages with the relatively mundane details of school life, occasionally punctuated by further illuminations of intent. For example, in the midst of an otherwise unremarkable discussion of the barn and a nearby foundation of an earlier barn now vanished, the reader suddenly learns that "One of the major projects of the second or third year of the school should be the rebuilding of this barn as a snug and roomy place to house the eventual herd from which the school should get its milk (when a small pasteurizing plant can be managed)." This would never come about. Instead, a few years later, that old barn foundation became part of a new headmaster's house – for David and Peggy Bailey.

Another selling point for the school was the idea of "The Grand Campus," not merely the school's own 40 acres, but the surrounding reaches of Vermont countryside, which was then much less populous than it is today (the original campus in now a suburban subdivision). In the forties, Vermont still had more cows than people, who didn't catch up till the sixties. Over the years, the land, the place, this "Grand Campus" (though few ever called it that) would make a profound impression on students, sometimes even more so than curriculum, peers and the rest of the school together.

According to the catalog, Woodstock's academic week would have six tightly scheduled class days. The class day would begin with wake-up at 6:30 a.m., breakfast at 7:30, followed by five classes between 8 and 1. After lunch, at 1:10 p.m., came a brief respite. But, the text ordered, "By two-thirty all students (including day students) will be dressed for the afternoon's activity, and should have reported to the person in charge. Varying with the season and the weather, these afternoon physical activities will include organized sports such as soccer, possibly football, skiing, skating and winter sports of all sorts; hiking, cabin building etc. Approximately three of the afternoons each week will be devoted to sports, two to various work projects. Saturday afternoon and probably Sunday afternoon will be free, with each student reporting to a person in charge what his intentions are." At 4:30 on class days, students were to be free to study, attend to their barn chores, get supper ready, take tea in the living room at Greenhithe, or just relax – "general reading will be encouraged." After supper at 6, a brief vesper service along Quaker lines was to be followed by "a general assembly for any matters of school life needing attention; often two or three good songs, and dispersal to evening studies; or in case of some outside speaker or some special program, the assembly may be replaced by this program. Bedtime will be eight-thirty for the younger students, an hour later for the rest."

Recognizing the demands that such a schedule makes on students and faculty alike, the catalog explained: "Each subject will meet <u>five</u> times during the six-day period, this with three purposes: 1. To enable each teacher to have one full 24-hour period free during the week, a time at which he should leave the place entirely, come back refreshed, eager to give his maximum. 2. To break to some extent the monotony of the week's classes. 3. To create some extra daylight study time. (Each student will take not over four courses, have one study hour each morning, two on four days of the week.)"

The catalog concluded with a brief epilogue: "Response both to the financial proposal and to the enrolment campaign – not yet really begun – has been so splendid that there seems little likelihood of our not having registration to the capacity of the present accommodations (including the remodeled barn)... A recent visit to two schools founded on the modern ideal of making sound scholarship vital and the whole educational value of the environment realized makes it appear even more certain that there is a grand place for a school like this, which while being tharoly [sic] modern and progressive academically, will still emphasize the religious values in the life of a growing youngster, and by reason of the unusually fine community of which the School will be a part, will establish a close relation with the activities and interests of the town."

All this describes a school that embodies Ken's values more than David's – particularly in its heavy emphasis on spiritual values and the idealization of physical work. Not surprisingly then, as Ken turned 43 that winter, he felt in control of his fate, his mood was close to euphoric, despite the workload that kept him chronically tired.

As he recorded in his diary, "This eighth of March I have no enthusiastic plans, burning ideals to set down. Probably it is because I am too well satisfied with the way life is going anyway, too busy working out some of these ideals of long standing. Matters I have still to work out, tho, are these:

"1.   How to keep life relaxed and joyous next year despite the evident demands on me. I will have to plan time off each afternoon; perhaps an hr. after lunch

"2.   To get my feet so comfortable that I can hike again.

"3.   A good, rugged, lithe, graceful frame, well muscled, obedient, joyous.

"4.   Most important: a radiant personality, result of morning watch."

The arrival of an early spring reinforced Ken's happy mood. By March 27, he was raking the lawn and tending flowerbeds at Greenhithe. Renovation of the barn had begun. Earlier in the month, the school had bought a house on the Green in the village to use for a boys' dormitory. David's return to Woodstock during his spring vacation prompted another round of board meetings to deal with necessary, but not unpleasant, details. At the end of March, Ken predicted the school would have 50 students in September, 40 boarders and 10 day students. He wrote, "we have 15 day prospects, 24 boarding, 12 of them very good."

But with the approach of summer, Ken's attention turned increasingly to his camps in Plymouth. Progress on the Country School slowed. In late June, now fully immersed in the seventh summer of Farm and Wilderness, Ken recorded one of his now rare trips to Woodstock in his diary: "Read mail, including one letter from [his friend and supporter] Tennien saying O.K. for $10,000 more. Praises be! Now our financial troubles are ended, for we can concentrate on enrolment; we can make the conversion to a non-profit; we can get in contributions from a wider area." As for enrolment, he noted there were now "about 16, or half" the students the school needed, a downward revision of his March prediction of 50. This was one of his last diary entries of any sort until the camp season was over.

In May, the board had decided to convert the school from a profit-making corporation to a non-profit, which was completed in August with Ken, David and Miss Johnson as the principle incorporators once more. The new articles of association stated that the Woodstock Country School, Inc., was formed "for the purpose of establishing and maintaining at Woodstock in the County of Windsor and State of Vermont a school for the education of boys and girls, exclusively for that public, and charitable purpose... The members of this corporation shall be the incorporators, the trustees when elected and such other persons as the Board of Trustees may from time to time elect to membership. This corporation shall have perpetual existence."

Coming home to Woodstock at the end of Lawrenceville's school year, David found himself more or less in charge of getting the school ready to open because Ken was busy running his camps. But Miss Johnson still provided guidance and support. As David recalled that summer, "I was always available for enrolment, for people who phoned inquiries or came there for interviews. I also supervised the alterations we were to make on Greenhithe and the barn. These included establishing one classroom for biology in the barn, and a second floor apartment where the groom's quarters had been, and then putting heat in the main building, Greenhithe. We also had to construct a two-story wooden stairway to run down to the ground as a fire escape."

David also hired the last few teachers the school needed and handled the details of buying the house on The Green that would serve as a boys' dorm and a residence for the Webbs. Meanwhile, David's mother and her friend, Mrs. Giles, worked long hours furnishing and decorating Greenhithe in the most tasteful and delicate fashion – so delicate, in fact, that most of their work would not withstand the normal wear and tear of the following year.

After the end of the camp season in September, Ken took stock, outlining a Five-Year Plan for the school, the camps and himself. Nothing in his plans suggests that he considered the possibility that he might be over committed. He wrote: "How different from college days and before, when I used to dream, but with a lurking sense of frustration because I couldn't see how to accomplish the things I dreamt of. Now I dream as much, but the foundations are laid for the realization of plans, and I have both the confidence in tested ability and the experience to know how to achieve what I wish... What are some of these dreams? First, that the School will prosper, will become one of the choice little schools of the country, will make a significant contribution to the cause of better education: classes designed to stimulate intellectual curiosity, to awaken interests which will lead to the continuing process of self-education; an environment rich and varied, designed to teach the dignity and the satisfaction of labor, the joy of wholesome activity in the out-of-doors; a spiritual life deep and true enuf to give youngsters the anchorage they so vitally need, to help in building a fine, noble, and useful personality, at peace with God and man."

By early September, the Country School was still far from fully enrolled, with only five students more than had signed up in June. That signaled potential financial trouble for the school, but there was real trouble at the camps: they had lost money during the summer. Yet Ken's optimism remained undaunted: "It has been a fine summer: boundless goodwill and prospects for another year. Only the finances are bad, but we'll get that fixed with this fall and plan for a $10,000 profit next summer. At the moment School enrolment looks good: 21 yesterday, with three or four more pretty sure, one visiting last night."

The Webbs spent as much of September closing up the camps and moving into Woodstock as they did setting up the Country School for its first opening day. Ken went on another trip to visit other New England schools to glean ideas for Woodstock. He was particularly taken by the weaving program at Fireside and a local bird identification project at Indian Mountain. Ken's diary betrayed no anxiety about the prospect, nor did he record many details of preschool activities. He stopped writing entirely the day before school opened. Only in the last week before opening did Ken immerse himself once more in the details of school business on campus. For three months, he had left all that to David so that, although the abstract plan of the school was still largely Ken's, its physical and practical realization was largely David's. Only in the final week before opening day did Ken and David truly begin working together, side by side, making joint decisions on a daily basis, which required mutual respect and understanding. Time and circumstance had robbed them of the academic equivalent of spring training and without it they found it difficult to remember always that they were supposed to be on the same team.

Evelyn Giles

Elizabeth Forrest Johnson with Lady

1946-47 student body at Greenhithe

Class of 1948 at Greenhithe
BACK ROW (l.to r.): Severn Darden, Jerry Hults, Kim Lau Kee, Dick Dunham, Morty Schiff, Jane Fisher. MIDDLE ROW: Carol Edwards, Bert Work, Janet Gay, Jerry Fox, Josephine Van der Gracht, Jim Barter, Gerry Freund. FRONT ROW: Nancy Boone, Helen Foster, Marion MacAfee, Kay Batten, Sheila Spenser.

CHAPTER TWO

# Fall 1945 – Spring 1948

**WCS Catalog for 1946-47 (selections), December 1945:**

WOODSTOCK COUNTRY SCHOOL

*A college preparatory school for boys and girls from the seventh through the twelfth grades.*

INCORPORATED 1945 NOT FOR PROFIT

*Board of Trustees*
*Owen Moon term expires 1949*
*Elizabeth F. Johnson term expires 1948*
*Lee Anderson term expires 1947*
*Evelyn Carter Giles (Mrs. Howard Giles) term expires 1946*
*David W. Bailey Vice-President of the Board*
*Kenneth B. Webb President of the Board*
*Ruth Schenk Hawkes (Mrs. R.S. Hawkes) Secretary of the Board*

OFFICERS

*David W. Bailey, Co-director*
*Elizabeth F. Johnson, Treasurer*
*Kenneth B. Webb, Co-director*
*Johanna S. Peterson, Secretary*

REFERENCES BY PERMISSION

*Other Friends of the School*
*Professor Joseph Albers, Black Mountain College*
*Samuel Barber, Composer*
*Ward M. Canaday, Chairman, Willys-Overland Motors, Inc.*
*Dorothy Canfield Fisher, author*
*Bliss Forbush, Friends School of Baltimore, Md.*
*Anne Bosworth Greene, Author*
*Mr. and Mrs. Owen Lattimore, Baltimore, Md.*

*Mr. George Mullins, New York City, N.Y.*
*Mrs. Elliott Speer, The Masters School*
*Dr. Charles C. Tillinghast, Horace Mann School for Boys*

*[This first list of "Friends of the School" also included 32 names of the parents and guardians of the first year's students.]*

## Location and Physical Aspects, WCS brochure, 1945

*Woodstock, Vermont, elevation 700 feet, population 1,200, is on Route 4, 13 miles from White River Junction, 36 miles from Rutland… There are five churches, three local doctors (with the modern Hanover Hospital 18 miles away) and three good inns.*

*The forty-acre tract of upland meadow and woodland, which constitutes the main property of the School, is situated about five minutes walk from the Green in Woodstock. On this land, besides the ski slopes, an outdoor swimming pool near the woods, pasture land and a garden area, there are two large buildings. One [Greenhithe] houses the girls' dormitory, dining room, infirmary quarters, office, faculty room, common room and – at present – all but one of the classrooms. The other building [The Barn], a roomy and picturesque barn, houses the science laboratory, a small gymnasium and theatre, a master's suite, and beyond a heavy sliding door, the quarters for horses, cattle, and poultry.*

*The School owns another piece of property on the Green [The Green], a large old double house with two beautiful fireplaces, which are noted in Woodstock. This building is the boys' dormitory and provides space for resident faculty.*

• • •

When the Woodstock Country School opened on September 26, 1945, there were 35 students enrolled. There was a senior class of three, there were one or two juniors who were also war veterans, and, contrary to the catalog, there was even a sixth grader. Some students had scholarships, but most were paying the full $1,200 a year fee for tuition and board (day students, $300). Most of them came from the Atlantic coast region, from Arlington, Virginia, to Maine. Several came from New York City, several others from Boston. They all came to this new and unknown school through networks of relatives, friends and colleagues that Ken Webb, David Bailey and Elizabeth Johnson had developed over the years. These contacts delivered a diverse group.

The first student on campus arrived well before the start of school, because she had nowhere else to go: Patience Malet, an English girl with her own horse, whose mother was an Army lieutenant in Denver. The three seniors were Phebe Brown of an old Boston family, Ray Carpenter, who was heading toward a military career, and Mary Lea Johnson of the Johnson & Johnson Company family (she came from an unhappy time at the Dobbs School, recommended to Woodstock by friends of Miss Johnson). Roger Phillips chose Woodstock because there was no formal dress code. Louis Wislocki, unhappy at Milton, found his way to Woodstock because his mother, Florence Clothier Wislocki, had been at Baldwin under Miss Johnson (who soon drew her into working on the school's behalf). Dr. Wislocki, who was by then a child psychiatrist on staff at the Home for Little Wanderers in Massachusetts, recommended one of her youngsters for the school: Jimmy Barter from Maine, remarkably bright, but with a Dickensian childhood that led to serious trouble with the law and state custody by the time he was 13. He agreed to accept a scholarship to Woodstock because its mattresses were better than the ones at the school he'd run away from. Harvey Tyler became the school's youngest student, a sixth grader, because his and David Bailey's families were old friends. Joe Bernhardt's father was in the U.S. Dept. of Agriculture in Washington. David Ezekiel's father was an agriculture specialist for the United Nations. Klaus Heimann, who fled Nazi Germany with his family in 1939, was having a terrible time in public school in Massachusetts until a friend of Miss Johnson arranged for him to have a scholarship to Woodstock. Mary Lou Doggett and Lillian Russell both came over from the Farm and Wilderness Camps, as did Ken Webb's daughter, Susan (Sukie) and his seventh grade son, Robbie. Helle Krafft came from Norway as a ninth grader, happy to get away from five confined years of war and her mother. Walter Walker's aunt, Helen Gahagan Douglas, knew the Baileys through spending summers in Vermont. And so it went. Whatever brought them to Woodstock, any students who thought about it certainly knew that their 35 places there were not won through fierce competition (there was not even an entrance exam then). But for most, that was just the first of the school's pluses, offering a cooperative respite from bruising competition. Even more important in 1945 was the newness, the sense of adventure and the growing belief that they were creating something of lasting importance, a school with humane values.

From the beginning, Woodstock was a place where a student could get another chance, socially, academically, emotionally. At Woodstock, a student's past didn't follow him or her as relentlessly as it surely would at other institutions. Instead of the ruthless, destructive competition of schools which created at least as many losers as winners, Woodstock's cooperative communal philosophy meant that the school tried to meet the needs of every student, regardless of how gifted that student might or might not be. Woodstock offered a refuge to all kinds of students, a place away from the "real" world or the "natural" family, at least for a time; a place where one could define oneself as one might – and likely be accepted for that. The school welcomed idiosyncrasy gladly, encouraged considerable experiment and expected hard work, both physical and academic. At the same time, the school expected students to progress, to mature in fairly traditional ways and while it put up with those who tested the limits of acceptable performance for a long time (some thought too long too often), it did not tolerate them forever. The inherent tension between these sometimes contradictory goals – providing sufficient relaxation to encourage emotional growth and, simultaneously, setting very high standards – gave the school its special dynamic. Not all of Woodstock's students were kids seeking refuge from one storm or another. Some were attracted by the sheer vitality of the place. When the school worked best over the years, it also had a solid minority of students who most wanted an academically strong school that would provide the intellectual challenges that they weren't getting where they were.

## Roger Phillips '49 interview, May 17, 1984

*It was an absolute lifesaver. I was there the first day of the school, which was in '45. The very first day. And I graduated in '49. I came out of a family that had – my father had been in the Second World War and, you know, he enlisted. He was old at the time, he had a First World War record. He enlisted in the Second World War thinking it was going to be over in six months and it wasn't.*

*It went on for four years. It really drained the family resources in more ways than one and home was not a great place for me at that time, and I wasn't reacting well in public school either. I don't know why, I think it had something to do with the fact that my father did go to war. It was just like losing a parent. You go crazy. I became kind of a delinquent. And then when I got to Woodstock, it was like finding a new family.*

FALL 1945 – SPRING 1948

## Susan (Sukie) Webb Hammond '50 interview, April 30, 1986

*I went because my father was starting the school. He believed in a truly academic education and, I think, had very creative ideas about education, very creative ideas which were grounded in a solid academic training, and it was the most obvious thing in the world for his children, then, to go to the school that he was heading...*

*I was in eighth grade, and it was a small faculty, obviously, so I had my parents from time to time as teachers, and I remember my father teaching a course called 'Modern Language,' which explored oral techniques we take so much for granted these days... I was a day student, but we were living in the boys' dorm down on the Green...*

*I don't remember the first day. I remember that first year we had World War II veterans... I had just turned 12, and to have somebody who had been in the war... and very much older, I suspect he was 19 or 20. It seemed a lot at the time... We were a fairly small group, we knew each other well. There was a sense of informality, a nice feel of informality, not informality to the point of sloppiness... Actually, the academic training I got at the Country School was really terrific, and I then sort of glided through my senior year at the George School, and certainly had no problem making the transition to college.*

## Helle Krafft Sorlie '49 letters, 1983-84

*I loved the school also, I came from Norway where we just had had a 5-year long war. It was rather fantastic to be able to buy and eat as many bananas and oranges and any other things you wanted. It was also nice to get away and to be by myself, I really grew up the one school year I spent there... I didn't know the language at all when I came to the school (I could say yes and no when I arrived), but everyone was very helpful and very eager to teach me English, so I learnt fast... My writing didn't come as easy as my speaking, so David suggested I write a diary and he would correct. That worked beautifully.*

*...about David and Mr. Webb – that's the way we addressed them, and that should tell you something about them... I remember David was very rude to me once and made me cry for what he said, and [a senior] Phebe Brown I think it was told me not to mind, that was just his way now and then. He took most interest in the elder kids, but usually he was nice, but a bit aloof. I liked him very much.*

## Jim Barter '48 interview, February 24, 1985

*I thought it was a school that was made up of misfits and people who had been thrown out of every prestigious boarding school along the East Coast. I'm not sure if that is actually true, but there was certainly that feeling about it. I was very unsophisticated when I came to the school. I was very much in awe of the kids, – I mean everybody there had a background – adopted daughter of a famous psychologist, nephew of a liberal politician, children of government officials – everybody had some kind of distinguished background.*

*But one was a dirty boy, there was no other way of describing him. He rarely changed his clothes, he'd wear his pants until they were stiff and dirty, he slept in his engineer boots – I remember him sleeping in his sheets and not changing them until they got black. He was just dirty. And I was this kid from a shack in the woods of Maine, or not very far from it, I had no claims to sophistication, but I mean, he never showered! We didn't even have indoor plumbing where I grew up. We had an outhouse, and bathed once or twice a month in a tub in front of the kitchen stove, where the water had been boiled to make a bath, so I wasn't the most fastidious kid in the world. But that one really was in a class by himself.*

• • •

In the midst of it all were Ken Webb and David Bailey, trying to work together to make sense of the variety of backgrounds, needs and expectations all tugging the school in different directions. At the same time, they were trying to make sense of each other as well, to make their arranged marriage work, as it were – but it made for an odd family to have two father figures and no true mother figure that first year. Most of the students were accustomed to odd families and this one had all those additional faculty aunts and uncles to help out (most of the time), so the school worked at least as well as some families and better than others.

Ken Webb, with two degrees from Harvard, was the most impressively credentialed member of the faculty, though several other teachers also had master's degrees. In addition to being the dorm head at The Green, Ken taught senior and junior English, Latin and Greek, and a course in General Language for eighth graders. He also wrote the school catalog and general publicity and supervised the student magazine, Symposium. His wife, Susan, was a part-time teacher of Latin and Greek and of necessity helped run the dormitory, where they lived with their three children (two of whom were day students). In the dorm, the Webbs invited the students in for snacks every night.

In contrast to Ken, David Bailey was always a little diffident about his academic achievements, in part no doubt because they were not remarkable, but also because he held other values, such as "good citizenship," at least as high as academic success. David had attended Harvard (1930-33) with mixed results, before transferring to Black Mountain College the year it opened. His two years at Black Mountain, from which he took his degree in 1935, were a transforming experience for him, full of energy, vitality and hope, all of which he wanted to recapture in different ways with the Country School. David taught Social Studies and English in the lower grades, as well as organizing athletics and social events. ("Ken didn't think much of me as an educator, so I was put in charge of recreation," David said years later). His wife, Peggy, was a part-time English and drama teacher, whose involvement was limited by a serious illness for which she was hospitalized that summer. She and David lived with their son, Peter, some distance from the school, in a house where Peggy felt isolated and alone, in part because "David was completely immersed. When school began, the school just drew him into it, and he became completely immersed in new faculty, new students and just keeping the school's head above water."

To instruct their disparate student body and to meet their sometimes greater non-academic needs, the co-directors hired a faculty of five full-time teachers, another six part-time teachers and a non-teaching staff of four (a secretary, a cook, a nurse and a maintenance man). The faculty and staff filled out a school family that included not only the "children" spread over seven or eight chronological and many more emotional years, but also the "parents" who covered three generations. The youthfully ubiquitous Elizabeth Johnson (she even became treasurer of the student magazine) was old enough at 64 to be the grandmother of Faith Murray, the 22-year-old art teacher who looked no older than some of her students. The core of this extended family was varied in age, gender, and experience.

• • •

**Edith Cochran:** Edith not only taught math at all levels, she was in charge of the girls' dorm in Greenhithe, where she frequently held afternoon tea parties for selected student guests ("a real aristocrat," David called her). She came to Woodstock with 20 years teaching experience and became one of the school's dominant personalities during its first six years. She had a graduate degree in Landscape Architecture and took care of much of the school's landscaping for the next few years. She had taught landscape architecture at Smith College for years, then taught at the all girls' school, St. Mary's in the Mountains, which was then a very strict, traditional place, but has since turned itself into the coeducational White Mountain School, with very much of a Woodstock appearance (if not the progressive substance). David recalled that "Edith Cochran's innovative course in geometry – she used no textbook but instead required the pupils to create a theorem book of their own slowly and logically. More than one non-math student was successful in getting through the course and thus receiving a diploma."

**Bob Lake**: Although Bob Lake was one of the younger faculty, he, too, was one of the school's first defining personalities. He was a veteran of the Tenth Mountain Division, the ski troops, though he had never seen combat. Ken Webb had hired him to work at the Farm and Wilderness Camps the year before the school started, then hired him again as the first member of the Woodstock faculty. A Dartmouth College graduate, Bob had three years' experience teaching at other progressive schools and had worked for the Vermont Soil Conservation Service. He taught Biology, Zoology and Farming, and lived with his wife and three children in the former groom's apartment in The Barn, the classroom building near Greenhithe. This made him generally available to students, whom he enjoyed immensely, which contributed to his becoming the central figure in a major crisis several years later.

**Faith Murray**: Faith, who taught art, was young and single and lived in Greenhithe, where she was Edith's assistant in running the dorm. Diminutive but dynamic, Faith worked with every student in the school, whether the student wanted to draw or paint or sculpt, or not. Busy as she was, Vermont was too remote for her and she left after a year. (David remembered her as "a young little girl, and I remember the students used to pick her up and carry her around." David had recruited her from Black Mountain, where she had studied with Josef Albers. He turned to Albers several times over the years for art teachers.)

**Bert Sarason**: Another one-year teacher. David hired him over the summer to teach Social Studies and English. He came to Woodstock after teaching in more rigid, impersonal places like the Harvey School (all boys, grades 4 to 8). A feisty New Yorker unafraid of speaking his mind, Bert was not always diplomatic about doing so. His students enjoyed his lively classes, including numerous digressions into school issues, even to open criticism of the co-directors.

**Alice Bianchi**: Alice, wife of a Woodstock merchant, taught French (her native tongue) and Spanish. Discovered and hired by David over the summer, she came to the Country School with 16 years of teaching experience at Dana Hall, National Park Seminary, and Central High School in Washington, D.C. Although she taught at Woodstock for three years, she remained relatively uninvolved in the community. The part-time teachers, in addition to the co-directors' wives, included Sue Beatty for music, Ted Gregg for religion, John Long for shop and Carl Voss for social studies – none of whom remained at the school after the first year.

**Johanna Pederson**: Although she was not a teacher until the second year of the school, Johanna Pederson contributed to the character of the place from the start, as the school's first secretary. She was the first of many secretaries in the school's history who served as an unofficial counselor, confessor and cheerleader for all kinds of students.

• • •

In addition to the personal enthusiasm most of the adults brought to the enterprise, Woodstock opened at a time of remarkable confluence of other energies. In the post-war world at large, there was a profound surge of hope and idealism that the world would become a better, more decent place. The idea of the school was a part of the greater optimism that more humane institutions could create more humane people and a more humane world, an optimism affecting students and faculty alike. The freshness of the freedom the school allowed its students added an exuberance to the usual restlessness of adolescents busy finding out who they were, exploring the larger world around them, testing their own limits, falling in love, falling out of love and generally feeling passionate about life in all its grand and trivial disguises. Focussing and intensifying both the global and the personal energies was the inherent dynamic of an institution being born.

For the most part, teachers and students alike threw themselves wholeheartedly into the task of creating their school, a task made much more fascinating and complex by the majority view that Woodstock should be a place which each new school generation could re-create for itself, to meet its own needs and perpetuate the energy of creation. Some even felt more strongly: believing not that the school could re-create itself, but that *it should have to re-create itself constantly* if it were to retain the vitality it needed to contribute to profoundly changing American education. Others, while wishing the school to be a shining example, also wished it to have a clear and more or less fixed definition. This philosophical tension, while always present, was rarely discussed directly, any more than fish discuss water. But because the tension was there, other, apparently less important questions generated emotional debate out of proportion to the importance of the nominal issue. In one such battle, the community decided it would be all right for the soccer team to have red and white uniforms, but only on the clear understanding that these were not the school colors, that it was not right for the group to choose school colors at all because that would bind future students to a choice in which they had no say.

While a school could survive quite nicely without having official colors, other issues required deciding on a more or less permanent basis – though deciding which issues should be decided could spark a lively discussion as well. Throughout that first fall term, throughout the first several years, the school hummed along on this vitality of shared new experience, the momentum of continual newness, the excitement of creating and controlling at least some of the terms of one's own life.

Academically, too, the school was full of ferment, with teachers pushing students to their intellectual limits in rigorous courses. Susan Webb recalled: "There was a great deal of challenge in the teaching... (and there was) the feeling of the school, that the students and all, and the faculty, were very supportive of each other. It was the first school some of these kids had ever hit where there was some sense of freedom to learn and not to be stifled by just sitting in a classroom and that kind of thing."

### Roger Phillips '49 interview, May 17, 1984

*The first day at the school, it was a beautiful day in September. There was no precedent, so no one knew what to do. We were all kind of milling around in front of Greenhithe, talking and sitting on the steps and this and that, and somehow we all gravitated – there were thirty kids, approximately, pretty near the whole school that first year – we gravitated to the hayloft in the barn. We were kind of exploring the buildings. But when we got to the hayloft we had a huge fight with the hay and jumping down off the rafters and, you know piling on top of each other, and that was the lubricant that got everybody going, that was the sounding of the gong. From then on, everybody was kind of loose and the thing really started. There was a huge amount of camaraderie in the first year because we all felt that we were sharing that experience... My room assignment was in the dormitory down on The Green, across from the Town Hall... I go up to the room, I'm rooming with some guy named Larry Hagman, and my sister and mother who were chatting as we went up the stairs, all of a sudden they're dead silent. I look back at them and they're staring at this woman I'd just passed, who was on her hands and knees on the floor – this flaming redhead – planing a bureau drawer. And that was Mary Martin.*

•••

Already a long way from her roots in Weatherford, Texas, with a string of Broadway and movie hits to her credit, Mary Martin acted like just another 31-year-old mother of a ninth grader when she came to Woodstock. On a visit the following spring, she gave an outdoor concert for the whole school on the hillside above Greenhithe. Accompanied by her guitarist, she sang a wonderful variety of songs, including a rousing version of Lullaby of Broadway. But such was the informality of the occasion that after awhile the students called for Larry to sing, too, so mother and son did a popular folk song together, after which Mary Martin said, "Larry, you have a beautiful voice. I had no idea."

Larry Hagman, the future J.R. Ewing in the Dallas series on CBS, had learned of Woodstock through his step-grandmother, who was a friend of one of David Bailey's cousins.

"He was 14 at the time or something," David said years later, "and I didn't realize what a terribly naughty boy he was at the time, but he was a very naughty boy."

Larry quickly became one of the stars of sorts in the school, where his willingness to try almost anything also led to his eventual forced departure. Larry is also widely remembered for his good-natured, though sometimes extreme, antics. Day student Margaret Nichols came to school by horse every day and, without asking, Larry would sometimes ride her horse around the baseball field trying to get it to perform rodeo tricks. Another time, perhaps apocryphally, Larry was on skis making love to a young lady, also on skis, when they began to slide out of the woods toward the lift line, so fell down on purpose, and told all their friends about it later. And Larry kept a striking photo of his mother on his bureau. One of his roommates, Jim Barter, who would become a nationally prominent psychiatrist, recalled coming into his room on the first day of school: "There was this showgirl in a very skimpy costume on the mirror and I looked at it and made some sexist gross remark... And Larry said to me, that's my mother.

I was rather backward, I'd never known anyone's mother ran around looking like that. But I don't think he was peeved, I think he was just setting me straight. It was an interesting picture for a kid to have of his mother."

Both these boys came from broken homes. Larry's father was still back in Texas, his mother was remarried, and Larry had become an unruly kid who was always getting in trouble, until the Country School recognized the charm in his excesses. Jim's father had simply disappeared. Jim had taken his last name from the stepfather who had been kind to him, but had died. He had nine half-siblings and another stepfather who beat him, and he had spent most of the previous two years in jail or corrective institutions. In contrast to Larry, Jim no longer courted trouble, but preferred lying low ("I tried to blend in with the wallpaper"), to the point of hiding in the closet one night when his roommates decided to drink. The fourth roommate, also from a broken family, was Walter Walker, a talented artist and, contradictorily, a big, combative kid unafraid of any situation, who won David Bailey's gratitude more than once by keeping marauding townies at bay. These three, together with Roger Phillips whose family was still together but unhinged, reflect the kinds of needs and desires that filled the school with energy and ferment from the opening day.

The physical campus, focussed as it was on Greenhithe, heightened the sense of shared experience, common enterprise, community. All the boarding girls lived there, as well as two teachers. Everyone ate three meals there every day, as well as morning snacks and afternoon tea, all of which were served and cleaned up by the students. Some of the classes were in Greenhithe, as were most committee meetings and all school meetings where the community debated and decided how best to express its institutional values. Most of all, Greenhithe was the school's social center, not just for dances and other Saturday night entertainments, but for all those in-between moments and hanging out which let young lives take their own forms.

The powerful sense of community that suffused school life fills the pages of Symposium, which began as a mimeographed, student-run publication of universal purpose: "Our columns are open to members of the faculty as well as persons outside the school." The March 1946 Symposium carried this brief, lead editorial: "This issue of the school magazine is somewhat different in that we have been able to afford to have it printed. Subscriptions remain the sole source of income as heretofore. Without endowment, and independent of the faculty, the Symposium is run by the students, and the articles and poems included in it are printed without censorship. For this privilege we are indebted to co-directors Mr. Kenneth Webb and Mr. David Bailey."

The earliest Symposiums offer a kind of literate, collective family album, reflecting the eclectic intellectual life of the school according to the taste of its continually changing editors. While including some of the usual precocious poetry and fiction of bright high school magazines, Symposium also included articles about the school, the town of Woodstock and the world, as well as reviews of plays, concerts and other cultural events. One report on the school listed the 103 books (79 titles) read by 22 students in grades 8 through 12 English classes during the fall term, adding: "The average number of books perused in this period is almost five per person. Some students, of course, read less than this average figure – but in no case less than three. Pat Malet, Walter Walker and James Barter devoured eight, twelve, and fourteen volumes respectively."

Some of the non-school subjects students chose to write about were the peacetime military draft, the Civil War battle at Chancellorsville, the Trusteeship System and the Mandate System, figure skating, the Lost Continent of Atlantis, Richard Wright's *Native Son* and deceptive political messages in comic books.

Among faculty, Ken Webb contributed an article answering the question "What Is a Friends' Meeting?" Bob Lake wrote about building the school's new ski tow and Faith Murray described some student artwork. In particular, she mentioned Walter Walker's explanation of a strange recent painting: "One late afternoon a friend of mine who was then quite young went walking in a graveyard. She wanted to see if there were any skeletons about. Suddenly she heard a mourning dove and it frightened her. I wanted to paint the way the mourning dove made her feel."

As well as the generally, much more playful and familiar work (landscapes, a dream of Indians, sculpted animals, a self-portrait and a Madonna and Child), the art teacher wrote about a student who had fled with his family from Nazi Germany: "During this past month Klaus Heimann has produced two pictures well worth mentioning – one of a very tough-looking helmeted God of War blowing an atomic bomb through a pea-shooter at the world, which hangs from a lamp-post; the other, just as dramatic, is of a bearded criminal being questioned under the strong yellow beam of a spot-light." Klaus Heimann also wrote a bitterly wry piece about the use of surplus war material. Among his suggestions: "Bayonets would make fine can-openers and they might be used by the enraged wife on her spouse."

Woodstock's first term ended with the school's first dramatic production, a short Nativity play put on in the back of the Barn, where a few students kept their horses and the school had some livestock, including a cow. Peggy Bailey wrote the script and directed it, Larry Hagman sang a Christmas carol and, with great serendipity, the cow lowed at the end as if on cue.

## Mary Lea Johnson '46, Phebe Brown '46, Jim Barter '48, editors of *Symposium*, December 16, 1945

*Dear Santa,*

*If you don't come down the chimney this Christmas, we'll understand.*

*There are others whose needs are greater than ours, Senators Bilbo and Wheeler, for example.*

*We know that your time is limited just a day's time; and there are always a few persons who require special consideration. But if you have a chance, won't you look in on Java, India, China, Greece, Middle Europe and certain South American so-called republics.*

*And if you have a moment to spare, won't you look in on our Oakies, our sharecroppers, our unemployed veterans, our Jews distasteful to Mr. Coughlin, and our negroes.*

*We hope you can make it now in December 1945, for, to tell you the truth, a lot of people in this world are losing faith in Santa Claus.*

## Ken Webb, WCS 1946-47 Handbook, summer 1946

*Woodstock has always looked with disfavor on the multiplication of rules, preferring to rely on the natural good sense and cooperativeness of boys and girls. Most of the procedure herein outlined should be regarded as the smoothest way, in the mature consideration of a number of people who have worked on the matter, to achieve that gracious and cooperative living with which our close-knit community can be truly happy...*

*Loss of privileges, penalties, punishments etc.*

*Smoking in or about the dormitories, except as it may be permitted by faculty members in their own rooms, constitutes a fire hazard which cannot be tolerated and will make a student liable to expulsion. Breaking the smoking rules in any other way will mean loss of the privilege for a definite time.*

*Having in one's possession or drinking any intoxicating beverage anywhere in Woodstock will make a student subject to expulsion.*

*Both of these misdemeanors are adjudged by the Discipline Committee.*

*THESE RULES REGARDING TOBACCO AND INTOXICANTS HOLD WHETHER SCHOOL IS IN SESSION OR NOT.*

*Lateness in getting to the dormitory in the evening, lateness to bed or talking after 'taps' will mean no snacks. Lateness to class or other school appointments, or coming to the table with dirty face or hands, will mean making up at a special Saturday afternoon study hall double the time lost in the tardiness or in washing up for the meal in question.*

*Messiness in the dormitory mill lead to an assignment of scrubbing the cellar stairs, the porch floor, or the brickwork of the fireplaces. Coming to the table with unsuitable or untidy dress will mean being sent away to change and the time thus lost made up in Saturday study hall. Going downtown with unsuitable or untidy dress will mean deprivation of the downtown privilege.*

*Clothing, books, or other possessions left around the building will be collected for the pound and redeemable for ten cents an article.*

*Borrowing of others' books, clothing or other possessions without express permission of the owner will be treated as stealing and dealt with by the discipline committee"* (comprising the co-directors and two other teachers).

• • •

Ken Webb wrote the first and only WCS Handbook to help new students get to know the school in the fall of 1946 and to remind old students of the rules and customs that had been established during the first year. The moral accountant style of this summary was never the actual style of life in the school. Nevertheless, the moral accountability implicit in the handbook remained part of the school's code for more than thirty years of its existence. The difference in this emphasis derived from the different styles of the co-directors. As Ken defined their relationship in the handbook: "The school is set up under a system of shared responsibility, David Bailey or Kenneth Webb being responsible for its entire administration except for the financial control, for which Standish Deake (see Chapter 3) as business manager and comptroller is responsible directly to the Board of Trustees... In general, David Bailey is responsible for students' individual problems, their daily program including sports and studies; Kenneth Webb for the curriculum, including study hours etc., for the work program, entertainment, lecture and conference program, 'public relations,' and for all publications of the school, including this handbook."

David generally accepted students for who they were, adolescents who were bound to make mistakes. He believed they needed the freedom to make mistakes if they were to learn from them. And he trusted most of his students would learn enough from their little mistakes to keep from making great ones. But he could, and did, deal strictly with those who pushed the limits too hard. He eventually expelled Larry Hagman for one offense too many, but it was both serious and a harbinger of future crises, although this one was relatively minor. There was a fire in the boys dorm at The Green, forcing a temporary evacuation, but causing only limited damage. As the story goes, several boys were smoking illegally in a bathroon and someone tossed a lit cigarette out the window. It landed in a gutter full of dry leaves, and caught fire. Larry Hagman, for whatever reason, took responsibility and was separated from the school. But for most of the students, the school's freedom was more intimidating than enticing and the system worked, or at least taught students as they matured that they could misbehave more or less at will so long as they were discreet.

"David's way of controlling was different from Ken's," recalled Gerry Freund '48, David's friend and admirer for 35 years. "David's way of controlling provided a tent within which you could operate with a lot of freedom," said Gerry. "Ken Webb's authoritarianism applied to every single piece of your behavior. But David changed during the course of the years of his headmastership and there was no consistency. There were times when David would tolerate and then there were times when David would excise students, sometimes in groups, simply deciding that they weren't for this experience. Nevertheless, he infected his students. He gave freedom. He was capricious. He was the arbiter of this school. It was a one-person school. There was never a possibility of anyone's competing for the center of attention. If they did, they would leave."

Perhaps the greatest expression of freedom during the first year of the school was that the students had some say in what the rules would be and much more of a role in deciding how they would be enforced. Years later, David described the results: "It was James Barter who with us adults helped to organize the first student government arrangement, the student council, which we thereafter felt was the most important element in all the years that we ran the school (until 1967). Right from the start, we set up a student council so that it directly represented their electorate. Each academic grade elected a representative and each dormitory elected one or more representatives, depending on the size of the dorm. This system prevailed for over 20 years. The student government system was not unique with us, but was indicative of the fact that our school was student oriented."

The student council's responsibilities varied over the years, but they generally included such jobs as running the dorms, supervising study halls and serving as the ODA, the OD's assistant. Each day a different faculty member was designated as OD, "officer of the day" in charge of running the school, responsible for making sure that students came to chapel and meals, attended classes and study halls and signed out for afternoon and evening activities – and sometimes more demanding, accounting for those who were missing. Much of this was delegated to the ODA, along with running errands, greeting visitors and answering the school phone after the secretary went home. In addition to this sort of helping to paint Tom Sawyer's fence, student council members were also expected to report any students they saw breaking rules, an expectation more honored in the breach than the observance by most students. The council was also called on to sit in judgment on its fellow students, even its own members, when deciding who should get special privileges. Council meetings almost always included a faculty advisor (usually David), and final judgment on council decisions was reserved to the faculty or co-directors.

The inherent contradiction in this arrangement (the shared illusion of student power without its real substance) would begin to undermine the school in the early 1960s, when students openly expressed their eternal reluctance "to be policemen." After several reorganizations aimed at maintaining some sort of student government, the whole idea vanished in the late 1960s. By then it was faculty members who were openly stating their reluctance "to be policemen," and the school had no coherent central authority remaining to suggest that maybe that was part of a faculty member's job.

During the first years of the school, the student council's functions were not yet fully defined, as Ken noted in the Handbook, adding that "it is part of Woodstock's purpose to give students as much practice as possible in setting up and administering their own democratic government, to turn over an increasing proportion of student activities to their control. The Student Council should not become merely a police force, but should continually be creative in its administration of student affairs." The student council was not created to be a legislative body, although it was encouraged to petition the faculty with its proposals. But even the faculty's legislative authority was sometimes ambiguous. Insofar as the school had a democratic decision-making process, it included the whole community acting in the forum of the weekly school meetings, of which the student council president was the moderator. This arrangement provided the students with some real if limited power over their lives when the institution was new and for most of the school's life in modified forms.

Any new institution struggles to make its reality live up to its ideals. Woodstock's struggle is described in the school's first formal catalog, written by Ken Webb with remarkable frankness in December 1945, after only one term of Woodstock life. The 16-page pamphlet systematically reviewed the school's goals and achievements, as he put it, in theory and in fact.

## Scholarship:

**In Theory,** Woodstock's ideal of Scholarship put a higher emphasis on intellectual integrity than was encouraged by more traditional schools (or the culture at large, one might add): "The school should stimulate intellectual curiosity, should create an interest in good reading, good discussion, in clear, independent thinking, and a desire to continue self-education. It must establish habits of sound scholarship, sure mastery of fundamental skills, and must keep in sight the objective of adequate preparation for college."

**In Fact,** Ken reported, "All the students do not study all the time, and not all assignments are satisfactorily prepared, but the gratifying amount of serious study which is being put into mastery of 'tool subjects' is done with an understanding and a willingness which imply that classes are stimulating. Students have read far beyond the requirements of courses. They have responded eagerly to informal talks and discussions by well-informed guests on a variety of subjects. The writing in the two issues already out of the quarterly mimeographed 'Symposium' shows a surprising breadth of interest, not only in things of the mind, but in the affairs of the world in general. If pupils have not all achieved intellectual curiosity in full measure, they have, as a whole, gained a remarkable degree of awareness of the immediate and the wider community of which they are a part." For most of its first 30 years, Woodstock rightly prided itself on its high academic standards, as it consistently sent its best graduates to the best colleges. But when the school ran into difficulty, declining academic rigor and achievement were among the clearest signs of other, deeper problems.

## Athletics:

**In Theory,** Athletics at Woodstock included regular vigorous outdoor exercise, activity that benefits every muscle and helps to develop a sound body, sports and games played for the joy of playing, team play in which one puts forth all he's got with no thought of self, the building of wholesome attitudes which lead one to value health and physical fitness."

**In Fact**, Ken reported, "Just the work of settling in during the fall term has provided much of our regular physical activity. There have been frequent 'pickup' games, no formal athletics." Eventually, Woodstock would play other schools in soccer, field hockey, ice hockey, basketball and tennis, which replaced baseball in the early 1970s. Woodstock teams usually lost and a .500 season was a rare accomplishment. There were occasional moments of glory, like the 1950 baseball game in which Dave Pope pitched the school's only no-hitter, but sports never became the focus of the school. With most teams having more positions to fill than good players to fill them, athletics remained a source of cooperation much more than competition.

### Religion:

**In Theory**, Religion was to be integral to Woodstock life: "Spiritually, the atmosphere of the school should be definite and vigorous enough to lead students to the conviction that the principles of Christianity are vital, that they afford a satisfying way of life, and that religion can be both a source of strength and a transforming force in individual lives and in society."

**In Fact**, Ken noted, "The attitude of students here in worship services, though often impatient of the formalism of traditional ritualistic worship, is not only serious but reverent. Visitors who have attended occasional Sunday vespers or daily chapel, both types of service conducted by the students, have commented on their feeling and sincerity." The brief morning chapel was usually nondenominational, if not nonreligious, led by faculty, students, or visitors who sometimes sang hymns and prayed and other times played jazz, read poetry, or talked about public issues. Vespers was likely to be more traditionally Protestant, as when Elizabeth Johnson gave her sermon titled "Get Thee Behind Me Satan," but it could also take the form of a Quaker meeting or a discussion of military conscription. However, no religion, not even Ken's Quakerism, ever became a focus for the school. Like sports, religion remained more an opportunity for communal cooperation than doctrinal competition.

### Esthetics:

**In Theory**, with Esthetics, "We would have students gain here a sensitivity to beauty and a realization that everyone has some modicum of ability which can lead to satisfaction in art and music. Everyone should do enough painting and drawing and sculpture to appreciate good art; everyone should know the joy of an hour around the piano singing."

**In Fact**, Ken wrote, "Every student has had the experience of drawing and painting, some of the boys most unwillingly at first, but later with an interest which has broken down barriers of diffidence, self-consciousness, and belief that such pursuits are 'sissy.'" Art and music, and later Drama, would continue to provide esthetic focus for the school for most of its life.

## Democracy:

**In Theory**, Woodstock was a strong proponent of Democracy: "Education to be fully rounded must include training in cooperation and democratic living, in the realization that each individual has responsibilities toward the community as a whole. Students should have the experience of governing themselves in the many areas where this is possible."

**In Fact**, Ken acknowledged, "we see many small failures in cooperation, in democratic procedure, yet necessary work gets done, someone is always ready to help when help is needed; and students are actually learning what democracy is, how it can be properly used, even what its diseases are, such as indifference, pressure groups, unawareness of the demagogue." Democratic processes and decision-making, and their implicit power struggles, would be an increasingly important part of the school for most of its history.

## Work:

**In Theory**, the school saw great value in Work: "The students should have the opportunity to do most of the work necessary to the daily life of the community. To strengthen and broaden this work experience, there should be a farm to teach responsibility, respect for work, and appreciation of the labor involved in the production of so many things we take for granted."

**In Fact**, Ken wrote, "The farm is full of plans, not achievement, at present. We have been able to give students opportunity for realistic work, even in caring for a cow, 3 goats, 4 horses, and a miscellaneous assortment of calves, turkeys, chickens, and pigs. This spring a large garden, mainly of fall crops, will be planted, and by next autumn, with somewhat more stock, we should begin to have a truly productive farm unit."

FALL 1945 – SPRING 1948

• • •

Woodstock's farm operation would never become a fully realized part of the institution, like the farm at the Putney School. What Woodstock maintained was a perpetual fantasy of farming, in the form of a peripheral farm operation, even after the school hired a fulltime farmer in 1958. Varying numbers of devoted students worked on the farm or in the stables over the years, but never involved the whole school. All students participated in a student work program, cleaning the school and feeding the community every day. Throughout Woodstock's history, every student had an assigned, rotating work job as well as assigned dorm jobs.

The first WCS catalog concludes with a characteristic Ken Webb passage: "This 1946-47 catalog of the Woodstock Country School was written at the end of the school's first term. A comparison with the [prospectus], issued before the school had started, will show minor changes in what we had hoped to do. The deviations from the script, however, are mainly the result of extemporization to meet an unforeseen situation and are proof of a desirable flexibility. Parents who wrote us or talked with us during the Christmas vacation were as enthusiastic as the students about a school where they treat you like human beings: you have some freedom, but you work harder than you ever did when everything was forced on you."

Being treated like a human being was always at the core of being at Woodstock, although its meaning was not constant. The real education, which the catalog only hinted at, was social, in the broadest sense. The egalitarianism implicit, for example, in calling teachers by their first names was a little unsettling for many students at first. Even in Symposium, the traditional "Mr." and "Mrs." prevailed for most teachers, but not all. The first name style was always one of the hardest aspects of Woodstock life for outsiders to accept. They usually complained that calling teachers by their first names demonstrated a lack of respect. Given time, they often came to understand that the opposite was true. The formalism of respect so ritualized in other schools often masked a profound disrespect of teachers and students for each other, behind a hypocritical façade of good manners, which bred cynicism. Seeking to avoid that, the first name basis at Woodstock, while expecting genuine civility, still left teachers and students alike free to win or lose respect on the basis of the authenticity of their actions and personal qualities. They were all directly responsible for their own behavior and so could learn to value others and themselves, not for the superficialities of age or rank, but for whatever goodness was in them.

Just as fundamental to Woodstock life was coeducation. The word does not appear in the catalog, which defines the school as "a college preparatory school for boys and girls" on the title page and then says no more about the genders. But there they are in all the pictures, boys and girls together, boys and girls very decorously together to be sure, but together in classes, together in meetings, together riding horses, together feeding turkeys, together singing around the piano. Some other "coeducational" schools of the time prohibited boys and girls from holding hands and even the Putney School kept its students tightly scheduled in an effort to keep their energies appropriately channeled. But at Woodstock, coeducation was an expression of sexual equality and integration, as boys and girls were together in every part of the school except the dorms. Yet, the catalog does not discuss the way coeducation suffused daily life at the school. Nor does it discuss the underlying reason: that emotional growth was just as important as intellectual growth, with the implicit corollary that to achieve real emotional growth, young people must be free to have real emotional relationships with each other.

This side of the school, the students' non-academic life, was David Bailey's main responsibility, by mutual agreement with Ken. David was more relaxed about it all than Ken would have been, so that even as Ken was summing up Woodstock's first term with public optimism in the catalog, he was already having private misgivings about his working relationship with David, and its effect, good and bad, on the school.

### Ken Webb diary entry, January 15, 1946

*Well, we got our school going, and then began the most grueling three months I've ever spent. Thank God the organization period is over now, and with the three wks at Xmas, I have been able to get rested. Arranged with David to handle by myself the promotion and town relations, to keep a voice in matters of major policy, teachers etc., and am now much happier, more relaxed, and interested again in the school. I've made adjustment to the different attitudes of David, and see how I can work around them, eventually bring the school out to about the position I want it to maintain. It gives me really exactly the position I want, for I am quite free, quite able to cultivate contacts on the outside without keeping my nose too closely to the grindstone. Then I have the camps in which to exercise complete executive power which is also pleasant. I really think that David's casualness is making of the school a more deliteful place for kids than it might have been with me. I guess not, but a splendid atmosphere has certainly been created.*

## Jim Barter '48 interview, February 21, 1985

*The school was pretty disorganized, I think. I came from a school which was very rigid, very organized, and I remember there were all kinds of problems in deciding what the rules were. I remember one of the big controversies early on was whether or not students would be allowed to smoke, and then where they would be allowed to smoke. The final compromise was to have a smoking area by the flagpole, so all the kids who smoked had to go up to the flagpole. Instead of making a rule that you could or couldn't smoke, what they did was to make smoking as unpleasant as can be. David smoked like a chimney, so he wasn't one who could enforce smoking rules, but Ken didn't smoke and I remember there was a real kind of democratic process that went on, meetings and discussions, and I think the decision about having a smoking area came out of these meetings. That first year there was a lot of that process, where things would be talked out and I have the sense that there was a lot of byplay between Ken and David about the way things should be run, and I have the sense that there were a lot of times when they weren't together.*

## Roger Phillips '49 interview, May 17, 1984

*There was tremendous rivalry between Ken Webb and David. Not any outright competition, just that they were very different people. Ken was kind of a square, he didn't smoke, he was a very different man from David. Ken wasn't at all interested in sports, although yes, he'd be outdoors chopping wood. David used to read the box scores as soon as he'd get the paper, the first thing he'd turn to would be the Red Sox. Most of the kids really liked David and didn't like Ken and it was kind of unfortunate, although David never slandered Ken at all. Never that I remember did he ever speak badly of Ken. But they were such different people that they were destined to part. I mean Ken Webb would seem so out of place at a cocktail party and David, that was David's natural habitat.*

## David Bailey self-tape, January 1981

*Listening, mostly silently, is such a valuable weapon, as it has been for all the centuries, not as a confessional but as a most useful instrument. It performs great service to school people, particularly in a small, informal type of place such as ours.*

• • •

Of all the differences between Ken and David, none was more important than the way they related to students. And probably no other factor contributed more to Ken's leaving the school. Ken worried in his diary about his relationships with students, he fretted about not liking them and their not liking him, but he was never able to resolve these difficulties, least of all to his own satisfaction. Ken was never fully comfortable with adolescents, he was not terribly sympathetic to adolescent problems, and he tended to prefer absolute solutions universally applied, rather than adopting a child-by-child approach that was, or might seem to him, inconsistent. Little wonder, then, that Ken was drawn increasingly to his camps in Plymouth, not merely because they ran only in the summer, and because they were dedicated to play – serious play oftentimes, but play nonetheless – most of all because they were populated by younger children, most of them pre-adolescent.

While Ken certainly had some friends among the students and was widely respected as a teacher, he was also the butt of communal jokes. No headmaster, least of all a co-director with an integral, powerful rival, can easily survive in such an atmosphere (as other heads of the Country School, even without rivals, would learn again in later years).

David, on the other hand, liked adolescent young people. He enjoyed their company, their struggles, their freshness, their difficulties and all the messy and charming loose ends that go with the age. He revelled in the challenge of getting a troubled child to come out all right and, most of all, he believed the school could do better with most kids than their parents could. Although he played games with the students, sports, parlor games, bridge and chess, as well as more complex mind games, he was never trying to be one of them. He always maintained a certain distance as the adult, the authority-figure, the headmaster, no matter how teasing and silly his behavior might get.

For many, perhaps most Country School students, David's character, with all its contradictions, surprises and inconsistencies, offered a vital, pleasant, or, at worst, neutral center for a school experience that was more exciting and varied than most students had ever thought possible. People who knew Woodstock in its best periods over 30 years commonly use words like "paradise" or "magic" to describe the experience. Even Peggy Bailey, David's wife, who sometimes considered David's flexibility in his dealings with the children too lenient, nevertheless acknowledged: "with all his faults, God knows we all have faults, David had this kind of magic touch with the young," which eluded her description and remained essentially mystical. (David Bailey's style is explored more fully in Chapter 3.)

For all his real or imagined inconsistencies and contradictions, David's values were universally perceived as different from those of Ken Webb, whether for better or worse. Their fundamental difference was that Ken believed students should be taught and therefore discipline should be imposed by others, whereas David believed students would learn to learn and therefore self-discipline should be encouraged, even at the risk of self-indulgence. In practice, their differences rarely seemed so stark, but were expressed in more subtle gestures of nuance and emphasis, of personal style. And it was David's style, his "casualness," that made Woodstock such a "deliteful place... (with a) splendid atmosphere," as Ken observed at the end of the very first term. Even then, Ken was giving ground to David's "different attitudes" rather than challenging them, though he still hoped to work around them to make the school conform more to his own vision somehow, some day. While it would be another two and a half years before he was fully separated from Woodstock, Ken would never again seriously challenge David's authority in the school. What is strange about their relationship is not that they should contend for control of the institution, but that the contest should be so covert between them and, at the same time, so keenly felt in the school community.

As Ken remembered it years later, real communication between him and David diminished to a minimal level within a few weeks after Woodstock opened. Ken did not write in his diary at all during that first term, but by the winter he was clearly detaching himself from too close involvement in the school. Only a few months before, his optimistic five-year plan for the school had been followed by a second five-year plan. By January 1946, he was thinking of five years as his maximum commitment to the Country School: "This five years will be very pleasant, I am sure, for David and I have found out how to work together. Then when the five years are up, I'll have a following to call on for help with the cooperative school" (which Ken planned for years at Camp Timberlake, but which never came into being)."

For all his repeated optimism about learning to work with David, Ken seemed more engaged in psychological cheerleading to keep his own spirits up than in making an accurate assessment of day-to-day reality, in which most of the school looked to David for the final decision in disputes. Insofar as Ken believed his own optimism, he was effectively denying his workday reality. By the end of that first term, the struggle for control of the school, which would seem to others to take years, was effectively over and David had won. Woodstock was becoming David's school.

There is no evidence that Ken and David ever made any serious, direct attempt to resolve their differences. Nor is there any evidence that Elizabeth Johnson, Owen Moon, or anyone else with influence with either man, ever sought to bring them closer together. There was no explosion, no confrontation, no effort to clear the air, not just in 1945, but also for the rest of both of their lives. As Ken put it, "We never had a fight, never came to blows, never had anything of that sort. We were just not on the same wavelength." And Susan recalled that "Ken was always optimistic that his and David's differences could be resolved, until he finally recognized that basically they differed too much." Ken and David went on working together like good, stoic New Englanders, they colluded in unspoken denial and carried on as if there were no differences between them, or as if those differences would somehow resolve themselves, or as if those differences didn't really matter. They acted as if no one could see the differences between them, when of course anyone who looked could see them plainly. While they might persuade themselves that they were keeping their conflicts hidden, it was an illusion to think they could hide that reality from 35 bright adolescents, many of whom had long since learned to sense much subtler signs of trouble in their natural families. While denying their differences allowed the co-directors to believe they presented the appearance of unity, in practice there was no way to neutralize their conflict as the community struggled to decide what kind of school it was. Among the issues that clearly put Ken and David on different sides were smoking and editorial freedom for Symposium.

Given his own way, Ken would have prohibited smoking altogether. But because David and other staff members smoked heavily, as did many students, and even more because Ken believed in the democratic process for the school, it was an issue he could not win. Nevertheless, he kept trying, recording in his diary on February 2, 1946, "The school meeting decided to shelve the constitution for two months at any rate, which gives us the best setting for the few but important changes which I feel should be made next year. One will be restriction of smoking to recess and a half hour after supper, and only on the porch [of

Greenhithe]." As it turned out, that constitution never came off the shelf and smoking was never so restricted.

As the faculty advisor for Symposium, Ken warned the students not to publish a mocking account of local Halloween festivities for fear of offending local sensibilities. From the start, Ken had been more worried about town relations than David. Ken wanted the school to play an active role in the community (though never quite spelled out how the school could do that). With the Halloween account blocked, the student editors appealed to David. He told them he saw no harm in it and had no objection to seeing it in print. Years later, this contradiction still rankled Ken, even as he acknowledged that he and David had never discussed the issue: "I never brought it up to him. It was done, there was no point in pursuing it. I didn't want to have an open fight with him. I wanted to get along as best we could. So I guess a number of times I gave in when maybe I shouldn't have. But it seemed best in the long run to do that. I didn't want to see the school go under when I left it."

When Ken and David did work jointly on a problem, there could be an odd tentativeness to their approach, as when they realized that each of them had independently decided they did not wish to rehire social studies teacher Bert Sarason. Although Bert was bright and able enough (he went on to a position as an assistant professor of English at New Haven State Teacher's College), the co-directors perceived him at 21 having a hostile spirit, a chip on his shoulder all the time no doubt having heard about his classroom digressions. When the issue first came up in January 1946, Ken and David merely talked to Bert about whether or not he should return to the school the following fall. A few days later, they talked to Elizabeth Johnson about the problem. Ken wrote in his diary, "She said definitely that we should make a change now without any doubt. So, we will... It is a great relief to me, for I had said that we should, but was uncertain whether to force the issue." Even so, they hesitated. Five days later, Ken recorded that he and David "decided definitely to refuse Bert a contract for another year. Feel better now that we have, tho also regretful." But it was still not finally done for another eleven days, having taken three weeks.

Another area of fundamental difference between David and Ken was religion. The Webbs were devoted Quakers and Ken surrendered the idea of having a Quaker school only slowly as his efforts at friendly persuasion proved fruitless. David was neither an anti-religious man, nor an overtly religious one. He was Episcopalian. As long as he ran the school, there was chapel every morning, vespers every Sunday and the usually mild, pro forma religious flavor common to baccalaureate, commencement and similar occasions. The chapels and vespers were sometimes traditional services with hymns and prayers, but perhaps as often they were taken over by faculty, students or visitors who talked about concerns that were not immediately recognizable as religious, things like jazz, poetry or military conscription. There was never any question that Woodstock would be anything but nominally Christian in a nominally Christian society. For David that meant a lack of insistence on ritual or dogma, a broad tolerance of diversity, the essence of the gospel of Mark 9:40, "For he that is not against us is for us." That spirit of confident acceptance has always been rare in religious or secular life.

When it came to enforcing school rules, this same tolerance on David's part caused constant friction with Ken. The issue almost came to a head in November of the school's second year, when Ken caught a trusted senior hunting deer at his camps in Plymouth. The student was Bob Green, the Navy veteran, who had taken on extra responsibilities helping to run the boys' dorm. Ken wanted him dealt with harshly. David felt otherwise and his more lenient view prevailed. (The following February, the faculty would vote 7-2 to expel another student and David would still keep him as well, albeit on strict probation.) Some weeks after the Green episode, Ken wrote glancingly about it and about the effort he was making to improve his relationships with students, concluding: "I like the kids better, like the chance to talk with them, and I think that gradually I am going to see a definite change as I see indications now of a change in attitude toward me. In fact, tho Susan and I were disgusted with the handling of the Green case and ready to quit the end of the year, this afternoon's faculty meeting with its struggle over the question of smoking rather restored our faith that all lesser problems can be worked out on as rational a basis. What I should like to do is stay with the school in present capacity one more year. Not only will I learn much more about the problems of a school, but it will be so good for me to work out my own problems of personal adjustment, and that problem has got to be worked out before we begin our school. I can have a radiant, gay, and loving personality if only I can let the best in me keep ascendancy all the time."

That was as close as the Webbs came to precipitate action. Their leave-taking from the school was long and gradual, so gradual in fact that Peggy Bailey couldn't remember, "whether it was at the end of the second year or the third year that Ken Webb withdrew from the school."

Even Ken's daughter, Sukie, a Woodstock student for the first four years, had no sharp memory of his departure. She said his leaving caused no significant shift in the school, that to her Woodstock seemed the same during all her time there. Others also have trouble recalling the chronology of Ken's leaving, and with good reason, since Ken detached himself slowly, by degrees, as he gave over the day-to-day running of the school to David, while focussing his own energies increasingly on program organization, public relations and fund raising (and he found even his work of choice becoming harder and harder during the second year). At the same time, he was increasingly distracted by the demands of his growing camps (there would be six in all).

In January 1947, Ken decided he would leave the school, in April, he formally resigned as co-director and vice president of the trustees. The board accepted his resignation and created the one-year position of field director for him for 1947-48, meaning he spent most of his final year with the Country School off campus, away from David and the students.

Thirty-five years later, after David's emphysema had forced his own early retirement; after the school had closed; after David had died and after the Webbs had retired from their successful camps, that are now run by the Farm and Wilderness Foundation, Susan Webb thought the most difficult difference between Ken and David had been their views of "discipline." In their joint interview, the Webbs summed up their Country school experience this way:

**Susan Webb**: *Ken's feeling was that if somebody was caught smoking, you might give them one chance to improve, but you didn't give them two. They went out. And we weren't afraid to. Ken felt strongly that if a person agreed not to smoke at the school but continually did it, that he was simply thrown out of the school. Just as we send a boy home from the camp here, because he knows he's agreed not to smoke when he comes and we find that he's doing it. He undoubtedly has other problems, too. But David wouldn't do that. David would not clamp down. And I think also that David was very popular with the students because he wasn't firm enough. When it came to that, he wasn't firm enough with himself, if you don't mind my putting it that way. And Ken is a very disciplined person.*

**Ken Webb**: *There were many ways in which we shared common ideals. But I did believe in discipline. I did believe in structure. And he didn't believe in discipline of any sort, apparently. Of course that's what finally did the school in. He believed in this structureless education with everybody doing what everybody wanted to do. I believed in structure. Not a repressive structure, but enough to keep things going along the right road.*

**Susan Webb**: *I've always felt that if I had been able to change anything, it would have been to put in a stronger feeling of Quaker leadership. Because I think then we would have had the strength of Quaker meetings behind us, and the Yearly Meeting,* *and we would have had certain standards that had to be met. And I think that would have been a good thing for that school.*

**Ken Webb**: *I would have changed the relationship between David and me. Instead of trying to be co-directors, which is impossible, we would have had it out as to which would be head of it. And I think that since, really, it was my idea and my reputation that got the school going, I would have insisted on being head, and having David as second in command, assistant. I think that would have entirely changed the character of the school.*

**Susan Webb**: *And I think we would have given more. You know, I always say that there are some things that you simply, you answer 'No' to, and you have to have the courage to do it.*

**Ken Webb**: *I think we had determined to leave because the camps were growing so, there were six camps, and we just couldn't manage all that and be proud of the school, too. So I thought it was foolish to bring this all to a head, since we had to leave anyway and I'd never change David.*

**Susan Webb**: *Yes, we had to choose. But I think, really, Ken was unwilling to open up all the disagreements, all the difficulties between him and David. It would have torn the school apart, not only the school but the town, we felt, because of loyalties to the Baileys and the whole situation there. And it would have been so difficult that it was easier for us, perhaps it wasn't the best decision, but it was the quietest and most sensible way as we could see it at that time. But I know it's worked out better for us in the long run.*
**Ken Webb**: *Well, of course I believe in calling a spade a spade, if you've got to go into that. But with us, we didn't see that we would gain anything by it, and it would probably destroy the school, because nobody wants to go into a school or put kids into a school where there's a row going on. And that was the reason I never went around to people who helped start the school to explain why I was leaving. And I've always felt guilty that I never cleared that with them. And yet I couldn't do it without seeming to be talking about a split in the school, and it wasn't that either.*

**Susan Webb**: *We didn't tell them all this kind of thing. But we never felt we lost by that.*

FALL 1945 – SPRING 1948

David Ezekiel  Thurston Anderson  Morty Schiff

John Miller  John Bulkley  Sandy Phillips

Joe Bernhardt  Keem Lau Kee  Michael Tucker,
John Sammis

WCS – WOODSTOCK COUNTRY SCHOOL

Rodney Cohn  John Blake  David Pope

Dusty Rhodes  Josie Van der Gracht  Nancy Pinkerton

Janet Gay  Anne Stanley  Violet McClusky

FALL 1945 – SPRING 1948

Nancy Bradley    Betty Sommers    Molly Blake

Harriet McMahan    Ann Coleman    Judy Fisher

Jackie Trask    Sheila Spencer    Jane Fisher

David Bailey

FALL 1945 – SPRING 1948

Geology field trip to Dartmouth (l. to r.): Mary Lou Dunker, Nancy Bradley, Polly Oatfield, Ann Rutherford, (back row) R. Jones, T. Weekley

Cellar hole swimming pool (l. to r.):
Ann Wycoff, Midge Murphy, Kay Batten, Lillian Russell, Polly Oatfield,
Mary Lois Doggett, Mary Lou Dunker, Veda Toucey

Mary Lois Doggett receiving diploma from David Bailey,
on Greenhithe lawn, June 1947

David Bailey (center) and Buffy Dunker (to his left),
surrounded by students at the WCS swimming pool in an old house stone
foundation, just up the hill from Greenhithe, circa 1947

CHAPTER THREE

# Summer 1948 – Summer 1951

### Buffy Dunker interview, May 2, 1983

*I know a lot of women had a crush on him, I mean I was just like gaga for about a year and a half, or something like that. He was a very sexual person. I mean the way he looked down at some of the girls – it would just send them. And the other part of his personality, particularly early on, was that he was what people felt was vague. Therefore, when kids got to the school, they used David for whatever figure they needed to relate to. He could become the stern father, he could be the inspiring older brother, he could be the loving, forgiving father to the Queen's taste – for lots of the girls that was true, and some of the boys – he could be a tremendous rival, any image that needed to be filled out for those kids. He could be any kind of father that the kids wanted, particularly because he only acted it out right there in the middle of the Common Room. He never acted things out in a way that upset those fantasies in a destructive way.*

## Obituary of David's father, Walter Channing Bailey, M.D., 67, died July 30, 1938

*Dr. Bailey was a good executive because he managed to do things in a smooth and effortless way, with a minimum of fuss and confusion, and a complete intuitive understanding of the people with whom he was dealing. Someone who loved him wrote, "He thought we were nice people, and so we <u>were</u> nice people." He brought out the best in all his friends and his family, and they, in turn, adored him.*

## David Bailey self-tape, January 1981

*This minor memorial should be graced with a title and I suggest we consider "Felicity Awhile" from the famous final death speech of <u>Hamlet</u>. The first word indicates that Woodstock was a happy community of old and young, of staff and student. The second word implies essence to the point of mortality. It is quite possible the school will never be duplicated, nor even well imitated. And now it is time to perhaps consider where its ideas came from, where they originated. I can state that there was not an educational philosophgy as such it its origin, rather it came from an amalgam of the influences on my life and those of Peggy.*

*To begin with, I emerged from an aristocratic family, which had interests primarily in people and their needs. My schooling varied, ranging from traditional public school in Vermont to a traditional prep school in Massachusetts, then to elegant Harvard, and it included various experimental and innovative integrating schools. For example, I began in southern California in Montessori kindergarten, which continued in Washington. Then I attended three schools in Switzerland, one traditional and two quite different, co-educational places. One of these, on the shores of Lake Geneva, was run by an English Quaker lady and a Swiss mathematician. They were both pacifists, of course, and the schol was started after World War I as an international, vegetarian, pacifist school. It was small, and co-ed of course, and lots of fun, and I got a great deal of profit from the experience....*

SUMMER 1948 – SUMMER 1951

> *But after Europe I enrolled in the Shady Hill School in Canbridge, which was one of the early so-called progressive schools under the inspired leadership of Katherine Taylor. This school was also smallish and innovative and very exciting. Its chief feature was top notch instructors. There I had my first contact with live music and with formal art, and with dramatics and with real attempts at literary study.... As a result I learned to recognize, though not to emulate, the quality of mind, of body, and of personal standards.*

By June 1948, when Ken Webb fully dissociated himself from the Woodstock Country School, it had long since become David Bailey's school – emotionally, philosophically and in mundane daily practice. Ken's departure merely made reality official, the same encroaching reality that Ken had acknowledged to himself during the very first term of the school. Since both Ken and David were determined that Woodstock should be student-centered and democratic, it was all but inevitable that David would emerge as the school's dominant personality, the benign and sometimes enigmatic dictator who defined the school's essential character.

"David had a genius for understanding adolescents," recalled Gerry Freund, who came to Woodstock as a student in 1946 and remained close to the school for the rest of its life, serving as a trustee for most of those years. "David was not an adolescent, except that he had something of the spirit of an adolescent. He was able to be an adult who could cool into adolescence. He played his role by playing chess in the common room and drawing people out over different moves. He played his role by being out on the soccer field, encouraging a girl who needed to wear off an enormous energy to compete just as heavily in soccer, I think of one girl in particular, the daughter of a professor at the time, but there were many others. He blew the whistle on people, kind of literally and figuratively, who needed to have the whistle blown on them. Of course, he made mistakes, here as with other things. But he was regarded by all of us as fundamentally well-intentioned and, in that sense, fundamentally fair. He was always pretty remarkably conservative, although for his time, remarkably radical."

David Bailey came by his contradictions honestly, from a mixed background of the restraints of old money and the provocative curiosity of visceral rebelliousness. He, his brother and two sisters grew up in a big house on Boston's Beacon Hill. His father came from an old Boston family, had gone to Harvard and Harvard Medical School, and he was a doctor, a chest specialist. David's father had rather traditional expectations of his children, especially that the boys should go to Harvard, which they did (as did David's son Peter years later).

But neither of the Bailey boys accepted these traditional expectations easily. His older brother, Tad, graduated from Harvard, he went on to art school and a lifelong career as an artist and social activist, very much at odds with mainstream American culture, but very mannerly in his opposition.

David's mother, Ruth Perkins Bailey, was a New Yorker whose natural style was already a bit much for her Bostonian circle. Even though she, too, came from an old moneyed family, had a father who had fought in the Civil War and had been educated at an exclusive girls' school, she was also an independent woman for her time. David's wife, Peggy, remembers her mother-in-law fondly: "She was an aristocrat and was used to having servants and money all her life. She was of an aristocratic family, but also an aristocratic inside, you know, as well. She didn't go on to college, she did the traditional trips in Europe with her mother, who was a very wealthy woman, and there she intensified her love of the beautiful and her taste for exquisite furniture and paintings and all this kind of thing which she collected greatly. She was also physically very brave, much braver than I. Once, as a young woman, when she was alone in one of the great houses that she lived in, a burglar came in and she chased him downstairs and out of the house."

From his mother, David got his independence, his love of the arts, his sociability, even his sense of humor. His father was a taciturn man, always beautifully groomed, very courteous, with great charm – but he rarely spoke. And he spoke even less during his long, lingering illness during David's adolescence and young manhood. Little wonder, then, that David's personal style should have been so oblique, relying as it did so much on sly humor, implication, nonverbal responsiveness and often leaving the most important things unsaid.

Ruth Bailey was devoted to her husband, taking care of him at their home in Barnard, until he died there in 1938. As a widow, she stayed on in Vermont. She took an active interest in local affairs, making friends with Elizabeth Johnson and encouraging the creation of the Country School. She cheerfully contributed her decorating talents, and much of her art and furniture, to making Greenhithe elegant for the opening of the school. "She had a wonderful sense of humor," Peggy Bailey recalls. "Tad and David would both tease her, and she was always good humored about it. Oh, she had, like all of us, she had faults. One of them of course was this extraordinary generosity which verged on extravagance. She was always giving things to people, incredible number of things. Not just to relatives, but to friends and not so good friends, but she was just like that."

David's early education reinforced his independence of character, particularly his years at the Shady Hill School in Cambridge. Years later at Woodstock, he would often draw on ideas and experiences from Shady Hill, adapting them to his Woodstock circumstances. He also went to a progressive, coeducational, vegetarian, pacifist boarding school in Switzerland when he was 16 and his father was one of Herbert Hoover's dollar-a-year men trying to help Europe recover from World War I. His brother and sisters went with him to the Swiss school, about which he recalled none too fondly, "The school was run by a Swiss pacifist – he used to go to jail every year instead of serving his military term. My siblings and I were the only Americans in the school. We used to walk four miles to get the school milk. We used to eat dried flowers. It was a vegetarian school." One of the reasons David was sent to that school was the hope that the rugged mountain regimen would help his tubercular condition, which did in fact clear up. For the rest of his life, he remained vulnerable to heavy colds, pneumonia, pleurisy – and finally the emphysema that cut short his career and his life.

David's increasing disenchantment with his educational experiences culminated at Harvard, where he did not do well and dropped out after two years, largely out of disinterest. About the only positive part of his time at Harvard was studying Shakespeare with the famed scholar George Lyman Kitteridge. Otherwise, he was not getting what he wanted or needed. At the same time, his health was somewhat frail, so that in 1933, when John Rice was recruiting students for first year of his experimental Black Mountain College in North Carolina, that sounded good to David as a fresh learning experience. Black Mountain also sounded good to his parents, as a way to get David into the high and dry mountain climate where his health might improve. There, as it turned out, he would also meet his wife.

### David Baily self-tape, January 1981

*This tiny, experimental place was so exciting and so endowed with brilliant teachers, including the two best I've ever met [John Rice and the painter Josef Albers], that I, and also Peggy, remained at Black Mountain for two years, until we married. It had high academic standards, brilliant art teaching, an appreciation of nature and beauty, and the delight of social communion among all the ages there, with people of different backgrounds and personalities. It was the most valuable and influential educational experience that I had. Its influence had many echoes in the Woodstock endeavor.*

*There was trust among us, and recognition of quality, and appreciation of techniques, an appreciation of the value of the individual, some skill in recognizing the value of different teachers. Here I relearned a precept of the philosopher Alfred North Whitehead, which was* **that the most important human talent and quality was friendliness**, *and of course Woodstock shone with friendliness from us all.... [emphasis added]*

## Hilda Loram (Peggy) Bailey interview, September 1982

*I was born in South Africa, in Durban, in 1910. My mother is Scottish, father was a Colonial. He was born in South Africa, but his family came from Devon. He attended King's College, Cambridge, and during World War I he took his PhD at Columbia, and my sister and I went to the Horace Mann School, which was then one of the very new places. I don't remember very much about that except playing in the sandbox and making plum puddings, which I didn't care for. Then my father, being a government servant in the education department, was moved from Durban to a much smaller town. Since the schools there were not very good, I was educated at home according to my father's plan, which leaned heavily on the humanities, art, music and not very much on science or math, at which none of as were very good.*

• • •

Peggy Loram had learned to read when she was very young and her father gave her the run of his study. "I read everything – a lot of stuff I probably shouldn't have read and I didn't understand, but I read it anyway. My father in some ways had very advanced views on education, in other ways they were quite traditional. But some of my earliest recollections are of my father reading to us at bedtime, which was a nightly ritual, to my sister and myself, and we got through the whole of the Iliad, and the whole of the Odyssey, which we enjoyed enormously. When we played games, my sister and I, we dramatized the Canterbury Tales, and Treasure Island, and things like that."

Charles Templeton Loram, Peggy's father, made his career in government education, starting as a teacher, moving up to school inspector, travelling around the country (often on horseback), eventually rising in the bureaucracy to become Commissioner of Education for South Africa under Prime Minister Jan Christiaan

Smuts in the 1920s. Loram's views on race were remarkably progressive for the time, as he strongly believed black South Africans could and should be educated, and that as many as possible should go to college. But he also believed blacks should be patient and not expect everything at once, that progress would be a long, slow process. Loram learned to speak the Zulu language and he had black household servants whose conditions and devotion recall the romanticized version of the antebellum American south. After Smuts left office in 1924 and the Conservatives started moving South Africa towards apartheid, Loram's politics became increasingly untenable. In 1931, he left his homeland and accepted appointment as Sterling Professor of Education at Yale, where he founded and chaired the Department of Race Relations — which lasted only until he died in 1940.

While her father was in government, Peggy went to a very disciplined and traditional girls' school in Cape Town, where she did well academically and was allowed to take special classes in ballet and art (she loved to draw). Upon graduation, she was accepted into the University of Cape Town, but her father thought she could get into Oxford if she had a post-graduate year in England. So, she spent a rather unhappy year at St. Swithins, a very traditional girls' school in Winchester, concentrating on the Latin, Greek and French, which had been the focus of her studies in Cape Town. In the spring, she took the exams for Lady Margaret College in Oxford. She did not do well enough to be accepted, but the college advised her that, with another year of study at St. Swithins, she would probably get in.

Peggy did not feel that going to Oxford was worth the price of another year in Winchester. Besides, by then her father was moving the whole family to the United States. Seeking the American equivalent of Oxford, Loram turned to Swarthmore, whose president had been his classmate in Cambridge. Travelling in England at the time, Swarthmore's president interviewed Peggy and accepted her as a sophomore, starting in the fall of 1929. "I gave up languages, much to my father's disgust," Peggy remembered, "but I felt I was just going to have to work too terribly hard at it. I went back to my old love, which was English. I inherited my devotion to literature from my father. His lack of knowledge and lack of skill in science and math, too, probably influenced me, although I'm sure basically it was just my incompetence in the subject. I hated math, I never had any real science courses. He himself had never been particularly interested in any of that. Books were his forte, not just the content of books, but the actual handling of them, the number of books, the amount of reading were part of my father's life and it influenced me enormously. For Christmas and birthdays, he always gave us books. I have some of them to this day, very worthwhile books, the old fashioned classics."

Peggy graduated from Swarthmore in 1932, in the midst of the Depression, with honors in English and no job prospects. Her father staked her to a year of graduate study at Columbia, where she earned her Master's in English (Victorian Literature) while finding the work there generally less rigorous than at Swarthmore.

The following spring, her father's old-boy network helped Peggy again as the Swarthmore president's brother-in-law broke away from another college in the south and set out to start his own. The brother-in-law was John Rice, the classics professor whose free spirit had disrupted Rollins College for three years, leading up to his firing and his subsequent decision to start Black Mountain College, taking several Rollins faculty and students with him. In the spring of 1933, Rice was recruiting faculty and the president of Swarthmore recommended Peggy Loram. "I saw him in New York and, after a very brief interview, I left, not knowing what was going to be decided, not being terribly anxious to go there actually it sounded all rather, it was rather, haphazard." Black Mountain hired Peggy at 23 to teach English and, because the college asked people to work for no more than what they needed Peggy (her father comfortably ensconced at Yale), earned $40 plus room and board her first year, $200 her second year.

Besides faculty, Rice also recruited students, among them David Bailey.

### Peggy Bailey interview, September 1982

*We were driving up to Black Mountain. The buildings the college had managed to rent for a mere song belonged to a church, a set of huge white buildings on top of a hill looking over the Blue Ridge Mountains, magnificent views, a perfectly beautiful place. Anyway, we were driving up there and we met this car with a couple of students in it coming the other way. The students in my car hailed these other students, whom they knew, and sitting in the back of the car was this tall, thin young man who was looking down rather menacingly. I learned afterward it was just because the sun was in his eyes and he couldn't see very well. We were introduced rather hastily, and then we passed each other and left. I was told afterwards, by the students in the car David was in, that David had said after we'd passed: 'Very attractive young faculty girl there – I think I'll make some time with her.' They all hooted with laughter, and that was that. Later on, David told me that he did see me very clearly and he even remembered the hat I had on. But here we disagree, because he said I had on a silly hat with a feather in it. I think I had on a large, plain, black, rather Garboesque job, just a plain black hat, one of the soft, floppy ones. No feather, it was quite plain.*

• • •

Even if it had been love at first sight, neither David nor Peggy was the sort of person likely to admit it easily, if ever. Love aside, considerable intimacy was inevitable among the faculty and students at Black Mountain, since it was isolated, small (22 students, 10 teachers and assorted spouses and children), and close-quartered (all but a few faculty families lived in the college's main building, which also held the classrooms and offices).

Peggy was the youngest faculty member and one of only three women instructors. At first she taught a single course, Victorian Literature, but later, despite her lack of experience in almost any phase of the theatre, she was drafted to direct a college production of Congreve's *The Way of the World*, the first play she ever directed (not counting those she put on with the coerced cooperation of her siblings). Finally, her duties included serving as an advisor to students and one of her advisees was David Bailey, who was also in her Victorian Literature class.

"I happened to be chosen to be his advisor, I don't know why, they just picked sort of at random and I was his advisor," Peggy recalled. Martin Duberman, in his history of Black Mountain, reported that the students chose their own advisors, so perhaps David was already "making time". Duberman also described Rice's attitude toward young people, an attitude quite similar to the way David would view adolescents at the Country School: "Adults tended to bring out the peremptory side of Rice more than students did. He showed greater patience with twenty-year-olds because he had greater faith in their ability to change, and where growth was possible Rice preferred to issue invitations rather than commands. He realized that many young people had already given up on themselves by the time they reached college."

David had certainly given up on (or rejected) Harvard and his own natural WASP milieu (though he would never move that far from it). Whether he had begon to give up on himself before Black Mountain found him is uncertaion, but he was surely drifting with no apparent direction in mind. As a student he could be distracted, as Peggy recalled: "It was hard for him to write papers, he took a long time about writing them, and he had to be sort of pushed, though they were good when they were written. He was a good student, but he wasn't always interested in what was going on. I remember one time when I was talking about something and he was reading a newspaper. I told him not to read the newspaper, but he went on. So I told him to leave the room, and he did. This was long before I got to know him very well. I just felt that I couldn't have him doing that. Actually, he read the newspaper because he was always so very interested in contemporary affairs and kept abreast of everything. Later on he came to my study and he apologized. He didn't read the paper in class after that."

When he first went to Black Mountain, David planned to stay only one year. Then, if his health improved and his studies were sound, he would return to Harvard, not because he missed it, but to please his father. His dislike of Harvard increased in the midst of the contrasting institutional freedom and intellectual ferment of Black Mountain. He was influenced, too, by John Rice, especially the philosophy of self-questioning and self-discipline that Rice emphasized in his course on the 18th Century (which David took). And then there was his developing relationship with Peggy. Towards the end of that first year, David decided to stay at Black Mountain for a second year. But to appease the family as best he could, he also decided to take summer courses at Harvard. He asked Peggy to come to Cambridge with him and, when she agreed, he made arrangements for her to live with a friend of the family there. They spent a lot of time together that summer, usually meeting on the steps of Widener Library.

Peggy was first drawn to David by his "enormous charm, a very quick, intelligent mind and an enormous aesthetic capability and appreciation of music and art. He was musical himself, he sang in a little group they had at the college. And he was terribly interested in art. Josef Albers had a great influence on him at Black Mountain, though he himself didn't draw. And then he had an extraordinarily wonderful sense of humor. And he, too, had been rather traditionally educated, that is a great many of the classics and things I'd read, he knew, too, they had been part of his upbringing. And then, of course, there was his interest in other people, which was all consuming – other people, all kinds, all ages, all grades, all ranks of society."

During his second and senior year at Black Mountain, David's interest in other people led him to volunteer as a student teacher at The Cottage School on the college campus. Organized by a faculty member for the younger faculty children, the school also accepted local children (according to Peggy: "the children of the really rural people, who lived up in the hills around us, who came to school barefoot and all this kind of thing"). David was intrigued by the whole experience, his first as a teacher, and he was particularly fascinated by the children's names, like Arlanda, which seemed to him almost Shakespearean.

But being an open, freewheeling Black Mountain experiment, the school soon reached limits beyond which the local children were not willing – or allowed – to go. When discussions of Darwin's theory of evolution came up, the local enrollment dropped off.

By the spring of 1935, David and Peggy had decided to marry, which they did in September. In the meantime, David took his finals, a process that included an all-day oral exam by an outside examiner, which anyone at the college could observe. He passed and graduated from Black Mountain. For the next ten years, David and Peggy Bailey lived the life of itinerant teachers. They went first to the Miquon School near Philadelphia for three years. There David taught fifth grade and Peggy first. The school was going through some hard times then and it wore both of them down. David was frequently sick with bad colds and bronchitis and Peggy eventually resigned with exhaustion.

In the fall of 1938, they returned to Black Mountain College, Peggy to teach English and David to do public relations. The college had never had anyone to do public relations and David persuaded the Board of Fellows to let him do it. By then, Black Mountain had gone through the first of the many purges that punctuated its 23-year history. The founder, John Rice, whom David had admired so much and whose philosophy had so influenced his own, had been forced to leave the college the previous year. Although Rice returned in the fall, he no longer ran the place but was more like an exiled ruler in his own land. With no one else at Black Mountain ready or willing to offer strong leadership as rector, the college chose Robert Wunsch, a rather uninspiring theatre teacher of whom David was much less enamored.

Even though Black Mountain had changed considerably from the place David had loved so much just three years earlier, he worked hard and travelled widely throughout the fall, wearing himself down, until he had to be hospitalized in Washington in mid-winter with pneumonia and pleurisy. "Those were the days when they put great heavy bolsters on either side of you to hold the lung in place," Peggy remembered. "That was when they first told him that he shouldn't smoke. Of course nobody knew anything about emphysema in those days. He tried to stop smoking by chewing gum instead, but then Mr. Rice objected to this, oddly enough, so David went back, very eagerly, to smoking. Oddly enough, Mr. Rice himself smoked a pipe, and he too died of cancer."

At the end of that school year, Wunsch let David go, but he didn't tell David himself, he told Peggy and left it to her to break it to her husband: "It was very hard for him. He was very good about it, but it obviously had hurt him a lot. I don't remember what David said. I remember his just sitting, listening while

I was explaining to him. I think his being ill had a lot to do with it, you see, because obviously he couldn't take the strain of this constant traveling. And then some of his ideas were quite innovative, and there was a certain element of the college that didn't approve."

For the next three years, they lived in New Haven, close to Peggy's parents at Yale. David taught in the grades at the Foot School, which catered primarily to the children of Yale faculty, whom David remembered as the brightest children he ever taught. Peggy did not teach during that time, though she tutored some. Her energies were directed mostly to their son and only child, Peter, who was born in May 1940.

The Baileys moved to northern New Hampshire in the fall of 1942, where David had his first job at a boarding school. They all had a terrible time – Peter had pneumonia, David was hospitalized with bronchitis and then Peggy was hospitalized for exhaustion. On top of that, they were unhappy with the school: there was no library, faculty quarters were meager, the school was poorly run, the faculty were uninspiring, there was a kind of timidity about the whole place.

And if all that weren't enough, Peggy recalled, "There was a terrible accident. David was out supervising a group of boys who were sledding on an icy hill and one of the boys turned over and the sled had those long runners and one of them went right into his head and David had to take care of him. I remember David's coming home with blood all over the front of his coat. David's not good at that sort of thing. He was very good at the time, but I think it must have been a horrible strain. The boy lived, but I think the sight in one eye was permanently damaged. He came back to school eventually and all the kids applauded him, but I think there was something wrong with him. It was terrible. But I don't think that's what made David leave the school. One of the interesting things about David was that he could go through some of these experiences and they would leave a deep mark on him, but they didn't seem to erode him, whereas those experiences for me, such as the five days in the hospital while David was dying, left a permanent mark on me. It will always be there. Now I sometimes felt that with David, he could put those kinds of things behind him and they didn't interfere with what was ahead, which of course was a very good thing to do. He had a resilience which I don't think I have."

The school wanted David to stay, offering him a raise and better accommodations. He was popular and effective with the students, the sort of teacher who can get kids to do almost anything. But he didn't want to stay, so he was once again without a job, which could have been worse, since it meant the three

Baileys spent the summer in Vermont, at David's mother's house in the hills of Pomfret. For Peggy, "It was a rough summer because there was so much uncertainty. Although David was anxious and concerned, I don't recall it ever – that's one of the extraordinary things about David – I don't recall it ever making him bad tempered, irritable, taking to drink, or anything like that."

Quite the contrary, in fact, for it was that summer that David first began talking about starting his own school with his friends the Deakes, with the two couples to comprise the entire faculty at first. But before the plan developed very far, David was offered a job at Lawrenceville and Stan Deake went into the Navy. Stan told David if he should somehow get a chance to start a school of his own, he should go ahead with it. Impelled by his increasing dissatisfaction with the traditional stuffiness of Lawrenceville, that is just what David did.

## Peggy Bailey interview, September 1982

*One of the basic principles was obviously coeducation. I was used to it – David was not, because Harvard was not in those days. But I remember at Black Mountain, Mr. Rice, who believed strongly in coeducation, used to say that you've got to regard girls not just as girls, somebody that you can have sex with or that you go out with to dances and see occasionally. They are human beings, and you have to learn to live with them. I remember David's being very struck by that...*

*Then there was a great emphasis, even in those days, a great emphasis on art, music, and eventually dramatics, all of which stemmed from Black Mountain, and which both David and I regarded as an enormously important part of the curriculum. We were one of the first schools, when we were at our height, who gave academic credit for drama, and the colleges accepted it. It wasn't heard of before, drama was one of those 'off' things that you did with little clubs.*

*We also believed in discipline, intellectual discipline, in writing, reading, and understanding – and also discipline in behavior, particularly as it affected the community; not doing anything that would hurt the community, by reputation and so on; not breaking any of its rules, which were common sense rules; not being a gossip or a talebearer; doing your utmost and then even more than you thought you were capable of to help the school.*

## David Bailey self-tape, January 1981

*Our student government system was not unique with us, but was indicative of the fact that our school was student oriented, that its government was jointly run by the whole school population, with great respect for each individual and that the adults were superior only in academic attainments. One of the earliest indications of this equality and freedom for all of us, young and old, was the first joint effort to write a school catalog. We had the usual difficulties creating such a feature. We had the same difficulty two decades later, without having any significant success in between. We did manage to write a few sentences about the type of school we were, namely, we were small, coeducational, informal, college preparatory and with unusual facilities in fields of the arts and the sciences. During all the years we were at the school, these elements prevailed as features, and they formed an institutional character that became known, mostly on the Eastern seaboard, but among the top-ranking colleges of the country. We were known as a person school, with a respect for the individual that was obviously carried out, and our change, our difference, from the traditional school was welcome and evident.*

• • •

The clearest sign that David was in control of the Country School by the fall of 1947 (as Ken Webb began his lame duck year) was that the school ceased to have a formal catalog. The three earlier catalogs were all essentially Ken's work, albeit revised somewhat and approved by others. While largely consonant with David's values, those catalogs have a literal-mindedness that David must have found uncomfortably constraining. He hated to be pinned down too closely for fear it would cost him flexibility later on when he needed it. No doubt he had been at least partly pleased that first fall of the school, when the community's effort to write a constitution collapsed, not only because David had a strong, anglophiliac sympathy for the unwritten rule, but also because he had experienced Black Mountain's determination to avoid codification, so that values might shape the institution rather than the other way around.

None of David's successors would understand the significance of the catalog question, all would belabor themselves and others to pin the school in print and none would really succeed, though one (Phil Hansen) came closer than the rest. Uncomprehendingly, David's immediate successor would boast that the school finally had its first catalog in more than twenty years, thinking this was a sign of order and progress, rather than mere mainstream banality. For the fact was the school had a catalog for many of those years, just not a traditional one. This catalog was a simple, 16-page photo brochure, supplemented by an annually revised Bulletin of Information. The only text, other than captions, in the brochure was David's brief summary of Woodstock's essentials: flexibility, atmosphere and good teachers (which appears in full in the introduction).

David's point about the catalog was process. Having students and faculty struggle with the problem of defining the school, articulating what was or should be good about their community, would move them all toward realizing it in day-to-day life. That was what was important. And if an actual catalog came out of the process, so much the better, but the catalog was never more important than serving as a screen for making it easier to talk about values that were often difficult to approach directly.

In a more intentional way, the student government system, which David called "the most important element in all the years that we ran the school," dealt directly with personal values and, by implication, with institutional values. The mechanism for this was the "group system," which consisted of five sets of increasingly broad privileges granted to students for what might as well have been called "good citizenship" in the Country School community. All students began with no group at all and had to apply to the student council one group at a time, starting with Group One, which allowed room-study instead of evening study hall. While groups granted by the student council could be, and frequently were, turned down by the faculty, it is likely the faculty rarely granted group privileges not first approved by the student council.

Even in the school's first few months, its government was not really "run by the whole school population," as David claimed. There were experiments years later with community meeting governance, but not while David was headmaster. Once he was in charge, he delegated much decision-making, but the community understood that all decisions were subject to David's modification or reversal – and not always on the more conservative side. More than once, the faculty was offended by David's willingness to keep a student they wanted expelled, just as there were times he expelled students they would have kept – but always he acted with the individual in mind, trying to do what would be best for that person under the circumstances. As a result, he was seen as trying to be fair even when he was obviously unfair.

For all his real or imagined inconsistencies or contradictions, David Bailey's values were universally perceived as different from those of Ken Webb. The Webbs put the difference in terms of "discipline" and there is some undeniable truth in that, but not the whole truth. David valued "discipline" too, though in different ways. The fundamental difference between Ken and David was that Ken believed students should be taught and therefore discipline should be imposed by others, whereas David believed students would learn and therefore self-discipline should be encouraged. Their differences were really matters of nuance and emphasis, which show up most clearly not in any abstract statement of principle, but in daily practice. Ken was generally predictable, David was frequently unpredictable. In that sense, the biggest difference between them was a matter of style.

### Peggy Bailey interview, June 23, 1982

*David used to say that Christianity was the most practical religion in the world. David went to church very seldom. He went to the Episcopal Church when we lived in Woodstock, because he sang in the church choir, but that he enjoyed, because he was a good singer, he had singing lessons when he was young and he had a very good voice. He didn't go to church as a habit at all, but he used to say it was the most practical religion there was – I think he meant this business of learning to live with other people, putting up with their faults, turning the other cheek, repaying evil with good, etcetera. All this, in the end, was a practical way of running a community. And David himself was, I think, extraordinarily 'Christian' in that he very, very seldom – in fact I can't remember his bearing a grudge even when people did things that should have embittered him.*

• • •

During the first decade and more of the Country School, those embittering things were for the most part still in the future. Throughout the forties, David's powers were waxing, the school was becoming more and more his, but more than that it was growing in size and reputation. As David's sensibility increasingly shaped the school's character, the codification of rules all but disappeared. Certainly smoking in the dorms and drinking were still unacceptable, and students were even expelled for either offense, but infractions like lateness were increasingly dealt with by those who were affected, or as they became a problem pattern in a student's behavior. Likewise, study hall was less used as anything but an academic punishment. This change recognized that it was rather contradictory for a school to send an implicit message that studying is a punishment. Study hall was used regularly as a fairly strict means of dealing with students who had poor study habits, or who tended to disturb others in unsupervised study. (The school's Bulletin of Information a few years later has no section devoted to rules, although the rules regarding smoking, automobiles, pets and firearms are listed separately at logical points in the text. There is no mention of study hall or other minor rules.)

Woodstock slowly but surely became a more relaxed place, not because of any loosening of standards as such, but because of a loosening of the means of achieving or enforcing those standards. David accepted students for who they were, adolescents who were bound to make mistakes, but he trusted them to keep their mistakes from becoming too serious. He could and did deal harshly with those who pushed the limits too hard. But the school flourished for most of its first twenty years. When it came time for David to leave, neither he nor the institution managed to figure out how to do that well. But that was in the late 1960s, the late 1940s were sunnier. The 1946 enrolment of 35 students rose to 61 the second year, 65 the third, to 70 the fourth, to 79 the fifth, where it leveled off for another five years.

Financially, the school finished in the black even for the first year, due in great part to the strict control Elizabeth Johnson exercised as treasurer. So strongly did she establish the principle of the school's living within its means that for its first 21 years of operation Woodstock showed only one deficit and was virtually debt-free in 1967. During the next 14 years, after David Bailey had retired, the school operated in the black for only two years and had debts of more than $800,000 when it closed in 1980.

"Certainly we built up a record of operating in the black in all the early years, the first two decades at least, without having the help of an endowment," David recalled. "It must be admitted that this was done at first because we took advantage of the faculty's willingness to work for very low cash salaries, way below national standards. To make that fact more palatable, we were a school in which the faculty enjoyed teaching. They got their reward largely through enjoyment of the quality of the student populous, the informality, the mutual respect, and the quality of the product. It also must be admitted that a large portion of the teachers these first few years had some income of their own to fall back on."

The teachers coming to Woodstock in those early years included a number who would help define the school for almost two decades. Of course, these included David himself – his favorite subject was geography, but he also taught English, Spanish, or whatever else was needed – and Peggy, whose senior English class was a Woodstock tradition from 1947 to 1967. But Peggy was never more than a part-time teacher, also doing Drama, and David was characteristically diffident about his own abilities: "I recognized my own intellectual shortcomings and was more interested in hiring qualified faculty and giving them freedom to teach as best they could, while I myself specialized in managing the institution, in the athletics, and in what farming we could do."

Three of the school's important teachers were hired for the start of the second year – Buffy Dunker, Mounir Sa'adah and Stan Deake. Buffy and Mounir would be part of the school's stable core faculty for decades, while Stan Deake and Bob Lake, from the first year, would be at the center of two very different early crises.

## John M. Bulkley, Jr., '48 letter in Continuum, Fall 1974

*Woodstock has meant so much to me, while there and since, that it completely turned my life around and probably did for most other students. From the mediocre, boring, and trite non-life most of us had experienced in the public school life, we were blessed with a 24 hour a day, male-female situation where we were gently molded into thinking individuals who could at least begin to solve our own problems, and perhaps those of others because David taught us how to care. Much has been written about the importance of the formative years, but no where near enough on Woodstock the "society." Unlike the six hour a day high school system, where a student could fake being someone else and then go home, by the very nature of the life at Woodstock, every student (and teacher) was forced into developing his own personality. That this is the ultimate in the learning process should be rather obvious if one checks the credentials of past graduates.*

*You may not recall, but in the 1940's, Woodstock was on a shoestring and most of us were not the greatest scholastic material. Yet together we all proved what the Air University has been teaching to our officers for years: problem solve together and derive solutions above and beyond the smarts of individual answers.... We didn't know about the technical aspects of problem solving in those days, but, consciously or not, David used them with the student council, while Edich [Cochran] forced them down our throats in her math classes. It would be many years later before I would realize just how effective David and Edith were.*

*To conclude the above I will only say that in the past twelve months I have had indicted a rapist and double murderer, and am about to sit back and watch one of our senior Senators indicted for accepting a bribe for clearing two companies with the SEC [Securities and Exchange Commission]. Concerning the latter, about nine people should receive sentences. All of this was the result of the technique called "problem solving."*

### James Barter '48 interview

*"Buffy was a blast. She really was. She went to Antioch before she went to Vassar, and apparently she had been a real rebel at Antioch, led a protest march down the middle of Yellow Springs, and was known as wild and fast. There was some of that kind of breezy attitude about her when she was at school. She had a sense of humor. I found her somebody easy to talk to and to confide in. A lot of kids did."*

• • •

Buffy's son once told another teacher that if Buffy had not found the Country School, she probably would have ended up in an institution. She started her first year at Woodstock as the school secretary. The following year, she began teaching music (she remembers David asking her to do it; he said she persuaded him to let her). She continued to teach music history and theory for 23 years. During that time, she also took on the duties of school bookkeeper, then business manager and treasurer. Eventually, Buffy would even be president of the Board of Trustees, but this was not until 1978, after she had been separated from the school for many years, during which she had achieved a certain celebrity in the Boston *Globe* as one of the few sexagenarian lesbian grandmothers playing softball and doing feminist therapy in Boston, so the school, much-changed since she had left, was no longer one of her highest priorities.

In 1946, Buffy was 41 years old, coming off a bad marriage that ended in divorce. One of her three children, Mary Lou, was young enough to be a Woodstock student. Buffy was without significant work experience and was casting about for something to do with her life. She thought she would like to teach math in grade school, but at a friend's suggestion she also wrote to David at the Country School. She didn't need the job for income – she was born Elizabeth Dennison, of the Dennison paper fortune – but she desperately needed the self-esteem.

"I signed my full name to the letter and David wrote me back and said he'd be happy to see me, and wrote by hand at the bottom, 'Are you by any chance related to Jimmy Dennison?' – who was a Harvard classmate of David's, and my brother, so of course that gave me status right away," Buffy recalled: "You know David's snobby. But I had to get the approval of Kenneth Webb and I snowed him I guess or something, because if he had known what I really was like he would not have hired me. I'm much too radical for him. He was so moral, you know he didn't approve of kids falling in love, necking, or anything like that."

Since Woodstock didn't need a math or science teacher at the moment, Buffy started as the school secretary, dealing with everyone and everything with humor, energy and openness that soon made her a favorite for many students. And for most of her years at Woodstock, Buffy was a reliable student confidante, even to the point of cliquishness for the musical ones among them. She delighted in hearing the details of their ups and downs and often shared freely of her own. She was a dynamo and threw herself into the life of the school with such energy and commitment that she soon became invaluable. After she retired in 1970, the work she had been doing turned into fulltime jobs for three men.

For many years, she was the regular Thursday OD, which meant she was in charge of the weekly all-school cleanup. She was also a fierce disciplinarian and grew more so with the years, as more than one girl came to feel her disproportionate wrath over an untucked shirttail. She could be cruel and arbitrary and there were always some students who were intimidated by her.

Perhaps her most enduring contribution to the school's institutional life was music. She not only taught music history and theory classes and led the madrigal chorus (in which David sang), but she embodied music as a central and vital part of the school. She assembled the school's classical record collection, housed and available to all in the Common Room. She made sure morning chapel usually included music. She offered "listener's music" in the afternoons and on Sundays. She took numerous school trips to concerts in the area and helped arrange recitals at the school by Samuel Barber, Gian Carlo Manotti and Pete Seeger, among others.

Most of all, students remember thinking Buffy was in love with David, frequently speculating as to what was really going on. Buffy says he held her hand one night as they walked from Greenhithe to the Barn, but never anything else. More importantly to the life of the school, Buffy soon became David's real second-in-command, regardless of who else might have the formal title. By virtue of her devotion to David, her endless energy and her willingness to spend most of her time in the school, Buffy became, in effect, David's professional wife. She played that role for more than 20 years and then, after he retired, she was for a while his professional widow. She retired at age 65 in 1970.

## Judy Fisher '50 interview

*The best teacher that I had, one of the high points of my life, was Mounir Sa'adah. He was terrific and he was probably the first teacher that I had who actually posed questions that made his students think and go beyond the boundaries of what they were already thinking. He was full of enthusiasm for teaching. He had those great, black eyes, and he was a funny, fun, very urban gentleman, but he used to ask these questions and you were never quite sure what he was asking and you'd think about it for a while. Of all the teachers there, he had a way of taking you further in your thinking, thinking about possibilities or alternatives or things that you'd never tried. I think he was a great teacher in that respect.*

• • •

A Christian Arab born in Damascus, Syria, in 1909, Mounir Sa'adah made his first Country School connection as a freshman at the American University of Beirut. His English instructor there was Ken Webb. That summer, when he was running a camp up in the Lebanese mountains for the children of victims of the Armenian Holocaust, Ken needed a native Arabic speaker who also spoke English to be a liaison between the camp and local communities. "So Kenneth asked me if I would be the public relations person to establish good relations with the villages and the people around, smooth any difficulties that arose and meet any guests that came. I went up and had a great time. They used to bring 150 orphans at a time up there and give them a good exposure to sun and fresh air and a change from orphanage life."

Ken returned to America that summer, but the two men kept in touch. Mounir went on to finish his undergraduate studies at the university and take a graduate degree at the Near East School of Theology. Then he taught at the American University of Beirut himself for 15 years before coming to the United States to teach at Western Reserve Academy in Ohio in 1945. "When I dropped Ken a note, which was forwarded three times, and he wrote back and said, 'I don't know why you're here, or what you're doing, or how long but don't engage yourself in anything that cannot be altered until you come and see the best school in the best town in the best state in the country that I just started.' "

Mounir visited Woodstock in March 1946 and found the school "very exciting – there was intimacy – they would sit around the piano and sing, there was a great deal of rapport between faculty and students, but they kept a high degree of respect for each other." During his visit, Mounir spoke at a school vespers service and gave a public talk on Middle East issues at the Universalist Church. The trip produced two jobs. The following fall, Mounir came to the Country School to teach history and philosophy. He also became the minister at the Universalist Church, positions he would hold until 1964, when he accepted the chairmanship of the history department at the Choate School in Wallingford, Connecticut.

For Mounir, running the Country School had no appeal, he did not seek that kind of power: "You see, I was so excited about my teaching there that I just sailed on and I did not know that there were politics in the whole situation. Politics is not anything I engage in. I talked my profession with everybody, I talked students with everybody, but it didn't occur to me that I might be stepping on somebody's toes or somebody was climbing and I was in the way, or something. I had no idea as to what the politics of the situation were, or what the realities were. I discovered only after I retired, politics is half of the life of private schools."

Mounir devoted his energies to his courses, which included Ancient History and European History, as well as two senior courses called Contemporary History and Problems of Democracy. The former was a current events course and was as unpredictable as the daily New York Times, which was the only text. Problems of Democracy, or P.D. as it was called, was a more reflective course that had little to do with democracy in the usual sense. The course changed almost every year, but always featured readings from the great philosophers beginning with Plato and Aristotle. It usually required each student to teach for a week in the spring, on a subject of his or her own choosing. Mounir also conducted numerous chapel and Sunday vespers services. In the early 1960s, he developed an Arabic language program, which the school, vainly, thought might get funding from the Central Intelligence Agency.

But in its early years, much of the Country School's excitement came from the sense of shared enterprise, of students and faculty alike helping each other make the school work. And Mounir remembers this both growing out of and feeding a remarkable generosity of spirit: "The faculty were really good people, who were dedicated. There was no question of time or anything that we weren't willing to give to the school. And then they gave us a free hand to do whatever – nobody ever told me what to teach or what not to teach. Just open it and find whatever there is in it – that was the great secret of the school. And David was able always to have people who, if they were left on their own, they did very well. I liked the school. I think it was a terrific place. I read more books, I studied more, I enjoyed growing with the school – after all, I had just arrived from the Middle East and the school just gave me an opportunity to grow into American life. I think everyone else felt the same way – that we were growing with the school."

Perhaps more than any other teacher from the early years of the school, Mounir embodies a critical distinction that would be vital for the school to survive. Long after the school had closed, many people, especially alumni and alumni trustees, continued to perceive Woodstock as an extension and expression of David's persona. Institutionally, the school's leadership collectively failed to see the school as Mounir experienced it: an independent, learnable, perpetuable educational structure.

Mounir was never terribly close to David. He described David as a man of the world who presented himself as unworldly. He liked many of David's personal qualities, but he was not seduced by David's personal style: "David had charm, there was no question. Where it was, I don't know, I never saw it. But he had charm, he could charm people. Even parents – some of them fell so much in love with him that they came to Woodstock just to be close enough to see David. And he told one of his secretaries once, when she wanted to resign, 'Every single secretary who has ever been here has fallen in love with me.'" While that may have been true of Buffy, it may be apocryphal for others.

Mounir and Buffy were always at odds, for 18 years as colleagues and beyond, and Buffy at least was never one to hide it very well (which may have helped protect Mounir's status in a perverse way). But just as Buffy was free to act as she saw fit because of her money, so Mounir gained a measure of independence and safety from being the Universalist minister, having a separate sanctuary and constituency. For a long time, this man who had few illusions about the reality of the school, and certainly no uncontrolled affection for the school's dominant personalities, nevertheless served as Woodstock's director of admissions. He did the job well, not least because of his apolitical posture, his willingness to bend with the wind and his own ability to be charming even to those he found distasteful (an important quality for any admissions director, not to mention any minister). But Mounir is also one of the few people in the school's history who was able to make clear distinctions between the qualities of the school as such and the qualities of the people who ran it. He was one of the few people in any position of responsibility in the history of the school who could explain those distinctions, define the differences and articulate the value of each. Perhaps none of the school's trustees ever achieved as much clarity, and few ever demonstrated they had any clue as to what really made the school work (when it did work). Even in 1978, when the Country School was slowly destroying itself in plain view of anyone who cared to look, the trustees turned to Mounir for an evaluation and recommendations. Characteristically, Mounir produced an atmospheric, apparently flattering document that was, at core, a devastating critique. The trustees misrepresented the report in their official minutes. Then they ignored it.

### James Barter '48 interview, February 24, 1985

*Actually the person I was closest to in terms of teachers was Bob Lake. Bob. I don't know if he adopted me or I adopted him. I think he was the father that I never had. I really idealized him and thought he was just a super, terrific guy. I got very interested in biology since I liked Bob. I got involved in all kinds of projects, I built bookcases for him, I did a mural for the biology lab, which must have been thirty feet long – a chart of all the philae, with representative drawings of everything from the single cells through the analids through the complex animals, with them all carefully labeled and so forth. That was a labor of love. You talk about hero worship and Bob could do no wrong in my eyes. He would take me skiing with him, taught me how to ski. He was extremely easy to get along with, very friendly, very outgoing, I can't remember his ever getting angry. I remember one trip we took together and we went to a floating bridge in Vermont, a floating bridge that you drive across, and we had been talking about frogs and frogs' anatomy, and he pulled the car over and we got out and caught a frog, and he dissected the frog right there on the spot and showed me the heart beating.*

Sex at the Country School was one of those permanent issues that many of the adults wished would just go away. Ken and David may have disagreed in theory about how much sex should be allowed among adolescents, but in practice they carried out a traditional conspiracy of ignorance: I don't want to know and you don't want to know. Years later, Ken and Susan Webb said if there was much sexuality on campus, they didn't know about it. While David may have known more, he didn't want to be perceived as knowing and Peggy certainly didn't want to know. But the children knew.

According to legend, one of the students, a drug fortune heiress, returned from the school's first Christmas vacation with a suitcase full of contraceptives for the girls' dorm: diaphragms and spermicides. Impossible to verify, but the company in question did in fact make those products in 1945. For the most part, despite the casual atmosphere, the school's sexual life was probably not so very different from what it was elsewhere: there were fast girls, there were predatory boys, there were loving couples, there were lots of virgins of both sexes, there was plenty of experimentation, there was discretion and there was lots of empty talk. For five years, the school avoided its worst nightmare, a public sexual scandal. In fact, for five years there appears to have been no serious private sexual scandal either. When the first one happened, it caught everyone by surprise.

By all accounts, Bob Lake was a charming, almost dashing young man. He was in his mid-twenties when he joined the Country School's first faculty in 1945. He came to the school from Ken Webb's camp, having previously worked for the Vermont Soil Conservation Service and having served in the Tenth Mountain Division (the U.S. ski troops) during the war. A Dartmouth College graduate, he was married, had three small children and gave every appearance of being a happy part of a near-perfect family. Certainly young James Barter thought so.

What Barter and apparently no one else at the school knew then was that Bob Lake had not seen combat, had not gone overseas with his division, but had been mustered out on psychiatric grounds. What people at the school saw – and believed to be real – was an energetic younger teacher whose classes in biology, zoology and geology were well run, popular and challenging. They saw a man whose interest in his students was strong, often intense, and whose contribution to the life of the school was varied and positive: he led field trips, he skied, he taught skiing, he built the school ski tow, he contributed to Symposium, he took lots of school pictures. His fellow teachers elected him to serve one year as their representative on the Board of Trustees.

"Bob Lake was a great teacher," Judy Fisher '50, recalled, "so casual, very warm, very quiet, very concerned. I spent a lot of time – I had a wildflower project and I used to go out horseback riding and I would get specimens and he'd help me find the Latin names for them and put the pressed flowers in a book. He really helped a lot of students develop an interest in the natural sciences just because he was so interested in them and what they were doing. I'm sure he'd seen six hundred projects like this before, but he just made the student feel like this is really something special – a very dignified, a very warm person."

Roger Phillips '49 remembered Bob as "kind of a square, Boy Scout type – clean shaven, sturdy, non-smoking, which wasn't such a common thing in those days." As far as anyone knew, Bob Lake was reliable friendly, helpful – year after year, he did his job and never caused any problems.

But by the fall of 1950, Bob Lake was deeply involved with Buffy Dunker's daughter, Mary Lou. Their affair went on for some time without anyone suspecting. Their time together was spent mostly in the privacy of cabins at Ken Webb's camp, which was closed and deserted for the winter. Then in November they had a problem, as Buffy recalls: "Mary Lou was pregnant by Bob Lake and he took her to Boston to have an abortion. I thought she was going off to visit colleges, which was just fine, it was the fall of her senior year. I didn't know she was pregnant and there was nothing to indicate to me that way, except that I knew that she and Bob Lake did a lot of work together."

When Mary Lou didn't show up at the time she was supposed to come back from Boston, the situation unravelled. The school's response, David's response, was swift and amputating. He fired Bob Lake immediately, giving him two days to vacate the premises and his family a month to follow. David paid him $2,432.50, but required him to sign a formal release (one of the few early documents to survive, since it was in the school's safe deposit box). Besides being a standard general release, the document spells out the terms of Lake's departure, as well as the promise: "I further agree that I will not communicate with the students, members of the faculty and patrons at the school concerning any matters involving the school and myself in any way to slander the school."

This was Thanksgiving time, the school remained in session and alumni often came to visit. James Barter came: "I drove up with a couple of friends, partly to see Bob, and when I arrived there was all this stiffness. I didn't know what the hell was going on. No one would tell me, except that Bob was leaving the school, that he had this terrific job at Dartmouth, just too good a job to turn down, and his wife didn't contradict the story. That was the cover story, David told me the same story. One thing that I do remember about that time was, and I remember the twinge of jealousy that I felt about this, was Bob raving about what a terrific student Mary Lou was, how she was the best zoology student he'd ever had." (Dartmouth College has no record of ever employing any Robert Lake and the school's $2,432.50 payment seems to support the inference that the story was a fabrication.)

As for Mary Lou, David would not allow her to return to the school and Buffy agreed with the decision: "Of course, we knew what we had to do – it was perfectly clear that you couldn't have the kid back among the other innocent children. So Mary Lou finished the year living with her sister Betsy, who was married and pregnant in Ithaca where her husband was still in law school." Mary Lou was bitter and angry about the way she was treated and years later Buffy would come to share those feelings when, under a different headmaster, another Country School student got pregnant, went home to have her baby and came back to school.

Bob Lake's marriage was over, his wife filed for divorce. Apparently Mary Lou was not his first such liaison. But she was perhaps his most serious. He was not allowed to see her for the rest of the school year, but some time after that he persuaded Buffy to let him talk to Mary Lou, with a chaperone, during a train ride to Boston. But instead of showing up for that meeting, he went to his ex-wife's house, where she eventually found him in the basement, where he had stood on a box with a rope around his neck and shot himself as he kicked the box away.

According to Buffy, Mary Lou's second and third husbands both looked like Bob Lake. His ex-wife gave his collection of Country School slides to James Barter: "The interesting thing is, Bob took pictures of girls. Some of the pictures are gorgeous, they really are, they're carefully posed. But as you look through the pictures – I have never done a frequency count, but I suspect that if you did a frequency count, you'd find that there are ten pictures of girls for every one picture of anybody else."

## David Bailey, earliest extant report to the Trustees, October 1950

*The School opens its sixth year with a good deal of optimism [before the Bob Lake crisis]. Several factors are responsible for this happy feeling. First, we have the realization that we successfully weathered a difficult season last year, overcoming both a bad morale situation and what might have been a disastrous financial story. The Treasurer's Report will attest that we once again finished our year's business with a margin. Also, our physical plant and equipment are in better shape than ever before, especially in such vital areas as heat and plumbing, and in kitchen facilities, though there are still some inadequacies.*

*Perhaps the most important fact that contributes to our optimism is our enrollment. We have 79 students, all but 8 of whom are boarders. This is several more than we have ever had and is 11 more boarding pupils than we has at this time last year. We are happy about this not only because of the financial return, which will make our lives easier this year, but we wre struck also by the quality and source of our students. More than one half of our new students came to us through enthusiastic reports from parents and alumni. Also it seems to us that the new students represent generally a higher standard than we have had, though perhaps there aren't as many exciting individualists as formerly.*

*This large enrollment is not an unmixed blessing. It had never been the headmaster's intention to have a school as large as this, but such a size may be financially necessary and even educationally desirable. All in all the school appears to be maturing gracefully. A great many more people are hearing about us, and we are more sought after and notices by our educational competitors and colleagues.* ***It seems that our school is fulfilling a real need. It has so far achieved a relatively rare synthesis of high scholastic achievement and informal, genuine living. Especially in this day of almost universal adolescent insecurity are we performing a service. For we function as a parent-figure or as a home for the majority of our students, and we can give them the affectionate firmness as well as the intellectual guidance which so many of them previously lacked.*** *[emphasis added]*

*It may be that we are merely on the high crest of a wave that will soon ebb, but none of us can look far into the future these days, so with what facts and judgments we have to go on we feel our optimism is justified.*

● ● ●

David's October optimism was soon tested by the Bob Lake situation that emerged less than a month later. While that was a profound, personal crisis for a few people, as it turned out, it did not become a serious institutional crisis. That was coming. Altogether the events of 1950-51 would make all the school's previous struggles seem trivial by comparison.

The morale and financial problems of 1946-49 derived primarily from underenrollment. The budget projected an increase of five tuitions that were not realized. In September 1949, Woodstock faced an estimated deficit of more than $9,000 on the annual budget of less than $100,000. To ease the situation, the faculty voluntarily and unanimously voted to take a ten per cent cut in salary, saving the school almost $3,000. Eventually late enrollments, close budget control, and unanticipated income (about $9,000) more than resolved the issue. Not only was full faculty pay restored in the spring, several unexpected, unbudgeted expenses were covered as well. The school finished $769 in the black.

For the faculty to vote to cut its pay on its own initiative, with no assurance it would ever be restored, is a measure of how clearly people then at the school perceived it as a shared enterprise, a fundamentally communal venture. The faculty voted to make its sacrifice despite some misgivings that the headmaster and the Trustees were not doing all they could and should to raise the money needed to run and improve the school. The 1949 faculty contrasted sharply with faculties of the 1970s, whose response to the school's growing financial difficulties was not to make any sacrifice as a group, but rather to compete individually for dwindling resources. Then, too, the faculty in the 1970s had little reason to believe that the school's fiscal policies, as set by the Trustees or carried out by the administration, were anywhere near as careful and responsible as they had been more than twenty years earlier. By the 1970s, the Trustees had put the school in a deficit-spending basis without any credible plan to offset the shortfalls.

Stan Deake, as the Country School's controller in 1949, exercised tight budgetary control over the budget to keep the school solvent. Stan also taught chemistry, physics, and math, and he ran the boys dorm at The Green. When Ken Webb disengaged in 1947, David named Stan Deake as the Assistant Headmaster. This seemed to bring the school close to what Stan and David had planned before Stan went into the Navy and David was partnered with Ken Webb.

Standish Deake and his wife Genevieve had joined the Country School in its second year, 1946, after Stan's discharge as a naval communications officer. He spent that summer building his own physics lab in The Barn, which was slowly being turned into Woodstock's main classroom building. Stan's previous experience included seven years as a state biologist in Massachusetts and five years teaching (two at Milton Academy), all of which contributed to David's calling him, years later, "a top quality teacher" and "a good professional."

At the October 1946 Trustees meeting, Elizabeth Johnson resigned as Treasurer so that Stan Deake, her chosen successor, could take over. Genevieve Deake kept the school's books. This was Miss Johnson's style of preparing for the future, leaving as little to chance as possible. She remained on the board, she remained on the executive committee, and she took on the newly created board position of Assistant Treasurer. During the cash-strapped year of 1949-50, WCS even managed to build itself a little, eight-bay library between Greenhithe and The Barn, without borrowing any money. It was named the Elizabeth Forest Johnson Library.

Stan Deake's manner was not as casual as most other Country School teachers. For a time he wore his Navy uniform at school. And like Ken Webb, he was the butt of considerable student joking behind his back. He was also well respected as a teacher and administrator. For his fifth year at the school in 1950-51, his salary of $3,500 was second only to David Bailey's $4,000 (with Mounir Sa'adah next at $2,750). Stan's budgets and budget reports were consistently clear, cogent, and humane – right through the spring of 1951.

Then suddenly he became dispensible.

"Stan was something else," Judy Fisher '51 recalled much later. "What would you call Stan? He would be the enforcer. Rules, regulations. Well one never knows how faculty decisions are made, but a number of my class was thrown out of school five weeks before graduation [June 8]. I always thought, well, that was too bad, but I think somebody had to be made an example of and so Stan was the faculty member who had to bring down the rules and regulations. And then Stan was asked to leave. It was just inter-personal relationships. A lot of people thought he was – well, there were rumors and innuendoes – rather unpleasant things were said about him, I don't know whether they were true of not. But he was not well-liked, which I don't know is particularly fair."

On June 20, David Bailey reported to the Trustees that: "The situation of the Deakes is still somewhat amorphous.... It is the opinion of the headmaster that, since May 21st, Mr. Deake has been given every opportunity to resign gracefully.... An alternative to such a resignation could, of course, be dismissal for cause, but this is an action we should avoid if possible." David here gives no hint as to the cause, nor why it should be avoided. No evidence of any offence has survived. Even the memories of participants and witnesses, like Judy Fisher, remained opaque.

According to Mounir Sa'adah decades later: "We got into a terrible situation and when there was trouble, I was always put in the middle of the situation to work it out. I had to tell Stan Deake his relations with the school ought to be severed. Basically he disagreed with David on administrative grounds, but that was not why he was dismissed. I don't think I want to put it on the record why.

Whether the problem was there or not I don't know. But I had to do the dirty job, had to go to Stan and tell him that. David wouldn't face it."

Thirty years later, David still wasn't fully facing it. He said that philosophical disagreements led him to fire Stan suddenly, and that both Stan and his wife had been shocked by it. David said he had made a mistake not having a talk with Stan, "and I'm really not over that yet."

Whatever the real issue was, Stan did eventually resign, after he was assured his salary for the coming year, or until he found work, whichever came first. He was also paid for his work as Treasurer during June and allowed to remain in his apartment at The Green until September. And for the second time in less than a year, the school required a departing faculty member to sign a comprehensive release, holding the school harmless for all time.

Given these circumstances, the school took no official public notice of Stan's leaving, in sharp contrast to the bouquets and gifts showered on Edith Cochran, who retired that spring after teaching math to Country School students since the opening day. The last, even semi-official public reference to Stan Deake appears with no apparent irony in the graduation issue of *Symposium*, June 1951, as part of a long sequence of word images catching essences of the school following "Woodstock Is… Stan, a steady figure in the tempestuous wind, a comfortable shuttle between the Barn and Greenhithe."

With Stan Gone, and with Elizabeth Johnson's blessing, Buffy Dunker took over as Woodstock's Treasurer and Controller, positions she would hold for the rest of David Bailey's tenure as headmaster. For David, Stan's departure meant that there were no more serious rivals for his power in the school. With the resignation of the original Trustees, including Elizabeth Johnson the following spring, David was in control.

Sara Dunham

1951 soccer team on the front steps of Greenhithe
FRONT ROW: Frank Wray '54, Dave Talbot '54, Cy Williams '52, George Bond '54, Jeff Mahlstedt '52, jack Merrill '52, Roger Condit '55, Jim Whithead '55 SECOND ROW: Coach Wendell Cameron, Charles English '54, Dave Beaver '53, Tony Newcomb '52, Steve Zachary '54, Bill Tyson '53, Dick Rodmn '53, Rodney Clurman '52. BACK ROW: Mason Barr '53, Sandy McLane '54, Dick Pettingill '52, Frank Buffum '53, Bruce Brockway '52, John Molholm '53, Mike Rich '52, Jack Briggs '52

Student Council 1951-52 (l. to r.):
Jack Briggs '52, unknown, Gay Schroeder '52, Helen Baldwin '55, Masom Barr '53, Jane Davidson '52, unknown, George Bond '54, Michael Schwartz '52, Charles English '54.

Parents Weekend 1953: Eleanor Roosevelt, at WCS to visit her goddaughter, stops in the kitchen with the school's cooks, "Pop" Landers and his wife.

CHAPTER FOUR

# Fall 1951 – Fall 1955

### Curt Hinckley interview, March 19, 1986

*I went to the interview [in New Haven in the early summer of 1951] to discover that David was in bed, sick with something and he interviewed me in bed. And I remember very little about the interview... I had the kind of academic background that he was looking for because he wanted somebody who could teach a number of the sciences and who was able to be in a dormitory and I certainly fit into those categories. And I hesitate to say with certainty, but I think when the interview was over that I had the job... I don't think it was a matter of well, we'll get back to you and let you know – first of all, that doesn't sound like David... It certainly was not the kind of interview one would have at Loomis or Exeter or Gunnery or one of the other prestigious institutions, where one would go dressed in – well, maybe not pinstripe suit and tie – but nevertheless dressed for the occasion and welcomed in proper fashion, not by somebody lying in bed. I can only assume that this may have had something to do with the subsequent development of emphysema, though it may have been quite a delay, but I think this was respiratory...*

*David certainly was different, there's no questions about it, different in the sense of – I realize the opposite of 'proper' is 'improper,' but that's not what I mean – I really mean not proper in the sense of formal, much more casual, today we would probably say laid back – vague, imprecise, and yet he captured so many people's spirits and high flying ideas just by the way he was... there were those qualities which came through it all which made it sound as if this might be something much more interesting than the traditional kind of setting.*

### Mounir Sa'adah interview, June 19, 1985

*Elizabeth Johnson got a huge kick out of the place she was running for years, at least the financial end of things. She was a no nonsense woman, a very strong woman – I remember David was [exhausted in the summer of 1951] and Elizabeth Johnson called me up and said, "You're taking charge of the place until David is able to handle things." I said, "No, this is one area I don't want to step on David's toes." She said, "Nonsense, we are to run the school." And she went over to David and said, "Mounir is in charge for the duration and to be paid pro rata ... "And David said, "Of course."*

### David Bailey report to trustees, June 21, 1951

*Because of the important changes in administration, and because of the several new, untried teachers, next year may be a difficult one. On the other hand it could, with its new spirit of enthusiasm, be our best one yet. We hope, however, that we can budgetarily manage a smaller student body, thus courting fewer problems...*

*It was requested and granted, at the May meeting, that the headmaster and his wife be given an opportunity for a summer vacation and a considerable absence from the school during the next academic year. Events have worked out so that neither of these is possible. The Trust-*

*ees should be aware that the school will open in the fall and continue through the year with the probability of both the Baileys more fatigued than ever. The headmaster has no suggestions to make and merely wants to present the problem, realizing there is probably no solution to it.*

• • •

For all the gloom of David's outlook in June, this would be his bleakest report to the trustees for more than a decade to come. Already his natural resilience was at work, aided by the elimination of the worst sources of tension in the school. He was helped further when the Trustees arranged for him and Peggy to go away in August for their first lengthy vacation in several years (in October, the board formalized a month's paid vacation annually for the headmaster).

More important, in the spring the board had begun a serious effort to build a headmaster's house on campus since David and Peggy had been living in different rented houses off campus since 1945. By August, almost half of the necessary $20,000 was raised privately, including a generous share from the students' annual gift to the school. But the local banks had turned down repeated loan applications. At the August 3 meeting of the Executive Committee, Elizabeth Johnson expressed the opinion of the majority – and a basic corollary of the principle that the school should always live carefully within its means – that they could not authorize starting the house until the full $20,000 was committed (just as the library had not been started in 1949 until the school knew how it would pay for it). The dilemma was solved by Buffy Dunker's offer to take a personal mortgage on a loan of $10,000, on the same terms offered to the bank. The minutes of the meeting note that David "expressed his objection to such a loan, but if the Trustees felt such assurance was necessary to get the house started, he would be willing to accept the assurance, providing that there could be some guarantee that the loan need not be made and the money obtained from some other source, whether by loan or gift."

The committee approved the financing on that basis and construction began immediately under the direction of Molly Gregory, the designer who had emigrated to Woodstock from Black Mountain and set up business as Woodstock Enterprises (of which David was the nominal president). In his fall report, David spoke of "the exciting and nearly miraculous advent of the new headmaster's house. This has been a concern and almost a crusade on the part of so many students and friends that it has had a spiritual value added to its obvious value to the future of the school. The financing of this project has also been unusually fortuitous, so that less than the anticipated expenses to the school will be necessary." In the spring of 1952, the Baileys moved into their new house, which was furnished in part by one of the largest student gifts in the school's history.

The new headmaster's house was a modernistic design with low, clean lines, built on the foundation of an abandoned barn. Set into the hillside, the house had entrances on both floors. "It was unique in being an upside down house, with the bedrooms, rather cold, on the ground floor and the kitchen and living rooms on the top floor, and the view from the balcony on three sides was an important feature," David recalled years later. "This building was our first real home."

Most importantly during the summer of 1951, Stan Deake's departure had left David thoroughly secure as the head of the school, without rivals, without even potential rivals, either as headmaster or as president of the Board of Trustees (he had assumed the board presidency in 1946, expecting to continue alternating annually with Ken Webb). That summer the trustees also abolished the position of Associate Headmaster (held by Stan Deake), dividing its responsibilities between two Deputy Headmasters, Mounir Sa'adah and English teacher Allen Weatherby, neither of whom had any apparent ambition to run the school. "There was no one around any more, in terms of strength," according to Gerry Freund '48 years later, "Buffy was the only one who conceivably had it, and she was so adoring that there was no worry there, either. People like Bus Talbot or Allen Weatherby, really remarkably fine people, but none of them had the spark in them of replacing David. He had no worry once Deake was gone... If there was anything to be fearful of, it might be an organized student body, which he didn't like."

In February, 1952, half way through the last year of David's first five-year term as headmaster, the trustees voted unanimously to reappoint him indefinitely, rather than for another five-year term as required by the by-laws, which they amended accordingly. The meeting minutes reported that "Mr. Bailey returned and accepted the appointment. He spoke of the special character of the school, and pointed out the taxing nature of the work of Headmaster as a reason for the advisability of not limiting the term of appointment to a definite number of years. He expressed the hope that he would be able to fill the job adequately and would be the first to recognize the time when it became too taxing."

With Elizabeth Johnson's full retirement from the board in the spring of 1952, there was no one left from the original school community but the Baileys. Roger Phillips '49 would come on the board as the first alumni trustee that fall, but neither he nor any other board member could match Elizabeth Johnson's authority, nor her willingness to confront David on issues of substance. The heady mix of strong and sometimes clashing personalities of Woodstock's first years was gone and the school's future success or failure would depend almost entirely on the style and values of its headmaster.

The underlying values beneath David's style, values that he rarely tried to articulate directly, were something he took as givens, the "eternal verities" as Peggy Bailey called them. David always disliked trying to articulate a "philosophy" for the school, feeling it ended up sounding like pontification, or just like the claims of the other schools, none of which could be lived up to because a school was just made up of people with all their inevitable human frailties. Peggy said she and David did not have long discussions defining their values because they both knew what the "verities" were already, that they included, among other things, "courage, steadfastness in the face of adversities, understanding of and sympathy with one's fellows, devotion to truth even when it meant hardship for oneself, and a belief in justice and disciplined liberty."

### Whitney Slater Tokunaga '53 interview, April 30, 1986

*I think I was very rebellious... There was the time that Peggy wanted me at rehearsal, and David said that I should stay at school because I had been bad. And I thought to myself, which of the two am I more frightened of? So I said, "Well, David – I'll stay here, I'll be glad to say here, but Peggy will be furious-- she wants me at rehearsal."*

*And he said, "You must stay here."*

*And I said, "Well, that's fine, will you explain to Peggy why I'm not there?"*

*And so of course he let me go...*

*I guess that was kind of mean of me. I was playing with him a little.*

### Sidney Smith '56 interview, May 16, 1984

*The reason I was interested in [the WCS history] is mainly, I realize that if you talk to a lot of people, most people are going to remember David and other people.... But the one who sticks in my mind is Peggy – more than anybody else – because I think that very few people liked Peggy, she wasn't a kind of agreeable sort of person. But I did, and she made an enormous impression on me.... She was very kind to me....*

*Peggy went out of her way to help me and encourage me, mostly in English class – and she was all excited about my coming to New York and [pursuing dance] and thought that's what I should do. And she was very kind. And I don't think she found it easy, herself, to talk to people, she's not a gregarious type of talker....*

*I simply liked her looks. I liked everything about her. I liked her, she was tiny and precise and neat and so different from David, who was kind of always gangly and hanging about.... I wish I had become closer but she was very hard to get close to....*

*She was my advisor senior year, and she was really encouraging about being a dancer, and she liked dancing herself.... I liked her enormously, I really did.... She never revealed anything about herself. We never had heart-to-hearts and she never told me about her experiences.... Peggy always impressed me as the kind of person who never had any men in her life. She seemed totally feminine in every way, what she wore was feminine... Don't forget to mention her, and her influence, whatever that was – mostly her work – not so much her influence, just her very tidy little way, every day, that she was – which kept the whole thing moving. I don't know if she was a happy woman, I can't tell – she may even be happier now that he's not here....*

*Whenever I'm in doubt as to how to handle a situation, I think of what she might do. She had great dignity and courage and I did admire her.*

• • •

Woodstock's emerging institutional character during its first decade is most clearly illustrated by Peggy Bailey's evolving role in the school. At first, Peggy had been reluctant to get involved. She had not taught at all the first year, though she directed two dramatic productions. She only reluctantly gave in to David's insistence that she teach eighth grade English the second year. But when Ken Webb stopped teaching in 1947, she took over senior English and that course rapidly became one of the Country School's truest institutions. For years thereafter, all seniors would spend the first week of the fall term struggling with their first assignment for Peggy, an essay on "How to Make a Bed." While particulars of the course changed over the years, Peggy was consistent in that she made her classes write often, she drilled them in vocabulary, she drilled them in comprehension, she tested them often and she was a hard grader – so hard that student mythology held that she never gave any A's (while Peggy said she gave "some"). At the heart of senior English for years were the central texts: *Hamlet* in the fall, a Victorian novel in the winter (often Hardy's *Return of the Native*) and selections from *The Bible* read as literature in the spring.

"I felt the children needed – a word which they hated and which some of the younger faculty resented – discipline," Peggy said years later. "Discipline in the written word, in the reading word, not this spilling out of stuff that some of them used to indulge in and which they then thought was a masterpiece. Make the word do what you wanted it to do. That's why they did the famous theme 'How to Make a Bed.' Then you could go on from there. I also felt there were enormous gaps in the American children's education, in their reading. They would sit down to read *Moby Dick*, shall we say, and the opening line – 'Call me Ishmael' – meant nothing to them. They were woefully ignorant about *The Bible*, most of them. I happen to be rather well read in *The Bible*. When I was a child I was given a book of Biblical stories and I sat down and read them just the way you read comics. So I felt they should study the classics, the Greek tragedies, *The Bible*, and other things, to get some background. I never thought of myself as having 'guiding principles,' as they say – but I was in love with my subject, and I wanted them to be in love with the subject, too."

Even more of an institution, eventually, was the Woodstock drama program. At first, as at most schools, the dramatics club was extracurricular, irregular and informal, even when Peggy was directing. During 1948-49, student enthusiasm and the increasing involvement of co-director Jo Oatfield brought drama activities to a level where the faculty approved drama as a course, for full or half credit, starting in the fall of 1949. David had come to appreciate the great value of theatre while he was at Black Mountain and was always especially proud of Woodstock's drama program: "I recall one year a candidate for Bryn Mawr had her transcript questioned because we had given her two years academic credit for dramatics. When I explained the content of our drama courses, Bryn Mawr had no hesitancy in honoring the credit that had been given." For years, he told people Woodstock had the best drama program in the country for a prep school.

By 1951, the basic structure of the drama program was well established and would not change significantly for another 15 years. In addition to the fall production for Parents Weekend and the spring production for Commencement, directed jointly by Peggy and Jo, the program included shorter, more experimental winter productions, often directed by students. Full credit students also took classroom sections on the history of the theatre, costume, make-up, movement, mime, acting, lighting and stagecraft, taught by Peggy, Jo and others.

"If it hadn't been for Jo, we would never have had a program at all – she had so many capabilities," Peggy recalled. "She originally majored in physical education at some exclusive women's college. That's where she got all her knowledge of folk dancing and all kinds of dance. And when she and her husband were living in England, they masterminded a kind of little theatre group there. Jo was extremely courageous about undertaking something that was almost impossible, and I was rather timid in that respect. She was a very good director. Her specialty was crowd scenes, she was wonderful at that. She was also very interested in spiritualism, ESP and all that. She felt she had some ability in this area. She had a great sense of humor, a bit on the wry side, and she was a very shrewd judge of human character. She was a very heavy smoker. She was a much more lusty person than I was. Not lustful, but lusty. She was extraordinarily sensitive to people's reactions and feelings and she was a great believer, as I was, in discipline. She didn't like all that soul outpouring that the young increasingly indulged in."

Joyce Oatfield, whom everyone called Jo, was a Country School parent from the first day. She started teaching in 1948 and stayed for the next 17 years. A heavyset English woman with remarkable energy and mobility for her 200-plus pound bulk, Jo met the world with a brittle British facade that kept most people from knowing her intimately. Educated in England, with a diploma from the Chelsea College of Physical Education, Jo had been a London Air Raid warden during the Blitz. She and her husband had worked all over the world, from the teak business in Burma to the citrus business in Florida, with periods of personnel training, department store merchandising and running an English nursery school – all while raising three children. The youngest of these, Polly, was at Woodstock (having started in seventh grade in 1945), when Mr. Oatfield died. With her family in difficult straits, David first offered Jo a job running the girls'' dorm, organizing the school's work program and teaching home economics, until she found her natural niche teaching English, French and drama.

From their first major production of *As You Like It* for Commencement in 1950, Peggy and Jo made the drama program a focal point of the school. Often involving as many as half the students on stage and off, Peggy and Jo mounted more than 30 productions over the years, ranging from *The Wind In The Willows* to T.S. Eliot's *Murder In The Cathedral*. They also directed Euripides' *Alcestis* and Anouilh's *Antigone*, Giroudoux's *The Enchanted*, Shaw's *Androcles and The Lion*, and Goldsmith's *She Stoops to Conquer*, as well as *A Midsummer Night's Dream*, *Romeo and Juliet*, *Twelfth Night*, and *The Tempest* by Shakespeare, although the latter was not completed for reasons beyond the directors' control.

For Peggy, the drama program was a paradigm of Woodstock at its best: "It embodied a lot of the principles that I believed in which not everybody did – immense discipline – extraordinary hard work, even drudgery – intellectual appreciation, aesthetic appreciation – opening up the horizons for the children. This idea of giving up your own desires, sometimes almost your own identity, for the sake of the enterprise that we were all working on. It embodied what I thought were the best qualities of the school."

### Student council minutes, February 11, 1953

*The student council met with the faculty at David's house at 2:45 p.m.*
  *General school problems were discussed.*
  *The fact that there has been less out-of-class contact with the faculty than in preceding years. This is largely due to the facts that there are fewer faculty living on campus and that all the faculty (offices) are in the Barn. Several suggestions were made to help overcome this: a) that the faculty attend more evening meals b) that the O.D. would always stay in Greenhithe, and c) since many advisees and advisors can never manage to get together, set periods for conferences might be valuable...*

### Peggy Bailey, Baccalaureate address, June 7, 1953

*Perhaps we know you too well to say goodbye to you properly – with the right amount of dispassionate affection... Perhaps, as Barrie said, you find yourself looking in the mirror and saying to yourself, "What an interesting face! I wonder what the owner of that face has been up to." But perhaps we know what you have been up to. We have known you in the spoken and unspoken word – the glance-- the brief silence – the shared laughter. David once said that he didn't know whether living with you kept him young, or aged him before his time. I think, by some mysterious alchemy, it does both.*
  *When you leave us, you do not leave us entirely-- in the flesh perhaps, but not in the spirit. Little bits and pieces of you are left lying around – thin ghosts lurking in the corners of the Physics Lab. Your moods of joy or sorrow – your disobediences, your immaturities-- your*

*kindness, generosity, enthusiasm and energy – the gifts and heritage of youth – linger around Greenhithe and on the slopes of the hills. We remember these things with occasional exasperation, and pride and thankfulness.*

• • •

In the fall of 1950, David had written wistfully of Woodstock's student body not having "as many exciting individualists as formerly," though he later called the class of 1951 "an exceptionally fine group of students who have gone on to about 15 different colleges." But in the fall of 1951, his report to the board again contained a note of disappointment: "This school year starts off with 76 pupils, apparently an innocuous lot." By April 1954, he had expanded his view into a cultural trend: "The student body as a whole is less creative, less radical, more conformist than at other times. They seem to represent their national age group quite accurately in a kind of unspoken apathy and unwillingness to be bold experimenters. Thus they have been somewhat easier to work with, but less inspiring... A uniform stiffening of academic standards is necessary because of the generally poor intellectual background of many of the students, the 'national youth' seems to be becoming less and less of a reading generation, and thus their general knowledge, mental discipline, and basic skills are weak."

No doubt, students in general were becoming less radical – or less open – during the early 1950's. Certainly, the worldwide surge of post-war optimism that had fed the vitality of Woodstock's early years had given way to widespread Cold War caution, fear and anxiety (which even found their way into the *Symposium* a couple of times). The school had only occasional brushes with the outside world's new mood. In 1948, a Woodstock student's aunt, Helen Gahagan Douglas, lost her Congressional race in California to Richard Nixon, thanks to his notoriously red-baiting "Pink Lady" campaign. The school's semi-official folksinger, Pete Seeger, was under suspicion and harassment, blacklisted, and convicted of contempt of Congress (later overturned). Even some Woodstock parents were put through loyalty checks (while David comforted their children). And Woodstock teachers were required to sign the State of Vermont loyalty oath by January 1, 1954.

Despite the nation's cultural chill, there must still have been a few American adolescents out there as vital and radical as Woodstock's mythical early alumni in and around the fabled class of 1948. After all, the school needed to fill only 25 or so places each year and David, who made all the final admissions decisions, would probably have admitted new iconoclasts if he had recognized them.

That the school didn't attract such young people, or perhaps didn't cultivate them, was another measure of its own gradual institutionalizing, toward relatively more conformist patterns. Later, after 1951, this drift showed up in the evolving faculty as well, as it slowly become more homogeneous, with fewer strong, eccentric, engaging personalities. While the faculty of the mid-'50s would make fewer waves in the school than that of the Deake-Lake era, it would also strike fewer sparks. Still, the potential for a headier mix of personalities remained, defined perhaps at extremes by Mounir Sa'adah and Buffy Dunker. Very different, always at odds, Mounir and Buffy were, from 1946 on, perhaps the most radical members of the Country School faculty – radical in their views, but radical, too, in their impact on students, in their ways of opening young people up to alternative ways of thinking and being.

Fundamentally philosophical and reflective, Mounir let students learn, often for the first time, that questions are sometimes more important than answers, that there are questions with many answers or none and that perhaps no answers are ever final. Further, he posed his questions in a powerful moral context, challenging students to confront the most basic problems of right and wrong. While moral behavior was a clear personal imperative for Mounir, he presented himself in a tantalizingly contradictory context in which no thought was unthinkable or undebatable. His method, in the classroom and out, was essentially Socratic, the authority-who-is-not-the-authority provoking conclusions that raise more questions. (He later described a wry example of the early faculty's willingness to test reality, "the time when we the faculty decided not to show up at the school for a day to see what would happen. Nothing! The young people ran the show smoothly and it was discovered that we were (the faculty) redundant." There is no indication this experiment was repeated.)

In sharp contrast to Mounir, Buffy at any given moment seemed to stand for one and only one particular politically correct way of thinking. But what Buffy found politically correct could, and did, change drastically over the years, highlighting her real message – the one that was received, if not sent – that, under the right circumstances, there was almost no personal behavior that was not all right, within fairly broad, essentially benign limits. There was a certain consistency to her contradictions: while Buffy was persistent, if not rigid, in enforcing the school's rules (often loudly demanding that a shirt be tucked in), she also spent most of her life outside of school challenging the rules of the larger society. The way she lived her life dramatized some fundamental, sometimes conflicting questions of honesty, loyalty and justice. In the mix of her intense enthusiasms, she illustrated the somewhat contradictory notions that to live a full life one must make limiting commitments; and that one must be willing to experience everything, while at the same time making choices.

For all their chronic personal friction, Buffy and Mounir complemented each other nicely within the school, providing two very different, usually responsible ways of approaching the world with boundless energy, Buffy's like a thunderstorm, Mounir's like the tide. They also served as extreme ends of a faculty spectrum, which allowed ample room for other individualities. And David continued to recruit others as idiosyncratic as those two on occasion, such as Jo Oatfield. More frequently, however, as the diverse and sometimes difficult characters of the early years moved on, David replaced them with people no less able, but with personalities not always so powerful or varied.

When Edith Cochran retired in June 1951, she was the last of Woodstock's founding faculty except the Baileys. She was honored at commencement with nostalgic comment and cut flowers and with a card signed by all the students. In addition, the student council established a book fund in her name, after deciding not to give her a hand-carved sign commemorating "Edith's Tea Shoppe." In some ways a strict and forbidding spinster, Edith had for six years opened her apartment to students for afternoon tea and discussion, a tradition that left the school with her. Acknowledging Edith's "extraordinary service," David said she had "given in devotion and work an amount that can neither be measured nor repaid."

Other striking personalities came and went more quickly during Edith's years – Bert Sarason, Miss Peterson, and intensely intellectual Jack Eichrodt and his darkly beautiful, caring wife, Grace. And then there was the tall and dapper Max Wilson – Maximilian William Wilson, Haitian and the son of an ambassador, working on his doctoral thesis. Wilson was Woodstock's first and last black teacher until 1972. "He was about six-two, very strong French accent – he was very black and very tall," Severn Darden recalled. "He was very erudite. He had read just about everything, spoke several languages, and he was very funny – he was always leaping out at couples that were kissing on the porch, and laughing." He left Woodstock before the end of school in 1948, when forced to leave the country by the State Department.

At the same time, David brought in two other men who had a quietly profound effect on the school while they were there:

- **George (Bus) Talbot,** whom everyone called Bus, ran the Country School's summer program in 1947 and 1948, before joining the regular faculty that fall. A quiet, powerfully-built farmer with a direct, no nonsense manner, he taught algebra and geometry and ran the athletic program, until his sudden death from a heart attack in the spring of 1954. A recovering alcoholic, Bus had been at the Derby School in Hingham, Mass., before coming to Woodstock. In early 1948, he bought a 100-year-old farm in nearby South Pomfret, where he, his wife and six children ran a family dairy farm for years. Hard working, intelligent and caring, Bus quickly became a trusted and valued member of the school community, someone both David and students turned to for counsel and support. Whitney Slater Tokunaga '53 said, "Bus was my advisor from ninth grade on, and I decided somewhere in the middle of ninth grade that if God had been fair he'd have let Bus be my father." As David wrote after Bus died: "He was not only a wonderful teacher and loyal friend of the school for six years, but he represented to many of us an example of the ideal man and father. We were fortunate to have known him." In tribute to his value to the school, the trustees offered full scholarships to his children. In all, six Talbots, from Stan in the class of 1952 to Elsa in the class of 1968, graduated from Woodstock.

- **Allen Weatherby,** so the legend has it, was happily enjoying a baseball game from the bleachers in Fenway Park during the summer of 1949 when he fell into conversation with an avid Red Sox fan beside him. That fan was David Bailey. And before the game was over, he had persuaded Allen to come to the Country School to teach English and foreign languages in the fall. A 1934 Harvard graduate, Allen had been West Coast editor for Doubleday before owning and operating the Hollywood Book Store for eight years. Friendly, but reserved, Allen had a brittle wit and some impatience with his slower Latin scholars. He was perhaps the most academically able member of the faculty while he was at the school, even winning a Fulbright Scholarship for study in Greece in 1952-53 (which ill health forced him to forego). During his five years at the school, Allen was one of its most popular and most demanding teachers, strongly reinforcing Woodstock's traditions of academic excellence with an 11th-grade English course that featured a close reading of *King Lear* and the requirement that each student write a lengthy autobiography. When he left the school in 1954, he returned to Harvard to get his doctorate and thence went on to college teaching.

After the Lake and Deake crises of 1950-51, David's hiring style grew more conventional over the next several years (except 1952, when he had no faculty turnover at all). He no longer recruited in sports arenas, but used more traditional channels with more traditional results. While these results were mixed, some new teachers found Woodstock quickly incompatible. These came and went with remarkable speed, including a math teacher with Colonial Virginia ancestry who returned to Virginia; an English teaching would-be novelist who felt D.H. Lawrence had a dirty mind; a descendent of a great New England naturalist who preferred playing basketball to teaching science; or a stiff and bullying Englishman who gave up teaching English to become a corporate lawyer. But others hired during these years, while not so obviously idiosyncratic as their predecessors, would nevertheless provide the school with strong academic standards and solid institutional continuity during the next decade. These included Curt Hinckley and Priscilla (Prill) Baird, who arrived separately in 1951, married within a year, and remained at Woodstock through 1959 (with a brief return during 1963-66, described in Chapter 6).

In the summer of 1951, when he had his interview with David in bed, Curt was just half a year out of Yale. He was in the last class of post-war January graduates, having served two years in the Navy hospital corps. When he met David, Curt was working as a psychiatric aide (orderly) at the Yale Psychiatric Clinic. At Woodstock – for $1,600 a year – he taught biology, zoology and chemistry, was the assistant head of the boys' dorm and supervised the school's fire protection procedures. When the demand arose, Curt offered informal sex education classes, with a basically biological orientation. He was, in different parts, replacing both Bob Lake and Stan Deake in the fall of 1951. The first student that David introduced Curt to was Cy Williams '52, who had pitched the school's only no-hitter (ever) and was the student council president. Cy's first words to the new teacher were: "Well, you follow a loser."

Prill taught art and one French course and ran the small girls' dorm in the Barn. Since graduating from Connecticut College in 1945, Prill had spent the next six years getting her MA from Columbia Teacher's College, teaching, and being a group leader for the Experiment in International Living for six summers. She was to become the first art teacher since the school began who would last more than one year.

"At the beginning, it was all pretty wonderful," Curt recalled, "it was all just an exciting, challenging, fabulous experience. It was a very easy place, easy situation to fall in love with... everything about it – from the geography of Woodstock, Vermont, to the climate, to the size, to the dedicated people who were in this with me, the faculty, to the students, who were a real challenge and very exciting, and as a result, when things worked, they really worked and were very, very rewarding."

After their marriage in 1952, the Hinckleys continued to run a boys' dorm and began raising a family, having three children in all. Strong-minded and disciplined people, the Hinckleys pushed their students hard, maintaining high standards of discipline and high expectations in the classroom and out. Curt, especially, kept his classroom so orderly that a fellow faculty member called "his chem and bio labs two of the showpieces of the school." Both Hinckleys also tended to bring a little clinical detachment to their non-academic work as well, practicing a kind of lay psychotherapy within the community and maintaining a sometimes-cool distance from their students/patients, or peers. This was more a matter of style than substance – both Hinckleys remained devoted to Woodstock and its purposes long after they left the school – but it was a style at variance from the intense spirit of communal engagement that so characterized the school's first years. Cy Williams made his comment – "well, you follow a loser" – out of that old spirit, while Curt expressed the newer mode by not chasing down the comment's meaning. Yet Curt, too, would look back at his early Woodstock years as a communal, we're-all-in-this-together kind of experience. Had it been just a matter of the Hinckleys' somewhat detached lifestyle, the question of student-faculty interaction might have not seemed important enough to David in 1953 to call a special meeting of the faculty and student council. But he had hired others who were also devoted and detached in different ways – and a school that meant to be a kind of family could not afford too many adults who were inaccessible to kids who needed them.

### 'Fun' Seminar Tried in Vermont

NEW YORK HERALD TRIBUNE, SUNDAY JULY 1953
*By Allen Weatherby*
*[Last February] an experiment was carried through at the Woodstock Country School, a co-educational boarding school in Vermont. Classes were cancelled, the schedule was scrapped, and the entire week devoted to "The History and Practice of Passing the Time."*

*Originally this investigation of the nature of entertainment was to have been a one-day affair, one of a series of monthly seminars. But, when preliminary discussions were held by the faculty on the "Fun" seminar, a week was set aside for it.*

*At first some of the children showed signs of uneasiness; others with the conventionally characteristic of twelve to eighteen-year-olds, were openly shocked. But, by the end of the week all but a mere handful of diehards were convinced that they had not heretofore given enough serious thought to the business of amusing themselves....*

*[Among the week's highlights]... faculty members read aloud from E.B. White, Dickens, "Saki" and Herman Wouk.... faculty members spoke on "the History of Entertainment".... a scene from "The Taming of the Shrew".... madrigals by a student-faculty group.... the diaries of Pepys and Parson Woodford, and the letters of Horace Walpole.... construction of homemade sleds.... A feeling grew that people used to have more fun in the days when activities were more active – before the passive enjoyments: TV, radio, comic books.... Parlor games – tiddlly winks, parchesi, rumor, charades.... making thins [from scraps].... the local movie was compulsory,... an indifferent picture,... a detailed analysis of the story, acting, direction, and meaning, if any.... a doubleheader basketball game, with both boys' and girls' teams participating.... dancing....*

*At the end of the week handicrafts got the most votes. But a change seems to have taken place all along the line. Students now ask whether the picture downtown is worth going to. The faculty has been asked to read aloud again.*

• • •

Until one day in early 1953, Rockwell (Steve) and Isabel Stephens, both in their fifties, had never heard of the Woodstock Country School. They were enjoying a visitors' lunch at the Putney School and David Bailey, sitting next to them, invited them to come to Woodstock in the fall. Isabel had just resigned from Wellesley College (where she had been head of the Education Department and served on the admissions committee). Steve had just closed down his ski business in Boston. They had not yet decided what to do next, but they knew they wanted eventually to retire to Vermont, so they accepted David's offer. They bought a house in South Woodstock and worked for the school for twelve years, until their retirement in 1965.

"I don't think that we realized, until the school opened in September [1953], just how dubious the faculty was about adding two more people to the faculty, when they could easily have split up those salaries among themselves," Isabel recalled years later. "And I don't know that they ever did know how little salaries we had. We took one job and never had more than that, just the salary of one job, which we split between us."

Isabel taught U.S. and English History and helped run college placement, which David had done mostly by himself before. Steve taught business math and mechanical drawing, ran the cross-country and downhill ski programs, and looked after school maintenance. Although Isabel impressed students and faculty alike as an intellectual powerhouse whose courses were rich and tough, she did not involve herself deeply in the school. She had expected, when David hired her, that she would be his assistant headmaster or the equivalent. She had not expected Buffy. These two strong women did not mesh effectively, so Isabel pulled back. Since she and Steve were both half-time employees, they fiercely protected their non-school hours. They maintained a careful separation from most of the non-academic life of the school, happy to leave most of those intensities to the younger, more energetic faculty. As Isabel recalled it: "Anyway, we always had that agreement, and it was one of the things that we both loved. And it was always recognized, in the sense that we didn't have a whole lot loaded on us. When David would say, 'Oh, of course you're going to coach (field) hockey,' I'd say, 'Of course I'm not, you know, I'm going home at two o'clock.'... David tried to persuade us to come to supper every night, but we didn't do that, we came by every third night."

Larry and Kilty Roberts came to Woodstock with the Stephens in 1953 and they stayed until David retired in 1967. Larry taught algebra, general science and physics, helped out with soccer and helped manage the school property. For more than a decade, he and Kilty ran a small girls' dorm, first on Linden Hill and in the Farmhouse at Upwey. A quiet, self-controlled young man, Larry graduated from Trinity College in 1944 (where he played varsity soccer) and earned his Master's degree in physics there in 1950. A Signal Corps instructor during the war, a summer physics instructor at Trinity, he had most recently worked as a ranger for the Connecticut Park and Forest Commission. Kilty Roberts graduated from Mount Holyoke College in 1951, with a degree in physiology. They had a very young daughter then, the first of their three children.

They interviewed as a couple and Kilty remembered David "had a casual air in his dungarees and open shirt – no tie and jacket, which was the thing I would have expected from the headmaster at the time, it was a lot more informal than the schools we'd had experience in." For Larry, the school required "growing and adjustments on my part – it certainly wasn't like a chain of command and getting orders like I did in the Forestry Department... and there was a very strong faculty, amazingly strong for a brand new school – and they were extremely capable, very vocal people with lots of interests... It was a good school for their kids to get an education – you don't often see that in schools." Of fourteen Woodstock faculty members in 1953-54, ten had sent, or would send, one or more of their children to the school (and the Stephens's sent two grandchildren). All but three of about eighteen would graduate. One of those two was the Roberts's oldest, Hannah, who spent 1967-68 at Woodstock, but by then her parents were gone, David was gone and the school was a very different place.

But in 1953, like the Hinckleys and the Stephenses, in different ways, Larry and Kilty held themselves at some remove from the heart of the school life. They were, by nature, somewhat reserved and therefore not at first inclined to plunge headlong into the hurly burly of community life. But they learned and grew and became much more involved over the years, as they, too, came to cherish the school and all it did to open their lives as well.

It would be easy to overstate the shift in faculty attitudes, for even a "detached" Woodstock faculty was intimate to the point of obsessive about the lives of students by the standards of 1953 America. But the balance had shifted away from earlier, deeper student-faculty involvement, to a mode of more limited exposure for the adults, many of whom were less sympathetic to, even disdainful of adolescent difficulties or enthusiasms. In the mid-fifties, some teachers found it tolerable not merely to call their students "children," but to treat them as children, thereby retarding or deflecting, rather than promoting growth. Certainly there is always the problem of keeping the distinction between students and teachers clear – answering the perennial question: who are the grown-ups here? But that can be done without creating a gulf between the sides, without creating sides. The changing tastes and attitudes of young people added to the problem, and David himself was not immune from seeming reactionary sometimes. He was openly and persistently critical of new tastes in music, not just rock'n'roll, but jazz – especially the saxophones of Charlie Parker, John Coltrane or Paul Desmond. It was not an easy time to be an adult or a young person. Working hard to be responsive as well as responsible, Isabel, Larry and Curt were all-important figures in the school for most of a decade. From 1954 through 1962, one or another of them was the faculty representative to the board of trustees – but none generated quite the devotion and affection the community gave their predecessors during 1948-54: Edith Cochran, Bus Talbot and Allen Weatherby. Moving the Country School toward a new flowering in the early 1960s, David turned again to hiring more charismatic, idiosyncratic teachers – and students grew less inclined to project authority on others just because they were older.

FALL 1951 – FALL 1955

## Curt Hinckley interview, March 19, 1986

*I think David probably served as a father image for me, just as he did for a lot of students. He seemed to be the all-knowing, somewhat mystical person who had an insight into adolescents and what they needed and how best to provide them with what they needed...*

*I think it was a very difficult situation to be in as a young, new teacher, because I think the greatest temptation is to emulate the master. However, the master was not interested in helping one learn how to do that, because that was his – pardon the pun – bailiwick... So the frustration I think that I experienced was that I saw what appeared to be some wonderful things happening, but I couldn't find out how to be more effective in doing the same kinds of things... And while it's wonderful to bathe in that mystique, I think it also leaves a lot to be desired. I think if one goes to study with the master, it would be awfully nice to be able to learn more from the master and not be thrown to such a large degree on one's own resources.*

## Sidney Smith '56 interview, May 16, 1984

*I threw a salt shaker at somebody once and [David] spanked me – put me over his knew and spanked me – and I thought later on, that dirty old man. But he could be quite cruel at times, if you were on his bad list, if he'd heard bad reports about you, or seen you do anything bad _ he could really make you suffer for it for quite awhile – just by looking at you, by staring at you....*

*It was his physical presence – he never really said too much – it was the way he looked at you. He had this kind of power over children. Some children got along very well with him and did everything he wanted them to do, and others didn't, and I was one of the ones who didn't, and that's why I suppose I didn't like him as much as I did Peggy....*

*[David] would give you a look that meant that you weren't exactly his favorite – but that's part of the mystique. That's why he was such a good headmaster, that he had this ability to frighten people – because if he frightened you and then he was nice to you, you felt all the better because of it....*

## Isabel Stephens interview, December 12, 1983

*I always thought that, while I was there, that David ran it and if you didn't like it, well then you could go somewhere else. But of course you took a chance [on the school]...*

*Some of the biggest issues in some ways sound small – like the smoking issue – which was quite bitterly contested in the faculty. Some of us thought that David used smoking privileges as a reward and, when you won smoking privileges, that you were somebody. And we always felt that this was exactly the reverse of what he could have done if he had wanted to, by making the non-smokers prestigious, without a whole lot of talk about it, of course, but making them feel individually that they were doing something quite brave in just not smoking... It was the sort of thing that came up over and over...*

*But when it came to the fundamentals of the school, what it was trying to do, I always thought there was unanimity. And I think they were trying very hard, on the whole successfully, to build confidence in children – who had brains and didn't know it, and those who were slightly less endowed but still fully able to be useful to society and get over their sense of inferiority.*

## David Bailey report to the trustees, October 16, 1954

*The start of our 10th academic year has not yet been marked by anything unusual. The enrolment is not perfect, but there are some good aspects to it. There are several more boys than girls – many of them large, healthy and docile. They crowd the dormitory and damage the food budget, but are otherwise a good asset... Through a variety of circumstances, we have one or two fewer girls than usual. The budget suffers but the living arrangements in the girls' dormitory are happier and neater.*

*The "old guard" of the faculty started the year in not the best physical shape, because nobody seemed to have a very restful summer...*

*Plantwise, the school is in reasonably good shape... Because we have inevitably pointed toward it, the acquisition of a new dormitory is all-important as a measure of our success... It is presumed that the Trustees will perforce spend the great majority of their deliberations on this subject. Suffice it to say herein that the Headmaster's schedule so far allows very little time for individual student conferences, and even less for extra-mural activities. [Isabel] Stephens is to help with some of the most burdensome administrative duties. She will be particularly useful in the college admissions work with the Seniors, so the Headmaster will be considerably relieved in the winter and spring of much paper work and consultation time. The future, therefore, looks better than the present.*

• • •

Nine years after its first opening day, Woodstock was gathering many of the attributes of maturing educational institutions. The recently formed Alumni Association (1951) and Parents Association (1952) were boosting morale by reinforcing the school's sense of community and continuity, while also making some contribution in fundraising and student recruitment. Physically, besides the two-year old headmaster's house, the school had managed to add other long-sought amenities, including an assembly room, a baseball field, a parking lot by Greenhithe (with a basketball hoop), a small carpentry shop building and a fire pond by the Barn. Not terribly impressive, perhaps, as traditional bricks-and-mortar monuments, but very practical and of added meaning because they had been put off so long by limited resources.

The school's somewhat offbeat style and substance continued to gain increasing visibility and acceptance among outsiders. The school community cheerfully welcomed such talismans of belonging as the wider world bestowed. The 1952 commencement speaker was U.S. Senator Estes Kefauver of Tennessee, then a Democratic contender for the Presidential nomination who had received national attention as chairman of a series of Senate hearings on organized crime. His visit to Woodstock was heavily if not terribly accurately covered by the local press (at the time there was no local radio or TV news). The Woodstock paper reported Kefauver's commencement speech on page one (in its own malaprop-heavy style): "The Senator agreed that the United States had made mistakes in China. But he emphatically disproved the underwriting of Chiang Kai Shek. 'A resolution is going on in the world,' he said. 'We must strive to attract that resolution in our direction and away from Communism.'" Another swirl of excitement and publicity attended the school's Parents Weekend in 1953, when Eleanor Roosevelt arrived to visit her goddaughter. Mrs. Roosevelt dutifully visited classes and had her picture taken with the school cook, "Pop" Landers, a deep-dyed old Vermont Yankee, charming everyone as she did. Less spectacularly, but more devotedly, since Pete Seeger first performed at Woodstock in 1950, his annual concerts became popular occasions in town as well as school life for more than a decade.

The school was celebrity conscious from the beginning, welcoming people as different as Alexander Kerensky and Mary Martin. Now David was learning to use the promotional value of these celebrities as well. As he told the trustees in April 1953, "an experiment in publicity will be our series of four ads in *The New Yorker* magazine. This is quite a departure from the usual practice of our school or any other, but we feel it's worth a gamble, especially as we think our present parent body is about 80 per cent *New Yorker*-reader-type." And at least one parent was a *New Yorker*-editor-type, Harold Ross, whose daughter Patti was in the class of 1954.

At the same time that so many small things were falling into place, the school was making little progress with the biggest item on its agenda – a new boys' dorm. State and local banks consistently turned down the school's request for a $90,000 mortgage, just as they had earlier refused to underwrite the headmaster's house, but this time no other source of money was readily available. In April 1954, even though he had made no fundraising assignments in his role as board president, David complained to the trustees, "Everybody's talking about a new dormitory building but nobody's doing very much. So far, no one has been directly solicited for a gift or loan... The students are naturally enthused about the project, though we have to some extent tried to restrain the zeal lest it be abortive. The money they secure (through the student gift) will not be important but the spirit exhibited will be, therefore there is hope for enough confidence from the trustees and from the administration to make a formal announcement this spring at Commencement... It looks now as if a decisive factor will be not so much the immediate financial prospects but the collective boldness of Trustees." The Commencement announcement made, the school started slowly to raise the needed money. By the October board meeting, the new dorm fund was over $26,000, but roughly $15,000 of that came from school reserves, with only $11,000 in gifts. In order to be able to break ground the following spring, the board voted to mount a short but intense campaign to raise the remaining $64,000 in four months – starting at Parents Weekend on November 5.

Early in the morning of November 4, the Barn, the school's main classroom building, burned to the ground. The fire was first reported at 1:45 a.m.

"About the middle of the night, Peter [Bailey, then 14 years old] came and woke me up, and said 'I think there's a fire'," Peggy Bailey recalled. "I thought he was having a bad dream, so I took him back to his room to tuck him up. Then I noticed his window that faced out onto the Barn, the shade was all blood red, so I pulled up the shade and there was the Barn, blazing. I put Peter back to bed and I had to go wake David. For a moment he could hardly believe it. It was our tenth year, and he was getting on (he was 42). I remember his sitting for a moment on the side of his bed with his head in his hands. Then he got up and dressed and went out. By this time the firemen were there and some students. Mercifully there was no one in the building."

By daylight, the building was gone. The physics and chemistry labs were gone, and biology lab with James Barter's zoology mural was gone. Several classrooms were gone, the art room was gone. Mounir's office was gone, with most of his books and papers. Student cubbies were gone with all their books, papers, projects and treasures. The drama room was gone with its few costumes and props. The student common room was gone, the faculty room was gone, the school store was gone. David's office was gone, Buffy's office was gone, the school office was gone – and with them all the school's student files, financial records, most of the institutional documents of a decade. The estimated replacement cost for the Barn was more than $100,000. The school's insurance covered less than $50,000. Most of the records would never be fully reconstructed.

Sarah Lorenz Mitchell was a senior then: "I woke up in the middle of the night and the barn was burning down, and I woke up all my roommates – all the girls in the senior class were in that big room (in Greenhithe) that looked out on the Barn. The next morning, I was on morning kitchen crew and we all had been up all night... I was the only person, nobody else showed up, going about getting the breakfast – and David walked in, and he looked at me and said what are you doing here? And I said, you know, it's time to get the breakfast, and he looked at me, and I understood what he was thinking, which was, that's right, and this is a young woman, this is what women do in a crisis, and I knew that he was paying me a compliment about what it was to be a grown-up, but nothing was said, it was just something that was understood. Then he pitched in, and other people came and so on."

The community absorbed the event quickly and remarkably calmly. Some people cried, some stared a moment in disbelief, then everyone went to work. Classes were shifted to the Greenhithe common room and dining room, to the Baileys' house, to Buffy's house, and to the girls' dorm down the hill. People made do, people pitched in, people rose to the occasion. By mid-morning, with the Barn still hot and smoking, the school was running on schedule.

One of the area's daily newspapers, *The Valley News*, reported, "Cause of the blaze is not known, Woodstock fire chief Eric Paige said this morning. Bailey reported he had passed the building at 11 last night and noted nothing unusual... A fortuitous shift in the wind may have saved the head master's house and other structures from damage... Despite the early hour, the blaze drew a large local crowd to the scene... Gingerly probing the hot wreckage this morning, school authorities discovered two large metal cash boxes, which had carried their contents unharmed through the blaze. They were waiting for the school safe to cool off before opening it. A chimney, the only remnant of the building left standing after the blaze, was pulled down to avoid the possibility of its collapsing later." After noting that the blaze could be seen as much as twenty miles away, the paper added, "Bailey said today that the school will rebuild its lost facilities at a future date."

Parents Weekend was held as scheduled. The building and fundraising plans for the new dormitory were announced as planned. Then the Parents Association expanded its goal, deciding to raise enough money to build both a new dorm and a new classroom building as soon as possible.

An article in the local paper, probably written at the school by David and others, describes the aftermath of the fire: "David Bailey, headmaster, spoke with pride and praise of the behavior of the 78 pupils. 'It was particularly difficult for them,' he said earlier this week, 'for there was really nothing for them to do but follow routine procedure at a time when they wanted to give constructive help.' Mr. Bailey and all members of the faculty have been deeply moved by the many offers of help and the replacement of supplies and equipment which have come in from people in this area; so deeply touched by the sympathy and helpfulness of the community that they feel at a loss for ways in which to express their gratitude."

### Alicia Burnham Winslow '56 interview, November 15, 1984

*The night of the fire I thought it was early sunrise. I remember seeing stuff dancing on the wall and I said, oh, here's another fire drill – I didn't know, I was half asleep. And we got out there and all of a sudden, there it was, a ball of flame – a bonfire – and everybody was sucking their breath in...*

*I remember we did get pictures and it was like a natural disaster... They were the only pictures, somebody took them, and they were lousy, and I remember them pinning them up on the board and numbered them and people bought them – I still have them right in my room here...*

*The foundation seemed to be so little. There was no foundation at all under the wonderful costume room... And the biology room – that was the room the little alligator was in – and the whole Barn burned and all people could think about was the alligator crawling in the water to get cool and burning up.*

FALL 1951 – FALL 1955

## Sidney Smith '56 interview, May 16, 1984

*It was in the middle of the night, about three in the morning. We were all woken up and we ran to the window. And everybody talked about the animals in the building, there was a lab in the building – all the guinea pigs burning up....*

*It was a huge fire, too, really. By the time we all woke up and were hanging out the window, it was really going. And the thought that it would catch the Library [nearby]. It was that bad. And the firetrucks were already there....*

*I'll tell you something that I remember very well – was seeing David the next morning. We were all sort of afraid to look at him – and he really looked dreadful. Been up all night, of course. But he was wonderful, calm – and we all sort of made do that year.*

## Isabel Stephens interview, December 12, 1983

*The fire was one of the best things that ever happened from that point of view, how they all pulled together. It was wonderful, I was impressed to death. Oh, I remember that year so well – my geography class met in one of Buffy's upstairs rooms in her house, which she very generously let us use, and David was full of scorn because, he said "there wasn't anyplace to put up a map or anything," and I said, "Oh well, we'll study other things" and he said, "Well what else is there?" Well, I said we could study the whole business of the solar system and how we happen to have seasons and what effect all these things make on industries and occupations and which areas will be agricultural and which won't and so on. Well, he said, "That's not geography, that's just a whole lot of bosh." I said, "Of course it's geography, it's very fashionable, I'll get some books on the effect of the environment on personality and they'll eat it up like anything." Well, he said, "When are they going to make any maps?" I said, "Maybe we won't make any maps."*

*He was horrified, really horrified.*

• • •

Seven months after David expressed his concern about "the collective boldness of the trustees," the board was only on the verge of starting a boys' dorm fundraising campaign, for which there was little preparation and no organization. At their May meeting, "after much discussion on how to raise the necessary money for the [boys' dorm], the trustees had agreed that [Elizabeth] Hitchcock would approach [her brother-in-law, Laurance] Rockefeller asking if he would be willing to endorse the loan at Chase Bank, [John] McDill would see some local friends of his and [David] Bailey and [Gordon] Gay would try to see one or two potential donors in Boston and New York to determine what their support would be if the building project is started." By October, the board still had not named a fundraising chairman, nor had strong leadership emerged either on or beyond the board, thus leaving David in charge by default (and probably by preference).

The passivity of the board had paralleled the subsiding of student and faculty energies from earlier years. Had the Barn burned down three years earlier, the school would have had an experienced and seasoned board in place to deal with the crisis. In the fall of 1951, Woodstock's eleven board members included three people who had shaped the school from its inception: Elizabeth Johnson, George Mullins and David Bailey. These three, together with faculty representative Allen Weatherby and Woodstock bank president Earl Ransom, made up the executive committee, providing the school not only with strong leadership, but with a reliable institutional memory as well.

By October 1954, they were all gone but David. At that year's annual meeting, almost all of Woodstock's eleven trustees had been recruited by the headmaster, who still served as president. Only Gordon Gay, a Pacific Mills executive who sent three daughters to Woodstock, had served on the board before 1950, although the new alumni representative on the board, Christian von Huene '50, had been a student during the early years. Only Bartlett Hayes, head of the art department at Phillips Andover Academy, and WCS faculty representative Isabel Stephens, had significant school experience, most of it at schools decidedly different from Woodstock. Of 11 board members, six had served two years or less and eight had no direct experience either with running a school or with Woodstock itself (although four of those eight were parents of Woodstock students). This board, coping only marginally with the school's long-standing need for a new dormitory, now faced the immediate necessity of replacing the main school building as well.

Looking for a more imaginative solution to the problem than just building two new buildings – and no doubt seeking some way to rekindle the school's early pioneering spirit – David turned to his network of local contacts to develop alternatives. He reported to the six other members attending the special board meeting of December 10, 1954:

"Mr. Bailey presented the building plans made by [architect Payson] Webber which consist of 24 double bedrooms, 15 x 10, with 75,900 cubic feet and would cost approximately $75,000. He also showed the trustees pictures of a Quonset hut, which has never been used and can be bought for $4,000. This is 100 x 40 and could be floored and heated for about $15,000. The dubious merits of investing that much money in temporary buildings were discussed.

"Mr. Bailey then dropped his bombshell: Upwey Farms in South Woodstock can be bought for $90,000 – 400 acres – many buildings.

"Mr. Bailey mentioned three problems which would confront him if the school were to buy Upwey: First, the intangible: Would the school change in character because of the physical set-up? Second, it would be difficult to arrange a "center" which is important. And third, his personal feelings about the present headmaster's house which was acquired through much sacrifice and effort. There is no replacement for it at Upwey."

The meeting adjourned until the next day, when eight trustees met in the hamlet of South Woodstock: one store, an inn and a few houses five miles south of Woodstock Village. The trustees spent an hour and a half examining the Upwey property before reconvening at Isabel Stephen's house, where they voted to empower David and Buffy to spend up to $500 to secure a first refusal on Upwey Farms.

Upwey Farms, with 400 acres and numerous buildings, including the large main house, had belonged to Owen Moon, who had made it a showplace in its day. In 1954, it was still pretty fancy, with several large barns, two additional farmhouses, a large stone amphitheatre and elaborate gardens among its perquisites. It was still a working farm, with an emphasis on horses related to the Green Mountain Horse Association next door.

## Larry Roberts, personal notes on faculty meeting, January 12, 1955

*Faculty meeting 12 January 1955 – #17. Upwey*
  **Mounir [Sa'adah]** – *thinks it would be a mistake to stay here [Greenhithe] for 50 years. Worried about water supply, flexibility*

**Prill [Hinckley]** – Worried about building here (Ivan [Shove, the school's builder] worried)
**Curt [Hinckley]** – On the fence, against size increase
**Peggy [Bailey]** – feels selfish (about headmaster's house)
Worried about extra plant load, hard to keep up spiritually and financially
**Jo [Oatfield]** – Philosophical either way – upkeep looks too expensive, should stay here happy and forget completely
**Herman [Einsmann]** – worried about flexibility, too large, upkeep, far from town, finance problem
**Steve [Stephens]** – worried about upkeep. Larger plant would be more attractive. Doesn't like centralization
**Ginny [Weeks]** – Worried about finances, intangible support and loyalty, keep same size, no view. Wonderful opportunity
**Buffy [Dunker]** – Working out of problems will be good for students. Be good to get off present shoestring, but not in any hurry. Doesn't like the road [main buildings close to Vermont Route 106]. Doesn't know enough. More first rate students. Scared to death of change and immensely attracted
**Shep [Smith]** – Starting a new school if we do go. Should be a place for boys to go to, not quite such centralization [as at Greenhithe]
**Isabel [Stephens]** – Will get fewer children that need to be patched up shortly. Want a place for students of happy homes that can help build. Want school this size or smaller – if we can't stay small, stay here. Doesn't want to live on flat with new road. Should have a good headmaster's house and good salaries. Will take 10-15 years, changing, creating and shifting...

Higher insurance rates
Less accessible to stores, library, movies, churches, recreation center, doctors, Dartmouth – less convenient for faculty
Lack of public water and sewer system – means increased maintenance problems and costs
Too great centralization
No good location for David's house
Maintenance costs will be higher because buildings are larger
Plantation (tree farm) is now about 30 years old and should have been thinned nearly 15 years ago. Not to be counted upon as a money making venture in the immediate future

*Will be a new school, not Woodstock Country School moved – in minds of present alumni*
*Too expensive to remodel for what we need*
*Because of physical layout, not much more room for future expansion than present site, even if no property sold*
*Higher operating costs will result in higher tuition rate and reduce number of deserving children that we can help with scholarships*

## David Bailey report to the trustees, January 15, 1955

*Obviously the chief consideration for us today is to decide what to build and where. Our investigations and thinking have brought us to where we should either build three or more structures on the present campus, or purchase the Upwey property and convert the necessary building there. There are of course drawbacks and advantages to both plans. Right at the start it should be said that in my opinion it would be feasible and quite satisfactory, certainly much easier, to stay where we are. On the other hand, the move to Upwey is a challenge and an opportunity, and the long range future of the school would be enhanced by such a move. The Upwey property offers graciousness and spaciousness...*

*Naturally one of the fears about the change is that we will become so involved with possessions that the fundamental educational process will suffer...*

*To sum up these ramblings about our dilemma, I must say that we can envision our future in either site. The Upwey property promises a more glorious possibility. It also means our gambling on our ability to cope with the various financial problems. My recommendation would be to take the chance, buy the place at once, so that we can be free of the present uncertainty and be able to start on specific plans and operations.*

• • •

Although he did not make it clear at the January 12 faculty meeting, David had already made up his mind to try to move the school to Upwey Farms, where he swam in the pond as a boy. At the special board meeting three days later, his view prevailed without strong objection, even though there was little solid information on which to base a decision. Even David and Buffy characterized their financial presentation as "fanciful." Nor had all the trustees yet visited Upwey. Nevertheless, when the board took a straw vote on the question after a couple of hours' discussion, nine of the eleven favored the move. Having decided the main question, the board then turned it over to the executive committee to carry out. The committee comprised David Bailey, John McDill, Ivy Thomas, Isabel Stephens and Frank Canaday (who, as the only non-Woodstock resident, missed all six meetings over the next two months). As the committee clerk, Buffy Dunker also took part in most of its meetings. By delegating its authority to the Executive Committee, the board effectively abstained from making any hard decisions on the questions that would shape the future of the institution in its care. The board did not organize itself into working subcommittees to examine the philosophical questions raised by the Upwey proposition, not even those David pointed out himself. Nor did it take a harder look at the "fanciful" financial projections on which the proposition was based. Instead, the board gave David what amounted to a vote of confidence in telling him to work it out however he thought best.

This was less an abrogation of collective responsibility (though it was certainly that) than a measure of the degree to which David had taken control of his institution. The trustees were not alone in believing David could, and would, bring the school out all right. Most parents, especially those most active in the Parents Association, were uncritically enthusiastic about the move. David found it easy to continue leading his "conformist" students, while he dealt with the alumni – who strongly opposed leaving Greenhithe – by leaving them out of the discussion. The effect of this non-discussion was sometimes almost surreal. For years, David had said he wanted no larger school each time it reached a higher level of enrolment. But when he worried aloud about the move changing the character of the school, especially by making it larger, the trustees dismissed the concern: "Whether or not the school would become larger is, according to Mr. Gay, an unimportant factor: if the school is to be kept small there is no reason for worry – just keep it small," the January minutes reported.

Gordon Gay, a lifelong business executive who had served as a WCS trustee since 1946, should have known better – the Country School, with no endowment to fall back on, was planning to take on a much larger physical plant which would be much more expensive to run, even according to the "fanciful" financial projections presented at the same meeting. The school could get that income from two places: fundraising, which had not been one of its strengths, or increased enrollment. The board did not confront this dilemma, but left it to resolve itself. Paradigmatically of the headmaster's relationship with the board, the meeting ended with David asking for "volunteers to draw up a statement on the fundamental character of the school," a task he had purposefully avoided doing himself for more than a decade.

During the next seven weeks, David worked diligently to dispel the uncertainty of the school's future, but always with Upwey as the favored alternative in his own mind. David had told the trustees, rather too sanguinely, that "while the student body and the parents are enthusiastic, the faculty has some reservations" about the move. The students, hardly enthusiastic, were putting a good face on their powerlessness. Led by Ellie Noss '56, they raised some money for "The Cause" by publishing an ad-filled tenth anniversary issue of *Symposium* that was profoundly nostalgic about the Greenhithe school. A majority of the faculty, on the other hand, was openly opposed to moving to South Woodstock for a host of reasons (see above), most of which would prove valid. They were also concerned that the cost of running the new plant would come out of teacher salaries, since the trustees had already cut back their commitment to the Scholarship Fund. But the faculty's resistance was not organized or effective, most faculty members saw more than one side of the question and none saw enough difficulty to resign over the issue. Mostly, the teachers were already stretched thin dealing with the seemingly endless academic and social improvisations necessitated by the fire that they had little energy left for confrontational politics, least of all for confronting a headmaster almost all of them fundamentally respected and trusted.

On January 20, 1955, David reported to the Executive Committee that the faculty was opposed to proposed plans for moving to Upwey in South Woodstock. Now, if moving from Greenhithe was necessary, they favored a third plan. (All of the faculty-proposed plans had in common that they tried to solve the problem of providing the school with a "center" – in the end, none of them was adopted.) The official minutes of this Executive Committee meeting, prepared by Isabel Stephens, suggested a congenial unanimity that did not exist in her unsanitized draft. There, after discussing the various plans, she recorded that John McDill asked "whether this shifting of plans was not disconcerting and whether it was possible to launch any sort of money- raising campaign if we could not ourselves decide whether the Upwey estate was usable by us... I had quite a time persuading Payson Webber [the architect] that we were sensible people this afternoon. I want to be perfectly sure that we are doing something we can manage. It seems risky. But on your [David's] assurance I am satisfied."

By January 26, another alternative had emerged – a third local property, closer to town than Upwey and more satisfactory to the faculty on other points as well. The faculty made this property on the River Road, the adjoining Lamb and Aycrigg farms, their first choice. Staying at Greenhithe was an acceptable alternative. The faculty rejected going to Upwey at all because it was too expensive. David reported this at the next day's executive committee meeting, along with the news that the school's $80,000 offer for Upwey had been rejected, although the owner indicted a continued willingness to dicker. The committee voted to withdraw its offer for Upwey and to seek instead to offer $80,000 for the Lamb-Aycrigg properties – "about 800 acres of fields, hills and woods, half a mile of river frontage, springs which supply plenty of water, a couple of small brooks and ponds, three houses, two large barns, and several usable smaller buildings," as David described them. The farms spread up a rolling hillside above the Ottauquechee River. They were a little more than a mile from the center of the village, close enough to walk, but far enough away to be a little less in the public eye.

In a letter asking authorization from the full board for the new plan, David reported on the developments leading up to it without quite hiding his disappointment: "Though these properties may lack some of the grandeur of Upwey, they are well endowed with beauty of locale and distant vistas, and with enormous quantities of sunlight. They will be relatively easy to maintain; they are more advantageously located in relation to Woodstock... I hope this shifting of gears does not indicate careless driving on our part. We really believe we are being both cautious and imaginative. At Upwey, the long-term prospects were exciting but the immediate future was seamy. At this new place, we can contemplate both futures happily."

On February 16, the Executive Committee authorized David to make the offer on the Lamb-Aycrigg properties. But David had not been waiting idly by for their decision. In good Yankee trader fashion, he had kept on dickering with Upwey's owner, Tony Farrell, until, on February 23, he reported to the Executive Committee that Farrell had accepted "a price of $79,000 and an additional $6,000 in 'other values'" which would be defined at a later date. On March 3, Farrell accepted $4,500 in cash and various farm equipment to satisfy the "other values" condition. On March 4, title to the Upwey property passed to the Woodstock Country School.

But that was not the end of it. David continued to talk terms with Tony Farrell, apparently without any awareness of the trustees. By the end of March, the Farrells agreed to buy the Greenhithe property for $40,000, including the Baileys' house, which especially appealed to Mrs. Farrell. The trustees were surprised, but not displeased. As Gordon Gay wrote David, "I'm not too sure that I understand why you had to move so fast with the sale of Greenhithe. Surely, we do not have the cash do we, to meet our obligations in connection with the purchase and the immediate building program? In view of the fact that this is a kind of a swap and a lot of details are being worked out personally, I would make certain if I were you that all understandings are carefully spelled out and put in written form within a short time after the discussion. Such details are usually the things that get us into trouble."

Details of the deal with Tony Farrell did not prove troublesome to the school. He and his family lived in the Baileys' house for a few years before selling the property and moving away. The next owners allowed Greenhithe to deteriorate, leaving it unprotected from weather, or vandals, or romantic local young people seeking seclusion. Yet another owner finally tore it down, leaving only a semi-circle of giant spruce to suggest its once lively existence.

David had solved Woodstock's need for new dormitories and a new classroom building by sheer force of personality. Despite widespread misgivings about moving to Upwey, no one in the school community could, or would, stand up to David in his determination to embrace the "elegance," the "spaciousness and graciousness," or the "grandeur" he saw in the school's future at Upwey. In time, that vision would be at least partly realized, the school would have some of its best days in South Woodstock. But by moving there, it had also brought a host of new problems, as most of the faculty's worries turned out to be well founded. In January 1955, when the school was then at its largest-ever enrolment of 80 students, David told the trustees, "Enlarging the student body is possible, but not desired by anyone – in fact if this were necessary, I think all of us would prefer to stay at Greenhithe."

That September, when the school opened at Upwey, enrollment stood at 93. Continuous pressure for more operating income for almost two more decades would eventually drive enrollment to 126. Only in 1976 would the school again be as small and intimate as it had been during its first decade – but by then its smallness was neither a matter of choice or principle, it was a sign of dying.

Early in the morning of November 4, 1954, the Barn – the WCS main building that held classrooms, offices, science labs, a common room and an auditorium – burned to the ground in a few hours. By morning there was little to look at but the smoking ruin. Here, Gary Plantiff '56 talks to David Bailey (long coat) and his brother Tad Bailey beside him.

David Stein '56 (with pickaxe), unknown (l) and Bill Kelly '58 (r)

Bill Hogan '56, Becky Hughes '57, Jon Nordheimer '55, and Muffy French '55

David Raider '57

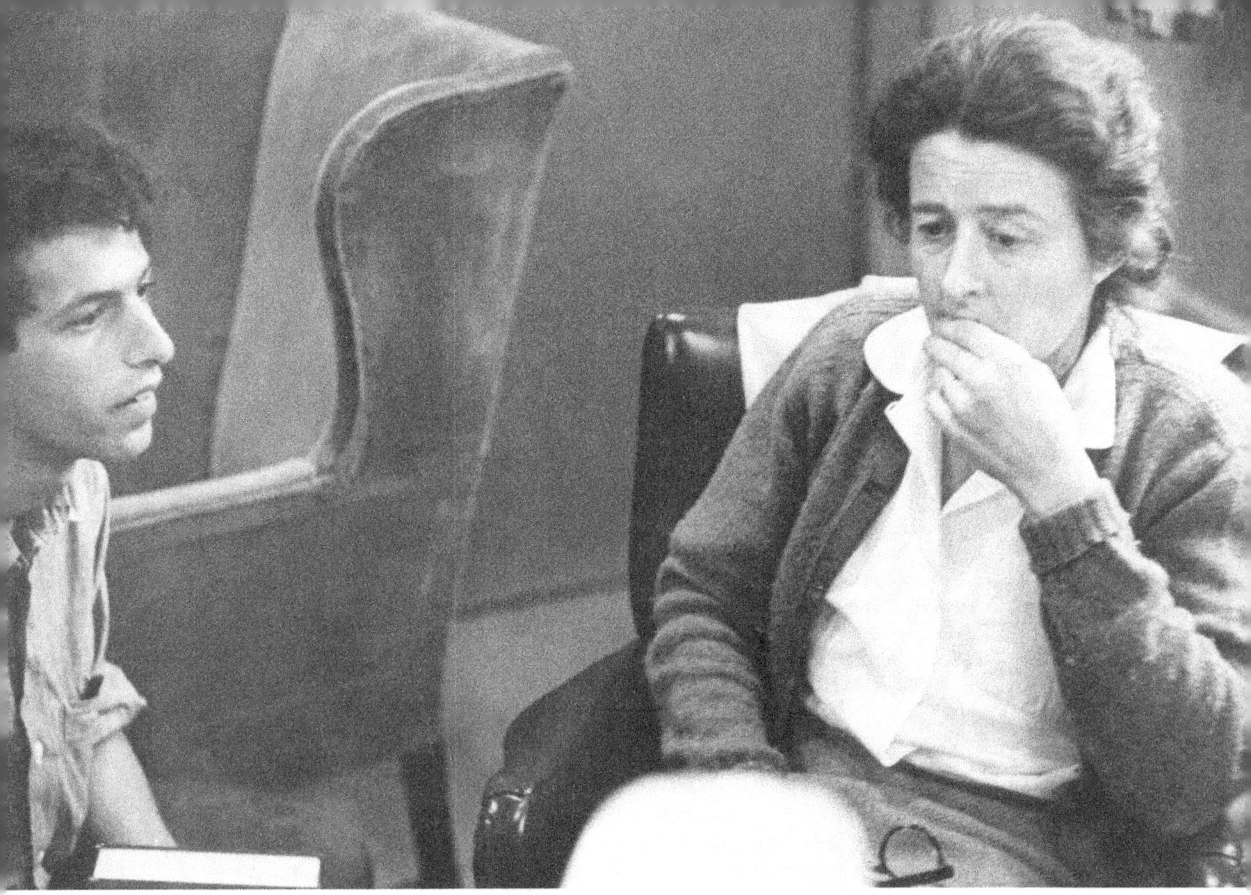

Henry Felt '60 and Isabel Stephens

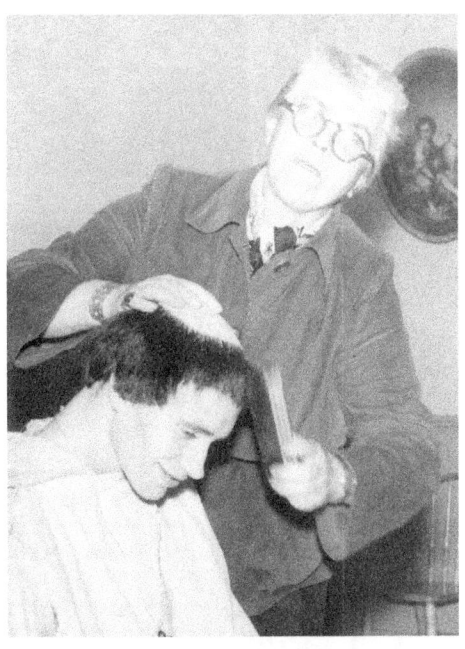

Backstage: Jo Oatfield prepares Bill Eva '57 to appear in "Murder in the Cathedral"

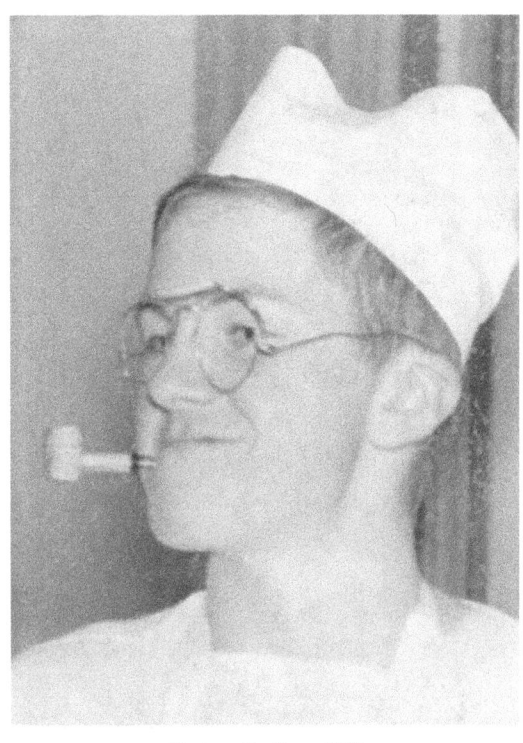

Peter Bailey '57

"The Devil Among the Skins" by Ernest Goodwin, winter 1960 (l. to r.) Gardner Garretson, Ed Shiller, and Gay Sweet, all class of 1960.

Retta Thompson '61

ANNE LEWIS '60

The Troll Hole – reputedly a former colonial root cellar, or an ancient astronomical marker, or something else, located near the top of Morgan Hill, the site of many WCS all-school picnics.

Farm Crew: Joan Hannah '57 (foreground), Jonathan Potter '57 (standing, right) in the garden uphill from Greenhithe

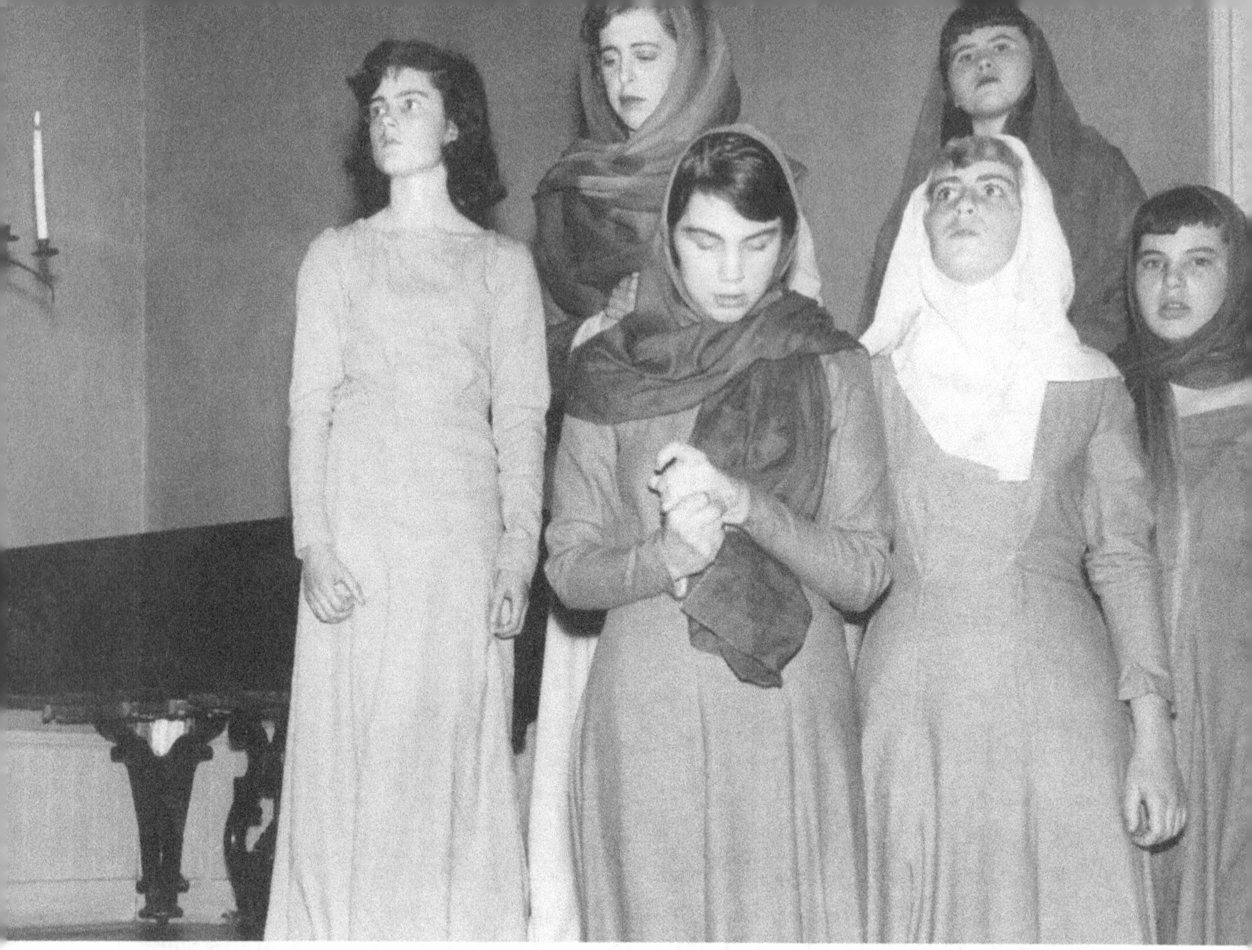

"Murder in the Cathedral" by T.S. Eliot – chorus:
BACK ROW (l. to r.): Sidney Smith '56, Heather Hoskins '55, Ellen Sheehan '56
FRONT ROW: Sarah Lorenz '55, Anne Adams '54, Debbie Moon '57
Performed in the Unitarian Universalist Church in Woodstock, fall, 1953

Sara Dunham

Shakespeare's A Midsummer Night's Dream in the amphitheatre, June 1956
From left: Laura McDill '57, Sidney Smith '56, and Judy Weil '58,
FRONT: Hank Savelberg '62

CHAPTER FIVE

# Fall 1955 – Spring 1962

### WCS brochure, Spring 1955

*Purchase of Upwey Farms gives the school a property of great beauty, with buildings ready for immediate conversion at less cost than all-new construction. More than 400 acres of meadows and woods include ample flat land for playing fields, excellent terrain for skiing, brooks and pond for swimming and skating... One huge barn will be converted to become the focus of the daytime and academic life of the school, with its many facilities under one roof: classrooms and library, assembly hall and student common room, dining room and kitchen, faculty room and offices, plus a great sweep of unobstructed floor space in the old hay loft for indoor games and square dances. Three science laboratories in their separate building, with their work rooms, will provide greater space and equipment for continuing and improving the school's unusual science curriculum... Upwey supplies an environment ideally suited to the kind of living and learning that the Woodstock Country School has always encouraged.*

## David Bailey report to the trustees, October 14, 1955

*Undoubtedly, there would have been easier ways to celebrate our tenth anniversary than the one we selected, but our move to South Woodstock, despite its enormous difficulties, has been a bold gamble which seems, so far, to promise success....*

*The first few weeks are always deceptively pleasant and problem-less, but it can be truthfully said that our start has been good – surprisingly so to many, both within and without the school, who feared the job would overwhelm us...*

*It is impossible to convey to the trustees the many serious problems which were encountered, conquered, and forgotten. A near-miracle has been wrought, and it was done by human endeavor – a noble thing indeed. Despite the obvious inadequacies and incompletions, we have a glorious plant to work with, and none of us can fail to see the vision of further exciting developments.*

*One former problem we do not have to worry about is enrollment. Like most schools today, we were deluged with applications this summer, three or four times the number we could consider. We opened with ninety-three, twelve more than ever before, and we're not sure that they make a proper sized group for us, either educationally or financially. Extra children were admitted late in the summer for the sake of the budget, so we'll just have to learn empirically what size group we can best handle. So far, it is working adequately, partly because we have been more on the alert and more painstaking in seeing that the essentials are attended to....*

*Before closing this inadequate report, I would also like to call your attention to the fact that the school, despite its excellent history of budgetary soundness, it's, nevertheless, a fiscal freak. The structure is supported by unsound foundations in one respect, i.e., that it depends upon a few key people who are doing the work of several and are not being properly paid for it. In other words, some time in the future, the trustees must face the fact that these key individuals will have to be replaced and the budget will, in consequence, suffer vastly. This future problem is, therefore, related to the size of the school, and some advance thinking on the subject will provide some insurance."*

## Buffy Dunker treasurer's report, October 10, 1955

*1954-55 operations produced a margin of $4,596.49. The margin was made up of small savings in many departments and represents a lot of self-denial from many people during a difficult year...*

*A budget for 1955-56 is presented herewith. Income is at a high point in our history, and so are expenditures. Several items, especially those for fuel and electricity, are frankly guesses, as there is no experience or rule of thumb to help us. We have doubled the size of our usual allowance for contingencies and in several items we have been quite generous so we are willing to risk these figures.*

## Anonymous student bulletin board posting, November 2, 1955

*As almost everyone knows, the fire was a year ago tonight, or tomorrow morning as many people wish to look at it. I don't know how many of you have thought about the tremendous transformation that has taken place the past 365 days; if you have you realize what an undertaking there has been.*

*For nearly eight months we lived closely, getting on each other's nerves at times, and faring the best we could under the circumstances. Graduation came and ended life for us around Greenhithe, but there are still many memories that will be talked about in the future...*

*Every one of us is new this year in a sense. The new students never lived at Greenhithe to know what it was really like. The remaining old students are about as familiar with these new surroundings as anyone else. We all can help to make this year and those ahead successful for David and everyone else by keeping up the intangible spirit which is the core of the school.*

• • •

For a while during the summer, Woodstock briefly recaptured something of the spirit of its early years. While Upwey was being remodeled, David set up a limited summer operation with a few staff members in Owen Moon House, the eighteenth century "mansion" which had an old warmth quite like Greenhithe's. Students and alumni, about twenty on campus at any moment, worked on the school throughout the summer, helping with the conversion of barns to school buildings. A few students were also on campus for tutoring or make-up work. Together, they made up a small, intimate, focused community whose intimacy was heightened by the leisurely pace of Vermont summer. But most of the school community never experienced this flashback. It was gone by September, the offices were moved to Upwey where they "belonged," the displaced old school was swollen with new arrivals, the physical plant was only partly ready to function as a community and the character of the "new" WCS was being shaped by housing the girls in Owen Moon House (an echo of Greenhithe), while the boys lived barracks-style in a single loft above the classrooms of Upwey (not an echo of the school's past so much as a hint of the possible military service looming in each boy's future). There was, as everyone knew in advance, no "center."

While much of the rosy future outlined in the 1955 Upwey brochure would come to pass in time, by the opening of school that fall it remained, for the most part, wishful thinking. The Upwey plant would be under construction throughout the school year, which made it much less than "ideally suited to the kind of living and learning that the Woodstock Country School has always encouraged." More problematically, the school was not only significantly larger than ever (with no increase in faculty), but almost half the students were new, stretching all the staff and older students that much thinner. And although Upwey Hall, the main barn, was a central building containing classrooms, kitchen, dining room, offices, common room and faculty room and boys' dorm, it was not a center for the school as Greenhithe had been. For one thing, Upwey was a hastily-converted horse barn, not a gracious, inviting old inn which had been welcoming all kinds of people for generations. For another, Upwey was not a girls' dorm, with all its attractions for both the girls who lived there and the boys who hung out.

Upwey did serve temporarily as a dorm, a little-desired, uncongenial, makeshift boys' dorm, with 35 boys living in an open hayloft, without heat for most of that Vermont autumn. In contrast to the way Greenhithe drew people in the school together, Upwey's effect was predictably centrifugal, since in 1955 most girls did not hang out in boys' dorms. So some of the boys would go to Owen Moon House where the girls were, but the boys weren't allowed inside; there was no common room. The rest of the boys were left to hang out in their classroom building, no longer able to escape to their own rooms in a dorm down the hill. Finally, Upwey symbolized how, in a very real sense, everything about the school was up for redefinition just because its location was so radically different. Geographically turned upside down, from being a school on a hill, looking out to the horizon across the restless tumble of Vermont hills, WCS had turned itself into a school in a valley, on a flood plain between the occasionally flooding Kedron Brook and Vermont state highway 106. At Greenhithe, the best vantage points were from the heart of the school or close to it, so that the countryside permeated daily life. At Upwey, where the main barns were handsome but undistinguished, it was necessary to leave the heart of the school to discover and enjoy the best of the natural place.

For awhile, at least, the newness, the closeness, the lingering sense of crisis and the growing sense of adventure, all worked in the school's favor, creating conditions to help put people on their best behavior. But that, too, was stressful, especially for adolescents. The steady press of reconstruction and reorganization drained off much of the school's energy into property instead of people, undermined the relaxed and constant buzz of personal communication that had made the school so comfortable in Greenhithe. Instead, the distance grew between adults and student. As early as the second week of the school, at the weekly senior meeting, Bill Hogan '56 urged his classmates to do more to keep student behavior in line, warning that the faculty was angry about poor study halls and slack obedience to smoking rules and that it blamed these on the lack of senior leadership. He urged his classmates to take more responsibility, but to be careful to avoid resentment and not to overrule the student body. "We have to move quickly," he said, expressing the incongruity of the situation. "We must form traditions."

David, who always attended senior meetings, supported Bill Hogan and encouraged group action of some sort from a fractious class that would never coalesce. David also lectured the student council for not doing its job, even though nine of the thirteen council members were new students who didn't have any good idea what their job was. In the middle of the fall term, another senior wrote in his diary, "Is the old Woodstock gone? The old students are wondering. The new students are at a loss, for they can see no 'Woodstock' to conform to."

The plaintive student appeal for "spirit" on the eve of the anniversary of the fire came in the context of widespread student anger openly directed at Buffy. The day before, she had unilaterally banned all smoking at Upwey, triggering an outcry by the smokers in the boys' dorm who faced having to go outdoors at night to smoke. The soccer team lost 5-0 that afternoon and the players blamed Buffy for their poor play. The bulletin boards in Upwey filled with protests, mostly anonymous. The next morning, when Buffy ran chapel, most students refused to sing the hymns; she professed delight. Appealing privately to David, who had been away from campus when Buffy imposed her ban, the student council president, a non-smoker, wrote: "As I remember, you said in council meeting that no action would be taken on the smoking problem until you had formally warned the school on Thursday." The same day, that senior noted, "the Dunker Act was repealed at supper by the supreme Bailey."

The students were not alone in feeling over-extended, confused by the move to Upwey. The faculty, too, was struggling with additional stress, but unlike the school's early faculties, this group did not choose to share its feelings with students, remaining mostly emotionally remote and, to some extent, in conflict with the student body. Instead of two overwhelmed groups providing mutual support to each other in useful ways, they retreated into the somewhat hostile, mutually suspicious camps all too resonant of a more traditional school. Though there were few at the school to remember it, this was in stark contrast to the early school's powerful sense of common enterprise and mutual purpose. Whatever the reason (personal inclination, pressured circumstance, or something deeper), too many members of the 1955 faculty tended to hide their own difficulties from the "children" and to blame the students when they acted like adolescents. A bitter irony at any time, it was more so at Woodstock when the school was over-enrolled and included more than the usual number of academically marginal and walking-wounded students, ten of whom (including four seniors) would not survive the year.

Even David failed to ameliorate the situation significantly, though he rushed around putting out fires (like Buffy's peremptory smoking decision) as best he could. Even though he complained publicly to the students about their shortcomings, he didn't level with them about why the grownups acted as they did, or how he felt about the faculty. Privately, at the end-of-term faculty meeting in December, David complained that teachers weren't doing their job either and that the school had drifted into a negative, "fin de siecle" mood. He complained that evening study halls were not well supervised, that attendance wasn't taken often enough and that faculty were too scarce around campus during the afternoons and at meals. He wanted to have more senior meetings, more student meetings, more bull sessions, or "just have something happen." But most importantly, he warned that some advisors weren't seeing their advisees enough and those who were didn't leave notes in his box. He also wanted teachers to let him, and the advisor, know whenever a student didn't do homework. He wasn't being kept well enough informed, he felt, and so was hampered in trying to head off problems before they became serious. In contrast, Isabel Stephens wanted it made clear to parents "that we do not guarantee miracles, colleges or anything else." Perhaps most tellingly, that same faculty meeting discussed Woodstock's first formal, outside evaluation for accreditation (see next section); yet even though the process emphasized self-evaluation, the faculty made no provision to include the students in any part of assessing their institution. Woodstock students in 1955 were in a very different school from the one their predecessors were part of, when they could believe that what they said could make a significant difference in the quality of their institution.

The teaching faculty was varyingly aware of morale problems, including their own, as their answers (or lack of answers) to the self-evaluation questionnaire would show (see next section). But there was no faculty consensus on a solution. In February, they considered having "more religious vespers" services; recent vespers had featured psychoanalyst Erik Erikson, literary Critic I.A. Richards, and two young draft resisters. Throughout the winter, the faculty discussed, without success, "ways to restore 'old spirit' without reducing enrollment." These discussions were complicated by the faculty's judgment that fully 30 underclass students – a third of the school – were "doubtful" for the following year, for academic, behavioral or other reasons. In March, after the first few boys had moved into French House, the new, partially-renovated barn on East Hill. They complained that their rooms had no doors, so they still couldn't get much privacy after months of barracks-living. The doors had been omitted to save money and David's response was to let the students buy their own doors at $15 each. There were doors (but no locks) on students' rooms in other dorms, just as there had been when the school was in Woodstock. In a faculty meeting, Mounir warned that the students "bitterly resent" the situation and Chuck Silliman, a first-year English teacher, warned of a split between the school and the students. In time, the doors were put in.

While it was a hard and grinding year, 1955-56 was a year without any great crisis, but without great triumphs either. In May, David reported to the trustees, "The first academic year at Upwey has, in many ways, not been as difficult as many of us feared it might be. Most of our worry has been provoked by the thought that the property itself would be too big to manage. So far, this has not been the case, despite the fact that many physical areas of the school have been in an unfinished state and the weather has treated us rudely for months" (including a baseball game snowed out in early May). But David also acknowledged deeper problems, including stronger ties to Greenhithe than he had expected from older students and alumni. How he missed this (if he did) is perplexing, since it was all but shouted at him from all sides (including students and alumni largely excluded from the decision-making process). In addition, David noted, "the potential of the Upwey property has not evoked as much enthusiasm from the students as expected. I think the staff has been perhaps overly concerned with the physical aspects of the place, with the public relations in the village and, somewhat, with the increased size of the school population so that we have been too cautious and have perhaps been relatively out of touch with the personal and spiritual needs of the children."

After suggesting his "gloomy view" was exaggerated in order to provoke better performances in the future, David added, "actually, I am perhaps being too self-critical, for the many visitors, officials and otherwise, whom we have had these past months have all remarked on the relaxed, happy and friendly alertness of the children. Considering the number of problems, especially physical and financial ones, that faced us in the past twelve months, we have not done badly."

The move to Upwey had proved disorienting in many ways for many people, faculty as much as students and the school as a whole was still somewhat disoriented as the year ended. David's report to the trustees offered a sort of soul-searching, but not one he had shared with the whole community. The early sense of a coherent community had faded, in part because the institutional school had taken on its new shape largely by being bent to David's will, without any meaningful community participation. Even during that first year at Upwey, the school made no considered effort to have the community self-consciously consider its own condition as a community. Perhaps the closest it came was accidental, a spontaneous collective response to a perceived injustice. In the early spring, someone violated the fundamental trust that allowed, among other things, the school kitchen to go unlocked. Someone one night went into the kitchen and made off with a gallon of strawberries. Or so the school was told the next day when assembled in the dining room where, David told them, they would remain until he learned who did it. The students, overwhelmingly innocent of any complicity in, or even knowledge of the alleged infraction, grew restless in captivity. In time, echoing the response to the paranoid Captain Queeg in The Caine Mutiny, students started chanting: "All right. Who did it? Who stole the strawberries?" Over and over, they chanted, until it seemed like all the students were chanting together in open rebuke to David's use of collective punishment to solve the disappearance of a gallon of fruit. David reacted badly. He got angry. He probably framed the issue as a violation of trust, but all the same most of the students were innocent of that violation. But the student protest worked, the forced detention ended and many students felt a quiet pride in their resistance, even if they never knew who stole the strawberries, if there were any strawberries.

That the school ended a difficult transitional year in reasonably good shape was a sign of basic institutional health and considerable luck. But the school's success remained rooted in David's energy and intuition, his tireless willingness to keep improvising until something worked. Such an oblique and flexible approach, no matter how successful, was no assurance that another more intractable institutional crisis could be slid past as gracefully without facing fundamental issues more squarely. According to the school's press release, Woodstock's two commencement speakers that year appealed to students "to equip themselves with the tools of communication required for life in a world beset by misunderstandings." The irony was presumably unintended.

### Anonymous bulletin board message posted by Don Cooper '57, November 1955

*Curling and winding around the poles of the (common) room are piddles of cigarette smoke mixing with the foul air molecules (very illegally, indeed). There is slight smell of dirty blue-jeans and unshaven males, whilst among them mingle the heavenly scents of thirty-seven females, which does purify things...*

*The bell sounds and the legal smokers trot in from the flagpole or butt area, and seat themselves without much dignity. The speaker takes his stand and speaks. His voice does not quite reach the back of the room because of the bubble gum smackers, and the non-bath itchers, plus of course the gossipers from True Romances. A hymn is sung cheerily by some, and not so cheerily by others. The amoebas shuffle off to a cold bench. And so the day goes.*

*And ten days later at a teachers conference in Montpelier, Vermont, hundreds of harassed educators sit around a table and try to find a reason for this sluggishness. The answer lies in a neat package in all of their minds, but they dare not speak the truth.*

*The Children are simply lazy, and it is the Age.*

## New England Association of Colleges and Secondary Schools, Fall 1955

*Statement of Standards*

*No school may be considered for membership until it has completed at least five years of successful operation as an Independent Secondary School, with the majority of its students enrolled for two or more years – and at least one third of the students graduating each year in the five-year period having been admitted to recognized institutions of higher education. No school which is wholly or chiefly a tutoring or a vocational school shall be eligible.*

*To qualify for membership and to maintain membership, each school... shall have a clearly stated educational policy. This statement shall set forth the philosophy underlining the educational program designed to meet the objectives of the school.*

## Larry Roberts, answer for evaluation, January 1956

*To develop to the utmost, the potential ability of each student by exposure to academic, social, and physical situations. For most this means leadership training through student government, intellectual challenge by extensive pre-college training, and ethical training by discussion, example, and experience.*

*The school has accomplished this in the past and I feel will again. However, in the past and one foot in the future, with too few thoughts for the present. As a result, too much is taken for carry-over. Perhaps we hoped for carry-over, or are unaware of carry-over. Thus it is necessary to start again to build traditions of achievement academically and cooperatively, of selflessness instead of selfishness, or leadership instead of follow-the-leadership, of constructive criticism instead of destructive criticism, of positive thinking and intellectual curiosity instead of negativism and passivity, of daring to make a mistake if honestly trying instead of silence due to fear of being laughed at, of working with the group rather than playing to the mob or shunning society.*

*Many of the time consuming and effort consuming aspects of making the Upwey move possible... are drawing to a close. This divided interest has not left the faculty time enough to discover the wealth of material in our midst.*

• • •

Woodstock had started the formal application process to the New England Association of Colleges and Secondary Schools (NEACSS) during the fall of 1955. David put Isabel Stephens in charge of preparing and coordinating all the paperwork, which included the statement of philosophy and objectives, a self evaluation and various informational statements. The application also required a two-day visit by a committee of evaluators from other schools, people who were chosen independently by the schools' association, but who also had to be acceptable to the Country School.

NEACSS, comprising virtually the whole known world of the region's education establishment, did not seek to make the evaluation process a high-risk venture, but by its very traditional nature it appeared more threatening to Woodstock than it really was. Accreditation, pro forma as it was in most respects, was important to the school in order to keep attracting able students. And for both the school and the associations, the essential value of the process lay in the self-evaluation – for each school was judged *in its own terms*. Being measured by how well it was living up to its own standards made it important for those standards to be clear and clearly stated. Clarifying those standards was meant to be at least partly a self-enforcing means of achieving some institutional integrity.

One of the first formal steps in the self-evaluation was a questionnaire for the faculty, filled out by 13 teachers, not all of whom answered every question. Larry Roberts tabulated the results in a tightly-packed, five-page report for the Evaluation Committee:

(1) There was strong consensus on the size of the school: nine of ten who responded wanted no more than 85 boarders (four wanted no more than 80), which was about the size of the school at the time.

(2) As for the faculty, six of 13 teachers had no comments; most of the others wanted no more work for teachers, no change in the number of teachers (but fewer part-timers), and modestly increasing salaries.

The salary range was then $2,000-$4,000, with the headmaster at $4,500.

(3) Four teachers wanted more faculty participation in administration, four did not, and four thought the current level was fine.

(4) There was strong agreement that the most needed additions were an auditorium-theatre and a shop, nine votes each, of eleven. The shop was already in progress. Sound-proofing the dining room was the third choice (four votes), followed by student work/hobby room, library expansion and audio visual aids (three votes each).

(5) There was no consensus, only scattered suggestion, for improvements in administration, athletics, academics, admissions, professional standards, or social life. Most of the suggestions were practical and positive, giving the impression that there were no serious difficulties perceived in these areas.

(6) While there was no clear consensus on the school's most serious weakness, the eight teachers who made comments all touched on their relationships with students: "babysitting difficult children and being unrealistic with weak ones," "inability to handle problems due to lack of training or inclination," "overlooking the middle and concentrating on the very good or very bad," "lack of contact with students."

(7) There was much more clarity about the school's greatest strength: three teachers named David, while seven others cited the "devotion and interest in the school on the part of teachers, students, and alumni," which implicitly included David.

• • •

"Discussion of size of school, budget, administration all rather hazy," Larry commented in his notes on the faculty meeting at which he presented his report. Also hazy was faculty perception of its relationship to David, which Buffy interpreted as "less load on Headmaster." There were also requests for "more complete delegation of authority, including spending of department budget" and "shorter faculty meetings and less haggling." Mounir recalled a time that a faculty vote was not carried out and wondered if faculty votes were advisory only?

The question hung in the air. Throughout David's tenure, Woodstock functioned without official faculty meeting minutes and often without formal votes. The faculty meeting that January had little desire to challenge the familiar process.

The faculty self-evaluation was one of the steps toward meeting another of the New England Association's evaluation requirements, preparing a statement of the school's philosophy and objectives. In early 1956, the Woodstock Country School had no clearly-elaborated educational philosophy. The idea of a school constitution was prematurely tabled in 1946 and the attempt to hold a school convention to define rules and policies in 1951 was voted down in a student meeting. David seemed to have successfully institutionalized his personal anathema to rational, self-conscious self-definition.

To meet the association's philosophy requirement, Isabel started by using David's 1950 brief from the picture folder: "There is no formula for education. No system will serve all times and all individuals. There is no such thing as 'new' education. We can only take what we have learned about the subject and apply it in such a way that it is suited to our times. Our education at Woodstock depends on three main ingredients. These are flexibility, atmosphere and good teachers. We are convinced that the members of our teaching staff are not only effective in the classroom, but are also people of warmth and understanding who are interested in the children as people rather than just as pupils. It is difficult to have a poor school with excellent teachers. But to make these teachers most effective, we believe they should be allowed to live and teach in a climate of friendliness, of freedom and of informality. The students also do their best learning and growing in an atmosphere of trust and group responsibility. Our flexibility is maintained so that we may remain receptive to ideas, and able to shift our methods to suit new demands and individual needs."

To this, Isabel added three more paragraphs, written in consultation with David: "As a preparatory school, we strive for intellectual achievement commensurate with the ability of the child and the demands of the colleges. Our curriculum is largely based on the offerings given in most preparatory schools, with a few unusual elements of our own and a high degree of flexibility in individual student programs. We purposely do not enroll only the most able students preparing for the top colleges. All our recommendations for college are made with the highest integrity and are not compromised on the basis of expedience. It is not our purpose to build the school's reputation primarily on its college admission record.

"It is more important to us that we become successful in equipping our students with the tools of learning, and that we bring forth in them respect for themselves as persons and the desire for the highest standards of individual and group behavior.

"For these purposes, we are more than just a school but we are, quite genuinely, a community, a group of children and adults sharing the intellectual, spiritual, social and physical experience necessary to community living. We are, hence, more informal and less artificial than most coeducational institutions. The atmosphere is one of friendliness and trust. Coeducation is an essential element and so is the work program. The many demands upon the students that require responsibility, whether through student government problems, committee work, the daily chores, or through the constant need to behave in a thoughtful and dependable manner in all areas are sometimes taxing but always valuable ways to learn. In short, we are striving for discipline within freedom."

Isabel presented the full statement to the faculty in mid-April and the faculty approved it without change. Neither the Executive Committee, meeting the next day, nor the full board of trustees formally discussed the school's philosophy during the evaluation process, nor did trustees take part in other aspects of the school's self-evaluation in any formal way. It is an accurate reflection of Woodstock's inherent contradiction in the mid-fifties that it should claim to be more than just a school, "a genuine community," even though that community's self scrutiny and assessment was largely carried out by a minority of a minority. That would be the handful of faculty members, without significant participation by the community's student majority, nor by the trustees, who bore the ultimate responsibility for the community's continued existence.

Indeed, in responding to the New England Association's questionnaire, which was to serve as the basis for the visiting committee's assessment of the school, David wrote: "No provision is made [for a periodic study and evaluation by the trustees and the faculty of the school's whole program]. The Headmaster writes at least two reports a year to the Trustees. Our small size seems to eliminate the need for a formal system of regular self-evaluation. Faculty meetings inevitably include some weekly re-examination."

For the most part, Isabel wrote the required report, relying heavily on Buffy for much of the information. Most of Isabel's draft answers became the final answers. For example, in answer to the question "Have the objectives of the school been re-examined or revised recently?" – Isabel wrote: "Not appreciably. They remain principally the two concerns – the development of mature and responsible persons and the achievement of a sense of satisfaction from hard work – intellectual and physical – within a framework of activities that allow for individual differences without catering to every whim and idiosyncrasy."

Only one of Isabel's answers was changed appreciably. In describing "any unique or unusual instructional equipment," she wrote accurately enough: "We have no physical equipment that is unique or even unusual. What is unusual is the combination of freedom and discipline inside and outside of the classrooms. Because the members of the faculty are well prepared to teach the subject they offer and because they want the students to feel that they are free to participate in discussions and planning, classes are sometimes informal, but the caliber of the work demanded is high and no student is permitted to do sloppy work or to produce less than he is capable of doing so far as the instructor is able to judge... It is very unusual to find a faculty so frank, so willing to be self-critical and so ready to take suggestions and try other ways to reaching a child where conventional means have not been successful."

Instead, the final version said simply: "Except for our location, four hundred acres of fields and woods, beautiful gardens, outdoor amphitheatre, and acres of fine playing fields, our 'instructional equipment' is not unusual. What is unusual about the school lies rather is our ability to 'make do' and learn from the experience." Elsewhere in the questionnaire, the school claimed it had a gymnasium, a pool, tennis courts and an ice rink "under construction," which was largely wishful thinking expressive of the Upwey grandeur syndrome. While the school had some access to such facilities, it would never have its own gym or tennis courts; a swimming pond and an ice rink remained a year or two in the future.

The New England Association's Evaluating Committee did not cavil at that small overstatement of facilities in an otherwise thorough and thoughtful presentation of the school's substance. Nor did the committee penalize the school for turning in part of its report late, apparently accepting that as part of Woodstock's "leisurely and casual" style. By the committee's own account, its two-day visit to the campus during the first week of May was pleasant and uneventful. Morale at the school was high, partly in response to the belated spring weather, partly in anticipation of Pete Seeger's annual concert later the same week. Then, too, a difficult year was winding down, the disruption caused by several runaways in April was fading and all the boys were at last moved out of Upwey and settled in French House, their new dorm in a converted barn on East Hill.

"Just last week, the Evaluating Committee of the New England Association came for its official visit to see if we are worthy of admission to that august body," David told the trustees a few days later. "There will be no formal decision made in this regard until early next winter, but we were led to believe that the Committee was favorably impressed with what we are trying to do... From an outside observer's view, the history of the last year must look like a real success story and though we know better because we see some weak spots from the inside, we must nevertheless admit that a surprising amount has been accomplished... mostly what success we have had has been due to the devotion and generosity and the intelligent energies of the staff, the Trustees and the various other friends of the school." For no apparent reason, David omitted the real and mostly willing sacrifice by more than a hundred students over the 18 months since the Barn had burned.

The committee's report, completed that summer, was, indeed, favorable.

### Evaluating Committee report, May 1956

*It seems to us that the primary purpose of the school is to be "another home" for the students, an evident need for some of them... The faculty admissions committee chooses candidates for whom they think the school can do the most...*

*The students gave the general impression of self-reliance, freedom, readiness to speak up for their point of view. Various school customs, such as calling teachers by their first names, were doubtless adopted for the purpose of breaking down the barriers between the generations and establishing a warm and comradely relation. These seem to do no harm provided they do not lead to confusion in the students' minds concerning conventional standards of manners and respect for the respectable in the world outside of school...*

*We were surprised to learn how relatively light the teachers' extra-curricular responsibilities are. The fact that classes meet only three times a week (an arrangement made possible by 70-minute periods) releases each teacher for a free day a week. Most teachers do not coach sports. Possibly faculty members are involved more than we know in supervision of projects on the grounds, but we understand that many faculty members are frequently free from two o'clock...*

*We were impressed, not wholly favorably, by the amount of free time available to the students. They have sports or work program tasks three afternoons a week [four, in fact] and are free during the other afternoons. There is no afternoon study hour. Students are free all day Sunday until the five o'clock vesper service...*

*Dormitory supervisors serve as counselors. All full-time teachers have a group of counselors to whom they give academic and personal guidance, and regardless of such assignment any teacher who makes rapport with a student stands ready to give him guidance. In view of the informality of the atmosphere and the relaxed relationships between the generations, it seems probable that much of the guidance takes place in casual or casual-seeming situations.*

*As we understand it, standards of conduct are not stated in a formal way, but the Headmaster, faculty members, and the student council exert pressure and make use of a system of penalties and rewards. A just evaluation of the guidance and discipline at the school would require a longer visit than we could make. We wonder, however, if explicitness as to what is expected would not be valuable...*

*Woodstock Country School seems to us a good school run by intelligent and sincere people. We have some questions in mind about the effect on standards and achievement of what struck us as a leisurely and casual approach to educational problems; yet we feel that the approach is positively related to the schools' philosophy and that granted the philosophy and the type of students in the group, the results are satisfactory. We hope that the officials will consider our criticism, but we unanimously recommend Woodstock Country School for membership in the New England Association of Colleges and Secondary Schools.*

## Paraphrase of David Bailey's talk, Parents Association minutes, November 4, 1956

*Mr. Bailey expressed his thanks for the interest of the partners in the school and said that he had been questioned as to the absence of the school catalog. He has never written such a catalog because he was at a loss to explain the philosophy of the school in precise terms. To set down exactly what the school was trying to accomplish, he felt it would first be necessary to define the child of today. Today's child, he said, was first of all an 'adolescent,' which in itself has become a dirty word...*

*Today's child is apt to live in a suburb, beset by many pressures. He thinks of himself as a cipher, a number without individuality or personality. He is at a loss for standards, and since he is apt to be aware of the difficulties and unhappiness of his elders, he sees no reason for growing himself. He cannot picture himself as ever being able to cope with the problems of which his parents and their friends complain. Unwilling as he is to assume the responsibilities of adulthood, he nevertheless clutches eagerly at the symbols of smoking, and drinking and driving cars.*

*Above all things he wants to be noticed, to be important and to be noticed, to be important and to belong. He sticks his neck out to accomplish this and when he gets slapped down withdraws and builds up walls to protect himself. Unfortunately, these walls protect him alike from the bad and the good, and so it becomes increasingly difficult to reach and communicate with him.*

*To the parent, this frightened unsure child appears selfish and rebellious, and the parent either becomes afraid of the child and does too much, or errs on the other side of nagging and becoming dictatorial. It is at this point that the professionals get called in and are asked what to do.*

*The professionals have an advantage over the parents in most cases because they are more patient and less emotionally involved, they can do things the parents can't. If the child is rude to the professionals, they are not terrified lest the child not love them. The professionals are not in a hurry; they do not set out on their task with a sense of having failed already.*

*Because the child has so often developed a suspicious attitude toward adults, the first name basis at WCS is valuable. It creates a feeling that we are all human beings together, and it helps the child to see the grown-ups as individuals like themselves. Since no one is in a hurry, there is time to treat each child as an individual case and so there are fewer hard and fast rules against which the child feels he must rebel on principal.*

*As the child finds the grown-ups treating him with liking and respect, he comes to like and respect himself and to gain a sense of belonging. This sense of belonging to something bigger than himself is the single most important aspect. Everyone needs this sense of group identification... The school gives the child a sense of belonging in many ways; there are the school work programs, the various committees to which they are appointed or elected, the special activities they can join and the sports teams. They learn that the standards they are expected to maintain have been established by themselves instead of being prescribed by others. They begin to relax and feel comfortable, and most important to find that it is pleasant and rewarding to begin to grow up and accept responsibility and to contribute to the group's activity and welfare.*

*Often the children need a firm hand and want to be guided. It takes constant vigilance to retain the right balance, to know when to let them go ahead and make mistakes from which they will learn, and when to apply the brakes. This is one of the great reasons the school must be kept small, since knowing when to go easy and when to be firm is entirely an individual matter. And above all the school wants to provide each child with enough room to find himself, to give him elbow room to make mistakes, to try out behavior patterns here among friends and to establish his own set of standards for dealing with later problems.*

•••

Despite David's reaffirmation to the trustees of his "belief that a student body of about 85 would be a preferred size," Woodstock opened in the fall of 1956 with 92 students, 34 of them new. Despite a strong faculty consensus in favor of a small school, and despite the formation of the WCS Planning Committee of Trustees and faculty to organize the school on the basis of an enrolment of 82, the school would not be as small as 92 again for almost two decades (its peak under David was 101). The faculty discussed the issue at length in an October meeting attended by Katherine Taylor, who had run the pioneering, progressive Shady Hill School in Cambridge for 27 years, including those years when David Bailey had been in grade school. She observed that, with a larger student body, the school would inevitably lose some degree of intimacy, though enlarging the staff would ameliorate that to some extent. She emphasized that the Trustees should raise the money to make a larger staff possible, that David should demand more from the trustees, and that he and the faculty should make sure the trustees really know about and understood the school. She was prophetically correct on all three points. But the Trustees would never achieve a reasonable standard of fundraising, not even from board members themselves. Rather than building a strong board, David kept control by keeping the board weak. And when the faculty started telling the board what the school was like more than a decade later, the honest message was bad news and received with disbelief and disdain.

David's report to the Trustees ten days later was only half-hearted. He noted that, although the sense of emergency of the past two years had gone, the need for planning was crucial "because almost every day we must make decisions which have long range effects." Describing without naming the effects of larger enrolment on the larger Upwey campus, David wrote: "Primarily there is an obvious financial aspect, for although we have always managed, as we will do this year, to operate in the black, we must realize that to add at least one more staff member as we should, and to raise the faculty salaries as we will, we are not going to be able to maintain operations in the black unless more income is provided. This will be especially true if there continues to be plant expansion which will cost more for upkeep and maintenance. We have provided some reasonably good salary raises this year but they must continue if we are to maintain the strength of the school, which is primarily in its staff."

On campus, the school's day-to-day life still suffered from some of the difficulties of the year before, especially those of transition and definition. In November, David spoke to the faculty of the "malaise of the school," but the intensity of the malaise was diminishing and the quality of the student body had improved. There was a growing, articulated sense that Woodstock was coming of age institutionally. "We're coming of age in a certain sense," wrote Larry Roberts in his notes in October on the discussion with Katherine Taylor. "We feel as if we are coming of age as a school," wrote David Bailey in letters to parents in November, inviting them to serve on the WCS Planning Committee the trustees had formed in response to his appeal. "Now that it has come of age, the school should act to consolidate its gain and make determined, long-range plans for the future," wrote David to the trustees in February, introducing the WCS Planning Committee's fairly modest recommendations, most of which were carried out over the next several years. "The implication of this report is that the school should not increase its enrollment, but should add to its faculty and non-teaching staff," David added. "We hope everyone will understand that the school is not trying to become fancy or larger, but is trying to improve itself qualitatively so that it can continue to be a worthy educational institution."

There were other good signs in 1956-57. One day in December, the seniors persuaded the faculty to stay home while the seniors ran the school – taught classes, supervised meals, ran special programs – all without a hitch. The abortive Hungarian revolution that fall helped, too. At the instigation of Roger Phillips ('49) and assisted by a $250 scholarship from the Woodstock Rotary Club, the school adopted an escaped Hungarian student, Stephen Imredy. He arrived in Woodstock in January 1957 with little command of English, but great energy and goodwill, which enlivened the school for the next two years. And beginning to loosen up and enliven the faculty, a process that would continue for the next five years, was the new geometry teacher, Lovett Garceau (also exceptional in that he was not known as "Lovett," because everyone called him "Mr. Garceau"). A Harvard graduate and inventor whose property adjoined the school's, Garceau quickly became one of the school's legends, for his brilliance and his absorption in his subject, even to the point of students slipping unnoticed out the window of his classroom while he outlined the intricacies of an arcane problem at the backboard. Affable and idiosyncratic, this part-time teacher was, in student myth, the quintessence of the eccentric genius. In fact, Garceau's medical inventions, including a heart pump, were eminently practical and profitable.

In the spring of 1957, the school was shocked by another political event in the real world. Woodstock's semi-official folk singer, Pete Seeger, was indicted for contempt of congress as an uncooperative witness in 1955 before the House Un-American Activities Committee, HUAC. (He would not come to trial until 1961 and would not be finally exonerated until 1962).

Pete Seeger, son of composer Charles Seeger and classmate of John F. Kennedy, Harvard '40, was a presumed Communist to some. But to students at the Country School, Pete Seeger was alumnus Mike Seeger's half brother, a musician in a family of musicians, and a former member of the Weavers, whose annual concerts had raised money for the school and enlivened the local cultural life since 1950. Despite his occasionally pointed remarks, Seeger's concerts were not notably political. "As a political radical, it was hard for me to sing anywhere in the fifties," Seeger recalled of the opportunity to sing at Woodstock, "I was grateful." He remembered his visits there being "like old home week," including joining Buffy's music classes where, one year, the group wrote the song "Full Fathom Five" based on a poem from *The Tempest*. So when the students heard about his indictment, they called a meeting, they discussed what to do, they passed the hat, they raised $80 for Pete Seeger's defense fund and they put his picture on the cover of the graduation issue of the *Symposium* (without a word of commentary inside). These student gestures, while tolerated, were not matched by the school as an institution, by the faculty or trustees – an accurate expression of Woodstock's ambivalence during the Cold War. While the Country School had not indulged the kind of political purges common to many American schools at the time (even Putney), the politics of intimidation nevertheless had an impact.

Just a year earlier, the faculty had fretted over the possibility of a member of the Soviet delegation to the United Nations coming to Woodstock as part of a Quaker conference on campus during the summer when school would not be in session. The issue was raised by two fearful trustees. Among faculty, David, Buffy and Steve Stephens favored the Russian's coming, Isabel Stephens thought the American Friends "are reddish and have already made the dangerous step, so it doesn't matter who the person is," and Peggy opposed the visit, "for the school's sake." As it turned out, there were no repercussions. As for Pete Seeger, he kept giving his annual concerts through 1965, once bringing a young protégé named Joan Baez. He sent a son and daughter to school as well.

Probably the school's greatest gain in acquiring the Upwey property had nothing to do with buildings or grounds, but was the accidental addition of two people who unexpectedly came with the property. Victor and Ula Savelberg had come from Germany a few years earlier to work for the Farrells, taking care of Owen Moon House. When the Farrells moved on, David hired Victor to do school maintenance, Ula to help in the kitchen. Friendly and easygoing, Victor and Ula quickly became essential members of the community – "they were so satisfactory, they became the heart of the school," as David put it. Their son, Hank Savelberg, graduated with the class of 1961. From the first, Ula's remarkable combination of affection and order helped make the kitchen a comfortable and efficient part of the school for students and staff alike. In 1957, David put her in charge and for most of the next quarter century she gave the school good management, miraculously good food and a generosity of spirit that included baking a cake for every student's birthday. By luck and flexibility, the school had turned its kitchen into one of its most significant areas of extra-curricular learning, providing a mix of friendliness, drudgery, responsibility and useful work that most students enjoyed, and some found vital.

As Tom Stokes '63 wrote years later, Ula "ran the kitchen. In many ways she was a key teacher. She was organized, unassuming, and by her cooperative and caring nature elicitive of student help. Escept for her days off, there was no other kitchen staff. Although her budget was seventy-seven cents a day per student, there was not many complaints. All birthdays were remembered with a cake, and on April Fools Day each table got a casserole consisting of snow topped with bread crumbs." (In later years certainly, and perhaps in 1963 and before, Ula had help in the kitchen. Agnes Barr and Rosie Guertler worked for years with Ula and both contributed to the warmth and comfort, the shelter even, that the kitchen always provided.)

In the fall of 1957, David revitalized Woodstock's art program by hiring Lowell and Virginia Naeve. Other than David, Lowell Naeve was the first strong, independent, idiosyncratic, adult male personality in the school since it had lost Allen Weatherby and Bus Talbot in 1954. Not that there hadn't been other perfectly decent, capable men on campus, but none had quite the personal vitality and spirit to counterbalance the headmaster's dominant presence, to challenge David without threatening him. During the same time, the growing distance between the so-called old guard and their students meant that Woodstock was evolving toward a more traditional, limited faculty-student interaction. By 1957, even Mounir and Buffy were less involved with students than they had been at Greenhithe. For Mounir, the increasing demands of his Universalist church parish in Woodstock and the increased distance to South Woodstock cut into his time on campus, though he continued to cultivate his special coterie of admiring youngsters. Even though Buffy had built her own house on the Upwey campus, she had allowed her circle of special students to dissipate, partly because she was immersed in the demanding detail of rebuilding the school, partly because she needed more energy to cope with complication in her private life.

Lowell Naeve hardly looked the Country School type. Crew-cut, thick-nosed, stocky, he could have been mistaken for a 40-year-old ex-Marine. But Lowell was an accomplished artist whose work was in the Museum of Modern Art, the United Nations and the New York Public Library. His wife, Virginia Paccassi Naeve, was a working artist in her own right. Two years earlier, they had both contributed to a gallery show held at the former boys' dorm on the Green, an exhibition organized by David's brother, Tad Bailey, to benefit United World Federalists. When David got in a bind for an art teacher, Tad had recommended the Naeves. For the next five years, Lowell and Virginia, but especially Lowell, brought a remarkable new energy to the school, reinvigorating the art department and making art central to Woodstock life in ways that it hadn't been since the earliest years of the school. The Naeves gave art the kind of place in the Woodstock community that David had seen it have at Black Mountain under Josef Albers, whom he considered one of the two greatest teachers he ever had (the other being Black Mountain's John Rice). Years later, David said, "The quality of Lowell Naeve, both as a person and as an artist, was such that both the drama and art department became even more important than music, so that over half the pupils were usually enrolled in one of the art programs, which was always on a college entrance level. This made us very distinctive among college prep schools, and our reputation was greatly enhanced."

Lowell and Virginia taught their students a traditional high school art curriculum heavy on drawing and painting, but they also introduced new courses using exotic materials. Virginia persuaded a large tile-making corporation to donate hundreds of pounds of colorful, scrap tile, which made possible her course on mosaics (which also gave the school some publicity). Lowell introduced courses in sculpture, photography and film-making – with such success that for a few years, student films joined drama productions on the annual Parents Weekend program. At other times, he offered courses in card-making (in which students designed, printed and marketed greeting cards) or architecture (in which students designed and built models of the house they would like to live in – with one of the models being so large and sturdy it was donated to the children's ward of a nearby hospital). Lowell also brought to his work a caring respect for the students and their work. Year after year, he would photograph each student with a prized piece of sculpture, a painting, a print, whatever the student valued. He kept the photographs in an ever-growing album which showed the continuity, variety and vitality of student art work.

Lowell brought the same kind of energy and commitment to the rest of his life. During his first term at Woodstock, he put in long hours building the school's skating rink. Then the student meeting, making an unusual gift to a teacher, voted to buy him a pair of ice skates. But the greatest difference between Lowell and the rest of the Country School faculty was that he had gone to prison for his beliefs. In 1940, when he was 23, Lowell refused to register for the draft. He had arrived at his conscientious objection alone, thinking it through in solitude and acting on it over the opposition of his parents. In prison for four years, he was surprised to find others who shared his beliefs, to discover that he was part of a long and honorable countercurrent in western civilization and that part of the citizen's responsibility was to question authority. (Eventually, the Naeves would move to Canada to help their son avoid the war in Viet-Nam.) In 1950, the Libertarian Press published Lowell's prison memoirs, "A Field of Broken Stones," illustrated by Lowell, with an introduction by Paul Goodman. In the fall of 1959, while he was still at Woodstock, Swallow Paperbooks reissued the book, which rippled through the community, offering rare openness and intimate detail about a teacher's private life.

In all of this, Lowell stood in striking contrast to most of the rest of the Country School's teachers, who valued privacy more than openness. Other teachers saw Lowell as more of a loner than a team player and they sometimes felt the art program took more than its share of the school's attention and budget. But Lowell's honesty and directness with his students were qualities that helped bring out the best in them. He was effective in dealing with "today's child," as David had described that child to the Parents Association. And as David hired other new teachers over the next several years, the best of them were like Lowell – not in personality, but in the sense that they were also people of energy, competence, principle and openness to young people. They refreshed a faculty, a school, that had threatened to grow stale.

FALL 1955 – SPRING 1962

## Russ Mead interview, March 1985

*When you describe the school to somebody's child who wanted to go there, you describe the faculty. That's what you could get hold of and knew. But at Woodstock, its communities [faculty, students, trustees] were not at all inviolate. There were many faculty, myself included, who had much more in common with the student role and were probably in as much need of therapy and maturation and teaching... There was never a sense that the faculty were in any way united or were in their own envelope. Those who didn't live on campus, in fact, rarely mixed with those who did, outside the classroom setting. I think that was good...*

*Before I was hired I went to Woodstock, I met with David and we walked around and we talked and he said, "Well, good then, you'll come here." I hadn't said. I didn't even know how much money was involved. Later I had to call him and say, "Did you offer me a job?" and he said, "Well, I assumed you were coming."...*

*That was really the only oblique part of it. He had great intensity about the school, great enthusiasm for what was going on there, but I think at the time of our meeting, he had enemies. I mean, by interpretation, was that he was recruiting allies, not in an overt sense of here's what I want, will you join the conspiracy? – but he wanted people who thought as he did, but who were bright enough and structured enough to be able to teach.*

*He talked about a number of the teachers, but somehow I had the feeling that the older faculty were as much antagonists of David as the younger faculty. I don't mean that in an unhealthy sense – but in some ways, David was just as much a student in the school as anybody else and was as willful and apparently immature – much more consciously, I think, than anybody gave him credit for until years later...*

*"Oh really, David?" was a very common thing for Peggy to say."*

## Tad Bailey, "A Sense of Human," 1970

*We must care for the humanity in ourselves by caring for that same humanity in everyone else. That concern must be shown not only for the life common to all human beings, but also for all the other forms of life that depend on us and on which our lives depend. This is neither an easy nor a rapid process. The only way it can be done is to ask people everywhere to examine and reexamine the values by which they order their lives. This kind of work is usually lonely and always difficult. Though decisions of this type must finally be made by each person out of his own personal conviction, we all need help in reaching these decisions.*

*We can give and receive that help by talking out our concern with others who care enough to look beyond the easy answers. We can form small groups of people among those who realize that we are dealing today with the basic questions of life. We can work our way slowly through the thickets of private interest and through the maze of our habitual evasions until we are strong enough to face our common needs. As we grow, we can develop communication and strength just by reaching out for more people.*

*This power is created and begins to grow as you consider your own humanity. It is cumulative power. It is permanent power, but only if we work fast enough to put it to work before the confusion of our world becomes disintegration... The real revolution is in the acceptance of our responsibility as human beings.*

• • •

Tad Bailey did not have an easy relationship with his younger brother, David, but he was often helpful and supportive. Tad was among the first to offer help after the Barn burned in 1954. There is a striking photograph of the two brothers standing with the same posture, staring with the same wordless expression at the smoking ruin, seeming to understand each other's hearts exactly. Tad's widow remembered them always "at each other's throats," never agreeing about anything. But they agreed about enough for Tad to be in and out of the Country School so often over the years, probably even he couldn't keep the chronology straight. He frequently tutored Country School students, especially those with reading difficulties, and he occasionally filled in as a teacher. Although never a full-time faculty member, Tad's most continuous and intense involvement with the school began in the fall of 1957, when he came in to teach French.

Tad's presence in the school always had a special, somewhat dissonant resonance, mysterious and fascinating to students, since Tad was so much like and unlike David, with that odd, affectionate distance between them, holding them both apart and together. Tad was much more direct than David, much more accessible as a person, much more willing to commit his convictions to paper and to communicate them to others as clearly as possible. Gerry Freund found Tad "an easier person to deal with but, in my experience, just as complicated as David. I wouldn't have called him accessible... Tad was crippled also... Thank God he had his painting." For Isabel Stephens, the Baileys' childhoods – their unhappy relationships with their father – were the source of much of their power as educators, as they tried to make up to others for what they had lacked themselves. She reasoned that David, and probably Tad, must have thought a lot about "what it is that helps somebody who feels kind of negative and a little bit foreign or neglected or dumped off in a school where he didn't want to get sent – because he and Tad have both spoken about the year they were sent to Switzerland. They really resented that, they felt dumped."

Tad generally confronted the world more directly than his brother, but he clearly drew on much the same values. As Isabel Stephens wrote after Tad's death in 1974, "Tad cared deeply about wasted human potential. He had, over the years, become more and more engaged in tutoring and helping young people to read and write and to use words effectively. He was often discouraged and became dissatisfied with standard methods of remedial teaching. He read extensively, trying to learn all he could about the human brain and how we learn. Finally, after spending a few weeks at the Institute for the Achievement of Human Potential, he started on his own initiative a tiny 'clinic' for a few children in Pomfret in the summer of 1967." (This soon became the Woodstock Learning Clinic, which, for more than 40 years, specialized in the prevention and treatment of learning disabilities in the central Vermont region.)

While inevitably sharing many of the childhood upheavals of the Bailey household, Tad somehow managed to grow up in an apparently more orderly way than David, graduating from the Belmont Hill School and Harvard College, 1932, followed by a graduate year at the Boston Museum School. But after a few years teaching at the Forman School in Litchfield, Connecticut, Tad gave up conventional orderliness in the world's eye to spend all his time on painting, mostly watercolors. That in turn gave way to the disorder of World War II in which, David recalled, "Tad became a member of the ski troop and an officer. He went through most of basic training with a broken foot, a fact that he concealed from everyone until he won his commission."

After the war, and because of his revulsion to war, Tad spent several years working for the United World Federalists, writing, editing and illustrating their publications. During the same period, he continued to paint, while also joining the Windsor County Mental Health Association, serving on the Pomfret School Board and teaching from time to time at the Country School. As one of Tad's colleagues at the Woodstock Learning Clinic wrote after his death, "Tad was a man of incredible energies and unshakeable belief in the innate goodness of man. He felt that education was the key: That knowing right, man would do right. He also believed very strongly that all of us must help each other by sharing time, ideas and knowledge. To him, a life ruled by self-interest was wasted: he was terribly impatient with people who lived for themselves, who would not take the time or trouble to share and help. One of the things that made him angriest was discussion of salaries at the Learning Clinic: 'You are *helping* people,' he would insist, 'why are you talking about money?'"

While David would never have expressed his own noblesse oblige so boldly, the same underlying value certainly affected the way he chose people to work at Woodstock and how much he decided to pay them. When Tad agreed to teach a single course in 1957, David agreed to pay him $400, but of course they both knew money wasn't the point of the agreement, the importance of the enterprise was. Having his older brother on the payroll symbolically certified the worth of David's school. More importantly, Tad participated in the community well beyond his contractual obligations. He teamed with Lowell Naeve to make movies and to support other art projects involving students. But more than any other teacher, Tad worked individually with students with learning difficulties, some of whom found him the best teacher they ever had.

### David Bailey report to the trustees, October 12, 1957

*So far our thirteenth year has started with reasonably good fortune. The large number, 98 pupils, has expectedly strained us a bit, but the quality of the school population at all levels seems superior... Inevitably, the school has become more formalized than heretofore, which makes the headmaster somewhat uneasy, but the greater numbers demand this approach.*

### Dinah Smith '59, Student Council minutes, February 15, 1959

*The meeting was called to order at 7:00 p.m. David Beatty presided, David [Bailey] was present. Dexter Cheney was 20 minutes late.*

*There was discussion on how to get rid of the two kittens who reside at the respective dorms. The one at French House, Asbestos, has been labeled pregnant and must be exterminated multo presto. David told a story of a previous somewhat similar situation of a school-cat that finally died and over whose corpse there was a great to-do because the Biologists wanted to dissect it and the Sentimentalists made loud protests. The cat was interred and dug up and re-interred etc. and the whole affair was very unsatisfactory.*

## David Bailey report to the trustees, May 2, 1959

The academic and social aspects of the school have functioned very smoothly so far this year, with no major crises or disasters. The largest difficulty that confronted us has been faculty illness – perhaps a sign that some of us are wearing out. [The most serious was Mounir, who was out for much of the year with back problems that required hospitalization.] It has been generally a happy year, with many extra events and offerings to enliven the routine and to keep our famed "flexibility" in trim. The Woodstock cliché, that we never have a normal week, has once more proven to be true.

## David Bailey report to the trustees, October 5, 1959

Nothing very spectacular, such as a fire, has been planned for the School which has entered into its 15th year. We expect a fairly normal year, but there will be a few changes from the past...

We have, of course, an over-rich curriculum as usual, but it is more costly this year, both because of salary increases and because, for the first time, we are numerically rich in staff. This is good for all of us if we can afford it. We are tidier about many little things just because we have more supervision... [but] we must beware of the usual dangers of becoming too routine. The vigor and excitement of the earlier pioneer years were important ingredients of the education at that time, and as we grow older and find easier and more systematic ways, there is the danger of some loss of freshness.

## VII

## Tom Edsall '59 interview, April 29, 1986

*By the standards then, it was quite progressive – all this teacher by the first name stuff, no coats and ties – but there was also a certain degree of required order [Peggy Bailey told boys when to get haircuts]... and people generally abided by that order...*

*We had a little drugs that were just starting, but they were not in school, they were on trips down to New York. This was sort of early on, but the Beat Generation stuff – this was 1958-59, down in Greenwich Village. [Two of my friends], early on, got to know people down there and we used to get marijuana, particularly around Christmas and summer holidays. I can't recall ever using drugs on campus.*

*I can recall having booze on campus, which a group of us started to do fairly commonly on weekends. Every Saturday night as I recall there used to be a dance where a lot of us were sort of hanging around in the Common Room, and then a group of about six of us used to drink secretively. David learned that there was some drinking going on and he came to the senior class [meeting] or something, and he said, "I have learned there's drinking going on, and this is my warning – no one's in trouble now, but if it goes on anymore, if anyone gets caught, they will be in trouble." And we stopped at that point. We were close to graduating, it was spring of our senior year, it would have been a disaster... So we stopped.*

*I mean, most schools ought to work that way...*

*That's one of the things that struck me about Woodstock, that there was sort of a line drawn, on how far you could go and what you could do – in a quite liberal context for its time. Afterwards that seemed to deteriorate and disappear. At any rate, I think there has to be some definition. The problem with most private schools was that they had very rigid definitions. I think David's virtue was that he defined things in a way that people – at least while I was there – would not have accused him of being unfair. It would have been a legitimate defining. It was not rigid. It was a subjective decision on his part, but not one that was viewed as arbitrary...*

*And I was comfortable in that atmosphere. And I have always, since then, worked much better where I did things on my own, not regulated by others. Woodstock was not a very regulated place, and for me, that was just what I needed, and it has always been since then... The only way I could write a book, or do some of the good stuff I've done for the Washington Post or the Baltimore Sun before that, was when I did it on my own, in an unregulated fashion, and I didn't do that much good academic work when I was in Woodstock, but that sense of freedom was very important, and was of sustained importance to me for the rest of my life.*

## John Maynard '61 interview, September 20, 1984

*A dorm raid. It was terrific. My junior year. We planned it very well. I think there was snow, at any rate it was quite cool. The guys in French House planned this – we may have had guys from East Hill – and we were going to raid OMH [Owen Moon House girls dorm] at midnight, something like that. Maybe it was even 2. We planned on how we were going to sneak down and run around the place and go in at certain entrances, and that was about as much as we planned. Nothing special was going to happen except a lot of yelling and carrying on and running through the place. I think we all figured we'd all go right back up the hill. And we just had an awfully good time doing it. And of course everyone admitted to doing it, and the next day the faculty were extremely sour – whether it was real or put on, I don't know – and the whole afternoon was shut down and we had special tough type punishment jobs to do...*

*The spirit of the faculty and the community was not that it was a community in that it was planned or that people even wanted it to be a community. It was a community inasmuch as it just happened, and I think partly as a result of that, there was nothing radical about the school. People I talked to at the time said, 'radical school, radical school' – one thing that was radical was that we did all the work around the place, except fixing boilers and pipes. As a social experiment it was really quite laissez faire. I think, now that's too bad.*

*I don't know whether, in their faculty meetings, [the teachers] did come together to bring some direction to the school, but I'm not sure I see the effects of anything like that... Some group process that gets people to understand something different about each other, which would take an awful lot of work among teenagers, but it would have been a very, very good thing to have... Thinking ourselves somehow into a community involves some kinds of things that we don't usually do.*

*Let me tell you something about gossip. There was a lot of gossip. We heard it. From the faculty to us about other faculty You know, so-and-so is crazy, that kind of thing… I remember Buffy saying some things about Isabel, I don't remember exactly, but disparaging… It's very difficult to stop that. But one way to do that is if there's some kind of, I don't know, purpose or some spiritual connectedness or something. I don't know how you do that, but that kind of thing would have been good for a place like Woodstock.*

## Isabel Stephens memo to the trustees, October 1959

*A year ago I wrote a memo suggesting that the school budget every year for some long term improvements in plant. I assume from what I glean that it has been done this year and that we are now, for the first time, coming up with a 'deficit budget' – i.e., we have put into the budget items that used to be left out and covered, if possible, from balance on hand at the end of the year. This is sensible.*

*I am, however, alarmed by the suggestion that the academic departments of the school cut back on their expenditures because we have a deficit budget. If it is really likely that the school will be seriously in the red next year, of course all expenses must be scrutinized again and again. But the school is full, classes are too crowded. Two teachers who expected to be teaching subjects only once each are teaching two sections… One teacher [Molly Plumb] has 54 science students each meeting for 4 hours a week, sometimes in small lab sections made necessary by scarce equipment and space – result: she teaches all but 6 of the class periods in the mornings, and of those has only two with her lab free for preparations. She does not complain. But she will need to spend money on equipment and materials for teaching and must not feel guilty in doing so.*

*Other departments have been resourceful in the past about getting supplies – maps, projectors etc. as bargains or gifts – but the expansion of the Art Department, no matter how desirable in itself and how good as a central project, in the heart of the school has resulted in great physical inconvenience. Maps are in rooms not used by the class needing them, but can't be moved because another class does need them etc… In other words, this is a very poor year to say to the social science teachers, go easy on expenses. We have been glad to be accommodating in doing the makeshift thing to expand Art without waiting to rebuild the whole cow barn into a wonder Art Center. We have been glad to wait for the desperately needed larger library until Drama* has a theater. But we shall insist upon pretty heavy expenditures for books for the library, and paperbacks for "teaching materials." We shall need more maps and charts. We shall want to rent more movies etc.

This is all very familiar. Every school and college worth its salt is full of teachers who try to love one another, but who fight for their own departments and their own interests. Nothing new here. But in most schools and colleges there is no question in anyone's mind about where the money should be poured. Tuition money should go into tuition. Board and room money into board and room. Any left-overs should go into long term improvement of facilities for teaching and learning, including of course athletics and other activities such as animals or forestry or anything else. First and foremost, must come the academic considerations.

Resentment begins to boil the instant any member of a faculty even suspects or half believes that money is being budgeted away from what he believes to be essential academic activities. It is right here that the rub comes. This member of the faculty is not convinced that money is not being wasted on the so-called farming activities. I want to see very clear evidence in figures that it is the increase in faculty salaries that creates the present deficit, and not expenditures for farm machinery, equipment, salary and living costs and heating etc., for the 'farmer' and his family etc.

Like all the other members of the faculty (I think all), I like the idea of shipshape property. I want to see the fields mowed. I want to see the fences either taken away or repaired. I want to have horses on the place and properly cared for. But I have not been shown comparative figures that convince me that these three things are being done in the best and cheapest way. I have not been shown figures to convince me that we should raise chickens...

All these things may be no affair of mine. Perhaps I should just take my salary raise and be glad to economize. But when that salary is raised even by the 'big jump' of $25 a month it does not quiet my malaise about the feeling that the faculty is subsidizing an uneconomical arrangement...

It was with considerable reluctance that we went along two years ago with the idea that a resident caretaker would improve the looks and value of the property... If a man could be found who would take on the property as his responsibility and relieve the headmaster of all worry about cattle, hay, horses, riders, orchards, dead trees, sloppy fences, *dilapidated and useless machinery etc., let's try it – not for profit, but as a necessary part of our maintenance costs in the huge property... So far I have encountered only discouraging figures... when we are convinced that every penny spent [on the farm program] pays off in improvement of the school as a school, we will be more eager to watch every penny we spend for books and charts and classroom space and shelves and ceiling for sound softening and darkrooms and practice space for piano players and places to put banjos and all the other things we think matter in our lives and the lives of high school pupils.*

### Helen Risom Belluschi '61 letter, July 18, 2016

*My personal experience with the Woodstock Country School? It was the first place where I knew that I belonged to something I liked.*

• • •

Although ostensibly writing to the Trustees, Isabel's real audience was David. Everyone knew perfectly well that the budget was created by David and Buffy, and that the Trustees merely tinkered at the edges if at all. Who knows if Isabel was aware of the irony of her concern for maps, given her blythe willingness do do without maps altogether after the fire in 1954. Her apparent resentment of a dynamic arts program smacks of unknown subtext. The snide remark about Drama clearly targets Peggy. And her protests about farming and chicken is a direct protest of one of David's pet projects. When she indicates doubts that the farm program contributes to "improvement of the school as a school," she seems to believe she's at a more traditional school than Woodstock. There's no record of a response to Isabel from the Trustees or David.

It's true that David's reports to the trustees during 1958-59-60 paid more attention to the school's property and finances than to students and faculty, even though both reached their highest numerical levels. Enrolment reached 101 in 1960, shortly after the trustees formed a committee to study the size-of-the-school question. Three years earlier, Isabel had warned in a faculty meeting that "the headmaster, in a year or two, won't have time to love a hundred children and see a hundred or two visitors." But there was nothing in the headmaster's reports (or elsewhere yet) implying that he felt increasing stress. Quite the opposite – he seemed full of energy, pursuing a variety of initiatives which were essentially problems of institutional success.

"The opening of our 16th academic year was one of the best beginnings we have ever had," David reported to the trustees in October 1960. "It seems to be due partly to the quality of the new students and partly to the efforts of the Student Council in organizing a different orientation period... The school staff, totaling 26, 18 of whom are teachers, has remained the same, with the exception of the loss of an extra hand in the kitchen. This continuity of personnel, as in recent years, has been one of the strengths of the school, and it does not lead to intellectual stagnation because the teachers so often find themselves with a program different from the one of the year before." David also noted that in the largest-ever class of 32 seniors, half "have IQs of 130 or better."

The pace of the school's material improvement was also picking up. The new theatre-auditorium in Upwey's Drama Loft, for which Peggy Bailey had lobbied the trustees two years earlier, was ready to use in the fall of 1960, complete with a lighting system planned by Broadway lighting designer Jean Rosenthal. A few months later, a new Art Loft was installed in the former drama loft (the former barracks dorm). And a few months after that, construction started on a new library in the nearby cow barn, bringing to a close six cramped and noisy years with a library in the middle of Upwey, next to the dining room. All this represented a change in longstanding plans to put the library upstairs in Upwey and to move the Art Department to the cow barn (over the maintenance shop and boys' locker room). In contrast to earlier years, these decisions were made without student participation, as John Maynard, who was then a senior, recalled: "The students were never asked. I may have been the only person who thought that was too bad, and said something about it, but by that time the decision had already been made... David announced it, but it was not something we were brought in on... Bringing the students in on other kinds of decisions was something that no one else [among the students] had ever done, nobody knew about it. No other schools that we knew of [did it]. I think Dewey would have let students make decisions."

But with the school thriving again, albeit in more conventional ways than a decade earlier – and despite the possible restiveness of the faculty suggested by Isabel's memo (above) – David was giving more attention than usual to longer term efforts to create institutional security. In varying degrees, he was working on the Endowment Fund, the Parents Association Annual Giving Campaign and the Capital Campaign, announced in January, to raise $50,000 for the theatre and library. But his relationship to the trustees remained contradictory and so, in some ways, self-defeating. At one moment, David would tell his board: "Sometimes I hanker for a bit more interference because the Woodstock Trustees have, for the most part, kept themselves in ignorance of the school."

But at other times, the headmaster and president himself did more to perpetuate that ignorance than to dispel it. (This is explored in more detail in Chapter 6.)

At the same time, since at least 1957, David had been under almost constant pressure from a few trustees to raise Woodstock faculty salaries. And while salaries had risen somewhat, there was still a strong case that the faculty was partly subsidizing the school. The 1960 faculty accepted this reluctantly, even resentfully, in contrast to the intensity of the commitment and belief that led the faculty of 1949 to take a voluntary pay cut in order to balance the budget. Helping to alleviate faculty salary problems was the Woodstocking Fund, established in strict anonymity in 1959 by the Sidore family (who had sent two sons and a daughter to the school). Strictly for faculty benefit, the Woodstocking Fund was a periodically renewed four-figure fund. It was established under David's administration, in his sole discretion, to make both loans and grants to help faculty members with mortgages, medical expenses and other pressing needs.

In 1960-61, none of the school's problems seemed unmanageable. Even though the school's tuition income was, for the first time ever, less than its annual operating expenses, the difference was less than $2,000 and not even a cause for formal comment, much less concern. On the contrary, with a student body of remarkably high caliber and with the nucleus of an exciting new generation of faculty members, the school's future had never looked brighter. David would eventually characterize this period, "my middle years at Upwey, [as] probably the best years socially and academically in school history."

On campus, the 1960-61 academic year had been one of the best in 16 years. The largest senior class ever, 32 graduates, was also one of the strongest, both in intellect and character. At Commencement, David commented on the class's loyalty and affection, for each other and for the school. Off campus, the school had drawn increasing financial support from the local community and especially from a more and more productive Parents Association and a growing alumni organization.

One measure of the state of the school was the students' choice of a school gift of 1960. "I think one of my nicest memories there was a school meeting going on after lunch and I was in the faculty room," Peggy Bailey recalled. "Somebody came in and said, 'I think you'd better come into the school meeting, so I thought there must have been some sort of crisis, so I hurried in, but it turned out that we were presented with a check for us to take a trip abroad, which had been given by the students and faculty. There was a little scroll made, and it was presented very ceremoniously, handed to David, who in turn handed it to me. Everybody applauded, it was very nice." A year later, an even stronger measure of the apparent state of the school was the Baileys' willingness to cash that check and take a trip. In the summer of 1961, the Baileys felt confident and comfortable enough to leave the school for extended travel in Great Britain. They stayed in London and went to the theatre, they visited friends and alumni in the country and they drove for almost a month through twenty counties in southern England, visiting Cambridge, Bath, Salisbury and the "Hardy Country."

"Wiltshire was our favorite country," Peggy reported in the school newsletter, "but everywhere we went we enjoyed the beautiful villages, castles and gardens. This was our first really extensive vacation since the founding of the school – and a most happy one."

## Patricia Jenkins Brenner '63 interview, Feb. 15, 1985

*David made me feel really shy, because, first of all he was so imposing physically, so big. And he always was really close when he talked. And his eyes – I always felt that they were inside of me, they were piercing through me, and it made me really edgy and uncomfortable, and then [he] would meet me with a smile and it was almost too close.*

*I think maybe my mother conferred with him, too, and he wrote a letter home saying, 'We would like Pat to come to Woodstock' and 'We hope she would like Woodstock, because we know Woodstock would like her.' And I did end up going there...*

*David had that piercing, penetrating look, always with a smile, a little bit with a twinkle. He was always slightly amused or bemused by me. And he said to me once that I never looked him in the eye, that I would begin to talk to him and I couldn't hold his eyes and I'd look down.*

*And he smiled, he laughed – it was by no means a put down, it was just a comment on his perception of me and he found that delightful, one more thing that made me special. It absolutely delighted him, and it mortified me! Because I realized it was true, that it was like he was undressing me, but in a kind of spiritual, emotional way, like he could read inside of me. And I was really afraid to let anybody do that because I was so unsure about what was there. He knew something that I didn't know, even about me. I mean, how did he know that Woodstock was going to like me, how did he know that I was going to like Woodstock? It seemed like he knew that, and that wasn't fair – I mean I didn't know that.*

*But it was just really special to be liked by David, because David was special. There was always this twinkle there. And I felt like a little girl around David."*

## Dan Seeger '63 interview, March 21, 1985

*Nobody was close to David. Everyone had a fear of him, you know... but he was actually a very kind person. I don't know whether it was his imposing size, or the fact that he had to be the ultimate disciplinarian that made people scared of him...*

*He was always trying to be a participant in everything that was going on, and obviously being unable to do it because too much was going on, but he did it in a very nice way. He was an eager substitute [teacher], when he didn't know a darn thing about what was being taught – and it worked, of course, because students would tell him what was going on...*

*Sports – he was always interested in sports; sports were very big to him. I think Cam [athletic director Wendell Cameron] was always disappointed that Woodstock's baseball team was the worst, and that was his game, of course, being an almost major league pitcher.*

*But hockey was the best. I was a little bit upset, I came back two years later and there was no hockey rink, it was totally gone. I couldn't figure that out at all, 'cause they had a championship hockey team. That was the game that they won at...*

*None of the teachers were that close to us. You know that school wasn't rooted in any kind of Summerhill-style therapy, so nobody got close to the students, there was no effort. If anybody was having any kind of emotional problems, I don't know if anyone on the faculty was either assigned or prepared to deal with it... you didn't get close to teachers, there wasn't really any closeness...*

*These are things that do anger me or else I wouldn't think of them to this day – there wasn't any communication. If a misunderstanding arises, people should work it out, they should talk about it, rather than jump to conclusions and act irrational and make a [snap] judgment like that. I guess that's what I reasoned about the Group System so much, or some kids who got arbitrarily kicked out of school... It was typical of the era that people didn't deal with people the way they do now. People are much more open now. I think at Woodstock in the seventies people would have talked about that.*

FALL 1955 – SPRING 1962

## David Bailey report to trustees, Oct. 11, 1961

*The academic year began quite casually this fall, mostly, I think, because none of us felt quite ready to begin. The combination of early arrivals for soccer practice and the fact that some of the buildings weren't quite in shape meant that we drifted into our start without the usual complete readiness. The new group, however, is rather a mild one and it caught onto the system quite easily. Last year was such an excellent one, academically and financially, that it may be that we were not anticipating, as happily as usual, the start of the new year...*

*At this Annual Meeting the Trustees will, as usual, have to concern themselves, primarily, with financial problems... money must be raised to fill the gap between capital expenditures and capital gifts... the operating budget, which is in balance only because of considerable sums from previous years' Margins and Gifts. This condition cannot continue year after year... we do have to plan on continuing annual salary increments and, of course, as the plant expands so does the cost of running and maintaining it... tuition increase of $200 next year.... Could more income be gained by using the plant in the summer, either by having some sort of summer session, or by renting some of the buildings?... the farm still manages just about to pay for itself... alumni should be making more of a financial contribution on a regular basis...*

*We also had requests from one staff member for permission to build a family fall-out shelter. This is a subject I'd rather not worry about at all, but it is incumbent upon the Trustees to consider whether some sort of shelter should be available, particularly for the students, to protect us from criticism...*

*In closing it is, perhaps, belaboring a point to state that the School is not efficiently administered. For example, not all the school personnel are used to best advantage; and perhaps, the educational offerings are unnecessarily rich, and the School doesn't profit enough from the talents and capabilities of the Trustees. Being a Trustee is a thankless task, but it would probably be less of a burden if the Trustees felt they were playing a larger part in the welfare of the School. The School is grateful for what the Trustees have done and would appreciate any suggestions as to what more they could do.*

For years before Trustee Joy Sweet's memo would prompt the Trustees to start to scrutinize the state of the school, David had been sending oblique distress signals. In the fall of 1961, when David observed that "none of us felt quite ready to begin," he partly meant that his own, sometimes uncertain health had become a growing burden. What he did not say directly was that he had been quite breathless that summer during his and Peggy's trip to England, that he had been too winded to climb hills or castle stairs. The following year, David would stop walking the hundred yards or so of almost level road between his house and Upwey. He drove back and forth instead. Peggy couldn't recall just when she first heard the word emphysema applied to David, but "I remember Hugh [Hermann, a Woodstock doctor] telling me about it with a kind of finality in his voice... David never talked very much himself about it,.. and I didn't go ferreting into it as much as I should have."

Dr. Hugh Hermann was a Harvard-trained surgeon who started practicing medicine at Woodstock's Ottauquechee Health Center in 1958. He said he first saw David as a patient around 1959 and he knew immediately that David had emphysema. (Years later, Aaron Cohen '68, a respiratory therapist in an intensive care unit for newborns, reported, "I've never seen anyone with emphysema like he had.") As early as 1959, David had the classic symptoms: barrel chest, chronic cough, difficulty with normal breathing and extreme dyspnea (breathlessness) from all but minimal physical exertion. Since emphysema impairs the ability of the lungs to function, it reduces the amount of oxygen getting into the blood stream, which in turn reduces muscle and brain function – all of which is made worse by smoking. Dr. Hermann compared having emphysema to flying at 10,000 feet without an oxygen system or a pressurized cabin. But as a young and somewhat cautious doctor treating an older man who was prominent in the community, Dr. Hermann was inclined to tread softly. Perhaps, as he remembered it, he did not mention emphysema specifically early on. He suggested that David stop smoking. He did not confront his patient squarely with the consequences of continuing that self-destructive behavior. Others had told David to stop smoking, but he kept smoking. He would say there was no point in stopping, that the damage was already done. Presumable he knew that was false.

In 1959, David did not make even the token effort to stop smoking that he had made in 1939, when he tried chewing gum after being hospitalized for pneumonia. By 1959, he had been smoking heavily for close to three decades, he was psychologically and perhaps physically dependent on cigarettes – and his persona in the school was strongly identified with smoking. In the memories of many alumni, David is inseparable from the cigarette in his hand or dangling from the corner of his mouth, or from his characteristic gesture of flicking its ashes into the cuff of his slacks. Moreover, he had shaped the school in part around the idea that smoking was a grown-up privilege that had to be earned. To acquire "smoking permission," Woodstock's 16-year-olds needed not only parental permission, but also David's approval. He used smoking permission as a lever of social control, a reward for good behavior, making it seem a tangible sign of maturity.

Even though David denied the efficacy of stopping smoking, the medical literature for the previous quarter century is clear and consistent that smoking can only make emphysema worse. Dr. Hermann eventually told David as much, but "he denied that smoking was harmful... David was very cavalier about his smoking. And I felt very unhappy that I wasn't able to help him... and it was out of complete frustration that I sent him to [a respiratory specialist in Boston]."

Dr. Hermann was emphatically clear that "David denied his illness, that's the bottom line." The doctor did not mean David denied he was sick – which became increasingly obvious – but that David denied the illness was important, that it could seriously impair his ability to run the school, or that his diminished capacity could harm the school. At the time, Dr. Hermann assumed that if David had made a list of everything that was wrong with him and presented that list to the board of trustees, he would be on Social Security disability and not headmaster of the Country School.

In attempting to confront his emphysema honestly, David's character put him in a double bind. As Gerry Freund '48 described it, "David, by nature, was infuriatingly unwilling to deal with matters that were important, that others considered important... David never wanted to be challenged by anybody about the leadership of the school." As the emphysema progressed, David talked to confidants like Gerry about not being able to get around the campus as much as he once could, and about not having as firm a grip on the school as he had once had. Others, especially David's most loyal supporters, discussed his condition among themselves and debated what, if anything, should be done about it, but the issue remained an oblique, unspoken subtext in official communications.

While it is clear in a general way that David's emphysema affected his performance as headmaster fairly early on, it's not clear what he knew about his disease or when he knew it, or what information he shared with others. Years after David died, Peggy Bailey refused to release any medical records.

She granted the author permission to talk to Dr. Hermann, only to rescind that permission a few days later after limited discussion. Peggy refused to grant permission to talk to any of David's other doctors or to cooperate in any other way to allow any clearer clinical understanding of his health. She explained her choice in terms of privacy: "I know that David himself would have been very, very upset about this kind of thing, inquiring into his health, which he was always apt to, tried to, well, not disguise, exactly, but to make light of, and I just decided that it was too much of an invasion of privacy." Alumnus and former Trustee Roger Phillips had already destroyed David's health insurance records, with Peggy's blessing.

The general prognosis for emphysema sufferers in 1961 was not hopeful, according to *Postgraduate Medicine:* "As you know, results of treatment of bronchitis and emphysema often are discouraging. Of great importance to the patient is the knowledge that his physician has an interest in him and in his illness and is willing to work with him patiently over a long period. The discomfort produced by the dyspnea, the necessary restriction of activity and the long course of the disease often lead to a sense of desperation on the part of the patient. Avoidance of irritants or dust in the inspired air is essential. The chief of these irritants, of course, is tobacco smoke... [since] continuation of smoking is extremely harmful once the disease is established." Similarly, the American Journal of the Medical Sciences pointed out that "the prognosis of the patient as a whole was somewhat more unfavorable in those who continued to smoke than in those who stopped smoking." And emphysema among non-smokers is rare.

Reflecting widespread uncertainty within the school community at the time, Buffy Dunker recalled the onset of David's disease: "When this emphysema first began to get David, it was very, very slow and very, very insidious... What happened to David was that he got very tired without being able to admit it. He did not have oxygen energy. So what happened was that he didn't make such good decisions. For instance, he was of course solely responsible for hiring a faculty. And he, in some of those years there, from 1962 on, instead of really picking a terrific teacher, he kept wanting to solve several problems with one person... [One teacher] was given more to do than was anywhere near appropriate... [Another], because he was a classical scholar, was put in charge of chapel services on Sunday... [A third was an] absolutely awful guy... What David was doing was playing chess with the things that the school needed, without looking to see whether he was getting an absolutely first rate teacher... the quality of the faculty deteriorated during [the middle 1960s] because of David's no longer being able to discriminate the way he could before, he lost the touch of his intuition, because it was hard work."

FALL 1955 – SPRING 1962

David Bailey and students, circa 1960

Eric Reisberg, Nita Werner, Bob Bewkes, & Lahly Poore in the WCS original production of the revue "Tried and True and Guilty" in 1974

Mounir Sa'adah

FALL 1955 – SPRING 1962

Mary Stewart '57, Drew Marshall '57, unknown, George Yeomans '58

Jo Oatfield

Sandy Bull '58

Pete Seeger

FALL 1955 – SPRING 1962

## Artist Lowell Naeve's pictures of his students with their work, 1961-62

Susan Cheever

Dana Emmons

Cassandra Hughes

Helen Risom

# FALL 1955 – SPRING 1962

Debbie Skinner

Penny Seeger

Wind ensemble (l. to r.): Sue Hay, Nancy Matthews, Lydia Lake, Buffy Dunker, Joan Newlon, and Penny Seeger

WCS Library (by 2016 it was a tack shop owned by alumna Laura Spittle, who keeps a WCS guestbook and welcome center)

CHAPTER SIX

# Fall 1963 – Summer 1965

### Peter Sauer self-tape, March 13, 1984

*I think I fell in love with the school even before I began my first interview for a job there [in 1961]. I had driven up to Woodstock and arrived in the late morning. I can remember David showing me a book of photographs of students in the school, and I remember him commenting that the lolly-columns in the common room were useful because kids like to swing on them...*

*I can also remember a faculty meeting in which we were discussing a particularly awkward child named Valerie, and John Greppin [a language teacher] made a long speech about Woodstock not being the right school for Valerie. She just didn't fit in here and it wasn't the right school. And David said "John, what is the right school for Valerie? Because that's what we're here for."*

*I know David was frustrated by teachers who were unable to understand that their individual relationships with the kids were equally as important as the subject matter that they were teaching... The school was, in many ways, a reaction to bureaucratic institutions. David believed that it should be individualized. David believed we should remake the school every time a new student walked in, just like Valerie.*

## Barbara Sproul '62 interview, August 2, 1984

*Woodstock was intellectually, completely different from anything I'd seen. Mostly I'd come from New Haven private schools where everyone was bored perpetually, and all of a sudden I was at a place where everyone was interested perpetually, and where the stars were people who could think and write and talk. People read the New York Times. Everybody read it every day... I was really out of my league, so that was fun, too, because I'd always been the smartest kid in my class, and all of a sudden no one thought I was particularly smart or particularly good, and it was wonderful. I got to start all over again, it was a whole new life...*

*As I say, intellectually, people were talking about real things, and abstract lessons were whenever possible, applied to real situations. Emotionally, sexually – if you got laid, you got laid. Nobody sat in the back seats of cars saying, "No, no," if they meant, "Yes, yes," It was so relieving. If you didn't want to get laid, you'd say "No, thank you very much," and nobody'd say, "Please, please, forever." There was just no nonsense about it. If you had a boyfriend, you had 49 friends who were boys. They finally became more of a learning experience than the boyfriend... it really didn't matter so much if you got laid later on in the evening, it was no longer the crucial issue. It started to assume what I think adults usually find is its appropriate place if it's allowed to be free – sexuality – so that it wasn't misfocused any more. People being warm, caring, loving, friendly, interested in each other, sharing things, talking to each other... assumed their proper places in a relationship.*

## FALL 1963 – SUMMER 1965

*Nobody ever got thrown out of Woodstock for sleeping with anybody, did they? People were reasonably sophisticated about birth control, and if you weren't when you got started, you got so there. Faculty seemed more interested in whether you were getting in over your head emotionally, whether a relationship was destructive psychologically.*

• • •

After a year without significant staff change in 1960-61, David hired Peter Sauer for 1961-62, to teach science and English, to help run the French House boys dorm, to help with weekend entertainment and, in time, much, much more. Just 22 years old, Peter had served six months in the National Guard after dropping out of graduate school in Florida, where he was studying marine biology. He wanted to teach because he had disliked school so much when he was a student at the Choate School. Visiting Woodstock, Peter fell in love with it because "it just felt like the right way to run a school – it was relaxed and comfortable, informal... [The way David talked about those lolly-columns made it clear to me] that he was concerned about what kids felt, instead of the curriculum... There was a balance between the cognitive and the affective in that school, to use a Bank Street phrase, and really what he knew was that human relationships are what matter."

Peter immersed himself in the life of the school, not just teaching, but taking students on jeep rides through the autumn foliage or snowshoe walks under a full moon. Later, he would also be the Director of Admissions (although David made almost all the final decisions). He would be twice elected as the faculty representative to the Board of Trustees and he would become increasingly involved in long-range planning for the school. "It was really like the fifties when I started," he remembered, a cohesive and creative school without a lot of serious problems – "I've thought that my first year was the last of the really good years."

But that year also saw the emergence of troubling new tensions within the school over a wide range of issues: student dress, hair, stealing, manners (especially during vespers services at the South Woodstock Community Church), and even over what music was allowed to be played in the student common room in Upwey. The student council grew increasingly ambivalent, wishing to be responsible for fellow students – worrying about "general feelings of apathy," but not wanting to seem like a police force. The council abandoned its responsibility for helping in the dorms, suggesting at one meeting simply that "co-ed dorms [might be the] solution to after-lights noise problem." One of the more unifying student activities during the year was the Peace Union group's campaign to ban the bomb.

On the other hand, the faculty wasn't having noticeably greater success with the same issues, or with trying to downgrade the status of smoking ("our attitude has changed in many cases," Larry Roberts noted in the fall). David complained that "this is the most conformist group of student I can remember," but when he suggested "a talk fest – break up into 4-5 groups with 2-3 teachers in each group and chat – find out what the students want, what they are mulling about," a majority of the faculty balked. In January, when dorm problems were at their worst, dorm head Wendell Cameron sympathized with the students living in over-crowded conditions: "it really isn't living up there." More typically, several older faculty called for exclusion of the trouble-makers, though some also suggested more positive ways to alleviate the pressure. When David later suggested the possibility of a small, student-only dorm of six to eight people, the student meeting enthusiastically adopted the idea for that year's school gift. When the trustees rejected the idea, the students chose no alternative, but set aside the money for some "future big project."

By the fall of 1962, the faculty decline that David predicted in his report to the trustees was already beginning. The nine full-time and part-time teachers who had been at Woodstock since 1954 or earlier (Buffy Dunker, Mounir Sa'adah, Jo Oatfield, Larry and Kilty Roberts, Isabel and Rockwell Stephens, and the Baileys themselves) still comprised the stable, core faculty, although some were approaching retirement. The new core faculty of younger teachers representing the school's future was not so stable. Old and new had in common the problems of low salaries, no contracts and more stressful working conditions – trying to teach a student body they still felt was too large, even more so now that it was unmannerly, unpresentable and inattentive in class because of unpoliced late night activities.

**II**

### Robin Maisel '62, *Symposium*, June 1962

*The crisis faced by youth today has been analyzed, psychoanalyzed and equated in formulae for the physicist and the social scientist. Yet the crisis remains as much an enigma as ever. This is not the crisis of a new order or an old order but the dangerous crisis of an order in transition. Any youth faces this crisis in the midst of anger from our elders and misunderstanding from all quarters. I can't define the crisis but I can state the feelings of an angry youth who believes he knows part of the reason why the crisis exists.*

*It is widely acknowledged that problems face mankind. The gravity of the problems is also [acknowledged]. But this does not answer the question of where the crisis of youth stems from... The cause of the crisis lies, to a great extent, in the fact that the people who make the decisions, the people who face the problems, are the old and the young. There is no middle group to take some of the weight of responsibility for man's fate off the hands of these two camps.*

*The last war devastated what would today be the vital middle group. They are the disillusioned ones. The revulsion of war, the incomprehensibility of nuclear holocaust, the economic problems which have not been solved and the sharpening conflict of east and west, have left the middle group impotent in action and thought... We, the young, not individuals but a block of millions, are carrying a double burden, of which at least half should be carried by our parents. It is not easy for us to point accusing fingers at our elders because we love them and understand with compassion the more than thirty years during which they struggled alone...*

*The old order lives in the demi-world of yesterday's solutions for today's problems... We, the youth of the world, have the insight, understanding and the fortitude to build life for the new order in the period of transition. We are angry with the tired radicals who tell us to go slow... We are frustrated by the older leaders' morality now out of place and immoral in today's world.*

*What, then, are we to do? We are training our minds and learning the skills needed to solve the problems. Youth took the initiative in the integration fight. Youth leads now in the peace race. Youth is determined to solve the problems left over from our parents' mistakes. We give you, our parents and grandparents, fair warning... We shall retire you eventually and we hope and believe that with our understanding and fortitude we shall resolve the crisis of our order in transition.*

## Tony Lowes '62, *The Independent*, June 1962

*AGAINST THE COUNTRY BEATS*
*Even a rapid glance at recent school publications gives proof that this community's writing is of a despairing nature. This is not to say that despair had not been expressed well, but rather that an entire issue of this introspective self-pity, general pity, and world wide pity is hard not only on the reader, but also on the aspiring writer...*

*Introspection, to some degree, is necessary, but a school, or a people, who can only look in rapidly lose their balance and their mire increases.... And they love it. They thrive on it, they re-digest it daily, they re-read it nightly, and they send it to their friends and enemies. They find it in books and pin it on their walls.*

*Yet they get drunk to escape from it. They would run away, they say, if they had the guts. They would smoke pot if they had it...*

*This is the state we have reached: moles are compared to people, maturity to hell, and the seasons to the second coming; we seem unable to thank anyone for our blessings; we are unable to look out of the window and see anything but rain or a mushroom cloud; love is now something to be suffered, and the well-intentioned people are 'old fogies.' ... Society here encourages introspection, the students encourage self-pity, and the world, through these eyes, encourages despair. Perhaps, realizing this, we can fight back to the day when milk was milk, not a bottle of Strontium 90, and when a tree was a tree, not a cross for yet another Christ.*

## Russ Mead, Baccalaureate address, June 3, 1962

A statement made by many of you [in the Class of 1962] is that nuclear war is a new threat, that you are the first to be reaching some sort of maturity with the scare of total disintegration hanging thread-like over you...

This senior class either isn't involved yet, or else it has become adult so quickly that its youth is unreal, its character a fantasy. Most of your actions seem vagrant and fleeting reactions to a despair that moved another time...

If you were an ordinary group of seniors, a typical blob, I would have to offer up platitudes of citizenship and proper use of ballot and so forth. But you are not ordinary. In your present condition as specially endowed, I charge you not merely with individual thoughtfulness, with preparing yourselves to be good citizens, but with readying yourselves to be rulers...

Four weeks ago, in vespers, I trod ever so lightly on the peace movement and a few other protests of yours. These are fine as measures of defiance, as gestures to inform the world strength is building, but these exercises in protest are only useful if they strengthen your muscles of organization and persuasion that must someday grasp, not take or receive, but grasp the controls of government...

*Seeing difficulty of other young people following immediately behind their parents, or in reaction to them, it is not for you in this room merely to argue and try to get signatures from people of like mind; it is up to you to see to it that when the mantle of rule descends, it falls on the shoulders of you in this room and not on those who are less qualified by perception and more bound by tradition... The way to build a proper world is not through petition to the old powers that be, but in being those powers...*

*If holocaust should strike, it is no different a death from that we all face. There are no degrees of death. But there are degrees of life, and it is time for you to rise above zero to the boiling point. Anger has infected many of you, but it is aimed at a generation powerless to act because it is tied to a time that is no longer, and for us never was. Your anger must be directed at those of your own time who wish to follow in the tired old ruts of perspective.*

### Minutes of the board of trustees, May 5, 1962

*Mr. Bailey presented his report orally, saying that in general the [1961-62] school year had been an average one, not as good as the previous year. Several students had to leave school for a variety of reasons: illness, studies, or discipline. Two disciplinary problems were cause for concern – drinking and petty vice. The former has become prevalent throughout the country recently, and Mr. Bailey pointed out that a new kind of morality was appearing in Eastern schools which had no respect for 'mine' and 'thine' and had an elusive softness about it that made it hard to attack and handle.*

*As for college admissions, most of the good students were admitted to their first choice colleges. Four students, however, did not apply to any college.*

• • •

In the spring of 1962, Russ Mead was the first of the younger faculty to leave. Three years after he had left Peacham Academy, Woodstock no longer felt like a vacation to Russ: "I was tired. And I had had it with living on campus – there just wasn't enough time to be with family and we lived in dorms, and I began to think that it was harmful for the children to see all that much of what was going on. I was tired of having to spend so much time on other people's personal problems, on teenagers' personal problems. I have got all of my own problems that I can deal with. I really wanted to get away from all that intensity. You can only have so many failures. I just thought of it as being tired. Looking back, I think I see it that the whole procedure was unhealthy. And I wasn't maturing any faster than the students." A year earlier, the students had dedicated the 1961 graduation issue of *Symposium* to Russ "in gratitude for his kind help and understanding."

Less clear about his own development at the time, Russ asked David for more money, and let that seem to be the main issue. Announcing Russ's departure to the trustees that spring, David said he "was leaving to continue his studies for his doctorate." Actually, Russ was applying to other schools for jobs, but only at girls' schools and day schools, eventually exchanging Woodstock's hurly-burly for the more sedate atmosphere of Concord Academy. Still, when he became Concord's headmaster several years later, most of the changes he initiated to make the school more humane and intellectually challenging were consciously derived from his experience at Woodstock.

In retrospect, it is clear Russ's leaving marked the beginning of what would become devastating faculty turnover at Woodstock. It didn't seem so at the time. But two other younger teachers with five years tenure each also left that year, one of them suddenly for personal reasons early in the fall term. And Victor Savelberg, Ula's husband, died that fall after a year's battle with cancer, to the great sadness of the community (and with the later consequence that Ula would leave the school, taking her warm heart, good cooking and sound management with her for a couple of years).

In the spring of 1963, two more of the school's best teachers, Molly Plumb and Lowell Naeve, also departed, as did Lovett Garceau, the eccentric part-time math teacher. Molly followed Russ Mead to the calmer climate of Concord Academy (having complained bitterly about living with no private bath and no privacy in the girls' dorm). Lowell left to pursue his art and his political odyssey, which would lead the Naeves to emigrate to Canada in 1965 to protect their sons from the draft during the Viet-Nam War. (Despite some very able successors to Lowell, Woodstock would never again have quite as vital, varied and sustained an art program). Tad Bailey also left the school in 1963 to devote his energies to his art and, increasingly, to the Woodstock Learning Clinic. Earlier that spring, Elizabeth Forrest Johnson had died on April 1.

As the faculty decline accelerated with further resignations, retirements and illness over the next several years, David was unable to replace these teachers with new ones of equal caliber, those strong and diverse personalities whose personal commitment to the school so characterized Woodstock in its best years. There were a few individual exceptions, but as a whole, the Woodstock faculty would never again be quite as cohesive and confident as it had been when David's leadership was strong and healthy.

## David Bailey report to the trustees, October 4, 1962

*It is fruitless to apologize for having enrolled too many students this year. Though we have broken the barrier [of 100], probably no dreadful harm has occurred and the quality of the student body seems normally adequate this fall... at the moment, the school has reached a new height, in both quality and quantity of personnel. It would also be my prediction that the future, in this respect, could very easily bring decline. We can certainly anticipate, in the next year or two, further losses among the more valuable faculty members due to retirement or increasing ineffectiveness. It may be that we will be forced to pare our extensive academic offerings and focus on fewer and better paid instructors. At present we are offering the students a far wider choice than a school of this kind should and we've been almost absurdly lucky in being able to have done this in the last few years...*

*I am reluctant to advocate any but the absolutely essential changes or additions to the plant while we have our past improvements unpaid for, but I think it might be wise to look a little further ahead to make an overall plan of step by step developments. In summary, there are many unanswered questions, and the administration does not feel on sure enough ground to make firm recommendation for action by the Trustees in many of these areas. It is agreed by all, I'm sure, that the school should move forward and not spend most of its efforts merely to maintain a status quo. Therefore, what is the best direction to take? Should we anticipate curtailment of certain aspects of the program, such as stopping Arabic or Greek or some of the science or riding? Should we try to diminish or enlarge the productivity of the land? Should we embark on a wholly new project such as summer school? These are all rather large questions and it's hard to see clearly in which directions the administration and Trustees should most wisely move.*

## Jim (Webbs) Mellowes '64, *Occasional Worker* student publication, September 19, 1962

### GUEST COLUMN

*No kidding. We have more control over the student body this year than last. It's really amazing how far you can push youth these days. I've just been waiting for 'em to picket the phonograph while playing "Bo Diddely" [sic] or some trash like that. Night before last, when I was OD, I thought it would be nice to hear some Mozart instead of that Ray Charles. So I conned someone into thinking it was only allowed before dinner. He actually believed me, so I put on some sweet Mozart to settle down and clean my pipe! Yeah you really can LITERALLY lead 'em around by the nose. Heck, if this record player deal keeps up I think we can eliminate their choice of music entirely. And then who knows what's next! The funny thing is that I'm pretty sure the phonograph was a student gift; and we control it! Yeah, it's really great! I think this school is beginning to take shape after all – last week I wasn't sure.*

## Jim Edlin '65, *Occasional Worker*, October 3, 1962

### VESPERS: THE OTHER SIDE

*Between last week's article and having attended at least two services, we have all formed some sort of an opinion about Vespers. What follows is mine – but I feel that a good deal of it is fact.*

*Vespers is, as stated last week, basically a religious service, and though the powers-that-be assert it to be nonsectarian, I feel that it mainly favors one group. For, to begin with, it is held in a church of the Universalist sect. In a place of honor in this church stands a cross, but I see nowhere a statue of Buddha. We sing hymns to the glory of God and Christ, but never face East and pray to Allah.*

*If you do not suppose it to be nonsectarian, then by demanding our presence, those in authority violate not only a basic principle of our country, but the even more sacred right of an individual to choose his means of religious expression.*

*Furthermore, this service does not fulfill the religious needs of some of us, yet forces others to do what is against their beliefs.*

*I have, from time to time, opposed Vespers on these grounds, but have been rebuffed (by those in control) with the answer, "It is not intended as a religious service as much as an intellectual experience." If so, why must a man, with something valid to say, say it in church as a preacher instead of in an auditorium as a speaker?*

## Student Council minutes, Gillian Lowes, secretary, January 8, 1963

*Chris [Morris '63] opened the meeting at 7:05 in the Physics Lab, with Molly [Plumb] and Teddy [LeComte] present, but not David.*

*The meeting was spent discussing plans to spark Woodstock. We want something really different that nobody has ever tried. The last all-school project was the library. We're established now, and we can go on as a regular co-ed boarding school, or we can do something new and different. Woodstock is living in the past. There has been a steady decline in enthusiasm and feeling in the school the last few years...*

### SUGGESTIONS:

- *... that five students visit each private school in the area (i.e., Stowe, Putney, Buxton, etc.) and about thirty students remain at home with the exchange students...*
- *Some new form of government. Honor System. Abolish (student) council...*
- *Sell the school and build another one. Move the school to the Rocky Mountains. The kids at Woodstock feel very secure. They don't have to worry about really working (except academics) at all...*
- *Rebuild the common room. The common room was a more interesting, ALIVE place four years ago, with dancing, folk-dancing, talking, cards and bridge, etc. Now there is just hush-hush talking, a cliquey kind of talking together in groups, or staring off into space.*
- *Dig a swimming pool...*

*The remainder of the meeting was spent discussing the Honor System. It is based on the idea that each individual is responsible not only for his own conduct, but also for everyone else's.*

> *Objections were that Woodstock has some "perverted idea" that squealing is not right. Students defend each other to an enormous degree. There is also a prevailing tendency to sit and ignore, rather than to act...*

• • •

School had opened in the fall of 1962 with 101 students, the largest enrolment ever, too many for the overcrowded dorms and too many for a teaching staff that was feeling more and more overworked, underpaid and at odds with the students. At the first faculty meeting in September, before the students arrived, Tad Bailey presented a plan to focus all the school's courses directly on language, in order to improve communication, to help students learn to recognize and correct their own misunderstandings and to develop their ability to analyze and choose effectively from the proliferating options the world would offer. Tad argued that the world seemed to be changing faster than when his generation was young, and students of the early sixties would face problems that were more numerous, more complex and more serious. He warned that these trends were accelerating and "we aren't coping very well." A few individual teachers tried to incorporate Tad's ideas and exercises into the curriculum during the first six weeks of the term as Tad visited every class. But the effort was informal, unstructured and petered out with uncertain results. Teachers were too little trained in the process, which was still experimental and largely unformed and they had mixed opinions about its value, as well as about the state of the school. "Thinking is in such ruts," David said in November. Isabel disagreed and the faculty reached no consensus on Tad's report and follow-up proposal in December. But in discussing Tad's ideas, they decided to produce "the Woodstock ECLECTIC Reader," based on a short paragraph by Peggy Bailey describing a typical Country School lunch. This appeared on the first page of the reader, followed by eleven pages of variations on the theme by other teachers. These included journalistic, scientific, musical and poetic treatments (the last a parody of Alexander Pope), as well as versions in French, German, Arabic and one by linguist John Greppin combining Latin, Greek, and Hebrew. The Reader concludes with a philosophical parody that turns out to be less the mocking epistemology of lunch than it seems:

"The problem of eating and the quest for food has occupied the minds of men since the dawn of history. Does man live by bread alone? Is he solely motivated by his economic needs? Are all his institutions, morality, art, literature and culture mere derivatives of his search for food?... In this school we propose a tentative answer to the question. We think that food is a common interest that brings people together at certain intervals. This occasion can be used to nourish our bodies with simple but well-prepared meals. It is also an opportunity to relax from the intellectual and physical strains of the day, to exchange refreshing conversations with people we are not likely to meet in any significant way during the routines of school life and to impart information [during announcements] that is of general interest to the school. Somehow, we attempt to make the 'feeding experience' a 'total experience' that will nourish the spiritual, moral, social, emotional and intellectual needs of the community. Have we succeeded?"

Tad's proposal provoked further discussion of setting up some day-long school project that would demonstrate his ideas in practical terms, such as making something and then writing instructions for how to make it. In January, after the student council announced that it wanted an all-school project that was "something really different that nobody has ever tried," the faculty started planning a mid-winter break that would give the students the experience of getting deeply involved in a long piece of work requiring intellectual discipline. Although the students were most interested in reorganizing school government into an Honor System, including judicial and legislative bodies, the faculty spent little time on the idea. They were caught up instead in David's suggestion, based on a similar experience he had at Shady Hill, that each student create an island country – providing some selection of its flora, fauna, geography, government, customs, costumes, art, dance, economy, horticulture, language, transportation, culture, history, philosophy, religion, currency, national quirks, or the like. During the ten days of the Island Project in mid-February 1963, most students produced illustrated papers on their countries, though there were also models, dances, a tape, a movie and a play. The refreshing break in routine was good for morale, but the faculty puzzled over assessing the educational value of the project, then let it go – along with any further discussion of implementing Tad's ideas. Frustrated by the impasse, Tad left the school at the end of the year.

During January, the student council's effort to re-make the school government generated a good deal of discussion, leading up to a school meeting on the proposed Honor System. But that meeting did not vote on the change. Although the council pursued the idea in February, the election of a new council toward the end of the month put an end to the idea. The initiative had produced one concrete change, suggested by David and approved at the school meeting, that all students serve as ODAs, rather than just council members. Isabel objected the next day in faculty meeting that such a big change should have been submitted to the faculty for approval, to emphasize its importance. But the faculty did not resist the change, which in any event soon proved impractical and was replaced by the old system. Nor was the council itself all that open to change. When Jim Edlin '65 and the other council members had been elected in November, Edlin proposed that all council meetings be open to everyone except for such business that needed to remain private (such as considering individual students for Groups and other privileges). Edlin's proposal lost by an 8-1 vote and he resigned, only to have the faculty suspend him from school a few days later for multiple offenses, especially for having defiantly sat in the church balcony during vespers. Nominally Jewish, Edlin asserted his right not to believe in any organized religion and defended his choice of seats as a constitutionally protected anti-religious protest against coerced church-going. "Mounir likens Edlin's rebellion to Gandhi, and in defiance he asked for severest penalty," Buffy wrote of the decision. Only Buffy and Lowell Naeve opposed Edlin's suspension.

For most of the year, the faculty's preoccupations were more mundane and immediate: manners, dress, cleanliness, table manners, courtesy, stealing – all continued to aggravate old and young alike. Even music became an issue of authority when the faculty, at its first September meeting, banned "that kind of music" from the student common room without clearly defining what "that kind of music" was. At the end of November, Laurie Friedman '63 wrote an open letter to the faculty in the *Occasional Worker:* "Perhaps there are those among you who feel that this issue is settled and no longer under discussion. You are very much mistaken. The student body, as a whole, has neither forgotten nor accepted the preposterous edict, which you have so dogmatically handed down as being infallible law. It is an insult to every one of us that this issue was not brought before a school meeting and then discussed among us all." She emphasized that the record player in the common room had been a student gift to the school for students as much as faculty use, adding: "I quote from one faculty member: 'Pete Seeger is alright but Leadbelly is not.' ... I have also heard it said that you are protecting those among us who find jazz and rock and roll offensive. But let us take a vote among the faculty and students and see exactly who we are protecting... You speak of inconsideration on the part of the students playing the music you so heartily dislike. Tell me, what could be more inconsiderate than imposing your taste upon us without our consent?" Her call for a general meeting to resolve the issue went unheeded. After a year of wrangling, the faculty was even farther from agreement, with Peter Sauer calling the music ban a mistake, while Isabel Stephens announced, "If I have to walk through the common room and hear that music day after day, I won't come back next year."

Another, lesser source of chronic student-faculty friction was the library in which hundreds of books still sat in uncatalogued piles on the floor a year after the library opened. Despite its poor lighting and too-expensive materials (the library was converted under the supervision of a professional architect during David's trip to Europe in the summer of 1961), the room was David's pride and joy. But it was noisy, hard to supervise and David complained that it wasn't popular enough with the students. Webbs Mellowes, who published a wicked parody of the library architect in *Symposium*, had another view of David and the school's priorities in the *Occasional Worker:* "He was building projects to improve the school, but his good teachers are leaving. His <u>main</u> concern should be the welfare of a good faculty, not of the Drama Department, the cleanliness of the front hall, the library, or the hockey team; for these trifles are replacing worthwhile individuals."

In October, on Jo Oatfield's suggestion, the faculty decided to have a "faculty table" at breakfast and dinner, even though David thought the psychology of it was bad. The student reaction was immediately negative, with the student council observing, "The faculty seem less and less present as members of our community, rather than supervisors." Larry Roberts wrote in his notes at the next faculty meeting: "talk at council that this school is getting more like public school – teacher more the enemy – also not around to talk to – resent faculty table – less communication – withdrawal." At the same meeting, Lowell Naeve suggested school meetings with freedom of discussion every couple of weeks, which was not approved.

Coloring the whole school year was David's obviously deteriorating health and his growing inability to respond as he once could to the demands of 130 or so people who looked to him as the final solver of all problems. By 1963, David's emphysema was worse, he was seeing a specialist in Boston and facing the prospect of major surgery in the summer. Though none of this was formally passed on to the faculty or students, they were all aware of its effects and made uneasy by the circumstance. At the same November faculty meeting that sent Jim Edlin home, David spoke obliquely of being "stuck with" the school and current criticism of it. According to Larry Roberts's notes of the meeting, "David would be happy to find another person to run this school. David has a letter that would make many uncomfortable if published. That the school does exist is very important to many alumni. If the school ceases or is greatly altered, many could be hurt. David, the person, is tied too closely into this picture."

In February, David met for two hours with the junior class (class of 1964), which was seen as causing much of the tension in the school. He said later he found them bewildered about the faculty's standards and afraid of change in the school. He added that he was hard on them for isolating themselves. By then, David was already looking for an assistant headmaster, a decision he discussed with the faculty in early March. A candidate visited the school a few weeks later, then decided not to take the job. David told the faculty he was relieved, content to maintain the status quo with the staff. But he kept looking.

### David Bailey, special report to the Trustees, March 1963

*The school is a going concern, a viable institution. In shape and size and basic nature, I don't see it changing much in the near future. It will and should, from time to time, change its academic emphasis according to the times or personnel. It is in a position to do larger and more exciting things in any number of fields: natural sciences, graphic and performing arts, foreign languages, etc. It is also in the position to be a project pilot in a number of ways besides the academic. In short, though it has some of the security of an established organization, it has tremendous flexibility, an asset which I hope it will maintain, though it should not, of course, be able to be blown willy-nilly by every changing educational breeze.*

*On the other hand, much of its current viability is dependant upon the impermanence of a few people whose skill and devotion have brought it to its present stage. There will be other such people in the future, but they are getting harder to find. They should be people who are excited by education itself in the broad sense, and by the values and opportunities as found here. In order to allow these people their fullest focus, they should be less burdened with personal discomforts. Of course, this means more money for better housing, for continued education for themselves and their children, more travel, etc. Similarly, the school itself is now ready for some refinements, which it has, heretofore, sacrificed in favor of certain essentials like the library, the laboratories, the theater, and other facilities. The children, and consequently, the staff, should be allowed to live here with more grace. We should not have to economize on so many small things. For example, the program of chores, which should never be abandoned no matter how much money is available, should include more constructive activities as well as the minutiae of daily living.*

*Though the concerns of the school should continue to include college preparation, that particular goal should take care of itself if the rest of the job is done right. There is something intangible here of great value. It has to do with the experience of human relationships, of tolerance, of self-knowing, of respect for and devotion to things of real worth, intellectual and social. It is almost a verity that most of the children will keep with them always.*

• • •

As his emphysema gradually, but relentlessly, limited his own capabilities, David was aware that maintaining the school's quality required the faculty and especially the Trustees to carry more of the load than they had in the past. In its earliest years, the school had a small, intimate, coherent group of Trustees, seven to ten people with at least an implicit understanding of their common purpose, guided by the direct, synthesizing outlook of Elizabeth Forest Johnson (who died in April 1963, unable to help David and the school come to terms with the emergence of their most serious crisis). Woodstock's early boards were characterized by mutual trust, communication and dedication to the shared goals of the school. This commonality of purpose helped contain David's and Ken Webb's rivalry within civilized bounds. It also motivated many of the early Trustees to spend long hours working for the school, from Elizabeth Johnson's keeping the books to John McDill's running a bulldozer to carve a soccer field out of the hillside next to Greenhithe. Most of those early Trustees joined the board because they liked the school, they felt it added something positive to the town of Woodstock, they believed in its educational purposes. They wanted to see the Country School flourish in its own terms.

By 1963, the nature of the board had changed, even though David had recruited every member himself, most of them in recent years. By then even the most devoted of the off-campus trustees rarely took part in the everyday life of the school. Some were passively uncritical. And others had serious reservations about Woodstock's basic nature, not always honestly expressed. Only Gordon Gay, Ivy Thomas (who was serving her last year) and David himself had been Trustees during the school's Greenhithe days, which ended in 1955. The board had grown to fifteen members and, starting in 1961, turned over an average of three to four members a year for the next decade (with only one, relatively minor member serving for the entire period). Despite his almost annual *pro forma* pleas to the Trustees to take a more active role in the school, David remained quite content to have Trustees who were mostly inactive, leaving him to run things as he saw fit. This was a fine and familiar way for a healthy headmaster to function. But by 1963, David was beginning to need substantial, reliable support from Trustees for the first time since the earliest years of the school. He needed their help more than most of them knew, but he wouldn't tell them why. And they didn't try hard enough to find out.

"One of the problems, I guess, was that David, being a one-man show, created a board that was pretty ineffective," recalled Roger Phillips '49, David's lifelong friend who had first served as the alumni representative to the board in 1952. An insurance executive who looked after David's life and health insurance needs, Roger also served continuously as a Trustee from 1962 to 1976. He found that his fellow board members "loved serving when [David] was making all decisions and the school was rolling along, and I'm as guilty as anyone, because I'm not really a great, innovative, take-charge person in a situation like that [when David began to need more help]. And even though you look around individually at the people on the board, and they're all talented... we didn't have anybody who was able to say, 'Wait a minute, the direction is not right.'... Nobody came in and said, 'This is what has to be done.'" And those who tried were divisive, he added. "They couldn't rally the troops."

In his special report of March 1963, David went on to write: "Now, how can the Trustees help? Of course, there is money, but the money will come only with involvement and with the faith and excitement of helping in a noble enterprise of providing 'infinite riches in a little room.' The Trustees should be so selected and so organized that they will happily and skilfully make the sacrifices necessary to keep this potentially precious microcosm lively and important. There should be more meetings both on and off campus. There should be committees at work investigating, searching, advising in areas where the 'educators' cannot or should not be primarily concerned... The work of the Trustees should alleviate rather than add to the burdens of the administration. Above all, it needs organization and an executive who will see that things get done."

Plans to implement the last point were already in the works. Gordon Gay, an executive with Pacific Mills, had considered accepting the presidency of the board in 1956, but a heart attack had prevented it. Seven years later, because of that same heart condition, he had slowed his working pace, had moved to a farm in northwestern Connecticut and had both the time and inclination to help the school that had done so well by the three daughters he had sent there. Having served on the board since 1946, the second year of the school, Gordon Gay had a strong sense of the institution's continuity and he was familiar with the current board. Gordon Gay was also familiar with some of the trustees' growing impatience with David's one-man-show style, which had contributed to at least two unfriendly resignations during the previous two years.

George Holton was elected to the Country School board in 1958. Holton was chairman of the board of Socony Mobil Corporation until 1965, when he retired at age 75 to the second home he had maintained for years in Woodstock. Asked principally to advise the school on investments, he attended four meetings before writing David a tentative letter of resignation in the spring of 1961: "I have been very much interested in the accomplishments of the school and greatly impressed by the intelligence, dedication and drive of your Trustees and faculty. However, I know so little about the operation of educational institutions and even less about current theories of education that I feel wholly inadequate to assume even the minimum responsibilities of a Trustee... Needless to say I have greatly enjoyed the connection over the past couple of years but I really wish that you would now accept my resignation and substitute in my place some one much better qualified to make worthwhile contribution to your effort. Speaking of contributions, [Trustee] Tom Debevoise's solicitations have been no factor in my arriving at the foregoing conclusions. I think the theory behind Trustee donations is sound. On the other hand, many people as they face retirement and living on a fixed income find themselves committed as far as their budget will permit to those charities and other giving which over the years have presented a special appeal. I am among that number..."

Hearing the former chair of a major oil company plead poverty, David declined to excuse his trustee gracefully from his commitments a year and a half before the end of his term: "I have been aware, of course, of your uncertainty about your value to us as a Trustee, but you need not have doubts about that because your wisdom and experience at meetings is helpful... As to the problem of Trustee donations, I think we are stuck with that. Each of us will have to give something, even if it is small, and I am sure there is not one of us who can't afford a token donation."

In reply, the former Socony Mobil honcho gave not an inch, nor a penny: "Please present my resignation at your forthcoming meeting. Please also express my regrets at severing this very pleasant association with a group of very nice and intelligent people engaged in a most worthwhile undertaking." Years later, when Woodstock students called for a boycott of some major U.S. corporations as a protest against the American invasion of Cambodia, George Holton protested this protest to one of David's successors, noting disingenuously in passing, "I am a former Trustee who resigned because of my inability to obtain, save through Mounir Sa'adah, information I considered desirable for any helpful functioning." (Holton wasn't the only wealthy Trustee to stiff the school on freely-made commitments during the 1960s, with Walter Paine and Judge Bill Billings among the others.)

A much greater loss to the board in 1962 was John McDill. First elected as a Trustee in 1953, he served on the executive committee for nine years and was David's vice president for eight years, working in every area of board activity. He sent two of his three children to Woodstock, he took the initiative to keep himself informed about campus life, and he took special interest in timber harvesting and the farm program (in which he was allied with David against sometimes considerable faculty and Trustee resistance). "You need a few people who can not only come off at the Trustees meetings, but come, stay a week or at least several days [on campus]," according to Isabel Stephens: "That's one reason John McDill was so good. He may have been around too much from David's point of view, but he was also around. Oh, yes, he really paid attention. But it is an awful job." In the fall of 1962, John McDill resigned as a Trustee just a few weeks after accepting re-election as vice president of the board and with three years still to go in his third term as trustee. Six months later, the minutes of the spring meeting report of the Trustees' resolution to send him a letter of appreciation and gratitude, while noting that David had not written him in the interim.

Eight years earlier, in the aftermath of the barn fire of 1954, John McDill had led the Trustees in the school's first major fund drive, the Tenth Anniversary Fund. He gave vigorous leadership to the campaign committee, with strong support from David and Buffy on campus, and from the Parents Association led by Mary Eaton (mother of Peter '56). Together, they carried it off with remarkable energy and enthusiasm for an institution they loved and wanted to see thrive. The Tenth Anniversary Fund went public in May 1955, with a modest little brochure announcing a goal of $65,000 needed to help the school set up at Upwey Farms. That move would cost $225,000 in all, but the school already had $160,000 in hand from fire insurance, previous gifts, reserves and the sale of other properties. Organized like most fundraising campaigns, with regional representatives, donor lists and the rest, the campaign resembled others also in its reliance on the energies and persistence of its committee members, especially the chairman. Writing to his top volunteers in July, John McDill reported, "Our general appeal for $65,000 in May brought in over $10,000 not too encouraging at first glance, but we feel that many of our prospective donors are awaiting developments before making their gifts. It almost requires a crisis such as now confronts us to bring people forward with aid. By mid-August our cash resources will be exhausted."

Not only were the school's cash resources not exhausted, but John McDill's prodding of all campaign workers helped push the total raised past $90,000 by

Parents Weekend in the fall. When the school closed the books on the campaign in February 1956, less than a year after the first public solicitation, it had brought in just over $108,000 against its initial goal of $65,000. "From the above financial statement," David Bailey wrote for the next Newsletter, "it is easy to see that there is much for which we should be grateful and proud. The school and its friends have outdone themselves. Each group has produced more than was expected of it: the one by contributing more than the minimum goal, and the other by keeping expenses below the original estimates. For amateurs, this seems like a fine performance all around, and we should all spend some time now patting each other on the back. If we pat hard enough, we may even shake more dollars from more pockets for, of course, there is a continuing need as described elsewhere in the Newsletter. However, even if we should not receive another dollar in donations, which is unthinkable, I believe a marvelous job has been done, and I want to thank everyone who has contributed so much. Particular thanks are due to John McDill, the Chairman of the Tenth Anniversary Fund," (When this appeared in print, the part about patting and pockets was omitted.)

The established relationship of Woodstock's headmaster to his board had long been the inverse of the typical relationship between boards and headmasters. Woodstock's board and headmaster were both used to having David run things. The board continued to set it up so that he *had* to run things, though perhaps the board made it easier. But if the trustees were sometimes tentative in their effort to relieve David of responsibilities that he was certainly not eager to surrender, the faculty as well, in its occasionally fractious way, was actively adding to David's burden. Whatever individuals may have known or observed about the headmaster's health, the faculty as a body, even more than the students by this time, continued to look to David as a final solver of all problems. When, at the last faculty meeting of the year, Isabel Stephens asserted, "we've been too soft the last two years," she was articulating a widely held view, especially among the older teachers who were dug in against the future. She was also expressing the shared understanding that it was up to David to fix it. Beyond the question of whether he had the energy to meet, much less hold back the rising tide of student activism in the country, there was the deeper question of his growing philosophical distance from his faculty (as the episodes of the faculty table and the new ODA system suggest). And complicating all his dealings with members of the school was David's basic nature, his obliqueness, his ability to deflect direct questions and to mask his own feelings, and his willingness to try to deny the state of his health. Among those involved with the school, perhaps only Peggy was close enough to David to raise delicate questions directly and, by her own account, she did not do so. For the rest of the Country School community in 1963, it was extremely difficult, if not impossible, to know with any certainty just how sick David was, how much help he really needed, or how tenaciously he would seek to maintain his grip on the school.

By 1963, however, Woodstock no longer enjoyed its once high level of institutional cohesion. The school suffered sometimes subtle, but increasing stress as all of its constituencies – students, faculty, trustees and even parents – came into conflict more frequently, and more openly, with each other and with their headmaster.

### Joy Sweet memo to fellow trustees, May 1, 1963

NOTES FOR THE TRUSTEES:
*These are all matters having to do with the transition of a very special institution from its pioneering to a more mature phase. The Trustees are essential to the process. They will actively support the exceptionally fine educational process at Woodstock which DWB [David] and the whole faculty have created and must continue to foster and develop. To give intelligent support the Trustees must now become an integral part of the total operation.*

*In a cursory review of the Trustee material from 1959 to the present date the following items call for further thought. They are all part of the picture DWB has raised in his memo: a picture of lack of communication and consequent lack of action. The reasons for this are on both sides but must rest primarily with the school, I believe, and the school must supply facts and demand solutions wherever appropriate.*

*In 1961 we agreed to hold sessions which would carry over at least from one day to the next, so that there might be time to assimilate information and reflect on it. We did this twice, only.*

*We have no notice as to who constitutes the Executive Committee of the Trustees. It was agreed in 1960 that all Trustees would receive minutes of the Executive Committee meetings. I think we have had none since May 29, 1961.*

*In 1959 we received a written report from the Faculty Representative on the Board. This was a great help. It is our only record of Faculty attitudes. Could this practice be renewed?*

*Who are the Development Committee?...*

*I note with concern that this year's record of giving is apparently the lowest in dollars and in number of parents represented since 1959...*

*Also in line with DWB's memo we must finally arrive at an overall, long-term plan, for the orderly development of the School including standards for salaries as requested by the Faculty in Oct. of 1959. Salaries must come first. If Parent giving has fallen off may it not be in part due to the suspicion that salaries are not going up fast enough – that in fact their contributions are only holding the line..."*

• • •

There is no record of anyone responding formally, or directly, to Joy Sweet's typed, single-spaced, two-and-a-half-page memo, which went on from raising broad issues to concern with such smaller matters as suggesting that "an Agenda for each Trustees meeting should be prepared and distributed well in advance." In his report to the board at its meeting on May 4, David responded only obliquely, writing, "Obviously, the Board has not been properly led or informed and, in consequence, they have not been as much use to the school as could have been the case. The Board should consider its own reorganization as to its personnel, its officers, its committees, its goals and its responsibilities, and the meeting this May should deal, to a large extent, with that general problem." In a small community like Woodstock's, there is something seriously amiss when problems like these become the subject of memos instead of phone calls or face-to-face conversations.

The transition to a more traditional, formal, active board of Trustees might not have been easy under the best of circumstances. It was additionally complicated by the loss of so many members who carried the institutional memory, as well as institutional affection. And it was made harder still by the accretion of new members who joined the board not because they really knew and cared about the school, but for some other motive: they felt a sense of social responsibility, or they were expressing friendship for David, or they saw the board as another networking opportunity, or they were acting out of their noblesse oblige, or who knows what. Some even seem to have seen being on the board as an opportunity to change the school to make it more "acceptable" and ordinary – which may have appeared much easier to do than the tenacious little Country School community would ever allow it to be. Having David continue as board president may well have outlived its naturalness and probably its usefulness institutionally. But who, on this dysfunctional board, could lead it to orderly effectiveness?

Joy Sweet, for example, would not seem a terribly likely board member at all. In the first place, her daughter, who spent four years at the school before graduating in the class of 1960, did not have a very wonderful time at Woodstock. Twenty-five years later Gay Sweet still held the school in a special contempt, even while acknowledging that it had been a better place for her to be than home. Gay's mother's memo, while presumably fully accurate in its particular complaints, also seems to draw its intensity from something more than the stated causes. One wonders why she did not simply pick up the phone and talk to David. If she was aware he was sick, then her memo seems callous to the point of cruelty. However, if he was not being forthright about his emphysema, then she and the rest of the board were in an impossible position, not having the crucial information that would allow them to understand and deal with real problems in their real context.

Beyond that, Joy Sweet's memo reflects a mind set that would bedevil the school for the rest of its existence. Having become used to a situation in which the board president and the headmaster were one and the same person, the one who took care of everything, the board found it difficult to take initiative, or to accept responsibility for taking initiative, or even to understand what initiative it should take (including fundraising). Always with some exceptions, the Trustees remained essentially outsiders, uninvolved in, even unaware of the real life of the school. To different degrees and in different ways, they accepted the us/them dichotomy so startlingly close to the surface when Joy Sweet wrote, "*the school* must supply facts and demand solutions," as if the school and the board were somehow separate entities rather than parts of the same one. Any board that asks the institution in its charge to "demand solutions" is a board that is not in control of its institution and it is a board that doesn't understand its own role and responsibilities.

That was a nettle of reality that the board chronically failed to grasp, and rarely made a perceptible effort to grasp. From the early sixties on, the Trustees as a body seem to have felt increasingly uncomfortable with the school's essentially independent nature, both philosophically and emotionally. This is evident not only in the later, unresolved struggle to define the school's philosophy after David had left, but in the more mundane and perhaps more telling details of erratic Trustee giving to the school (rarely even close to 100 percent in any given year). Even worse was the unreliable Trustee attendance at trustee meetings – at the May 4, 1963, meeting, the first meeting after David's urgent special report in March, five of thirteen members were absent and a sixth was late. That left the other eight to try to do something to help the school cope with its very sick headmaster who wouldn't talk about his illness directly.

FALL 1963 – SUMMER 1965

## David Bailey report to the Trustees, May 4, 1963

*This year events have so combined themselves as to confront the administration with the realization that some changes must be made in the method of operation. No longer can so much be expected to be done by so few. Age withers and custom stales. Better organization should produce more help and, therefore, greater effectiveness. The Parents' Association, the alumni, Trustees and the staff could all be more properly used. So, without having the pendulum swing too far toward organizational top-heaviness, it is time to tidy up and streamline and derive more benefits from our assets.*

*The staff, as usual, has been most helpful. Here again some of them could have been more effectively used. Certainly more of the day-to-day decisions need not be made at the top, and the Headmaster has found himself increasingly neglectful of important areas because of his daily absorption with the problems of individuals. In view of this, he has, at last, felt the need of an administrative assistant. The only good candidate he has found in his brief search was not quite suitable and will not be coming in any case, so this newly created position will remain unfilled for a while. A fuller search in subsequent months should produce the right candidate...*

*Staffing the school for the next academic year has been more complex than usual. We will probably have a surplus of people. This is caused somewhat by trying to insure ourselves for the year after, also. At least two other key teachers retire a year from now. We will be particularly rich next year in the drama, art and science departments...*

*It is still hoped that a plan can be adopted for a regular and income-producing activity in the summer. The favorite plan at the moment, and it's only in its beginning stages of thinking, is the year-round school set up either on a three term or four trimester basis. This proposal has many educational and financial advantages and probably it's better adapted to a college than a school, but if the logistical details of it are really practical, this particular school would in many ways be ideal. A faculty committee has been exploring the idea, and it would be necessary for a policy committee of the Trustees to look into it further.*

*Next year's schedule is planned so that it would be possible to install such a program within the coming year...*

*We have just had word that Curtis Hinckley, former science teacher and dorm master here, is available next year or the year after. It is recommended that the position of administrative assistant be established for either year and that appropriate salary and housing be provided."*

∙ ∙ ∙

With David's health as a constant, but *unarticulated* subtext, the meeting turned first to the question of an administrative assistant, before going on to reorganizing the board and more routine matters. The trustees "decided that if Mr. Bailey was sure that Mr. Hinckley was the man he wanted for an assistant, the sooner he was employed the better, and that the Board was cognizant of the financial involvement of such an appointment. Mrs. Sweet was emphatic that the time had come when goals should not be sacrificed because of finances, and that the two should be separated. It is the consensus of the Board that financing could be managed when goals were legitimate and clear." With no recorded dissent, the board voted to re-create the position of Assistant Headmaster, providing David with his first such assistant since Stan Deake left the school twelve years before.

Having provided David with help in the day-to-day running of the school, the trustees next approved a plan for relieving him of the duties of serving as president of the board, to go into affect at the annual meeting the following October. The previous week, a committee headed by Paul Newlon and including Gordon Gay and Joy Sweet, had met in Danbury, Connecticut, with fellow Trustee John Verdery, headmaster of the Wooster School (who was unable to attend the Woodstock board meeting because of one of his own). The committee's report, which was implemented in toto, largely reflected Verdery's experience with mainstream institutions and the tested technique they had found useful in surviving for several generations. The committee recommended that "the Board should be made into a working unit, carefully chosen for its contributions to the school, and organized in such manner as to be able to relieve the school administration of having to see that the Board is operating. Up to the present this body has not been an active group, mainly because it has not been asked to do so." The committee insisted that "the Headmaster should not be President of the Board. He should be relieved of all supervision of the board and it should be somebody else's concern to crack the whip when necessary. The Headmaster should be in a position to delegate work to the President rather than do it himself." The committee also recommended forming the usual sub-committees to carry out the board's responsibilities, including an Executive Committee comprising the committee members, as well as Walter Paine (whom the board elected vice president) and David Bailey.

The board took no action on the idea of a year-round school beyond referring it for further study by the newly formed Policy Committee.

Even though David's health had not been mentioned on the record and wouldn't be until he mentioned it himself in his report to the board in October 1963, everyone at the meeting should have been acutely aware of it, whether admitting it or not. Unable to deal directly with the main issue, the trustees found themselves coping with its effects: the implications and ramifications of a headmaster who had once done whatever needed to be done to keep the school going, but was now able to do only a fraction of what he had been able to do and would, in the future, be able to do less and less. David would never again be able to do the whole job as David himself had defined it in practice.

In particular, where the school's primary fundraiser from year to year had once been David, drawing mostly on his ties to family, friends and parents, now the school needed to figure out how to fend for itself financially in a consistent and adequate way. Money had not been a huge problem for the school for its first 18 years. With a combined strategy of living frugally, running on a balanced budget, relying on staff willing to work for less than they were worth and depending on a small but close network of donors to help in emergencies, Woodstock in 1963 was not only operating in the black, but was only five years away from paying off all its debts – all this with little help from the trustees as a group (although individual trustees had contributed greatly). But with the larger plant at Upwey, the inevitable and chronic need to pay higher salaries and the desire to live with more "grace" as David put it, all meant the school would have to learn how to raise more money. Under the circumstances that should have been clear to everyone, that meant the trustees would have to raise money – or the money wouldn't be raised. The board's untested skill, consistency and effectiveness in fundraising – not to mention its energy and enthusiasm – had become a crucial element for the school's survival.

One measure of the board's collective sense of responsibility and willingness to take responsibility for "the general management and control of the business and affairs" of the school, as provided in the by-laws, showed up at the same meeting. When the board considered current fundraising efforts, the board punted. In the May 1963 minutes, the *entire* report on fundraising by the Trustees states: "It was briefly discussed whether the Trustees should set themselves a dollar goal to achieve by contributing themselves, or by finding contributors, and whether the contributions should be solicited for a definite purpose. Members would like the school to provide names of possible donors. It was pointed out that the Trustees themselves had not even been solicited this year." The passive voice here masks the reality that the board wasn't even able to solicit itself. The trustees let it go at that, they did not then take the obvious first step and solicit themselves. Not an auspicious start for an organization supposedly moving into what Joy Sweet said would be "a more mature phase."

## VI

### Larry Roberts and Buffy Dunker, combined faculty meeting notes, May 29, 1963

*Faculty Meeting*
*Current enrollment*
*43 girls – 3 day students – OK*
*57 boys – one day student – <u>too many!!</u>*
*96 boarders is impossible*
*(suggestions for alternative housing, no decision)*
*Cut some? Who should <u>not</u> return?*
*Must break this clique [seven names, all juniors] – NIHILISTIC – the rest of the school resents this little group*
*Non-producers shouldn't be allowed to return? Also get rid of those who refuse to dress well and get haircuts?*
**Isabel Stephens**: *would like David to speak to the entire student body and tell them what next year is going to be like and they can leave now or act as told on our terms. Letter should go to all parents.*
**Mounir Sa'adah**: *we can't continue walking through corridors and not seeing things.*
**Jo Oatfield**: *It is emotionally tiring for a few teachers to keep trying to get students to do things when other faculty are ignoring or not acting.*
*Much yak.*
**Ben Holden** [math teacher and John's son]: *kids think ODA and such jobs are because of faculty laziness.*
**Jo**: *abolish student council!*
**Isabel** *especially stated in all her years of teaching, she had not*

*encountered the attitudes, the nihilism of this last spring.*
*Discussion about music, haircuts, standards.*
***Molly Plumb*** *[who was not returning]: as long as you have young faculty members who condone this, the problems will remain.*
***Peter Sauer****: long gulf between faculty and students – banning of music in fall was a mistake.*
***David****: We have to set standards even in the face of declining national standards.*
***Isabel****: time students found out courtesy is not an old fashioned word.*
*A special group, which is small, sets the tone – should we try to reach them? Most are the good students. David will meet with all juniors to give ultimatum.*

## James (Webbs) Melowes '64, *Symposium*, spring 1963

A SOCIETY OF DIRTY OLD CLOTHES AND TOTAL ILLITERACY
I can't help suspecting a slight tone of animosity in the voice of his majesty on the subject of appearance. The appearance not of himself, oddly enough, but of those within his kingdom. But this suspicion of hostility must be false, for how rare our king is. On the subject of haircuts and clothing he is not self-centered; he is genuinely concerned with the general appearance of each one of us. Unlike most selfish tyrants of today who are only worried about their own elegance – he is not. He thinks for the good of his underlings. Just the other day he said that we looked terrible and that something must be done about our filth.

Yes – shameful as we look – we must face reality and for once consider the true importance of our society. His Royal Sir is to be admired for admitting this flaw in his own people. Along with this, our King is honorable enough to tell us openly that we are illiterate. He has the strength of mind and body to take the action necessary to solve our problems. He has said that we must first learn to dig holes; and to a few of our citizens lacking in rural training, carrying logs will help. Through these rather crude beginnings we shall emerge from our – actually his – distressed citizenry. Champion of our decadent and illiterate lives, our king will bring new hope. Well read, he will lead us on – like the dumb animals we are-- to unified, content, secure living among the animal world, and teach us to follow the laws of *the jungle. Through the dignity of proper appearance and literacy – not yet achieved – we will learn to follow. Undoubtedly there will be problems; but his honor will drown out us long-haired and arrogant-tongued ignorami, and replace us with good citizens who will wear nice clothes and dig useless holes.*

*So let us not take his capricious outbursts as insults, or call them irrational: our King and his Magistrates speak for us – not against. We MUST follow the advice of our superiors, for we are only the illiterate hole diggers.*

## David Bailey report to the Trustees, October 12, 1963

*From early evidence this school year promises to be a somewhat better one than the last. For various reasons, there was a considerable slump in morale last spring, but a change for the better is noted. The student body this year does not appear to be an especially able one, but it has many strong attributes of civilization. The new students are more cheerful than is customary and perhaps this is significant. The teaching staff has been enlarged in excess of need. This was partly accidental as we tried to safeguard the school against any gaps in essential departments both for this year and the future…*

*It seems unnecessary to remind you once again that running a school is serious business, and the Trustees, being the highest authorities in the matter, should devote more time and attention to the school than they sometimes have.*

*Speaking only as a Headmaster now, I welcome being relieved of the responsibilities of President. Even more I welcome the advent of an Assistant. Mr. Hinckley started his duties September 1st, and has been a tremendous help already. His office has been arranged as the College Guidance Center. He's teaching an advanced biology course which is filling a real need, and he is bearing much of the heat and burden of each school day… this year would be unmanageable without him. It is hoped that when my full health has been restored that more time can be spent on specific educational details, many of which have been ignored in recent years.*

FALL 1963 – SUMMER 1965

• • •

The "various reasons" for the "considerable slump in morale last spring," as David put it, were both unmentioned and obvious to anyone who cared to see them: his worsening emphysema and his decreased ability to put out little fires before they got serious. In August, David had major surgery in Boston, having one lung scraped and repaired as much as possible. David had been reluctant to have the operation when it was first recommended, then changed his mind and decided to get it over with quickly. Afterwards, the surgeon told Peggy he had done all he could for David, but that he was going to have trouble again. David's other lung also needed surgical repair, but his doctors were afraid the first was too weak to carry him through another operation, despite his relatively remarkable lung capacity from vocal exercises he had done as a young singer. After he was released from the hospital, David rested for a week or so in a Boston hotel, then returned to school. "He more or less plunged back into things," Peggy recalled, and even though he started taking a day off each week for the first time, "everything was harder for him." David knew perfectly well his relative improvement was only temporary, but he rarely discussed it, even with Peggy. He went back to being headmaster, he continued to sneak cigarettes in the boys' john at Upwey, and he acted in many ways as if nothing had changed. This became the official line, as the Parents Association reported briefly in its December 1963 newsletter, in a brief item buried on page 3: "[In August] David underwent a lung operation. His slow pace last spring and this fall was because of this trouble. He assured us he's feeling fine now and is resuming his normal pace." This was false assurance.

David was not resuming his "normal pace" or anything like it. He hadn't been able to sustain his normal pace for at least two years. And even though he expressed his hope to the trustees "that *when my full health has been restored* that more time can be spent on specific educational details, many of which have been ignored in recent years," that was only an unrealistic hope. Realistically, his "full health" could not be restored, the effects of the emphysema are irreversible. The headmaster, who had once been able to pick up almost all of the loose ends of school life, was now able to manage only a fraction of all he had once done with so little apparent effort. In the future, he might, for a while, manage to do a larger fraction, but he could never again be expected to do the whole job as he himself had defined it in practice. To respond effectively to its new reality, the school community needed some reassurance that David would be well enough, if not completely well, to continue to lead the school for a while. Even sick, he remained the powerful, charismatic center of the school, the person without whom many people could not imagine Woodstock existing. With that limited reassurance, the school could at least attempt to address its most serious problem, the inevitability of David's succession. Insofar as anyone believed in the literal truth of David's "normal pace" or "full health" restored, that person was divorced from reality. There was no light at the end of that tunnel of fantasy. And the vital search for David's successor was not even on the table for discussion. Because David was in denial about his disability, everyone in the hermetic Woodstock community faced an impossible choice: either join the denial or force a confrontation with the charismatic central figure about his incapacities. David's operation gave him, the school, and the Trustees in particular, breathing space, to deal realistically and responsibly with the paused but inevitable decline of the headmaster. Consciously or not, they chose to do otherwise, reinforcing the collective, self-destructive charade.

Hiring Curt Hinckley enabled David to mask his own incapacities awhile longer. David acknowledged that "this year would be unmanageable without him." And the rest of the school seemed to take that at face value. But Curt's experience as David's assistant was difficult and frustrating, because David did not delegate significant authority. David did not always share information. David did not confer with Curt or confide in Curt, or begin to groom Curt to take over the school even though it was widely assumed that Curt was David's heir apparent (the previous spring, Jo Oatfield had objected to the trustees' creating the Assistant Headmaster title precisely because it created that expectation with a sick Headmaster). Having been a strong advocate for an assistant for David, Peggy discussed these problems with him at the time, but she had little success in persuading David to confer more with Curt. While Curt did not complain publicly about his administratively emasculated position, other faculty couldn't help but notice and wonder. But there is no record of anyone one ever formally questioning what was going on.

Curt had returned to Woodstock for three main reasons: his wife was unhappy with their situation at Colorado Academy, they both had strong, positive memories of their previous eight years at the Country School and the assistant headmaster job would give Curt his first administrative experience, in surroundings with which he was already familiar. "Of course I didn't realize how much David did not want an assistant headmaster," Curt said years later, "since letting go of any part of the reins was something that was pretty foreign to him, and the thought that anybody could take over any part of what he did was not an idea that he entertained lightly. It was a real struggle. And I had the feeling that these are the things I ought to be doing, but I knew that I really couldn't make any decisions that were of any significance – because the final decision would always be made by David – and therefore, what was I doing?"

What he ended up mostly doing was college placement, in which he had no experience, so he ended up relying heavily on Isabel Stephens (who was in her retirement year) and on David, who had been doing it right along. David also asked Curt to run the Vespers program, finding speakers for the unpopular Sunday night event. And Curt insisted on continuing to teach one science course a year (biology, zoology, or chemistry) while taking his share of ODs, advisees and other regular faculty duties. Yet for all that he continued to feel "sort of useless" and was unhappy enough in his position to start looking for something else less than two years later. In an early example of the way its institutional denial was eroding Woodstock from within, Curt never sought to clarify his situation in any direct discussion with David (any more than David did).

In the four years Curt had been away from Woodstock, studying at Harvard and teaching in Ghana and Colorado, David had changed from the headmaster Curt knew in the 1950's: "I would say there was a world of difference, he had no energy, he was a typical emphysema person, where he spent a great deal of time just wheezing... And then of course everybody knew what he was doing [still smoking covertly] – that contrast of a little boy and the master – because there is David – Peggy has just walked into the office – he's sitting there in his chair, there's Jean Zeller [the school secretary] sitting behind her desk, he has been in the process of dictating or talking to her about something, and the minute he knows that Peggy is walking in the door, the cigarette goes underneath the chair – so there is the smoke curling up around the chair... Everybody knew that he was smoking, everybody knew that he was a plain fool – but what do you do?... I don't know how he rationalized what he was doing to himself."

But Curt did not confront David with the contradictions of his self-destructive behavior, nor did Curt call David a "fool" to his face, nor, apparently, did anyone else connected with the school, except perhaps Peggy, privately. But nothing she was able to say kept David from smoking, undermining his authority with the students just when he was warning them against other drugs and expelling some for smoking marijuana.

Curt felt the school, too, had changed dramatically in the four years he had been away: "My impression was that it was a very different kind of situation, just right across the board. It was much more difficult for me. Of course I'd had such continuity before, eight years. But I had difficulty re-establishing what I remembered as the sense of we're-all-in-this-together kind of feeling with the students. I had much more of a sense of us versus them... I don't remember having much contact with the Trustees at all, [even though] I was the clerk... But as far as interacting with the Trustees as I imagine an assistant headmaster interacts with Trustees, no. That's clear."

Another science teacher, John Pierce, came to Woodstock that fall of 1963, replacing Molly Plumb. John was 49 then, just two years younger than David, and he had lived and taught in Vermont schools for many years before coming to Woodstock. A burly, quiet man with an alert presence, he was active in Rotary (like David) and the Stellafane Telescope Makers Club in Springfield. He loved teaching and, during the next seven years, his classes became legend at Woodstock, especially his natural history class that required each student to stake out a small plot of ground and observe it closely through the seasons, observing all its changes in a journal. Slow to emerge as a leader in the school, John would eventually become one of the few to carry the school's institutional memory beyond David's eventual retirement four years later.

Although the more wearing issues of the previous year did not go away, 1963-64 was a less confrontational year in the school (helped by a *modus vivendi* on the music issue). Not only were there more teachers than ever, 23, there were more who were young and sympathetic. At the first faculty meeting, Buffy noted that David "warned that kids' feelings get hurt and confidence damaged by our facetious remarks. Also be around and show that we like them." While student appearance and manners continued to rankle many teachers (Peggy refused to allow the messy ones in her classes), others like Isabel found the nagging less and less worth the effort, while younger teachers like Peter Sauer and the new drama teacher, Bill Tyson '53, announced in a faculty meeting they could no longer support the school's haircut policy. That policy was enforced, as it had been for years, by Peggy's making a weekly list of boys who had to have their hair cut. For the time being, the students were less confrontational in testing limits. At an October faculty meeting, David observed, "there aren't any delightful screwballs [among the students] – they are closed in, constipated, can't move." Another teacher reported, "our kids are accident prone, and are losing many books and papers." A third observed that "the children are monosyllabic with each other as well as us." The 29 seniors were mostly C students (only one graduated with Honors) whose college-acceptance record was weak. Few of them took very active roles in the school, positive or negative. There were so many students needing therapy (especially those from families with drinking problems and divorces) that David suggested possibly having a psychiatrist on the staff and raised the question of just what kind of school Woodstock should be (a question that came up several more times, with no clear answer by the end of the year). The student council minutes described the students' self-perception:

"we are children (most of us) of self-indulgent parents – when we come here we are looking for new heroes."

Whatever pain and numbness the students brought to the school from their own lives was intensified by the assassination of President Kennedy that November, an event that most in the community seem to have experienced in solitary despair or with just a few friends. Peter Sauer was off campus with his wife, Ruth, celebrating her birthday, when they first heard the news: "My immediate reaction was to get back to the school and the dorm and see how everything was. And I remember going by Sam Sweezy's room and he had his phonograph on playing quite loudly some rather raucous-sounding guitar blues and I stopped in and I said, 'Sam, I just feel that music is – is inappropriate.' And he burst into tears and said that for him it was appropriate, it was important to play that music at that time. And I realized that – I went upstairs and cried, too, after he said that, and I think I realized that he probably had more political understanding of what the hell was going on in the country at that point that I did."

Except for a mundane memorial service several days later, Woodstock didn't mourn as a community, nor did it attempt as a school to assess the consequences of the president's death. In a faculty discussion lamenting the students' reluctance to read 19th century novels, the faculty generally agreed (according to Buffy's notes) that in the student's world, "kinetic expression of emotion is forbidden – note apathy of mourning for Kennedy, and some wanted to dance – so they can't talk. They feel that we look down on them and don't understand them or take them seriously, so they distrust us." In the same context, David questioned whether recent authors wrote well and commented, "I'll be caught dead before I read Camus" (to which Isabel, Mounir, and Buffy all responded that he was missing an important writer).

In the spring of 1964, following several years of making unremarkable school gifts, the Woodstock students raised a small amount of money ($132) "to start a scholarship for an underprivileged student, preferably a Negro." The Civil Rights movement had never been strong at the Country School. While Woodstock had black students (and even a black teacher) from its earliest years, the school had not considered racial integration one of its fundamental goals and so rarely had more than one or two, usually exemplary black students at a time. Woodstock's essentially paternalistic attitude toward race was captured nicely in the October 1961 Trustee meeting minutes: "David had promised the students last year to secure the enrollment of an African student for the current year. That project failed, but a good American Negro candidate had applied and had to be accepted with no strings attached to his ability to pay tuition. It turned out that he required almost full scholarship."

By 1964, Woodstock students were increasingly conscious of and self-conscious about their collectively white, affluent, sheltered life-experience. They wanted to change it. But nothing was done with the 1964 school gift for a scholarship. The following October, the student meeting voted to give the money to a tutoring agency for minorities, since "last year's plan of a scholarship for a Negro student seems impractical." Nevertheless, David took the hint. When the ABC ("A Better Chance") Program was organized that same year, to offer bright minority kids a private school education, Woodstock was one of the first schools to participate. The students voted to dedicate the 1965 school gift to supporting the ABC Program.

Probably no one tried harder to dispel the perceived Woodstock malaise that year than senior Henry Howell. In his fourth year at Woodstock, he had grown increasingly disturbed by the community's apathy and negativity. When he accepted at-large election as Student Council president in February, he said he wanted to promote a policy that would "make students' lives meaningful and worthwhile at this trying and difficult stage of growth. Corollary: to increase students' enthusiasm for their studies and private hobbies." Acknowledging that he wouldn't achieve his goal in the time he had left at school, he sought to enlist the faculty in making it happen after he was gone. For his final paper in Mounir Sa'adah's P.D. (Problems of Democracy) class, he wrote about "The Change in W.C.S. Attitude from 1946 to 1964 And What Should Be Done About It" (no longer extant). His research included a questionnaire for the faculty which pointedly focused on student pessimism and faculty lack of involvement. From the faculty's responses, he wrote a 1,200-word report – "Notes To The Faculty" – which was incorporated into the official record of the May trustees meeting.

Henry Howell was not a particular faculty favorite, despite three years as an honors student. When he first took over as head of the council, the faculty was indulgent of his agenda for change. "The council still has large ideas," Larry Roberts noted in mid-February, "still pushing for more communication between faculty and students." Isabel Stephens and Jo Oatfield thought the barrier was only natural, but Mounir Sa'adah saw "something basically unwell about the situation" and David supported Henry with practical suggestions. After four months of his agitation, the faculty view was less kindly, according to Larry's notes in mid-April: "Henry Howell – dictatorial complex? Sent letters to all students to bring back rifles and bows (for the Fish and Game Club suggested by David) – questionnaire (for his P.D. paper)... officious and emotional at Council."

All this was in sharp contrast to the response of his peers. In January, before he was a member, Henry Howell applied to the student council for Group IV (the right to study anywhere on campus). The council, noting that he "studies. Funny. responsible. Would not abuse privilege," granted him the group, as did the faculty. At the end of May, after Henry's term was up, the council freely recommended him for Group V (the highest, including the right to cut classes) with an 8-0 vote and this assessment: "does what he thinks is right – not power crazy, worked thoughtfully on council, Fish and Game Club, and Ski Club, and he did it for the general good." They might have mentioned, but had the discretion not to, that Henry had been one of the organizers of a "dorm sneak" at the end of April, when about 70 students gathered at the school picnic ground at the top of Morgan Hill and partied from midnight to three a.m. The faculty rejected Henry for Group V by a 5-7 vote, while approving another student who had fewer council votes, but who had also made no discernible waves.

In his report to the trustees in early May, Henry Howell suggested that "to give the students a sense of accomplishment and self-esteem… not only must there be a far closer association between the faculty and the student council, but a greater understanding between the whole student body and the faculty. So far this year little effort has been made on anyone's part to bridge the now widening gaps of communication. We are two separate factions: one growing restless through ignorance; the other too unwilling to express themselves. I do not claim that the faculty misunderstands the students, but as a student representative, I am positive we greatly misunderstood and misinterpret the faculty."

Referring to the faculty's responses to his questionnaire, he noted: "Many of you consider the lack of enthusiasm to be a direct product of the unsteadiness and uneasiness in our age created by <u>the bomb</u>; that because of the pessimism reflected in authors, politicians, philosophers, teachers, etc., young people have nothing to believe in, nothing worthy of their commitment and wholehearted effort." He challenged this view, citing several recent school projects (a bobsled run, the ski team, student-produced plays), which had generated substantial student enthusiasm. These, he suggested, had succeeded at least in part through faculty participation, whereas most student activities were moribund or defunct: "The reasons for these failures vary, of course, but I think they are mostly the result of antiquity in the committees, few student leaders, lack of definite goals, lack of something worthwhile to grab hold of, seeming disinterest of the faculty, cynicism of the Seniors, and most important – no one who will listen, sympathize, work very hard or smile."

In his four years at Woodstock, Henry Howell had been slow to emerge as an active leader, nor was that leadership expected, even though he had always been respected by peers and adults alike (his previous school reported he was academically average in his class, but "in personal integrity and ethics he stands at the top"). For most of his time at Woodstock he had kept to himself, concentrating on his school work, playing soccer, doing his work job and generally being a reliable citizen – but always most enjoying his solitary horseback rides through the surrounding countryside. The school was good for him, it had allowed him time and space to grow and he understood this, and he understood that it was important for the school to survive and do the same for others.

Whatever Henry Howell or other individuals may have known about David's health or trustee commitment to the school or faculty unrest, or any of Woodstock's other problems in the spring of 1964, almost everyone was uneasy about the future. The students knew something was very wrong and they were afraid, afraid they were losing the school they loved, the school that had become home and family for so many of them. Again, it was Henry Howell who expressed this fear and longing, in "A General Plea" to the community in mid-May:

"We are all physically, if not mentally, exhausted, and some are ready to give up caring. I do not believe more than a couple of people will say this was a 'good' year. It has not been, and might have been so predicted several years before. But such a conclusion is only superficial. The school is in a state of flux... The faculty are somewhat confused. They are groping in the dark to find new footholds. They have argued, been depressed and exasperated. The students have lost unity, become apathetic and thought the faculty and themselves good-for-nothings. We are still two opposing factions...

"Woodstock has been imbued with a permissiveness of spirit that allows and encourages Jerry Bermans, Wendy Joneses, Zito Plans, temporarily partitioned common rooms, student-led seminars, an Independent Magazine, workshop plays, and Island Project Weeks. These people and activities have in common complete originality. They rise not out of programmed curricula, but rather from an unleashed desire to experiment... The school is going in some direction: a few say up, many say down... The path we are now following is not that of the old versatile Woodstock, but rather the way to stringent discipline and unquestioning belief in tradition. Fortunately, these ominous shackles are not yet fastened to us – the Senior class prevented such catastrophe. They might have grabbed a banner and shouted, 'Let's go!' but that would have been utterly incongruous. Instead the protest remains silent. They are perhaps a calm preceding the storm. A paradoxical harbinger which foretells transition and aspiration."

Despite his own recitation of the evidence, Henry Howell predicted that the worst was over and that Woodstock would soon regain the vitality it had when he first came there in 1960.

Although Henry Howell did not graduate with honors, David's final comment honored him all the same: "Over all a very fine year, I believe. Henry made a marvellous effort for general community benefit. If there were some errors, he learned from them, and there were plenty of successes, too. The experience in leadership was invaluable to him, and he stuck his neck out often, where he could not have in the past. I do hope he feels much was accomplished and that he was greatly appreciated, even by those who may have disagreed with his judgment. His interest in music is deep and genuine, as he is himself."

## Anonymous parody, May 1964

<u>COUNCIL NOTES</u> – Saturday Night

*The council met tonight in Uncle Tom's Cabin at 1:00 A.M. All the members were present and Kurtz was absent. He showed up sometime later which greatly altered our discussion. "The horror! The horror!"*

*We discussed all that we failed to accomplish during our so-called term. We hope that the next council will carry out some of our unfinished plans. They are the rejuvenation of Dodge City, the "joint" meetings, obscene language labs, and the dealings from the bottom of the pack of groups and privileges.*

*Soon will be time for a decision on the student gift. The council thoroughly discourages any suggestion as we would like to get the fool business over with.*

*Haphazardly, Henry Hovel, Ex-President, Nana Greene, typist*

## David Bailey report to the trustees, May 4, 1964

*The current academic year has been only so-so, certainly not our best one. The quality of work done by the students has been distinguished primarily by dullness, and even in the creative fields there has not been much of our usual exciting production. Possibly some of this has resulted from our increasing conservatism, especially in the admissions department... Despite the fact there have been some student departures during the year, the conduct record has been one of our best, once again be-speaking a docility and kind of uniform dullness... There has been undoubtedly a combination of reasons for this rather pedestrian year but I don't expect that it is more than a phase; next year things will sparkle again, I am confident.*

### David Bailey report to the Trustees, May 10, 1965

*As I try to report on the school's 20th year of operation I feel as if I'm doing so with unclean hands. The year has certainly not been a good one for us, and, because I am not sure why this has been so, I will just report on some of the facts without much attempt at interpretation. During the year, a number, large for us, of our students have departed for reasons that range from withdrawal for academic cause to dismissal for the use of alcohol or marijuana, and departure for marriage or romance. Most of the students in these categories were marginal ones and were here because of our kindness.... Also, the fact that several of the teachers were new this year made for poorer supervision and control. There was also less of my personal close watching and hand tooling than usual. I feel guilty that all these conditions were conjoined to produce such poor results. The fact that many other schools have had similar or worse problems this year is small comfort, but it does indicate that some of the problems can be assigned to the non-civilization of the time – the strange unease, distress, and general breakdown of standards that all can see in the youth of this country and all over the world.*

### David Bailey report to the Trustees, May 7, 1966

*Instead of an inadequately written and explained report on the academic year I would prefer to speak a few words about it at the meeting or at least answer questions. Briefly, it's not been a good year, and the college admissions results are a little poorer than we expected. The administration's focus has, of course, been on the [Twentieth Anniversary fundraising] Campaign and on the 4-term plan so that the ordinary attention given to the operation of the school and the welfare of its members has been minimal."*

FALL 1963 – SUMMER 1965

• • •

Woodstock opened with 96 students in the fall of 1964, fewer than planned because three dropped out just before school opened. Although this caused some budget-tightening, David told the faculty, "qualitatively this looks to be a better group than last year – it's good to be smaller." He also briefed the faculty on the medical restrictions that would further limit his activities as headmaster: under doctor's orders, he was to do no lifting, he was to go home and rest for an hour after lunch, he was to have no appointments between lunch and 3:30 p.m., he was to be in bed by 10 p.m., and he was to take Thursdays off. It was recommended that the faculty not bring small problems to his attention. His emphysema was now compounded by a related heart condition, angina, a disease marked by spasmodic attacks of intense suffocative pain, precipitated by deficient oxygenation of the heart muscles."

The school year did not "sparkle again" as David had optimistically predicted in the spring. All the same issues of recent years remained and new ones were added, as the student council sought to share the faculty's power to make rules and, failing that, seemed to disintegrate by the year's end, when the faculty expelled the council president (having deposed another one a year earlier). But the council seemed more a victim of apathy and irrelevance, as its own minutes became less and less reliable, then stopped altogether. In November, the council fretted, "there is a lack of a coherent feeling in the student body: need ways to solve it. If we felt some pride in our community spirit, the community would improve... There is not only a lack of coherence but a lack of consideration – in the dorms, etc." Increasingly, students were leading double lives: a usually acceptable if unremarkable public life (grades were overwhelmingly Bs and Cs that year), while privately and discreetly they did as they pleased. Those who were caught were sometimes (but far from always) dealt with harshly. By the end of the year, 21 students, more than a fifth of Woodstock's enrollment, had been permanently separated from the school for behavior, academic failure, or psychological reasons, and several others had been suspended at various times.

The faculty also lacked coherence, as fewer and fewer of Woodstock's rules and customs seemed settled, even within the faculty itself. Isabel and Rockwell Stephens had retired, Mounir Sa'adah had gone to the Choate School to head the history department and Woodstock had five more new, young teachers in their place that fall. Disagreements about the nature of the school grew more frequent, sometimes sharp. In October, David said at least five teachers were creating unnecessary tensions in the school, even deliberately upsetting students. He warned them all to try to keep students unaware of problems if possible, but otherwise to know the facts and tell the truth. Buffy's and Larry's faculty meeting notes reveal an increasingly indecisive faculty, split several ways, reconsidering more and more aspects of the school, but unable to reach consensus. In early December, more than a dozen students were thought to be involved with marijuana, diet pills and alcohol – for which six students were expelled. Some wanted to blame outsiders. Larry noted, "at least three doctors [in Woodstock] knew about the situation and did not inform the school – at least two parents knew." But Buffy noted, "Jo [Oatfield] wonders if it isn't our fault. David says, 'What shall we say to people who ask about the firings?' Be simple and honest, but not hysterical. Jo wants us to police ourselves, and when I laugh, she's nasty." Wendell Cameron, the athletic director and dorm head, told the same meeting (according to Buffy) that "the locker room was reeking [of alcohol] last year... [and that] he has heard about drinking but doesn't tell David because David doesn't do anything." In February, when David sat down with a cross-section of students to discuss "the general malaise," he found they complained of "monotony and dissatisfaction with courses... We don't praise and encourage enough. The faculty's own complaints depress them." Even so, this faculty felt it necessary to protect student innocence from the corruptions of Federico Fellini's *La Dolce Vita* (1960), forbidding them from seeing one of the profoundly moral films of the decade. Only in June did the faculty realize that some, and perhaps many, students knew more than the teachers suspected about their disagreements and vacillations – because "this notebook [Buffy's faculty meeting notes] has been regularly read by some male child" who, for two years, had come into the faculty room late at night to accomplish that bit of original research.

Not only was the school going through a decline on campus, where the uncertain quality of administration, faculty, and students fed each other's dissatisfaction in a familiar pattern of institutional stress across the country in the 1960s – Woodstock's off-campus support systems were also in difficulty. The trustees were still groping for effective leadership, the Alumni Association was more a name for shared sentiment than a reliable resource, and the Parents Association, once devoted and effective, had begun to atrophy. From the Barn fire in 1954 through 1962, the Parents Association provided the school with a vital and reliable source of income both directly, through contributions, and indirectly, through referrals of students. In 1954-55, with the seemingly tireless leadership of Mary Eaton, the parents not only helped make the Tenth Anniversary Fund a success, they were also working to maintain the school's revolving fund for scholarships. In 1957, with Jane Wylie (mother of Bob '57) at the head, the parents initiated the school's endowment fund, in addition to the annual giving program. For several years, these campaigns grew with the help of many parents, but especially because of the efforts of people like Jens Risom, Howard Johnson, John Morris, Donald Miller, Hugh Smallen, William Gillespie, Robert Brinker, Paul Newlon and Joy Sweet (the last two going on to serve as trustees as well). By 1964, David was having more difficulty each year finding good parental leadership, telling the faculty in January 1965 that he thought the current chairman was "literally disintegrating."

The Parents Association had come about as the result of a trustees' initiative in the fall of 1952, when the board pointed out that for seven years the school had been subsidized, in effect, by its faculty: "Our salary budget this year for eleven teachers, exclusive of office and house personnel, is $28,800. This is an average per teacher of $2,600 per year. Those of us who are in businesses and professions and who are employers know that this is less than we ourselves have to pay office personnel. We have been very lucky in this school. We have been able to attract qualified teachers with graduate degrees who are willing to teach here because they like this kind of school and because they like working with David Bailey. We do not know how long our luck will hold. We do know that we have no moral right to expect well trained people to teach our children for salaries that are less than good stenographers get."

In 1952-53, its first year of annual giving, the Parents Association surpassed the $4,000 goal the trustees set for it, then fell just short of the goal the second year. After donations dropped off sharply during the Tenth Anniversary Fund campaign, the parents' scholarship fund raised more than $7,000 in 1957-58, gradually climbing to its peak of $14,381 in 1959-60. There it hovered for two years, before going into a decline that paralleled David Bailey's health and the amount of energy he could give to guiding the parents' efforts:

    1960-61 – $14,029
    1961-62 – 14,255
    1962-63 – 11,793
    1963-64 – 7,901
    1964-65 – 6,744
    1965-66 – 5,000
    1966-67 – 4,888
    1967-68 – 3,589

And even these figures are sometimes too rosy since, for example, out of the 1964-65 total of $6,744, more than $3,000 came from just five parents.

Parents' giving almost doubled in 1968-69 and rose as high as $8,400 four years later, but never came close to its previous highs in the late fifties and early sixties, when parent involvement with Woodstock and its headmaster was at its most intense.

Like the parents, the trustees had always derived much of their direction and inspiration from David. Unlike the parents, the trustees remained responsible for the school's welfare regardless of David's ability to lead them. They had begun to take some of their responsibility seriously in 1963, as David relinquished the presidency of the board, but they were often hindered by lack of information, sometimes abetted by inadequate questioning, on a range of issues of varying significance. Most importantly, the board did not have an accurate, detailed understanding of their headmaster's health, which set the context for everything else they had to consider. Not all board members knew the extent of David's emphysema at the time, some knew nothing of his surgery till afterwards, some didn't know at all. The result was a tragically childish game of irresponsible non-communication. Some players kept secrets, but then sulked because others weren't sympathetic to what they were going through. Other players did little serious investigation on their own, but sulked because others didn't tell them the truth. Making this charade more complicated and poisonous, an unspoken rule forbade the players from openly acknowledging the community's conditions without risking ostracism.

The first serious trustee-led fundraising campaign was the three-year Capital Fund Drive (1961-64) led by Trustee Tom Debevoise, then Vermont's Attorney General and a Woodstock resident. The Capital Fund sought $50,000 to pay for the new theater, art studio and library, which were estimated to cost $51,000 but were completed for $46,000. When the trustees started planning the Capital Fund in 1960, they already had $10,000-plus in hand to pay for the theater renovations, which were to be completed that fall. The drive raised about $35,000 more (apparently no formal final accounting was ever made). The drive also revealed weaknesses in Woodstock's fundraising approach. When the campaign went public in the spring of 1961, the first and only letter of general solicitation went out over David Bailey's name, even though the chairman was a well-known public figure whose name might have helped tap new sources of income. Debevoise promised the trustees that a second letter would go out before the end of the school year. Debevoise did not produce a second letter then, or ever.

In his final report on the Capital Fund Drive in May 1964, Debevoise discussed some of these anomalies: "The only reference I can find in the minutes of Trustees' meetings to the origin of the subject fund raising drive is a very cryptic reference in those of October 8, 1960, which authorizes the Executive Committee to decide on a means of solicitation of funds for the theater-library project. This cryptic reference had been thought to signal a change from the past practice of the school, which had in effect reserved fund raising for David's selective solicitation of particular individuals. That same meeting authorized the building of a new library. Although the minutes do not mention it, I was asked to undertake Trustee leadership of the drive, and it was expressly understood that David was not to be burdened by the drive."

The campaign began as planned, Debevoise reported: "The period of the drive was to be three years and follow-up solicitations with brochures were to be used during this period to solicit new parents, alumni and past parents and friends who had not already contributed... In my letter to the Trustees asking them how many individuals they would undertake to contact personally, I stated that they would have a list of prospects by return mail. They never got such a list because I was unable to get one from the school. David evidently decided that the personal approach by him was the proper way to handle it as it had been handled in the past... No further general mailing was made, and for this reason, we must have on hand a considerable number of the brochures. The lack of follow-up is all my fault."

During that same period, Debevoise completed his term as attorney general and moved to Washington to enter a private law practice with the newly-formed firm of Debevoise, Liberman & Corben. Admittedly out of touch with life at the school (he was emphatic in 1986 *that he had never known about David's lung surgery in 1963*), Debevoise was optimistic in his conclusions: "I believe there is significance in this our first attempted, general drive [it was the second]. The Trustees, thanks to the generosity of few [sic] of them, exceed their goal [as a board] and provided almost a third of the funds raised, almost as much as was obtained from past parents and friends. The record also shows that most of the funds which were collected came in the early part of the drive, indicating that if there had been any general follow-up and continuous pressure throughout the three-year period to March of this year, considerably more might have been raised from certain categories of donors... In conclusion, I would suggest that, if we have a worthwhile goal, we have the ability if we plan thoroughly and carry through to raise substantial capital."

This summary does not address (except through Freudian slip) the sad implications of trustee giving: a few trustees contributed some $15,000, but several gave nothing. Debevoise apparently never asked for full participation. At that May 1964 meeting, absurdly but consistently with institutional denial, Trustee Paul Newlon suggested each board member write "a list or statement of his ideas for goals for the Country School" and send them to Tom Debevoise to "abstract and synthesize" them. The ten trustees present approved the idea and set a one-week deadline for their comments. Board president Gordon Gay wrote to an absent trustee inviting his "ideas of what the goals for the school should be for, say, the next ten years. This should be comprehensive enough to include such matters as Capital additions to plant and equipment, educational aims including teaching and teachers, endowment for scholarships or other purposes – in fact, anything [that] should be accomplished in the given period… [and] to indicate just how such goals could be implemented and achieved." As the trustees were well aware, this was not just an exercise in wishful thinking, but the school's first attempt at long-range planning since the Planning Committee of 1957 (see Chapter 5). More importantly, this was the board's first step in setting its priorities for the 20th Anniversary campaign, which it planned to begin in 1965.

Tom Debevoise received four letters from people on campus, not all of them trustees. Of the eleven off-campus trustees, only five, including himself, had anything to say about Woodstock's future. There was no follow up asking for more. Debevoise dutifully synthesized the nine letters he had. His synthesis would not mention that none of the letters mentioned a failing headmaster, or the school's need for a healthy one.

## Tom Debevoise report to the board May 25, 1964

*Let me say by way of introduction that nobody suggested any radical changes in the school size or plant.*

*The most mentioned goal is faculty excellence. The letters suggest, however, that this is not <u>solely</u> a matter of good salaries; indeed, faculty housing was mentioned more frequently than salaries. The totality of the physical plant is apparently considered important in attracting and keeping faculty, although this idea was not expressed explicitly.*

*From an analysis of the letters, it is also apparent that while everyone for the long term is concerned about teachers and students, the most immediate capital requirements (and they are large) are for the plant. In this regard, frequent reference is made not only to the desirability of faculty housing, but also to the overcrowding of the student dormitories. The present infirmary is not working well, the science laboratories are inadequate, there is a need for a music wing and additional provision for athletics. Not as glamorous, and perhaps for that reason not mentioned as often, is the known need for an ample water supply, and, probably even more expensive, a matter which will be imposed upon the school by state law in the near future, more adequate sewage disposal facilities. One thing not mentioned, but which I feel we should be more informed about since we do not take or accumulate depreciation, is the estimated requirement for repair, maintenance and replacement of existing facilities (piping, heating, roofing, et al) during the next ten years.*

*Concern for the future student body was expressed in terms of the desirability of ample scholarship funds. In this regard, as well as in connection with fund raising, several persons mentioned the value of improved communications between the school and the rest of the world for the purpose of recruitment from a wide range of desirable students.*

*As far as a capital drive is concerned, I would analyze the writers' desires to favor*

*(1) an endowment fund for teachers' salaries and benefits,*

*(2) an endowment fund for scholarships, and*

*(3) capital additions to faculty housing and student dormitories –*
    *with a majority placing them in that order...*

*Of perhaps equal or greater importance to the future of the school are numerous other comments in the letters concerning its managerial organization. There is considerable sentiment expressed for several types of business manager, someone to be in charge of improved communications with the outside world, the daily trades people, maintenance men, community, alumni, parents and the rest of the world. The need to assign full-time responsibility for an attractive, regular and well-written publication as well as record keeping and personal communication with alumni, parents and friends is a recurring suggestion.*

*I believe it is important that the Trustees meet to effectuate such organizational changes immediately and prior to the start of any anniversary fund raising drive. Additionally, I believe it is important for the Trustees to meet immediately to decide on such policy matters as campus housing for the faculty and to initiate such a program this summer if it is adopted.*

## Mark Hurwitt '65 interview, March 24, 1986

*I think that this was the big watershed period, 1965, this was when things really changed – when it became obvious that things had to change because something was wrong. What was wrong? I don't know...*

*David, Peggy – Isabel and Rockwell [Stephens], Jo Oatfield, Buffy – there was this old guard... and they'd really been involved in this too long to be flexible to changes and by the time my sister Jan went to the school in 1971 the whole faculty that she had was totally different from the one I had, even the young people that were teachers when I was there in '65, none of the same teachers were there... So things changed – the people changed, the rules changed. But you know, we fought a war for that... The world was changing, all that stuff like long hair and pot smoking was becoming commonplace – but in David and Buffy's minds, they were still back in the fifties, where this was considered intolerable behavior...*

*I definitely knew that they were running on some information that was no longer pertinent to the situation – that [the old guard was] out of touch with what was happening at the time. I could tell that they really had been dynamic people when the school started. I could tell that David had been something at one time, that David was great, but when I got there David was in bed. David was sick, physically, he had emphysema, doctors were telling him he shouldn't smoke... Saturday nights we'd have a dance in the common room, kids would have a dance and there'd usually not be faculty around except there'd be one person who was assigned to be on who kind of breezed in every half hour, just to take a peek, and walk away – and David would come down from his house... and sit down next to you and bum a cigarette. And here'd be the headmaster, and you'd be in a position where you wouldn't want to tell his wife that he was... bumming cigarettes off students – because it was David. When he did these kinds of things he was kind of lovable – David, face it, that man was a charmer and a manipulator, and he could pretty much get whatever he wanted out of somebody...*

*At other times of the day, David was seen in the smoking area – they had an outdoor smoking area... and David was observed out there picking up butts...*

*[When he came over at night] his mood was different, he was kind of chummy, kind of sit there next to you and be your friend, bum*

*a cigarette, and in the daytime he would not be like that – he'd be cold and sort of – actually, now that I'm thinking of him, I think I kind of liked the old boy. He was kind of a special case... David was fun to play with – even though we were antagonistic – David was fun to play with, he was a charmer.*

• • •

From the earliest planning, there was confusion about the best way to mark the school's 20th anniversary. At the May 1964 trustees meeting, David said he felt "the principal value of the anniversary was spiritual," somehow helping to restore the school's weary spirit. Others thought some sort of public celebration was the thing to do, primarily for its public relations value. Still others wanted the focus to be a fundraising campaign, which led to Tom Debevoise's effort to bring some clarity and order to the board's and the administration's thinking.

Meeting at the school in mid-June, David Bailey, Curt Hinckley, Buffy Dunker and Peter Sauer agreed the 20th Anniversary Campaign's goal should be $900,000, more than twice as much as Woodstock had raised in all its fundraising efforts since 1945. The administrators decided the 20th Anniversary Campaign should run five years, 1965 to 1970, until the 25th Anniversary Campaign began. With the slightest acknowledgment of the problems of past campaigns, they recommended a resident fundraising administrator, "preferably an alumnus who had been trained by a specialist." They assigned half the $900,000 goal to capital improvements: three small dorms (8 to 10 students), two for girls, one for boys; an infirmary, a sports building, and additional space for science, music and art activities; a fresh water supply and sewage disposal. They assigned the $450,000 balance of the 20th Anniversary Campaign goal to endowment, primarily for faculty salaries and student scholarships, but also for additional personnel, including a business manger, librarian, alumni secretary and fundraising administrator.

Later that month, the board's executive committee met in New York City with a professional fundraiser who pointed out that Woodstock's campaign would need a longer lead time than most because the school had never systematically assessed its prospects. According to the minutes of the meeting, Carl Kersting of Brown & Co. also advised that "an inventory of our resources is needed to find out a possible goal. In large campaigns professionals make studies of potential givers before they are approached. They expect to approach and really work on about four times as many people as eventually give large gifts. Experience shows that 10 donors will provide 40% of the goal, 100 more donors will provide 30% more, and the balance will come in small amounts from all the rest of the possible donors. WCS should get full information on some 400 large donors to have a chance of raising 70% of the goal... The headmaster's job is to set the goal and purposes of a campaign. The Trustees support and implement fundraising... Professional fundraising is not advisable for a list of prospects as small as WCS has."

In July, the executive committee used this advice to set a tentative Twentieth Anniversary Campaign goal at around $520,000, not $900,000 proposed by David and his staff.

Inexplicably, with so much uncertainty about priorities, with such limited fundraising success in the past, and with decidedly limited resources in the present, the executive committee voted at the same meeting to commit the school immediately to a $300,000 capital program, which had never been discussed at a trustees meeting and about which a majority of the board was uninformed. This was the Vermont Scholarship program that was to underwrite two Vermont students a year (up to a total of eight), starting in the fall of 1964. This was the brainchild of Trustee Walter Paine, the independently wealthy publisher of The Valley News, the region's daily newspaper in Lebanon N.H. Walter had moved into one of Woodstock Village's more lavish houses with his wife and eight children and stepchildren. He was then turning many local heads with his real and promised largesse. Paine pushed the trustees hard for the public relations value of the Vermont Scholarships, saying the program could well raise $200,000 – which some, no doubt, expected to come from Paine himself. Paine did not support the program, nor did it bring in contributions on its own. The program become one more drain on the budget and later competed with the 20th Anniversary Campaign for contributions. In March 1965, after Pete Seeger gave a benefit concert for the Vermont Scholarships, David told a faculty planning group the program had "no money on hand except $350." He added that by then he was beginning to wonder about Walter Paine. A year later, the Vermont Scholarships had simply disappeared without a word.

In the fall of 1964, Walter Paine had another suggestion for the Country School, to hire his friend Ron Salk to handle the school's PR, and the board promptly complied (choosing among one alternative). Salk, whose brother Jonas discovered the polio vaccine, had little success publicizing Woodstock's programs and fundraising efforts. Two years later, he was gone, with board president Gordon Gay commenting tartly, "I don't think a good job has been done."

Walter Paine himself was not around by the time his recommendations turned sour. Having joined the board in 1961 and served as its vice president since 1963, he resigned in November 1965, just a month after he had accepted a second four-year term and re-election as vice-president. What is striking in all this is not that Paine failed to fulfill his freely chosen obligations, but that the Woodstock board had been so easily charmed into making such quick, unexamined, poor decisions on his recommendation. The trustees continued to treat him with unusual deference long after he had resigned and had reneged on two-thirds of his $3,000 pledge to the 20th Anniversary Campaign. (By then Walter Paine had also acquired Greenhithe, and torn it down, and replaced it with a brightly lit paddle tennis court.)

In September 1964, the institutional disarray of the Trustees and administration also contributed to the resignation of one of the board's hardest workers, Joy Sweet. Part of her effort had been tacitly acknowledged in that June 1964 campaign goal of a $450,000 endowment for scholarships and faculty salaries, two of the school's most chronic financial needs. The issue of faculty salaries was as old as the school itself, though in the beginning it was mitigated first by those staff who had other income and, perhaps equally, by the staff's sense of shared endeavour, (the faculty of 1949 taking a voluntary pay cut to help balance the budget). That sprit had waned under the pressure of perennial sacrifice, of growing families, of the need for retirement security and of a diminished sense that the school was any more a truly cooperative effort.

With so many issues vague or out of control, Joy Sweet resigned less than a year after she had accepted election to a second four-year term. When David tried to entice her back, she responded, "I have resigned. And I have resigned largely because I no longer wish to take part in a situation in which I feel the Board does not receive the cooperation necessary for it to function effectively. If this reflects rigidity on my part, all the more reason for me not to be there."

Ignoring the cooperation issue completely, David replied with a pleasant, chatty letter, in which he commented: "Needless to say, I'm tremendously grateful, as are we all, for the many good things you did on our behalf. The salary levels would not have reached their present comparative respectable heights if you hadn't exerted the constant push and efficiency." (Without that constant push, David dispensed with written contracts the next year, much to the professed surprise of some continuing Trustees.)

The 1964-65 school year would have been difficult enough if its main problems had been the tension among and between students and faculty. But despite this continuing unraveling of the school at its center, David did not husband his resources effectively and focus his energies on revitalizing campus life. Nor did David and the board coordinate their efforts to set the school's priorities and develop an effective plan to meet them. Instead, he drew the faculty into a circular discussion of summer activities, adding a major new variable to the problem: the idea of a year-round school.

## David Bailey report to the Trustees, January 19, 1965

PROPOSAL FOR YEAR-ROUND SCHOOL

*The plan is to have four terms of ten weeks each, separated by four vacations of three weeks each. It is mandatory that the faculty members be absent one term per year, and the student attendance is optional for any number of terms. Each course, in academic terms, would be valued at 1/3 credit, so that it is theoretically possible for a child, in continuous attendance, to complete a high school program in 3 years. Every course currently given and imaginable is divisible into ten-week segments. It would also be possible to receive course credit for some work done in absentia, for example, certain types of purposeful travel or for special projects pursued off campus. Replacing absent teachers when necessary could be done by use of visiting instructors, such as retired teachers and professors.*

*As far as I know, such a year-round scheme is not yet being attempted by any ordinary boarding school. Some colleges are trying it, and I believe it is the 'wave of the future' at the secondary school level.*

## Peter Sauer report to the Trustees, January 19, 1965

*The consensus of the meeting of the faculty on January 13th was that we are in favor of the 4-term plan. Each of us has found some strength or advantage that makes it appealing. It allows flexibility in course planning and material. It will lead us to new teaching methods and changes. It allows a young teacher a term to study in the winter when far more courses in Graduate schools are available than in the summer. Besides the flexibility it provides, the 4-term plan will make the school community – for students and faculty – more exciting and dynamic, providing a turnover of interests and experiences throughout the year.*

*As enthusiastic as the Faculty may be toward this plan, we do see difficulties. Faculty families have many other ties in Woodstock than just their teaching jobs at the School; there are young children in school and working spouses. These ties would make it difficult and expensive for many to take any term but the summer off, if taking a term off would mean moving out of a house, which is considered home. It was the consensus of the meeting that married full-time faculty members would not be asked to vacate their apartments for their terms off unless they wished to do so even if the apartments were adjacent to dormitories. The discussion touched on other important disadvantages and difficulties in this plan, which are discussed in David Bailey's Proposal. Although we are most divided on the weight and importance of these difficulties, it is my impression that most of the faculty would like some of these difficulties settled before the operation of the 4-term school began.*

## Larry Roberts, interview, November 13, 1985

*I think one low point in the faculty was when they were aware that David was ill and wasn't going to get better... Another low point as far as I was concerned was when we had spent months; perhaps years, discussing the Four Term Plan, deciding to go into it, and the Trustees [took] it out of our hands. The trustees said it was such a good plan, start it now – and we had, in faculty meeting, voted that we would get a coordinator and have him on the grounds a year and line up off campus jobs and off campus positions for faculty and so forth, and then go into the Four Term Plan. And we were not allowed to do that for some reason or other. We were told to start it in October or whatever it was, that fall. And so when the coordinator was hired, he didn't know what was coming off and he had to be coordinating without any advance research time... So we had a lot of idealistic thoughts, the great possibilities, and then the nitty-gritty caught up with us.*

• • •

David had first started exploring the idea of turning Woodstock into a year-round, four-term school around 1960, discussing it informally and sporadically with the faculty during the next few years. After the failure in 1962 of the "Summer for Advanced Study" on campus, David grew more serious about a year-round school. In a January 1963 faculty meeting, he sketched out a plan with four 10-week terms and three-week vacations between terms. He suggested that no teacher should teach more than seven terms in a row and he acknowledged difficulty with faculty housing. The following month, he persuaded the faculty to approve a 1963-64 schedule with three 10-week terms separated by three-week vacations. In May 1963, David told the trustees, his "favorite plan" for producing summer income was a year-round school. A faculty committee was beginning to examine the idea, the headmaster added, and he suggested the trustees also name a committee to consider the proposal. They did not do so, nor did they act on the implied invitation in his comment that "next year's schedule is planned so that it would be possible to install such a program within the coming year."

Following David's lung operation that summer, the Year-Round School plan lay dormant for more than a year. Then in January 1965, as the trustees were beginning to focus their attention on the 20th Anniversary Campaign, David again brought up what was now called the Four Term Plan. A close reading of Peter Sauer's self-contradictory report on faculty discussion of the plan supports his memory years later that "I was against the idea... I didn't know what kind of a market there would be for the idea. And I didn't like the idea of a school in the summer, to teach at or to go to." But even a close reading of Peter's report does not reveal the extent of faculty reservations about the idea. Like Peter, the faculty as a group wanted to support David as much as it could, despite the everyday frictions of school life and so found it difficult to fight with him over an idea so long dear to his heart. Despite Peter's report of "consensus," the faculty at that January meeting saw mostly problems: coming and going of faculty and students, need for more fulltime teachers, concern about the response of current students, need for special housing for transient faculty and the need to have enough money in hand to carry the project through several years without budgetary distortions.

Although David's report took the plan's overall value for granted, he went on to discuss particulars of some presumed advantages and disadvantages. He wrote that the plan would give the school an estimated $25,000 to $30,000 more income each year, that the summer term's student labor would make the farm more efficient and profitable and that "educational advantages are not provable but probable. The greater flexibility of the year's schedule gives opportunity for all kinds of extra learning experiences." Among the additional difficulties David discussed was the need to hire a coordinator to keep teacher and student traffic flowing smoothly, to organize the proliferation of courses into orderly schedules each term and to make sure each student's accumulation of courses could meet Woodstock's diploma requirements and also add up to an adequate college preparatory record. David also acknowledged other problems: providing language and math sequences to a constantly changing student body, increased wear and tear on the plant and equipment, and "the hazards of substitution of personnel." But he remained sanguine about the whole project: "The usual birth pangs will occur, particularly in regard to the cultural lag before this system is fully accepted by patrons, colleges and other educational authorities. All these anticipated difficulties seem solvable, for I cannot think of any one of them that is by itself inhibiting." He did not consider whether all "difficulties" together might not be inhibiting, or at least cause for more caution.

David concluded by arguing, "the relationship between this plan and money raising is quite obvious. National rather than just local publicity should ensue. Appeals to foundations would be reasonable... All other sources of support could be approached because of it, since it will be, if it starts soon enough, unique and a fairly visible pilot project for the nation... In fact, I would say that in regard to the magnitude of a fund raising goal, we could not easily anticipate, without some such plan or its equivalent in excitement and novelty, a sum much larger than one-quarter of a million dollars." Given these reports that were so provocative but incomplete, and knowing that the uncertainty of David's health presented another, more serious difficulty with the plan, the trustees approved "in principle year-round operation of the school" and authorized further study of the question.

### Peter Sauer, "The Woodstock Plan," March 1965

*Before 1840, most urban schools in the United States operated on 11- or 12-month 4-term programs, while rural schools operated very short agriculturally-oriented school years. In the 75 years following 1840, the need for child labor in cities, and the concept that child labor was good for both child and economy forced urban school systems to shorten their school year. At the same time, with an increase in farm machinery and the enactment of state minimum education laws, rural schools gradually lengthened their school years. Eventually short Christmas and Easter (rural "mud season") vacations were added. By 1915 most of the nation's schools operated on a nine-month school year.*

*Renewed interest in year-round schools followed both World War I and II. Since 1960, school systems in California, Connecticut, Massachusetts, New York, Maryland and Arizona have studied or experimented with 12-month plans with varying degrees of success.*

In March 1965, in an effort led and coordinated by Peter Sauer, the faculty completed a preliminary study of the plan, now called "The Woodstock Plan." Peter also did most of the preliminary research on the Four Term Plan and wrote the 35-page summary that would serve as the basis on which the trustees would make their decision on the plan. In the "Historical Background" section, Peter discussed several public school systems that experimented with year-round schooling and found it wanting for a variety of reasons, high among them cost. Phillips Exeter Academy in Exeter, N.H., was "the only other independent school we know of that has studied the year-round school," but in 1958 Exeter had rejected the idea for educational reasons, fearing that the increased turnover would exhaust the vitality and capacity of teachers and students alike (Exeter decided against year-round operation again in 1965). This section concludes that the inherent problems of year-round schooling are public resistance to the idea, an administrative complexity that might limit rather than enhance flexibility, and the likelihood that it will lose money.

The rest of Sauer's report outlined Woodstock's Four Term Plan and assumed its success, since "it [is] essentially different from any other Four Term Plan we know of." Written during a year when Woodstock was losing a fifth of its students, the report resolved Exeter's concern over increased traffic by viewing increased turnover as an asset, a source of "variety and enrichment." The new four-term coordinator would maintain Woodstock's traditional flexibility (how was unstated). And Buffy Dunker's financial report began by apparently promising profitability, even for an under-enrolled school: "The Minimum Budget shows that the school would not lose money with as few as 55 students for a fourth term (assuming the usual 90-plus enrollment for the other three terms), unless heavy carrying charges for capital improvements are incurred." The budget projections assumed there would be one new dorm built. The academic planning projections assumed that there would be two new dorms, as the Trustees were then planning. The budget showed the fourth term as profitable; it showed also the four-term school year running a deficit of $40,000-plus. That was several thousand dollars more than the school's current, projected three-term deficit. "Naturally all figures are compromise guesses," Buffy warned. But, she added, "the large deficit indicates foundation help could well be sought, particularly for special personnel and for scholarships."

By the spring of 1965, a year after Trustee Tom Debevoise's memo on priorities, there was, if anything, less certainly than ever about what should be done first. Acknowledging this and the other stresses of the year, David told the trustees in his spring report, "I am perfectly willing to admit that I may be too old or too old-fashioned to be any longer the right person for the position [of headmaster], and it may behoove the Trustees to meet in camera to consider this whole question." By now David had been losing ground to his emphysema for at least four years. Not surprisingly, the board did not take him up on his offer.

In April 1965, the Fund for the Advancement of Education, an offshoot of the Ford Foundation, had awarded the school a $2,000 officer's grant for further study, including visits to schools with relevant programs. At the May board meeting, the trustees spent little time on the Woodstock Plan: "Mr. Bailey said that the only Trustee action needed was an expression of interest and support. He said that with these it might be desirable to announce the Plan at Commencement." The board voted "to support enthusiastically continued study of [the plan's] operation."

Peter Sauer, who knew more than anyone else about the details of the Four Term Plan, both strengths and weaknesses, suddenly resigned from the school in August 1965. He had run the ABC program at Woodstock so well that Dartmouth College hired him to run the program there. For Peter, this was a better job with a much better salary. During his four years at Woodstock, Peter had accepted so much varied responsibility that some at the school had begun to think of him as David's possible heir. Peggy was one of these. She even discussed the possibility with David, but nothing further came of the idea. As it turned out, Peter was one of the last extraordinary teachers David would hire. In addition to teaching English and science, running a dorm and frequently serving as a link between older faculty and students, Peter served two years as faculty trustee, ran admissions and did most of the administrative work on the Vermont Scholarships and the ABC Program. Peter also did most of the preliminary research on the Four Term Plan and wrote the report that would serve as the basis on which the trustees would make their decision on the plan.

During 1964-65, his last year at Woodstock, Peter was under increasing pressures. He had a young and growing family (and his second daughter was a Downs baby). He found himself in growing disagreement with David in faculty meetings on issues ranging from individual students to policy questions like the Four Term Plan. His relations with some students, mostly the older boys in his dorm, were increasingly difficult. And insulting graffiti about him appeared around the school and in *Symposium*. In late spring, a student put sugar in Peter's gas tank (for which the student, the president of the student council, was expelled). Peter felt the school was not as good as it had been, the faculty was not as good as it had been and David was not as good as he had been: "I don't think he rebounded after his operation [in 1963]. I'm trying to think about how I felt about leaving the school. I don't feel as though I was fleeing a sinking ship. I really don't."

John Pierce in science class

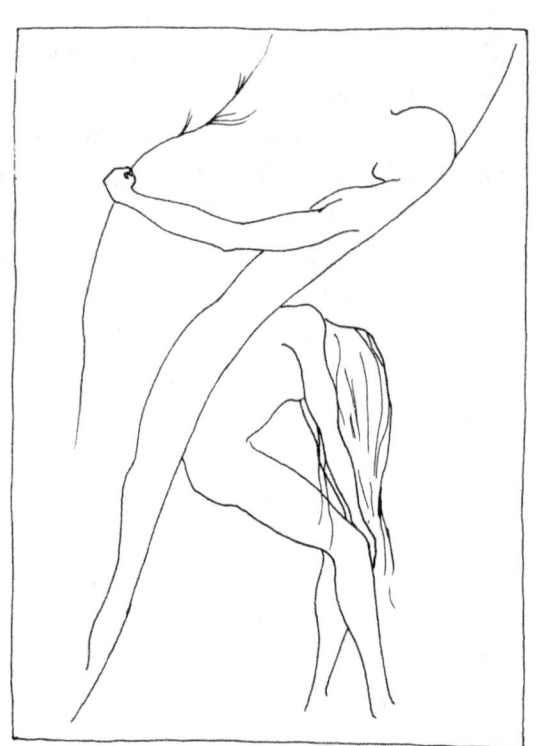

Apple Barn

Arthur Keggereis '80

Dharani (Liz) Burnham '73

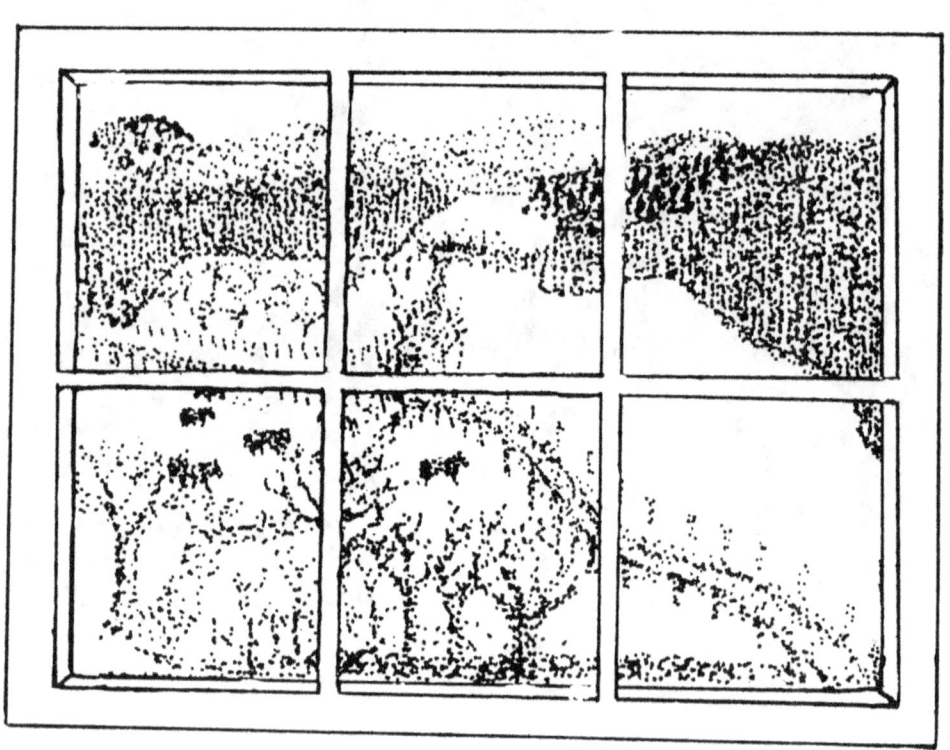

Bailey House boys dorm, apple orchard in foreground, East Hill farmhouse boys dorm to the right in the background

WCS campus – Upwey in the foreground, up the hill are Bailey House (left) and the Acorns

CHAPTER SEVEN

# Spring 1965 – Spring 1967

### Owen Coogan, professional fundraiser, report to the Trustees, May 10, 1965

*This survey by Hogan Winters and Company, Inc., was conducted at your request, to determine the attitude of the Woodstock Country School "family" toward the school and the extent of support that might be expected for its contemplated development program... Nine members of the Board of Trustees were interviewed. The total number of persons interviewed was 37, representing parents of students, parents of graduates, alumni, and former trustees. All interviews were conducted on a confidential basis to encourage frank and candid expression of views....*

## THE IMAGE OF WCS

*Both educators and laymen considered the School excellent from the academic standpoint...*

*The administration of the School in non-academic areas was generally accepted, but with some reservations as regards the disciplinary program....*

*It is interesting to note that a few persons expressed concern over the fact that the School presents a balanced budget each year, despite the fact that there is an apparent decline, in that part of its revenue which is provided on a voluntary basis. These persons felt that this did not necessarily reflect a favorable financial position, but might indicate curtailment of some desirable elements of the School program in order to accomplish this feat.*

*The Woodstock Country School is almost universally regarded as the creation of the Headmaster and its image is a reflection of his character, personality, and ideas. This was evidenced by the general and genuine concern expressed for his health and for the future of the School if he were compelled to limit his participation or to withdraw. It is safe to say that people are wondering if there could be a Woodstock Country School without Mr. Bailey....*

## LEADERSHIP

*This is the major problem facing the Woodstock Country School in terms of a capital fund program. In such campaigns, leadership usually comes from within the "family," starting with the board. It can be said that the Woodstock Country School seems to have a representative board, interested and capable, as far as guiding the School as a sound educational institution. In our opinion, however, if a campaign for capital needs is undertaken at this time, the leadership will have to come from groups outside the Board. It is not readily apparent, either, that the Board will provide a financial stimulus to the campaign through large gifts....*

## FINANCIAL SUPPORT

*While we cannot make an absolute judgment as to the reasons for the decrease in the amounts of money raised by the Woodstock Country School in its annual fund-raising programs among both alumni and parents, it is a factor which must be considered.... Concern for the Headmaster's health and for the possibility that the character of the School may change if he leaves is a problem. Serious consideration should be given to this question so that, if a capital funds program is launched, a definitive answer will be available.*

• • •

David himself had initiated the 20th Anniversary Campaign in October 1963, when he appointed lawyers Tom Debevoise and Paul Newlon as a Trustee committee of two "to investigate the organization of a special fund drive." Their work had led to the Debevoise summary of suggested changes in the school, to the $900,000 wish list and to some cold advice from a professional fundraiser in 1964 – but not to any organization. It wasn't until January 1965 that the board decided it would seek professional help, designating Gordon Gay, Paul Newlon, and John Meek as the trustee committee that brought in Owen Coogan.

In April, Paul Newlon had written forcefully to Gordon Gay, "So that nobody will be surprised when I say so bluntly at the May 10 meeting, I want to say now that in my opinion, this project is not for amateurs or occasional operators." He defended Coogan's firm's fee of $30,000 as a reasonable cost for raising $500.000, or even $300,000, a view that prevailed at the meeting. But Newlon's letter continued, "I am totally convinced that we do need a full-time director and associate director throughout the campaign, except in July and August when, as Coogan thought, we can probably manage better on a half-time basis. The School Administration cannot supply the necessary direction. It must run the School as well as help with this program. Besides, it is not expert in this kind of operation. Nor is Mr. Salk. Of course, he should be used and to the best advantage, but only under Coogan's direction. If he can provide materials or do other work, which will save some expense without reducing effectiveness and results, that should, of course, be done. So far as I am concerned, however, I would follow Coogan's advice on this, whatever it may be. It would be pretty silly to hire professional counselors and then not follow their advice."

In May the board accepted Coogan's findings without challenge and voted accordingly to hire him to set up a campaign that would publicly begin in January 1966. All the campaign-related votes were unanimous, but the minutes note, without explanation, that the votes "carried with Mr. Bailey pointing out that he had not voted on any of these three motions." A year later, when the campaign was faltering, Gerry Freund said if David continued to resist asking for money in the Woodstock area, the campaign could not reach its goal – to which David replied that he had not voted for that goal in the first place (before Gerry was involved). Trustee Paul Newlon told David he was burying his head in the sand, that Woodstock had to be a major base of support for the school if it was to prosper. Although the board was willing to hire Owen Coogan despite David's passive resistance, it was not yet ready to satisfy Coogan's request for a "definitive answer" to the question of the headmaster's health.

The school did not hire a fulltime director, associate director or even a secretary for the campaign. On the contrary. In June, Gordon Gay asked Owen Coogan to change his summer schedule for organizing the campaign as the trustees had voted, because David and Buffy would be away for most of August and would not be able to work on the campaign, which remained leaderless. Coogan had emphasized this in his report: "We are concerned over the fact that none of the interviews produced the nomination of a single person who might serve as general chairman of this campaign. As a result of our interviews, we are able to indicate to the Board only one individual with the interest and enthusiasm for the Woodstock Country School to be sought in a chairman."

Later that summer, David recruited Gerry Freund to serve as the chairman for the advanced gifts phase of the 20th Anniversary Campaign, the phase that would, theoretically, bring in the largest single gifts and 40% of the campaign's total goal. In accepting the assignment that August, Gerry wrote Owen Coogan, "I would be happy to serve as chairman of this phase of the drive within the limits of the time I can make available. To this I should add, what should really be perfectly obvious, that the time and energy that any individual devotes to this purpose would only be worthwhile if the drive is properly organized with clearly established techniques and fund drive priority goals." He went on to mention specific organizational tasks that needed doing and required David's help, including regional committees for Boston, Washington, New York, Cleveland and Woodstock. (The Woodstock committee, that Walter Paine had agreed to organize in 1965, was not formed until the summer of 1966. Paine had resigned from the campaign in November 1965.)

Bringing Gerry Freund '48 in to help made a lot of sense. In the 17 years since he had graduated from Woodstock, Gerry Freund had become one of the school's star alumni. In 1965, he was an associate director at the Rockefeller Foundation, where he started as a consultant in 1960. After Woodstock, he had gone to Haverford College, where he was Phi Beta Kappa and graduated magna cum laude in History in 1952. He went on to Oxford University as a Fulbright Scholar, earning his D.Phil. in 1955. During the next several years, he worked at St. Antony's College, Oxford, as a research fellow; at the Institute for Advanced Study in Princeton where he worked with George Kennan; at the Council on Foreign Relations; and at the Washington Center of Foreign Policy. He was an assistant professor of history at Haverford for two years. And he published two books on modern German history, as well as chapters of two other books and a variety of reviews and articles. In 1956, Gerry had married another Woodstock graduate, Jane Trask '51 (and Radcliffe '55). Of their three children, born from 1959 to 1962, two would eventually attend the Country School. In addition, Jane's sister Jacky '49 was an early organizer of the Alumni Association, a job that Jane later took over, serving as the alumni representative to the Board of Trustees from 1958 to 1961.

Wherever he went, Gerry had stayed in touch with David, one of the most influential people in his life. Gerry also stayed in touch with Roger Phillips '49, a trustee who by 1965 was a successful young insurance broker, also with a young family. The Freunds and the Phillipses had vacationed together in the school's East Hill farmhouse in the summers of 1963 and 1964. After David made his Four Term Plan proposal to the January 1965 trustees meeting, Roger shared it with Gerry. Characteristically, Gerry made inquiries on the school's behalf from his vantage at the Rockefeller Foundation. He summarized his leads in a long letter to David (cc Roger), which led to a meeting with, and the eventual $2,000 grant from, the Fund for the Advancement of Education. As an early volunteer in the 20th Anniversary Campaign, Gerry was enthusiastic about the Four Term Plan, not only because he believed it would distinguish the school, but also because he thought it would help with fundraising.

Setting a campaign goal proved difficult. Owen Coogan noted in his report in May that any amount of money would be difficult to raise without significant trustee giving – and that the trustees had "shown no enthusiastic willingness to participate in a capital program at this time – with two possible exceptions. A goal of $500,000 for the Woodstock Country School would seem to be an extremely ambitious one without significant generosity on the part of those who have the ability to set an example for others to follow... It is therefore our professional judgment that an objective of between $250,000 and $300,000 would be an attainable goal..." While the trustees voted to hire Owen Coogan for six months to set up the campaign, they did not set a goal in May (though the minutes indicate they still believed they could raise $500,000), nor did they set any goal for trustee giving. At their next meeting, in October 1965, the trustees voted to adopt Gerry Freund's statement of the campaign goals; that the school expected to raise $800,000 over the next three years, of which $300,000 should be in hand by May 1, 1966. However, in January 1966, when the campaign case statement came out, the campaign goal was $350,000 – but the list of projects included most of those in the $900,000 wish list that David, Buffy, Peter Sauer and Curt Hinckley had drawn up 18 months earlier.

Organization of the campaign turned out to be at least as daunting as defining its goals. Regional organizing was slow to non-existent, approaches to foundations and corporations were less productive than anticipated, volunteers did not always work and clerical support was unreliable. With no fulltime director of the campaign on campus, most of the follow-up effort was up to David, who was neither willing nor able to support the campaign wholeheartedly. In December, Trustee and fellow headmaster John Verdery gently suggested the importance of organizing the school's primary constituencies, especially in Boston and Woodstock, as well as nurturing its important benefactors, like Laurance Rockefeller. Nothing changed. On December 30, David wrote to Gordon Gay, thanking him for his pledge, but also mocking the school's new "Coogan-construction" pledge cards – then adding, with consummate detachment, "I get the impression that the fund drive is beginning to move though there's a lot of stumbling. Presumably some discussion and possible clarification will be held [at the board meeting] on Thursday next."

### Gerry Freund '48, appeal to T. Mellon and Sons, November 30, 1965,

*I am writing to you, not in the capacity of a foundation officer but as an interested party in a school from which both my wife and I graduated, the Woodstock Country School in South Woodstock, Vermont, which is attempting what is to my knowledge a unique educational experiment. Because of your experience in the field of private philanthropy I am turning to you for counsel regarding possible sources of assistance to the school for certain substantive educational costs during the take-off period of the experimental program.*

*The Woodstock plan has been under study for over a year. The investigation has been helped by a small officer's grant from the Fund for the Advancement of Education. In October the school's Trustees with the backing of the administration, faculty, the students and their parents, decided to put the new plan into effect beginning with the next academic year [1966-67]....*

> *Henceforth the Woodstock Country School will make full use of its human and physical resources the year-round with a full complement of students and faculty on campus in each quarter of the 12-month academic Year....*
>
> *The plan will make it possible to bring university professors to the school during sabbatical years or for the regular full scale academic program each summer quarter to give courses that cannot ordinarily be offered at secondary schools. Such university personnel will be able to combine limited teaching with on-going research and writing, using the nearby library facilities of Dartmouth College....*
>
> *Under the plan qualified students at Woodstock might accelerate the completion of college preparatory work, while other students can be guided to spend a longer period at the secondary level developing talents and gaining maturity through more prolonged participation in community projects and employment....*
>
> *This amounts, I believe, to a revised conception of secondary education. The relative success or failure of this plan could, therefore, be of significance to private schools and public school systems elsewhere.*
>
> *It is typical of the Woodstock Country School to attempt a pilot project effort which may be of significance to the nation. Throughout its 20-year history under the leadership of Headmaster David W. Bailey, one of the co-founders, the school has fostered individualism and social responsibility of young people in a country environment and has offered high standards of college preparation. A spirit of innovation and willingness to experiment is typical of the school.*

• • •

During the summer of 1965 there had been no significant further development of the plan. By September, having lost Peter Sauer, who knew more than anyone else about the details of the plan, David wanted to hold off making any decision on it. Facing a new year with eight new teachers at the school (in addition to five new teachers the year before), David openly begged the board not to plunge ahead recklessly: "The busyness of the opening weeks of school is only one reason why it is felt here that there should be a slowing down or even a slight moratorium in the making of decisions about some of the very important matters to be considered at the October Trustees' meeting. There are still enough unknowns so that hasty action would be unwise. The prospect of ownership of the Giles House is one such unknown [Mrs. Giles had died in April, leaving her large house and nearby property to the school]. The possibility of purchase of the Doscher property is another. The new dormitory designed by Ulrich Franzen is another. And the slow but continuous investigation of the 4-term year-round school is a fourth. All of these are involved in the campaign for fund raising and therefore in the Statement of the Case for this campaign, particularly with regard to Gerry Freund's role in the Advance Gifts Program, and the enrollment of regional leaders... If slowing down delays the full start of the campaign, this may make the work of Hogan and Winters, Inc., [campaign consultants] more complicated, but what other harm will ensue? There is too much iffiness, as suggested above, and the danger of poor decisions too quickly made are apparent to us here."

A month later David had changed his mind and was proposing that the trustees put the Woodstock Plan into effect "in somewhat the same form as originally proposed. The problems of curriculum, academic credits, staffing and housing seem to be pretty well provided for in our thinking, and therefore, we would not be fearful of committing ourselves to a start in the near future" – just as he had suggested more than two years earlier. David's rationale was that: "The near prospect of the Woodstock Plan is becoming more and more a major factor and attraction in the campaign for funds. Rightly or wrongly, it promises to have an allure beyond the bricks and mortar needs that would interest only the existing school family. At the January 1966 board meeting, which alumnus Gerry Freund of the Rockefeller Foundation will also attend, there will be considerable, in fact, major discussion of the place of this educational idea in the total."

The faculty had briefly discussed the Four Term Plan in September, noting "the problem of no group continuity with people coming and going," but without proposing a solution. In December, preparing a draft for a press announcement, Ron Salk observed, "the vaguest part of the plan is what is happening next fall." In January 1966, David told the faculty to "start conditioning the students." The students had played no part in developing the plan and felt no great need for it. David suggested that teachers "talk in detail at length with advisees about future plans as if we were in the Four Term Plan,... collect the questions and bring them in." Faculty discussion raised a variety of questions: what courses to teach, what content, how to section them, whether to have English every term and what should be required?" At the same meeting, David explained that he had returned $800 of the $2,000 grant from the Fund for the Advancement of Education because it hadn't been needed for further development of the plan.

Meeting for two days in January 1966, the board first postponed any decision. As the minutes put it, "Mr. Debevoise and Mr. Meek both stated they thought it was most desirable that a clear statement of the Woodstock Plan be made so that all of the Trustees would have clearly in mind the nature of the Plan." The minutes show no further elaboration or clarification of the plan and no written statement. Nevertheless, the board voted unanimously the next day to put the plan into effect at the start of the following academic year, in October 1966. The board's resolution, drafted by Tom Debevoise and alumnus Gerry Freund, said in part: "The Trustees are convinced that this Woodstock Plan will encourage the students to gain educational experience not otherwise readily available to them, that it will enrich the intellectual atmosphere at the School, and that it will permit the School to continue to serve the broader function of testing new methods with which to improve the educational process. They solicit the support of the School family and all others interested in these goals." In other words, led by a Washington lawyer and a New York foundation officer, the board members all voted to implement a plan they didn't fully understand and was nowhere clearly defined, but would surely be a good thing, they hoped.

The trustees made no provision for any further development of the plan, although they discussed their desire to time its public announcement very carefully (even though a detailed announcement had already been the page one story in the school's public newsletter the previous summer and there had been coverage in the local press the previous spring). When the "official" public announcement was made in February 1966, it generated no national publicity, or regional publicity either. Nor were foundations responsive to the school's appeal, despite numerous approaches by David Bailey and Gerry Freund.

At the January meeting, the trustees voted unanimously to start building a new girls' dorm in the spring. The board also decided to use Giles House for at least a year. And the board decided to hire a Four-Term Coordinator to run the Woodstock Plan. That would turn out to be Jim Young, who would live in the Giles mansion, the best housing WCS had to offer.

## Gerry Freund '48, letter to David Bailey, January 7, 1966

Dear David:

After yesterday's meeting of the board of Trustees, I feel exasperated and deeply concerned about future prospects.

The lesser problem is raising money for buildings and equipment, although you gave no undertaking to have the school function less chaotically in this difficult process. Far from it. Although significant funds are expended for professional help and a number of us who are at least as busy as you are work long hours to raise funds, you continue to reiterate that the school does not really need money. Although lack of organization prevented the school from raising significant funds over the years and presents a major problem now, you belittle the efforts to create some lasting semblance of organization. You point to the dribbles of voluntary contributions over the years as if they were unusual and ignore the fact that this easy charity prevents significant giving. Far from acknowledging the effort of others which extend even to writing letters and making appointments for you [which Gerry Freund had done], you imply that all the accomplishments so far are yours and attribute the mistakes that have been made entirely to others. You complain about the costs of professional help but do not give Owen Coogan the chance to earn the fee he is paid...

I am even more troubled by what now appear to be the prospects for the Woodstock Plan. I believed that this exciting venture could also serve to rejuvenate the school. But what is called the Woodstock Plan, rightly because Woodstock is the one school committed to it, is of greater importance than this one school itself. Your conception has unique secondary features; but the basic plan has been discussed by responsible educators for years. Because Woodstock is willing to try it out, you are attracting the attention and possible support of institutions concerned with mitigating or solving crucial problems of secondary education. They will not shrink from participating in an experiment which may fail more than it succeeds. Those are the risks of an experiment, but unless the plan is developed and implemented in a thoughtful and conscientious manner employing such extra and high caliber talents as are required to give it the best possible chance of succeeding, it will *fail and in the bargain the school will get a bad reputation and quite possibly even become a laughing stock.*

*Your expressed attitude and activities to date concerning the hiring of the needed coordinator make me pessimistic about the outcome of the experiment. Not the least of the school's current problems is its selection, quality, and turnover of teaching staff. If you really seriously consider a person off the highway for the coordinator job, if you fail to canvass as widely as possible to find the best possible person for this job, how can the Woodstock Plan possibly succeed?... Nothing said yesterday or that has happened previously inspires confidence that this recruiting job will be done on a level that the national importance of the Plan deserves.*

*Almost a year ago, on January 28, 1965, I gave you the names of six educators who investigated and developed year-round school plans, who clearly have data of various kinds that could be helpful in implementing the Plan in Woodstock. To the best of my knowledge there has been no discussion with any of these individuals...*

*My concern is for the school, but it is also for the school's honest service in meeting the country's educational needs. Moreover, as one who is professionally active in this general field, I have no intention of being involved with a half-baked venture that, instead of serving educational needs, risks setting back the efforts of those who are seriously concerned about them.*

• • •

If addressed to a healthy man who was being willful or obtuse, this letter might seem reasonable, though not as reasonable as an actual, face-to-face conversation. Addressed as it was, to a man slowly dying from emphysema and in denial about it, the letter is so drenched in denial that it is divorced from reality to the point of seeming almost deranged. What good could possibly come of such a letter?

Gerry Freund had agreed to become general chairman of the 20th Anniversary Campaign in December 1965, as his commitment to the advance gifts phase ended. The campaign was not meeting its goals; early gifts were well below expectations. As of the January 6 board meeting, the campaign had only $50,000 in gifts and pledges toward its $300,000 goal in May. In addition to all the organizational difficulties at the school, Owen Coogan emphasized that the drive had been hampered by a lack of "exemplary" gifts, especially from the trustees. Gerry sent copies of his January 7 letter to the Trustees committee to which he was responsible – Gordon Gay, Tom Debevoise, Roger Phillips and John Verdery – as well as a blind carbon to Owen Coogan. In his cover letter, Gerry told the trustees, "I must add to what is not explicit in the letter, that I cannot further involve myself on behalf of the school with foundations, corporations, individuals... if there is not every evidence to show that a serious effort will be made to plan and implement the year-around plan in an honest and conscientious manner seeking and employing the highest standard personnel that can be attracted to assist David with this task... In adopting the Plan the Trustees took on a responsibility for more than one school. I ask no more than that the Trustees now live up to that responsibility."

In a memo to Gordon Gay in mid-January, David responded to some of Gerry's accusations with a partially irrelevant rebuttal: "The six names referred to in Gerry's letter were all written to over a year ago, with meager replies. I also wrote Gerry at that time that I had done this. None of them was a person to be considered a coordinator anyway."

Compounding David's willfulness and unwillingness to share authority was the inability of the Trustees, collectively, to set clear, constant priorities for their school. The January 6 board meeting minutes illustrate this, as Trustee Irene Crowe, for years one of the school's most generous benefactors, said she "hopes that Mr. Bailey's time and energy will be freed to work with the students and with the development of the Woodstock Plan. Administrative problems should be tackled with this in mind." A few days later, Mrs. Crowe wrote to Gordon Gay (who passed the message on to David), "I do not exclude the possibility of increasing this amount [her campaign pledge] depending on development of basic structure within the school which will permit the Plan to succeed."

At the end of February, Owen Coogan concluded his full-time service to the school. He wrote a formal report for the trustees in mid-April. By then, the 20th Anniversary Campaign was effectively over, though it would drag on in name for another three years. The treasurer's report in April 1968 shows the campaign having brought in $191,000 in cash, in-kind gifts and pledges ($10,000). This total probably included some annual giving since, by then, there had been no formal campaign activity for more than a year. The campaign had reached $125,000 by May 1966 and $152,000 by September 1966, when its third and last report was issued. There were no corporate or foundation contributions.

"The results to date are indeed disappointing," Owen Coogan wrote in April 1965. He concluded there were ample numbers of people who supported the school's program, but "there has not been adequate solicitation of those with a definite interest in the Woodstock School...." As his last recommendation, Coogan urged that, even though the campaign had become dependent, largely by default, primarily on mail solicitations, nevertheless a mail follow-up to David Bailey's March appeal should go out no later than April 29. It went out in early September.

In retrospect years later, Gerry attributed David's unreliable effort in fundraising to his dislike of any competing power structures in the school. Gerry recalled that in the late-1940s a parent who was an experienced fundraiser offered to raise a substantial endowment for the Country School, but David turned it down for fear he might lose control. More than a decade later, when David and Gerry together approached that same parent for help raising money for the school, he turned them down flat. Ultimately, Gerry concluded, David's attitude toward fundraising compromised the school's future.

Additionally, from the first, the Four Term Plan rested on contradictory and unreconciled assumptions: that it would make money for the school and that it was an experiment that needed significant start-up funding if it was to have any chance of success. Gerry Freund took the latter view, as his letter to the Mellon fund went on to explain that the school needed $75,000 over two years: to hire a four-term coordinator, to defray the costs of guest scholars and artists, to provide appropriate housing for these guests and to bring educators, foundation officers and other visitors to the school to see the plan at work. Gerry would write such letters for more than a year, as he pushed David hard to see that the school would have enough money to give the Woodstock Plan a fair chance to succeed or fail on its merit alone.

In June 1966, Jim Young, the new four-term coordinator, met with the faculty to decide what courses would be offered in the fall, to define course sequences and pre-requisites, to establish a tuition payment schedule, to plan off-campus term requirements and settle other loose ends. He prepared a 17-item checklist of details for the faculty to complete before his return June 20 (when the faculty would be gone until September). The checklist covered the most basic parts of school life, including course offerings and descriptions, graduation requirements and athletics. In discussing what remained to be done, a teacher noted that students and parents needed this information to plan for next year. When the question of Parents Weekend came up, David just said "to hell with it."

That was the end of another grinding year at Woodstock. Although the school did not lose as many students as in 1964-65, nor have as many in therapy as in 1963-64, still the 1965-66 school year had its share of both, as well as the continuing chronic struggles over music, clothes, hair, manners, alcohol, drugs and authority.

## IV

## Larry Roberts, faculty meeting notes, April 20 and 22, 1966

*David brought Tony [Roland, the student council president, against whom students had started an impeachment petition] into Faculty meeting. David told him charges sounded quite serious in basic human ways – tried to get Tony to "sit where he sat people at dorm." Tony wouldn't sit anywhere, said he didn't make anyone sit anywhere they didn't want to...*

**David** – [you were] twice off on weekends, tried to do something clever, dishonesty of a sort, trickery area, artificial phone – all, tried to gyp airlines.

**Tony** – "I don't know a parent that doesn't gyp the airlines..."

**David** – We're getting lots of stories about your "reign of terror" or bullying in the dorm... what about head counts?

**Tony** – that happened two or three times, pretty pathetic, not harmful. I'm not the judge, just part of the mob.

**David** – Is there a purpose?

**Tony** – I don't know.

**David** – why are the kids mad at you?

**Tony** – I don't know. I guess I don't tell them very much. Don't see any end in sight. We cracked down a little bit, tried to make it look good to faculty without bothering students much...

**David** – why did you deny drinking last fall?

**Tony** – Self-protection.

**Steve [Dunning**, philosophy teacher] – What do you think of visiting OMH (Owen Moon House, a girls' dorm)?

**Tony** – I have no one to see there, so I wouldn't go. I don't see how you can get any moral obligation about it, there is very little moral [behavior] in school...

**Steve** – there's no question of communication between faculty and students, even you as council president don't try to communicate... Are we stuck with this?

**Tony** – until Roland, Chapman, Jeff Eaton, Van Kirk, etc., go. Everyone talks on a superficial level...

**David** – would it help this impasse if you were absented from school or impeached as the petition suggests, or some of both?...

**Steve** – is there no alternative to getting rid of your group?

**Tony** – *I don't think so, and there are others coming along to take our place. Coffman's a good spokesman, but an anarchist. Seniors don't know how to help. The disease is in its last stages. Don't know what the standards are. People leading the influence are the so-called negative people.*

**David** – *[there have been] at least two attempts to abolish council. Should system be changed?*

**Tony** – *a period of respite. Probably incredibly tough for faculty...*

David – *Visitors seem to sense an atmosphere that they like. How can they do this when students are reportedly completely unhappy?...*

**Larry [Roberts]** – *wondered about Council and Council President's actions and condoning of hell raising Saturday night at OMH [Owen Moon House girls dorm]?*

**Tony** – *I was pretty high Saturday myself and could do nothing.*

**David** – *OK, Tone, we'll call you if we need you further. (Roland leaves.)*

**John [Pierce]** – *I sense something stern, strong and powerful, with lots of good will toward men. How can we hold our breath and our noses at the same time long enough to graduate him?*

**David Horan** [English teacher and dorm head] – *lots of things he's done at the dorm have been appreciated...*

**David** – *If he is sent home, I must send a telegram. His father's still recovering from a heart attack. Shirley [his mother] is in England also. He would have to go to the Peckermans, where he went last weekend. What should the telegram say?*

**John [Pierce]** – *(thinks David is confused.)*

**David** – *I'm not confused; I may be 19th century.*

**John [Pierce]** – *I think the boy is a bully and a threat to the school...*

**Ron [Salk]** – *He is a danger to the population of the school.*

**Nat [Carter]**, Spanish teacher] – *He's getting worse, not better.*

**David** – *I want agreement, consensus for the records, for the future, college, FBI. Much stems from environmental influence both in N.Y. and England.*

**Curt [Hinckley]** – *He was in the girls' dorm, where and when he was not supposed to be and was in a position of trust as Council head at the time...*

[The faculty voted to send Roland home, but a special faculty meeting two days later continued to consider his case.]

*Various teachers spoke about talks with Tony since last meeting, each reported Tony denied each charge, especially the bullying.*

**Steve [Dunning]** *– lots of talk saying Mackintosh was the bully, not Tony, in regard to dorm actions, opposing petition, to impeach Tony...*

**David** *– we know he has lied on at least two occasions...*

**Chris [Magriel**, *math teacher and girls' dorm head]* *– kids think Tony gets away with murder with the faculty.*

**Bob [Smith**, *history teacher]* *– kids curious, wondering what's going to happen to Tony, not incensed the way they were when Lehman-Haupt left [expelled in January]...*

**John [Pierce]** *moved that Tony Roland be informed that he is not to return to school while it is in session and that he will be given the opportunity to satisfy his academic requirements... [and] get his diploma by mail. Passed.*

*[Because Roland had the lead in the graduation play, Shakespeare's "The Tempest," it was cancelled, but he managed to squeak through his exams and earn a diploma.]*

## Anthony C. Roland '66 letters to David Bailey, June 11 * June 17 * Aug. 10, 1966

*Dear David,*

*I wish to thank you for your help last week. It was very kind of you to allow me to take those exams when you were all so pressed and harried. I am very grateful...*

• • •

*Next year sounds very exciting and I'm jealous. It's all your work and despite some pretty dastardly impediments you'll succeed for many young people.*

*Thank you again for your help with my college dilemma...*

• • •

*Otherwise, I'm set up in London in the Fashion Photo world, making too much money for anyone my age and wondering how I can break all the ties, connections, and business prospects I have accumulated in this short time. I feel I must go to College, just as I should have gone* to High School and work out these problems. They certainly don't find themselves in this hipster-fantasy world I'm in now...

Yours, Tony

### Tom Debevoise report to the Trustees, May 25, 1964

*One interesting suggestion, which I had not heard before but which obviously has been discussed at the school, is for building one or two small dormitories to house a faculty family plus eight to ten students. The idea rather appeals to me, particularly in a building designed for this purpose. While many schools have such a living arrangement, to my knowledge it has usually come about to make use of available houses and has not resulted from a planned building of such facilities.*

### David Bailey report to the trustees, October 10, 1964

*No critical situation with the plant. Everything that we need is here and, of course, we have more and better facilities in many areas than lots of schools have.*

### Trustee meeting minutes, October 10, 1964

*Mr. Brooke Fleck [an architect on the board] reported on the results of his committee's work on planning changes and additions to the Country School and showed a drawing which was most helpful in envisioning what the School might look like in a few years. There was a discussion of new dormitories, their layout and location; of an addition to the Science building; of the rearrangement of use of present buildings; and changes in the grounds which would make a more sensible whole, taking all of these alterations into account.*

### Trustee meeting minutes, January 19, 1965

*Plans were presented by Brooke Fleck for a new girls' dormitory which would house a faculty family and eight to ten girls, building costs being estimated in the neighborhood of $17.50 per foot. Neither a specific* *date on which the construction would start nor construction types, materials, etc., had been established...*

*Roughly the following priority of projects was established as to importance in the dispersal of funds:*
- *a. Girls' dormitory with faculty quarters*
- *b. Alterations of Owen Moon House [girls' dorm]*
- *c. Boys' dormitory*
- *d. Increased space for science...*

*The motion was made authorizing the drafting of specific plans for the girls' dormitory, to be presented at the May meeting, whose construction will begin as soon as weather and finances permit in the Spring... and unanimously passed.*

### Trustee meeting minutes, May 10, 1965

*Mr. Bailey stated that the plans for a new dormitory were to be available from Mr. Ulrich Franzen [an architect whose son was at WCS] within a week or so...*

*[The board voted] that the officers and headmaster be authorized to borrow up to $75,000 to finance construction of a new dormitory.*

### Tom Debevoise memo to the Trustees, April 29, 1966

*As things now stand, the only comprehensive plan for developing the school plant to meet the future needs of the school is that presented by Mr. Fleck at the October 1964 meeting. As I remember it, there was no indication of crowding, and the separate groupings of boys' dormitories, girls' dormitories and school buildings appears appropriate and well planned for convenience, maintenance and development of the property currently owned by the school.*

### Trustee meeting minutes, October 1, 1966

*Mr. Debevoise moved that the School plan and build immediately a new girls' dormitory on the School's present property, subject to the findings of the Finance Committee and considering the obligations arising under the Woodstock Plan. This motion was seconded by Mr. Newlon, but was not passed.*

SPRING 1965 – SPRING 1967

• • •

In 1962, when the school had completed its new library in the cow barn and the drama and art lofts in Upwey, Woodstock had no further pressing need for new buildings other than dormitories. The main dorms, especially French House with 40 boys and Owen Moon House with 35 girls, were consistently overcrowded. The smaller dorms, converted farmhouses, were more manageable because of their size, but also provided very close quarters. In addition, all the dorms needed substantial repairs, particularly Owen Moon House where, for much of the winter, there was ice under the windows inside the girls' rooms. The solution, discussed sporadically for years by trustees, faculty and students, was new small dorms. Building a large dorm had not been seriously considered since 1955, when the school was still at the Greenhithe site. By 1957, Isabel Stephens was promoting small dorms, by which she and everyone else generally meant dorms for 8 to 12 students (usually 8 to 10), with one or two faculty apartments. In 1962, when overcrowding at French House seemed unusually onerous, the students petitioned the trustees for a student A-frame, a small dorm near French House for 6 to 8 older students (but without faculty). Although the students had voted to give the school gift that year to help pay for the A-frame, the trustees were not yet prepared to consider seriously the idea of students living in an unsupervised dorm. They turned it down without the possibility of further discussion.

The school had no long-term plan in 1962. The projects recommended by the Planning Committee five years earlier had either been completed or dropped, but they were not part of a comprehensive plan in any case. In 1962, the daily life of school was beginning to feel the early effects of David's emphysema as well as the increasing challenge from less compliant students. Lacking a clear plan, the school continued to make ad hoc decisions on its buildings, reacting to problems as they became too serious to ignore. For example, in 1964 the school built a fine little pre-fab house for its beloved cook, Ula Savelberg. Recently widowed, she had been living in a trailer that was no longer offering sufficient protection against Vermont winters. The school borrowed $12,000 to pay for the house, which was completed in November. The amount was not significant, but it reversed the budgetary trend of debt reduction, which could have left the school debt-free in 1967.

In the spring of 1964, the Trustees had started working on a 10-year plan for the school, as part of their planning for the 20th Anniversary Campaign. Only five off-campus trustees joined in the initial planning – Tom Debevoise, Gordon Gay, Joy Sweet, Roger Phillips and Brooke Fleck. All but the last had taken an active interest in the school for years. Brooke Fleck, an architect in nearby Lyme,

N.H., had joined the board the previous fall and quickly developed a fondness for the school. Basing his work on the priorities he had heard discussed, Fleck made a number of plans and drawings for the October 1964 board meeting, showing what the school might look like in ten years. The projected map showed a variety of new buildings, including two small girls' dorms, two small boys' dorms, four separate faculty residences, a science wing, a music building, an infirmary and an athletic building (most of which the trustees formally adopted at the same meeting as 20th Anniversary Campaign goals). In November, still acting on what he thought were shared priorities, Fleck presented drawings, floor plans, elevations and specs for a small dorm to house eight girls (each with a room 11' x 18') and a three-bedroom faculty apartment – for an estimated total cost of $76,000. At the January 1965 board meeting, Trustees Paul Newlon and Dr. Charles Foote made a motion, which passed unanimously, directing that Fleck draft construction plans for the girls' dorm and that "construction will begin as soon as weather and finances permit in the spring." Reporting on the meeting to the faculty, David said, "a couple of trustees rammed through a girls' dorm... Brooke Fleck has sort of been chosen to do the plans... Is this $75,000 building what we really want?" Two weeks later, the faculty learned that Fleck had agreed to step aside if David could persuade a more prominent designer to "volunteer" to design the new dorm, even though that "doesn't necessarily make it cheaper." Shortly thereafter, Ulrich Franzen, an accomplished Manhattan architect who had a son at Woodstock, agreed to design the school's new dorm. Harvard-trained and apprenticed under I.M. Pei, Franzen was known for creating "fortresslike" buildings in the Brutalist style. In the spring, the trustees decided to borrow $75,000 to finance the dorm, planning to pay off the loan with proceeds from the 20th Anniversary Campaign. The first problem in working with a busy, national-class architect was that he didn't make a little school in Vermont a high priority in his practice. Construction on the Franzen dorm began a year later, in May 1966, and the construction drawings were completed some time after that. Although the 20th Anniversary Campaign was already slowing down by then, it had raised more than enough to pay for a $75,000 dorm. The school did not have the money in hand to pay for a fancy architect's much more expensive building.

"We tried to talk David out of building that crazy damn dorm," contractor Ivan Shove said years later, referring to the reaction he and the supervising architect, Ralph Brieling, had when they first saw Franzen's plans for a dormitory that looked like a military stronghold. Ivan Shove had been part of the Country School since 1954 when he built the shop at Greenhithe. In South Woodstock, Ivan had supervised construction in Upwey Hall, the French House dorm, the library and many smaller projects. Ivan knew and liked the school, and his daughter graduated with the class of 1960 ("Sally did well at the Country School, and liked it – and I think it was a great thing for her"). As soon as he saw the plans for the Franzen dorm, Ivan knew it would be difficult and expensive to build. The design, a somewhat castle-like semi-circle of specially-colored cinderblock, was replete with odd angles and varied levels which made it slow and difficult to build. The cinder block construction made the building hard to heat and hard to insulate, while the "crenellated" floor outline created a much higher percentage of exterior wall exposed to Vermont winters.

"It didn't make sense," Ivan told David at the time, "but I think David felt that, because he was getting a gift of those drawings – and because it was different – that it was a great thing. But the school couldn't afford that kind of dormitory." Driving the cost up further was the delay in receiving the plans, causing construction to continue through the winter and requiring more expensive procedures to be able to keep laying cinder block during cold weather. "It was a miserable thing to build," and it took almost 16 months, Ivan said: "What they should have built was just a regular plain thing with a corridor in the middle and rooms off each side of it, which they could have had [Fleck's design]. We both [Shove and Brieling] thought they could have had twice the building for what [the Franzen dorm] cost." The Trustees later named the Franzen dorm "Bailey House."

While the school was waiting for the Franzen dorm to get under way, one of Woodstock's earliest benefactors, Evelyn Giles, died. In her will, she left the school her home, an ample Georgian town house called Four Square, to be used "for some dignified purpose," by which everyone knew she meant a house for the headmaster. Not surprisingly, David said the place was too grand for him and Peggy to live in, much to the disappointment of Gerry Freund and others. But that still left the problem of finding some other dignified use, a problem made more difficult by the house's elegance – Mrs. Giles had employed three fulltime caretakers – as well as its location, a five-minute walk down a state highway from the rest of the school. Although the trustees gratefully accepted the bequest in October 1965, for some time they found little use for it other than their own meetings in the grand, two-story living room.

At the same time that the school was inheriting Giles House, David had decided there was another property the school should acquire. As he reported to the trustees that fall, "In early summer we were informed that we could buy the adjacent property of the Photography School [owned by John Doscher]. Because it was felt here that such property could serve the school in many ways, including a possible girls' dormitory, we shifted our plans and decided that while the Doscher property was a possibility, we would change the original plans and have the first dormitory designed by Mr. Franzen sited on the opposite hillside and used for boys. Naturally this has caused many delays and we're only now ready to start on the latter facility." (In other words, although the ground breaking for the Franzen dorm was still seven months away, this unilateral announcement reversed the board's decision the previous January to build Brook Fleck's girls' dorm. The board did not challenge David's decision and Fleck resigned from the board early the next year.)

David argued that the Doscher property "would be most valuable for the school to possess. There are about 100 acres, including a half a mile contiguous with the school's southerly border. It possesses what seems to be a more than ample supply of fresh water up-hill from the school (as well as a swimming pond). There is an abandoned tennis court that could be re-activated. There is the two-story laboratory building which has some 2500 feet of floor space. Most appealing of all is the handsome Georgian mansion and its wing, containing enough rooms and baths for at least twelve girls and a faculty family... So, if the Trustees could see the way to acquire the property, perhaps on some time-payment basis, it is recommended that this be done."

At the same meeting, the trustees adopted goals for the 20th Anniversary Campaign that included two new dormitories (twelve students each), additional science space, new music space, new sources of water and additional recreational space, including tennis courts. The Doscher property contained all of these except the second dorm and the music building. The Trustees agreed to seek an option, but "due to the present fundraising campaign it was agreed that the School was in no position now to purchase the property."

The main objections to the Doscher place were that it was far away (about a mile from Upwey up a dirt road), that it needed significant repairs and that it would be bad public relations for the school to take yet more property off the local tax roll. As Tom Debevoise argued to the board in a subsequent memo on the subject, "I do not believe that the school's public relations are so good that we, as Trustees, can afford to ignore any potentially adverse effect on them, locally or away from Vermont. The school family is small.... The school shares the Woodstock area with many people of wealth, many of whom have helped the school financially and in other ways in the past, including many who have served on the board... Unless we can demonstrate that the Doscher property is needed as an integral part of our operations, the local public relations effect will undoubtedly be very bad." David continued to recommend buying the place through 1967, without success. He believed until his death that not buying the Doscher property was "the greatest financial tragedy, in fact, educational tragedy, that was suffered at the school while I was there."

By the spring of 1966, the board had made other decisions which would be much more obviously and immediately damaging to their school than deciding not to buy the Doscher property. They had decided to implement the Four Term Plan before it was fully thought out and before it had the advance funding most of them believed it needed to have a fair chance of succeeding. They had launched the 20th Anniversary Campaign without the staff support most of them believed it needed to succeed. The campaign was already falling significantly short of its goals. And they had approved building the Franzen dorm for 18 boys that was wildly inappropriate to the style of the school and the harshness of the Vermont climate. It was cramped and dark and ugly, offensive to many South Woodstock neighbors and expensive beyond all projections. The Franzen dorm cost $200,000, wiping out everything the 20th Anniversary Campaign had raised and leaving no financial cushion for the Four Term Plan.

More fundamentally, the board still had not seriously addressed the question of who would follow David as headmaster, or when, or how to make the transition, even though it was clear David was having increasing difficulty running the school. Instead of planning as orderly a transition as possible, the board was allowing David to make institutionally destructive decisions unchallenged. Curt Hinckley had long since ceased to be anyone's heir apparent and left the school in June 1966. His successor as assistant headmaster was Jim Young, the new four-term coordinator. Few people, if any, thought he was a good fit for the school, certainly not appropriate to be David's successor. Among board members, there were even sharp disagreements about just what Jim Young's duties should be.

### Curt Hinckley interview, March 19, 1986

*I became aware of how much information, was not available to me... What's the purpose of asking somebody to do a job and then only giving them part of the information that they need to do the job? Is that a matter of control?... It functions as control...*

*As far as getting any kind of training, either from some outside agency or some agency coming in to talk to faculty about any issues – suicide, drugs... The withholding of information played such a critical role – one would hear, for example, that so and so was in the infirmary or [the hospital], and the details were never forthcoming. One would never be filled in with what led up to that. [And] there was never, to my knowledge, any protocol discussed or established about any of those situations... and no attempt, as I say, to grapple with the problem head on...*

*I suspect that a lot of other people were feeling the same kind of frustration that I was – of David's lack of leadership and direction at that time – that he couldn't do it, but he couldn't get other people to do it either.*

## Gerry Freund '48, letter to fellow Trustees, January 8, 1966

*... I cannot further involve myself on behalf of the school with foundations, corporations, individuals such as [education specialists] Keppel, Howe, Conant, if there is not every evidence to show that a serious effort will be made to plan and implement the year-around plan in an honest and conscientious manner seeking and employing the highest standard personnel that can be attracted to assist David with this task.*

*... Can you as Trustees afford to have the school become "visible," so to speak, with personnel hired exclusively from among those who happen to walk in from the highway?*

*In adopting the Plan the Trustees took on a responsibility for more than one school. I ask no more than that the Trustees now live up to that responsibility.*

## Tom Debevoise memo to the Trustees, April 29. 1966

*In the last year [1965-66] we have all learned much about the school's strengths and weaknesses. Relating what I have learned back and rereading all of the material I have accumulated in the last six years as a school trustee, I find one thing above all else which I believe has been detrimental to the school administration during that period...*

*Like many other people, our headmaster is unable to delegate administrative responsibility and to accept administrative recommendations and plans proposed by others.*

*The list is growing of both Trustees and faculty who have left the school for the very reason that, after being asked to do a job, they found they were prevented from effectively accomplishing it, agreed upon courses of action were changed unilaterally after having been initiated, their recommendations were rejected and their decisions were reversed without explanation.*

*I have never talked to Curt [Hinckley] about his experiences at*

*Woodstock and do not know his personal reasons for leaving. In February, when David told me that Curt might leave, however, I responded that I thought it was the best thing Curt could do for himself, since it seemed clear to me that David was not permitting him to do the job for which he had been hired. At the January Trustees' meeting, I stated that I, for one, did not want the [four term] administrator who was hired to be another Curt Hinckley in the sense of someone hired to do a job but not permitted to do it. It was at that time that we made the selection of the administrator subject to Trustee approval...*

*In February, I also suggested to David that, if he were planning to try to keep control of every decision, to keep every decision flexible, and to control all outside contacts that will be required in developing The Woodstock Plan, as he has in connection with everything else in the past, I thought it would be better for him to accept an emeritus position to teach and work with the students at the school, or to retire. Many administrative decisions will have to be made without time for lengthy consideration. Many other matters will have to be followed up promptly. Decisions, once made, will have to be permitted to stick. Unless there are some radical changes in the way things have been run at the school in the past, I see no alternative to some change in David's relation to the school administration, if The Woodstock Plan is to have a fair chance of success.*

*These remarks are not intended to downgrade what David has accomplished administratively – they cannot. Everyone in administrative positions has certain weaknesses as well as strengths. The administrative abilities and strengths that are required to build a school up from nothing and carry it through its first twenty years are surely great. They are not, however, necessarily the same administrative abilities and strengths that are required as a school reaches maturity, young teachers replace the original faculty and plans must be made to turn an experimental into a perpetual institution.*

## Topher Delaney '66 interview, March 15, 1985

*Woodstock was a terrible school... It was a real easy school to get into, and I wanted out of where I was going, so I just applied there. I was going to Colorado Rocky Mountain School [CRMS]... I graduated from Woodstock in 1966 [with honors]. I had some very traumatic experiences at home... and I was not in boarding school out of my own will...*

> *I was used to John [Holden at CRMS] – John was a straight shooter... I always thought David [Bailey] had a lot of agendas going on – and what the agendas were, it's never been clear to me – but I thought the school represented the confusion of agendas. Because it was not a cohesive school... He pitted kids against each other, and I didn't like being in that position... There were a lot of troubled kids when I was there, lots and lots of problems going on – really disturbed families, kids badly treated, parents not there, parents remiss, difficult... There were kids who'd been in trouble all their lives... They were generally bright kids, [who] would have done better with more care. At that time David was old. He wasn't young and there was just too much work... I mean he was a tired guy... [David was 54 years old.]*
>
> *I just felt that I was in the middle of a breakdown. I saw the school breaking apart. I didn't know why it was breaking apart. I didn't know what was going on with the school, it seemed to have had better days...*
>
> *I was on a path, and I was going somewhere – a lot of kids weren't going anywhere... they weren't going to college, they hadn't thought about it – I don't know what they were doing. I had to study hard and I had to get good grades... Most of the kids did not feel good about themselves... That's what it was about David – he didn't make me feel good about myself. In talking to him, I mean... I was feeling straight and good, and I felt that really, in his heart, he liked the people who were getting in trouble and all this stuff but, because he was headmaster, [he] really couldn't say that was okay, but he really thought that troublemaking was a neat thing to do – and I think in some way he encouraged that... I think he loved the wildness... I mean they were always taking in these little lost rats [in mid-year]... rejects from other schools".*

● ● ●

During 1965-66, Woodstock took in more than its usual number of mid-year students, perhaps ten in all, including a boy who followed Topher Delaney from Colorado in November. In December, when the faculty considered the sixth late admission of the fall term, a sophomore already in therapy, Buffy and others objected... Buffy had not changed her mind about Woodstock's traditional willingness to take a chance on young people in trouble (after all, Roger Phillips and Gerry Freund, for example, both felt Woodstock had saved their lives). But with all the pressures from trying to raise money, organize the Four Term Plan and re-build the campus, all the while with David's health deteriorating, Buffy felt the school was at it limits: "we've tried too much rescuing this fall already."

In his memo to the trustees in April 1966, Tom Debevoise was responding to the same institutional problems, including his perception of Buffy's declining influence. He had viewed Buffy as very practical and businesslike, despite her protectiveness of David: "I think we all had confidence in Buffy keeping him in line... I think she had more influence than the board of Trustees had in those days." Tom's confidence wasn't shaken so much by reports of problems with students and teachers on campus, as by David's own actions. One reason for the bluntness of Tom's memo was his view that David had sabotaged a local fundraising event in April, as well as all efforts to organize any fundraising in Woodstock. "In no fund drives would David cooperate at all," Tom said years later, recalling as well his own frustrations trying to lead the Capital Campaign for the library and theatre.

By April 1966, Tom was also aware that David had ignored the vote of the trustees to build a small girls' dorm and had gone ahead with the boys' dorm designed by Ulrich Franzen: "That was without consultation with the Trustees." Further, there was his strong displeasure over David's treatment of Curt Hinckley, as well as his stronger fear that David would treat Curt's successor no better and, thereby, undermine the future of the Four Term Plan: "I was right – they should have had the administrator that we'd promised." But because Tom had planned to attend the April 30 fundraising dinner in Woodstock, he had made unalterable plans for the following weekend. With Tom absent from the trustees meeting and unable to push his arguments personally, the board let most of them go unaddressed. The minutes of the meeting reported simply on the issues raised in "Mr. Debevoise's Report: Mr. Debevoise had circulated his reports on delinquent accounts, on the tax situation on the Doscher and Giles properties and on the 4-term Year, and Mr. Gay asked that they be made a part of the record." There is no record of any discussion, no record of any action. At least some of the trustees were keenly aware that they faced problems they were not even beginning to resolve. Four months earlier, in January 1966, Gerry Freund wrote to Trustee John Verdery: "from my private conversations with David I have gathered that he is [as] frightened of hiring a first rate person for this job just as he is of getting high-standard teachers. Gordon [Gay] and Tom [Debevoise] wrangled with David and insisted that the Trustees should have a voice in selecting the coordinator, but past experience leads me to fear that David will go off on his own hook and face the board with an accomplished fact." Neither Gerry, nor Tom, nor anyone else proposed taking any action to head off what damage they believed the headmaster would continue to do to the school.

The particular concern, which triggered Tom's April memo, was a letter from board president Gordon Gay, reporting, "We have hired Jim [Young, the new four-term coordinator] on an annual basis – like David's – at $11,000. He will be about the busiest man on the place, with all the duties of coordination for the Four Term Plan plus many of Curt's (who will not return since he is going back to [Africa], as well as teaching math and some dorm duties." Tom's response was direct: "To me the loading of Jim Young with any regular duties other than those of the administrator will completely destroy his ability to give his best to the job for which he has been hired." He cited the school's public and private representations that the coordinator job would be a fulltime one, with which dorm and teaching duties will be in direct conflict. Typically, the issue was settled if not resolved outside the board meeting, as Gordon Gay stated in his president's report to the board in May: "David and I, and Jim, himself, are positively convinced that his success as a coordinator will be dependent to a large measure upon his success as a teacher. In a school of our size, we need some Indians along with the Chiefs and I doubt if anyone of us wants to get into detailed organization of workloads so long as the definition of Jim's job is clearly defined. That has been done with an express stipulation by me when he was hired, that although he is to report to the Headmaster on all matters, if he is unable to produce results for which he was hired for any reason, he is to call for a meeting with David and me or your executive committee." This implicit, but unintended, division of authority and loyalty was further reinforced by the compromise that allowed Jim Young not to run a dorm, but to live in the headmaster-intended Giles House. As a symbol, this choice was an excellent geographical expression of Jim Young's emotional and intellectual separation from the Country School in almost every way that mattered most.

The situation was loaded: the four-term coordinator was expected to create a new program that would affect every aspect of the school, but to do so without changing the school's basic nature and without challenging the authority of the school's aging headmaster. To succeed in such a difficult task, anyone would need great empathy and maturity. Jim Young had neither. Chosen by David, approved by the board, Jim Young was quite unprepared, by training or temperament, to cope with the Woodstock Country School as it was in 1966, or as it had been for the previous 21 years. A thirty-year-old Dartmouth College graduate, he was blond, athletic, naive and thoroughly conventional. Despite his ample energy, intelligence, and eagerness, he was too overloaded with teaching and counseling to be able to put what he felt was adequate time into scheduling, curriculum planning, developing off-campus opportunities and recruiting visiting teachers. All his own teaching experience had been at day schools, in Bloomfield Hills and

Cleveland, where he also coached soccer, wrestling and baseball. He had nothing in his background to prepare him for dealing with the Byzantine complexities of someone like David and his relationships to students, teachers or trustees.

In early 1966, the Trustees began to consider what they would provide for David's retirement, which they still considered a distant prospect. Tom Debevoise had suggested an early retirement for the headmaster, with little support from the rest of the board at its January 1966 meeting. After that meeting, Roger Phillips had discussed the question with the Baileys, to determine their needs and assets. In May, the board formed a Bailey Retirement Fund committee comprising Roger Phillips, John Verdery, headmaster at the Wooster School, and Stephen Delano, David's Harvard roommate. In October, Roger reported to the board that David had a small annuity income and about $40,000 in securities. The board resolved to work on this until the Baileys were assured of a livable retirement income. David had also found a modest house he liked, about 20 miles away in Wilder, for sale at $30,000. After almost two hours of sometimes strong disagreement over who should ultimately own the house, the school or the Baileys, the board voted to make "an immediate contribution of $3,000 towards the purchase of the property," allowing David to make the down payment. The board also conditionally voted to have the school guarantee the mortgage, though this was "the School's intention but not obligation." Still there was no urgency to this planning, no date had been set for the Baileys to step down and one trustee even spoke of David's staying at the school for another decade.

The Baileys' retirement package was approved by the board largely through the effort of the three trustees who were alumni. They were Roger and two others elected earlier that day, Gerry Freund '48 and, representing the Alumni Association, Barbara Sproul '62. Barbara was then 21, just graduated from Sarah Lawrence College and enrolled in graduate school at Columbia where she would earn her Ph.D. in religion in 1972. A cousin of the family that built Sproul Plaza at the University of California, Berkeley, Barbara loved Woodstock, where she had been one of David's favorites. Barbara, Roger and Gerry comprised the "David faction" on the board, not so much in the sense that others were against David, but in that they could not match the young alumni's devotion to their headmaster. Insofar as there was another faction, Tom Debevoise and Paul Newlon were among those who, when forced to choose, tended to be more concerned with the institution than any single individual in it. These were loose and shifting groups of individuals, not voting blocks, but the philosophical differences they implied were real enough. While these were clear divisions in the board in the fall of 1966, the distance between members was not yet great and Gordon Gay worked hard to bring the board along as a group on as many issues as possible. Even at that October 1966 board meeting ten days before the start of school – and the start of the first term of the Four Term Plan – the board split down the middle on whether to build the new girls' dorm, which had been its top priority three years earlier. David was again urging the board to buy the Doscher property, to use the Doscher house for a girls' dorm. Gordon Gay, Tom Debevoise and Gerry Freund all favored building a new dorm instead, but the board voted 6-5 against it, and did nothing further. The board needed to step up. In addition to personnel questions involving David Bailey, Jim Young and others, there were also the cash drain of the Franzen dorm under construction, the decline in the Parents Association's annual fund drive, the continuing cash drain of the Vermont Scholarship Program, the effective end of the 20th Anniversary Campaign little more than halfway to its goal, the lag in Four Term Plan organizing, the projection of Four Term Plan deficits as high as $100,000 a year, and uncertainties about the school's re-evaluation – for which none of the requisite reports had been written with the evaluators' visit less than a month away.

## VI

### Jean Zeller, WCS secretary, letter to Gordon Gay, September 16, 1966

*Buffy has brought to my attention that official notice of the October 1st meeting of the Trustees has not gone out. I guess in the rush of leaving for England [for his son Peter's wedding] it slipped David's mind... David has not had time to write his usual Headmaster's report, either... This new Woodstock Plan has certainly kept everyone busy [trying to get ready for the start of school October 10].*

### Gordon Gay letter to Jean Zeller, September 18, 1966

*So many decisions are coming up at the last moment, shall not try to write a report but will give mine orally, if it appears necessary. I hope David will try to have one written by the time of the meeting. I'm sure most of the trustees will want to be 'filled in' on four term progress, etc.*

### Jean Zeller letter to Gordon Gay, September 27, 1966

*This has been such a hectic time. If we live through this week, I have hopes for the future.*

SPRING 1965 – SPRING 1967

## David Bailey report to the Trustees, October 1, 1966

*There's not much value in continuing to anticipate the launching of our Woodstock Plan, since it's still in prospect, except to say that we are excited and a bit awed by the experiment...*

*Our absorption in this has not made us lose sight of the fact that the re-evaluation of the school by the New England Association of Colleges and Secondary Schools will take place in about three weeks. That, of course, is of extreme importance for the school's accreditation no matter what system we're operating under – old math, new math or Casey Stengel math. The month starting this first day threatens to be the busiest in the history of the school. Once it is survived without disaster, the future should be comparatively easy sailing, but always with challenging and exciting newness because of the frequent changes of personnel, young and old, with their concomitant variety of perspective and activity.*

*We have some caution about the success of the Plan this year if only because many of our present parents may, in the final analysis, be too conservative and unadventurous. We also have reason to worry about money for the first year or two of the experiment. There are so many unknowns even about this fall term where at least the enrollment is determined. Although we are probably overstaffed, we know that we cannot this fall offer two such key subjects as chemistry and dramatics. It is hoped and even assumed that the Trustees will be optimistic and bold as they've been in the past in committing the school to deficit financing. The prospect of greatly improved school economics is one of the lights over the horizon that is leading us on...*

*In general, we are so well organized for this year that it's terrifying.*

## Trustee meeting minutes, October 1, 1966

*4-Term Administrator's Report: Mr. Young talked about the progress and problems of establishing the Woodstock Plan, noting that many of the parents are not familiar with its possibilities yet [because no detailed information was available to them until early September; that included a course syllabus for fall and winter terms, but not spring or summer].*

*A general discussion of policy about enrollment for the summer term brought out two points of view: the financial and prestige advan-*

tages of full enrollment, and the possible monetary risk of seeking quality students and high caliber teachers. The consensus favored taking a chance on the latter course.

### Jean Zeller letter to Gordon Gay, October 18, 1966

*We're busy beyond belief here... David really doesn't know what to do first some days – everything's pressing. Do bear with us. As he said in his Headmaster's Report, if we get through October we may make it.*

### David Bailey letter to Trustee Dick Day, October 20, 1966

*Jim Young is a bit overwhelmed with the complexities of our new plans but his energy and computer mind are going very well.*

• • •

The Saturday before the five-member committee from the New England Association of Colleges and Secondary Schools arrived at Woodstock for its ten-year re-evaluation visit, a student driving a school truck ran into another student, hospitalizing him with a broken arm and ruptured spleen. The injured student returned to school the following Wednesday, the day the committee arrived. Just the day before, another student had stolen some arsenic from the chemistry lab and taken it in a suicide attempt. "The student was hospitalized, and was still alive at the time of our departure. He had received a telephone call from his mother, telling him of the separation of his parents," the committee reported, apparently unaware of this student's series of previous suicide attempts. Despite these events and the school's hasty preparation for the visit, Larry Roberts wrote afterwards to Gordon Gay: "The evaluators are gone and we can breathe a sigh of relief. I don't know what the outcome of the visit will be, but the people were pleasant and the school [was] at its best."

Within fairly broad limits, almost any reasonable school could win accreditation from the New England Association in 1966. The accreditation process was not terribly demanding or onerous, relying as it did on each school's own definition of what it was about: "a concise, clearly written statement of objectives and philosophy should normally be presented at the time of application. This is a critical part of the evaluation because the school is to be (re)evaluated on the basis of its effectiveness in carrying out the statement of philosophy and objectives." The first time the school was evaluated, in 1956, when Isabel Stephens wrote most of the reports, the school presented a brief, reasonably clear statement of philosophy (see Chapter 4). Ten years later, David wrote the statement of philosophy, which comprised only eight typewritten lines about the school: "It was incorporated, not for profit, in 1945. It is for the sole purpose of the education of boys and girls. No philosophy has been expressed in the catalogue, but we do state that college preparation is one of the purposes. More important to most of the staff, however, is not just the large college admission record, but it is rather the general development of the child leading toward adulthood. The emphasis is on the intellectual, but, of course, the spiritual and physical well being of the Students are also attended to. We want to help each child 'put his center in the middle.'" Despite such diffidence, the committee did not cavil, but stated in its report: "The committee reaffirms its strong sympathy for the philosophy of the school which, though nowhere stated succinctly, is apparent everywhere."

In early October, David had assured the trustees there would probably be no problem with re-accreditation. According to Jim Young, "I didn't know anything about [the re-evaluation] until I got to school in the fall... David didn't seem particularly uptight about it. I don't think David felt there were very many problems." At the end of October, one member of the re-evaluation committee stayed with the Youngs in Giles House, "quite a conservative lady, and so she really had lots of questions about what was going on," Young recalled; he was not protective of the school and the re-evaluation "did not go well." After the committee's visit, David was worried enough to follow-up with Ralph West, the school association's administrator, and with Miss Dora Palmer, the committee chairman and head of the English department at the Northfield School for Girls (who had, during the committee's visit, assured a faculty meeting, "we are not exterminators"). David wrote to Gordon Gay that his later conversations with these two had made him "feel better about the outlook." But in December, the association met and, in accordance with the visiting committee's recommendation, voted to table Woodstock's re-accreditation while the school adjusted to its new year-round schedule. In its formal notification to the school, the Association explained: "It further voted that a full evaluation of the school will take place next year and that continued membership in the New England Association of Colleges and Secondary Schools will be dependent upon the correction [in the year's interval] of specific and serious areas of deficiency."

The association's official letter, from Edith Phelps, headmistress of the Dana Hall School, concluded: "We earnestly hope that there can be immediate consideration of these serious weaknesses and that some action may be initiated to alleviate and to correct them. Woodstock is too fine a school to allow a lowering of its standards even in its preoccupation with its new program. And a personal word of best wishes, David, to you for a happy holiday season!"

Initial reaction at the school was mostly anger and denial. David sequestered the report in his office, requiring faculty members to make an appointment with him to see it and forbidding them from discussing it with anyone, even each other. David and others disputed the accuracy of the committee's report. Jim Young, having privately shared his own misgivings with one of the evaluators, felt the committee report was fully justified. But Young wasn't trying to fix anything and he wasn't sharing his concerns with others at the school, least of all with David, because "I didn't really know enough." Reacting to the committee's assessment of the school, neither David in writing to the trustees, nor Buffy in eight pages of handwritten notes, specified *any* major shortcoming of the report. At the same time, they and others also realized that, despite numerous factual errors, the report's overview was rosier in some ways than the school's actual condition (Buffy's notes show that, at an executive committee meeting in December, "David notes weaknesses that were missed. 'Don't tell 'em,' says Tom Debevoise").

The report's major points were:

1. **Quality of faculty** – "Basically, the faculty is a competent group from the point of view of academic preparation and, therefore, technically able to cope with the great freedom and flexibility within the instructional framework required by *the generally excellent and interested student body...* [emphasis added] There is a nucleus of thoroughly experienced and enthusiastic, dedicated teachers, but the larger number have taught from one to five years. Ten out of a total of seventeen teaching faculty fall into this category. Of the ten, six have taught only one year prior to this one and one has no prior experience." The report might also have added that there were only four teachers, including David, who had more than four years experience at Woodstock – Buffy, who was two years from retirement; Larry Roberts, who was in his last year, and Peggy Bailey, who was only a part-time English teacher, having given up her drama work.

    "The greatest criticism is the lack of a dynamic interaction between the students and some of the faculty... a lot of rote, unimaginative classroom teaching, despite the obvious sincerity of the teachers involved. This situation is saved by the individual concern given each student... Taken as a whole, the faculty is woefully weak in performance." Basing its conclusions on classroom observations, but without using names, the report cited half a dozen teachers as particularly weak, three as particularly strong, and three more as strong but with weaknesses. What the committee probably didn't know was that, of that faculty of 17, at least half a dozen teachers of both genders and very different ages had more or less widely known personal problems with alcohol, drugs (mainly marijuana), and/or sex (including several student/teacher affairs). Common knowledge of this adult behavior in the midst of demands for higher student standards caused predictable tensions on campus. One teacher was dropped at the end of the year because of his misbehavior, but others went unchallenged. According to Jim Young, David was aware of a female teacher having an affair with one of her students, but never intervened. Gerry Freund challenged David about the flagrant activities of another male teacher, who nevertheless remained at the school, unreformed, for several more years.

(In this litigious age, even the certainty of truth about these situations, from the mouths of participants or from firsthand observation, is not enough to persuade a knowledgeable author to say more. Suffice it to say that some of the best, as well as worst, of Woodstock's faculty were involved and that it was a time of active student initiative, which created a remarkably intricate, moral Gordian knot: one rather open student/teacher affair, of which David took no official notice, had the express approval of the girl's father.)

2. **Faculty Turnover** – "We hope that the school can be given time to recover from the widespread change of faculty, which resulted two years ago from retirements and normal shifting of jobs." The committee showed no understanding that faculty turnover had been going on for five years, following a period of remarkable stability. In fact, more teachers had left the school in those five years than were on the faculty in 1966. The average faculty tenure by then was only 4.4 years, with 11 teachers having been at Woodstock two years or less. The committee did not probe the causes of this turnover, nor the almost as rapid turnover among trustees.

3. **Faculty salaries** – "Salaries range from $3,200 for a teacher with no experience to $9,000 for a teacher with twenty-two years' experience. Despite the fact that these salaries include housing and meals and the excellent perquisites of Blue Cross, TIAA, plan for substitute teachers, etc., the Committee feels that the salaries themselves are far too low and does not see how the Headmaster can get outstanding, or even, perhaps, adequate teachers at these figures." The trustees had been fighting sporadically with David about salaries for more than a decade. The school's self-evaluation reported both its high and low salary figures were $200 higher than the high and low of the previous year. According to Buffy's notes, comparative figures for similar schools "for 1964-65 show 'salaries for instruction' lower than ours for 10 schools, higher in 6."

4. **Quality of students; admissions policy** – Curiously, while the association's official letter from Mrs. Phelps made this a major concern, Miss Palmer's committee report had almost nothing but praise for students it found to be "generally excellent and interested." Elsewhere, the report typically said, "the students reflect a positive attitude toward the school and demonstrate enthusiastic support of the school's philosophy... The majority are [sic] well motivated, and both in words and action, demonstrate in study hall and classroom situations, their seriousness of purpose in pursuing academic goals. The school is to be recommended for the creation of this spirit through its philosophy of putting the burden of responsibility squarely on the shoulders of the individual student." More problematical, as the school's self-evaluation shows, Woodstock was accepting more than fifty percent of its applicants, an admissions ratio significantly increased from five years earlier when Woodstock was noticeably more selective.

5. **Seemingly "lax" tone of student body; need for definite standards** – What truly bothered the committee and Mrs. Phelps, apparently, was the style of the students. The report complained about too much lounging in classrooms and the need for a more ship-shape appearance around the school. As one of the "two glaring weaknesses in the overall picture of the school" (the other was faculty weakness), the report cited moral guidance: "no proper attempt made to guide the students in the vital field of spiritual values. They are taught to question, but no

real help is given in finding answers. Consequently, students tend to show this questioning in a surface lack of courtesy and an initial inability to meet strange adults on easy terms. Their world seems to be purely a world of youth, and they seem isolated from and suspicious of the larger world." Not only was this complaint rooted in a philosophy very different from Woodstock's (for which the committee avowed "strong sympathy"), but it suggested a touching unawareness of that "larger world" beyond schools. This was, after all, 1966, when strange adults were turning more and more to violence to solve their problems, whether in Mississippi, Berkeley, or Southeast Asia.

That summer had seen the first and only Woodstock alumnus killed in Viet-Nam. The U.S. government gave Merriman Smith, Jr. '56 a widely publicized state funeral, not because he was an especially good helicopter pilot, but because his father was a senior White House correspondent for United Press International. President Johnson's cynical use of Smitty's death to promote the growing war was just one more example of untrustworthy people over thirty feeding the growing sense among young people of isolation from and suspicion of the larger, "adult" world, a national mood that was adding to the very local distance between older faculty and their students.

6. **Precarious financial situation** – Although the committee demonstrated striking sloppiness in getting most of the details of Woodstock's financial situation wrong, its conclusion was correct if somewhat self-contradictory: "The overall financial picture is, of course, extremely precarious... However, the school seems to be on a sound enough financial basis to survive." The committee noted the deficit budget problem (while not understanding that it was a new problem), but it missed the additional financial difficulties relating to the Four Term Plan, the fundraising campaign and the new dorm-building program.

David had provided a much better but somewhat misleading summary of the problems in the self-evaluation report: "The first 10 or 12 years the school operated without a deficit, but we took much out of our hides to do so. If we had about $25,000 a year more money, we could be surer of building once again a really superior staff. Over the years we've not paid much attention to money campaigns, to Alumni organization for support or to publicity, and we're just now trying to accustom ourselves to a more formal organization that will increase our financial resources. The Annual Giving, directed by the Parents' Association, has not produced very much in recent years, and our current 3-year 20th Anniversary capital campaign has thus far only produced about half of its goal of $350,000. The local community, which is also the Headmaster's hometown, has not been solicited for support lately. For one thing we do not always receive 'golden opinions' from the neighboring citizenry both because of our tax-exempt status, and because the students have looked a bit bizarre and over-casual in appearance. The Trustees have been patient but not happy about this nor about my resistance to soliciting for money in Woodstock. By and large, the Trustees over the years have not been a money-raising group, but when from these three obvious sources of financial support – parents, alumni and Trustees – we get the normal amount of dollar help, there shouldn't be any problem for us." (But David offered no answer to the question: How was the school going to get to "the normal amount"?)

Despite various corrections of the committee's error-filled report, the reality of the school's financial condition did not change. The following spring, the trustees heard again about Woodstock's "precarious" finances. According to the May 1967 board meeting minutes, "The treasurer reported her deep concern with the size of this year's deficit and consequent shrinkage of resources... the school's cash position during the summer [the first summer of the Four Term Plan] will be precarious." (By its own calculations in a grant application to the Charles F. Kettering Foundation, the Country School would need an additional $196,500 to support the Woodstock Plan over its first three years. The money was not forthcoming, from Kettering or anywhere else, but the school went ahead anyway, in effect assuming an unacknowledged debt for which there was no apparent income. The school mitigated this somewhat by doing without air conditioning ($27,000) and tennis courts ($5,000).)

7. **Fire hazards of physical plant** – The committee concluded: "More attention should be paid to making sure that the fire hazards are reduced to a minimum." No one at the school disagreed, but they wondered what the committee was talking about since the self-evaluation pointed out that school buildings were protected with sprinkler systems or Protecto Wire, as well as fire extinguishers. The trustees noted the last state fire inspection had turned up no problems.

8. **Absence of drama teacher** "in a school in which dramatics has been such a distinguished and major part of the program" – Simply translated, this meant that Jo Oatfield had retired, that two younger drama teachers had moved on and that Peggy Bailey lacked the strength to carry on alone. David would hire a new, young drama teacher for the spring term.

Forwarding the committee's report to the Trustees in late December, David wrote in a richly ironic cover letter, "Frankly, I am a bit shocked, ashamed and angry, particularly as I don't think I've been well enough informed, but no matter, our main purpose, naturally, is to take the necessary actions and to remain in the good graces of the establishment, the NEAC&SS. As John Milton said, I will be 'calm of mind, all passions spent' by the time of the meeting, and I will see you there."

At the January 1967 board meeting, David agreed readily that the first three criticisms concerning faculty "deserve a lot of attention." As for the quality of students and "lax" tone, he said that was "definitely our business, certainly more than it is the [association's], but it is an area which we want to improve in some ways but not necessarily in the ways that the 'establishment' would wish." David called the precarious financial situation "arguable and probably erroneous," but said "fire hazards" were easily fixed and suggested the absence of a drama teacher in a school in which dramatics had been such a distinguished and major part of the program was "hardly a criticism."

Surprisingly, the school association's official summary letter to the trustees had ignored two of the committee's more probing critiques, both crucial to the rationale behind the committee's recommendation to table Woodstock's re-accreditation in order to give the school some time to resolve its difficulties.

First, the committee report said of the Four Term Plan: "Three problems become immediately apparent: (1) Will the students choose their 'off' terms in reasonably regular numbers to allow for provision of a full school in each of the four terms and so pave the way for additional faculty who must be hired to cover the extra teaching? (2) Is the present inexperienced faculty capable of managing the longer and more frequent class periods and generally different approach that the new system requires? (3) Is it, the school, chronically short of ready cash, capable of withstanding the ups and downs the program will surely face in the future? No judgment can be given on the program at this time, since it has been in operation for only two weeks... it would appear that at Woodstock the broad goals were considered carefully, but specific problems were not sufficiently considered and worked out. Such working out, will, we believe, take at least two or three years before the effectiveness of the plan can be determined."

The second and more important issue raised by the committee was David's health: "The Headmaster is ill with emphysema. He himself told us of this obvious difficulty and stated what was apparent to the Committee: He is no longer able to maintain the strong personal control of the entire school which has been one of its greatest strengths in the past. He feels that this situation, together with a less than satisfactory Admissions check, has resulted in a serious slipping of the overall performance of the student body... All the factors noted in this section strongly indicate that final judgment of the school at this time is not valid."

### Nini Petrullo Rikoski '65 interview, April 19, 1985

*The whole school kind of ran around David, probably too much so. And clearly, when the school didn't survive too well after he was gone, that to me sort of proved it. But his moods tended to infect the whole school. If David was having a bad day, things didn't go OK. If David was having a good day, things went OK. It just kind of permeated things. A lot of students didn't like him, or didn't seem to, and I don't know whether that was because they had a problem with him, or because it was an age where they had problems with parent figures and authority figures anyway and he was the ultimate one there.*

*One of the things I was always quite sure about with David was that he was really interested in all of the students that were there. I had a sense that David's basic criteria for deciding whether he wanted someone there or not was whether he thought they were interesting. Whatever the formal criteria may have been for selection, it really came down to whether this was somebody David thought would be good for the school or the school would be good for them... it was people he wanted who came there, and some of the people he wanted were pretty bad news, because I think in a way he was attracted to problem kids, because I know that some of his favorites were some of the ones that gave him the most trouble...*

## SPRING 1965 – SPRING 1967

*[After David's lung operation in 1963], Peggy told us all [individually] that he was not supposed to smoke any more... We weren't supposed to give him cigarettes. And one of the things that would happen was that he would ask the kids that smoked for a cigarette, and most of the time they would just give it to him. But occasionally he would get somebody who would say, 'No, you're not supposed to have a cigarette.' And he'd get really angry. That was a hard one for some of the kids that really liked him. They wanted to do what he wanted but they didn't want to do something that was going to hurt him... But that was one of the sources of some of his anger later on, the cigarette thing...*

*It was a little bit scary to watch him cough, because he would get started coughing and would have trouble catching a breath. And that big, tall frame of his – when he'd get really doubled over – that was memorable."*

### David Bailey speaking at the dedication of the Franzen dorm as Bailey House in the spring of 1967, as remembered by Myron Grauer '67, October 15, 2016

*When they saw what we planned to build here, they said we were crazy.*
*Well they were right, we were crazy.*
*Or maybe I was crazy. You're crazy. We're all crazy.*
*The only way creative people make progress is to be a little crazy.*
*So all of you should go forth in the world,*
*and wear your craziness with pride,*
*and be creative.*

### Sarah Howell Skarrow '67 interview, June 13, 1986

*David denied he was sick, definitely... whenever he spoke in the common room – he could have had someone else speak for him, but he was going to do it himself, even to the point of not being able to get his breath – he was going to stand up there in the common room and say what he had to say...*

*There was always a butt in his hand. He shouldn't have been walking around the school, and he was, going about his regular duties. I think Peggy [Bailey] would have preferred him not to do so much, I sort of remember that. He'd walk and talk and smoke like nothing was – like everything was hunky-dory. I mean his hard, laborious breathing just stands out in my mind... gasping for air and he was still walking around the halls... He would show up at school on days when he was supposed to be home resting...*

*He was harder to hear the second year [1966-67] than the first. The first year he was sort of gruff and then the second year he was sort of whispering. I mean everybody had to be really quiet to hear him...*

*I went through the same thing with my brother... and there was that same sort of denial with him, as to when he should stop, and the company [that he founded] suffered. I mean he was just not mentally capable of handling everything, keeping it under control, and things were slipping. But the people who worked for him were crazy about him and just hung in there with him...*

*I think a few students felt that [David] couldn't handle it any more, that he should turn it over to somebody else. Maybe there was a sense of a loss of control. I felt bad for him. I remember seeing him in the halls and I felt, oh, God, this guy's going to die – and then what? It was kind of scary – 'cause I liked him.*

• • •

In November 1966, between the re-evaluation committee's visit and the release of its report, Woodstock's board president, Gordon Gay, suffered a debilitating stroke while staying at Giles House. He returned to Connecticut in an ambulance to spend several weeks in a hospital near his home. A month later, his condition remained so delicate that David did not send him the re-evaluation report, and even in January the trustees agreed to share only as much information as doctors approved. Gordon Gay had been David's friend and a Woodstock trustee for twenty years, the last three as more or less David's surrogate as president of the board. Although Gordon Gay would live another twelve years, he was unable to renew his work for the school and retired officially in May 1967, when the board voted a resolution of appreciation for his services. The business of running the board fell to the vice president, Tom Debevoise, who served as acting president from November to May, when he formally succeeded Gordon Gay as president of the board.

At their January 1967 meeting, the trustees concentrated on issues raised by the re-evaluation committee report. The discussion focused on the quality of faculty and students (and "the number of 'problem children' or 'children with problems' now enrolled"). The board addressed the question of raising faculty salaries despite projected operating deficits and the dwindling of fundraising, without reaching a firm conclusion. The board asked David to provide regular reports "concerning the composition of the faculty" and to draft an admissions policy as a first step toward improving the quality of students at the school. The board also asked Tom Debevoise to write to the New England Association "expressing surprise at some of the errors" in the report. The trustees agreed that, for the next visit of the re-accreditation committee, some of them "should be present, if possible."

The board did not discuss any further details of David's retirement package. Privately, several board members were feeling increasing urgency about the state of the school. Gerry Freund especially pursued David about most of the issues facing him and the board. In February, still hoping to revitalize the 20th Anniversary Campaign, Gerry Freund wrote David outlining all that needed to be done and concluded, "I will make time available to pursue the fund drive effort, but first I want there to be a clear and firm understanding about the steps to be taken including priorities among them, and second I want assurances of active assistance from other trustees and effective cooperation from the school."

At the same time, Jim Young was not only quietly looking for another job, he was also sharing his dissatisfactions with the school with others, including trustees – but not including David – behavior Gerry Freund later called a "hatchet job." Jim Young's approach may have been devious, but his concerns were real, especially drug use, which he feared would lead to a State Police bust. He was also bothered by the school's sexuality: "the dormitories were really in a shambles that year,.. we really didn't know which was the boys and which was the girls." But beyond his prudish objections to life at the school, Jim Young simply felt out of his depth: "I couldn't handle it. I felt that some of the emotional and psychological problems of the kind, and their needs, that the school just was not coping with them properly... I felt I was in over my head, I didn't see things happening that I felt were going to make it any better." Jim had been something of a protégé of Dick Day, then the headmaster at Phillips Exeter, and Jim had managed to get Dick Day elected to Woodstock's board that fall, before the term had started. So, when Jim was having difficulties with Woodstock, he talked privately about them with Dick Day and Tom Debevoise (just as he had talked privately with an evaluator). He made a special trip to New York City to meet alone with the two of them. On that same trip, Jim Young met with the headmaster of the Hawken School in Cleveland to see if he could return there in the fall, which he did.

On March 3, 1967, Tom Debevoise sent telegrams to his fellow trustees calling a special meeting for Sunday, March 12, in New York City. The agenda: "the question of school behavioral and academic standards and their implementation." The urgency of the problem at this moment, as Debevoise explained it, derived from "a talk Dick Day had with Jim Young at my request. Jim is seriously considering leaving the school [a fact he had not shared with David] because of the school's standards [subjects which he had discussed with David]. I have not heretofore delved into the subject of the school's behavioral and academic standards, for which I am at fault, and so have no expertise thereon, but I very much need reassurance after what I have recently heard and seen. As a small 'for instance,' insignificant perhaps if isolated, after talking with David last Saturday, I visited the library. On the sign behind the desk listing library regulations was scrawled what I take to be a vulgar epithet. In the little room next to the rear exit of the library were myriad cigarette butts stamped out on the floor with no attempt at concealment of what I understand is illicit smoking. The small room also smelled of paint fumes from several partially used gallon cans." Tom said he requested reports on the state of the school from David, as well as Jim Young, English teacher Dave Horan, and Larry Roberts

Independently discussing the same issues, Gerry Freund wrote to David on the same day: "I feel the present situation is a dangerous one, dangerous to the present and future welfare of the school. In my judgment, your voluntary or involuntary leaving of the headmastership at this time would be injurious to the school, and, on personal grounds, I want you and Peggy to be in no doubt that I have argued this point vociferously with those who, for a variety of reasons – though I believe entirely with good intentions – express to me the need for immediate changes." Acknowledging the seriousness of the questions, "some of which may even stem from personally ambitious individuals," Gerry emphasized, "there is no doubt that the questions will have to be answered and that certain obvious weaknesses about which I have been candid with you for a long time will now have to be met with decisive action on your part. This especially in the area of faculty weaknesses. The area of student behavior, discipline, academic atmosphere is not in my opinion the most important, but clearly the most dramatic – especially in the eyes of individuals whose background and predilections and unsubtle understanding of adolescence leads to unwarranted comparisons and conclusions. I hope that you will marshal your wits, energies and convictions to give the board as utterly convincing a defense of the school's policies of admission and treatment of youngsters as you gave me at dinner the night before the January meeting. I advise this... because of my belief in the essential 'philosophy' of the school and fear that while a change in the balance of faculty and student composition is called for, the board in its concern may precipitously act to emasculate the essential strength of the school through radical action."

He closed his letter by explaining, "I did not immediately contact you after being called into the alarming discussion with Tom and Dick Day [because they felt] that you should not hear of their worries either helter-skelter or indirectly but from a personal conversation with Tom. The same, by the way, holds for Roger [Phillips] and Barbara [Sproul] whom Tom asked me to inform and counsel to hold off contacting you until he had visited Woodstock." During this same period, according to Gerry's then wife, Jane Trask '51, "Gerald [and others on the board] really forced David out. David was not ready to retire, but... [Gerald] did a lot of talking to me about how David has got to go... I felt badly about it, and I think David felt badly about it, too. I think he would have been happy to stay there a few more years... Gerald was just adamant that David just had to go." Years later, Tom Debevoise agreed David had been forced out and said, "a lot of the agitation was from Gerry." According to Tom, Roger Phillips and Barbara Sproul were more reluctant, but eventually "the young alumni just buffeted him [David]... I don't think they were going behind his back... They just told him it has to be... I don't remember reactions on his part."

In March 1967, responding to Tom's request, David's 1,000-word report on faculty and student behavior sounded rather sad and tired, often defensive: "Sometimes we get misled by parents who neglect to tell us that the child is adopted or has had a nervous breakdown at the age of 10, and sometimes another school successfully takes advantage of us... The appearance of the students is not an ipso facto indication of moral attitude or conduct. Quite often, the opposite is true. I do not consider that our children have morals inferior to most. If I'm wrong about this, I would welcome evidence." Shifting the focus somewhat, David concluded, "Obviously, the chief concern of the present situation is the possible loss of Jim Young. It would be regrettable if he should choose to leave – 'rash, ill-advised, sudden.' Some of his disaffections are legitimately felt, some are due to his particular background. He has no evidence to have confidence in our eventual results of our rather peculiar methods. Though I'm a reasonably pleasant guy to work for, apparently I'm hard to work with, mostly because of my strange, imprecise, and indefinite way of operating, and because I assume an empathy will bring results without instructions. My comparative ill-health has not allowed me to pick up the pieces and shore up the cavities that I used to do all the time. Surely a livelier guy could do a better job. The Trustees, as the appointees of Jim and myself, have serious decisions to make. I'll be glad to help and as honestly as I can. I certainly don't want to get in the way... I fear me this has not been a satisfactory answer to your many concerns, and, of course, I expect further serious questioning. I didn't cut any classes to come here, and I have the time and the willingness to be at your service on the occasion of this [Trustees] meeting."

David was too kind to Jim Young, or possibly unaware of Young's behavior. Before he had been at Woodstock for six months, Jim Young had surreptitiously found another employer for the following year. With no further commitment to Woodstock, he helped bring about the crisis that would finally break David Bailey's stranglehold on the school. "Young exacerbated the whole situation," according to Gerry Freund years later: he said, hyperbolically, that Young was on the golf course as much as he was at the school, that he would regale people at the Country Club bar with stories of the school, especially sex, and especially sex between faculty and students. Gerry, who learned this from friends of the school who worked at the Country Club, said, I wasn't alone in insisting that this guy get out as soon as possible." Having enjoyed the second highest salary at the school and the best housing, Jim Young would still be unable to manage a graceful exit with a modicum of loyalty. If he wrote the report Tom Debevoise requested, it has not survived.

Of the other reports Tom requested, only Larry's is extant. More than twice as long as David's, Larry's report presents a school out of control: "We need someone to set faculty standards of quality, preparation, and action. David could do this, but won't. Jim can't do it over David... Four Term Plan – we are not getting off the ground. Jim is so involved in other things that he gets almost no time to plan ahead – as of March 1 we just decided what courses [are] to be offered spring term... Philosophy – In the past, written or unwritten, there was a philosophy and a set of standards. Although students were allowed to express themselves in a variety of ways, when these limits were reached it was made clear to all that, for the good of the community, certain contrary conditions could not be tolerated. The last half of this idea now seems to have disappeared and students just express themselves... There is small wonder that the students are torn with the schism in the faculty. The standards perfectly acceptable to part of the faculty are anathema to another part. These differences include all the problem areas of dress, haircuts, language, manners, social behavior and smoking. At times when rules are decided by majority vote in faculty meeting, the dissenters do not support them..."

On March 12, 1967, after David left the board meeting at which no minutes were kept, the nine trustees present (out of 14) voted unanimously to send the Baileys on an off-campus sabbatical year with full pay for 1967-68. The board also voted unanimously to establish an advisory committee on faculty hiring (with "a request to the headmaster that he consult with the committee chairman prior to making any new faculty appointments") and a search committee to find an acting headmaster. Within three weeks, the search committee headed by Gerry Freund had hired John Holden, the retiring head of the Colorado Rocky Mountain School, as Woodstock's headmaster for the coming year. It was time. Myron Grauer '67, who was at Woodstock just one year, remembered being in an office with several people, including David, who was smoking. When Peggy walked in, David hid his cigarette in his tweed jacket pocket. Peggy didn't stay long. When she left, someone said, "David, your pocket is on fire." It wasn't ablaze, but smoke was pouring out from the cigarette smouldering the fabric.

Announcing the decisions of the trustees had no immediate, dramatic impact on the school. At the faculty meeting three days later, Buffy recorded the discussion briefly: "Dissatisfactions: DWB [David] not precise enough – some don't do what they are asked to do – some of present mess due to sloppiness and lack of standards – students exploit weakness of administration... Girls and boys come to Upwey for lovemaking [before 6 a.m.]." Responding promptly to improve standards, the faculty voted that no students would be allowed to leave their dorms before 6:45 a.m.

In his spring report to the board, David wrote, "This has been a most difficult and confusing year for the Trustees, and I am most sorry that any of the troubles have occurred – Mr. Gay's illness, the accreditation difficulties, Mr. Young's departure and many others. The offer to the Baileys of a full year's sabbatical was a stunning response, literally and figuratively. Mrs. Bailey and I are most grateful for as well as needful of the sabbatical and are so happy that we have it to look forward to, particularly as we have a place to go [the house in Wilder], also with the help of the Trustees. We can last through the year and the summer term, and we'll do our best until the Holdens take over. It is impossible to express appreciation in proper terms."

At the May meeting attended by nine of fifteen trustees, Tom Debevoise announced that David had officially resigned, effective at the end of his sabbatical year. In his letter to the board, David cited "health uncertainties" and the likelihood of a second lung operation (which he never had, since his doctors felt his "repaired" lung was not strong enough to carry him through such lengthy surgery). The board unanimously adopted Tom's resolution accepting David's resignation, then wrangled over when to announce it. David favored delay, waiting for some Associated Press story already a month overdue, but the board decided it was best not to wait.

With David out of the room and Paul Newlon on his way back to New York, the seven remaining trustees spent another three hours trying unsuccessfully to decide how to assure David a decent retirement income. The "David faction" (Trustees Gerry Freund, Roger Phillips, and Barbara Sproul, plus Treasurer Buffy Dunker) dominated the discussion, seeking to commit the school to supporting David at a long-term cost estimated at as much as $175,000. The first question was whether David was eligible for Social Security disability, which seemed likely. Roger Phillips wanted some trustee to get Peggy's permission to talk to David's doctor to get the facts. David's known problems included hyper-tension, high blood pressure, a shift in EKG and emphysema, Roger said, adding: "I had a conversation with David, I think he feels disabled for this job." Gerry Freund challenged this, saying Roger's story "sounded different the last time you told it." Gerry expressed reluctance to call David "disabled," for fear of hurting his feelings and his chances of future employment; Gerry also objected to seeking information from David's doctor. Tom Debevoise emphasized the board's primary responsibility to the institution of the Woodstock Country School, warning against taking any decision without knowing the facts of David's health, of his other resources, or of alternative sources of income and other details. Tom also cautioned the board against the legal hazards of "an improvident act," such as committing resources the school could not afford, especially in light of the treasurer's report of a substantial deficit for the year. Barbara Sproul said that in 1963 David's doctor had told the trustees David was able to handle the headmaster's job, even though privately the doctor didn't believe it was true. Barbara also worried that a commitment of $175,000 could break the school. Gerry Freund argued $175,000 wasn't worth discussing against a man's life. He and that Buffy believed that amount could be raised (even though it was more than the 20th Anniversary Campaign had raised by then). Gerry said that he wanted the school to suffer more, if necessary, for David to suffer less. When the full board reconvened the next morning, it approved a resolution reaffirming "the school's responsibility to provide for the Baileys' future financial security" and appointed a committee to find the best way to do so.

There was little reaction in the school when David announced his decision. Some of those who were there remembered, more than anything, feeling relief at the arrival of the inevitable. The school's group system went through another reorganization, the Four Term Plan maintained its disorganization and the student council continued to decline, to the point that David suggested it be appointed by the faculty. Commencement that June featured three speakers:

Gerry Freund, Tom Debevoise and Philip H. Hoff, then Governor of Vermont, all paying tribute to David's accomplishments. The three had been invited, apparently, with no thought that all three would accept. The graduating class of 23 included eight with academic honors, despite David's year-long complaint that grades were too high.

When Israel's Six Day war started on June 5, 1967, Myron Grauer '67 cut classes to keep up with the news. Among the classes he cut was Peggy Bailey's senior English. It was an unusually hot day with a baseball game scheduled, as Grauer remembered it: "I was sitting at David and Peggy's table at lunch that day and Peggy confronted me at lunch about cutting her class. David then instructed Cam [baseball coach Wendell Cameron] that I was to wear my catching gear throughout the game except when I was batting, and that I was to play the entire game. I almost passed out from the heat!" Years later, as a retired law professor, Grauer remained somewhat ambivalent toward the WCS system of justice, but glad that he remained conscious.

## David Sloan Wilson '67 letter, February 23, 1987

*My memories of WCS are intensely ambivalent. Some very good things existed there, but in the middle of an extremely hostile, lord-of-the-flies social atmosphere. I don't feel injured by the experience, and I suppose even benefitted, in the spirit of the old saying "that which does not kill us makes us stronger." I did see some people made thoroughly miserable, however, and others transformed into nasty streetwise little assholes just so they could survive there.*

*For me, WCS represents a world made by adolescents without much adult guidance or control. An idealist such as David Bailey thought that control shouldn't be necessary and that guidance would be sought by the adolescents. At first he was right, but both he and WCS were unprepared for 1960's, and adolescents who rejected both guidance and control. WCS's basic philosophy made it powerless against such students.*

*During my years there the faculty became increasingly superfluous to life at the school. Classes were in chaos during my senior year. I have vivid memories of students setting fire to toilet paper rolls and jumping in and out of windows during geometry class! Virtually everyone was smoking marijuana and several were rumored to be on heroin. Social cliques roamed the halls like street gangs, hurling abuse at each other that fortunately was only psychological, and students that didn't join a clique were doomed to the life of a social outcast. In many ways WCS was a self-created ghetto school, situated in rural Vermont, that affluent families spent thousands of dollars for their children to attend. It is hard to feel nostalgic about it, and part of me celebrated when it collapsed.*

*As I read over this letter I wonder if I am exaggerating, and how I can reconcile this image of WCS with my more pleasant memories: of long walks through the Vermont countryside, of fishing in the stream and a secret pond that only I knew about, of the great teachers such as John Pierce and Buffy Dunker, who really did influence my life, of my wondersul adolescent romances that now warm the heart of an old fart, and four or five really good friends that I always will think warmly of.*

*Somehow they get lost in my sense of outrage at what a mean world arrogant adolescents can make for themselves when provided the opportunity. Perhaps I accentuate my outrage the way others accentuate their pleasant memories into the warm glow of nostalgia.*

## David Bailey self-tape, January 1, 1981

*Shortly after our good days at Upwey began to decline in the quality and morale of the student body. I think this came down to us from the college level. Protests against the Vietnam War seemed to affect everyone and at about this time we lost some of our best teachers for economic reasons, and their replacements were not able to redress the quality we had had. We still ran a quality school and had excellent eating and living conditions, but somehow our very best days had disappeared and we took comfort in the fewer high quality students that we were then getting. I was aware of this slow decline and there were hints reaching me that maybe I, too, had had my best days and perhaps I should consider stepping down.*

*To complicate my situation my health also declined and I had to have a serious surgical operation involving the scraping of my lungs followed by a too short recuperative period so when I finally returned to school I was less able to handle any emergency problems that arose. I was reluctant to step down because I had no financial security of any kind so I couldn't afford to leave. But, when later I was assured that financial help would be given me, I planned to resign....*

SPRING 1965 – SPRING 1967

• • •

Fully unpacking the denial in David's brief reminiscence recorded after the school had closed would be a reiteration of much of the previous two chapters. "Our very best days" didn't just disappear "somehow." Briefly, David's emphysema was compromising his ability to function no later than 1961. Russ Mead left in 1962. David's lung operation was 1963. Molly Plumb left in 1963. Mounir Sa'adah and Peter Sauer left in 1964, as did Lowell and Virginia Naeve. Viet-Nam War protests didn't reach significant intensity until 1965, when the Naeves emigrated to Canada. The Woodstock Plan had served as a diversion from the school's most serious problem for years. By 1967, David and Peggy's last term at Woodstock was also the "summer of love" that proved far more culturally challenging than anti-war protest (fifty years later, war has become cultural wallpaper but lifestyle still starts fights). That first summer term of the year-round school, underenrolled as would become chronic, was in many ways quiet and pleasant, almost wonderful. The school was small, 44 students, there was little tension and Vermont was green. It was not unlike the school of 1945. But marijuana use was increasing at Woodstock, as in the rest of America. When a large group of students was caught smoking, it created a crisis and led to a marathon faculty meeting to decide what to do about the offenders.

"David, in his exhaustion, wanted to throw anybody implicated out, that was his response. He felt betrayed by the kids," recalled Jody Horan, who had come to Woodstock to teach drama in the spring of 1967, fresh out of college. "It was a real battle as a faculty, with people divided right down the middle and it ended up going to a majority vote. And the vote went against David, and my recollection is that he wept. I remember him crying... It was definitely a vote against his point of view, and it was sort of the end of him... Nobody was doing it to be against David, they just felt he was wrong. And knowing the way those faculties were, they cared for and they cared about the kids and what was right for the kids. And so David – and this is, I think, probably the point of my story, not that the drugs were wrecking the school – David went out and spoke to all the students and represented a vote, that he didn't believe in at all, as his own. And I just remember feeling that I was in the presence of a real giant... representing our decision as his own, as only David could do – that wonderful face – you are my children, and this is what we're doing."

What the faculty had decided was to deal with the problem by talking about it openly and appealing to the students' sense that Woodstock was their school as much as anyone's. The school had a bonfire and burned a lot of marijuana, and the community reached a public agreement that they wouldn't smoke marijuana on campus, and that it was primarily up to students to keep each other in line. The summer term ended in September, the first year of the Woodstock Plan was over. John Holden had already arrived to take David's place for a year. There was no formal observance of the Baileys' departure. David and Peggy went quietly away to Lavenham, their house in Wilder. David was 55 years old.

"He gave no acknowledgement that he wasn't functioning as well as he had," Dave Horan remembered. Jody Horan agreed: "He couldn't talk about it, say anything about it, God forbid he should hold a party over it. He didn't want to leave, he made that very clear, he made it very clear to us that he had been thrown out… That's what made it so tough, that we all as a faculty knew he should not be there… But I just remember very clearly his telling us that the Trustees had done it, and that he felt very betrayed, and everybody universally feeling, how can he not see it? How can he not know?"

Peter Dembski '72

SPRING 1965 – SPRING 1967

Aggie Barr

Earl Barr

Stuart Cudlitz '71

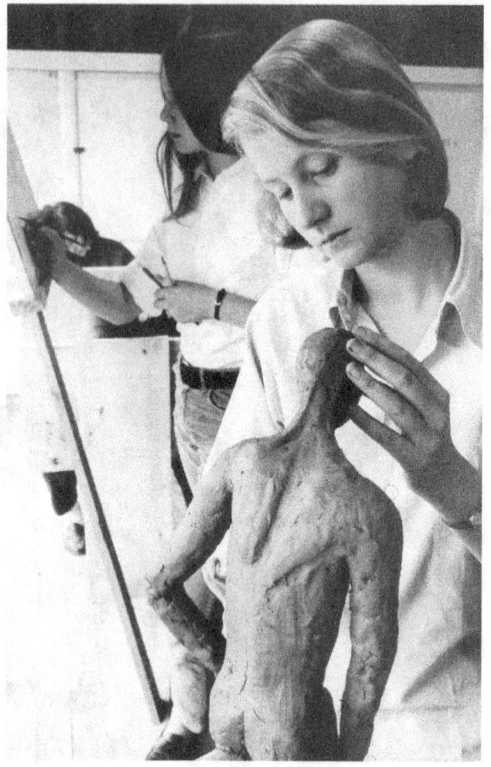
Kathleen Tomlinson '65

Todd Brief '69

SPRING 1965 – SPRING 1967

*Chloë Johnson*

Charity Hardison '68

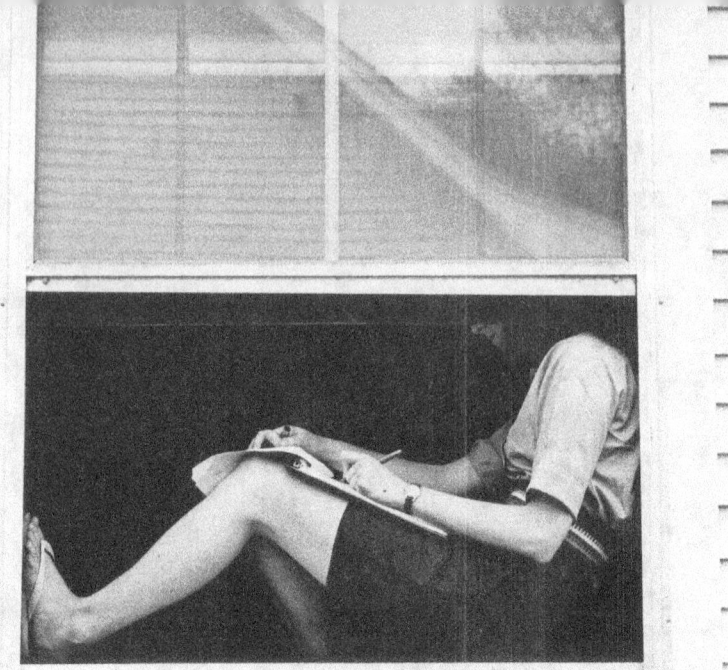

WCS horse barn: Becky Fairweather (front) and others

CHAPTER EIGHT

# Fall 1967 – Summer 1968

### John Holden letter to the alumni, September 1967

*Dear Alumni,*
*I'll need your help when I take over the helm at Woodstock Country School next month. What was the magic ingredient in your education? How is Woodstock unique? What are the most important aspects of the school to preserve for future generations? I know what a rare, mature kind of loyalty most of you have to this school. You, alumni, can give me the clues that will help me to preserve the best of the Woodstock tradition and to move ahead in the right direction.*

*The real test of a school's worth is the story of what its Alumni are doing with their lives. Woodstock Country School has already proved itself in this way and that, plus our long association and friendship with David Bailey, was the deciding factor in bringing Anne and me here.*

### Mary Lois Hamilton Bertram '47, reply to Holden, September 15, 1967

*As a member of the class of 1947, I feel as though I might be speaking from behind the moon... You want to know why we have such deep loyalty to Woodstock, for us that were so early in the establishment, it is hard to put into words. I think it was David Bailey for the most part. He taught us to think. He had a way of shaming us when we didn't. He had a way of teaching you self-respect.*

### Sally Streeter Harrison '49, reply to Holden September 16, 1967

*It is always a risky business to ask advice of anyone, but especially of such a motley crew as we WCS alumni. In this case it is like the second wife asking the first wife the secrets of her success. I am afraid that we feel quite a sense of possessiveness about David and Peggy and WCS.*

*I see that you have already gleaned the fact that most of us have very personal feelings of loyalty to the school and to David and Peggy, who made it what it is. You seem, however, to assume that we want you to be a similar success in the same job, a very generous thought on your part, indeed. Slightly presumptuous, maybe. Why would we want you, a perfect stranger, to succeed in the same shoes where David also succeeded? Who are you? We don't know you. You had better be good. You will find that David and Peggy have left you some pretty big footprints to fill. (Color us hostile.)*
*RUN A TIGHT SHIP WITH A LOOSE CONTROL WHEN AT THE HELM...*
*I can see by your three paragraph letter that you are a blunt kind of man, a person who shoots straight from the hip. This is a good quality to have because no one is misled about what you are, but only if it is tempered with patience, humility, wisdom, and frequent self-re-examination. I hope that you have these qualities, Mr. Holden, and that if you don't, that you are willing to seek them out...*

FALL 1967 – SUMMER 1968

## Philip S. Castle '54, reply to John Holden, September 13, 1967

*Three words best characterize the uniqueness of the three years I spent at WCS: experimentation, innovation, and flexibility. Many school systems pretend to aspire to these habits, and administrators devote much talk to the virtues implied in them. Very few schools actually do something positive in this direction. There are three schools that did: Woodstock, Colorado Rocky Mtn., and Putney... It is a source of comfort and reassurance that you will be there to ensure the continuance of Woodstock's progressive spirit.*

## Ellie Noss Whitney '56, reply to Holden, fall 1967

*Woodstock? It meant David, Buffy and Mounir, whose impact on my life will never wear off, for good or ill.*

*It meant trust and freedom, as much of both as I could take. Being trusted, where in other schools a student would be watched, we strained and stretched, some of us, to be worthy of that trust, and so grew more than we would otherwise have done.*

*It meant work: the dish crew, the library, enough responsibility and initiative for each student to find a place and a job that was his own, that he could take pride in.*

*It meant faculty meetings, where each student's name was brought up individually for privileges and discussed by all. I know of no other school where this is systematically done.*

*Of <u>course</u> it meant good teaching (Peggy, Jo, Curt, Alan Weatherby, Isabel). But if I had to pick one thing that was more important than any other at Woodstock, I'd have to say, the opportunity to grow my own way, under the eye of teachers who knew that each of us was different from all the others.*

## Robert Helfman '64, reply to Holden, September 1967

*Woodstock was a good school for many reasons, the best of which are certainly hard to define. The atmosphere gave an opportunity for a relaxed mingling of many influences. Educational, of course, but there is a transcendental and most important first – the environment...*

*One last and fervent hope. That Woodstock can learn and perhaps discover its essential value before hate and war have destroyed all that is beautiful in humanity, and that the school can relax, cease to strive and impose false, unnecessary values, and <u>trust.</u> Trust life in its innate, spontaneous invention...*

## Anonymous reply to Holden, September 27, 1967

*Time. Mostly time. Time to take good, long, hard looks, time to spend within one's self, time to piece things together, all the time in the world. And the chance, let's call it opportunity, to be angry, to demand, to fight and be rotten, to make the mistakes, the choices, to realize the unique other-individual, to be able to shamelessly get rid of all the crazy chaos and illusions and by doing to begin the discovery of that 'separate peace.'*

*Woodstock itself was somewhat of an illusion: a womb, a big, bullet-proof shield, an air-tight oasis set down in the midst of a magnificent valley, far from the big city and the vast and complex machinery of the outside world. And this, I feel, is dangerous, though not easily avoidable...*

*I wish you luck.*

## John Holden, Independent School Bulletin, October 1974

*Let's face it – there is a certain mystique about the position of head of any school. The head is variously the despot, the ogre, the inspiration, and the laughingstock. When the old head retires and a new one is appointed, tongues begin to wag, nerves begin to go taut, and the new person is looked on as much more of an ogre, much more a cruel despot. But when the school's board hasn't had time to find a permanent head and appoints an interim person, what then?*

*Well, I happen to have been that interim person for two very different schools in two very different parts of the country... Against the obvious fact that the interim head is temporary, one can weigh the freedom from worries about being fired and the courage one has to face the board and criticize when needed, to zero in on faculty who have been coasting on their past records, to remind alumni of a proud heritage that recent years have befogged.*

FALL 1967 – SUMMER 1968

*When I started in at [the Woodstock Country School], I made some terrible mistakes that cost me dearly. But inspired by my wife, Anne, I did do one thing right before that fall term ever opened. We had a wing-ding of a party for [the Baileys] and invited most everyone who knew and loved them from as far away as New York. The toasts and tributes were beautiful."*

• • •

When John Holden arrived at the Country School in 1967, the first summer term of the Four-Term Plan was still in session and David was still headmaster. John and Anne quietly settled in as the first headmaster family to live in Giles House [when Gerry Freund's committee hired John in March, it thought it was also getting Anne Holden, John's co-founder at the Colorado Rocky Mountain School; but Anne made it clear she would work only if she were paid independently, which the board declined to do]. As soon as the summer term was over and John was in charge, the Holdens organized a dinner party for David and Peggy, a gathering of some 60 people in Giles House. Since the students, the faculty, the trustees had all allowed the occasion of the Baileys' retirement to pass without ceremony, this was the Baileys' only formal send-off. This was also a characteristic, perhaps instinctive, John Holden gesture, at once generous, thoughtful and shrewd; at once honoring his predecessor's service to the school and underscoring the reality of his separation from it.

During the summer, many of the trustees were concerned about how David would handle the transition. Visiting the campus in late July, Dick Day had a long talk with David and found him "terribly tired, almost completely without energy." Less than three weeks later, Roger Phillips wrote Gerry Freund that he found "David looking and sounding healthier than ever. (I feel so guilty about David – until I remember that the three of us could not have changed that decision)." But David did leave quietly, as Buffy Dunker reported to Gerry in September; "from what DWB [David] has said to John S. Holden, and what JSH has said to me, our worries about DWB's being able to let go are no longer appropriate. David's working himself around to the sensible thing."

"When we took over," John Holden recalled, "David simply said, 'You're experienced, you do it your way.'" David also sent them a little key, for a padlock or strongbox, about which he wrote: "The enclosed is a little thing with much meaning. It is the key to the school, used at Greenhithe and at Upwey. In fact, it has opened many doors and hearts. For me it is the greatest of pleasures to turn it over to you with my blessing and gratitude. You too heard the need and you were willing, as you always have been, to pick up the burden. I know you will carry it with skill and devotion. You have come at the right time and everyone has full confidence."

The interim headmaster's charge from the board was no more explicit, but he understood his most important task was to get the school safely through its still-pending re-evaluation (which he managed to postpone again, until the spring of 1968, allowing time for the school to accomplish the detailed self-evaluation it had omitted in 1966). A few weeks after the start of school, Holden wrote to a colleague, "I think that my primary responsibility is to bring the school through this evaluation. There are some fantastic strengths in the school and some glaring weaknesses. It's a real challenge, but there's a wonderful faculty and a wonderful student body to work with."

By 1967, John Holden, like David, had devoted 32 years to progressive education. John's career began in 1935 at the Putney School, where he went after graduating from Bowdoin. During his 17 years at Putney, John first taught English and later took on administrative duties – "I was sort of an errand boy, right-hand man" – as an assistant to the then headmistress Carmelita Hinton. He had often traveled to Woodstock to see his sister (whose daughter was WCS '68), as he later wrote: "Among our particular friends up here were the McDills, Tad Bailey, and David and Peggy. I remember sitting on the terrace at my sister's home in Prosper in the summer of 1943 and discussing at great length with Peggy and David their plans for starting this school."

In 1952, John and Anne Holden moved to Carbondale, Colorado, to start the Colorado Rocky Mountain School (CRMS), "which we carried to its capacity of 120 through fourteen exciting years until we felt we would be better suited to promoting this kind of education further."

CRMS was always more like Putney than Woodstock, more traditional, more tightly organized, but all the same, more like Woodstock than, say, like Deerfield, St. Paul's, Hawken, or Fort Worth Country Day. Although John was always a strong advocate of coeducation, he saw himself as less permissive than David: "I think I was pretty much of a Puritan when it came to boys and girls in bed together and we tried to make them feel that sexual intercourse was the ultimate intimacy, that you don't go into it in any casual way, that it may be better to wait until you're really ready, although I don't think we ever expelled anybody for fornication at CRMS. But we hoped that they would put it off until the right time. They didn't always, I'm sure... But everyone knew where we stood."

John contrasted his view with what he took to be Woodstock's attitude toward student sexuality in 1967: "Buffy took me up in the woods and showed me the little cabin... you couldn't stand up in it, but you could lie down. I don't know who built it, it had been built some years before, but apparently it was known about by everybody on campus and any students who wanted privacy. I have no idea of whoever used it, or whether, but there it was, apparently with David's blessing... He knew about it and didn't do anything about it."

Almost as tall as David, John had always been more rugged, a football player where David's most intense sports had been tennis and volleyball. Even as young men, they had almost opposite outlooks on nature. John was an avid skier, hiker, rock climber and camper all his life. When he later served as interim headmaster at a school in Chicago, he established an outdoor education program there and was the first to rappel off the roof of the school auditorium. John expected his students at CRMS to cope with the outdoors whether they liked it or not and most of them did, or learned to. This outward-bound style was one of the most distinguishing characteristics of John's school, it was one of the main reasons he set it in the Rockies rather than Vermont. But if nature was an opportunity for challenge or conquest to John, David had a more Wordsworthian view in which the natural world was a source of beauty, contemplation and poetry, a realm in which students were encouraged to roam and discover, but not necessarily conquer.

Just as John's face was open and classically handsome compared to the craggy complexity of David's physiognomy, so too was John's personal style, including what he called his occasional "nasty temper," much more straight-forward than the Cantabridgian intricacy of David's obliqueness. To people at the Country School, John seemed to epitomize the blunt-spoken westerner; to them he was an outsider. John knew that and went to work at once reaching out to all the school's constituencies, balancing as best he could a decent respect for Woodstock's past against a realistic assessment of its present. He had to maintain a delicate balance, muting his bluntness without becoming inauthentic. He expressed this in a letter to Gerry Freund at the end of October: "I can't emphasize the weaknesses all the time without outraging everybody, but must overcome them if we are to come through the evaluation."

## John Holden letter to students, September 1967

Dear Students,

    In this interim three-week vacation period lots of things are happening here at WCS. David Bailey retires for a well earned sabbatical. And I will try to live up to the high standard of understanding and appreciation of youth that he has set and maintained at this school. Some changes will have to be made. I won't pretend that I can do everything the way he does. I will confer with students and faculty, however, about changes that become necessary...

    But what we (Anne and I) can do for the school in the year or two that we will be with you depends on each of you, on the faculty and the alumni as it does on us. The magnificent spirit of the place can't really be improved if last spring's art exhibit and sale for Vietnamese refugees and the door-to-door canvassing leading to the meeting to discuss Viet-Nam are typical. But efforts of this kind would be more effective if the school, the faculty, and the students began to have a new look, a new hope for the future, a new story to tell the world. A few superficial things will make all the difference, though some of us will hate to admit it. If the Ruth Perkins Bailey alcove in the library were kept picked up, if there were never any milk cartons around the entrance of French House, if students would really make an effort to look neat when they come to supper or go to town, if dormitories were always sacrosanct, we would never have to defend our reputation. All this has a double importance when we realize that we will soon be re-evaluated by the New England Association of Colleges and Secondary Schools and that the school's accreditation will depend on the success of the evaluation. In a sense we are working for the cause of liberal coeducational boarding schools everywhere, not just for Woodstock. We believe we can trust you to persuade the local people, the colleges you apply to, the world in general that the school that David and Peggy started in 1946 [sic] is the best kind of school for today and tomorrow.

    I am confident that you will sacrifice some of your personal pride in superficial symbols in order to re-establish your pride in this school. We know how idealistic you are and that you will respond to the right stimulus. With the faculty giving their all, and with you proving that you *can be trusted to accomplish more than you thought you could in this informal coeducational environment, we should not only pass the evaluation but surpass all other types of schools.*

*This thing is bigger than any of us, but it is the kind of challenge we can all live up to.*

## Student representatives, letter to all students, September 14, 1967

Dear Students,

*As you may already know, during the summer term, the entire student body and faculty, working together, arrived at an agreement beneficial to all of us. The agreement was that the students would stop using Marijuana and other drugs while at Woodstock. The reason behind this agreement was a realization by the students of the position in which this puts Woodstock, and all other people related to the school. Should the school be investigated by Federal authorities, and should drugs be found, the result could be a closing down of the school, or at least, a blow to the school's reputation. This would also be a blow to the reputation of each student, and could affect his, or her, college admission.*

*The major result of this agreement has been a general relaxation of the tensions between student and faculty. Now that a new term is beginning we, as representatives of the student body, would like to stress that this agreement must remain, and so we are asking you to give a great deal of consideration to the situation at hand. If you feel that you cannot do without drugs, please do not come back to Woodstock. The trust that has been established is a great improvement over the old system, but one person can destroy it; there will be no second chances. We hope that you agree with us and that you will want to return to Woodstock this Fall."*

## Aaron Cohen '68 & Owen Bangs '68, letter to all WCS parents, October 11, 1967

Dear Parents,
*As many of you know, on October 21 there will be a mass mobilization in opposition to our policy in Viet-Nam, in our nation's capitol. Many students at the Woodstock Country School are strongly opposed to*

*this policy and feel called upon to express their opposition. We feel the mobilization is a valid method for expression of this dissent. Therefore, the Woodstock Country School Chapter of Students for Democratic Society (SDS) is working to get as many students as possible to the mobilization. For this your permission is needed.*

*Please fill out the form at the bottom of this page and return it as quickly as possible...*

## John Pierce end of term comment on anonymous student ("Phil"), December 1967

*Phil's personal management seems adequate to the task of seeing him through each day with some work done, some play, and just enough triumph to suggest that he waken the next day to continue. However, it is a rather low-voltage life he leads. He's a good fellow because he isn't a bad one. He doesn't flunk, because he passes. He's disinclined to lend his opinions and his emotions to the formation of a Community Government here, but he'll probably go along with whatever someone else produces. I'd like to hear him cuss once, or laugh, but if that isn't Phil, so be it. Meantime, he's doing fine, indeed.*

• • •

"We had no idea we were moving into the first private school to boast an SDS chapter; truly the Woodstock Country School was the only school that had a chapter in the Students for a Democratic Society at that time," John Holden recalled years later. "I don't have any very explicit memory of Aaron Cohen... He was very bright, very quick, but he accepted totally that whole SDS idea that you had to be 100% with them or that you were totally against them... And I always thought you had to be able to sit down, listen to the other fellow's side, have them listen to yours, and then come up with a conclusion that was acceptable to everybody..." John put that principle into practice almost immediately when he learned that some of the older students had been offended by his letter to them (above), especially his comments about appearance. John met with them to hear their complaints and seek a *modus vivendi*. The next day, he told the faculty the students' concerns were superficial, but "change is everywhere, so we will not demand something unreasonable." But he also said he had told the students he would have a hard time raising money if they didn't improve their looks.

## FALL 1967 – SUMMER 1968

For a fresh headmaster, the Washington anti-war demonstration could have been a much harsher test. Instead, it too served to demonstrate John Holden's reasonableness in dealing with a potentially divisive issue. John opposed the war, but he couldn't responsibly allow it to consume the school. By treating the demonstration as a school-sponsored event, providing a faculty escort for the trip and allowing any student to go, with parental permission, he effectively removed the school from the crossfire of any argument that ensued. But this arrangement also depended on the reasonableness of students who were more interested in change than confrontation, as the letter home attests – the revolution starts this weekend, if you want to take part bring a note from your parents.

The October 1967 Moratorium was the first massive anti-war demonstration in Washington, when Abby Hoffman and the rest of the Yippies were going to levitate the Pentagon. Woodstock students went down in buses with college students from Dartmouth, Goddard and Franconia to join the mass chronicled by Norman Mailer in "The Armies of the Night." But while Mailer was shuttling back to New York for his dinner party that night, most of the students stayed to surround the Pentagon, where they were tear-gassed, beaten, arrested and jailed if they stayed too long. "The troops marched in, dragged them off – one or two people – and they learned quite a good deal," John Holden recalled, "I didn't object to that."

At about the same time, he was dealing with a more protracted domestic crisis, which was equally testing of a new headmaster. One of the senior girls, widely respected on campus by students and faculty alike, was in trouble. She was one of David's favorites – he once said, "If I were to start another school and had the chance to take one Woodstock student away with me, I would choose [her]." She and her boyfriend were viewed by many of their fellow students as something of an ideal couple. During the previous spring, she got pregnant. During the summer, when she was on campus, others began to suspect her condition, but no one did anything. At the end of the term, with apparently unconscious irony, David wrote in his brief final comment for the girl, "She has been a great help to our first summer term with her calm graciousness and good taste. During the coming year, [she] should take a term off campus to do something meaningful to her."

When the possibility of pregnancy came up in an early fall faculty meeting, the girl's advisor (herself just out of college) attacked her colleagues for having dirty minds. Besides that, the girl was one of the school's most loyal, upstanding citizens, a work job supervisor and a frequently-elected council member. She was one of the authors of the letter reminding other students of their collective pledge not to use marijuana at school. During the break between terms, she had written John, "I am deeply fond of David. I know that no one could fill his place, but I know that you will do your best. I think that we may have a few hard times. I will be as helpful to you as I possibly can with hopes that we may all learn from our success as well as mistakes."

A few weeks into the term, John could no longer avoid reality. In 17 years at Putney and 14 as head of CRMS, John had never had to deal with a pregnancy, had never been aware of one at either school. He spoke to the girl directly: "When I asked her she at first denied it and said, 'Oh, no, I gained weight this summer, I'm going to try to diet.' And she came back about an hour later and she said; 'You know, John, I am pregnant.' So I said, 'what do you think we ought to do about it? And do your family know?' She said, 'No, they don't – please let me tell them.' I think she was afraid I was going to tell them. Of course I was glad to let her do it. And she went home, in the middle of the fall, to have her baby... She was back in school in January and the baby was put up for adoption. She had thought it out before I called her in as to what she was going to do with the baby. It was much too late to have an abortion. She was very mature in the whole thing – for a 17-year-old girl she was extraordinarily mature in my estimation."

When her boyfriend heard of the girl's decision to leave school, he, too, volunteered to go home, which was not near the girl. Estranged, they both returned for the winter term and eventually graduated, he in June, she in December. Ironically, what many students remember most about John's handling of sexuality issues is a kind of embarrassing ineptitude, particularly a public discussion of his own sex life in excruciating detail. Even those who knew the details of the pregnancy (everyone knew about it in general), did not make much of John's basic decency and compassion in handling it, or of the courage in his willingness to invite both students to return. Partly, this came out of many older students' determination to dislike John no matter what he did, which was reinforced by his unfamiliarity with Woodstock lore and sometimes by his own mistakes. As he wrote later: "In spite of the fact that I had sought to learn what were [the Country School's] greatest strengths from alumni, I began to impose my own standards much more than I realized. I made a terrible mistake by having shown, at a time when we had to be away for a day, a movie that had been made at Colorado Rocky Mountain School the year we left there. Implied in that were standards we never dreamed of imposing at [Woodstock]. But at the next school meeting, the seniors got up and ramrodded through a vote to disband the student council before I knew what was happening."

FALL 1967 – SUMMER 1968

Led by the SDS students, who wanted some form of participatory democracy at Woodstock, the school spent much of October and November establishing "a governing body known as the Woodstock Country School Community," comprising the school's students, faculty and staff. The emergence of this new governing body left the powers and prerogatives of the faculty and headmaster unchanged, while making appropriate obeisance to the trustees and to the State of Vermont. While explaining his formal obligations under law and contract, John seemed to welcome this revitalizing recreation of the school's self-government. First, there really was no other school government by then; second, the idea of developing a community government and a constitution offered a useful way to channel student energy; and third, this was the kind of government John preferred anyway. At Colorado, and before that at Putney, John had enjoyed the community council government in which everyone was represented – faculty, staff and students. The community council idea was implicit in the community meeting proposal and, more than likely, would be discovered as the community meeting grew more unwieldy. John was willing to wait, encouraging that evolution.

Much of the fall term was taken up by community meetings to establish the community government. Many participants recall the meetings as long and tedious. Attendance levels varied, but the meetings served as a safety valve in a volatile time (at one meeting, the community discussed the case of a very popular senior boy who had been sent home for forcing his attentions on a new girl in the infirmary), and much energy was diffused. Some of the more traditional teachers opposed any form of community meeting (power sharing), but two of the teachers who mattered most in the school's small constellation, Buffy Dunker and John Pierce, both actively supported the experiment. Buffy was elected community secretary and wrote effusive, enthusiastic minutes of the meetings. John Pierce told students about the Town Hall style government that ran Goddard College for ten years and helped Woodstock model its system after Goddard's. Virtually the entire school, 98 people, attended the early November meeting which approved the new form of government by an almost 2-1 margin (56 for, 29 against, 13 abstaining)

Behind the questions of form and organization, however, were all the longstanding issues of standards (hair, clothes, "drugs"). On the evening of November 20, a group of 19 students met with John Holden and Buffy at her house and drew up "A Proposal for Basic Agreements" for the community meeting to consider. A year earlier, Jim Young had put out a sheet of "Rules and Responsibilities" which emphasized attendance, appearance and other outward signs of obedience. The student-generated "Basic Agreements" of 1967 focused on substance, presenting broad principles which covered all the earlier rules, as well as some important areas that had been omitted, including fire safety, work jobs, personal hygiene and consideration for others. Completely new was the brief student preamble, in which John's and Buffy's guidance seemed evident: "One of the most important aims of the Woodstock Country School Community is to provide a good education for all, including the chance to learn by experience in so far as possible without jeopardizing the school or infringing the rights of others. Therefore, any student coming to the school commits himself or herself to certain basic agreements which will establish and maintain conditions conducive to health, safety and serious study." The communal nature of these ideals was expressed in practice through the creation of a judiciary committee of five students and two faculty members, all elected at large from the community, whose job was to hear and decide disciplinary cases. Final authority was explicitly left in the headmaster's hands. With this work essentially completed by the end of the fall term, political ferment at the school subsided. Woodstock had evolved into the general form it would maintain with variation for the next decade. Bill Obrecht '68, who arrived at WCS in David's last term and graduated under Tawny Kilborne ("reviled headmaster") considered John Holden a "wonderful guy," a cross between Lyndon Johnson and Euell Gibbons.

In retrospect, John Holden recalled, "Each term was different and each term was more fun, really, as they got more used to us and more relaxed with us, more interested in what we had to say. The frustrations weren't all that bad, but the fall term was the worst... [and] I contributed to it by making some damn fool mistakes... It was frustrating for me because it wasn't my baby." By the end of the fall term, he was frustrated enough with the students to warn them to commit themselves to living up to the Basic Agreements, or else not to come back after the Christmas break. His frustrations did not lead to serious attrition. Only a handful of students were separated from the school during the fall (and of those two came back, another graduated). John Holden's year was nothing like 1964-65 when the school dispatched fully a fifth of its population.

During the summer and fall of 1967, the Trustees' Search Committee intensified its search for David's permanent successor, under increasing impatient pressure from other board members, particularly board president Tom Debevoise. The committee comprised five members, including two headmasters – Dick Day of Exeter and John Verdery of Wooster (who had deferred his resignation from the board only out of consideration for appearances and David's feelings). The committee's three Woodstock alumni were its more dominant participants. Among them, both Roger Phillips '49 and Barbara Sproul '62 deferred in great part to the chairman, Gerry Freund.

FALL 1967 – SUMMER 1968

## Gerry Freund '48 letter to Tom Debevoise, September 29, 1967

*In some quarters there is also misunderstanding about John Holden's status. For example, yesterday my wife met the parent of a child to be enrolled this year, who asked whether John Holden has as yet agreed to remain permanently as headmaster. At the fine occasion for the Baileys last weekend, there seemed to be a tacit assumption on the part of at least some Woodstock area guests that the Holdens do not wish to remain indefinitely. I know that the Holdens do not wish to stay on. We would be fortunate if they agreed to a second year should we need them. But for their sake and for that of the school, it should be made clear to everyone that they are there for an interim period until the Board succeeds in finding a new headmaster.*

### Search Committee report to trustees, October 14, 1967

*The Committee has not identified a person it wishes to recommend for the headmastership at this time. Members of the Committee are unanimous in wanting to continue their intensive search activities and expect to make a recommendation to the Board at a later time.*

### Gerry Freund '48 letter to John Verdery, October 20, 1967

*The Search Committee's report was accepted by the Board at its recent meeting without discussion except that Tom Debevoise [the President] stated that the Board looks forward to a recommendation at its next meeting scheduled for January 18th in New York... The school year seems to have gotten off to a good start [on October 7]. There is a generally healthy and optimistic climate.*

### Gerry Freund '48 letter to John Holden, November 13, 1967

*Sending home a pregnant girl and the boy involved must have been a painful responsibility. Schools such as Woodstock and CRMS are leaders of independent coeducational schools because they exercise primary responsibility towards the needs and plights of individual young people rather than towards the hollow images of prestige and status of establishment-minded schools... no part of a school benefits when a student is expelled. Measured in terms of the objectives of a school like Woodstock, the event has to be taken as a failure, for all of us... I am convinced that schools merit full respect only if they are not afraid to meet head-on the needs, problems, and crises of the young people they admit even when these prove awkward to handle and when the school's image is in danger of being tarnished because the surrounding community demands banishment.*

*The work you are doing this year is vital to the future of the school. Alone the prospective re-evaluation insures that. I am also focussed on the school's future leadership. So much depends, I'm sure you agree, on our finding a headmaster and through him a faculty who can actively express the sympathetic yet realistic understanding of adolescents that David gave and you are giving, along with qualities of vision and imagination to let Woodstock, and through it other schools, contribute to the changes in American secondary education that are even more critical now than when you and David and Mrs. Hinton and others made your most significant contributions. Capacity for leading a vigorous academic program, something Woodstock has never had except in the classroom of a few teachers, is as far as I am concerned an inseparably important qualification for a new headmaster for the kind of school we seek to build. That is why I am willing to... put first a capacity for visionary, imaginative, and energetic moral, social, and intellectual leadership. Many schools pay lip service to this ideal, but few live up to it. I hope we won't be afraid to do so.*

## Gerald Freund '48 letter to John Verdery, November 15, 1967

*I have heard that there are definite problems at Woodstock this term. Students have been dropped; others have left. There may be, there appears to be, a problem of leadership. This points to a very important task for the new and permanent headmaster: to improve the faculty. I am quite sure that a number of faculty members must be dropped, the sooner the better, and replaced by far better people. For a new headmaster to do that fairly quickly requires self-confidence as well as good judgment, and especially in a very small school, ruthlessness.*

*Though I know him little, I think [one candidate] has it and that it is nicely wrapped in kid gloves...*

*By about the middle of December, I hope our Committee can meet [to decide] to recommend [an] appointment at the January meeting or whether we prefer to have John Holden remain a second year while we continue the search.*

## Gerald Freund '48 letter to Barbara Sproul '62, November 30, 1967

*I talked last night with [assistant headmaster David] Denman, Holden, and Debevoise. I think I told you that Paul Newlon is worried about the way the school is being led, and there is almost daily more evidence of difficulties. It is very likely that more students will be dropped and others will drop out before the end of the term. It is interesting that Buffy is John Holden's strongest supporter in his quite strict application of discipline.*

*From my conversations with John, I got the impression that he is far more sensitive, sympathetic and understanding of student and faculty problems than his letters would lead one to believe or, for that matter, than at least some students and faculty think. At least part of the problem seems to be in the way he approaches individual and school-wide problems. Even if many of the criticisms of him are valid, and I'm not sure of that, I do not think there is any reason for us to opt precipitously for a new person for next year.*

*Tom [Debevoise] is not as much out of touch with events at the school as I had been led to believe, but he is satisfied to know only the superficialities and is inclined to think that whatever Holden is doing is right. That may be overstating it, but it is his tendency."*

## Trustee Thomas Debevoise letter to school constituency, January 16, 1968

*The Board of Trustees takes pleasure in announcing that at its meeting on January 11, 1968, William Skinner Kilborne, Jr., ["Tawny"] was appointed headmaster of the Woodstock Country School, beginning with the fall term 1968. The unanimous decision of the Trustees followed the recommendation of their five-member Search Committee...*

*[At that time, Tawny had visited the school once, in December, during vacation, and had met no students and few faculty.]*

### Gerald Freund '48 letter to John Holden, January 23, 1968

*I was glad that the Board made a responsible decision, that is, I felt that by the end of the afternoon, each person there knew enough about Kilborne and the view taken of him by other Trustees so that their votes were taken thoughtfully with a real sense of the pros and cons. It was a firm but not an enthusiastic decision not only because there are drawbacks but, in my opinion, because everyone there valued so highly the job you are doing and would have found it easier simply to ask you and Dave [Denman] to continue shouldering the burden."*

### Gerald Freund '48 letter to Trustee Paul Newlon, March 21, 1968

*The minutes of the last Trustees Meeting recently sent to us give a fulsome [sic] recapitulation of our discussion about Bill Kilborne... with the number of copies floating around and the traditional laxity about who sees the minutes, they are bound to come to Kilborne's attention and to that of others. Thus, the purpose of the final formal unanimous vote has been undermined... I don't blame Barbara for submitting her full notes (although she knew that I disagreed with her interpretation of my reasoning), but it was irresponsible of Buffy and John Holden – apparently without further consultation – simply to publish and disseminate Barbara's notes.*

• • •

The *eventual* official minutes of the January 1968 board meeting reported the selection of Woodstock's next headmaster – William S. Kilborne, Jr., familiarly known as Tawny. In the traditional custom of boards, the minutes recorded that the vote was unanimous and without significant misgivings. Had this been a traditional board, such a traditional fiction might have been appropriate and effective in easing a difficult transition – especially if the misgivings were to prove groundless. But if the misgivings were well-grounded, Woodstock's board was ill-prepared, since the trustees continued to be erratic, unreliable and divided.

Only nine of 16 trustees attended the May meeting, which approved the January minutes which included at least two patently false statements: that "Roger Phillips, Barbara Sproul, John Verdery and Richard Day then commented on Mr. Kilborne's qualifications and *recommended his appointment*," and that "a vote on the resolution was called for, and it passed *unanimously.*"

The original official minutes, written by Barbara Sproul, with heavy editing by Buffy Dunker and others, accurately conveyed significant misgivings about Tawny, but falsely reported a unanimous vote. Even Barbara's unedited version of the minutes had a unanimous vote, though it presented a greater range of misgivings.

However, in Buffy's *unofficial* personal notes, the trustees' misgivings are presented in still greater detail and the vote is clearly *not* unanimous. There were two strong dissenters, Barbara Sproul and John Pierce, the faculty representative to the board. (John Holden, who had no vote, also had serious reservations about Tawny). Barbara Sproul and John Pierce, a generation apart in age, felt strongly enough so that, when the question was re-voted to make it unanimous, they both insisted on abstaining. They continued to abstain even when Gerry Freund suggested a resolution of the board's *full* support for Tawny.

Tawny's credentials were pretty good. There was near-unanimity that he was bright, able, confident and qualified to be a headmaster somewhere. As Paul Newlon pointed out, Tawny came from a socially prominent family in which his father was in *Who's Who in America,* his mother had been head of the Junior League and both had inherited wealth. But Tawny had rebelled against his background by going into teaching and going to Texas, where he had become assistant headmaster of the Fort Worth Country Day School in 1965. His own schooling was traditionally upper class: Allen-Stevenson, Hackley, Westminster and Yale '58 (B.A. in History, Debating Society, Yale Record, Elizabethan Club and St. Vitus senior society – all the while maintaining a gentleman's C average). Tawny's class rank at Yale was 549 out of 736. He failed two courses the first term of his freshman year, but thereafter avoided any serious academic difficulty or distinction, though he later earned his M.A. in English from NYU. Tawny had also served in the Hawaiian National Guard and taught at the Salisbury, Kew Forest and Searing Tutoring Schools before going to Fort Worth in 1964. But perhaps most impressive to the Woodstock board, Tawny had just won a prize for an article describing his "ideal school," which happened to feature high academic standards and year-round education.

Tawny' s professional and personal recommendations were excellent, as were the reports of most Woodstock board members who interviewed him. A few said at first they didn't like this somewhat combative bantam rooster of a man (he was 5'8", 160 pounds, in 1968), but later warmed up to him. Several mentioned his youth (he was just 31) as a drawback, though they were pleased he was married, with two children, a five-year-old boy and a four-year-old girl. Everyone, without exception, was impressed with his wife, Irene, a trained musician and music teacher of considerable poise and intelligence.

Those with misgivings acknowledged Tawny's strengths. Almost a month before Tawny's election, Barbara Sproul wrote the other members of the Search Committee conceding that Tawny "has many good qualities and qualifications... [including] his facile intelligence, wit and humour... he comes from a solid and conservative educational background from which he seems to have retained the best things and discarded many of the more useless accouterments. He has a marked concern for maintaining a high level of educational quality... one could hardly deny that he would make an excellent headmaster."

But, Barbara wondered, would Tawny be an excellent headmaster *for Woodstock*? She noted while he had worked at all boys boarding schools and coeducational day schools, he had neither attended nor worked at coeducational boarding schools (an experiential handicap which had proved disastrous in Jim Young's case just a year earlier.) Tawny did not just lack experience, he had, in fact, openly expressed serious personal and philosophical misgivings about such schools (as well as saying he would prefer Woodstock students call him "Mr. Kilborne" rather than "Tawny," although he wouldn't make an issue of it). Barbara added, "while I feel no qualms about Kilborne's imagination in dealing with educational issues nor about his sensitivity to philosophical questions concerning young people in general, I do feel uneasy about his imagination and sensitivity – empathy, if you will – in dealing with students themselves."

"Woodstock is a very special school," Barbara reminded the committee. "Its very unique strength (and perhaps simultaneously, its most vulnerable point for criticism in its potential for failure) is its concern for, and general success with, troubled children. Kilborne often speaks of academic excellence in terms of students who are 'successful' in conventional terms. It seems to me that any good administrator can, with bright and 'normal' kids, create a good and even experimental school. But Woodstock would then become a sort of second-rate co-ed Exeter; it would lose that rather indescribable character it has had in the past and which I feel is essential to its contribution to the general field of education. More concisely, what I fear with regard to Kilborne is that he would use Woodstock to further his educational dreams while disregarding the unique qualities of the school."

The other members of the committee were not persuaded by Barbara's argument. But others expressed misgivings at that January board meeting. John Holden doubted Tawny's commitment to the student work program and worried that he would turn Woodstock into an urban school in a rural setting, which "would be devastating." When John Pierce also worried about how much Tawny might change the school, Tom Debevoise assured him all major changes would have to be approved by the board. He did not explain what "major changes" might mean, or how this traditionally detached, absentee board would manage to control any changes.

Gerry Freund acknowledged, "If Barbara is right, we are making a mistake," but he concluded that on balance the choice was good even though the school would be different.

Roger Phillips said he was sold on Tawny and, if he was misled, Tawny could lead the school far astray; but Roger was willing to take that risk.

John Verdery of Wooster said he wasn't afraid of mistakes Tawny "will certainly make," since he didn't think Tawny would "take the bit in his teeth and run away from us."

Dick Day of Exeter advised the board to accept the reality that the school would be different.

Judge Bill Billings of Woodstock, who had questioned the Country School's first-name business when he joined the board the previous fall, said he was favorably impressed with Tawny's more traditional conception of the school.

Tom Debevoise again assured doubters the board wouldn't give Tawny "carte blanche for change – he must consult with us... He wants consultation and advice." Tom said he was sure Tawny would learn quickly on the job. After the vote, Tom telephoned Tawny, who agreed to take over as Woodstock's headmaster in September 1968, at a salary of $14,000 a year (which was $4,000 less than John Holden was then getting, but $2,000 more than David Bailey was paid in his last year).

Looking back on the choice years later, Tom Debevoise remained detached. He said he had no misgivings about Tawny at the time and Barbara's doubts were "very subjective, not elucidating," that it would have taken much more clear cut problems to block Tawny's election by the time it came before the full board – "Barb either had to win earlier, or lose." Tom also said as board president he relied on his search committee, dominated by the young alumni, to find the right candidate. "The search was so thorough and then they picked someone who didn't like kids."

Tom accepted no responsibility for the collective mistake he joined in making. He had no explanation for it. But it wasn't that hard a call, really. Susan

Webb, Ken Webb's wife, wasn't involved with the school at all by then, but she still knew Woodstock better than its Trustees. She knew Tawny slightly: "I met him out at Fort Worth. I know I was very much surprised when I heard that he was coming here because I would never associate him and his patterns of education and all the rest of it somehow with this school."

### Tom Vickers '68 interview, March 18, 1985

*Now we're talking summer of '67 – Sergeant Pepper's Lonely Hearts Club Band had just come out, the Grateful Dead and all the San Francisco groups had just started to hit – all of a sudden pot was like everywhere, it was Timothy Leary, it was acid, it was speed, it was all these drugs which I didn't really know that much about and by the end of that so-called 'Summer of Love,' not only did I know a lot about it but so did everyone else. When we came back to school in the fall, what had been a very kind of tentative situation now was full blown... And [my best friend] was kind of the ringleader of this little coterie of drug users, and it put me in kind of a double whammy position because I was elected to the student council or whatever it was, and I was given notice by a couple of teachers that... there was a genuine fear that we would be busted...*

*Now at this time it wasn't just a harmless maybe two or three people smoking pot, it turned into 20, 30, sometimes 40 people a night going up to Dodge City [by the amphitheater] and smoking pot, and it would be like you walk in there and the place would reek. I mean we're talking <u>outside,</u> but you could still smell it, and everybody's blowing pot – it was like it got out of hand...*

### John Holden interview, April 15, 1985

*It was like quarter past one in the morning, phone rang, phone by the bed, and I picked it up and said hello and [the dorm head] said, "John, I've just been all through French House and there's not a single student anywhere to be found. I think we'd better go down to Upwey..."*

*So I got up, put on my clothes, rushed over to Upwey – here's the whole school and they were giving it the cleaning of its life, and I mean mops, pails, every inch of the damn place was being gone over. By this time it was two o'clock in the morning and there they were. Of course they'd broken the rules by leaving the dorm in the middle of the night, but they'd done it for such a good reason that we couldn't exactly throw the book at them. That left a really good feeling for awhile... I was glad we didn't jump to any conclusions but went over and found out what was going on... Apparently it was a tradition...*

## Gerald Freund '48 letter to Tom Debevoise, February 26, 1968

*The Baileys had heard... that there had been another marijuana mess at the school with apparently several students directly involved and others upset by the handling of it all. Just what that was I am not sure except I know that David made brief critical references to John Holden's excessively lenient treatment of students, in this case apparently only suspending the kids involved rather than dismissing at least the "ringleader" who apparently is [a board member's] nephew. I don't know the details and do not intend to become inquisitive about them but as you know, my own attitude regarding the school's treatment of students who use marijuana as opposed to more dangerous stuff and also as opposed to individuals who sell and otherwise influence other students to use it is that they should be dealt with in terms of primarily their own problems rather than primarily the community problem they cause. Therefore, I do not think that anything like outright dismissal from the school should be an automatic consequence...*

## John Holden report to the trustees, May 4, 1968

*Ever since we came in the fall, I have been telling the students that they would have to handle the drug problem. We don't want to be policemen; if they don't handle it properly, it can destroy the school. We know there had been some marijuana used here toward the end of the fall term. I warned everyone that if they returned, it was with the tacit understanding that they wouldn't use drugs at the school. Shortly after we returned for the winter, a number of our more conscientious students asked for the help of some key faculty members, because they knew that some students had disregarded the agreement. The faculty still asked the students to deal with it...*

Tom Vickers was one of several students who came to assistant headmaster Dave Denman during the winter term, worried about student drug use (which was not unusual for the time; primarily, though not solely, marijuana, with LSD and other psychedelics becoming more common. Some uppers, fewer downers; rarely, if ever, was there any heroin or cocaine at that time). Tom was on the student council, but he wasn't trying to be a policeman, any more than the headmaster or the faculty were. But Tom was worried about the consequences of doing nothing; "I felt that if we didn't police ourselves, we were going to get policed – and if we got policed then it was going to be a lot worse than if we policed ourselves. So we had a student meeting first – where we had kind of the main core of hard core pot smokers et cetera and just said, hey, look, you know this is a very real problem and it's not that we don't like you or care about you or respect you as people, but what it comes down to is if we get caught, this place closes, trustees don't give money, it gets real ugly and will mean the end of the school, as we know it. Now I really like it here and you really like it here, you don't want to see this place closed down, so let's cool it. And that worked for awhile."

In one of the student meetings with the headmaster, another student asked John Holden why he didn't just kick out all the dopers, as other schools did. John wondered what that would accomplish – "then we talked about the alternatives, and the thing that we all agreed on was if we could really get students talking with their parents so that they and their parents were really communicating again, then a lot could happen. And some day we might find a way of dealing with this really incredible problem." So John wrote letters to the parents of the fourteen or so known drug users and got mostly positive responses. In the spring, he reported to the trustees: "We are still working with these people, still communicating and what is more, so are their parents communicating – for the first time in years, in some cases."

Communication wasn't always enough. When the inevitable next episode came to John's attention some weeks later, he decided to expel "the two habitual [marijuana] users, who were also the most articulate advocates of the habit." But before he could act, the community meeting presented an alternative plan "for dealing with the situation without expulsions. Many of the most conscientious students were behind this. They wanted to work with their friends, much as Alcoholics Anonymous people work, to rid them of the habit. After thinking it over, I agreed; but one boy, a senior, needed something more. I sent him home for the rest of the term to communicate regularly with his parents, to finish his assignments, to get some help from a psychiatrist. He's back now, along with all of the others."

John told the trustees in May that he believed the school was "clean," though that belief probably represented equal parts of wishful thinking on his part and serious discretion on the part of students and faculty. In retrospect years later, John had no better solution; "I'm not sure we did the right thing, but we seemed to have solved the drug problem certainly. The school really turned around from the fall until spring as a result of our getting together... That, I think, was perhaps the most valuable thing that we did, was to generate a situation where really the students and the parents had to sit down together and talk these things out... Our way of dealing with the whole situation was to try to trust them, and to trust the majority of the students – and to put it up to them to live up to the best that was in them..." He reiterated his belief that drug use at Woodstock that year was largely limited to marijuana – though he was always savvy enough to acknowledge there could have been things going down that he didn't know about. Tom Vickers remembered the school remaining relatively abstemious until late spring, when "it was scary – people were taking acid, people were tripping on mescaline, it was really extreme out-there stuff... and graduation day everybody was stoned out of their gourd."

By the time of graduation, most of the school was in a celebratory mood after surviving a long, uncertain, sometimes difficult year. The community was beginning to realize that there could be a Country School without David Bailey after all, that it might be a somewhat different place, but it could retain its humane values and strong feeling of family. The community was developing a new sense of itself throughout John Holden's interim year and it expressed that sense most clearly through the re-evaluation process. Working out the Basic Agreements in the fall, creating a workable system of government, confronting drug use – for John Holden "it all stems back to the evaluation. The lack of this kind of thing <u>was</u> mentioned in the previous evaluation and the students were a little nervous about what was going to happen. And they were very much aware by that time it was up to them whether the school passed the evaluation or not."

Similarly, with the faculty: "Those teachers who had been through it were very much more aware of their weaknesses and their problems than I was, even though I'd read the report. When they saw I really was concentrating on doing right by the evaluation, they were all cooperation. And one of the things I was able to do was to persuade them to disregard the attitude that David had toward the whole thing and really look at it as the best opportunity for us to see what was really good about the school."

## John Holden letter to all at WCS, April 1968

When I came to WCS I was ignorant of what was really unique and great about this school... In the months since I took over I have seen great strengths that must be preserved and demonstrated, first to the evaluators and then to the new headmaster. The evaluators are here only from a Sunday evening through a Tuesday, so that we must help them find these strengths in a hurry. If possible, we must acquaint Mr. Kilborne with them before he gets here.

See if you agree with me that these are some of this school's greatest strengths. First is the student run work program – a really unique feature. Second is the fact that students are given a chance to learn from experience, to learn from their own mistakes and failures. Third, students have the freedom to speak out, in meeting, in the dining room, on the bulletin board. Fourth, students have taken initiative for many necessary improvements in the school. Fifth, people who have never been interested in school before may find a challenge here and take off into the orbit of successful academic achievement, and sixth, faculty, students, parents and trustees are anxious to have the school experiment in meaningful ways with the academic program. Examples of this are the students who completed geometry in five weeks, and the group who are studying Eastern Thought with a student leader...

We all have to do what is right to preserve the basic philosophy of the school. Where I have set limits, it has been because I know that schools without limits are doomed. You may have trouble understanding why I am anxious to allow a freedom of dress and hairstyles that clearly says, 'This school is in rebellion against a U.S. policy that drafts young men at eighteen but won't let them vote or drink until they are twenty-one' But then I say, 'you are campused if your hair is below your collar, your eyes or your ears.'

What I am really trying to put across to you and to the world is that WCS is an activist school: 'We believe in the right to object to what is wrong in our society. But we have our limits. We stop short of LSD and 'pot,' and free love and complete anarchy'

Non-profit independent schools depend on contributions in order to exist. Tuition fees never do pay for buildings, only for operational *expenses. The school would soon cease to exist without financial help from outside, and there's very little chance of getting financial help unless a school can show that it has a disciplined program that proves successful...*

*Remember that the Board of Trustees is committed to preserving the basic philosophy of the school, at the same time it is pledged to improve the school's academic standing. The new headmaster was chosen with that in mind. I am pledged to you and to the Board to try to make the transition as easy as possible for all concerned. Perhaps if we keep our eyes on the overall goals, we won't mind the little things so much, and we'll be willing to make some sacrifices for the school we want to preserve.*

### Buffy Dunker, first WCS Alumni Newsletter, spring 1968

*John Holden's year here has been very good. We've learned from him and he from us. We miss David, of course, all the time, but since we can no longer turn to him for advice and approval, when we turn to John we find him always ready to discuss things with as and encouraging us to solve our own problems.*

### John Holden, Independent School Bulletin, October 1974

*The interim head really did nothing but hold a mirror up to the school, let everybody see what it was really like, and then encouraged everybody to make it the best school of its kind in the country. Everything good about it was already there. I was able to remind the board of what it was they were trying to perpetuate. When we left [Woodstock] after a year, we felt a warm sense of identification with the school, its philosophy, the faculty and the student body. If we had to stay another year we might not have been quite as objective about it all.*

• • •

John Holden had started preparing for the re-evaluation early the previous September, meeting with Ralph West, Director of Evaluation, for the New England Association of Colleges and Secondary Schools, to review Woodstock's previous bad report and to discuss ways to improve the school. Enlisting West as an ally, Holden persuaded the association to accept someone from outside the region as chairman of the evaluating committee, Henry Scattergood, principal of the Germantown Friends School in Philadelphia. "After hesitating because I have never attended or taught in a boarding school and, therefore, would probably not be sufficiently sensitive to some of the problems and issues that administration, faculty and students face in a twenty-four hour/day situation," Scattergood accepted the job.

When Ralph West visited Woodstock in November, his easy-going, matter-of-fact manner helped to dispel much of the fear and resentment left over from the previous year's evaluation. For his part, West expressed optimism to John Holden, "it's hard to put one's finger on, but I sense a more positive atmosphere about the school than I did on my last visit this past January. They are fortunate in having you with them." West later wrote to William Barclay of the Commonwealth School in Boston, a member of the 1966 evaluation committee, asking him to serve again and noting John Holden "has made the evaluation of Woodstock in many ways the focus of his activities. A permanent headmaster has been selected, and I think to a great extent the resolution of many of Woodstock's concerns are the direct result of the committee of which you were a member."

Scattergood, meanwhile, visited the school in December, both to meet with John and two trustees, as well as to accept John's invitation for a two-family get-together. John also arranged for a Vermont Department of Education representative to take part in the evaluation. On campus, all of the faculty and many of the students took part in the formal self-evaluation. In mid-March, with everyone and everything apparently in order, John invited the evaluators to join the Holdens and as many Woodstock trustees as could make it (in all, ten trustees took part in the evaluation) for cocktail and dinner at the Giles House on Sunday evening, April 21.

All this careful cultivation bore fruit as intended. Despite last minute changes in the committee membership – including the loss of the carefully cultivated Scattergood because of illness – the committee's visit went smoothly. The new chairman, George St. John of the Cambridge School of Weston and a long-time friend of the Holdens, indicated before the committee left campus that its report would be positive. As John Holden wrote to a trustee, "I have no doubt at all about the outcome." The next week, he read the trustees part of a letter from George St. John: "It doesn't always happen that an official task becomes a heart warming, happy, and significant personal experience. That's what came about in this visit of mine under your roof and in your office, John, and in the school… To pull things together at the school, set some high standards and persuade older and younger to live by them – and to do it without abrasive jolts and collisions is a superb achievement. I like the way you have tried to connect David Bailey's best insights and hopes with the ongoing thinking of the school. So – my hat is off!"

When friendly Ralph West unofficially sent along a copy of the committee's report before the association acted on it, the good news was confirmed. The minutes of the first faculty meeting of the summer term noted, "In connection with the evaluation, John Holden felt that we had done something of a 'snow job,' the report being perhaps more favorable than it should have been. However, the report caught the essence of the school which is very important." John also "emphasized that there is still a great deal to be done to make this a really good school." When Buffy Dunker saw the committee's report, she wrote John; "You are right about its being too nice to us – but I like that so much better than the opposite. When it can be sent to others I very much want David to get a copy. He'll be so pleased to see that this committee understood what we say and do."

The committee's report, officially accepted by the association in mid-July and formally approved in December 1968, presented a thorough and largely complimentary overview of the school. The report also noted continuing under-enrollment, budget deficits, some weakness in the faculty, difficulties with the new pass-fail grading system (which would last less than a year) and problems with the Four Term Plan, as well as the absence of any formal school government and the need for a more clearly articulated philosophy.

The report added: "Mr. Holden seems to us to have built in a few months a remarkably close relationship with the students and faculty. He has guided the students gradually to a better awareness of their own and the school's best standards and to a greater acceptance of their own responsibility for the whole school community and for each other. It is fully true to the spirit of the school that Mr. Holden has not imposed a new pattern superficially, but has helped everybody to break through to new understandings by patient, open discussion. Faculty and students have been able to face difficult situations as partners, with mutual respect and a shared sense of obligation. It will of course be Mr. Kilborne's and Mr. Denman's task to continue and strengthen the positive spirit which seems to be clearly alive in students and faculty right now."

One reason for this positive spirit was John's ability to engage students, to respond to them well or badly, but always as human beings. In this he was like David, or any other effective headmaster, although John's style tended to be blunter than most. He had frequent confrontations with Aaron Cohen, the SDS leader, who was a constant irritant (as Cohen pretty much described himself). After one row in the spring, John wrote Aaron: "I'm sorry for both blasts I aimed at you last night; and I don't know why I went back to that happening of over a month ago. Actually, I couldn't help burning from the insults you leveled at me last night. They hurt particularly deeply because they hit right at the heart of the thing I've been devoting my life to for the last thirty years, HELPING BOYS AND GIRLS build their own ideal schools, both the buildings and the rules. I agree with so many of the things you are fighting for, but I do so hope you'll be a builder, not a destroyer. Most students I've talked to believe that this school is a lot nearer to their ideal than most. If so, it is worth working for. We welcome constructive ideas as well as constructive work."

John said the same thing publicly, once in Look Magazine in response to the White House's annual, cliché-ridden congratulations to high school graduates. Answering President Johnson's platitudes about individuality, independence and liberty, John Holden wrote: "This doesn't sit well with the eighteen-year-old who has just registered with the local draft board and found that he is now a slave to a system that may dictate his life for ten years... If he protests having to fight in a war he doesn't believe in, he is subject to a procedure which is entirely extra-legal... Liberty? They can't even vote for another three years. They are considered traitors for objecting to a war that they feel is immoral. The fact that they can't have any feeling of independence as long as these things are true is the biggest reason for the sit-ins, the uprisings and the riots. It is the fuel on which the violently anti-American student organizations exist. When the Government ends our participation in Viet-Nam, changes the draft procedure completely and allows the vote to eighteen-year-olds, you'll see an immediate change..." (John was unexpectedly right, the majority of those early-emancipated young voters supported Nixon and Reagan and their values, not the humane idealism he'd hoped for and expected.)

Privately, John Holden was more ambivalent. As Susan Webb recalled, "John and Ann Holden, whom we had known when they were first at Putney and we were at Vermont Academy, came to dinner one night, I think it was just after, it was either while they were there that one year in the school, I guess it was then, we had a great time swapping stories of our first experiences of teaching in schools and, you know, all this sort of thing. But they were simply – I think John just didn't want to cope. He couldn't feel that he had the kind of – I got the impression that it was just a job he didn't want to take up from where he'd left off because it was just going to be too much to try and do it and he probably might not succeed.... He did the one year interim and didn't want any more.... I think they felt quite floored with the situation. My impression was they just thought it was too big a job for them to want to be able to even take it on permanently in any way."

## FALL 1967 – SUMMER 1968

With his essential re-accreditation job finished, John Holden continued to disengage himself from the school during the summer term (including a two weeks' absence to go to his son's wedding in Ireland). The school presented him with no new crises or severe challenges. With too many problems and too little coherent support, John had begun to pull back even in the previous fall term, retreating into his professionalism and achieving what he could. The symbolic key which David gave John in September had not been enough, the school to which it belonged no longer existed and John did not pass the key on to his successor. In June, he wrote Ralph West: "I have one term to go at this interesting school. I am glad to have had the experience, but I have to admit that I will be glad when it is over."

Buffy's harpsichord: when Buffy Dunker retired in the spring of 1970, the Trustees held a party at Upwey at which they gave her a harpsichord.

WCS student body Fall 1968: each and every student drawn by Mark Smith (front row, fifth from left)

Girl-eyed
Gatherer of daisies

FALL 1967 – SUMMER 1968

Phil Krauss '72, Joe Danciger '71, David Petit '72

Malcolm Clark, Alonzo Whitehead

Peter Clemons

Woody Urban '72

Dinah Prince '71,
Karen Sanderson '71

Pauline Pharr Chinese teacher

Jeff Peabody '72, Tootie Alderson '72,
Jeff Greene '72

FALL 1967 – SUMMER 1968

Carly O'Donnell '72

Virginia Wood, English teacher

Farm crew: Bruce Fairweather (left) and students

Soccer players from front, l. to r.): Robert Poore '73, Robert Demuth '74, Dana Good '72, Bobby Silverman '74, John Williams '72, and (foreground) Marty Fisher '74

Bruce Fairweather, Tootie Alderson '72

JDI (Jim Ingerson), music teacher

French House boys dorm burning, April 7, 1969

CHAPTER NINE

# Summer 1968 – Summer 1970

## I

**Tawny Kilborne, letter to Search Committee, January 3, 1968**

*Essentially it strikes me that the philosophy and spirit of the Woodstock Country School coincide remarkably with my own. In this respect, I would be far more inclined to fight for continuity than to make radical departures. The school's intense awareness of the student as an individual, its sensitivity and respect for the painful questioning and rebellion that many adolescents, especially the interesting ones, go through – its courageous willingness to experiment and to blaze trails that others may follow – these are the qualities that have given the school its distinctive flavor in the past and that I believe should continue to distinguish it in the future.*

*Transition years are always rough, no matter how competent the interim administration, but they can serve as a useful buffer to a new head. It is my feeling, and I believe the Board's, that after this year the school needs clearly formulated policies and firm leadership in their orderly implementation...*

*In brief, I would hope to bring to Woodstock somewhat more rigorous academic standards and sound, stable, efficient administration. I would try to retain at Woodstock the profound, personal concern for the welfare of each student, the close relationship between students and faculty, the notion that education is more exciting and productive when it springs from a dialogue between faculty and students rather than from faculty pronouncements, the esteem in which all kinds of artistic creative activity appear to be held and an atmosphere that not only permits but encourages innovation.*

### Tawny Kilborne, letter to John Holden, April 29, 1968

*It struck me that one of the most attractive features of Woodstock is the marked independence and individuality of everyone associated with it – I think your advice about the dangers of getting too specific too soon is absolutely sound. There's no point in intensifying the instability that everyone feels when a new man takes over and besides, nobody likes the idea that somebody else is out to "reform" either him or his institution. Thus, if people ask me to talk about my plans for the school's future,* **I'll be properly evasive and vacuous – qualities people are quite accustomed to and comfortable with during an election year.** *[emphasis added]*

### Roger Phillips '49 fundraising letter, May 8, 1968

*One of the high points of the weekend [May 4-5, 1968] was a question and answer exchange between the new headmaster, William Kilbourne [sic], and the students. I had to return to New York and could not attend but when I called Buffy the following evening to get a report on how it went, her reply was 'fantastic.' She went on to say that Mr. Kilbourne's responses to students were very well received and after one answer the audience broke into spontaneous applause. The student body was very anxious to know what kind of a guy they would be confronted with next year and it is so good that this dialogue engendered respect and enthusiasm on both sides.*

### John Holden interview, April 15, 1985

*When [Tawny] came to the school and talked to the students in the spring, he didn't sound authoritarian. He sounded as though he heartily approved of the way we were doing things, the openness and the letting the kids have a voice. But in the fall he immediately rescinded the goodness that I think the students were very proud to have gotten out of the community meetings... I think that if there was 80% of the faculty and 80% of the students in favor of something and I was against it, I would have to bow to the majority... But he had to have the final veto. The students didn't like it one little bit when he immediately changed that, and they felt that he had misled them in what he said when he came in the spring.*

### Buffy Dunker interview, June 1, 1986

*That spring I pushed [Tawny] a little about his relationship with the students and the student council, and consulting with the students, and backing them when they proposed something. And he made all the right answers. He just said all the right things, and I remember that very clearly, but I did push him about it, because that was where my doubts were, and he answered in the way I would have liked to have him answer, so I thought he was going to be OK. And that's why it was such an incredible shock to me in the fall when he, before the kids even got back, was making changes that applied to them... without any consultation. That was a big disillusionment for me... I remember talking with him before the kids came back, when he was talking about the changes, and I said, "That's not fair." But that made no difference to him.*

• • •

Tawny's being less than straightforward with the students and faculty curiously mirrored the way the Trustees had been less than straightforward with him. The day before he met with the community in May 1968, he had attended a board meeting where he learned to his surprise that the school was not in as good shape, especially financially, as he had been led to believe. The 1967-68 budget approved by the board in October had a projected margin of $1,785. By May, that surplus had become a projected deficit of $28,302 (and would become a final deficit of $32,117 – more than eight times greater than any previous Country School deficit). The projected deficit for 1968-69 was $43,140, almost one tenth of the operating budget. Woodstock had recorded deficits only twice in the preceding 21 years – $3,992 for 1950-51 and $2,713 for 1966-67. In great part the new deficits were caused by the Four-Term Plan, particularly by under-enrollment by almost 50 per cent during the summer terms. John Holden had improved overall enrollment somewhat and summer enrollment by half. He left Tawny with a full school in the fall. In her treasurer's report, Buffy observed the added costs of the Search Committee and the re-evaluation would not be repeated, but nevertheless added that "it is obvious that we must seek additional operating funds for next year."

The only action the board took was to send out a fundraising letter signed by Roger Phillips (excerpted above), which asked for money almost as an afterthought, with skimpy results. Several Trustees promised to do some serious local soliciting over the summer, but the results of those efforts were equally skimpy. Although general giving to the school had improved during John Holden's year, the total number of gifts continued to decline due to the collapse of the 20th Anniversary Campaign (which also showed a deficit). The Parents Association Annual Giving total of $3,589 was less than at any time since the parents were first organized in 1951. And Larry Roberts's last report as business manager reiterated the need for hundreds of thousands of dollars in maintenance and new buildings, particularly repairs to the dorms and Upwey, as well as a new infirmary, music building and dorm. The school would have been in much worse shape had not David, before he retired, arranged to sell off some land to Trustee Irene Crowe, whose property abutted the school. Mrs. Crowe bought 60 acres on Morgan Hill, a back pasture area, for $40,000 (somewhat less than the estimated market value since Mrs. Crowe agreed to certain development limitations and to let the school to continue to use the property). When the sale was completed in early 1968, the school used the proceeds of $40,000 for operating expenses.

Near the end of his first Woodstock board meeting, according to the minutes, "Mr. Kilborne pointed out that the deficits could be decreased in various ways, such as by raising tuition, increasing enrollment, and/or cutting down the number of faculty" – all three of which he would soon do, or try to do, with sometimes fractious results. Buffy wrote in her personal notes that Tawny "didn't expect the seriousness of the financial picture – next year's deficit is mostly salaries." She also foreshadowed a dominant theme of Tawny's headmastership: during a discussion of foundation support for a national conference on the Four-Term Plan, Tawny thought it best to "wait for support for 4TP until school and Headmaster are united in one direction."

The following evening, after the dedication of the Franzen dorm as the David W. Bailey House ("such a marvellous symbol of David's vision and pioneering spirit," said Roger Phillips), Tawny met with the Woodstock community. He was "properly evasive and vacuous" as he had promised John Holden (see above), creating widespread expectations of a relaxed and open style of leadership when he took over the headmastership in the fall.

### Tom Debevoise letter to all Trustees, September 9, 1968

*I talked to our new headmaster today, his first day in residence (his furniture arrives tomorrow)... Bill [Kilborne] seemed well pleased with the outlook on students and faculty for the fall term and eager and anxious to get to work. Let me remind you all that it will be truly remarkable (and probably unprecedented) if his administration does not run into some rhubarbs and rough weather the first year or two, but I have every confidence in him and for the future of the school under his administration and I know you will all stand behind him if difficult times are encountered.*

### Tawny Kilborne, letter to fundraiser Robert Torrence, September 17, 1968

*Many thanks for your letter of September 10th and your offer to come to the school to discuss the services that your firm might offer us. However, the timing is wrong. Before giving any serious attention to fund-raising, I want to make sure that there is perfect agreement between the Board and me about the direction that this school is to take in the future. Naturally, a general philosophic agreement was reached before I accepted this position. However, there are one or two important points that I wish to take up with the Board at the annual meeting on October 5th and in committee meetings during the succeeding months. In short, I want to find out precisely where the school is going before I even begin to worry about how to raise the funds to get there.*

## Tawny Kilborne interview, July 27, 1984

*What attracted me to the Country School was really the opportunity to implement my own philosophy of curriculum. I really liked the Four-Term Plan, I really liked those focussed units that could take sort of a deep slash out of a cake instead of just skimming the frosting off the top which is the sort of thing a survey course does. I really liked the idea of being able to institute courses in music history and art history, in psychology, economics – areas that I think everybody should be exposed to at the secondary level and then they can choose whether or not to pursue them further in college. That's probably what primarily attracted me to the school...*

*My charge, I felt, was to clean the place up, to strengthen the faculty, to put the school on a sound economic base, to get rid of the rampant drugs – generally to tighten up – and I felt that the Trustees gave me a really free hand...They were very supportive during the first year chronicled on [my] calendar, which shows at least a major crisis a week.*

## Tawny Kilborne memo to all students, September 24, 1968

*School administrations are often too quick to take upon themselves responsibilities that can, in fact, be discharged only by the students. For example, an administration can force all students into four hours of supervised study halls, but only the students can accept the responsibility (and the pleasure) of working and learning. If the students do not accept this responsibility, the study halls are futile; if the students do accept this responsibility, the study halls are superfluous and an affront. Nor can an administration be effective chaperone or policemen. Here again, the students must regulate themselves and either accept the ethical and social mores of the community, or leave the community. Enforcement of these mores is everyone's responsibility, the first term ninth grader's as much as the headmaster's, because the very life of the school depends upon everyone's acceptance of certain minimum standards of conduct.*

*In May [1968] I said I preferred rules to be few in number, but that these few be enforced with great thoroughness. I haven't changed. I would like to see students responsible for handling their own time wisely. However, I think the school is obliged to help those who fail by structuring their day for them, but this is a last resort. Perhaps this kind of student belongs in an environment more structured than any of us want WCS to be.*

## SUMMER 1968 – SUMMER 1970

• • •

During the September vacation, Tawny decided to abolish the group system (which was barely functioning anyway), to reduce student sign-out procedures to a minimum, to return to a numerical grading system, to re-organize the work program and to institute a formal system of daily, written reports on students. He also created the new position of Dean of Students so that, as he put it, "the students will have someone to turn to who has the wisdom, the time, and the inclination to counsel with them."

Drawing a distinction between the headmaster's work and counseling students was something new to Woodstock, where the family feeling of the place tended to make the headmaster the inevitable counselor of last resort. Since the Dean of Students was also expected to handle discipline, too, it was structurally dysfunctional, requiring one person to dispense both punishment and advice based on mutual trust. Only one person managed to do both with some balance and she did it for only one term years later. The Dean of Students position also undercut the Woodstock tradition of shared responsibility among faculty members, especially through the advisor system, in which each faculty member was expected to develop as full a relationship as possible with a handful of students. That system was always something of a gamble and it had worked less and less well with a weaker and weaker faculty during the middle sixties. But its fundamental premise of expecting personal responsibility from the adults as much as the students remained a sound basis on which to build, or re-build, a healthy community.

Tawny chose Buffy to be the first Dean of students, hoping to make the most of her 22 years of Woodstock experience. She was then the last of the old guard that had, in 1963, formed the backbone of the faculty. Larry Roberts had left the school during the summer of 1968, unwilling to take a chance on the possibility of still more years of turmoil with an inexperienced headmaster. Even if Buffy hadn't been inappropriate by age, interest and instinct for the job, the Dean of Students would still have been a confusion of reality for any small school where the head is inevitably the dominant figure and the final arbiter of all important issues. As a result, the Dean's job soon became just another level of bureaucracy that, while clerically helpful, also distanced Tawny further from students.

When he announced these and other changes to the faculty two days before the fall term began, no one objected. Tawny further informed faculty that they could not grant incompletes in any courses without his approval, that they could not dismiss classes early without his approval, and that he expected them to wear "appropriate clothing" at school – all without incident. He introduced "Commendation and Warning" slips, multiple-carbon forms intended to help keep track of a student's performance, with copies for the student's file, the Dean of Students, the student's advisor and the student's parents – but no copy for the student. The only question on which Tawny invited the faculty's deliberation was what to do about the Pass/Fail grading system. Even there he made clear his intention to re-establish numerical grading for college application purposes at the very least.

On a Sunday evening two days later, Tawny met with the whole school for the first time as headmaster. Neither Buffy's private warnings, nor anything said in the faculty meeting had prepared Tawny for the students' reaction to his decisions. Tawny saw himself just doing his job, perhaps even being too liberal about it. The students, especially the older students, saw his actions as arbitrary and reactionary, attacking the school's longstanding community involvement in running itself. Tawny hadn't seen it coming and years later still didn't seem to understand why he should have.

"That meeting was at the Giles House, all the kids were in that huge room," Tawny recalled. "One of the kids... explained to me that the way things worked at the Woodstock Country School is that we have a community here and it's one man, one vote – every teacher has a vote, you have a vote, I have a vote, and it's a democracy, and we make the decisions about how the school is run. This is the way things are done. And I took about 20 seconds to ponder that before responding. I said, 'Now I'm going to announce my first administrative act.' I said, 'I hereby, forthwith suspend all powers of the community, the community no longer has the power to legislate anything.' And in that way, in one master stroke, I won the animosity of the entire student body in five minutes... I think there was silence. There certainly wasn't shouting and waving of fists or anything. I think it was just a sort of shocked silence."

Tawny's misperception then, as well as years later, was that the students had been allowed to run the school. Yet he had the records to the contrary, the minutes of the community meetings of the fall of 1967, which described a very different reality. Tawny would later turn this record over to a psychiatric colleague who was analyzing the school at Tawny's request. Whatever the subtleties of the community meeting, John Holden had always been clear about his ultimate authority as headmaster and had never relinquished his veto over the community, no matter how loath he may have been to exercise it. In July, just before Tawny took over, the community meeting had approved a proposal, submitted to the faculty for approval, to establish a system for overriding the headmaster's veto, but no such system was ever enacted. At the same time, in the midst of an apparent drug emergency that summer, the faculty, too, was so deferential to the headmaster that it decided it couldn't set policy because John Holden was away and the new man had not yet taken over. In other words, Tawny was reacting to a challenge that didn't exist, defending his authority when there was absolutely no serious challenge to it.

Meeting with the trustees the following weekend, "Mr. Kilborne requested that the Board adopt a statement he had prepared on responsibility and authority in the Woodstock Country School. He stated that the purpose of the statement was to have in writing a specific policy in regard to authority in order to resolve the confusion among students and faculty which has resulted from action taken by the previous headmaster" (Tawny himself later excised this dishonest reference to John Holden from the official record). Tawny's statement of authority read: "All responsibility and authority in the Woodstock Country School rests with the Board of Trustees, which has delegated to the headmaster the responsibility and authority of carrying out its policies and directing the administration of the school. The only responsibility and authority that students or faculty have is the responsibility and authority the headmaster delegates to them, and he may withdraw such powers as well as extend them. The Board understands that the headmaster is eager to delegate authority to both students and faculty, but the Board expects the headmaster to move cautiously in these areas, since the Board has entrusted the headmaster with the administration of the school at a very critical time in the school's development."

The trustees, many of whom were still attuned to taking their cues from their headmaster, reluctantly approved the statement "to be used at the discretion of the headmaster." The draft minutes of the meeting added: "The Board expressed a desire that the headmaster attempt to clarify the policy verbally [sic], using the written statement only as a last resort" – but Tawny excised this from the official record as well.

At that same meeting, Tawny suggested the school increase its enrollment to meet its budget needs. The board refused. Tawny recommended some radical changes in David Bailey's Four-Term Plan. The board reaffirmed its faith in the plan, but formed a committee to study it. Tawny urged the board to raise enough money to pull the school out of debt. The board approved an immediate fundraising letter, as well as a major campaign in 1969 to be headed by Trustee Johnnie Mayer (a fancy financier from Greenwich with a house in Reading, Vermont). Mayer promised Woodstock much, including $100,000 from an anonymous donor, but he resigned halfway through his term without delivering anything. Finally, Tawny pleaded with the board for active leaderships: "The school's greatest needs are a sense of direction and a sense of reality, and only the Board of Trustees, determining what it wants the school to be in five or ten years, can give the school this sense of direction."

Perhaps this collective mishegas could have been avoided had Tawny been less "evasive and vacuous" during his hiring process. Or the board might have actually listened to Barbara Sproul and John Pierce when they articulated what turned out to be accurate misgivings about Tawny. But this was a board with very limited experience actually taking responsibility for the school for which it was responsible. The established pattern had been for the board to take its direction from an experienced, self-assured headmaster. With an evasive headmaster who lacked experience and required reassurance in black and white, a school that had prided itself on not needing a written philosophy was especially vulnerable.

### III

### Gerry Freund '48 letter to Tustee Paul Newlon, October 30, 1968

*The more I hear, the more convinced I am that Tawny is doing an excellent job despite difficult circumstances. Candor and mutual trust are leading to an understanding with students who seem to respect his authority. He has given students new freedom, defended their choice of dress and hair length, and seems to be satisfying their need for setting definite limits on behaviour.*

### WCS students strike manifesto, November 14, 1968

*The Nitty Gritty #1 – from the Benevolent Society of Anarchists*
    *A CALL FOR JUSTICE*
*"For we wrestle not against flesh and blood but against principalities, against the rulers of the darkness of this world, against spiritual wickedness in high places." Ephesians 6:12*
    *STATEMENT OF PURPOSE*
*We, the students of Woodstock Country School, having attempted to make ourselves understood through the legal and prescribed channels, and having failed, now have no alternative but to employ underground and, we hope, more forceful methods. Utilizing full powers of TRUTH*

*tempered with satire, we urge the realization of our ideas on the administration of our community. These being: that power unacknowledged is no power at all; that we are attempting to create a NEW society, a workable utopia; that we refuse to be subjugated by a society that we reject; that we are human beings to be dealt with as such. And furthermore we feel that it is better to reject those things which may be good than to employ those things that may be bad...*

"It's trembling on the brink / One push and down it sink" – Wm. Burroughs

### Tawny Kilborne report to trustees, February 6, 1969

*The strike, though a harrowing experience for all concerned, nevertheless resulted in substantive and needed improvement in communications. After the strike, everyone was elated, from the most liberal student to the most conservative faculty member. The fundamental source of student dissatisfaction was, I believe, my remoteness, my unavailability relative to the omnipresence on campus of both of my predecessors. This is not a dilemma susceptible to easy solution. I feel that I must spend more time on organization and administration than have my predecessors, and I am unwilling to sacrifice the time any father owes to his small children (at home). This term I have been able to counsel more with individual students than last term. Nevertheless, I feel I will never be able to give the students the time and attention that they want and that they are accustomed to.*

• • •

Just two weeks before the student strike, Gerry Freund's unintentionally hilarious letter to Paul Newlon vividly illustrated the wishful thinking, the denial even, that the Trustees needed to delude themselves. "Candor and mutual trust" didn't exist between the Trustees and their headmaster, never mind between the headmaster and the student body who no longer believed his "evasive and vacuous" political lies. Tawny's calling the strike "a harrowing experience for all," reflects his own need for self-dramatization more than any other reality at the school. Student strikes in 1969 were something of a fad, after all. This headmaster had expressed his own sense of the time by coming to soccer practice in his Army fatigues, which might have been cool had he done it with any sense of irony.

The student strike began early Thursday morning, November 14, 1968. At least two faculty members knew it was coming the night before and they called Tawny, but neither he nor they did anything to head it off. In February, some trustees criticized the teachers, but not Tawny, for their inaction. Exeter headmaster Dick Day argued: "it is the responsibility of a group of teachers to redirect this kind of dissension. The effect of allowing a strike encourages this kind of a solution to a problem and makes a recurrence likely... It is essential that the initiative and control be in the hands of school authorities." Gerry Freund disagreed; arguing that the strike was a positive event and Tawny and the faculty had behaved with the right mixture of patience and authority. Tawny said he didn't think another strike was likely and he was right. He had promised immediate expulsion for any future strikers.

Far from "a harrowing experience for all," the strike was cheerful and relaxed for most, a pure non-violent direct action, not an attack but a refusal to participate "tempered with satire." As the students made explicit, "This strike is entirely internal in nature... All of our demands are flexible in form." Instead of going to classes, all the students gathered in Owen Moon House to discuss and formulate proposals. If any students did not join the student meeting, they laid low, for none was seen in the main building. Contrary to late-sixties rebellious vogue, Woodstock's students did not "occupy" the dorm, they threw up no barricades, they destroyed no property. Faculty members freely came and went all day, some even took part in the discussions. But Tawny was not one of them. He refused to visit the students in Owen Moon House, remaining holed up in his office, talking only with intermediaries.

In his frequently unreliable account to the trustees in February, Tawny portrayed the strike as much more of a confrontation than it was. According to Tawny, the strike began at his front door at 6 a.m., with strikers tacking up their statement. Kathy Cronkite (daughter of Walter Cronkite) said she was one of the "strike ringleaders" and said of Tawny that he was "not the school's finest hour as far as I was concerned." (In March 1969, faculty meeting minutes complained of her: "Won't wear shoes in Upwey.") Without naming any students, Tawny included most of the strike manifesto in his report to the trustees in February – *omitting* the parts italicized below, in effect denying the students their authenticity:

"This strike, by members of the Woodstock student community, is meant to bring about a change from politics of power, to those of sharing and limiting that power. It is not directed at any individual, but at the roots of problems which we feel are deeply hurting the school. These problems include a lack of understanding for the individual, dehumanization, and an antiseptic, remote view of the philosophy of the school. We understand that the administrative and financial problems of the school are pressing, but are they any more pressing that the needs of the students. *We recognize the importance of such matters as eased relationships with the town and the public in general, attention to academic records, and campus maintenance and improvements; but certainly these needs have less significance than the need to provide students with an atmosphere in which problems can be confronted and solved, in which they can prepare for life other than merely for college.* This morning, student meetings are being held to discuss specific ways to solve these problems. We will present our proposals to you as soon as possible. We hope that they will merit your closest attention, *closer than our advice has received in the past.*"

That "past," less than seven weeks long, had not produced much mutual trust, starting with Tawny's confrontational stripping the community of any power. Typical of miscommunication in the school were the "Commendation and Warning" slips. Only eleven days into the term, they had "caused such an uproar at Community Meeting" (according to the faculty meeting minutes), that the faculty voted to make them strictly internal: no copy to parents, no copy to the student's file, but a copy to the student after all. Similarly, when the Community Council proposed to revive the "sleep-through" privilege of a few years before, allowing students to sleep through breakfast until their first classes of the day, the faculty fretted about students staying up too late already, then approved it anyway. By the following week, as a result of the strike, breakfast became optional for everyone (and later supper also became optional). There were also unresolved, running struggles over most of the usual issues, including dress, study halls, table seating and stealing. The students wanted locks for their rooms to prevent stealing, the faculty refused fearing locked doors would conceal illicit sex and drugs.

The strike lasted most of the day on Thursday, during which the faculty met twice without deciding on any course of action. Once the students finished their two pages of "Ideas for the Humanization of the School," they left the dorm, came down to Upwey for supper and study hall more or less as usual and waited for the headmaster and faculty to respond to their "demands," which included the re-establishment of student-faculty judiciary committees first set up a year earlier. Tawny accepted these as advisory only, along with advisory committees on curriculum and admissions. In February, while accepting no responsibility for the effects of his slash and burn approach to the school fabric, Tawny assured the trustees with bland tone-deafness that he had not relinquished any power.

The more philosophical questions raised by the student strikers were not included in Tawny's report to the board and Tawny seems not to have understood either the intensity of the students' feelings or the deep roots those feelings had in Woodstock's history as an alternate home for its students. For example, Tawny believed any student who ran away from school should be expelled. But the students asserted that: "Running away is a problem, not a crime. Often times its causes are completely outside the school. It should be dealt with by communication by student, his parents, and those members of the faculty and the student body who the student feels are concerned." Illustratively, one of the strike's leaders had run away twice during his first term, just to go to Greenwich Village and hang out during the summer of 1967, when David Bailey was still headmaster. Twice, David accepted this bright, creative boy back into the community without severe punishment and in time he graduated and went on to a career in avant garde music.

Similarly, the students argued "Drug offenders should be considered individually by the [major rules] committee, to determine whether their problems can best be solved in the school or outside it. If the latter is the case, the student should not be suspended or expelled, but rather asked to withdraw until such time as he and the committee feel that he is ready to return. The student should, if he wishes, be the one to notify his parents of his offense. No stigma should be attached to a drug offense." *(Tawny's comment; "What, exactly, do they mean by 'stigma'?")* Likewise, "A student's sexual life is, simply from a pragmatic point of view, his own business. While rules about boys in girls' rooms and vice versa, must be maintained, no policy can be set about the students 'private affairs.'" In these and similar expressions of concern about their own lives, Tawny found material for his own odd psychodrama, concluding that: "The fundamental source of student dissatisfaction was, I believe, my remoteness."

Despite the strike, and despite some increased concern about drug use in early December, Woodstock ended its fall term placidly. Attrition had been twice as high as in John Holden's first term a year earlier, but this time provoked hardly any trustee reaction. Tawny reported to the board: "Eleven students left during the fall term. Five withdrew voluntarily, four of these for psychological reasons. Four were expelled, three of these for drugs. Two were suspended, one of these for drugs."

Reflecting the values expressed in the strike, the faculty in early December reached an apparent consensus on a new response to student drug use: "Individual counselling and concern was encouraged rather than an 'inquisition type' approach." At the first faculty meeting of the winter, this was stated officially;

"Drugs Policy – encourage dialogue and counsel with complete immunity for students. Punishment only when caught red handed. All faculty are obliged to report to Head observance of use or possession of drugs by students." Sensible as such an approach was in principle, Woodstock's young and inexperienced faculty was not well equipped to carry it out. By the end of 1968, more than five years into the school's struggle with drugs, there was still no one on the staff with any formal training in recognizing drug-influenced behavior, much less anyone with any training in counselling drug-using young people, or working to develop a nuanced understanding of "drugs" and being able to distinguish among marijuana, LSD, heroin, and the rest.

### Tawny Kilborne report to the Trustees, March 12, 1969

*I was OD [faculty member managing Upwey] the morning the students left for spring vacation. A group of students were pressing around the front desk trying to get me to check them out. One student said he had lost the permission slip his Dorm Head had signed. I told him he would have to get another slip or have his Dorm Head call me. The student started to give me an argument. I said, "There isn't time to argue or explain now. Simply do as you're told because I tell you to."*

*A girl standing near-by responded from deep in her psyche by suddenly smiling with both eyes and mouth and saying totally without sarcasm but rather with a kind of naive and happy wonder, "Yes, Daddy."*

### Students in French House boys' dorm, excerpts from a list headed "21 points" (numbered 1-23, skipping #11), probably winter 1969

*[Tawny] sits in office. yesterday I saw him for first time in three weeks. comes to meals for 4 seconds. shouldn't use semantics on ignorant people. he's slick, we can't trust him. too much academic pressure. trying to change basic philosophy. No communication to parents from Tawny. I admire him as a person, but not as a headmaster for WCS. Make school meeting meaningful. Most of faculty is not behind him. Tawny does not give me the security I want...*

### Tawny Kilborne letter to WCS parents, April 7, 1969

*Sometimes I think that the guilt we rightly feel as we confront the rebellion of the blacks is subtly transferred to our feelings about the rebellion of that other large disenfranchised segment of our society, the young, with results that may prove disastrous.*

### Tawny Kilborne report to the Trustees, May 13, 1969

*Immediately after the explosion at Harvard [April 9] the Woodstock students began simmering. I noticed from my office window on a Saturday afternoon knots of students with black armbands moving ominously about the campus. The O.D. ran into my office and told me he would not be responsible for anything that happened that day. I walked around Upwey, and on returning to the main corridor across the hall from the dining room, found a clot of students, some seated with their legs across the hallway, and some standing, blocking my way. I asked them to move. They did. I turned to one boy – a leader – and asked what was going on. He shrugged, "There's something in the air, that's all." I said, "Come on in my office and let's talk about it, all of you." Within two or three minutes I had forty kids in my office and we talked for three hours.*

*The conversation was a good honest exchange. The students objected to my remoteness ("We want you, Tawny, we want you more than anyone in the world," one girl said); partially in response, Irene [Mrs. Kilborne] and I have been having eight kids to our house for dinner every week."*

● ● ●

Early in the 1969 winter term, the faculty's most serious concern was that the students were exhausted by overwork. Still trying to make the Four-Term Plan make sense, the faculty now required all students to take five courses each term, where before they had taken only three or four. In rationalizing and tightening up the schedule, Tawny had persuaded the faculty to have classes meet every day for five days of the week, with Saturday given over to the newly compulsory fine arts courses, which all students were expected to take every term. This also eliminated the faculty's usual second day off each week (besides Sunday). At the February trustees meeting, Exeter's Dick Day wondered if such a full schedule might be a factor in the school's morale, noting that at his school, classes met for 50 minutes only four times a week and that upperclassmen took only four courses.

But by then, as Tawny told the board, he and the faculty were near panic over "the drug scene which has reached crisis proportions... the school is going through a real identity crisis – three headmasters in three years. The school is now depressed and demoralized... There has been a crisis every week, the staff is exhausted." Having initiated a policy of openness and counselling just a month earlier, the faculty found itself unable to cope effectively with what it learned, or thought it was learning. And the school had no rational process available to faculty or students to try to sort things out in a mode short of panic.

Woodstock's near-chronic sense of crisis and the insecurities of a young headmaster were both exacerbated by two inexperienced, impulsive young women who were both in their first year at the Country School. Ann Griffiths and Liz O'Donovan both taught English and shared responsibility for running the Owen Moon House girls' dorm, of which they had lost effective control by winter term. In January, under the new faculty policy of openness, they had tried to assess the range of drug use at the school. They found what schools all over the country were finding then: widespread availability and use of marijuana, hashish, LSD, speed and, occasionally, STP. They classed a third of the students as non-users, a third as casual users and a third as "druggies." Two other teachers made less assiduous assessments, but presented comparable results.

Describing her and Liz's effort to deal with the problem, Ann Griffiths wrote to the trustees for their February 6 meeting: "One by one we visited several of the dormitories and made the appeal. We presented the problem, discussed its ramifications in a school community, and offered solutions. The students chose to set a deadline – one week – for the clean-up. We were surprised and thrilled by the positive reaction to the proposal. Some students were so ecstatic that they danced about shaking hands and proclaiming that they were going straight... Our meetings were successful only in that we brought the problem out in the open and saw for the first time the depth and severity of the problem. Most of the students involved have returned to drug usage a mere two days after the deadline. During the clean-up period, at least ten students chose to get rid of LSD by taking it internally..." Ann concluded her report by recommending what even she called "police state" measures, such as "dismissing, ostensively [sic] for medical reasons, the heavy drug users... placing the more cooperative group of students in various positions of leadership and responsibility... inspecting all incoming mail... searching students' luggage and persons... hiring a person especially trained in drug detection..."

Liz O'Donovan's report in February was more hand-wringing ("Something must be done") and more anecdotal (including a story about students coming to her for help with a boy who was shooting heroin, which they considered beyond the pale). She also seemed closer to some understanding of the contradictions in the problem: "The presence of drugs in their lives means that they live with something no other generation ever experienced or could ever understand. It is an underworld which for many of them is the real world... A large proportion have not had an emotionally very stable upbringing... Speaking as one who is fond of some of the druggiest students – I find it intolerable to watch the position in which the less drug-ridden are made to feel themselves social outcasts, and in which a school, which should exist because of the love and enthusiasm of its pupils, is forced to sink into disciplinarian strictness in order to keep functioning at all."

Faculty response was hysterical and hypocritical. During two days of meetings, February 2 and 3, the faculty ignored the major rules committee, reneged on its new policy of counselling and immunity and voted to separate ten students from the school, frequently relying on information identified as privileged in the teachers' reports. Buffy's notes captured the faculty's mood: "What to do? Separate those who don't perform in classes or work jobs – without reference to drugs. Why lie? Problem of 'immunity' – how to use the information we have... Tawny wants a stoolie detective type, instead of our searching rooms etc. [Student M] very good in courses... can we keep her if all know she freaked out? John Greppin's information is *not privileged*; Fran [Rohr] insists we *are* using privileged info – we must be clear that decisions were from observations of behavior, corroborating our own hunches." The quality of deliberations was such that a student who was voted out the first day was acquitted the second, whereas another was fired after first being acquitted. (Years later, Tawny expressed satisfaction at expelling a total of 26 students during the winter term, believing that had solved Woodstock's drug problem.)

Two days after the marathon faculty meeting, Tawny met with the trustees in New York City and presented them with a picture of a school in crisis. Some trustees expressed surprise at Tawny's report on drugs, particularly about the presence of heroin on campus, but their surprise was mixed with skepticism about the faculty. "I think they were panicked, I think Tawny was the one who panicked," Tom Debevoise recalled, "[he] didn't know how to cope." The board's only action on drugs that day was to hire a nationally respected drug expert, Dr. Helen Nowlis, to study the problem. At the same time, several trustees criticized Tawny for his limited communication with students. Board president

Paul Newlon told him, "You cannot be locked off the way you say you must." Exeter's Dick Day said, "As a parent I would think that my child would get a lot of attention from the headmaster of such a small school. That would be the reason for picking Woodstock."

Relations between the headmaster and the board were uneasy for other reasons as well. Paul Newlon told Tawny he had not called on the trustees as he should, only to learn that Tawny had called on a local trustee and been rebuffed. Likewise, Paul, having replaced Tom Debevoise as the board's president in October, had then turned his attention elsewhere for the next four months, calling no executive committee meetings and following up on little of the board's business. He apologized to the board for his "lack of participation."

Throughout the winter on campus, the faculty's frantic behavior was fed by the teachers' own job insecurity. During that term, Tawny was purging his faculty, as several board members had long desired, firing many teachers and encouraging others to resign. Of that winter's faculty of 17, only four (including Ann Griffiths, who proposed the "police state" methods which characterized the school's treatment of students for awhile) would remain at Woodstock in the fall, in the meantime creating conditions for defiance, sycophancy and confusion. In March, at the last faculty meeting of the winter, "all faculty agreed that they are ready for complete change – will go along with new standards – they do not feel that the way things have gone for the past three or four years is good, deterioration has gone too far."

Tawny wrote a bitter winter's-end memo to the faculty and trustees, enumerating 20 recent, upsetting episodes which led him to conclude "that we have been taking students from liberal, permissive homes where they were often neglected and that we have been giving them precisely what they do not need, another liberal, permissive environment. Fear that we have nurtured the disorientation to the real world of some students and, even worse, that we have disoriented other students who, if they had gone elsewhere, would probably not have been so influenced. For example, one of the girls who has been wearing drama costumes stolen from the school's supply is a very straight, conscientious, and attractive young person. I feel that such an action would not have occurred to her in another environment."

The disconnection in all this is that, from the moment he started dismantling the school's systems the previous September, Tawny himself had been the prime mover in accelerating Woodstock's "permissive environment," often abetted by faculty and students. The headmaster and faculty created further stressful discontinuity by their inconsistency on policies ranging from breakfast to drugs. Tawny's example of the drama costumes illustrates the school's level of confusion. By Tawny's own account, the costume closet had been looted at will all term, mostly by the girls from Own Moon House, and no one was held accountable. This helps to explain why a "straight, conscientious" girl steals costumes, as well as the disorientation she might have felt knowing what she was doing, knowing her teachers and headmaster knew what she was doing, and knowing that none of them were doing anything about it. Such an occurrence is unthinkable in David Baileys school (or John Holden's) not merely because Drama was important to David, but because he was clear in his verities that stealing was wrong and destructive to a community.

Tawny had rushed Woodstock into a permissiveness that no one was demanding. For all that the school's structures were few and shaky when he took over, Tawny set about reducing them further. He eliminated the group system, most sign-out procedures, attendance at breakfast, daytime study halls, participation in afternoon activities or sports, attendance at supper and evening study hall, as well as student authority in the work program, in the dorms, or on disciplinary committees. More importantly, by insisting on his unchallenged authority to veto community decisions, he made it all but impossible for any but the most optimistic or obtuse students to feel they had any significant influence in their community or control over their lives there. Rather than dealing with the contradictions creating chaos in his school, Tawny turned to blaming the victims. He wrote angrily to parents and students, outlining school rules in a memo Gerry Freund, among others, found "shameful." And he began enlisting allies who agreed with his assessment that Woodstock was a lunatic asylum – contrary to the re-evaluation committee's assessment of the students less than a year before.

### George St. John Jr., re-evaluation report, June 1968

*One's first impression of the student body upon arriving at the Woodstock Country School is one of sloppiness and acted-out rebellion. Boys tend to have long hair (in a few cases down to their shoulders), some have bushy side-burns and boots or sandals. Girls go for jeans and work shirts in considerable numbers, a kind of camp or country dress. Yet none of the stereotypes fit. The students in general do not put on airs or affectations. They are polite, friendly, articulate, interested and interesting, and very much involved in their school community. They are certainly eloquent spokesmen for that cornerstone of the school philosophy, belief in the worth of each individual as he is, and in the value of an atmosphere within which each person can explore his relation to the community and to himself. The students react positively to the sense that they can try many things, that they can afford to fail, and that learning and growth can come from failure as well as success. They take a great deal of responsibility and initiative in the present life of the school. They organize and run the Work Program, sweep and clean all the school buildings, serve the meals and wash up dishes and pots and pans. They have established a code of behavior known as the Basic Agreement. They have worked hard among themselves to control marijuana smoking. They feel they have a hand in making the school and are proud of their role...*

*Many students feel that at Woodstock for the first time they have been treated as intelligent, responsible persons who can and must find the shape and direction their own lives should take. Particularly impressive is the way in which students respond to this challenge with a sense of social responsibility to the whole school community and not just with an egocentric concentration on their own development.*

*To a great degree this is what real education is all about, and at Woodstock it occurs significantly."*

## David Perkins '71 letter to Trustee Barbara Sproul '62, early March 1969

*As I write this letter, I reflect upon my past experience of the three terms I've been here at Woodstock. When I came here [in the summer] I got a feeling of friendship and warmth. There was also a sincere desire, and struggle to learn.*

*"When Mr. Kilbourn [sic] first came, I felt that he could be good for the school. Gradually he started making little changes, and giving token freedoms in return. As the term continued I felt an uneasy tension I couldn't really put a finger on. Slowly I realized that Mr. Kilbourn (sic) was trying to make this <u>his</u> ideal little school, and he would do it at any cost. An example of this was the expulsion of the students this term. True, a school can't exist with drugs, but expelling a student two thousand miles away, when he wasn't even taking this term (on campus), just doesn't make sense..."*

## Tawny Kilborne report to the trustees, May 13, 1969

*We have only five returning teachers, one of whom is presently off campus. And some of the [twelve] lame ducks are very bitter.*

*Forty-two students have left the Woodstock Country School since September for reasons other than graduation. Small wonder those who remain feel insecure and threatened.*

*Dr. James C. Miller, the Yale [associate professor of psychology] who has been consulting with us, made a fascinating observation of the school in general: 'The Woodstock Country School is a place where discrimination on the basis of merit had become taboo.' I have made discriminations on the basis of merit; I have expelled students who refused to abide by the rules of the school (and the laws of the state); I have flunked out students who refused to work; I have not renewed the contracts of teachers whom I considered ineffective. The result has been outrage and shock – in that order. Many students still perceive me as heartless, or at best 'wrong for this school,' but I sense that an increasing number feel that I do care about them, after all. I hope this is not wishful thinking.*

## Ralph O. West of NEACSS [schools association] letter to Tawny Kilborne, May 15, 1969

*Certainly my brief visit was not enough to qualify me to place judgment in detail on the school operation. I was distressed to hear of the disastrous firethat destroyed one of the boys' dormitories. It is significant that steps have been taken to assure safety in so far as is humanly possible of the other buildings. Certainly the present girls' dormitory [Owen Moon House] needs some attention both in terms of aesthetic appeal as well as safety. As it presently exists, I would call it less than satisfactory. Certainly something must be done to assure adequate infirmary facilities and health care for the student body.*

## Dr. James C. Miller report to the Trustees, July 1969

*Our first and most lasting impressions [during two visits to the school in April and May 1969] concerned two related areas: (1) the amount of change which had occurred at the school over the past 2-3 years and*

*(2) the degree of uncertainty, instability and anxiety which characterized nearly all activities at the school...*

*From what we learned in talking to people who knew about prior years at the school either first-hand or from oral history, the primary task of the school has subtly shifted in recent years from an emphasis on experimental, liberal education to an emphasis an maintaining and developing personal or community living skills...*

*We believe that the evidence for this change is abundant. Students generally told us they want more freedom to form relationships, explore 'hang-ups', 'turn on', change their society etc. and want less of any curriculum outside this. Faculty generally confirmed this both by describing classroom apathy or dependence and by describing the amount of time they spend in counselling or administering daily activities, crises etc.*

*Two aspects of this picture impressed as with respect to current conflicts at the school: (a) student beliefs and norms vary little from dissent, (b) many of the students, possibly up to half of the total student body, seem relatively unable to cope with community living in any form. In other words, the WCS student community is (a) largely defined by its opposition to authority and yet (b) populated with a large number of students who cannot cope with the responsibility such opposition might bring them. Our estimate is that about one-third (about 25) of the students at WCS appear to have psychotic or borderline psychotic impairments...*

*On all of our visits we were impressed by the sense of disjointedness and disorientation present in the school. Students and faculty alike seem pervasively anxious, and somewhat depressed.*

## Barbara Sproul '62 letter to Tawny, August 7, 1969,

*REFLECTIONS ON MILLER'S REPORT:*
*I found throughout a kind of either/or thinking, employed first in his statement that the school had changed from being a liberal, educational institution to being one whose main emphasis was on developing community living skills. Though I am not at the school at the present, I have been there in the past long enough to know that this is not the case. Being a small, co-ed, experimental school, it had always reflected a blend of these two attributes...*

*Miller also mentions that in his view one-third of the school student body is psychotic, or have borderline psychotic impairment. I find this fact to be quite fantastic and incomprehensible in the light of the fact that the basis for this estimate were not elucidated. It would seem that he feels this way because of their challenge to authority and their simultaneous inability to accept responsibility for themselves. If that is the case, then I dare say that most of the valuable and creative children of the country should be considered psychotic in their teens...*

*Obviously, we don't want lunatics in the place: we don't want kids who can't perform and who can't do the work. But I think two things must be retained of the school's philosophy: 1) that its experiment in learning not be strictly interpreted, that it continue to take risks on kids who have done poorly elsewhere who can do well in a different and creative environment such as Woodstock's; and 2) that it remember that teenagers are there to learn more than academic subjects in an academic way, that it is a factor in their age and stage of development that they are there to learn much more both in the classroom and outside of it, and the school has a responsibility to teach them in all things at all times, positively, openly and creatively.*

• • •

In the spring of 1968, according to moderately traditional George St. John of the Cambridge School of Weston, Woodstock's 94 students were above-average adolescents who cared deeply about each other and their school. A year later, in the spring of 1969, according to personally conservative Trustee Tom Debevoise, Woodstock's 78 students were good and decent kids who still cared about their school. In between somehow, according to professionally conservative Yale psychologist Jim Miller, a third of Woodstock's 78 students had suffered psychotic or borderline psychotic impairments. The *Rashomon* effect, the perception of reality shaped by the observer's predominant interest, was described in simpler terms by one of Woodstock's more brilliant and difficult students of the time, Jerome Berryhill'72, now a theoretical physicist, who was fond of remarking about Country School life, "Reality is a variable."

In the midst of the winter drug "crisis," Tawny had called Jim Miller, his former Yale roommate, and asked for help on that issue. There is no record of their considering the possibility of a conflict of interest, or the appearance of one, or the likelihood of bias that would lead Miller to tell Tawny what Tawny wanted to hear, or what Miller thought his fellow Yalie wanted to hear. Although Miller was not much involved then with individuals or drug-use behaviors, he agreed to visit Woodstock with some colleagues to evaluate the school in terms of his marginally-relevant professional focus at the time: the structure and dynamics of social service organizations. Until Tawny called him, Jim Miller had never heard of the Woodstock Country School, but he agreed to consult at the school, charging no fee other than travel expenses, on the basis of friendship and curiosity.

Long before he ever saw Woodstock, Miller reasonably warned Tawny "that drug-taking should not be labelled a symptom of some sort of disability, either individual or group." The psychologist also suggested his Yale group might be most useful in educating the faculty: "I really think that drugs are just one aspect of the student revolt. The implications for the school of demands for the 'new freedoms' could be discussed, and faculty could be encouraged to see drugs in this context. I strongly believe that they are competent to deal with even severe cases if they see the relevant social issues and don't prematurely think of illness and doctors... The school not only sounds fascinating, and a microcosm of what's happening in many aspects of society today, but also you have a *total* social environment that is at the same time small enough to be understandable (at least I hope to God for your sake it is understandable), and tractible. What would be really interesting, in the long run is to see if we could work together in understanding the 'group dynamics', if you will, of your school, perhaps as it continually relates to problem outcomes like drug-taking."

This rational and reasonable tone is typical of the professorial Miller, a tall, large-framed man of affable manner. In person, as in print, he strives to be responsive, fair, open to other points of view. He provided school documents from this period that were not available elsewhere. And yet his assessment of the school was more than passing strange, as if to demonstrate that there was more in heaven and earth than is dreamt of in modern psychology. After several visits to Woodstock in the spring, Miller presented a report to the board, which emphasized "the sense of disjointedness and disorientation," the Yale group observed on each visit. Miller attributed this sense to student psychosis and pre-psychosis, but nowhere in his report did he allude to any of the stress and turmoil of Tawny's first two terms detailed in this chapter. He simply ignored the fresh disjointedness and disorientation that Tawny created in the community. Miller did not need to resort to psychosis to explain why students and faculty seemed depressed and why "many of the students, possibly up to half of the total student body, seem relatively unable to cope with community living in any form."

On April 7, less than three weeks before the Miller group's first visit, the French House boys' dorm burned to the ground, displacing more than a fifth of the school – seventeen students and three faculty families. All of them lost virtually all their possessions, but there were no injuries or loss of life. The students were moved into other dormitories that were already overcrowded. Nine days after the fire, after the initial coping was over, Buffy reported to the faculty, "many kids are still upset and uprooted by the fire." Miller didn't address the destruction of the school's second largest dorm, upsetting and disorienting as it was. As far as Miller's report was concern, it was as if French House never burned down.

In the fall of 1954, when the Barn burned on the Greenhithe campus, David Bailey seized on the moment to rally students and faculty to a common cause. The school community responded to the crisis then with a sense of common purpose, determination, mutual support and considerable pride in carrying on. In startling contrast to the school's response 15 years earlier, Tawny and others treated the French House fire as something of an emotional non-event, not an opportunity to bind and heal the long-stressed school community. Nor did Tawny or others publicize the fire or make any emergency appeal for contributions, even though this was a disastrous financial event. The French House was insured for $77,500, but would cost almost four times that to replace. The Miller report contained no reference to the fire, or its effects on the school or individuals in it. In fact, the report referred to none of the daily context of the school despite Miller's stated belief that "mental illness is not something that happens in a vacuum – so the more disordered the social environment, the more disordered the individual will be."

There was additional, immediate stress on the community just three days before the first visit of the Yale group, when the faculty again grew anxious about drugs in response to shrill reports from the same women who had catalyzed the winter crisis. This time the faculty moved more judiciously at first. The Yale group arrived for a day of largely uneventful and somewhat unfocused small group meetings, primarily intended to allow the psychologists "to obtain information from all members of the WCS community about current concerns." Miller's colleagues met for an average of two to three hours with ten, generally well-attended student groups which, to judge by the group leaders' notes, provided a collage of impressions that captured the school reasonably well (even identifying one of the faculty hysterics). Questionnaires filled out by 60 of the school's 78 students provided confirmation that drug use at Woodstock conformed to typical patterns of the time: heavy on marijuana, light on "hard drugs," which the scientists did not define. The questionnaire also showed that two thirds of the students liked the school, but not with the passion typical of Woodstock students over the years, or even of those that George St. John met during the evaluation just a year earlier (see above).

"We saw the faculty as the most stressed group," wrote Miller, who met with the teachers in two small groups, then met separately with the headmaster for several hours. There was no questionnaire for the faculty, therefore no comparable assessment of faculty drug and alcohol use; but the latter was serious enough during that period that students complained about it to Tawny and assistant headmaster Dave Horan, leading Tawny to warn the faculty on April 30 to control its "drunkenness." The two faculty groups meeting with Miller were drawn up by Tawny: those who were remaining at the school (plus one of Tawny's friends who was leaving), and those who were leaving, willingly or otherwise. As Miller wrote, "we came to refer to the remaining group as the 'teachers' and the departing group as the 'parents'... [The first] group had as its primary task the teaching of students at the school, and was, as a result, quite critical of any behavior on the part of the students or the faculty that interfered with that task. The other group seemed to be more concerned with the personal welfare and personal satisfaction of the students." In other words, students who had come to Woodstock in many instances to escape destructive home lives now faced, by Miller's own metaphor, the additional, double trauma of losing their new "parents" and being abandoned to something akin to less caring, more remote foster care.

Two days after the Yale group's visit, ten faculty members met in a rump session to discuss six girls suspected of drug use and cigarette smoking in the Owen Moon House. The group considered circumstantial and hearsay evidence, but heard neither witnesses nor the accused before voting to suspend two of them for the remainder of the term, by a vote of 6-2 (with two abstentions). Two days after that, following a surprise room search which turned up some marijuana, Tawny unilaterally expelled one of the suspended girls and reduced the other's suspension to two weeks. Many of the students on campus objected to the "police state" style of the room search. The faculty, too, was divided over the morality of the room search, as well as the "Star Chamber" quality of the rump faculty meeting. Under this pressure, Tawny declared new policies, which provided reasonable due process for room searches and for "major offense" cases previously heard by the disbanded major rules committee. The episode did nothing to reassure the community about their headmaster's fundamental fairness or consistency.

By Miller's own assessment, the Yale group's second and last visit in May was a failure. Designed as "an inter-group exercise, where we asked students to plan the kind of school community in which they would like to live," the exercise did not help the school begin to solve its problems. The structure of the exercise worked against its purpose in two striking ways. First, the Yale psychologists role-playing as "the Administration" took a passive position in the faculty room, waiting for the students to come forward with proposals – an eerie echo of the futile student strike five months earlier. Second, the faculty and headmaster were relegated to silent observers in the exercise, while the students had to play themselves in dealing with the Yale psychologists as a fantasy administration. This, in turn, expressed the conscious or unconscious bias of the Yale group that problems in educational institutions come from the students and it's up to them to shape up and accept whatever the "grown-ups" decide for no better reason than that the grown-ups are grown-ups and that's what they decided. The exercise fell apart, students and faculty alike were confused about the rules and their roles – to the students the experience was "depressing" and frustrating; to the faculty, "make believe made it a game;" and to the Yale group, "we had set the conditions for students' chaotic reactions, and both the students and ourselves were, from that point of view, anxious to bring the exercise to an end."

No wonder, then, that Miller's report focused on the erratic and fragmented behavior of the students, not on the inconsistencies of an unaccountable and arbitrary authority that shaped their experience. Miller's report omitted any mention of the student's only significant proposal, the re-establishment of a major rules committee as a precaution against arbitrary and unpredictable administration of justice. Miller missed it, but others appreciated the bitter black humor of proposing a committee that had been formed twice before in the previous 18 months, only to be ignored or disempowered. (When he later discussed this student proposal in his book, Miller still omitted any of the context that gave it meaning and resonance in the life of the school.)

Inchoate as they may have been as a group, Woodstock's students were nevertheless fighting in the best ways they knew how to preserve what they valued most in what they still considered to be their school. Throughout this period, at least since early winter, unorganized but consistent student signals, like David Perkins's and others' letters to trustees, had accumulated sufficiently so that the trustees agreed to meet with students and faculty in five small groups on the evening before their May 13 board meeting. In preparation for those meetings, and in response to a request from Barbara Sproul, the Community Council prepared a one-page memo "to give you an outline of the issues, and areas we might discuss." The issues included control of students, support for students, problems with the Four-Term Plan, isolation, handling ABC (minority) scholarship students, the need for meaningful work and the school's financial future – but the underlying question for all the rest was, "What continuing general characteristics of the school can the students look forward to in the immediate future?"

At the board meeting the next day, Tawny reported that Woodstock had lost 42 students since September "for reasons other than graduation" He misrepresented Miller's opinion that "one-third of our students are borderline psychotics" (a view he shared with the faculty as well). The board was not impressed and requested a written report from the volunteer consultant (who was not present to correct this exaggeration of his view). Tawny also warned that "the intensity of the environment might lead many [students] to become more unstable" (echoing Miller's acknowledgement of the possibility of environmentally-induced psychosis). "The Students are simply confused. And I don't blame them," Tawny told the board, since "perhaps the primary source of their confusion [is] the faculty... We have only five returning teachers... and some of the lame ducks are very bitter." Despite everything, the students had gotten the board's attention, first with their persistence, then with their responsible and responsive behavior the night before the board meeting. A majority of the trustees agreed when Barbara Sproul reminded them that the trustee-student meeting of the previous evening should not be a one-shot matter, but should be the start of a continuing dialogue. By this time, both she and Gerry Freund were gaining support for their suggestion to have students on the board.

But the trustees were having troubles of their own which, if the Yale group had examined them, might have provided a fuller, clearer picture of the group dynamics of the school. Paul Newlon's leadership of the board in the seven months since he had replaced Tom Debevoise as president had been largely *in absentia*, for which Paul frequently apologized. During the May meeting, Paul turned to Tom and asked him to lead the campaign to raise enough money to replace the French House dorm that had just burned down, even though he had recently arranged for the school's largest gift up to that time, $50,000 from Laurance Rockefeller. Tom, slightly hung over, responded angrily as he recalled: "that burned me so much, after all the time and energy I'd put in on the school, that I stood up at the meeting and said I never should have done it. 'You are, in effect, asking me to take over as president and I'll be glad to if I have the resignations of all the Trustees in my hand.' I was mad. He hadn't done a damn thing, New York lawyer, could never get hold of him... and I was busier than he was... [But] nobody else was prepared to do the job." The rest of the board caucused, agreed to make Tom president and offered to resign. Tom turned down that offer, but he took over from Paul in mid-meeting and set about running the school as it had never been run before, establishing a board authority that had been impossible with David Bailey or John Holden as headmaster.

Regardless of the board's internal dynamics, Tawny continued to approach it in the confrontational style he had established at his first meeting in the fall. At that May meeting, Tawny particularly challenged the basic Country School premises of small size and small dorms. He recommended expanding the school to 120 students and building a new dorm for 48, twice as many students as any Woodstock dorm had ever held (except for the temporary 40-boy barracks in an Upwey loft in 1955). "As I see it, we have two choices: expand or perish," Tawny asserted, arguing that only a larger school would be a financially sound school: "The sacrifices we all may have to make to get there may be enormous, but surely the school will have taken a significant step forward if the Trustees determine where they want the school to go, and begin to move the school decisively in that direction."

The Trustees were not persuaded that Tawny's direction was the right direction and rejected both proposals. For all the anxious over-reaction of Country School adults, the school's year had not been nearly as "wild and whirling," in Tawny's phrase, as a good many other campuses that year, including nearby Dartmouth College where 40 undergraduates had been arrested and jailed for occupying the college president's office. Woodstock's spring term ended without incident. In late May, Jim Miller completed the Yale group's program, meeting with the faculty in an uneventful review session. He was joined in that meeting by a drug expert, Dr. Helen Nowlis of the University of Rochester, with whom Miller had consulted during the Woodstock experiment. She counseled caution and patience. In June, CBS News anchorman Walter Cronkite, a year after bad weather had prevented him from speaking at Woodstock's 1968 commencement, made it on the second try and delivered some traditional platitudes to the Class of '69, which included Kathy Cronkite. ("My daughter has been so happy here," the newsman told a reporter).

With the graduation of 33 seniors, in addition to the departure of 42 other students and 12 of 17 faculty members, Tawny had largely repopulated the school during his first academic year and looked forward to the summer term in what was now essentially "his" school. In his book, "Reparation and Change," Jim Miller put it much more bluntly than Tawny ever had: Tawny "felt that he had inherited a hospital, and he moved to eliminate both doctors and patients... He wished to act quickly and decisively to make the school his school, and not the founder's inheritance." To complete Miller's analogy,

Tawny the administrator still had to master the hospital board before the institution could be truly "his."

Shortly after the May board meeting, Gerry Freund wrote to David and Peggy Bailey, commenting on Tom Debevoise's sudden re-ascendancy, which Gerry viewed as improving chances to strengthen the school. "There are, of course, fundamental problems of leadership, philosophy, even ability," Gerry wrote, "and on these Tom and I do not necessarily see eye to eye. He is not consistent. I bank on his getting the picture in focus as a result of more intensive contact. I believe there will be board consensus for a change in headmaster unless there is consensus that we are prepared to husband a school fundamentally different from the one Tawny was hired to develop."

### Jim Miller, *Reparation and Change* (Chapter 7), 1978

*An unconscious agenda was set in terms of a set of role demands on [David Bailey's] successor. On the one hand, his successor would be asked to carry on, indeed to buttress, the traditions of freedom and the development of creativity in the school. On the other hand, he would have to be less than totally effective: he could not be the man the founder was, in the interests of preserving the founder's image; he could not be authoritarian in the manner of the founder, for that was a side of leadership at the school that was increasingly questioned; and finally, but perhaps most importantly, he would somehow have to express the guilt about the overthrow of the founder... It is indirectly a tribute to the founder of the school that the difficulties of defining his succession could not be discussed, to say nothing of understood, when they were each central issues over several crucial years in the school's history. Our analysis led us to the conclusion that it was essential for successors to be found who were "not right for the school."*

### Meeting minutes, Trustees and consultants, September 20, 1969

**Judge Billings**: *"Suppose a student says he wants to use drugs?"*
**Jim Miller**: *"Students might be learning from them. The question is – how can you help students?"*

**Helen Nowlis:** *"Jim is stating a value. Are you going to decide what education is or let the public decide it? Educators must stand up for what they believe and educate the public..."*

**Judge Billings:** *"If there's no policy in the school and then there's a raid – there's a mess."*

**Tom Debevoise:** *"There's nothing wrong in having a rule if it's derived correctly."*

**Nowlis and Miller:** *"Better not to have the rule. If you have the rule – you have to enforce it."*

**Tawny Kilborne:** *"A definite stand by adults is important."*

**Jim Miller:** *"We're not recommending an absence of policy. You could base a workable policy on good use of drugs – not pressing things on others – keeping up in work."*

**Tom Debevoise:** *"Having to decide whether a student has the maturity to use drugs – that's impossible."*

**Gerry Freund:** *"Of course it's easier to have hard and fast rules about these difficult things – but at what cost?"*

**Roger Phillips:** *"We need continuing help of this kind that we're getting here."*

**Gerry Freund:** *"We should consistently be involved with this kind of thing – and not only here."*

**Tom Debevoise:** *"Our policy now is: If you get caught, you go."*

**Helen Nowlis:** *"You're saying to the kids that the most important thing is not to get caught."*

**Paul Newlon:** *"We have a policy that's black and white..."*

**Tawny Kilborne:** *"Using drugs is destructive of the institution."*

**Helen Nowlis:** *"The primary goal is not being destructive of the community – not because there's some law."*

**Tawny Kilborne:** *"Expulsion can be educative."*

**Barbara Sproul:** *"What we're telling students is we can't offer you the educational experience of drugs, but we can offer you the educational experience of expulsion... Our policy is that behavior inimical to the school as a community will not be tolerated."*

The trustees thanked Dr. Nowlis and Dr. Miller for their tremendous help and guidance and for coming to the meeting to report and they then left the meeting. Miss Sproul said self-awareness as a policy might be self-defeating.

SUMMER 1968 – SUMMER 1970

## Jim Miller, *Reparation and Change* (Chapter 7), 1978

*The content of the [September 20 Trustees] meeting, at the manifest level, was ritualized and perfunctory [at first]... our [Dr. Nowlis and Dr. Miller] principal value from the beginning lay in our agreement to come and to help save the school from its real and imaginary catastrophic problems...*

*We were finally asked specifically what we would recommend with respect to the drug problem. In retrospect, what was wanted was an affirmation that it should and could be effectively banished or cured. Instead, what we said was it was a highly complex problem, involving legal, social and psychological consequences. While we made clear we thought we were not competent to comment on the legal consequences, we did feel it was not sociologically and psychologically a wise ground for policy making. We described the familiar studies on marijuana (raising doubts that it was any more harmful a drug than alcohol) and we discussed our clinical views on psychoactive drug taking: arguing that such drug effects, good or bad, were relative to the user). We commented that in our view any policy should be related to the school's goals of learning and/or social living. Thus, if a student is capable of taking drugs in a manner that furthered his own and others' interpersonal and cognitive learning, or did not interfere with it, this should he a matter of the student's individual discretion. He or she would of course have to take the consequences of whatever legal enforcement was imposed.*

*"This consultation led to a rather lively and hostile questioning of our assumptions... The 'drug-abuse' consultant [Helen Nowlis] essentially counseled moderation but did not take a stand... Two or three more liberal members of the Board who might have privately agreed with our opinion found the opportunity at this point to reunite with the more conservative members against our "radical" position... Moreover, the Board could unite momentarily around the Headmaster, whose position was against drugs and in favor of educational excellence. He had affected, it appeared, a magical, if predictably short-lived, solution to an aspect of the difficulties confronting both the Headmaster and the Board at this meeting. As clinical evidence of this, we felt we were thanked well beyond our contributions as we left."*

"Good news from Woodstock," Tawny wrote Helen Nowlis in mid-July. "Three new faculty members have settled in; they are splendid teachers, and the kids love them. Virtually all of the students who strongly objected to what I have been doing have left; the new students are enthusiastic and bright; we have more applications for admission than I dreamed we would at this time. Woodstock Country School is a happier place than I anticipated it would be for another year."

The students were indeed quiescent for the rest of the spring and into the summer, despite their nearly unanimous dislike and distrust of Tawny documented by the Yale group. With only 44 students on campus during the summer, the school enjoyed the intimacy of smallness, as it had in the past. Even so, the faculty still felt the need to hold an open faculty meeting to address the "trust problem," without much success. And for the moment, the school was ignoring the additional debt created by this under-enrollment, since a balanced budget required 100 students. Tawny told others the summer term "is an extraordinarily happy one" and "I frankly never anticipated that the upturn would be so rapid" and "the school is very clean, a little pot probably – but [drugs are] not a way of life."

Despite this optimism, Tawny was facing a much more serious challenge from the Trustees, who were expressing deep-seated reservations about his appropriateness to the Country School. Tawny himself had set the stage for a confrontation by telling the board's executive committee in March 1969 that Woodstock "as it is now performing ought not to exist." Preparing for that meeting, Tawny's personal notes list his third agenda item as "Our Greatest Needs" (the first two agenda items are "The Changing Status Quo" and "Drugs"). The greatest needs listed by Tawny are (A) "A more stable community" and (B) "An adequate physical plant, i.e. making what we have habitable." Under (B) Tawny listed four "Worthwhile Means" to achieve an adequate plant: "fundraising, using endowment, selling off land, further indebtedness." Under (A), to achieve a more stable community, he had nothing.

At the March 17 executive committee meeting, Tawny suggested that the solution to the school's difficulties was to accept only stable students who would not need "mental health attention." During its meetings with the community in May, the board's reluctance to blame the students for leadership failures was reinforced by the students' restrained and rational discussion of their concerns. Gerry Freund worried about the approach of the June board meeting, about "holding David's hands" and "containing my anger at Tawny's leadership." The latter had already led to sharp exchanges with the headmaster, as well as Buffy Dunker, who was almost reflexively protective of any Woodstock headmaster. Gerry told Barbara Sproul, "it is an absolutely critical moment in my judgment inasmuch as only a few alterations in the board can tip the balance in the direction of a largely non-caring or insensitive group who would be content to make, as in your phrase, a 'second-rate Exeter' out of the school." Barbara Sproul, unable to attend the June board meeting, wrote to Tom Debevoise of her doubts about Tawny, essentially restating with fresh evidence the reasons for her original vote against Tawny's appointment, which she now asked to be made explicit in the official board records.

At the meeting, with Tawny present, Tom read parts of Barbara's letter aloud: "My feeling [is] that the school is in terrible spiritual shape (and I use the term loosely); from the meeting of students at the last board meeting, from general communication with the students, and most recently from your summary of the school in a letter to [Laurance] Rockefeller, I feel that the people responsible for the school and its direction have no faith in it or understanding of its real character. There is a negative and apologetic attitude which I find most distressing. The school is a fine one and the kids are terrific. What is missing is active, competent and believing leadership... There is an enormous fear on the part of the administration... [and] I am particularly disturbed when I see this fear and misunderstanding reaching the board... [in its concern for] externals and course titles, rules, dress, administrative positions rather than for educational content, communication, responsibility or community."

Gerry Freund added his own "reservations about the spiritual health, general environment, and current leadership of the school," concerns which were echoed in varying intensities by Trustees William Speer, Judge Billings, Irene Crowe and Dave Horan, the faculty representative. While none of the eight trustees present challenged the validity of these misgivings, board president Debevoise conspicuously withheld comment. His public position, however, in letters to Laurance Rockefeller and other benefactors, was that "I am convinced the school has turned around and is headed uphill to a position of strength and leadership under [Tawny's] direction."

The board's lack of consensus, as well as most board members' innate caution, left the issue to fester. Writing about the school's lack of action on fundraising efforts, Gerry Freund told Exeter's Dick Day, "we are trying to help Tawny and the school, but find it virtually impossible to get cooperation... If there is one thing the school can take less readily than another change in leadership, it is a lack of leadership." Barbara Sproul wrote Tawny directly about alumni fundraising, complaining at length: "I just can't understand why nothing has been done." Tawny's brisk reply reported that everything was now getting done, that others had let things slide, that "sometimes when I delegate a matter, I forget about it." He reported that "last night two girls ran away... I wish I knew why." And he concluded with a rebuke: "Perhaps sometime when you are upset about the way things are going I could hear about it directly from you instead of via Gerry or via Tom... I am frankly disturbed by the discrepancy between what you have said directly to me... and what I have heard that you have said or written to others."

Barbara replied that she regretted having to send her views via letter to the June trustees meeting, "However, I had previously expressed to you, in our discussion after the Student-Trustee meeting, my feelings that there were severe disturbances in the school community which had not been successfully dealt with. I referred then to the atmosphere of fear and distrust which I felt pervaded the school, the emphasis on rules rather than community and cooperation; in essence, the emphasis on form rather than content... As you know I have always felt that the first responsibility of anyone in charge of a school – especially one like Woodstock – was to the whole being of the kids."

At the same time Barbara wrote Gerry Freund, "Would you believe that bit in [Tawny's] letter about not knowing why the girls ran away? He just has no idea of what he's saying, no self-consciousness about not being in touch with things." Dick Day, who was getting copies of much of this correspondence (as were Roger Phillips, Irene Crowe and Paul Newlon), assured Gerry Freund that "I also am worried about Tawny and the general lack of a sense of urgency which seems to characterize all he does. I also wish that his first reaction, when posed with some job or problem, were not that of asking for an addition to the staff... [During Tawny's recent visit to Exeter] one of the points which I stressed rather heavily was that it was essential he win the backing of his trustees." (Day suffered a heart attack in August and was no longer able to help the school regain its balance).

Tom Debevoise wrote Barbara and Gerry, seeking to build support for Tawny through a combination of criticism, conciliation, and faith: "I believe that WCS, under Tawny's leadership, has the potential to help and inspire adolescents in the future on a basis at least equal to David Bailey's best year." Tom's letter aroused "so much hostility" in Gerry that he couldn't answer it at once, he told Barbara, adding, "No doubt about it, Tom is doing things that have long needed doing and the fact that he was once the most irresponsible Chairman we had should not be dragged up. But he knows next to nothing about education and, most of the time, his ideas for the school are simply a more polished version of Tawny's. Suffice it to say that I would never again participate in the kind of kangaroo court proceedings that precipitated David out under Tom's board leadership; but... I shall continue to raise and, if necessary, precipitate the critical question concerning Tawny's tenure, if what is most vital about the school is at stake."

Meanwhile, Tawny responded to Barbara: "Although I was familiar with the [psychiatric] backgrounds of both of these girls [who ran away], I do not know what triggered their departure. If the Trustees see the headmaster's primary responsibility as knowing such matters (I gather this is what you meant by saying that the head's first responsibility is to the student's whole being), then I have seriously misunderstood both the purpose of the school and my proper role in it... Prior to my coming here, I stressed my central academic interest and warned Trustees repeatedly that there would be an enormous amount of flak during the first year. The job to be done was a difficult and unlovable one. The worst is now over; the spirit of the school has changed with almost miraculous speed. I feel you are now reacting to a situation that no longer exists."

Replying to Tawny in a much less combative mood, Barbara said, "I think it is most definitely within the realm of the headmaster's responsibility to listen and guide – to be the adult in residence if you will." At the same time, she told Gerry Freund, "I don't think [Tawny] likes me much any more and I'm sure he doesn't understand a word I'm talking about. He keeps assuming that if you talk to a kid for a minute about something not appropriate to the classroom, all academic standards are going to collapse." For his part, Tawny was telling Jim Miller that "Sproul and Freund are the two real Trustee malcontents." And contrary to Tawny's assurances that all was well on the Woodstock campus, Gerry wrote Barbara that Tawny's assistant headmaster, Dave Horan, had phoned: "He is disturbed, fed up, and would like to leave."

Into this poisoned context Jim Miller delivered his seven-page report suggesting Woodstock might do better as a psychiatric treatment school – but that in any event the school would not be able to do anything effectively until it clearly defined its primary purpose. At the September board meeting Miller and Helen Nowlis attended (see above), Miller backed off from his "psychotic" labeling of the students (though he later reasserted it in his 1978 book, as well as in his teaching and interviews almost twenty years later). Nowlis, who had spent some time on campus, but less than Miller, took issue with the label, called it "jargon," and advised against "rushing in a battery of psychiatrists." Privately, Miller had talked with Tawny about Tawny's being too rigid to be effective at Woodstock, a perception Miller recalled Tawny accepting intellectually but resisting emotionally. Miller omitted this issue from his report, along with his concern about the effects of a divided board of trustees on the school. However, the consultants were in solid agreement about the school's need to clarify its values, a position that embraced all the sub-issues.

Nowlis took the lead in urging a solution in having a sense of community as a goal. "Assume that with every problem you're going to consider the community... for every problem, bring in the community," Nowlis urged. "Your best defense [against a school in disarray] is meaningful activity in a community that means something to them." In other words, she was recommending a return to the approach John Holden had used (as had David, more constrictedly), and which Tawny had so emphatically rejected only a year earlier.

Faced with that conundrum, the board formed a committee. With the understanding that Gerry Freund would lead an effort to discover the values important to the community and present them in a statement of policy, the board unanimously approved a resolution, seconded by Tom Debevoise, creating "a committee to involve members of all parts of the school's community... [in a restatement of purpose] for adoption by the board and all members of the community."

Eliminating any ambiguity that this was tantamount to putting Tawny on probation, Gerry named Barbara Sproul and Bill Speer to his committee and together they started visiting the school regularly to meet with students, teachers and staff alike. At the same time, Tom Debevoise had taken control of important aspects of running the school, simultaneously supporting and controlling Tawny in many areas. With this assertion of Tom's authority, Tawny's combative approach to the board disappeared. Before Jim Miller left the meeting, it seemed the board was indeed finding a "magical" solution in rallying 'round the headmaster. Had he remained longer, he might have decided that the board was not rallying 'round so much as surrounding the headmaster. But that might not have changed his opinion that the solution would be short-lived.

Evidence of that possibility followed within days. Publicly, Tawny was telling anyone who would listen that "things at the Country School are good, exciting, and very much alive." Publicly, he was not telling anyone that the faculty member he'd come to trust and rely on most, his assistant headmaster Dave Horan, had suddenly and angrily resigned in frustration and disgust. Dave, who had a well-deserved reputation among students and faculty alike for calm, deliberate, sensible action, had replaced Peter Sauer after his sudden (but not angry) resignation in 1965. By 1969, Dave had become one of the new "old guard" from the Bailey days, along with John Pierce, Richard

Montagu and Buffy Dunker. No other teachers and few of the staff had been at Woodstock more than two years. Tawny had increasingly turned to Dave for help in running the school during 1968-69. Tawny formalized that working relationship in February, when he named Dave assistant headmaster (in addition to Dave's other work as an English teacher, college placement advisor and later helping run the Four-Term plan). The faculty elected Dave as its representative to the board of trustees. And Dave was widely liked and respected within the school community.

Dave later characterized his resignation as "impulsive," but the pressures leading up to it were rooted in his devotion to the school and his desire to see it become healthy again, which so much depended on Tawny. "Tawny and I [had] reached an understanding, the effect of which was that I was going to take care of the domestic affairs and he was going to worry about bringing in a lot of money, and communication with the Trustees – and not worry very much about discipline and schedules and stuff," Dave said years later. "I just remember feeling that, well, let's give it our best shot and see what comes of it, suspend judgment. I think there was quite a bit of skepticism among the faculty... one had the sense that almost everything he did was contrived... I remember feeling that I had to set or assume a role of buffer between Tawny and the rest of the school, sort of interpret his remarks, his thinking, to others – it might seem worse than it really was."

Even before he became assistant headmaster, Dave had begun to lose faith in Tawny. Early in the 1969 winter term the headmaster had asked Dave to decide which English teacher to fire, Dave recalled: "He said we've got too many English teachers, I want you to put the finger on somebody." I just had never done that sort of thing. He tried to persuade me that was part of being head of the English Department, what a ridiculous title [there were three other English teachers, all of whom had other responsibilities outside the 'department']. I guess I probably said that I would think about it, but eventually I said I can't [fire anyone]."

While Tawny was reporting that "the summer term was a joy," Dave was having an altogether different experience. "All during the summer I was just feeling really strung out with the amount of work I had allowed myself to take on. I was doing Four-Term stuff and college stuff and teaching a full load and trying to work with Tawny and feeling very demoralized and still trying very hard to have relationships with students... and just feeling that I could no longer be in that position of supporting him. I'd just gotten myself around to the point where I couldn't believe in him... So I very precipitously just quit, I just wound myself up and went in and said I just have to do this, I can't do all this stuff any more, and I guess he was delighted because he said OK and didn't try to persuade me otherwise."

Contributing to Tawny's presumed delight at Dave's departure, was the simultaneous departure of Dave's wife Len, a powerful, feisty woman who identified strongly with Janis Joplin's music and whose own emotionally energetic directness contrasted sharply with that of Tawny's remote propriety. She disliked Tawny so intensely that she loudly criticized him in the school dining room, knowing her insults could be heard by anyone who wished to hear. Tawny replaced Dave with himself as chairman of the English Department and as college placement advisor, hiring his wife Irene to help with the latter.

The school's official explanation for Dave's resignation, according to Buffy at the time, was that Dave had decided he needed a break and, with two small children to think about, driving a local public school bus was just what, he needed. Tawny made no reference to Dave's leaving in his reports at the time (nor did he remember it years later). But certainly Gerry Freund's committee, if not other trustees, were well aware of the causes of Dave's disaffection, since he and Gerry had been talking about their views of the school for months by then and remained in touch after Dave left. During the fall, the Horans' house in East Barnard served as a frequent gathering place for several teachers who needed a comfortable place away from school, where they could occasionally enjoy a toke of home-grown marijuana. At some point, the second-term science teacher, Rick Farrar, whom Tawny hired because he was a "trained psychologist," got wind of the Horan-parties and reported them to Tawny. Tawny immediately branded the Horans persona non grata and forbade his faculty to associate with them, or risk their jobs (though some, at least, ignored the ban). Soon thereafter, Tawny named Rick Farrar assistant headmaster, but he had sown a bitterness that would divide the faculty for years to come.

For the moment, as the 1969 fall term began, all of the school's constituencies – the students, the faculty, the trustees – were quiescent, allowing more measured attention to long- term planning. After the French House dorm had burned in the spring, Tawny had pushed the trustees to expand the school to 120 students. At the next meeting, he recommended the school be stabilized at 70 students. He presented the board with a deficit budget based on that assumption, which particularly offended Dick Day and Tom Debevoise. Tom took charge and solved this dorm/enrolment problem with one of the most creative and satisfactory decisions in the school's history. In place of the converted barn, which had housed an average of two dozen students, two faculty families and a faculty bachelor, Tom proposed half a dozen Acorn structures, pre-fabricated one-family houses, which could be quickly assembled on temporary foundations. His plan – to have five student Acorns (with five students each) and one faculty Acorn – was approved in August by a group of students, teachers and trustees and approved after the fact by the whole board. The Acorns were ready for the fall term and, for the remainder of the school's life, provided Woodstock's most popular housing.

Tom's financing scheme was equally creative and effective, especially for a deficit-hounded school with no effective fundraising programs. The school bought two Acorns outright, for $9,900 each. The school sold the other four, three to individuals, the fourth to a consortium of eight investors. The owners retained all real property interests, including the tax advantage of depreciation. The school had the use of the buildings and the capital in exchange for a rent equal to a ten per cent return on investment. The school had the option to buy back the Acorns after three years, at a depreciated cost and wound up receiving substantial portions of the value of the buildings as gifts. Tom was particularly pleased that he had made all the arrangements locally, which seemed to him to disprove the school's long-held conviction that it couldn't raise money in the town.

Such serendipity did not bless plans for the new, 48-student, co-ed dorm that Tawny had proposed in May. Before there was a chance for any serious discussion on campus, Tom authorized the architect to start drawing up plans for a 30-student dorm with two faculty families. When the trustees and the headmaster got around to consulting the faculty late in the fall, the faculty expressed clear, adamant opposition to so large a dorm – just as very different faculties had done every time it was asked about dorms during the previous decade. By December, the faculty realized that, if there was to be a co-ed dorm, then all the school's dorm rules would have to be reconsidered. Meanwhile, the executive committee expanded the planned dorm to 44 students. In January, the faculty strongly and almost unanimously objected to the large, co-ed dorm as being not only unmanageable, but destructive of the scale and intimacy that characterized Woodstock at its best. Three days later, the trustees unanimously approved the 44-student dorm, adding a third faculty apartment to make the place "more manageable." The decision was guided primarily by Tom's determination to expand the school to 120 boarders. A few days later, before these plans were presented to the Community for their approval. Tawny wrote to Tom Debevoise urging deception: "I was talking with Phil [Hansen], and he suggested that if we are building a 'coed' dorm with only a common room to be shared we say we are building two dorms each with its own name but connected by a common room. Seemingly silly semantic fine points can so easily become causes celebres; Phil's nomenclature might make clear that the new building does not represent a departure or a radicalization of the lifestyle of the school, at least not yet."

For Tawny, however, and for his relationship with the board, the most important building issue was the future of Giles House. The board, quite aware that David had declined to move into the place, had no special attachment to the elegant, but remote, Georgian mansion. At its September 1969 meeting, the board expressed a desire to sell Giles House eventually. But Tawny and Irene loved living there, to them it was an integral part of being Woodstock's headmaster and Tawny considered it one of his contractual perquisites. So much so, in fact, that at the next board meeting two weeks later, Tawny engineered a change in the September minutes to reflect his personal interest rather than the board's explicit expression of the school's interest. According to the revised minutes, it was "the headmaster's impression when he was hired that Giles House would be his permanent residence." The Trustees reversed themselves again in January 1970 and voted unanimously to sell the place as soon as it suited them.

As the 1969-70 school year progressed, morale declined among both faculty and students, leading to a reduction of the course load from five to four and complete elimination of the creative arts requirement, undoing policies that were only a year old. There were more instances in which broken confidences became an issue, when Tawny sent some students home as the result of information provided by other students. Drinking and theft increased during the fall, as did complaints of student-to-student cruelty, until the faculty finally acquiesced to the students' repeated demands for locks on their doors. With the cold weather, drug use moved indoors and seemed to increase, only this time there was no panic. Instead, when a faculty intern on an off-term from Bennington College suggested that everyone in the school was avoiding the drug issue, the faculty denied the charge and dropped the issue. Student attrition rose again, though not so high as the year before. Five faculty members also decided to leave before fall, but none was fired. Gerry Freund's committee on the Woodstock philosophy visited the campus frequently, but stirred up no trouble. The school's surface calm suggested that perhaps Tawny was settling in and learning to live with Woodstock, if not as Woodstock – and that Woodstock was learning to live with him. But none of the underlying conflicts had been addressed, much less resolved. For science teacher Pat Lee, the school felt all year like "a ticking time bomb."

SUMMER 1968 – SUMMER 1970

## Tawny Kilborne reports to the trustees, selections, 1969-1970

*I think that the Woodstock Country School is the most exciting educational institution I have ever been professionally associated with. The faculty feels the same way. Most of the students do too. I look forward to a very good year here. [October 1969]*

*This last fall has been an extraordinarily happy term at Woodstock... On the last day of school, over half the students showed up for a voluntary Christmas service at the South Woodstock chapel, after which everyone (even some who did not attend the service) ate cookies, drank punch, sang Christmas carols, and danced at the Giles House. The new spirit and sense of direction that began in the summer of 1969 appears to be growing in an exciting, healthy way." [January 1970]*

*I have never seen the students at Woodstock as happy as they are at the time of this writing. Those who wanted another kind of school have, for the most part, departed. There will be rough waters ahead, as there were this past winter, but no one is worried about the ship's foundering, and just about everyone knows we're sailing with a compass." [May 1970]"*

## Tawny Kilborne report to trustees (Appendix A), April 1970

*In the formulation of rules and customs in an independent school, I believe that two abysses yawn between which a headmaster must walk with care. On the one hand, if a headmaster tries to create a utopia he may provide students with one to four years of heaven but in so doing he may unequip them to deal with the realities of living outside this utopia, where people are held accountable for their actions, where promotion is denied on the basis of non-performance, and where sympathy is less in evidence than impersonal appraisals of the job done. It is the responsibility of the headmaster to help educate students to deal with these realities. On the other hand, if the headmaster simply holds a mirror up to society and tries to recreate its strengths and weaknesses, he provides students with no vision of a hope for a better future, and turns himself into a mere apologist for the status quo...*

*There is often no logical place to draw the line in these matters, yet lines must be drawn if the school is to carry out this part of its educative function... Implicit in many of our rules and customs is the assumption that the school should prepare people to live and work in society as it is, so that it can be transformed into something better...*

• • •

David Bailey had always resisted the inflexibility implicit in codifying Woodstock's rules, even on the rare occasions that students requested such codification. But he never resisted having rules, they were discussed in school meetings at the beginning of every school year, they were scattered but clearly stated in school brochures of two decades, and students were generally clear what the rules were, if not the consequences for breaking them. Jim Young was the first to pull all the rules together, in the spring of 1967, in a list more concerned with haircuts and bras than the sense of community responsibility the rules were meant to serve. That effort was so quickly ignored that by the following fall John Holden was unaware of this list as he worked with the community to adopt the Basic Agreement, a framework for behavior much more consonant with the school's unspoken philosophy.

In the spring of 1969, Tawny had distributd an angry memo full of Jim-Young-style rules, adding to several of those rules the promise of expulsion (other rules were listed without punishment). Appearing in the midst of more immediate and traumatic events, Tawny's memo went unprotested; nor did he repeat it in the catalog that summer, in part because Gerry Freund and other trustees reviewed and moderated the catalog copy line by line. This apparently settled the question of reliance on rigid, written rules. But in the spring of 1970, Tawny included in his report to the board his strongest statement yet of Woodstock's "Rules and Customs," numbering 34 in all, each with its likely punishment and Tawny's rationale. While these rules were mostly traditional and unexceptionable, this sudden escalation of codification by the headmaster was unique in Woodstock experience, and signaled a controlling point of view harsher than any in the school's first 23 years. Emphasizing the philosophical distance between himself and the rest of the school's experience, Tawny promised expulsion for a first offense in six areas: stealing, drug use, personal violence, willful property damage, "sexual behavior that flagrantly violates our culture's mores" (not more objectively defined) and, almost laughably as an expulsion offense, "running away from school."

These "Rules and Customs" went to board members in advance of their May 1970 meeting, raising anew all the doubts they had about their headmaster's leadership a year earlier. "I remember thinking, well, good luck to you," Tom Debevoise recalled. "If you need something like that, this isn't the place for it." But the Trustees' first order of business "was the budget, and Tom's prompt rejection of Tawny's proposed Operating Budget for 1970-71. Tom publicly criticized Tawny for merely increasing line items from the previous budget, rather than using more rigorous zero-base budgeting to justify each item in its own terms. Tom also criticized Tawny for not presenting a balanced budget, since the school was almost fully enrolled. Moreover, Tom had promised the bank that the school would run on a balanced budget as part of his application which secured a $260,000 loan to build the new dormitory. Tawny was humiliated and hurt, particularly since he had come to respect and rely on Tom's leadership: "Tom launched a totally unexpected attack upon me for the way I was handling the school's finances, which I thought was one of my longest and strongest suits, and it was this astonishing, out of nowhere, vituperative attack. I was just dumbfounded and said, 'Well, Tom, if you feel this way, why haven't you indicated this to me before?' During lunch, Gerry Freund and Roger [Phillips] expressed their horror that he would do such a thing."

But Tom was also reacting to Tawny's bulldogged refusal to drop a number of budget issues. One of these had produced a running battle with Tom over his insistence on including capital expenses (in particular, the cost of paying off the new dorm mortgage) in the operating budget. In his report to the board that spring, Tawny referred pointedly to these mortgage payments: "It was my understanding that the Trustees were going to raise this money." Tawny also challenged Tom's request to cut almost a third of Woodstock's none-too-large scholarship budget (then $32,250, compared to Putney's $100,000). And even though Tom had embarked on a building program that would enlarge the school to 120 boarders, Tawny recommended the board raise an additional $20,000 by increasing enrolment to 126, arguing that "to enroll fewer would seem to reflect an attachment to a round figure (100) that borders on numerological superstition."

And if this gratuitous slap at David Bailey's legacy hadn't been enough, Tawny had already pushed Tom too far once before. Tawny had written Tom the previous fall, referring to the 1969-70 budget (which eventually ended in surplus): "The projected deficit is $15,708. This includes David Bailey's retirement and the interest we owe on our loan (as you know, I have always questioned whether these expenses should be charged against the operating budget)." Tom replied that school obligations were not severable, no matter how the accounting was handled: "In regard to the budget, I am aware of your feeling in regard to David's retirement and interest, but I really don't want to hear any more about it."

The trustees proceeded with their May meeting, referring the budget questions to the Executive Committee for resolution, then disposed of several routine matters, including lunch, before taking up Tawny's "Rules and Customs." Roger Phillips immediately disagreed with the principle of formulating and promulgating such rules. Half of the ten trustees present objected to various aspects of the document and the absent Barbara Sproul criticized it sharply in a letter. Only the faculty representative, John Pierce, openly sided with Tawny, arguing that under David Bailey, the faculty "held to the idea of never dismissing a student." Roger Phillips said there seemed to be a basic difference in philosophy between Tawny and the board and asked the headmaster not to disseminate the document. Tawny refused, noting that it was already in circulation in the school and in use in admissions. Tawny explained, according to the minutes, "he felt that the students and administration were now close, while the trustees were deeply divided. [That he] thought more and more this was not a Board for which he wanted to work much longer, and that the trustees should look for someone else at the end of his contract [in July 1971]. [That the] school was now a healthy and going concern. He foresaw the undoing of this and a return to the school's former state in the Board's divisiveness." According to Tawny's recollection, it was moved and seconded "that the rules and regulations document be suspended by order of the board, and it was just about to come to a vote, and then somebody said, 'Well, let's ask Tawny – what will Tawny do?' And I said, 'I'll resign. Today.' So they didn't bring it to a vote."

Now taking a conciliatory tone, Tom Debevoise suggested a compromise, which Tawny accepted, whereby the "Rules and Customs" would not be withdrawn, but neither would they be further disseminated off campus. At Gerry Freund's suggestion, the board scheduled a special meeting for July 17, "to elucidate the school philosophy and, to the extent found appropriate, to adopt new programs and procedures to implement it." Tom appointed Gerry to head a committee to draw up an agenda. Earlier in the meeting, the faculty trustee, John Pierce, suggested having student trustees (without having mentioned the idea first to Tawny). The board invited the students to consider sending an advisory group to the July 17 trustees meeting.

Tawny's lame duck status for the coming year became common knowledge within a few weeks. And despite his assertions of a close-knit campus community, no segment of the school rushed to his support; not the students, not the faculty, not the parents and certainly not the alumni. After almost two years as Woodstock's headmaster, Tawny had no significant constituency of support, only a few individuals with little influence, with no voice and less impact. The overwhelming majority of people at the school seemed happy enough to see him go when his contract was up. According to the minutes, Tawny told the faculty meeting on June 3, that his "decision to resign was not a hasty one. He has had a growing awareness that he is not as happy in a boarding school as in a day school. He wishes more time to be with his family. Tawny is not an administrator for hire." At the same meeting, the faculty established a volunteer faculty committee to deal directly with the trustees concerning the July 17 philosophy meeting – the volunteers were Richard Montague, Peter Holland and Phil Hansen.

"Faculty unease has been considerable recently," Tawny wrote in a disjointed letter to Tom Debevoise two days after the faculty meeting. "Essentially, the Faculty feels a bit at sea not knowing what to expect in the immediate or distant future... The faculty has elected a committee of three to communicate directly with you and the rest of the board on matters that concern the faculty and that pertain to the possible changes in philosophy and the definite changes in administration for the school. I specifically asked not to be consulted in the communications with you and the board, though I believe I will be informed."

## Tawny Kilborne letter to Tom Debevoise, June 7, 1970

*I should like further to explain my resignation.*

*My first letter to you on the subject, written with the thought that you would probably duplicate it and send it to the rest of the Board, was circumspect, truthful, but significantly incomplete. The decision I reached some time ago – to resign after a four- or five-year hitch here – was motivated by essentially the personal priorities to which you alluded in your letter. My decision to resign at the end of my contract in the spring of 1971 was a direct result of the last Board meeting. That meeting made distressingly clear to me that the Board was probably too deeply divided to function effectively and that I personally do not wish to be accountable to the individuals in either faction.*

*The philosophic cleavage between a sizable segment of the Board and me to which I referred in my earlier letter does not include you. You may recall that Gerry, Roger and, I believe, others, justified the discussion of the "Rules and Customs" on the grounds that this document expressed a philosophy that was repugnant to them. As Board members, they felt they had a right to be concerned, and I agree with them. If the question had been merely a matter of implementation, then that prolonged discussion should not, in my estimation, have been allowed to run on...*

*Philosophically, I think a sizable segment of the Board wants the school to be more progressive than I do. Many of these Board members do not really know what they mean by 'more progressive,' but their feeling that I am too conservative, too little concerned with people and too much with the institution, is a reality with which I have grown increasingly impatient. This faction I see as well meaning, passionately vague, strongly influenced by the school's past, and fundamentally impractical. The other faction, led by you and dominant at the moment, strikes me as philosophically sufficiently close to me for me to be able in all good conscience to implement their policies, though one financial tenet held by this contingent seems to me most regrettable. I understand how you prefer your ideas in this regard be expressed: that the overall financial responsibility for the school is jointly the Board's and the headmaster's. Practically, this policy has meant the inclusion of capital expenses in an operating budget. Such a practice is exceedingly rare in independent schools (you are welcome to check this out; I have). It is a distinctive trait that is a contributing factor to the announced resignation of the present headmaster, and will, in my opinion, make the search for a successor significantly more difficult. It is certainly the Board's right to establish such a policy; I want to be sure you understand the price tag.*

*Perhaps the single most important factor in the advancing of my resignation date is intensely personal: the deep hurt and disappointment that you caused me by the gratuitously cruel way you handled the rejection of my budget. I still cannot understand it or reconcile it with the warmth and friendship I have often felt from you. I hope you will not indulge in the conveniently handy rationalization of ascribing to my defensiveness, or sensitivity to criticism, a situation that has developed as a result of your unkindness. Other Board members have spoken to me of their shock at the way you leaped for the jugular. For you as Chairman of the Board I see a dilemma: you require of the headmaster a high level of competence, which in this job means, among other things, a lot of guts, and at the same time you will not permit any questioning of your authority. I'm afraid you can't have it both ways. Certainly, if I treated a good teacher in faculty meeting the way you treated me last Board meeting, I would expect him to resign...*

*I profoundly wish that I did not feel the way I do. All that has happened has much saddened me. I have, as you pointed out, learned much from my total Woodstock experience, much that will serve me in good stead for the rest of my life. I hope the Board has learned too. I hope, also, personally, that we will have a chance to talk out, one-to-one some of these matters. It is because I perceived you as a friend that you were in a position to hurt so deeply.*

*Finally, please understand that I firmly believe that a year ago you saved both the school and my career from what could have been a devastating setback. I am grateful to you for giving me the time to accomplish whatever I have accomplished here. Subsequent events have not changed that feeling of gratitude.*

● ● ●

But the following week in faculty meeting, without sharing his letter to Tom, the headmaster was playing off the faculty against the trustees, telling the faculty he wanted to put pressure on the board in their consideration of the school's philosophy. Tawny encouraged the faculty to demand direct participation in the process, even making a motion (approved 9-6) that the faculty write the board a letter saying, "We hope that the trustees will formulate the school's philosophy in consultation with all of the school's constituency" and outlining procedures the board should follow in doing so. Tawny drafted the letter himself.

At the same time, Tawny wrote again to Tom asking that the board consider the headmaster's 1971-72 contract at its July 17 special meeting: "The timing is right, and would be even if I were not having serious doubts about the wisdom of continuing here... If I am going to move on, the Board needs to know right away so that it can begin to energetically hunt for a new man, and I need to know so that I can energetically hunt for a new school. Should the Board see fit to make me an offer for 1971-72, I will make up my mind by the end of July."

Meeting with the Executive Committee the day after Commencement, Tawny found Tom making "every conciliatory kind of effort" in working out the budget problems much to Tawny's satisfaction. Tom had good reason to be conciliatory, with his school divided every which way and approaching the loss of its third headmaster in four years. On top of that, on June 1, Tom had announced the school's 25th Anniversary Fund Drive, a three-year campaign with a goal of $400,000, but with no organization in place. Tom was then the de facto chairman and had raised almost $40,000 in advance gifts, but $35,000 of that had come from Laurance Rockefeller.

Just a week before the July meeting, Tom wrote to the board: "After the Spring Trustees meeting, evidently substantially as a result of the apparently rough going-over I gave him on the proposed budget, Tawny wrote me to say that he wished to resign a year from now, accelerating his plans to return to working with a day school. I talked with him briefly after graduation and ascertained that June 1971 was not necessarily the latest date he would consider – depending on arrangements after June 1970… We agreed that the Trustees should decide at the next Trustees' meeting their desires in connection with his move."

At the same time, Tawny himself instructed the faculty to meet without him in early July, directing it to come to some consensus about the direction of the school. When the faculty partially fulfilled its charge, Tawny rejected its conclusions, but refused to join its further deliberations, which were to be free form and philosophical – "you want a series of meetings of a kind that I am neither able nor inclined to chair." So the faculty went ahead and held these meetings without their headmaster.

There is no record of the board deciding, or even discussing, the future of Tawny's contract at its July 17 meeting. Instead, the trustees, with selected faculty and students, took part in a wide-ranging discussion of the school's psychic and philosophical distress, which Tawny had been publicly denying for a year. At their next faculty meeting, the faculty, many of whom felt excluded from the process of deciding the school's future, voted 12-2 to censure the trustees for not listening to the faculty and not wanting to come to grips with "the real problems of the school." The faculty's criticism appeared in the meeting minutes published in the school. Three days after the trustees meeting, Tom Debevoise wrote to all who took part in it, suggesting a community meeting two weeks later to discuss the issues raised before the trustees and "to reach a consensus on appropriate guidelines for the community." He also suggested he moderate that meeting himself: "Recognizing that I will not be directly affected by the decisions of the community, anymore than I have been by the rule of the school in the past, I believe I can play a helpful role as an Independent moderator."

Tawny resented Tom's proposal, "I thought he was out of line, any board chairman would be out of line doing that." With no vote of confidence from the trustees and no other constituency of support, Tawny suddenly resigned at the end of July, on two days notice, with eleven months to go on his contract. Having made his decision, but not announced it, Tawny went to Washington to discuss it with Tom who, Tawny felt, "took a fatherly tone" but assured him the school would go on. Tom felt Tawny was scared, "scared of the kids," scared of something, "he had to get out."

When Tawny discussed his resignation, "I said fine," Tom recalled, "I just listened. I made no effort to persuade him to stay, that's not my way." Tom felt that Tawny, in his unsettled state, wasn't doing the institution any good, so he might as well resign: "I don't remember any great surprise. I don't remember being upset. I don't see how he could have been helped." Tawny returned to Woodstock and publicly announced his resignation on Monday, August 3, blaming the trustees for undermining his authority. Years later, Tawny said there were only two people in the world he would cross the street to punch in the nose and one of them was Tom Debevoise (the other was a theatre director who mangled one of his plays). In 1970, Tawny punched Tom and the school in the nose metaphorically by ignoring Tom's advice and sending out a long letter of self-justification to the Woodstock trustees, former trustees, other headmasters and dozens of friends, colleagues and educators who might someday help him.

## IX

### Barbara Sproul '62 letter to Trustees, May 6, 1970

*I won't be able to attend the Board meeting this weekend....*

*I was greatly disturbed by the tenor of the headmaster's report [received today] because of its seeming emphasis on administration rather than education....*

*Appendix A to the report disturbed me even more in that its underlying thesis seemed to suggest that one of the fundamental ways in which Woodstock could help its students was to "adjust" them to the "realities" of our society....*

*The real responsibility we have as a school to the society is to provide a place where education can take place – where children can come and grow creatively, where they can learn....*

*And lastly, in connection with this second assumption in Tawny's report [that WCS is just a college prep school], I would like to comment on his asertion that "simply being at Woodstock is a privilege" – a privilege which should be earned. Being a school is also a privi-*

lege; having these kids at school is a privilege. Both, too, are privileges which must constantly be earned. Sand the responsibilities we have to these students and to those who follow them are far greater that the responsibilities they have to us. We exist for them, for these kids; we are responsible for their education and growth; we have no other reason for existing. If we solve _our_ problems with rigid and petty rules and requirements and do not solve _theirs_, we fail.

## Tawny Kilborne letter to all concerned, August 3, 1970

*I am resigning as headmaster of the Woodstock Country School effective immediately.*

*When the Board hired me, my charge was clear – to make coherent a potentially exciting academic program, to strengthen the faculty, to bring the school from enormous operating deficits to an operating surplus, to increase several fold the applications for admission, to make practicable the Four-Term Plan – in short, to make the school a healthier, happier place to learn and live. Students used to run away from Woodstock with some frequency. The school may not be paradise yet but we haven't had a runaway in over a year, and last term, for the first time, no student withdrew, was expelled or flunked out. Between September 1968 and May 1970 I felt I understood what the Board wanted, and I believe that the school met, and often exceeded, the Board's expectations.*

*In the May Board meeting, 1970, the board expressed its intense dissatisfaction with my codification of the school rules. Despite ample evidence that the rules were interpreted very flexibly, the Board felt that they were rigid and contrary to the school's traditions. The Board's feeling quickly became common knowledge, and as a result opposition from students and faculty was generated and then cited by the Board as evidence of the community's unhappiness with the rules. I began to feel that the Board was dissatisfied with the very order it had hired me to bring to the school. I therefore announced to the Chairman my resignation effective June 1971.*

*The seeds of discontent, however, had been sown. Suddenly, the order that I had worked so hard to bring about was questioned in all quarters. As I entered my lame duck year, it appeared to many students and faculty that the Board, from whom a headmaster derives all his authority had backed away from the Headmaster, individual Board members gave that impression in informal conversations with students and faculty. When the chairman [Tom Debevoise] wrote to the four students, the two faculty members [plus the headmaster], and the trustees who had attended the special Trustees' Meeting on July 18 his letter of July 20, 1970, calling for a Community meeting on August 21 "to reach a consensus on appropriate guidelines for the Community for the Fall term" and suggesting that this meeting be moderated by the Chairman, he reinforced the notion that the locus of decision-making power at the school had shifted. In the Community Meeting, July 19, one student who had attended the July Board meeting asked whether the community could be accountable to the Board rather than to the Headmaster. In the preceding community meeting, another student suggested that the school might operate better without a headmaster. Students began to get out of control, in community meetings and in the dining room. Faculty politicking became savage, and students and faculty began vying for power. For me, the situation became intolerable, and, I feel, terribly unfair. I hold the Board responsible."*

### Jim Miller interview, May 2, 1986

*I met with the board of Trustees. That was where I first learned about this feature that was still, I think, the most interesting single piece of data we got, and that is that, at the board meetings, there was always this chair left open – they sat in this U-shaped arrangement and left the center chair empty. And Tawny, as the headmaster, sat outside. In the old days, [David] Bailey would have sat in that center chair and, at all the meetings I ever attended, it was left empty."*

● ● ●

The *Rashomon* effect, perceiving reality according to one's personal needs, may have contributed to the self-serving inaccuracies and omissions of Tawny's letter (above); to which Tom Debevoise responded, "No worthwhile purpose would be served at this time by my answering what I believe to be the many, many distortions in it."

The *Rashomon* effect is perhaps the only explanation for the appearance of the ritualized empty chair Jim Miller saw at a trustees meeting (the record is clear that he attended only one, in September 1969, when his work at the

Country School was over). In his book, Miller wrote: "Our conversations with board members convinced us that the reparative functions of this perceived fantasized 'death' of the founder were still strong by the end of our consultation. They took the form of constant reminiscences, of overt expression of guilt about his removal, of deprecatory comparisons with his successors, of repeated alumni news about his whereabouts and activities, and finally the symbol of the empty chair at meetings of the board." Miller's assessment of the basic psychology of some board members was consonant with a shared sense of having deposed a father figure. But even in that, Miller was startlingly wrong in his depiction of events, reporting that "the founder of the school, then over 65 years of age, began to become physically and mentally less able to run the school" when the much more traumatic reality was that David had been forced to retire at age 55 after at least five years of growing debilitation from emphysema.

Tom Debevoise's reaction was emphatic: "There was no empty chair, I'm sure that didn't happen. I have no recollection of any such sentimentality." Gerry Freund, Roger Phillips, Barbara Sproul and others were equally certain that no such ritual was ever enacted. Certainly, it would have been out of keeping with Woodstock's powerful traditions of informality and change. Moreover, the trustees held their meetings in many different rooms in several different states, which could have meant carting "David's chair" back and forth, suggesting a level of organization beyond the board's consistent capabilities during those years. But does that mean Tawny's "best friend" Jim Miller was hallucinating? Probably not. Miller probably did see an empty chair at that trustees meeting. But the reason there was an empty chair was Tawny purposefully refused to sit within the trustees' circle, maintaining that his job was not to shape policy, only to carry it out.

At a deeper level, then, Miller's perception was metaphorically quite right, there was an empty chair where the headmaster should have been, a chair that had not been fully filled for the better part of a decade, a chair that had to be filled for the school to survive.

Commencement 1970: Student speaker Phil Krauss '71 (white jacket, above) talked about his shoes. He talked about where his shoes had been and gone, and then he set them on fire (below). Also on the podium are headmaster Phil Hansen, guest speaker, and moderator Stuart Cudlitz '71. The pail and barrel to the right are an excess of fire protection.

Gerry Freund '48

Jan Poore, dance teacher, at her faculty Acorn

Amy Wallace '72

Dan Richardson, business manager & basketball coach (above), with Erin Ervin '74

SUMMER 1968 – SUMMER 1970

Kitchen crew: Dianne Davis '71 (left) & Bridgette Chace '69 (whose mother went to WCS in its first year)

E. Rebecca Silliman, French teacher and Bailey House boys dorm head, 1970-71

Rosanne Pyfrom '73

Torsten Bodecker '73

Peter Dembski '72 testing water quality in the local Kedron Brook as part of Rick Farrar's science program that helped persuade the Village of Woodstock to install a sewer system that helped clean up the Ottauquechee River. Rick Farrar (in background) also ran a student-based bird banding program that evolved into the Vermont Institute of Natural Science that he co-founded with WCS support.

Didy Lyman '72 at Owen Moon House

SUMMER 1968 – SUMMER 1970

Richard Man '73

Phil Hansen, headmaster

Charles Halty '74

Catalogue shot: unknown, unknown, Dana Good, Bryant Urban, unknown, unknown unknown, unknown

Phil Hansen, headmaster

Peter Holland,
English teacher

WCS Library in the Kedron Brook flood of June 1973

CHAPTER TEN

# Summer 1970 – Fall 1973

**I**

**Trustee meeting minutes, discussion of WCS philosophy, July 18, 1970**

*A student felt that the faculty had been divided among themselves and that the students certainly had been divided, seeking their security in small groupings, alienated from the school administration. A student felt there was no pulling together of the community or real sense of community recently, after Tawny had announced his intention to move on in June 1971, that the faculty had finally gotten together... A student [felt] that the current structure within the school community, with an ever-felt, ultimate veto power in the headmaster, was dividing the* school community instead of assisting it to pull together. Community meetings, the students felt, were aimless because the students had no sense that decisions which might come out of them would be sympathetically considered and implemented... It was also brought out that the school does not have or plan any buildings except those essential for eating, sleeping and leaving [sic]...

## Gerry Freund '48 letter to Lori Bloustein '72, July 19, 1970

Dear Lori,

All four of you [students at the Trustees meeting], but you especially were often deeply effective and convincing in yesterday's often agonizing discussion, and at least some of us understood that you were also conveying problems and feelings that were not made explicit.

You have to believe that, though trustees may view what is going on differently and have disparate ideas about the timing and methods needed to end the painful loneliness and insecurity that grips so many at the school, all present yesterday realized that something needs to be done. This is an important step forward; and it is very substantially due to your efforts that the pain and need for attention were conveyed to people whom some of the rest of us have failed to convince of this over several years.

In this most difficult of times for the school those of us who feel the urgent necessity for fundamental non-violent change in the structure and style of the institution are bound to be frustrated by the more conservative judgments that prevail. But one cannot be sure who is right. Moreover, adding to the already prominent divisiveness would bring even greater insecurity to all concerned...

In this period all lines of communication should be kept open and the best way of doing that is to use them. Now that you have met them, you have trustees as well as teachers like Phil [Hansen] and John [Pierce] and others to resort to, and I for one would welcome keeping up the dialogue provided students and teachers realize that a trustee has the responsibility to support a school administration in its day-to-day decisions.

SUMMER 1970 – FALL 1973

## Tom Debevoise letter to WCS constituency, August 5, 1970

*To Alumni, Parents and Friends of the Woodstock Country School:*

*As I informed you in June, the Woodstock Country School is in the process of reviewing, rethinking and re-enunciating its philosophy. Last Friday [July 31], after scheduling a two-day period for self-study by the students, Tawny Kilborne announced that he wished to step down as headmaster. He was able to do this because he knew that Phil Hansen, who has played a large role in the re-evaluation, was equipped to carry on without loss of momentum. The executive committee has complete confidence in Phil, who has the background and has demonstrated the ability and the concern for individuals in the community and the school as an entity, which it wants in a headmaster. Accordingly, the executive committee was pleased to appoint Philip H. Hansen III Headmaster of the Woodstock Country School, until further action by the Board, and he has taken charge of the school as of the beginning of the month.*

*"I met with both students and faculty today and found them involved in and excited by the self study process. More about that later; but I did feel you would wish to hear immediately about the change of leadership. While dramatic in its suddenness, it leaves the school moving ahead with confidence and vigor."*

## Phil Hansen letter to WCS constituency, August 11, 1970

*I'm sure that many of you are wondering at this point about the meaning of the sudden change that has taken place in the leadership of the school. I am therefore writing you about a few of the basic directions and priorities I see for the school in the immediate future.*

*First of all, I feel that the school has a need for continuity and stability. This does not mean that no changes will be made, but that we need to avoid the psychology of siege and emergency. I have no intention of undoing the consolidation and stabilization which Tawny brought about. Tawny's contribution was the development of a strong and viable institution, and it is the existence of this institution which now permits us to take new directions. I believe that growth and change are at the heart of the educational process; chaos and anarchy are not. We will avoid violent lurches to the left or to the right, and seek to evolve in such a way as to create conditions favorable to future growth.*

*For the present, I see three major areas in which change is needed. First, we need to re-assess the quality of our community life. A school is a community of growth and learning, and students learn at least as much from the values by which the school lives day by day as they do from the classroom experience. A particular aspect of community life which has troubled us has been the schools' code of conduct [Tawny's "Rules and Customs"]. I am particularly concerned that we evolve a code to which all members of the community can commit themselves. We must avoid, on the one hand, rules which cut us off from dealing with the real problems of students. On the other hand, we must stop pursuing the mirage of permissiveness which always promises a paradise of freedom beyond the next horizon, and which ends up making us wanderers in a moral desert. The code of conduct has been the center of concern for too long. Our preoccupation has prevented us from facing realistically and compassionately the real problems of drug abuse and sexual promiscuity with which "the rules" are supposed to deal.*

*Second, we need to make our decision-making processes reflect more accurately the reality of a democratic educational community. This means that many bodies – the community meeting and its committees, the Community Council, the Major Rules Committee, the Faculty -- must be given more real authority and responsibility. The decentralization of the decision-making process will proceed as fast as these bodies can learn to participate effectively in the process. Eventually, I hope to see a growing consensus emerge as the diverse elements of the community learn to communicate and work together.*

*Third, we need to expand the range of the educational experiences available to our students. Without sacrificing the integrity of our academic life, we need to find ways to help students train their hands and bodies, and to develop the conviction that they are really responsible for themselves and their brothers. We need to take them more seriously as whole persons, and see them less as minds encased in extraneous tissues.*

• • •

In his first days as headmaster, Phil moved quickly to empower the school community, just the opposite of Tawny's first official act of suspending all the community's powers. After two years of inconsistent authoritarianism, Woodstock was more or less back where John Holden had left it, seeking to deal with problem behavior through a mutually reinforcing combination of collective and individual responsibility. Board president Tom Debevoise could almost have been quoting John Holden when he told the faculty that "the working out of guidelines should come from the community. The headmaster has residual authority... The faculty can best serve the school by working together with the students towards consensus. The faculty is an essential and vital part of the community. The measure of a headmaster is how few times he has to exercise his authority."

This was very much the attitude that Phil took toward the self-study and toward the rest of his headmastership. He wanted the community to work together, with his guidance, but without his having to bark orders. He made clear that he had to approve all policy decisions before they went into effect, but he put the emphasis on discussion, in which he participated and in which he made his views clearly known, thereby minimizing later surprises, disappointments and angry reactions.

Obliquely but unequivocally, avoiding the appearance of a personal attack, Phil rejected Tawny's policy on rules, his policy on power-sharing, and his policy of narrowly defined academic learning. Phil rejected them all on the same basis: that they were destructive to the development of whole persons. What Phil inherited from Tawny was a school that he had made bureaucratically more efficient in its fiscal control, record keeping and daily management, though he had lost ground in athletics, the work program and the coherence of community life. Beyond the campus, Tawny had made little progress in improving off-campus term opportunities for students, less progress in fundraising and none in alumni relations. Tawny had also reorganized the Woodstock faculty, leaving behind a smaller, more academically focused group of teachers, many of whom, like Tawny, were little interested in working with students beyond their academic needs.

During the summer of 1970, as open conflict at the school increased, Phil had publicly stood by Tawny, hoping and believing that Tawny could weather the crisis and remain an effective headmaster. Phil had not expected Tawny to resign. Phil had not expected Tawny to recommend him as the next headmaster. But Phil refused to take the job for less than Tawny's salary and he almost refused to take the job at all. Not yet 29 years old, Phil had a total of two years' teaching experience. He had been at Woodstock a year and a month. But he liked the school and, more importantly, the idea of the school. The school seemed to like him. It seemed to be a good fit. And Phil was flattered to be asked to be headmaster, he liked the challenge it posed and he was pleased by the prospect of exercising some authority. Besides, Tom Debevoise, acting on behalf of the Executive Committee, was persuasive, insistent and impatient. So Phil accepted the job, but only for one year and only on the condition that the board immediately start to search for his replacement.

Phil had come a long way from his first faculty meeting a little more than a year earlier, when he had been startled by an intense discussion of whether girls should be compelled to wear bras, or boys to wear shirts while playing tennis in town. He had grown up on a farm in Jefferson, Maine, the oldest of three widely spaced children in a broken home with an alcoholic father. He went to Bowdoin College on a State of Maine scholarship, graduating cum laude in 1964 as a history major, with minors in English and philosophy. He went on to Union Theological Seminary in New York City on a Rockefeller Brothers Theological Fellowship. After two years of seminary, Phil went on leave to work as executive director of the South Yonkers Youth Council in Yonkers, N.Y., which he described as "a depressed urban neighborhood involved in the crisis of ethnic change." His work ended suddenly a year later when a New York taxicab ran him down and broke his leg. After several months' recuperation, he took a teaching position at Kimball Union Academy, a traditional boys' boarding school in Meriden, N.H., which supplied Woodstock with several teachers over the years, starting with Dave Horan, who had, in turn, first piqued Phil's interest in the school. The following year, Phil returned to Union Theological to complete his work for his B.D. degree, writing a thesis titled "Aristocratic Self-Consciousness as a Mode of Personhood in Education Theory," which he described as "a thesis in the field of educational theory and adolescent development, focused on the ideas of Erik Ericson and Edgar Z. Friedenberg."

Looking for work in early 1969, Phil wrote Tawny, "I am interested in teaching some combination of English, History, and/or Religion, but I am more interested in becoming involved in the life of a creative school community than I am in teaching any specific subject. I am drawn into education by a growing fascination with the process of adolescence and a growing concern about its fate in our society. My experience during the past two years has convinced me that the most meaningful points at which I can be involved with young people are in the area of education. I am particularly interested in the nurture of excellence, both intellectual and personal. I am seeking a school which is approaching that task in a creative way, and which intends to treat adolescents with affection and respect. The many favorable things David [Horan] has told me about Woodstock and my own visits to the school last year [when John Holden was headmaster] indicate to me that Woodstock is that kind of school."

When he started at Woodstock in the summer of 1969, Phil thought of himself as a radical, though others were not so struck by it. English teacher Peter Holland, another Kimball Union transplant and Phil's closest friend on the faculty, spoke right to the point, as usual: "Phil claims to be a Marxist, and I find that amusing." Insofar as Phil had been tested by events, his radicalism emerged as largely theoretical and low key, remaining well within the American mainstream of acceptable dissent. He actively and openly opposed the war in Viet-Nam and served voluntarily as Woodstock's draft counselor, but he did not advocate draft resistance or draft card burning. (Though less openly, Tawny, too, opposed the war and he sent Phil to a draft counselor training conference at school expense.) In the spring of 1970, in the wake of the American invasion of Cambodia and the killings at Kent State, Phil worked hard at keeping his expressions of outrage within responsible boundaries and he encouraged Woodstock students to do the same. This was made easier, Phil recalled, since Woodstock joined the nationwide strike movement as an institution, probably the only school in the country that both went on strike and stayed open that spring. Woodstock's strike activities were pervasive and Phil was at their center: he helped students organize teach-ins and canvass the school's neighbors and try, unsuccessfully, to organize a boycott of prime military contractors – all with Tawny's blessing.

As Tawny recalled it, he and Phil had found each other instantly sympathetic at their first meeting. Phil interviewed him more thoroughly about the school than he interviewed Phil about his qualifications to work there. Tawny and Phil were quite alike in many ways, both bright, intellectually combative, quick to pounce on the minor solecisms of others' errors (they had both been debaters in college). They were both short, unathletic, tending toward pudginess. During 1969-70, Phil and Tawny had grown increasingly close: Phil took over the drama program when the need arose and he took over college counseling when that part of Dave Horan's job became too much for Tawny. Phil slowly became both Tawny's advisor and his interpreter to the rest of the school. At the same time, Phil was popular with the students, teaching the most fully-enrolled course the school ever offered, "Afro-American History", with 72 students ("I taught Black History from what I felt was a black perspective, as nearly as I could do that"). By the end of winter 1970, when Tawny and his official assistant headmaster, Rick Farrar, were barely speaking, Phil had become Tawny's closest confidant and his unofficial assistant headmaster, whom Tawny left in charge of the school when he was away. Among Tawny's supporters on the faculty, Phil was the only possible choice for a successor.

Quickly after Tawny's departure, the school relaxed more than it had at any time since he took over. One of Phil's first actions as headmaster, purposefully meant to signal change, came after he returned to his dorm one evening and found three students smoking marijuana. Instead of expelling them, as called for by Tawny's rules, Phil sought to communicate greater flexibility by suspending the three until the winter term. Phil didn't see himself as any less anti-drug than

Tawny, but as more open to listening to student views: "If kids feel that you love them, you can do a lot of things."

At the end of Phil's first week as head, the self-study to re-integrate the school began in an atmosphere of optimism and cooperation typical of the school's better times, though few there then had even known John Holden or David Bailey. For three days (Thursday-Saturday), all aspects of the school's life were up for discussion in four broad areas: Academic, Community Life, Rules and Customs and the Four-Term Plan, each of which was assigned a half day except Rules and Customs, which got all day Friday. A shifting population of about 60 students (out of 107) and a dozen faculty members (of 16) took part in these discussions, generally reaffirming Woodstock's ideals or realities. For the most part, the issues were only discussed, with no formal motions and votes.

The exception was Rules and Customs. Instead of taking one full day of meetings, Rules and Customs took a day and a half, in which 16 motions and numerous amendments were discussed and voted on, re-defining the whole question of Woodstock's rules. The community voted without dissent to scrap Tawny's codification of the rules. The community then approved nine Major Rules, which were largely consistent with Tawny's priorities (with the notable exception of running away), but without any prescribed punishments. The new rules covered the behavior that any community needs to address: stealing, vandalism, brutality, consistent lack of cooperation and consideration, "booze and dope," firearms/bombs, sex, and smoking, as well as a catch-all dormitory regulations clause. These rules passed by a vote of 34-2, with a lot of people abstaining and even more just absent. So far as the record shows, those abstaining or absent did not express articulated dissent.

Despite having only minority support, in a formal sense, the new system was widely accepted in practice and worked reasonably well for the next six years. Acceptance of the system was reinforced by community elections (each member having one vote, assuring a student majority) to choose the members of the student-faculty committees that would enforce the rules on a case-by-case basis. What made it work was the common sense and communal basis on which it rested. The first motion approved in the self-study was "that a standard of conduct at WCS be based on mutual consideration among individuals and a consciousness of the needs of the community as a whole." The most important factor was that Phil was not Tawny. Phil was willing to trust students, which made them inclined to trust him. But what was true for Phil was not so true for the rest of the faculty and Phil saw his most important goal as establishing trust and reconciliation between students and teachers.

SUMMER 1970 – FALL 1973

## Faculty meeting minutes (K' Williams), August 12, 1970

*Phil wants the faculty to look at the self-study proposals in terms of what it will mean in the way of faculty responsibility. Is it practical for the more permissive measures to go through? Will the faculty have too much responsibility?*

*Phil is also concerned about the confidence relationship between student and faculty. The student should be free to talk to a faculty member with the feeling that his conversation will not be shared with others unless there is a clear and present danger to an individual or the community. Students now feel distrust for the faculty. They seem to assume that faculty members are obligated to tell confidences to the headmaster and the faculty.*

*Phil will formulate a measure of reaffirmation of faculty confidences.*

*The discussion pointed out that some faculty members feel they are spread too thin to be good counselors. The Dean of Students [Marc Hurlbut] is gradually getting to be a counselor too. It is an important aspect of his job. It was decided that faculty members should give students a slight push to help their peers, especially in academics.*

*Phil felt that the self study was a good learning experience but expressed concern that it was not well attended by the faculty. 'The code of conduct should reflect the needs of the community' is a statement that originated in the last faculty meeting [actually a consensus on July 12], yet many faculty members were not at the self study to see that their own needs were reflected.*

## William Ballard, father of Madeleine '72, letter to Tom Debevoise et alia, September 1970

*During the past winter and spring [of 1970] I accompanied Madeleine on interviews to several boarding schools in New England. All of them had outstanding physical plants, large faculties, very good past records and cheaper tuition than Woodstock Country School. But, and this fact was most important, both to myself and my daughter, they all appeared to be rather dead in the water – very well maintained boats going absolutely no where primarily because there was no captain at the helm.*

*Upon our first visit to Woodstock last spring [While Tawny was still headmaster] Madeleine and I were very favorably impressed on two major counts: first that it was a very serious academic institution – and certainly not a custodial one. Second, and I think equally important to both my daughter and myself was the fact that there were definite rules of conduct and behavior that would allow the students to know exactly where they stood in most areas of potential conflict between themselves and school authoriues.*

*No pretense. No mysteries. No stupid moralizing. Just a series of simple, easy to understand rules of behavior....*

*[Despite Tawny Kilborne's resignation] it is my very strong hope that the school continues to be run by adults who are not afraid to be adults – who can listen and accept the criticisms of responsible teenagers, at the same time not at all abdicating their responsibilities as adults and teachers to provide very clear cut leadership and direction.*

## Dave Horan, English teacher, letter to the author, November 12, 1970

*Well now, while Phil is not particularly impressive initially, I'm convinced that he's good. He's not a David, but he's better than Tawny, or Holden or Young or Denman. Phil is quiet, sensitive, incredibly perceptive, articulate, an excxellent teacher (still teaching) but not a professional educator. The school still faces many of the institutional and contemporary problems suggested in your letter [to the Trustees]; Phil recognizes all these and that the way one approaches solutions is as significant as the solutions themselves. Having already been around as a teacher and having done considerable counselling, he already has developed the necessary rapport with the students that Tawny never really perceived was essential. He'll do well.*

## Phil Hansen, "A Code of Conduct," fall 1970

"The Major Rules Committee:

"The Major Rules Committee shall consist of seven members: three students elected by the community; three faculty members elected by the faculty [later by the community]; and the Headmaster ex officio. The Committee shall decide penalties in each individual case *for violations of major rules. The Committee shall reach its decisions by consensus if possible. If there is no consensus, and if there is a tie vote, the Headmaster shall decide the penalty. The Headmaster shall not vote unless there is a tie. His task will be to help the Committee reach consensus.*

*"The Major Rules Committee is responsible for making decisions which will promote the education of the offender and the welfare and preservation of the community. It shall strive for consistency and fairness, tempered by compassion for individuals and an understanding of their needs."*

## Jerome Berryhill '71 interview, May 1984

*Getting suspended kind of depressed me... Phil Hansen caught us smoking dope down in our dorm room. But Phil and I had a very close relationship. I think he regarded me, not as a protégé, but he'd taken me under his wing or something. He was all broken up about [punishing us], but he didn't see what else he could to... It's amazing when you consider he was younger then than I am now, I mean several years younger. I think he was too young for the job, basically. I think it put quite a strain on him...*

*I don't know if he had any conception of how many people were taking drugs on that campus... everybody but the Jesus freaks. Smoking dope all the time. A lot of people taking acid. And drinking whatever they could get their hands on... Daily. Certainly for me and the people I hung out with. In retrospect, one thing I didn't do at the Woodstock Country School was go to school.*

*One time Tawny Kilborne put me on academic probation. He called me into his office and said that I'd been missing way too many classes and I said, "Well, look, I'm passing all my classes. So what does it matter if I don't go?" He said, 'Well, passing isn't good enough. If you don't get A's in all your classes, we'll expel you.' I had to work hard to pass calculus. I remember for three days I took speed and sat and worked integrations [until] I'd gotten to where I'd sit there in the smoking area and I was, like, hallucinating equations. You know, functions would float by me in the air and I would integrate them on the fly. I was an integrating machine at that point. I went in and took the test and aced it.*

Tawny's recollection, that 1969-70 was "really such a good year except for the board," was essentially a fantasy shared by few others who lived through it. His legacy was not the healthier, happier school of his imagining but a school in which essential student life was driven underground by the threat of punishment. All the behavior that had produced the crisis of Tawny's first year continued through the second and would go on during Phil's headmastership, since the students were part of cultural change that would take its course regardless of the response of a little school in Vermont. But that school, like the larger culture, could still choose to respond to the behavior well or badly. For Phil, it had become clear that a moralistic and punitive approach created new problems without solving old ones. Worse, that approach had failed to ease the pain of children who were hurting, while it allowed the adults in the community to deny the problem and pretend everything was all right. Phil found this unacceptable, but he had few faculty allies.

The Woodstock faculty proved to be Tawny's most difficult legacy: close to unanimous in wanting change, but deeply divided as to whether that change should involve more "structure" or less, a harder line toward students or a gentler one. Tawny had inherited and largely cleaned out the relatively weak faculty of David Bailey's later years, which improved the school's academic quality, but left it with few reliable links to its better communal past (especially after Buffy's retirement in the spring of 1970). Tawny left behind a faculty that was young, ambitious, inexperienced and seriously divided philosophically. Purposefully seeking diversity, Tawny had hired 13 of the 16 faculty members who were on the staff in the summer of 1970. Conventional wisdom within the school community, shared by Tom Debevoise and Gerry Freund, was the early perception that Tawny had hired good teachers with strong personalities.

While there was some truth to that perception, it was also true that among the teachers Tawny hired (as well as among those he retained), there were a majority who had problematical behavior patterns. Among these were alcohol abuse, drug abuse, manipulative Christianity, sexual identity conflicts, emotional and threatened physical bullying and sexual adventuring – all of which involved students. Only a handful of these teachers were reliable truth-tellers in any circumstance. Compounding its individual difficulties, the faculty as a body was remarkably self-involved, especially in comparison to the students and the trustees. While the faculty's professional territoriality remained a problem throughout Phil's tenure, it was never more clearly expressed than in July 1970, when Tawny sent the faculty off to meet without him "to address itself [to] where the school should go from here."

The faculty did not address that question substantively, though it suggested Woodstock should not be primarily college-preparatory and that the code of conduct should be reviewed by a student faculty committee. But instead of taking a comprehensive, broad view of the school less than a week before the trustees meeting on the school's philosophy, the faculty passed just two unanimous motions. The first, "that all faculty members should be encouraged to take every eighth term off campus with remuneration," was equivalent to a 12.5% faculty pay raise, or another $20,000 on the school's annual salary budget. The other unanimous motion was "that faculty members be accorded authority commensurate with the responsibilities they carry in the community," hardly bespeaking a faculty brimming with self-confidence and the ability to lead.

When the trustees remained focused on the good of the school, not just the faculty, the faculty reacted with unprofessional pique: "A faculty member stated that obviously the Trustees didn't wish to hear the faculty… [Apparently] they do not have the desire to come to grips with the real problems [not specified] of the school… If Trustees aren't interested in faculty proposals, what kind of trustees are they? It was pointed out that very often schools are able to make progress in spite of their boards." At the same meeting, "a faculty member added that the Trustees are never going to solve our problems for us. He felt that there was a willingness on the Board's part not to obstruct. Essentially the ball was placed in our hands. Is the above delusion?" The faculty chose not to take on such responsibility, instead voting 12-2 to send the board a statement of its displeasure. This querulous temerity grew out of the faculty having felt "in limbo last year – not until this term has the faculty felt they had a real say in the larger issues."

Phil's relationship to the faculty was uneasy from the first, since it included people who thought they should have been headmaster in his place (Tawny offered, as his last official act, to fire assistant headmaster Rick Farrar, but Phil declined the offer, eventually having to do the job himself). Phil, already enjoying something of a honeymoon with students and trustees, soon sought conciliation with his faculty, writing Tom Debevoise: "The highest priority, as I see it, must be assigned to the needs of the faculty. These lie mainly in two areas. First, in order to maintain a stable and competent salary scale, while keeping salaries within a relatively narrow range. As faculty members gain seniority, however, their salaries must continue to rise. Provision must be made for a larger total amount to be devoted to salaries each succeeding year until a desirable balance of senior and junior faculty has been attained. Since all but [two] of our faculty members have come to the school in the last two years, this process will obviously take a number of years. Second, provision must be made for faculty members to take terms off campus in order to gain needed respite from the continual rigors of the four-term plan."

Even though the trustees implemented both requests, Phil continued to have difficult relations with his faculty, always expecting more than some of them were prepared to give, often holding up his own intense involvement with students as a model for them to emulate. However, like Tawny, many of the teachers he hired felt that their work should be largely limited to the classroom, leaving the rest of student lives to be looked after by others, or to be ignored until a crisis arose. Other teachers understood, with Phil, that much of what the school had to do was to rediscover a new version of its once better self – with close counseling of students, not college preparatory for everyone, emphasis on personal accountability and responsibility to the community.

Understanding these values, Phil provided the school with coherent leadership for the first time in several years, since David Bailey's denial of his emphysema first started having serious institutional consequences. The zeitgeist helped for a change, too, as the school benefited from another deep shift in American culture. Just as the emergence during the mid 1960s of marijuana, long hair and independent protest combined with David's weaknesses to compound the problems of his emphysema, so now, in 1970, the sudden, almost universal campus quiet in the wake of the National Guard's random execution of innocents at Kent State helped give Woodstock a breather in which to put its pieces back together.

In another stroke of luck, it happened that Tawny had just hired Dan Richardson to be Woodstock's business manager, starting in the Summer of 1970. Like Buffy Dunker before him, Dan was a dynamo. Not only was he cheerfully able to manage all the details Phil hated most – drawing and managing budgets, maintenance, even fundraising up to a point – he had energy left over to help coach soccer, help run the farm, serve as O.D. *every* morning and teach a course or two. Although many students at first distrusted his outspoken "conservatism," the result of fairly traditional schooling and little experience with adolescents, they quickly learned he had integrity and that he cared about them personally as much as anyone. Students also learned Dan could grow and come to value Woodstock's strengths, though he never stopped believing the school was too "permissive." Between them, despite their philosophical differences, Phil and Dan, with strong backing and support from Tom Debevoise, pulled the school together and made it run well and efficiently. Woodstock was once again a good school, where most of the students had a good experience and started to grow in healthy and creative ways that would continue for the rest of their lives.

SUMMER 1970 – FALL 1973

## Phil Hansen, "Theories, Goals and Strategies," October 12, 1970

*The Woodstock Country School is a community in process. Over the last few years, we have been forced to come to terms with, and finally to affirm, the reality of constant change. The impulsion to do so, which at first seemed to come from circumstances beyond our conscious control, has recently begun to appear more clearly to arise from the deeper traditions of the school. The school has traditionally been responsive to the needs of an evolving culture and society. Because we often deal with individuals whose relations to the dominant culture and society have reached the stage of crisis, the school has tended to relate to the rest of the world in terms of crisis. In the 1940s and 1950s, the point of crisis was the survival of the individual identity in a depersonalized mass society. While this crisis is still unresolved, it is being overshadowed today by the crisis of the disintegration of the social forms and institutions – the family, the local community, the school. Because the individual cannot survive in a social vacuum, we are now becoming increasingly aware of the possibilities of the school as a community, of the shared aspects of our life as well as the private aspects of our lives.*

*The fact that we are, and intend to be, in process, on the move, constantly responding to new insights arising from our experience, makes the task of formulating a "philosophy" difficult and a bit artificial. If we seek to freeze a moment in time and describe what our means and ends are at that moment, our formulation will go out of date even as we articulate it. Concepts broad enough to include all possible changes in direction and emphasis are likely to be so vague and abstract as to have little meaning. What I have tried to do in the statement which follows is to locate some of the consistencies which underlie the process of continual change, and to describe the major directions in which we now seem to be heading...*

## Amy Wallace '73 interview, March 11, 1985

*What's so great about Woodstock is that it hit this incredible middle ground between these liberal fuck-up schools where everybody didn't have to go to classes, didn't have to be aware, could do anything they wanted and get really sensitive and, you know, have encounter groups. That's one extreme. And the other is any number of conservative schools, including a school in Putney, where everybody is too conservative, too restrictive, et cetera. And Woodstock hit the most extraordinary balance between these two things. In other words, you had to go to class, or you suffer punishment – there were rules, but you could break them, and therefore you had a sense of rules, which I think is important. And the kids that I've known – this is based on my own experience knowing people who went to super-free schools not having any academic skills, not having any intellectual skills, it's really tragic – they just joined an encounter group and when you live in Berkeley, you don't need to do that in high school. So Woodstock is a magical school. I've never heard of another school that had this balance.*

### Alice Parker ' 74, poem in memory of John Pierce, *Symposium*, Winter 1971

*there was a moment of shock, there, this morning*

*i've never known my mouth*
*to drop open and not feel it*
*not feel it but in numbness*
*cry… fold over in cry…*
*i saw three weeks since i'd cried hello John!*
*a hand when it reached to comfort me*
*was one i had not known and i thought, i have discovered as i rode the dumptruck away i saw*
*the web he had helped me first to see*
*and the trees he had known from the twig on branch*
*away to immense forests of growth*
*life*
*i didn't do my homework for class yesterday,*
*i had meant to make up and come in full of questions*
*i've heard there is never a second chance*
*i've heard that we'll all burn in hell together…*
*but i know that where you are*
*somebody is opening their eyes… and SEEING… and*

*LISTENING*
*and probably yes most likely they are LIVING*
*for the first time...*
*there are those of us still living as we walk through*
*the forest on a path you pointed out maybe*
*with the warning not to stop noticing*
*along the way*
*i won't leave my sleeping bag in the pound anymore,*
*John*

## Phil Hansen letter to Tawny Kilborne, April 13, 1971

*Dear Tawny,*

*First of all, let me apologize for my long silence. As many other friends of mine would tell you I have never been the world's best correspondent and, for some reason or other, I seem to have had even less time in recent months for letter writing than I have ever had before. I thought perhaps I would see you and Irene at [the National Association of Independent Schools conference] ... Many people asked for you there, and many others in this part of the country would like their greetings conveyed.*

*We seem to have survived the winter in reasonably good health. While winter term wasn't exactly joyous, attrition was way down from last year. Now the snow has almost melted, and we're expecting seventy degree temperatures today. Everyone is feeling exuberant and at the same time a bit lazy. I have even taken to running two miles every morning before breakfast, urged on by [students] Woody Urban and Philip Krauss, who always seem to finish five minutes ahead of me. Personally, I have increasingly good feelings about the school and what is happening here. After eight months I am beginning to feel reasonably comfortable with where I am and somewhat more effective in what I am doing.*

*You may find it a bit ironic that I hired Dave Horan [to replace a teacher fired in January for dealing and taking drugs with students], although the Horans are not going to be moving onto the Campus. I had a certain amount of hesitation about this, given the history involved, but so far things are working out very well."*

• • •

By October 1970, the trustees had been working on the problem of expressing Woodstock's philosophy for more than a year without result. So the board seized on Phil's 10-page essay ("Theories, Goals, and Strategies" above), made a few minor changes and adopted it "as expressing the Board's consensus as to the school's philosophy." A few days before, the faculty had also accepted the paper "as a valid statement of the school's philosophy." Both votes were tantamount to a vote of confidence in Phil's interim leadership of the previous two months. His philosophical essay not only succeeded where all other recent efforts had failed, but it expressed essentially the same spirit of flexibility and personal concern contained in David Bailey's 1951 statement ("There is no formula for education... "), albeit Phil expressed it at twenty times the length. This was more than merely a difference in personal style. For Phil, the embrace of constant change was a learned response, not a natural one. Philosophically open to experiment and flux, Phil had an emotional temperament that needed order. As a result, after embracing new approaches to school problems (the self study or the Fine Arts Week break in the winter term, for example), he tended to institutionalize them with a rigidity that some of his teachers at Union Theological had warned about in their otherwise praise-filled letters of recommendation.

In the two months since Phil had agreed to become headmaster for a year, on the clear condition that the trustees immediately start searching for his successor, they had done nothing about it. At the October board meeting, with Phil out of the room, Tom Debevoise moved that the board make Phil the permanent headmaster. Ten of the eleven trustees present voted in favor. Barbara Sproul, without expressing the same sort of strong doubts she had had about choosing Tawny, insisted that her abstention be made part of the record. She then proposed a committee "to review the continuing leadership and programs of the school," which was defeated by a 7-3 vote. Bowing to the board's determination to pull back, she joined in a unanimous resolution expressing the Trustees' encouragement of and pleasure with Phil's actions and promising to "give him their full support." Despite his earlier misgivings, Phil decided to accept permanent appointment. He was feeling good about himself and the school, he felt he could do the job and "the school was the happiest I'd seen it since I'd been there." In retrospect, he said he had never seen a school make more progress in such a short time.

SUMMER 1970 – FALL 1973

## IV

## Phil Hansen letter to returning students, June 1971

*During the past year, many changes have taken place in the school. Some of you who have entered since last summer were not involved in the beginnings of these changes, but all of you have helped to create whatever has happened. There have been times, especially recently, when I have been forced to question the extent to which I have entrusted responsibility to students individually and collectively. The faculty and I have also been talking seriously at recent meetings about our responsibility for the quality of the experience students have at Woodstock. Many of us have begun to feel that we should take a more active role in helping students to determine the direction of their lives here. Nevertheless, we don't wish to overprotect and overdirect, or to resort to authoritarian cop-outs instead of confronting students directly with our concerns.*

*Among the issues about which I am personally concerned are... the extent and irresponsibility of drug use... [and] the tendency of some students to use the freedom they have here to do as little as possible and to allow their lives to degenerate into an endless round of evasions of opportunity and responsibility...*

*I continue to be troubled by the extent to which students seem unwilling to recognize that the ways in which they live from day to day substantially contribute to the happiness or misery of others. People who create their own private hell through drug abuse, indifference, self-contempt and cynicism cannot help but include increasing numbers of others in the terrible universe which they are making. Self-destructiveness almost always includes destructiveness to others. I think that one of the jobs of the school is to help students to learn to care enough about themselves so that they can care in a positive way about others also.*

*I want Woodstock to continue to be a school where students are free to direct their own lives in significant ways. I cannot accept, however, the concept, which some students seem to have, of the school as a jungle in which only the fittest deserve to survive. This summer about thirty new students will be entering the school... I am not willing to stand idly by and allow these people to be subjected to the many unnecessary torments and pressures which old students have used in the past to separate the fit from the unfit. Therefore, I think the time has come for the adults of the community to take a more active role in shaping the school's atmosphere and direction.*

## H. A. Riegelman, father of Sarah '74, letter to school, August 25, 1971

On all of my visits to the school [four in the last six months] I have been overwhelmed by the <u>filthy</u> conditions in the student living areas. While I recognize (very vaguely) that student self-determination is an important element of the Woodstock experience, the obvious results of such permissiveness indicate to me that the experience is not creating the desired result.... The slovenliness of the students I have observed, both with regard to living areas, personal dress and personal cleanliness, is nothing short of revolting....

Secondly, although <u>Sarah</u> didn't report this to us, on at least one occasion, a male student entered Sarah's room in the middle of the night with sexual intentions. Other factors involving this boy contribute to my concern. I have kept silent while Sarah was still attending the summer term to avoid undue agitation. However, this sort of conduct is completely unacceptable to me and does, in fact, constitute a criminal act under Vermont law.

## Stuart Cudlitz '71, *Symposium*, summer 1971

*Early evening rain, summer bright grey sky. A young man motionless in the rain, standing in an overgrown garden by a stream. His hand is in a raspberry bush, motionless. Red shirt, green trees, red berries, green coat, muted by a falling rain, illumines through the clean contrasting grain of the air. His hat drooped bent, and his pants speckled by dark drops. His shoes worn and mud covered wet, the pad washing away, and washing away the heavy humid air-sweat from his forehead and collar. Cleaning tangled hair and loosening the knot of tension between glazed sad eyes.*

*His hand in a raspberry bush, motionless, not reaching for a berry, rather clasped around a visible circle of events. By his hand are hornets, eating raspberries, slowly they are exploding, red, the bulbous taut juice. Their bodies black and white striped symmetrical. Wings buzzing quietly through the rain with the drone of a laborer's songs. Flying about the young man's hand, motionless.*

SUMMER 1970 – FALL 1973

• • •

Phil had good reason for both his expressions of anxiety and enthusiasm about the quality of Woodstock students experience in 1971, for the school was succeeding as brilliantly with some students as it was failing dismally with others; and doing brilliantly or dismally with the same student at different times. Despite the mixed results, Phil looked back on his first year of running the school as a success. The place had become more relaxed, students and faculty alike were feeling less threatened by each other. While student life was still veiled by discretion, there were signs of growing trust between most students and faculty. The faculty, too, was stabilizing. For the first time in a decade there was no significant change among the teachers, though there were some temporary faculty adjustments to accommodate the Four Term Plan and the new sabbatical program. Philosophically the faculty was deeply divided, especially on such issues as hitchhiking and allowing 18-year-olds to drink (which became legal in Vermont that summer). The faculty was young, most were in their twenties and early thirties, and many of them often seemed defensive and fearful in dealing with students. Student behavior was provocative enough that, at a community meeting in mid-August, Phil suggested that if students couldn't obey the rules, maybe the school should close. The same day the faculty discussed a wide range of sexual issues raised by Hillary Martin, '68, who was working in the library for the summer. This discussion included a recent Major Rules case that had embarrassed Phil and made the school's rule on student sex look absurd. Addressing such non-academic issues at the Trustees meeting three days later, Phil said he planned to bring in some specialists in "personal growth and human relationships."

The following Thursday, two of Woodstock's ABC Scholarship black male students blindfolded and raped a local white girl who had been brought to the New Dorm by her Native American boyfriend, a former Country School student, who was too drunk to take her home or to protect her. For two tense days, while the assailants were unknown, the Vermont State Police questioned people on campus and rumors of a drug bust had students hiding their illegal drugs. In the course of routine questioning, one of the black students confessed, implicating the other. They were arrested in Upwey and taken away in handcuffs as dozens of students and teachers watched. Although Phil considered closing the school immediately, eight days before the term ended, his calm and measured leadership over the next several days helped make such action unnecessary. Others were even relieved to see the two black students gone because they had been bullying some of the younger and smaller students. At Phil's direction, the school provided legal counsel for the black students, charging the $1,434 fee to the scholarship budget. One of them was a school leader, a conscientious student and a student representative to the board of trustees. He had also instigated the rape. He pleaded guilty and was sentenced to two years in prison, the sentence immediately suspended on condition he serve out his probation in the custody of an aunt and uncle in New Jersey. The other black student, a freshman on academic probation, pleaded guilty in juvenile court and was sent to the Weeks School, then Vermont's reform school. He remained there for a year, until Phil helped him get into the Hoosac School, on another ABC Scholarship. Reporting to the trustees two months after the rape, Phil emphasized that it was an isolated act by "a few individuals," but suggested the school was also guilty because of "certain failures of sensitivity and communication on the part of myself and others." Combined with his determination that student life not be governed by the law of the jungle, Phil's sense that the school was at least partly to blame for any jungle behavior made him all the more determined to provide Woodstock with a strong element of affective education.

Phil's interest in affective education – personal growth, human potential, sensitivity training, et cetera – had blossomed in early 1970, when Tawny Kilborne sponsored him and another faculty member for participation in a workshop. They returned full of enthusiasm for the whole faculty to try it, only to face the absolute refusal of the headmaster and strong resistance from most of the rest of the faculty. Nevertheless, as soon as he became headmaster himself, Phil brought in a sensitivity team for the 1970 Faculty Week before school opened that fall, with unfortunate results. During blindfold "trust" exercises, at least two married male teachers took the opportunity to make crude sexual advances on one of their unmarried, young female colleagues. In one of the group "honesty" exercises, the interaction produced a public exchange of memorable bitterness among several teachers who felt betrayed by each other in various personal and professional ways. In particular, those who were reported for partying at the Horans' house months earlier made bitter assessments of born-again Christian and science teacher Rick Farrar. They all remained part of the faculty as the fall term began.

Faced with such vituperative and deep division among the teachers, Phil drew back on affective education for a while (the fall 1971 Faculty Week would be devoted to more traditional school business). But Phil continued to want a more sensitized faculty, especially after the rape, so he hired a consulting psychiatrist who visited the school once a week, primarily to talk to faculty members about students' problems (without the students). He also hired a short-lived, black "race relations expert" whose main contribution to campus harmony was to sleep with willing students of any ethnicity. Certainly, increased sensitivity was something the school needed in 1971, though force-feeding was hardly the way to achieve it. But sensitivity training was also a way for Phil to try, indirectly, to meet his own needs as he found it increasingly difficult as headmaster to ask for, much less accept personal support, or even to talk about a mistake that was as obvious to everyone as the "race relations expert." In the months following the rape, more open and supportive communication might have helped Phil avoid needlessly offending most of the women on campus when he seriously considered inviting one of the rapists to return to school as a fully enrolled student. He abandoned the idea only after several women teachers and students heatedly tried to make him understand that the idea was simply unacceptable. Phil's difficulty in understanding women showed up even more vividly in his attitude toward the rape victim. Writing to Woodstock parents about the rape, Phil gushed that the state police investigation "was absolutely thorough and responsible, exemplary in every way," by which he meant that the criminals' rights had not been violated (even after they had been sentenced he was still calling their crime "alleged"). He dismissed the girl by saying only that her "presence in the dormitory was a clear violation of school policy." He expressed no concern for her rights, nor the gratuitous cruelty with which the State Police had treated her. Nor did he ever seek to help her in any way (personally or through the school), though she was even then being victimized by men for the third time in the event, this time by her father who threw her out of the house as unclean, tearing up the rest of his family in the process. Even years later, Phil seemed baffled by the idea of helping her, saying the school wasn't asked to do anything for her and, in any event, the girl "hadn't been injured."

For the most part, daily life at Woodstock went undisturbed by these issues in the fall of 1971, as the school experienced a remarkable relaxation after the tensions of the summer. The student trustees reported to the board, "Student morale is at one of its higher points in recent years. New students are adapting well... there has been a great drop in hostility between old students and new students... students seem more productive and there is a healthier academic atmosphere than in past terms." Looking at the same school at the same time, Phil wrote, "Once again this fall, students have returned to their schools depoliticized and introspective... A new inwardness, a preoccupation with the vicissitudes of self now prevails... The landscape is bleak, but not quite desolate... The mood is cautious, realistic, uncommitted... Personally, I find this atmosphere more bracing, if less intoxicating than that of the recent past. Students seem more accustomed to disillusionment, less overwhelmed and benumbed, than they did a year ago."

In fact, the most honest and effective emotional leadership in the school then came from a few students.

## Amy Wallace '73 talk to the community, November 1, 1971

*I've wanted to talk about this for a long time, so that's what I'm going to do. OK. Now, although this is, right, a liberal hippie-type school etc., etc., I still think that men here still treat women as sex objects and that women allow themselves to be treated that way. And it manifests itself much more subtly here than it does in the 'real' world. But I firmly believe at this point that it still goes on. I've been trying to think about how I wanted to present this so as not to alienate people, and I think one of the best ways to do it is through personal experience. And for obvious reasons it's difficult for me to talk about, but I'm going to do it anyway, and it's the way that I began to understand this.*

*Now in a number of relationships at this school, I feel that I have fallen into the passive role as the passive woman and allowed myself to be dominated by my lover (I'll use that term), and there was no one to tell me otherwise, and I'd been raised just to believe that that was the way it worked. And I would say that I catered to the interests and the trips of my gentleman friend to the point that in a certain sense I just would become an extension of his personality. And I was depressed by it, but I thought that was the way it was, and I was definitely very dominated and definitely very passive and definitely allowed myself to pretend to be interested in things that I wasn't and so forth, all just for the sake of this role. And I will say that I was intimidated sexually, as I believe many women are here. The fact that we've been raised to believe the male egos are very fragile, to the extent that you can't say, "This doesn't turn me on," or you can't say essentially what you want, and so there's a lot of rape going on. It's a very strong term, but I think so. And I also feel that I've gone through fidelity and jealousy and possessiveness crises that were made worse by my unawareness – everyone goes through those, right – but unawareness of my role as a woman, so it was much worse. And the thing that happened was all really terrible, and I knew the whole time, I knew instinctively that there was something wrong, and that I was being wronged as a woman, but I was afraid to admit it because that would be very devastating to my ego – it would be an incredible blow – it would shatter what I'd been living with, and what I'd been raised to believe, and so I just would always write it off to a personality conflict. And finally when I left here and got back to Los Angeles and started talking to women friends and things, I figured out what was going on for the first time, and I feel that it's really important for women to talk to other women, and men, of course, but there's only so much you can do yourself, and I believe that. I just knew what was going on here, and I consider myself a fairly intelligent person, but I needed some help to figure it out. And I know this is a very crude way of putting it, but I think I was raised, as most of us probably were – females – to believe that these male beasts are going to lust after us, and we've just got to sit tight and wait for true love and it will come and everything, and that's really a hard thing to get over – liberated as we may be – it's difficult and I went through a lot of trauma. Now as far as the Woodstock Country School, I think that some very sick things still go on here, and I'll begin with the easy-lay syndrome. And I know that that's very crude, and I know that we're much too sophisticated, that males here are much too sophisticated to actually use such a crude term as easy-lay, but I think that that feeling really prevails, I really do. And in my experience here it has, and it's just very sick, and it's not nearly so blatant as it is elsewhere, but I really feel that it still goes on. And another thing, see, that supports it, is what I term the foxy sex-kitten syndrome. A lot of men play stud, as it were, for the purposes of what I think is stroking their egos, and the easy-lay thing etc. But women support it by being foxy and cute and allowing themselves to be treated as sex objects because it's easy and it's safe and it's secure. And it's a role that you're familiar with, and there's a lot of peer-group pressure, and also because at this school and this generation, we feel that we have to be loose and hip and liberated and everything, and we gotta Do It – and so it's really a very sorry double bind because the women who don't know any better are supportive of the men who are into this very sick role. And I believe that's all I have to say, I think we should have a question-and-answer period or a discussion or something, but that's the extent of my outline.*

## Comments provoked by Amy Wallace's talk, fall 1971

*"Who ever heard of a promiscuous man?"*
*"I couldn't have a relationship with her, she's too good a friend."*
*"If I want to be tight with them, I can't be tight with you."*

*"The thing is, who wants to be an Adult?"*

*"My father once told me, 'If I ever find out you're having a relationship with some guy before you're eighteen, I'll take him to court.' He never said that to my brother"*

*"I've seen the light, I'm turning into a Puritan."*

## Phil Hansen report to the Trustees, May 13, 1972

*A year ago, my report emphasized primarily what I felt were the school's long-term problems. These were: (1) Insufficient authentic communication between faculty and students; (2) The lack of a common commitment to which faculty and students feel bound; (3) Our isolation from the outside world; (4) Tensions between Black and White students and faculty...*

*This spring, it is possible to report substantial progress in overcoming all of these problems. The experience of the past seven months has certainly reflected much more cohesion and commitment, a stronger sense of inner order than the school has known for several years. A number of strategies have been employed to bring about this change. I think that the establishment of clear and regular decision-making procedures, in which everyone can participate, has been particularly important in overcoming our former alienation. A heavier stress on the sharing of achievements, both on and off campus, has helped to support the idea that each individual is important and has a worthwhile contribution to make. A greater realization by the faculty that students need support as they search for a sense of worth and distinction has influenced both the quality of personal relationships and the direction of curriculum change. Certainly, the development of stronger, more consistent leadership within the student body has been an important factor. Equally important has been the increased self-assurance and effectiveness of the faculty in dealing with students from day to day...*

*Drug use by students has been reduced to the point at which it now constitutes primarily a problem of individual students rather than a threat to the school as a whole. Most important, in my opinion, is the gradual emergence of a broad consensus which students and teach-*

*ers can share regarding appropriate conduct and the purposes of the school. This growth is particularly remarkable in view of the fact that my discussions with headmasters of other schools indicate that this is not what is happening in most of them...*

*As a community, we have succeeded in taking control of our situation. The confidence which this control gives us is a substantial basis for the exhilaration we feel as the school year draws to a close."*

## Tam Stewart '73, student Trustee report to the Trustees, May 13, 1972

*The primary intent of this report is to shed some light upon two areas of importance. The first regards the present dormitory arrangement...*

*The New Dormitory is coeducational and predominantly comprised of newer and younger students. This has resulted in quite a few difficulties. Among these, complications between the sexes and heavy drug involvements have been the most serious. The overall sentiment among the occupants has been discontent and unhappiness.*

*The Bailey House and the Owen Moon House are not coeducational and contain fewer and older students. The result here is relative contentment, though many still prefer smaller accommodations. Problems of noise, major rule infractions and sexual abuse are lessened to a great extent.*

*The Acorn/East Hill complex provides individual, small-group sexually integrated living. [Individual Acorns were single sex.] Each building is self-sufficient; that is, each contains kitchen, bathroom, bedrooms, storage space and common room, resulting in near bliss...*

*The second point of interest is optimistic and indicates that much of the afore-mentioned difficulties will soon be resolved. I refer specifically to a growing community awareness within the community of the community... This awareness, optimism or concern, is clearly reflected through a new and socially accepted academic enthusiasm. In fact, the student trustees could not think of any area of school life which did not reflect this change. To conclude, it seems that a vital and long awaited element has as last begun to appear.*

### Phil Hansen comments to the faculty, November 22, 1972

*My relationship with you as a group, which I think is a problem area... There are fundamental differences between the way I think things should be here and a majority of the faculty... This is not personal, but a question of policy and the basic purposes of the school... I seem to be acting as if there were a gap between me and the faculty. My job is to worry about the whole, your job is to worry about the parts... I became headmaster much against my will... I recognize your concern about how much the school should impinge on your personal lives... I think that a certain amount of tension between the faculty and the headmaster is probably a good thing – but it's in no one's interests if you're all nervous wrecks all the time...*

### Phil Hansen, Essay in *Continuum*, winter 1972

*Aristotle remarked [Politics, Book 1] that "one who is incapable of association with others, or has no need of such association, is no member of a community, and must be either a beast or a God." A society which detaches education from its natural and necessary context in community condemns its young to the chilly loneliness of beasts and gods. They may be free to follow where instinct leads, or even to create worlds for themselves. But they will not have the power to be human. They will not know the liberating humility of accepting their own creaturehood, nor the exhilarating possibility of transcending it through communion with other men.*

### Amy Wallace '73 poem, *Symposium*, spring 1972

*A truly erotic poem would be*
*the softness of your belly*
*your smell*
*such long fingers*
*That I wonder why you don't sculpt*

*It would not be a love-poem*
*then we would all wince with boredom*
*It would be a lust-poem*
*A hymn to your shoulders*

## Phil Hansen comments at faculty self-study, January 14, 1973

*For the students we're dealing with now, and probably will be in the future, the art and music departments are more important than they have been... There is a need for faculty to relate positively to kids on their level... I don't think most kids want teachers to be their peers, but they can't relate to them very honestly except as peers... Loneliness is something adults can relieve if they take the initiative... I'm under great pressure from Gerry [Freund] to do more fundraising, last week I was recruiting new trustees, my annual report is late and is due this week, I have twenty-six college applications to complete this week. I'm not complaining exactly – or asking for sympathy – I get paid more. But I won't give up my relationships with students, I won't give up having advisees. That's one of the few things I like about my job and find rewarding... I find myself all the time dealing with people's fantasies about me... All these are very human things and when I'm in reasonably good spirits I can see them that way... I really don't know what to say about the 'guilt injections.' You all relate to your students that way. I'm becoming a little more comfortable with tension, because I believe certain tensions are creative. But I seem to be rambling, I guess, and I should stop.*

## Elizabeth Polchow '73 & Ed Flores '74, report on the student self-study, January 16, 1973

*[Of Woodstock's 107 students that term, 28 took part in the self-study.]*
   *Fear and distrust is generated in students by faculty circulating in dormitories. Students feel their privacy is being violated... Since no one objected to any of the rules, it was obvious that there were no reservations concerning the necessity of the rules... The students generally feel that they have the right to break the rules without faculty enforcement... Concerning Phil's role in the community, the group felt that both faculty and students had difficulty communicating with him...*

## Anonymous teacher unfinished appeal to trustees, January 18, 1973

*The faculty is torn and, as a body, largely unconfident and on the defensive. A number of faculty members seem to dislike the students... At the same time, the headmaster seems at bay, in some way blocked from positive, decisive action. He seems perhaps intimidated by a faculty he does not seem to like, either as a group or, for the most part, as individuals. He is not happy in his job and his unhappiness pervades the school... While the school is not at (nor will it necessarily reach) a crisis point, it is nevertheless near one, and has been for most of the time since last August. Somehow, if the school is to be a happy, healthy and creative environment, the tensions must be relieved... [The Trustees need] to reaffirm the nature of this school as a place where people share the ideal of being open, accessible, flexible, and trusting with one another....*

## Barbara Pollitt '73, Mark Shapiro '73, Dion Mallory '74, Marie Miller '74 – student Trustees report to the board, January 20, 1973

*Most diverse are the opinions expressed on the extent to which the faculty lives up to the claims made by the school's catalog concerning its support and guidance... Almost all the students feel, however, that there is a dichotomy between the image of faculty giving students support, projected by the school in its admissions procedure and its actuality. The school's philosophy as read in the school catalog presents a misleading ideal...*

*There seem to be factions developing in the student body that are gaining definition. Although this might be an oversimplification of the real situation, it seems that on the one hand a group wishing to retain the school's present emphasis on academics had developed in contrast to a group, represented by the recent emphasis on personal growth and development. The school obviously has obligations in both these areas, and must be attuned toward defining and maintaining a proper balance.*

SUMMER 1970 – FALL 1973

## Phil Hansen report to the Trustees, January 20, 1973

*I feel strongly that the time has come for the board to spell out more clearly what it expects of the headmaster. I am rather confused about what decisions I can make independently and in what matters I must consult the board. I find myself asked to do too many things, and must often choose between neglecting some of my duties in favor of others and doing all of them superficially. Even with a vastly improved administrative structure, I usually find myself mired so deeply in day-to-day details that I have little time or energy for the long-range thinking and planning which I must also do. Even though I spend most of my time talking with students and faculty, I am criticized as being "inaccessible" because I cannot possibly meet the demands of all those who wish to see me. The school has had four headmasters since 1966, and cannot afford to change leaders at such a rate... Therefore, without calling undue attention to myself, I must suggest that the board has no more important task than to make the position of headmaster viable, whoever may occupy it.*

*It is after 2:00 a.m. Again I have run out of time. Another job has been completed too hastily and too late. Tonight my body is obedient to my mind's commands. I have learned recently that I cannot take this obedience for granted. I am listening again to the opening passages of Beethoven's* Missa Solemnis, *music, which speaks of joy and hope in the face of adversity. It was not performed on the grand occasion for which it was commissioned; Beethoven would not allow it to be performed until he was satisfied that it was perfect and complete. The art of the headmaster does not permit such liberties. I am not bitter; I love the school more than ever, despite the terrible trials of the past two and a half years. Despite my many weaknesses, I feel that I have grown into the job, and have fulfilled my task creditably. But I am very, very tired. I feel my capacities as a person, capacities for love and job and thought and feeling just those qualities which I want most to impart to our students, being drained away. I am of little use to the school as a martyr, whatever gratification such a role might give me. People have begun to feel sorry for me; I find this demeaning. How can students and teachers draw strength from one whose distress is so obvious?*

*I feel that my greatest strengths lie in two areas: (1) my ability to relate to adolescents, and to help them relate to ideas; and (2) my capacity to formulate and articulate coherent philosophical and ideological positions. I am not a master of the details of day-to-day administration. I know and care little about financial management, despite a certain inherited Yankee shrewdness. I know even less about the fine points of fund-raising; my capacity to meet the needs of faculty members for affirmation and support is clearly limited, as is my ability to perceive those needs. I don't answer letters very promptly, and I tend to be over-awed by people of sophistication and wealth.*

*I feel that the board should weigh these strengths and weaknesses, and consider the question of whether I am still the most suitable person for the headmastership. The conditions under which I came into office were coercive both to me and to the board. The shortness of my tenure still represents an element of coercion. But plans for an orderly succession could be made, beginning now.* **I am willing to continue to serve, but I will not become a full-time fundraiser or a professional bureaucrat. I will not give up teaching or working directly with kids; if I can't do these things here, I'll do them somewhere else.**

*One option to the board is the formal appointment of an assistant headmaster who is strong in the areas where I am not....*

*I do not wish to preoccupy the board unduly with my personal difficulties. Unfortunately, I have learned only too well the sensitivity and centrality of the office I hold. I feel it would be unfair and dishonest of me not to share these reflections with the board. Perhaps with your help I can regain and retain my effectiveness as the school's leader."* [emphasis added]

## Phil Hansen private letter to Gerry Freund '48, April 27, 1973

*I have decided to notify the Trustees of my intention to resign, effective August 1, 1975....*

*What really motivates this decision is my feeling that the job is simply destroying me as a person. I am becoming a self-caricature. I can't think what, if anything, the future holds for me, but I can't go on like this. The date is chosen so at I can fulfill the obligation I have taken on for the education of my younger brother here [Mark Hansen '75], as well as for the reasons vis-à-vis the school which we have discussed before.*

*I feel totally drained and unable to go on unless I have a termination date to work towards. I am simply not adequate to do what (I guess) needs to be done. I think it's time to stop complaining and do something about it.*

*I thought you should be the first to know.*

## SUMMER 1970 – FALL 1973

• • •

Throughout the fall of 1972 and winter of 1973, affective education remained a focal issue at Woodstock. As the student trustees made clear in January (see above), the issue was particularly divisive for students. Clearly, many students shared their headmaster's perception that most faculty members failed to provide the quality of human support promised in the school catalog. Some of these students sought this support from Mary Louise Shoolery, whom Phil had engaged as a humanistic consultant. But other students found her "touchy-feely" approach repugnant and feared that Phil's apparently unshakable commitment to her was a sign of declining academic quality at the school. This fear was reinforced by many of the new faculty. Almost all of them offered "New Age" type courses, which valued the experience of a subject over any rigorous understanding of it. (In some cases, this was merely a matter of youthful style. Debbie Calloway, for example, after two relatively mellow years at the Country School went on to law school and a professorship at the University of Connecticut Law School. Others, however, dropped out of teaching altogether after Woodstock, going on to carpentry, crafts or running affective education workshops.) Although the school seemed to be drifting away from the kind of academic discipline Phil had always stood for, there was no formal plan to turn the Woodstock community into a hippie commune. In fact, there was no plan of any kind for the school's future and so no reassurance that it wasn't changing radically.

That lack of clarity was Gerry Freund's primary concern in October 1972, as he succeeded Tom Debevoise as president of the board. At his farewell dinner, Tom spoke of his image of himself as the lone lawman who rides into town to set things right, then goes on his way. Tom was on his way to becoming dean of the Vermont Law School and establishing it as the first law school in the state. But things at Woodstock were not even close to right as Tom rode off into the sunset. The school community was more stable under Phil Hansen than it had been for many years, but that stability was only relative. The Four-Term Plan continued to be a management nightmare, while disrupting the community every three months. Although the school was as full as it had ever been, with 121 students for the fall term, it still faced a budget deficit for 1972-73 (Dan Richardson was predicting a surplus by the end of the term, but Buffy Dunker called his figures "sleight of hand" and was worried because "the school always lets things go till it's too late"). The $300,000 New Dorm, of which Tom had been so proud, remained a social disaster and a financial drain. Fundraising was moribund. The headmaster was an invalid. Student Trustee Barbara Pollitt '73 told the trustees they needed to learn more about the school. All of this led Gerry Freund to recommend that the school re-examine itself, "where it's going and why it exists."

As president of the board, Gerry Freund was not a calming influence. He soon became one more source of tension for Phil Hansen. Phil and Gerry had already had testy dealings on at least two earlier occasions, once when Gerry felt he should have been informed more promptly of the rape in 1971. Besides that, Gerry had his own yen to be Woodstock's headmaster. In 1967, Tom and other board members had asked him to take over for David and, though tempted, he had declined, just as he later resisted encouragement to apply for the job directly in 1968. But in 1970, when Tawny resigned, Gerry had thought he might take the job after all and had resented the quickness with which Tom persuaded the Executive Committee to name Phil. Even in retrospect years later, Gerry seemed unresolved about this conflict of interest that permeated his relationship with everything and everyone at Woodstock.

By 1972, Gerry was himself an academic administrator, Dean of Arts and Humanities at Hunter College in New York City. He soon began pressuring Phil to put more time and energy into his administrative responsibilities, especially fundraising, which Phil approached reluctantly and behind schedule, with poor results. As Phil had made clear both in his remarks to the faculty and his report to the trustees, he loathed such work, leading Gerry to tell one faculty member that he couldn't afford to keep Phil on in a purely pastoral role. But Gerry, despite his years of experience in foundation work, made little effort to help Woodstock create the kind of development office common to most schools and colleges.

With Dan in charge on campus, school morale was high as the 1972 fall term began. One of the high points of the term came at the end of October, when almost the whole school, 98 people, attended the Duke Ellington concert at Dartmouth's Hopkins Center, a trip made possible only because Mike Bonnell '73 and John Bean '73 went to Hanover at 4 a.m. to be in line when tickets went on sale later that morning. Students were also continuing to work on their relationships with each other; after a hiatus during the summer, the women's group resumed its meetings and included men, but limited the group to students only (reflecting the student trustees' views reported in January (see above)). But the events that caused the most reaction were Mary Louise Shoolery's Celebration of Life weekends, "group experiences for the development of your inner potential, sessions of trust, understanding and growth" with no pretense whatsoever to academic content. Basically harmless in themselves, even observably beneficial to most of the 25 to 30 students who took part, these off-campus workshops served as the center of a sort of counter-clique in the school, a group in which students could feel a sense of belonging even though they were not part of "the elite," as the school's dominant students called themselves.

Since many of the "Mary Louise" students were also often among the less capable students academically or socially, their finding a positive way to take part in the community was, potentially, a powerful, healthy and integrating experience not otherwise available to them. There was no inherent reason for others to feel threatened by Mary Louise, since even in the fall it was clear she was not a powerful intellect, nor a charismatic leader who could take over the school, much as it seemed she sometimes tried. And experience bore that out, as even those students who were most fond of her, and most helped by her workshops, also soon outgrew her often controlling behavior and, in some cases, came to resent her resistance to letting them go their own ways.

In other words, Mary Louise represented a perfectly manageable, if not very exciting experiment in affective education, the kind of experiment that was then faddish even in mainstream schools at the time. None of her weekends was compulsory, so anyone who wasn't interested in her work could avoid her easily. What made the manageable unmanageable was Phil's unexplained, uncritical and insistent support for what she was doing – even though he did not take part in her weekends or workshops himself (though several other teachers did). Just as he had failed to clarify the values he wanted the faculty to share, so, too, Phil failed to convey to the students just where he stood on the question that concerned them most: what kind of a school was Woodstock trying to be. But he sent the community a powerful signal when he appointed Mary Louise as assistant Dean of Students. Dean of Students Marc Hurlbut openly refused to have anything to do with her approach, saying he preferred "professional relationships" while demonstrating his inability to have one with her. This standoff went unaddressed and unresolved.

Phil's absence and illness had done nothing to help improve his dealings with the faculty. This became clear in the faculty's reaction to Phil's plans for another self-study on the same January day as the Super Bowl. About a third of the faculty had made plans to watch the game in a room at the Woodstock Inn. When Phil scornfully derided such an activity, they angrily counter-attacked, led by Marc Hurlbut, and bullied Phil into adjusting the self-study schedule to accommodate the Super Bowl. These same people, and much of the rest of the faculty, were openly critical of – but given the chance to express their concerns to him directly in the self-study, few of them did so. Nor had they mentioned the Super Bowl in Community Meeting, when Phil first suggested a self-study generally focused on his own role in the school: "I would like to be much clearer about what you all (students and faculty) expect of me." The students took the self-study even less seriously (see above), only 28 of 107 even came to the meeting. But some teachers tried to tell Phil the truth in a helpful way, just as some had tried to talk to him privately. He wasn't hearing what was being said; when one teacher suggested that Phil intimidates teachers but does not support them, Phil noted that he was "intimidated" himself.

The self-study failed to clear the air or increase communication. Faculty relations increasingly turned on hidden agendas and special deals with the headmaster, who created an "administrative team" of four teachers who served as buffers between him and the rest of the faculty, without improving morale. While faculty meetings did not again reach the intensity of the Super Bowl fight, they remained tense, frequently acrimonious gatherings for two more years. While the grown-ups fought, the students avoided getting involved. Phil interpreted this as apathy, demanding more faculty intercession, without success. Sympathetic as most teachers were to Phil's struggle with his illness, they resented its interfering with the school or being blamed themselves for its manifestations. In time, amidst a long, twilight stalemate, Phil moved on, without having made peace with most of his peers, or himself. He resigned officially in April 1973, to be effective no later that September 1, 1975. By that April, he came to feel that the job of headmaster was destroying him as a person and turning him into a self-caricature. He felt drained and despairing and unable to go on.

### Phil Hansen letter to Gerry Freund, May 1973

*Dear Gerry:*

*I am writing to submit my resignation as headmaster... I have reached this decision with great reluctance after several months of serious thought...*

*First, I feel that I have led the school effectively as far as I can. As my vision of the school's needs and my philosophy of education have developed over the past year, they have led me to adopt priorities not shared by the majority of faculty and students. These divergences have led to an increasing number of confrontations between me and the faculty. Basically, I have come to believe that, as traditional social institutions like the family continue to disintegrate, residential schools will increasingly be called upon to replace those institutions which have in the past nurtured young people and permitted them to clarify their values and self-images... Increasingly, adolescents will depend on residential schools as sources of their sense of worth, their capacities to learn and love, as their spiritual "homes". I do not believe the college preparatory school as we have known it, even in its most 'progressive' incarnations, has a future... Rightly or wrongly, the majority of faculty members is committed to relatively traditional institutional forms, distinctions between the academic and non-academic, and between young people and adults which seem to me increasingly irrelevant...*

*The second factor weighing in my decision is the increasingly clear conflict between my personality and the needs and the role which I am called upon to play as 'headmaster.' I do not thrive on power relationships. I find that in the end whoever has power over others is both feared and manipulated by those subject to his power. As headmaster, my life is increasingly defined in terms of such relationships. I find myself dehumanized and cut off from those who mean most to me... my life in the school is, for me, an unremitting process of pain, loss, and destruction... I doubt that I will ever again care as much about an institution or a community as I have about Woodstock. But I have nothing left to give...*

*I feel that I have earned the right to a dignified exit, and I think it would be in the school's best interests and my own if I were permitted one."*

## Andy Gordon '72 story in *Continuum*, winter 1972

*A FABLE*

*Once upon a time in a deep dark wood lived an evil Magician. His name was Mexor. He was very smart but he didn't know up from down or in from out so he was always doing evil things. He would take little animals from the woods to his cave, where he would poke their stomachs and tickle them. The animals would laugh and giggle and smile. He would feed them and make them fat and put them next to his fire and they would get all warm and say that they never wanted to leave. Inevitably the magician would tire of his toys and put them out in the woods where they came from. He would say, "Goodbye little animal. Be glad that I fed you and kept you warm and remember that I was good to you." But the little animal would begin to shiver and feel cold, he was so used to the fire. He would decide to run to keep warm and find that he was too fat to keep moving, so he would lie down and cry. When the magician would see one of his old toys lying on the ground crying he would say, "What's wrong, little animal, don't you have a place to go? You are a cute little animal, why don't you find a cave to live in?" But the animal would just cry because in all the woods there were no other fires like the fire that the magician had. So the evil magician kept taking little animals into his cave to entertain him and all the little animals wanted the magician's fire, but they prayed that when their time came he would let them stay.*

### Elizabeth Polchow Livingston '73 letter, October 3, 2016

*I am someone only tangentially connected to this story, having been there only a year and feeling as though I just sort of passed through without such an intimate sampling of the garden of delights. But it was nevertheless, a garden of delights for me and just what I needed at the time. Of course, I wish I had never left.*

### Phil Hansen response to an inquiry, June 21, 1973

*A year-round program, whatever its advantages, is extraordinarily draining for teachers and administrators. This summer will be my first extended vacation in four years, and it doesn't come a moment too soon. I think the usual intensity of a boarding school situation is even further intensified by the continual turnover of faculty and students involved in a four-term program. This is one of several aspects of the program which we will be looking at as we seek to make a comprehensive evaluation of our experience with it in the near future....In general, I think what we have done is to prove that a year-round program is feasible, and very advantageous, at least for us. The question we need to ask is, "Is it worth it?"*

• • •

The spring term, like the winter, was uneasy and fractious, but without significant explosions. The closest came when Phil felt compelled to persuade the Major Rules committee to suspend two popular students, Mike Bonnell and John Bean, for riding on top of the school bus. Explaining the decision to the community, he referred to the offenders as "unsafe baggage." Students were offended by the episode, but their resistance took the form of satiric ridicule, silk screening dozens of tee shirts with a picture of Mike and John framed by the words "Unsafe Baggage." Pamela Fischer, the art teacher, resigned suddenly during the term and Phil incurred further faculty resentment by paying for her trip to Europe out of the teacher substitute fund. For the most part, tensions were rooted in old business, persistent but low key. "Despite the usual minor crises and catastrophes, which seem to be an inevitable part of boarding school life, Phil told the trustees in May, "the year has, in general, been a good one for the school." The term ended quietly with author Irving Wallace, Amy's father, speaking at commencement and warning the graduates not to accept the unexamined claims of authorities as gospel truth.

The question of affective education remained divisive and several students insisted on bringing it to the trustees again at their May meeting. "There is talk among students and faculty of a 'division' caused by the presence of the 'Developing Personal Potential' program in the school," Phil reported to the board, falsely asserting that no one had talked to him about their objections (some of which were included in the student trustees' report). The board, finding its members divided on the program, left it to the headmaster to decide its future. He, in turn, put the question to the community meeting, which voted to have "Personal Potential" as an extra-curricular activity and to let the curriculum committee decide on any academic courses. At the end of the term, Phil tried to persuade the faculty that the community didn't understand what it needed. But the faculty couldn't decide the issue and didn't even vote on the community meeting proposal. By this time, Mary Louise was losing her influence and left the school feeling unsupported and embittered. Phil soon went on summer sabbatical with two recent graduates. He and the boys drove to the West Coast, but declined an invitation to stay with Amy Wallace at her Berkeley commune, which Phil found distasteful. He never sought to revive the "Personal Potential" program and, years later, reached the conclusion that "Mary Louise conned me."

The spring term was also Dan Richardson's last term at Woodstock, and when he left a great part of the school's heart went with him. He was involved with almost every aspect of the school and every person in it in ways no one else there could match, or tried to match. Perhaps only David Bailey and Buffy Dunker had achieved greater personal involvement before. Dan cared about people and the school. He was rarely holed up in his office, but mostly out in the school dealing with people and problems, teaching classes or coaching sports, baling hay or snow-plowing driveways. Unhesitatingly, he spoke his mind, but even when he was angry he was not vindictive. He could accept fundamental disagreement without equating it with disloyalty, or using it as a basis for guilt injections. He was direct, he was honest and he had a relentlessly raucous sense of humor about himself as much as the rest of the universe. He not only let people know just where he stood, he respected them enough to tell them why. He also knew how to listen and was perhaps the most trusted teacher on campus. Although he was part of Phil's "administrative team," he publicly mocked such incipient bureaucracy openly, calling it "the Big Four" and "the Quad." He was also the last administrator in that group who was always straight and a reliable truth-teller. The others, if not deceitful, were surely full of intricacies. When he left, there was no one left in a faculty meeting who would say, as Dan did in the heat of the Super Bowl spat, "no football game is worth, to me, the heavy emotions going around here." For three years, while Phil was busy being the head of the school, Dan had casually become a significant part of its heart.

Dan and Phil did not part on good terms. Dan, working more closely with Phil than anyone in the school, believed Phil was doing the school serious, perhaps irreparable damage. With considerable misgiving after he had gone to Costa Rica, he shared his worries with some trustees he believed were open-minded; they accused him of wanting Phil's job. Phil believed Dan was personally disloyal to him and that was the same as being disloyal to the school. Phil had almost nothing in common with Dan, who somehow found time, energy and enthusiasm for his wife, his three children, sports, partying and doing the work that several people took over when he left. According to Phil, Marc Hurlbut said that Dan slacked off on his job as his departure for Costa Rica approached. Dan later acknowledgfed this was true, that in the spring of 1973 he was definitely "losing altitude," as the curent phrase had it. But Phil let his conflict with Dan spill over into his relationships with those he saw as Dan's allies, seriously damaging the school in at least one instance.

In August 1972, Dan had hired Patricia Heffernan as his assistant business manager and bookkeeper. She not only brought order and reliability to her work, but a caring attitude, which showed in her willingness to deal patiently with students and to brighten the business office with plants and flowers. Before he left, Dan tried to persuade Phil to name Pat as the school's business manager. But Phil wouldn't consider her as Dan's replacement. Delaying until Dan was about to leave, Phil hastily hired a man to do a fraction of the work Dan had done, but none of the extras and no relationships with students – all at an added cost of $6,000 per year. This man would be fired, perhaps unfairly, by Phil's successor two years later. To get him, Phil had to pass over Pat Heffernan, whose competence was certainly unquestioned by Tom Debevoise, who soon hired her to run the Vermont Law School as his assistant dean for seven years. Pat was not only one of Dan's people, she was an open, direct, self-confident woman – and Phil had chronic difficulties dealing with strong women on an equal basis. Pat had already complicated that problem by refusing to allow Phil to claim he hadn't been informed about financial issues, which she or Dan had brought to his attention in a timely fashion during 1972-73. It is likely that, with Pat Heffernan running the business office and managing the budget, Woodstock would not have stumbled so blindly from one financial crisis to the next for the next seven years.

Out of these antipathies, Dan became the scapegoat for Woodstock's long-burgeoning financial problems. The cash flow problem that the re-evaluation committee had predicted in 1966, calling the school's finances "precarious" because of the vagaries of the Four-Term Plan, had grown steadily worse in the succeeding seven years. At the end of 1972, the trustees had authorized Dan to borrow $25,000 to cover cash-flow contingencies. At their May meeting, the trustees called the cash flow problem "serious," and decided to discuss it at their August meeting. By the summer of 1973, the short-term shortfall was estimated at $68,000. Board president Gerry Freund called the situation "unprecedented" (which was hardly true) and blamed it on the New Dorm debt put in place by Tom Debevoise (which was only part of the problem). Phil professed complete surprise when he learned about it months later. Dan's successor as Director of Operations, with no prior experience in educational institutions, thought it meant the school would have to close before the fall term started. In fact, the school had been facing cash flow problems ever since the first summer term of the Four-Term Plan had been under-enrolled in 1967. Buffy had raised the issue and Dan had continued raising it since his arrival, with increasing insistence during 1972-73 (as the trustees' board meeting and executive committee minutes show). The executive committee responded as it always had, by raising the school's debt ceiling, this time to $70,000.

Woodstock was finding it increasingly difficult, but not yet impossible, to attract able students. The summer term was under-enrolled, adding to the budget deficit. At the end of June, before school re-opened, the Kedron Brook overflowed, flooding the basement of the library and part of the science building, but damage was limited. Having a lame-duck headmaster added to uncertainty in an already unstable school. But as the summer term began, Phil Hansen was on sabbatical, reducing on-campus tensions somewhat. The faculty remained splintered and at odds. Marc Hurlbut was acting headmaster and played a lot of tennis. It was not his style to get significantly involved in students' lives, nor to build bridges among faculty members. That was another quality Dan took with him when he left.

Early in the term, Marc and the Major Rules committee faced a possibly difficult drug case. Over the break, a faculty member on the committee had found a hollowed-out book with two hypodermic needles in it. In the back of the book was a list of 10 student names. He brought the matter to the committee, which spent several weeks in closed meetings trying to determine what it meant, causing significant tension in the school. As it turned out, the needle-and-heroin-user had graduated. So had most of the 10 named students, who were amphetamine buyers, listed in the book by the dealer. For a while, the identity of the dealer was unknown, even though he was a student on campus. His faculty advisor, Bill Meyer, had been advising the dealer to lay low. Other students, angry at what the school was being put through, came forward and identified the dealer. The committee expelled him and set lesser penalties for the others involved. The faculty member who had found the book went before an all-school meeting and, with others, answered student questions until there were no questions left. There were no repercussions for the faculty member who had protected the dealer.

Until the drug case was publicly resolved, the Major Rules meetings had seemed a little like the school's version of the Watergate hearings going on that summer. Several faculty members and students responded to Watergate by holding a Watergate Day of presentation and discussion of the facts (as known) and context of Watergate. Watergate Day was open to the public and well received.

The "sudden" cash flow crisis at the beginning of the summer had little impact on school life. It was was largely the result of recent decisions of the board and headmaster to spend money beyond the budget, such as paying for Phil's sabbatical ($3,200), hiring Mary Louise as an assistant dean ($2,000), paying the moving expenses of the director of studies ($2,000), hiring a new art teacher ($2,000-plus), setting up the headmaster search committee ($1,000), Dan's sabbatical ($3,000-plus), flood damage (about $5,000), and Giles House renovation ($4,000) – more than $22,000 in this partial list of unanticipated expenses. For all of that, cash flow difficulties were still contingent primarily on admissions (and aggravated by the absence of reliable budget controls). When the school was under-enrolled, the money came in more slowly than anticipated, and the school spent next term's tuitions (payable in advance) to pay for this term's expenses. With a continuously full school, no problem, but every time Woodstock was a little under- enrolled, its current expenses ate deeper into its future income, with crisis inevitable without some other source of income. The Trustees executive committee met in late August and made $17,000 in budget cuts, including $10,000 from the 25th Anniversary fund-raising campaign. In a cover letter that went out with the committee's minutes, Gerry Freund wrote inaccurately "that we are in an unprecedented cash flow bind." The cash flow bind was not unprecedented, it was perennial. What was unprecedented was that the board and administrators took it seriously, if only briefly and ineffectively.

As a practical matter, the cash flow "crisis" of 1973 ended almost as soon as it began. When acting headmaster Marc Hurlbut reported that the school's summer term was under-enrolled by 11 students (actually 18), the executive committee recognized that more students would help and authorized $2,600 worth of advertising. For the first time, Woodstock advertised for students with an ad in the New York Sunday Times Magazine. The ad ran four times that fall, starting in September. A full school would ameliorate the problem, not solve it. To underline that reality, *Continuum*, the WCS alumni magazine, ran the ad across the full cover, front and back – in red ink. The two-month-long admissions drive produced a full school by October 8, turning up 53 new students of remarkably high quality under the circumstances. Woodstock started that fall term with 126 students (110 boarders and 16 day students), five more students than its previous high the year before and, as it would turn out, its largest enrolment ever. The cash flow "crisis" promptly abated in the minds of the school's leadership if not in reality.

### WCS ad, New York Times Sunday Magazine, September 9, 1973

*"Vermont Farm Setting – WOODSTOCK COUNTRY SCHOOL - Pioneer of the Woodstock Plan of year-round on-campus and off-campus terms, the Woodstock Country School is a progressive, coeducational boarding school of about 100 students. Founded in 1945 and located on a 300-acre farm, the school offers a full elective academic curriculum with special strengths in the humanities, arts, music, drama, the environmental and natural sciences as well as opportunities for independent study. OPENINGS FOR FALL TERM – BEGINS OCTOBER 7"*

## Trustee Jim Sunshine, description of ideal WCS headmaster, July 11, 1973

*We are looking for a man or woman, minimum age 35, maximum 55, optimum 45; not necessarily from the field of independent secondary schools or even education at all, but from almost any professional field so long as he or she has the other requisite attributes and abilities; this person should be able to serve above all as a role model for the students, and hence should be a mature, stable married man (preferably with children), someone who has the strength and sentimental level, not someone who seeks to ingratiate himself with students and teachers but someone who can command honest respect; in academic terms he should not be a faddist, a sentimentalist, or a fake, nor should he be a member of the encounter group cult, although he should be aware of its uses and values; he should be intellectually competent, and he should be able to provide evidence that he has run other people and other institutions and organizations; he should be, as we are, fully cognizant of the non-academic aspects of boarding school life.*

• • •

Dave Horan, the faculty representitive on the headmaster search committee, read Jim Sunshine's description of the "ideal headmaster" to the faculty on August 1 and invited the faculty to make suggestions to the committee. As faculty members quickly recognized, all the description really said was: "we don't want someone like Phil" – or more accurately, we don't want somone like the caricature we think Phil is. The description, written by an experienced newspaperman with little love for or understanding of the Country School, was fundamentally obtuse. The description was itself a barrier to finding an extraordinary candidate (if any existed). The description asks for someone safe, not someone inspiring; someone pedestrian, not someone inventive; someone conventional, not someone imaginative – all in all, someone inappropriate to Woodstock at its best. The board was offering the headmastership to someone from "almost any professional field," not necessarily education even, but someone who was "as we are, fully cognizant of the non-academic aspects of boarding school life." That's a near-impossible formulation that rested on untruth: The board was not even close to "fully cognizant" of boarding school life. With this outline as the search committee's guide, how could it hope to find someone good for the Country School?

In October, Phil had returned from his sabbatical. Even before the students returned, another nasty faculty week re-established an atmosphere of tension and hostility, this time stirred up by the supposed cash flow "crisis" and amplified by Phil's two-hour lecture to the faculty about its responsibilities to the school, a massive guilt injection to which the faculty responded with total silence. None of it helped. The school leadership maintained a crisis atmosphere, later reinforced by the Arab oil boycott. Phil and his administrators spent hours of the faculty's time during faculty week and faculty meeting presenting incomplete and misleading budgetary information, requiring austerity and blaming Dan for it. Phil particularly blamed Dan for the 1972-73 budget deficit of $45,095, claiming it was a "surprise" even though Dan's budget reports during the year showed the projected deficit of $5,000 growing to twice that by January and almost twice as much again by May, after which most of the unanticipated expenses pushed it up further. Even twelve years later, Phil maintained that the auditor's "discovery" of the deficit, as well as the larger deficit of 1971-72, came as a surprise to him. It seemed never to occur to him that a headmaster has an affirmative duty to know his school's financial condition, at least in broad terms. As officially explained to the trustees in October 1973, almost half the deficit came from overspending the scholarship budget by $21,000 at Phil's direction; most of the rest was attributed to inflation ($14,700). The real surprise is that none of these reports caused significant comment or action when they were presented. At its October meeting, the board formally took control of the budget, requiring the headmaster to seek the trustees' approval for any significant, unbudgeted expenditure, compounding an awkward school administration with absentee management.

For the remainder of 1973 and all of 1974, the school would be in a holding pattern. The quality of life would change little. Tensions persisted between the headmaster and the faculty, but Phil no longer tried to change Woodstock to fit his vision of a spiritual home for its students. The students remained quiescent, discreet, their social life largely free of adult observation or interference. Phil had sufficient goodwill in his relations with students that he and they were content to coast through his lame duck terms with as little friction as possible in a community of adolescents, which now included Phil's younger brother, Mark Hansen, (whose presence was an added incentive for restraint). The trustees held their breath, hoping Phil could summon the strength to function until his successor was ready to take over. In some ways, board president Gerry Freund was trying to run the school *in absentia*. Jim Sunshine had joined the board in the fall of 1972. He had taken over as the fourth chairman of the 25th Anniversary Campaign – the first active one – and started despairing as the campaign lost momentum after Dan's departure. "By all means try Phil once more on the foundations," Jim wrote Gerry in November 1973. "We have to keep some motion in all this [the campaign], and we have to get some work out of Phil while he is here."

As for the quality of the school as a whole, Jim Sunshine had little hope for any immediate improvement. "I still think the answer is in getting a replacement for Phil who has the strength and desire to administer the school. I don't think Phil does, in fact, I think he hates the thought of it. Administering the school does not mean flying into a rage over something you don't like, or ignoring things you don't like, or just doing the things you like doing. It is leading people to want to do what you know must be done, showing them how to do it, helping them to do it, and providing them with what they need." Sharing this assessment, and concerned about Phil's stability, Gerry was prepared to have Marc Hurlbut step in on short notice. And to this end, the two trustees enlisted Marc to report to them regularly on Phil's emotional state, all unbeknownst to Phil. Phil's leadership had brought the school back from the edge of chaos in 1970 under Tawny, when some felt the school was like a mental hospital. Few if any thought that in 1973, not about the students at any rate. But in the process of restoring the school, Phil seemed to have lost his own way. Now he had become the most closely watched inmate of the institution he still titularly led.

Mark Bueide '74 & Bill Dwight '74

SUMMER 1970 – FALL 1973

Mike Bonnell '73 & Scott Eccleston '74

New Dorm, coed, built 1970

Lynn & Greg Vennell, science teacher

Mary Gafford '76,
Dennis Bivings '76

New Dorm, by Mark Beuide '74

Lisa Nelson '75

Les Rodriguez,
Spanish teacher

Commencement 1971: guest speaker Edward J. Bloustein,
WCS parent & president of Rutgers University with (behind him on the stage
l. to r.) headmaster Phil Hansen, moderator Faith Warner '72,
and student speaker Jeff Greene '72

Ken Seggerman '70

John Williams '72

Commencement rehearsal 1974 (l. to r.) Liz Burnham, unknown, Judy Kristl, Mark Hansen (Phil's brother), Dion Mallory (kneeling) and Patrick Stranahan (all class of 1974)

WCS students cruise for credit: in November 1974, history teacher Bob Williams (assisted by art teacher Bob Kissane) led his Ancient Civilizations class of 15 on a cruise of the eastern Mediterranean (the cruise was the second credit of the double credit course). The cruise on the SS Nevasa comprised some 900 students and 100 leaders from all over the world. WCS was the only US non-parochial private school. Above, at the pyramids, is Bob Williams (center with beard), flanked by James Mulligan '76 (left) and Chris Bacher '75.

Drawings by Betsy Rosenwald, Vivien LeMothe, Jeff Greene, & Torsten Bodecker

Headmasters' body language: David Bailey, Phil Hansen, and Walter Hill in the amphitheatre, spring 1974

CHAPTER ELEVEN

# Fall 1973 – Summer 1980

### Phil Hansen report to the Trustees, October 10, 1973

*We are facing a world in which social engineering is replacing self-determination, in which schools are more and more factories for the replication of interchangeable economic ciphers. At the same time, alienation, boredom and bottomless despair are more than ever dominant modes of feeling. Because the kids are quieter than they were, it doesn't follow that they are happier than they were. They have lost the language of protest, but voices still cry out in the night, louder and more desperate than before...*

*There are few places in which the fragile and tentative individuality of adolescents can be nurtured as it is here, and there will be fewer. I am impressed at every commencement with the number of students for whom Woodstock has proven a place of healing and a resource for personal wholeness. If the world beyond the school has little respect for this wholeness, we must (and can) teach our students to provide their own self-respect... I think that this school is needed, and deserves to survive, because of the values for which it stands and has always stood, in and out of season. For the Board or anyone else to give less than the best effort they can to assure its survival would be tragic desertion of these values.*

*In choosing a headmaster, I hope that the Search Committee and the Board will keep in mind above all else the question of whether the man or woman chosen can make a full commitment to the person-centered and humane values which are woven so deeply into the school's traditions. Competence is necessary, but not sufficient. The school must not only be managed, it must also be led. Direction is more important than administration, even now. If these thoughts seem sentimental, please indulge me. I am wont to be protective of fragile and vulnerable things which I love and believe in. Aware as I am of the school's fragility and vulnerability, I am even more conscious of its incalculable value. I trust that the Board and, eventually, my successor, will cherish it as much.*

## Nils Sundquist '74, tribute school farmer Bruce Fairweather, July 31, 2000

*Bruce Fairweather taught me to plow across a sidehill so that the soil from each furrow folds over uphill. The logic is that soil naturally moves downhill, so we could move it uphill when we plow in order to maintain soil cover on the slope.*

*Today, after ten years of moving soil uphill each time I plow, our garden has a significant ditch at the bottom edge that has never filled back in.*

*Such is the sublime influence of Bruce Fairweather, and, I should add, many others who taught me at Woodstock Country School. Twenty-six years after he taught me to roll the soil from each furrow uphill, the ditch at the bottom of our garden is the legacy of his lesson.*

*If I had plowed from the other direction, dumping the soil from each furrow downhill (this would be the easy way), I would eventually have stripped the upper slope of fertility, and piled it where it wasn't needed farther down.*

*Thanks to Bruce's teaching, our garden is productive along its entire slope, top to bottom. I can live with the ditch.*

*Thank you to Bruce, and the rest of my teachers, living and dead, for your lessons.*

### Phil Hansen report to the Trustees, October 19, 1973

*Thus far, morale within the school seems to be high... This year's faculty is the strongest I have worked with... [There is] increased unity concerning general school policy... The tensions between faculty and myself seem to have subsided to a considerable degree.*

•••

With the faculty invited to the board meeting on October 19, board president Gerry Freund did his own version of Phil Hansen's two-hour guilt-injection monologue at faculty week two weeks before. With almost no direct experience to base his opinions on, Gerry took more than an hour to criticize the faculty in sweeping generalities, with Phil beside him sitting silently red-faced and leg a-twitch. The board had requested this meeting, Phil had told the faculty, "To ask what we're doing and why. We can also tell them our concerns." At the beginning of the meeting, Gerry Freund announced that no one should take notes. Gerry's attack on the faculty was so unspecific that two other trustees, Jim Sunshine and Dick Nolte, challenged him to speak to particulars, but he didn't. Jim later told Gerry, "I called for the specifics as a sort of signal to the faculty that we would be willing to hear the other side and were not simply coming down on them with a mass of pre-judgments. I have found that the worst way of gaining a man's cooperation in an effort to improve what he is doing is to tell him he's doing a rotten job. A few people respond to that kind of treatment, but most just turn sullen and have to be fired." Jim seemed not to have understood that he was describing what had actually happened, and that his own obliqueness was part of the problem.

Unlike the response to Phil's faculty meeting lecture, this time several faculty members spoke up in the faculty's defense, while Phil remained silent in apparent assent to the board president's views. Nothing was resolved, no specifics were identified, the board offered no way forward. Most, if not all, the faculty remained resentful and generally distrustful of Gerry for months, even years afterward. (A faculty member's private, after-the-meeting notes summed up the meeting: "Gerry alienated a lot of people (what he did was behave like Phil) – he lectured a lot, not very concretely for the most part (rather subtextually), he didn't seem fully prepared. Nolte challenged Gerry to come out front; so did Sunshine (who came late). Nolte, afterwards, noted that the faculty had leapt to its own defense, but the headmaster had said nothing (almost literally, though his foot was excessively busy).... Buffy [Dunker] asked for a piece of paper and a pen to send a note to tell Gerry to shut up (but she didn't send it))."

The faculty's anger only increased in a faculty meeting a few days later, when Phil told them he disagreed with Gerry, but had said nothing because Gerry had asked him not to speak. So intense were the faculty's feelings that Phil and faculty Trustee Marc Hurlbut felt compelled to defend the faculty publicly with a memo to the board that was more defensive than defensible. It claimed, for example, that "The tendency of the past three years has been the deliberate introduction of more direction and structure rather than less." He sidestepped the reality that during that period the school had also sanctioned drinking by 18-year-olds (to conform to Vermont law), allowed almost unlimited inter-visitation in the dorms (driven by the co-ed New Dorm's architecture), dropped almost all institutional concern about sexual conduct and lowered academic standards at least to the extent that there were several new teachers who rarely flunked anyone for any reason, while Phil himself doubted that honors grades always reflected honors work. The school's financial condition, invoked from time to time for leverage, continued to go unaddressed in any systematic, effective way. The new business manager, Mort Rosenstein, told a November faculty meeting: "I want to say for the record – that we are dealing with a situation we aren't capable of dealing with." In December, Mort's report to the trustees was that "everything is in control now." Gerry Freund's letter urging Trustees to raise money for the school elicited only one response.

Phil lost control of himself frequently during his last five terms at Woodstock, screaming at students, using faculty meeting as a confessional, yelling and pounding his fist on the table in discussions with teachers, snapping pencils in half and frequently slamming his office door in anger. He concluded one argument with Pat Heffernan about business practice by slamming her door so hard he broke the hinges. In his calm and lucid moments, Phil acknowledged his condition and spoke of maintaining the illusion that we "still have a viable headmaster." He could do little to defend himself from the Trustees, but Phil sought distance and protection from the faculty by creating the position of Dean of Faculty and appointing Dave Horan to fill it. Dave was one of the older, more experienced and respected teachers, capable of calm, rational discussion with almost anyone. But Dave was also quiet and reserved by nature, not an active mediator of disputes. No doubt, he played a helpful role, but Phil was still the one who made the final decision in most matters.

In January 1974, the student trustees reported to the board, "Following the influx of approximately 85 new students over the past two terms, the student body seems to be arriving at some point of unification. There have been few crises equal in dimension to those that took place in the spring and summer [of 1973]." But they spoke too soon. Student behavior, in particular drinking, was largely out of control during the winter and 40 students (a third of the school) failed one or more courses. At the end of the term, Phil reported it had been "extraordinarily difficult... [and full of] tensions and irritations." Phil had several painful run-ins with students, making it "one of the least pleasant [terms] in recent memory."

In the spring of 1974, the school was under-enrolled by 10 boarders. In the fall, Phil had warned that such under-enrollment would trigger another budget crisis. But in the spring, there was no institutional response, nothing happened. There was no public discussion. The school did not even advertise for the chronically under-enrolled summer term. The summer term was under-enrolled by 17 boarders. In late July, the Trustees' Executive Committee decided to advertise again for students. The fall term began with full enrollment, but the shortfall of the previous two terms had not been covered. The school finished the fiscal year with a deficit of $29,435 but no sense of crisis. According to the minutes of the October board meeting, Trustee William Rose [faculty member Barbara Henderson's father] was concerned by the auditor's report, pointing out the practices of recent years: "Accumulated, unfounded, annual cash deficits were causing the school each year to meet slightly more of its current operating expenses with cash provided by tuition paid in advance for subsequent terms, i.e., anticipated rather than current income. While the situation was not yet alarming, he commented, it could soon become so if deficits were not ended and offset by surpluses."

For all their *deja vu*, the same circumstances in 1974 did not produce a cash flow "crisis" as they had in 1973. Quite. On November 10, 1974, the Executive Committee decided there was a looming deficit of $60,000 for the year, but felt no need for urgent action. On November 10, the board's Executive Committee minutes reports "income continues to run below projections... Income could fall short of projections by as much as $60,000 for the year." On November 11, Phil unilaterally froze the school's budget and sent an urgent memo to the staff: "our current enrollment and application figures dictate the most extreme pessimism about the school's financial future. Only your fullest cooperation in every way will assure the school's ability to operate beyond the current year." The next day, Phil issued another memo in which he took it all back: "It is the unswerving intention of the Board and Administration to assure the school's continued operation next year and for many years thereafter."

In the same memo, explaining the lack of community involvement in budget issues, Phil wrote: "I don't feel it fair to engage in community debates and discussions when the results are foregone conclusions. Sooner or later, headmasters have to choose between autocracy or fraud."

The emotional climate of the school had changed little in two years. Even though there had been no faculty week in 1974, the faculty was as divided as ever, which gave special nuance to Phil's assurance that headmaster-elect Walter Hill's "ideas coincide with those of this faculty." In mid-October, Phil reported that the school was "tranquil," the students highly motivated and clear about their priorities. The student trustees reported student "apathy and self-concern," adding: "In our quest for student opinion concerning school philosophies and policies, we encountered a total lack of interest." By the end of the month, there was widespread concern about school morale, much of it provoked by parents worried about the prevalence of drugs, alcohol, loose sex and anomie.

In June 1974, the trustees had announced their unanimous choice of architect Walter Hill to take over as headmaster in January 1975. The community was hoping the new man would be able to pull it all back together again. At graduation dinner at the end of the fall term, several recent alumni returned to give Phil an oil painting of himself and themselves and views of the school. Marc Hurlbut announced that the New Dorm would, henceforth, be called Hansen House (which the trustees, who had not been consulted, promptly reversed in hopes that some big donor's name would adorn that dorm instead). And Phil, speaking to the students for the last time as their headmaster, wished them well. Of his successor, Phil said only: "Please, please, please be kind to Walter Hill."

Walter Hill was 49 when he took over as Woodstock's headmaster. Most people called him Walter or Walt. His wife Pat called him "Bunk," as in "Bunker" Hill. For the previous four years, he had been vice rector for student affairs and long-range planning at St. Paul's School. Before that, he was on the faculty of Harvard's Graduate School of Education, and before that had his own architectural firm, Hill and Associates, in Cambridge. He and Pat had been married more than 25 years and had two nearly adult adopted children, a girl attending

Middlebury College and a boy who lived at home and worked at the nearby Kedron Valley Inn. Pat, who had been active in New Hampshire mental health and child advocacy programs, soon took over Woodstock's off-campus term program. Not only did the Hills look good on paper, they seemed to have all the personal qualities the Search Committee wanted as well. Unlike 1968, when Barbara Sproul and John Pierce were adamantly opposed to Tawny Kilborne, and unlike 1970 when Barbara alone raised doubts about Phil Hansen, this time there was almost untroubled unanimity. Barbara had some slight doubts, but she was losing interest in the school, shifting her energies to Amnesty International. Jim Sunshine had vague dissatisfaction with Walter as well, he recalled years later, but couldn't articulate them and so put them aside in the face of everyone else's enthusiasm. Besides, Russ Mead, who had become the headmaster at Concord Academy since he left Woodstock in 1962 and was now a Country School Trustee, had asked his Concord students to ask their friends and siblings at St. Paul's about Walter – and his report of their reports was glowing. There was also widespread enthusiasm for Walter among faculty who had met him, which some took as a warning signal. The different expectations of these faculty members, especially those with "administrative portfolios," were far too varied to be met by one school, much less one man.

### William Boardman '56, unanswered letter to search committee, April 26, 1974

*I hope you and your committee understand just how important it is that the next headmaster be someone who has a comfortable strength and knows how to relax the people around him (her). If he has this quality, and a reasonable intelligence, but no expertise in budget management, fundraising, or even education, the school will be a better place. Lacking that, even if he has the rest, I fear we will continue to boil and roll over at an unhealthy rate.*

*In almost any boarding school, but especially at one as small as Woodstock, in many ways the headmaster is the school. His presence is a dominant characteristic of the school, even if that presence is largely an absence (perhaps especially then). Your committee seems to be focusing on great cosmic criteria, but the school is defined daily by the way the headmaster walks down the halls (if he walks down the halls), by the people to whom he speaks (if he speaks), by the way he touches people (if he touches people). It's not just a semantic wriggle to say that we need not someone to fill the role of headmaster, but someone to be the headmaster....*

### Walter Hill comments during a visit to WCS, May 1, 1974

*Education is a continuum.... As a generalist you have got to understand the budget.... Ninth graders grow up too fast.... Everybody's into sumpin'.... I would also hope the headmaster would be considered a member of the faculty.... One of my best friends is a black in the south....*

### Barbara Sproul '62 letter to Jim Sunshine, May 28, 1974

*On the whole [Walter Hill] seems fine to me: fairly perceptive, likes kids, intelligent, personable. I find the same things objectionable about him that I did on first meeting; the cuteness of phrasing, the "I-don't-really-know-why-kids-like-me-so-much-but-they-do" attitude, and one other thing that mildly bothers me – I find I forget him almost immediately. (But that last complaint may say more about me than him, so I suppose you should ignore it.) But none of these is very serious. He does (underlined) have the required qualities, he is (underlined (I feel)) sure of his authority with kids and I suppose I think that is most important.*

### Phil Hansen, at faculty meeting, September 24, 1974

*I have every reason to think that Walter will involve all members of the community in the planning process, as I have."*

### Eve Holberg '75 & Tom Laskin '75, *Workers Literary Guild*, October 25, 1974

*It becomes more and more apparent, through personal experience and seeing the experience of others that the Woodstock Country School experience is one of general manipulation (asskissing) and pretend games...*

*What I mean by a solidified unit is more than the coercive social body we have now in the form of a bureaucratic state in miniature...*

FALL 1973 – SUMMER 1980

## Walter Hill's bumper sticker on his yellow jeep, 1975-76

*"I'd Rather Be Sailing!"*

• • •

In January 1975, there was no school ceremony to mark the occasion of changing leadership. Phil Hansen was gone. As Walter Hill succeeded him as Woodstock's headmaster, the school was eager for positive changes after two uneven years. The Trustees had been uncertain of whether Phil could make it to his retirement date, but they made no effort to provide him with useful support. What they did was arrange, unbeknownst to Phil, that Walter Hill would take over on short notice in a crisis. On January 5, 1975. at Walter's first community meeting, the students were full of manic energy and enthusiasm, animated by anticipation and release. The enrollment was 109 boarders, 6 day students. Students cheered frequently during Walter's brief talk, which ended with the old saying, "Don't walk in front of me, don't walk behind me, walk with me." That meeting turned out to be the peak of Walter's headmastership. Walter never truly connected with the students, the faculty, the trustees or the abiding spirit of the school. By the time he quit under fire in the summer of 1976, he had no constituency whatsoever – not students, not faculty, not Trustees, not even his wife, Pat, who stayed on without him, insisting the school honor *her* contract regardless of what Walter did.

Apparently, no one closely involved with the search process had had any substantial misgivings about choosing Walter. Ten years later, search committee chairman Jim Sunshine was still saying wistfully, "I did it all correctly, by the book." He never seemed to wonder if that wasn't the heart of the problem – doing it by the book, *at the Country School*? Jim had first come to know Woodstock in the spring of 1969, when the school served as a safe haven for a rebellious daughter who could no longer stay happily at home in Providence R.I. "By the time I got there the place was an insane asylum" in which the #1 activity was doing drugs, Cathy Sunshine remembered, "but I didn't have anywhere else to go." She graduated in June 1971 with a lot of animosity for the school; "I got out without frying my brain cells too badly." But her father was ambivalently grateful for whatevergood the school did do (he wrote in 2016 about "my daughter, Cathy, who hated WCS but who apparently learned enough there to get through Oberlin without difficulty, go through the Peace Corps in Africa, and is now a very successfulk free-lance editor in Washington"). Jim Sunshine served as head of the parents' association and helped revive that organization as a source of contributions and general support. That led to his becoming a Trustee in the fall of 1971 and taking over as the fourth chairman of the 25th Anniversary Campaign in the fall of 1972. He eventually succeeded Gerry Freund as president of the board as the school was beginning to unravel in the fall of 1975. Years later, Jim wondered out loud if Gerry had set him up for the collapse, since "Gerry was a past master at getting his ducks in a row."

Walter's early enthusiasts ranged from Dean of Students Marc Hurlbut, who felt the trustees should give top priority to building a gym, to Spanish teacher Les Rodriguez, the school's self-styled radical who spoke openly in faculty meeting of smoking dope with dinner because wine upset his stomach. Could Walter Hill shape Woodstock into the ideal school for both these men, or those who had still other visions? The expectations were unreasonable. What was surprising was just how fast Walter's headmastership came apart. He was in trouble within a month. By the end of May, it was clear Walter was not resolving the two-year crisis he had inherited from Phil, but was deepening it. He had made his first serious mistake just three weeks into the term. In consultation with Marc Hurlbut, whom he had made assistant headmaster and put in charge of "all aspects of student life" even though Marc really didn't like student life. Walter unilaterally changed inter-visitation to a major rule again, ignoring the school's community government system, as well as the faculty, not to mention the long-standing emotional explosiveness of the issue. In that single inept gesture, like Tawny, he had reinforced the students' worst fantasies about Woodstock becoming another St. Paul's and re-opened old, deep divisions among faculty members. When he later claimed he hadn't understood the process of going to community meeting with issues of school policy, he only compounded the community's distrust. Why had he not done his homework? At the same time, Walter was challenging the faculty about sending "confusing signals" to students, but not dealing in specifics. The return of the guilt injection revived the grim bickering of faculty meetings during Phil's last three years. And Walter wasn't sending the clearest signals himself, such as re-arranging the opening schedule of the summer term to accommodate assistant headmaster Marc Hurlbut's competing in a tennis match.

More disturbing, and incomprehensible, Walter's 19-year-old son lived on campus with his parents, but was not bound by school rules. His strange behavior included howling outside girls' dorms late at night, but he was not held accountable. Apparently, he was troubled, but Walter never shared any relevant information or guidance with the faculty.

Walter sent his most confusing signal near the end of the spring term, after five months of urging the faculty to clarify its expectations of student behavior. In late May, he unilaterally sanctioned student drinking at an off-campus overnight party at the home of a day student. About a third of the students went to the party. Some faculty were also invited, but only Marc Hurlbut and his wife attended, giving the occasion added sanction. Predictably, the party degenerated into an all-night drunken, stoned, violent, ugly scene in which at least one unwilling young girl had public sex with a drunken senior boy (the girl subsequently withdrew from school). Institutionally, the school made no response to any of the behavior at this officially-approved debauch, although Walter later gave the faculty a guilt injection for losing the girl. Not that the faculty was very clear about its own values, refusing to drop a student who had stolen, photocopied and distributed a final exam because, as one teacher put it "I would feel uncomfortable expelling him because he had no way of known it was wrong."

By the end of spring term 1975, Woodstock was more out of control than ever. The question once frequently asked in faculty meeting – "Who are the grown-ups here?" – no longer seemed to have much point. During the summer board meeting, Gerry Freund said the school was experiencing a crisis of responsibility and was over-managed. Jim Sunshine said the school was floundering. The news from outside was no better. The board had quietly closed its 25th anniversary campaign after it had raised a little more than half its goal of $401,000 in five years and all it had raised had been plowed back into operating expenses. At the same time, the board quietly initiated a capital funds drive with an unofficial goal of $900,000 that would not be mentioned in any of the campaign literature or publicity. The new drive was to be headed by Nell Richmond, a former parent from David Bailey's time, who couldn't recall whether she loved David or the school first. She remembered the extreme warmth of the school in those days, a warmth she didn't feel by 1975. Nor apparently did other friends of the school, as the Executive Committee minutes in July show: "Mrs. Richmond has talked with major prospects who are parents of graduates of many years ago; the responses have been negative. She said the school does not have loyal constituencies... She is distressed by the lack of response." So much so that she soon resigned from the campaign, leaving it to drift into oblivion.

As old friends were turning away from the school, new friends were harder to come by, not only donors but students. More and more students rejected Woodstock because of its campus life. With the school under-enrolled by 10 students in the spring of 1975, Walter told the faculty "this represents a serious crisis... we cannot afford under any circumstances not to be full in the summer."

But the administration made little extra admissions effort for the summer, which was then under-enrolled by 40 students. This was the smallest summer term enrollment in six years. Even then, the school did not make as much of an admissions push as it had in 1973, when much of the board and the faculty were also called on for extra help. In the interim, Walter had changed admissions directors, removing Bob Williams, a pleasant salesman with a low-key approach in favor of Peter Holland, who had a much more direct, even abrasive, manner, but was not noticeably more hard-driving. The results were not wonderful. Enrollment jumped in the fall, as always, but still the school was under-enrolled by 13, the smallest fall term since 1969. Winter was worse, only 85 boarders, and spring was down to 74, the smallest spring term enrollment since the 1950s. By the spring of 1976, not only were students telling admissions prospects that Woodstock was not a good school, admissions director Peter Holland was encouraging parents to take their children elsewhere.

Two occurrences during the summer of 1975 combined to extend student and faculty anger during the next school year. First, Walter turned over the job of revising the WCS catalog to his wife, Pat. She then set about re-writing the school's philosophy on her own, without consulting the community or the trustees, disregarding the years of effort it had taken the board, two headmasters and several generations of students and teachers to reach consensus on the philosophy as stated in the catalog. Second, in what Walter justified as an effort to control the budget, he reneged on several staff and faculty contracts. A quarter century earlier, when Woodstock was young and short of money, the faculty then voted to cut is own pay across the board in order to help the school survive. In 1975, with the school's survival equally if not more at stake, it seemed, such unanimity of self-sacrifice was out of the question. Walter consulted with his administrators – Marc Hurlbut, Bill Meyer, and Peter Holland, all among the highest-paid faculty members, none of whom volunteered to take a cut. Together they approved cuts that fell on lower-paid and part-time people. The heaviest of these cuts fell on Bob Henderson, the college placement advisor and history teacher. In mid-September, two days before the first faculty meeting of the fall term, Walter told Bob of his decision to cut Bob's $8,000 annual salary by 25% – with no reduction in Bob's duties. Bob had a wife and baby, with a second on the way, as well as an ex-wife and two small children living in Chicago.

Saving $2,000 this way in the face of a $60,000 deficit impressed no one, fiscally or morally. And it made an already deep morale problem that much greater. Walter's selective cruelty was not only futile, but self-defeating in the long run. Woodstock was approaching its third re-evaluation for re-accreditation by the New England Association of Colleges and Secondary Schools. Walter had already appointed Bob's wife, Barbara, one of the smartest and most capable members of the faculty, to manage the school's year-long self study, which began the re-evaluation process. She had only to do her job with integrity, thoroughness, and a few careful committee appointments and justice would be served. The result would make Walter's treatment of Bob look really stupid. In April 1976, when the school received the self-study reports, one of them emphatically rejected Walter's right to make unilateral changes in the school's philosophy as printed in the catalog. That report was tantamount to a motion of no confidence in Walter. Community discussion made the lack of confidence clear and the report was approved by a community vote of 74-1. Walter was not even the lone "No" vote. Walter had been on the committee that produced the report, but abstained from voting. He and his administrators (Hurlbut, Meyer, Holland) all abstained in the community vote. None of his administrators defended Walter in the community discussion.

The previous September 1975, two psychotherapists had attended a faculty meeting. Afterwards, Drs. Thomas Singer and Stuart Copans, had commented that the faculty was not sure of the headmaster's values and that made them feel variously guilty and/or anxious. They might have added angry and/or opportunistic. Before the meeting started, the therapists had placed an empty chair at the center of the faculty circle so that each faculty member faced it throughout the meeting. The therapists explained that the empty chair was symbolic, that faculty members were caught in a situation in which the center was empty, in which it was dangerous to make their own values clear because no one seemed to know what the headmaster's values were. One of the therapists suggested there seemed to be important value differences among faculty members and leaving values unclear was a way to avoid confronting the underlying differences. The faculty seemed to be pretending to believe in the same things, when in fact that was a fantasy. Walter did not respond to any of the observations related to values. He seemed not to have heard them. At about this time, one faculty member described an attempted confrontation with Walter as being "like fighting feathers in a dark closet with a fan on – mostly we just hit blank walls." Seven months later, when Walter faced that no-confidence report from a committee of which he was a member, he seemed genuinely surprised by it and by the discussion it provoked. But his response then was still no more effective than feathers in a dark closet with a fan on.

During the summer of 1976, Walter seemed surprised again when the faculty passed another no-confidence motion at a meeting he purposely set up for the faculty to evaluate his leadership, without his presence (he had not told them he had already resigned, effective June 30, 1977). He seemed surprised that the secret ballot vote was 16-0 against him (with one abstention), even though half a dozen of his most severe faculty critics had left the school in June. He seemed surprised that the vote to replace him immediately was 15-3 (with two abstentions). He continued to seem surprised when the school came apart around him and he peremptorily picked up and fled the campus a few weeks later.

### III

### Walter Hill report to the Trustees, June 27, 1976

*Attached you will find my best judgment of a "keep the doors open budget." This open door budget will, in my view further cripple the school. I am convinced that it would result in substantial further deterioration of our facilities. I am convinced these two situations would have a substantial effect on the morale and tone of the school at the very time when, with new faculty arriving, we are in a position to move the school forward and thereby, once again, attract the kind of students who we can help to prosper.*

### William Boardman '56 letter to teacher Dave Talbot '54, August 21, 1976

*I am still having trouble assessing what is going on [at school], but if you, Elizabeth [Miekeljohn, math teacher], and others are now fighting for the kind of school that I assume we would both like to see, more power to you.*

*I have never had many illusions about the difficulty of the fight, nor who the key people were. But I have never been able to exert much effect on those people and their closed view of the school....*

*After that meeting of the school and Trustees last spring, [Trustee] Jim Sunshine and I talked for half an hour or so and, at least for a few minutes, he dropped his defensiveness. I said some very strong, direct, and clear things to him, none of which would have been news to you. Jan [Poore] was there, and told him that everything I was saying was true. Rebecca [Boardman] joined us and added some more (from her experience as Dean oif Students). Jim seemed slightly shaken, somewhat interested – he said he'd like to talk to me at greater length. I'm still waiting.*

FALL 1973 – SUMMER 1980

## Executive Committee minutes, August 21, 1976

**Motion:** Mr. Nolte moved that the Executive Committee of the Board of Trustees recommend to the full Board of Trustees that the School will not open in October for the Fall Term unless, by August 28, 1976, sufficient cash and savings can be realized to carry the school through June 30, 1977.
  Seconded by Mr. Hill and unanimously passed (5-0)

**Motion:** Mr. Cheney moved that the Executive Committee warn a meeting of the Full Board to consider alternatives for the future of the Woodstock Country School, including liquidation, and such other business as is deemed appropriate. Such meeting will take place Saturday, August 28, 1976, at 9:30 a.m. at the Woodstock Country School. Seconded by Mr. Nolte and unanimously passed.

## Charles Halty '73, personal appeal to WCS alumni, August 23, 1976

Dear Alumni:
  Do you know what a 36-point 8-column headline looks like?
  It's big – but not as big as the end of the world. The one in last Friday's (August 20) Rutland Herald looked like the end of the world for the Country School, however:
    WOODSTOCK COUNTRY SCHOOL TRUSTEES DUE
           CRITICAL WEEKEND
The first sentence of the article read: "The headmaster of the Woodstock Country School denied Thursday reports that his institution is in dire financial straits and in danger of closing."
  There have been other stories since – in the Herald and on page one of the Valley News.
  Rumors are flying thick and fast tonight. The Trustees can't say what they decided last Saturday, but they're meeting again this Saturday. Perhaps (and I don't think I'm being melodramatic) for the last time in charge of a functioning institution and family.

*Let me be as clear as I can about what I think I know:*

*On Saturday, August 28, 1976 – this Saturday – the Trustees of the Woodstock Country School will meet to decide what action is to be taken. There are several options: to continue their present policies, to change leadership, to close the school, or to do something else I've neither thought of nor heard rumored.*

*The single, simple purpose of the letter is to get you – all of you – to respond by Saturday. A telegram, mailgram (only $2) – a letter or a visit to the school.*

*Let the Trustees know that the School's alumni care – that you care – for our Woodstock School community. Are deeply____? and will fight to keep the school alive.*

*Be positive.*
*Be critical.*
*But RESPOND – even by phone – by Saturday!*

## Florence C. Wislocki, MD, past parent, letter to the Trustees, August 30, 1976

*Though I very much want Woodstock Country School to open and to continue, I cannot believe that a week-end or a few weeks of frantic fund-raising in the form of contingency pledges can put the school on a sound financial basis. It is very doubtful that crisis emergency fund-raising efforts can even ensure sufficient financial support to carry the school for a full year. Even more tragic than not opening in October would be bankruptcy during the school year – an injustice to students and to faculty.*

*I believe that alumni/ae, parents and friends of the school should be (or better should have been) honestly informed of the situation and of realistic plans for the future of the school – which was once an idealistic and magnificent enterprise.*

• • •

When veteran *Rutland Herald* reporter Barney Crosier started calling Woodstock Country School officials on August 19, he knew only that the school was in serious financial trouble. He didn't know that Walter Hill had submitted a crippling budget to the board. He didn't know that the faculty had formally voted no-confidence in Walter Hill. Nor did he know that Walter had submitted his formal resignation to the board. But school officials didn't know what the reporter knew. So when he called, they stonewalled. Walter Hill lied. Marc Hurlbut refused to comment. Even Jim Sunshine, himself an editor on the *Providence Journal*, lied. The reporter resented the lies and put them in the paper. They were the same old lies the school had been telling itself for years, but somehow they weren't as comforting or persuasive when they appeared in print. In the days that followed, Walter avoided reporters as much as possible, except to announce his immediate resignation. Trying to undo the needless self-inflicted damage with the papers, Jim Sunshine started telling more of the truth about the school's condition, trying to elicit sympathy from reporters who were not hostile to begin with.

Charles Halty's appeal to the alumni got wide and sympathetic press coverage in the region. In three days it brought in pledges and some cash totaling more than $26,000, several times the annual alumni giving of recent years, but hardly enough to offset the estimated $200,000 shortfall for 1976-77. Still, the response was heartening. "I didn't think it could be done," Jim Sunshine revealingly told a reporter (Jim hadn't done it as campaign chair). And the emotional support, more than the money, gave the board some incentive to find a way to keep the school alive.

On August 28, when the trustees met as scheduled to consider liquidating the school, their first order of business was to accept Walter's resignation, which they did unanimously. This promoted assistant headmaster Marc Hurlbut to acting headmaster. He immediately expressed concern about his legal liability and the trustees immediately absolved him of any, since he was only "acting." At some time during this period, Jim Sunshine offered Marc the headmastership, but Marc turned it down. He had enough of boarding school life and already had other plans. Phil Hansen had gone to teach at the Roxbury Latin School in Boston, where he found Marc a job to teach and coach. Marc called Pat Heffernan to see if she would be Woodstock's headmaster, and others were sounded out as well, but there were no takers.

An unexpected result of the publicity about Woodstock's plight was that a Woodstock friend, Roger Smith, reported the news to the chairman of the board of the Stowe School, Robert D. Leaver (known as "Robin"), who contacted Walter Hill, who referred him to Jim Sunshine, who invited Robin to the board meeting. Woodstock Trustee Georgina Williamson of Sotheby Real Estate reported that a quick check showed Robin Leaver to have impressive credentials. Before Robin arrived at the meeting, several Woodstock Trustees fretted about whether Stowe's philosophy would be compatible with Woodstock's. Marc

Hurlbut warned the board that Stowe had real leadership problems and lack of authority and he wondered about the quality of their students. Finally, Gerry Freund brought the group back to reality: what better choice did they have? Eventually, by a 10-0 vote (with three abstentions), the Woodstock Trustees agreed in principle to merge the Country School into the new Stowe-Woodstock School.

At that meeting, Robin recalled, "I first saw that there might be an opportunity for a merger. I raised the subject with my fellow Stowe board members, Jan Robison and Carolyn Roberts, when we caucused, then raised it for discussion in the afternoon meeting." As Robin saw it, Stowe was operating in the black with full enrolment, but needed a better campus – and Woodstock, operating in the red and under-enrolled still had a wonderful campus. After further discussion, the Stowe board made a formal proposal on September 4 to merge the two schools on the Woodstock campus. The two boards announced the plan in a press release and their representatives, with their lawyers, set about working out the details. On September 25, the boards of both schools met to approve the final plan. In Woodstock, the Country School board spent the morning working its way through the legal steps of merger with a series of unanimous votes (recorded as 13-0, with 12 members present). Then they waited, and waited, recessed and reconvened. In mid-afternoon, the Stowe chairman called with bad news. Stowe's faculty and students were strongly opposed to the merger. The Stowe board had voted 8-5 in favor of the merger anyway – but they believed the merger required a two-thirds majority, so the motion failed by one vote. After the result was announced, the Stowe board realized that its by-laws in fact required only a majority vote to approve their merger, but decided not to retract its publicly, erroneous position.

Stowe chairman Robin Leaver, an entrepreneurial businessman with degrees from Brown College and Dartmouth's Tuck School of Business, had a different reaction: "I felt badly about our failure to muster the necessary vote for the merger at Stowe, and responsible to the WCS community. I had no desire to leave my business, move away from my children, or become a headmaster. I offered to become headmaster for one year, at a concessionary salary of $18,000, out of a sense of obligation." Robin conveyed this offer through one of Woodstock's newest Trustees, Garry Bewkes, vice president of the board of Norton Simon, Inc. As Bewkes reported it to the Woodstock board, Robin would take on the headmastership and board presidency of the Woodstock Country School (remaining for a while as Stowe's board chair as well); he would bring several Stowe board members with him, on the promise that Bewkes would raise $50,000 from the school's New York constituency and that Georgina Williamson would raise $50,000 from the Woodstock constituency (both over and above the $50,000 request to Laurance Rockefeller that was already pending). Late in the day, the Woodstock board accepted the offer, leaving it to Jim Sunshine and the school's lawyer to work out the details in Boston the next day, subject to subsequent, formal ratification by the board.

### Robin Leaver letter to alumni and friends, early November 1976

*Something magic is happening at your school... Our commitment is to building a new School, rooted in the principles of our predecessors, but responsive to the youngsters of today and tomorrow... Climb aboard the <u>Vision Express,</u> which is going to take this School from the edge of extinction to the full bloom of life...*

### Robin Leaver letter to alumni and friends, December 1976

*This is the first of a series of monthly letters to keep you apprised of the progress of the Vision Express... One of the first things we did was to abolish most rules. We have not only not lost any students, we have had no disciplinary problems... Perhaps the greatest catalyst has been caring. We literally keep in touch. In October I hugged a boy. His eyes filled with tears. Yesterday I saw that boy put his arm around a new student. His laughing eyes said come and play with us...*

### Robin Leaver letter to Laurance Rockefeller, January 5, 1977

*I believe that we should help people to learn to work hard and effectively in their respective lives, but also to be able to reflect on their labor and themselves... We attempt to provide a secure environment where young people are given intense personal support. Where we do that successfully, students become willing to take risks. As they risk, they grow, they self-create, they begin to be heroes...*

The new Woodstock Country School opened on October 4, 1976, with 44 boarders and 3 day students, almost as small a school as it had been when it started in 1945. The new headmaster told the faculty of 11 (only 6 full-time) that they would have to carry many of the responsibilities usually carried by the headmaster. Robin said if the faculty took responsibility for running the school, he would take responsibility for keeping it alive. Robin started by eliminating the hierarchical administrative structure that had served the school so badly. The first faculty meeting voted to eliminate the position of Dean of Students, which had proved so abrasive to students and divisive for faculty under both Buffy Dunker and Marc Hurlbut. Robin left it to his new assistant headmaster, Bill Meyer, to coordinate with the rest of the faculty whatever needed to be done. After a couple of weeks of school, Bill believed Woodstock "now has a realism and a lack of portfolios." Robin took over as moderator of community meeting, making it the school's governing body and eliminating the bicameral system (although the faculty continued to decide academic issues). Robin also moved to simplify the school's rules – but required all students to be at lunch and dinner, with assigned seats (except) on weekends. Robin put out new admissions ads which began: **"Be Yourself – Become Whom You Wish"**, adding that Woodstock "stresses letting you choose what to study and how... it is a close-knit community that is self-governing... a secure place where a boy or girl can risk doing new things and by risking, can grow." Robin also allowed the community to decide on re-admission of students who had flunked out or been expelled. The first former Woodstock student to go through the process was approved by a majority, but failed to get the necessary two-thirds vote to get back in. In all, the community re-admitted only 3 of 15 who applied.

On October 30, 1976, the Woodstock board ratified Robin's takeover of the school. Half of the alumni Trustees (Barbara Sproul, Roger Phillips, Dexter Cheney and John Morris) had already resigned. Gerry Freund and Anita McClellan (and less actively, Peggy Herschel and Bill Oram) remained on the board representing old Woodstock, along with David Bailey and Buffy Dunker on the Advisory Committee. The majority of the board was firmly behind Robin. He hand-picked his executive committee, which effectively ran the school: Jan Robison, whom he had brought in from Stowe; Roger Smith, a Dartmouth classmate and Woodstock businessman; Garry Bewkes; and Georgina Williamson, who had been on the board since 1973. Robin invited Gerry Freund to chair yet another headmaster search committee (since Robin intended to stay only a year).

The committee had hardly begun work when, in January, Georgina Williamson led an effort to keep Robin at Woodstock for a second year, recommending to the board that "the Headmaster receive an annual income of between $30,000 and $40,000, thus enabling him to spend more time at the school." At its August 20, 1977, meeting, the board voted to raise Robin's salary to $35,000. As Robin reported, "I was given a one-year contract and the responsibilities to find and hire my successor and raise 'an additional' $100,000.'"

Throughout the fall of 1976, Robin was full of energy, confidence, enthusiasm – and much of it was contagious. He wrote to reassure one parent, "we are re-defining our purposes and regaining our vision, we are meeting regularly as an entire family... There already exists an energy, a positivism and a joyfulness which is unlike anything I have ever experienced." He enlisted the faculty to manage their own salaries, within the instruction budget of $100,000 that needed to be cut to $60,000 by January 1977. Robin said, "I wanted them to be clear about the severity of the school's financial crisis, and that the crisis was the adversary, not their new headmaster." He told a newspaper reporter, "I don't know how much money was lost between June and October – the records are in incredible disarray... I think the Country School has been rife with inept management." He explained to Laurance Rockefeller, "We are doing away with rules for children and drafting agreements among adults... The Woodstock Country School has never been stronger."

When Walter Hill became headmaster, he had had his office walls painted white and had a student mural in the hall of Upwey painted over with white paint (causing another early backlash). Robin invited students to paint whatever they wanted on the "institutional white walls" of his office. He observed at the time, "Real participatory democracy only functions properly when it's being sheltered by a benevolent dictator, and everyone knows that." To a friend, Robin wrote: "I, personally, am having the time of my life and am finding it most exciting... I am sure we will emerge by the end of this year with most of our problems behind us." To another friend, he wrote "There is no question, I do get stratification from 'hanging tough' when others head for the hills." And to a third, he said, "I am learning that headmastering is one of the most rewarding and demanding jobs around. I wonder why it nurtures my spirit and depletes my sex drive at the same time." In the student report to the Trustees at the end of October, according to the minutes, Steve Power '77 said: "He saw a positive attitude among the students and attributed that to fewer rules and fewer committees... He added that the students have an enormous trust in their Headmaster and like having him here."

For most of those on campus, the fall term was difficult but wonderful, such a change and relief after the years of tension, confusion and double dealing since 1968. Robin generated tremendous trust among students and faculty alike. Of course, it was too good to last. For one thing, despite his manifest energy, Robin could not be expected to keep up the pace. He had other demands on his time and energy: he remained chairman of the Stowe board (some Stowe board members contributed to Woodstock); he had other business commitments, although he cut them back significantly; he travelled every other weekend for visitation with his two young sons; he travelled as necessary to raise money for the school. And still he tried to be the emotionally supportive headmaster both students and faculty desperately needed in Woodstock. There was a lot on his plate and the community understood that he was over-committed. For a while, he made it seem as if he could do it all, even if he was doing it with mirrors. But it felt like a honeymoon while it lasted.

In the winter term, Woodstock's familiar problems re-emerged, never having really gone away: student drinking and drug use, sexual promiscuity, community apathy, faculty incomprehension and exhaustion and community meeting complaints that "Robin is not around enough." At the January 29 board meeting, faculty Trustee Bill Meyer told the board "that things are different and difficult this term, more than ever before." Meyer elaborated, according to the minutes: "He pointed out that the student body was larger (enrollment was 62) and the faculty smaller than it has been in the past. He also noted that the faculty is fatigued from the fall term. He added that the students who are not contributing to the community are of great concern to the faculty as well as the student body. With all of this, he nevertheless felt that everyone was pulling together and there is a strength present, the likes of which he has not seen since he has been teaching at Woodstock."

Meyer's comments, and those of the student trustees, reflected the sense of a community meeting four days earlier: "This is a community, we all have to take our share of the load. We can't expect our parents to take care of us. People have lost the energy. Robin's energy is needed... People aren't being given enough direction... The people who were here before this term are an inner core who carry the spirit and we haven't spread it to our newer students, we haven't included them within our aura." At this meeting, as a morale booster, Robin suggested the school have a Winter Carnival, "the biggest party northern New England has ever seen." The carnival of February 25-27 was, in many ways, similar to previous winters' Fine Arts Week (aka "Five Rats, Eek!")

## Brad Lewis '59 letter to Isabel Stephens, November 6, 1976

*Thanks for your recent letter. I am glad to hear that you are involved with the school again, at least in an indirect way. A large part of Woodstock's difficulties has been the loss of experienced and knowledgeable educators to guide it through these times of transition...*

*David [Bailey] once called me the school's resident archconservative. However, the strength of Woodstock lay in the fact that intellectually it was founded on very conservative notions: a free intellectual environment predicates a highly disciplined mind; for teenagers just learning to study that discipline must be applied externally before it can grow internal...*

*When I returned to the school for a visit in 1973 I was appalled at the total collapse of even the vestiges of organization. The dorms were pigsties, the commons and classrooms both ratholes, and the students and faculty drifted about, like war orphans of some bombed-out town...*

*When a group of the alumni confronted Phil [Hansen] with our appraisal of the situation, he became very defensive. We were "outsiders"; the school was really very healthy; we were not able to see the real community at work. In three years of visits to the school I never saw that "community."*

*A group of us among the alumni have tried for some time to make the board listen. It adamantly refuses to see the facts. This is why I called for the total resignation of the board in my previous letter. For ten years it has guided the school by a policy of cover-up, neglect, mismanagement and deceit. I don't know who the power behind the board is, but whoever it may be has led Woodstock to the brink of extermination by insisting on a fiction that has long since ceased to convince anyone.*

## Robin Leaver letter to Trustee Jim Sunshine, June 12, 1977

*All things considered, it looks like it's going to be a summer of hustle. You know something? I would never do this for money. There just isn't enough.*

## Trustee meeting minutes, August 20, 1977

*Mr. Leaver said that after a great deal of thought he has decided not to continue as Headmaster after August 31, 1978. He said he had had a love affair with eighty students and he could not sustain that for more than two years..."*

## Robert Leaver letter to trustees, December 13, 1977

*I have not raised any money to speak of this fall... We are still facing $150,000 to $170,000 deficit this year. "El Rocko Grande" [Laurance Rockefeller] is giving us $50,000... About a month ago I began to realize that I was not going to be able to accomplish my objectives as a lame duck headmaster. Accordingly, I made the decision to continue as headmaster for an indefinite period of time until I feel that I have done what I am setting out to do... I will be disbanding the Headmaster Search Committee for the time being.*

## Trustee Jim Sunshine's note to Gerry Freund on resignation letter, December 28, 1977

*I'm not sure Robin really needs a board but if he does, he needs someone who knows more than I do. When he gets them, perhaps he will consult them before raising tuition. Anyhow, I'll miss you and Georgie [Williamson] especially. I know Robin saved the school where we failed, but I liked it better when you were president...*

## Robin Leaver memo to the author, August 15, 2000

*I was always told I wasn't around enough. I neither wanted to leave, nor did I enjoy my trips. I was not off on junkets. The students were my foremost interest and concern as headmaster. I can document the dates of the vast majority of my many fundraising trips. They were invariably difficult for me, and usually only marginally productive. The fact is that over the four years I spent at the school I worked myself into a state of physical and emotional exhaustion because of the time I spent calling and visiting people for money in addition to my duties at the school. I have correspondence describing my exhaustion, including a note from a Trustee confirming it.*

FALL 1973 – SUMMER 1980

## Betty Ferguson, WCS parent, letter to Robin, Good Friday, March 1978

*It was wonderful to see you again... I'm really worried about you. You seemed so sad and lonely. Your falling in love with a student could be a symptom of your loneliness.*

*By your Herculean effort you saved the school and now the school should make it possible for you to have the time to be with your children and your lover. Why should you put all your time, effort, and love into saving our children and your own children get left in a void? Like the shoemaker's children who go barefoot.*

*Robin you are physically very attractive & you have amazing personal charm. How has it happened that you are so lonely? Perhaps you have become a workaholic in order to avoid the possible pain of really close personal relationships?*

• • •

When Woodstock struggled to survive in the 1940s, it had no debt, it operated in the black by foregoing much and benefiting from much self-sacrifice by those who believed in the school's basic principles of freedom and responsibility. The move to Upwey changed the fiscal nature of the institution, but the school continued to flourish despite slowly-growing money problems until the headstrong and fiscally irresponsible decisions to build Bailey House (by David Bailey) and New Dorm (by Tom Debevoise) on credit – with no credible plan to manage the debt, other than to include it in the school's operating budget. The school Robin came to save carried a merciless heritage of fiscal irresponsibility by a board that never seemed to understand what it was doing, and not doing. By 1976, the sitting trustees had no fight left. Robin needed new board members who were his committed allies if the school was to have any chance of survival.

The school abandoned the Woodstock Four-Term Plan as an expensive and destructive failed experiment (then revived off-terms as Quest Terms in 1979). Enrollment increased slowly for a couple of years, to 89 (47 new students) in the fall of 1977, and then peaked at 96 in the winter of 1979. A year earlier, Robin had told the board that enrollment needed to be at least 130 to operate the school in the black. For fiscal 1976-77, Woodstock had a budget surplus of $112,000 – but that included the sale of the Giles House for $125,000 and unrestricted gifts of $153,000. At that time, the school's overall debt was just under

$400,000. The deficits for the next three years would total more than $440,000 even though the school was raising more money than at any time in its history. There were no easy solutions. There was too much to fix and too little time, with too few people, to fix it all quickly.

And then there was the New England Association of Schools and Colleges (NEASC) re-evaluation that was still pending. Walter Hill had started the process in 1975. The process was suspended during the turmoil of 1976 that ended with his departure. Robin re-started the re-accreditation: "I embraced the process because I wanted to leave an accredited school behind when I left. I even recruited new, specifically qualified Trustees to help us. I also tried to get Mr. Laurance Rockefeller's staff involved." In planning the logistics with NEASC official Ralph West, Robin assured him in May 1978 that: "Structurally, we are the same school you evaluated in 1968..." The re-accreditation committee that eventually visited the school in the fall of 1978 was appalled by what it perceived: "The Committee is seriously concerned with and disapproves (a) lack of attention to or attempt to control or educate students regarding the use of alcohol by minors (b) the absence of any program or standards relating to illegal drugs and (c) the amoral and casual attitude toward sexual promiscuity among minors... The evidence available to the Committee during its visit supports the conclusion that Woodstock Country School either ignores or absolves itself of any responsibility in these most important areas." The committee recommended that Woodstock have one year's probation during which to clean up its act.

Robin angrily objected, as he recalled: "The NEASC stated that they would evaluate our performance relative to our stated philosophy and goals. They did not do that. Rather they evaluated the school relative to *their* philosophy and goals. I protested, they revisited the school the following year, and we were re-accredited for three additional years." Later that summer, with no reference to the NEASC visit, Robin wrote the school constituency: "When we imposed stronger expectations on behavior, such as keeping dorms clean and attending morning meetings, most people were relieved. This year we have decided to be clearer about our expectations." The new NEASC visiting committee of five men came to Woodstock November 5 to 8, 1978. Around the same time, Robin was assuring Trustees: "Here we go again. Another year is off and we are stronger than ever." He also wrote to parents: "We are off to a great year, better than any since I have been headmaster."

When the NEASC committee wrote in mid-December advising that the school was once again to be put on a one-year probation, Robin did not respond.

The committee wrote again in January, inquiring as to the school's response. In early February, NEASC voted to put Woodstock on a one-year probation. At the Woodstock Trustees meeting on February 10, Robin reported being "disgusted with the entire exercise." The board, after considering having the school go without accreditation, voted to appeal the probation. On April 23, the NEASC accreditation committee again visited the campus and suggested tabling Woodstock's case to allow the school to address basic issues. As Robin put it to the trustees, their "concern is that we not condone inappropriate or illegal use of drugs or alcohol, or mislead parents concerning our commitment to their children." After further exchanges, NEASC wrote in late June to say that Woodstock would continue to be accredited for three years. NEASC made this official in late September 1979.

### Robert Leaver, draft statement (unpublished), December 1978

*The Woodstock Country School has no educational ideals, for it believes ideals impose limitations on experience, and anxiety on the individual, both of which are counter productive to personal growth. The school faculty tries to respond to the individual on his level. It emphatically resists the tendency to impose its, or society's, values on the individual. It refuses to condition students for society by the imposition of its own conditioning.*

### Robin Leaver, community meeting minutes, April 1979

*The most important trait is freedom... But this is not working, people aren't responding to absolute freedom without help from external authority. We want to help you reflect on past experiences. None of us really enjoy taking responsibility, but we must learn to.*

### Statement for NEASC in Trustee minutes, May 5, 1979

*In its role **in loco parentis** the Woodstock Country School accepts its responsibility to operate within the framework of the laws of society. While we do not condone the illegal use of drugs or alcohol, we recognize that experimentation with such substances is a widespread* *cultural phenomenon. The school confronts students with the consequences of their actions within the context of their developing value systems as well as the law. It addresses legal and moral problems openly and in an atmosphere of trust, avoiding punitive measures whenever possible. In order for this process to work we expect parents to accept the occasional need for confidentiality between faculty and students. We believe this gives us the flexibility to fulfill the intent, as well as the letter, of the law.*

### Robin Leaver letter to trustees, June 25, 1979

*I am concerned about the state of our board. Not only did we fail to gather a quorum for our May meeting, but so far only two of you have made contributions to the school this year... I am frankly not very productive because I am tired and disheartened... Only two Trustees came to graduation, one a parent.*

### Robin Leaver letter to faculty, July 5, 1979

*I believe I have been negligent... [announces few faculty raises] I will guarantee that no fulltime employee will be released for economic reasons between now and June 30, 1980. We are in a state of crisis.*

### Robin Leaver resignation letter to Stowe board, December 5, 1979

*Stowe has had a first priority in my heart... I had more fun, received more nourishment, and was more challenged personally as a trustee of the Stowe School than in any other involvement in my life... The Stowe board has become one of the strongest on which I have served.*

● ● ●

One faculty member who taught at Woodstock for the last few years, and also took on administrative responsibilities, remembered his birthday in the summer of 1979, when students gave him three lines of cocaine as a birthday present, because that's what his friends told them he'd like. He said he "indulged, mainly because I didn't want to hurt their feelings. He also said, "I was referred to as a fascist," and that there was a graffito saying he made the trains run on time. "I compromised much more that I should have," he said, adding that he would just like to forget. He summed up: I was far and away the most responsible, ethical member of that faculty.... I was the closest thing to a sane adult... [And] I was a jerk, too."

When the 1979 fall term began with 87 students on campus, Robin was insisting that he expected students to develop more "self-reliance, self-governance and self-discipline." But in conditions sometimes approaching absolute freedom, the students found themselves seeking protection in logical, but somewhat bizarre ways, as in their community meeting decision in October 1979: "Zippy [Borock] rule on bad drugs – Proposal: Misrepresentation of drugs will result in suspension for duration of the term determined by community meeting. Students are responsible for drugs sold by guests. PASSED: 40-1-12." There's no record of faculty or administration support for "Zippy's Rule," nor did anyone apparently ever call for its enforcement. As Robin viewed it, "it was an acknowledgement of student responsibility when drugs were sold and no faculty member was around to prevent it."

Two weeks later, according to the board minutes, faculty Trustee Janet van Sickle "reported that many faculty have been ill this fall and this has left many of the faculty dragging. There is also a sense of dispiritedness that everyone didn't get a cost of living increase this year: the faculty and staff feel that more than ever they are overworked and underpaid... There is also a concern about the direction of the school: an increased tension between faculty and students is occurring due to the tightening-up of rules and the imposition of structure."

The Trustees, too, were struggling to keep their collective footing in a fluid situation. In October 1978, after two years as his own board president, Robin had stepped aside in favor of Buffy Dunker, then 73 years old, who felt coerced into taking the position. Robin continued as a board member (and was still on the Stowe board). Garry Bewkes resigned four months later. In May 1979, the annual meeting of the Trustees lacked a quorum and was postponed until August. According to the minutes, Robin told the board: "The school has never been in better shape." Robin, who was projecting a surplus of $38,000 for 1978-79, had not prepared a 1979-80 budget. According to the minutes, "Leaver stated that this year's budget is equally applicable to next year" and the board voted level spending, pending adoption of a budget. In June, Robin revised 1978-79 to show a $60,108 deficit (later revised to $75,000). Robin also presented a budget for 1979-80 with $811,000 in expenses and a $2,471 surplus (later revised to a $9,000 deficit).

Buffy had taken over the board with great reluctance, she told close friends, mainly because she felt pressured by Gerry Freund and David Bailey. "I don't have time to be chairman of the board," Buffy said at the time. She expressed enthusiastic confidence in Robin, but she had little time or energy to devote to the board and she flatly refused to help with fundraising. While Buffy was one of nine Trustees present for the annual meeting in May, there was no quorum and no official annual meeting could be held until fall. After a year of accomplishing little, Buffy stepped down at the 1979 fall meeting. Replacing her as board president was her longtime nemesis Rhoda Teagle of Woodstock, who belonged to neither the Robin faction nor the old Woodstock faction of the board. Rhoda had no educational qualities useful to the Country School board (in 1970, she had expressed approval of the Kent State shootings). But she was married to Frank Teagle and was presumed to have some access to his substantial Standard Oil inheritance (the presumption of access proved largely illusory). Rhoda had also sent a daughter, a nephew (the author) and a niece to the school in the late 1950s. She harbored a deep-seated antipathy to the school and especially David Bailey, for what she perceived the wrong inflicted especially on the niece (even though she graduated from and loved the school). Rhoda had joined the board in the summer of 1977 and served quietly, hiding her feelings. Rhoda had disliked Buffy, at least since the 1950s, a dislike that turned to open disgust when, in 1977, Buffy had come out in the Boston Globe as a lesbian. By the fall of 1979, Rhoda was embarrassed by the Country School and was writing in her trustee meeting notes about Robin: "He'll be reverting to his old business – why should he still be headmaster then?" – to which another hand responded: "This year we have to have status quo."

At that same November Trustees meeting, Robin announced he would not serve as Headmaster beyond August 31, 1980, little more than nine months away. If all Rhoda wanted was to see Robin gone, she had only to wait. But Rhoda was not committed to seeing the school survive (though she kept that to herself). As Robin recalled, "I recruited Mrs. Teagle to serve as board chair. Until the spring of 1980, she and I were of one mind, worked closely together and shared a mutual respect." Once she was board chair, Rhoda made a greater effort to understand the school's reality by talking to other people. Unsatisfied with what Robin was telling her, she soon came to believe that assistant headmaster John Chater was a more reliable confidante than Robin. Chater came to the school in the spring of 1979. A native Vermonter who had helped set up the state's community college system, John had applied to be headmaster of the Stowe School, getting to know Robin Leaver first as a Stowe Trustee. When Stowe chose someone else, Robin offered him the Woodstock job.

By the middle of the 1979 fall term, Chater was getting disillusioned: "Right from the beginning I spent a lot of time getting to know the kids and talking with kids and seeing what they felt about how things were going... and I felt they got the short end of the stick because of the inability of the faculty and Robin to get it together, and the lack of direction on the part of the board, to let students know what the school was all about and assure the students that there was some stability around. The kids were often the most stable thing in the school. Often I felt that the kids had fifteen or twenty permissive parents [on campus], each of whom came up with a different solution, and were never in agreement about anything, and always made everything a big issue... The kids never had straight answers or any strategy directions. There were always different opinions. The rules were always changing and expectations were always changing, and if the faculty up held a rule... Robin would overturn it. There was always constant confusion and chaos, which I think wore the kids out. It certainly wore the faculty out... Robin loved to set the kids off against the faculty."

During the summer of 1979, twelve faculty members (not including Chater) signed a statement of what they called the "Preferred State" of WCS. The statement's recommendations included: (1) the Faculty Select Committee should review any new positions before they are filled, (2) the Headmaster should not over-ride decisions of other school bodies without consultation, and (3) the Headmaster should work through Community Council to deal with issues before they become crises. The statement also said: "Given the present financial condition of the school, the size of the Headmaster's salary is a matter of concern to the faculty."

### Robin Leaver memo to author, August 15, 2000

*I suggested the board have my replacement onboard by the end of April 1980. No action was taken. At some point, Mrs. Teagle decided to close the school. I opposed her efforts in the hope that a solution would be found. In early 1980, seeing me and my allies on the board as an obstacle to achieving her goal, Mrs. Teagle began looking for ways to discredit me. She did this by holding meetings to which I wasn't invited and attempting to elicit allegations of misconduct, which could be used against me.*

### Rhoda Teagle letter to Trustees, January 17, 1980

*The time has come to take a careful, serious, immediate and loving look at the Woodstock Country School. We cannot wait until the meeting planned for the end of February... At this time, there is not enough money to carry the school through June.*

### Trustee meeting minutes, February 1, 1980

*Leaver says we have gained a reputation for being able to turn difficult kids around; we are no longer known for the excellence of our academics.*

### Rachel Kaufman '80, letter from Brown University, September 1984

*I'm writing in response to your letter of a year or two ago.... I was there only three months, just before the school closed. So I can't offer you much in the way of memories – the spring of 1980 was a sad time for everyone at WCS except, perhaps, me – I had just arrived & was very much in need of the space and freedom I found there... I wish I could help, but the most I could offer you would be an angry treatise on American public education.*

### Gerry Freund '48 letter to Anne Adams Bross '54, February 12, 1980

*I am just out of a four-hour session in my office [in New York] with Rhoda [Teagle], Steve [Pollan], Russ [Mead], Peter [Sauer] which began with an updating of finances which makes matters even worse and the crunch more imminent than we thought at the Board meeting. I can't understand how Robin could not have known that it is mid-February, not mid-March that we are out of money... No matter, it is the facts, whatever they are, we have to deal with, and it is quite wonderful that the likes of those with whom I met this morning are utterly devoted to maintaining the school...*

*Among other responsibilities I am hell bent on finally giving David and Peggy some security and, equally, on having Robin come out of present circumstances not only looking good but feeling good."*

FALL 1973 – SUMMER 1980

## Robin Leaver memo to author, August 15, 2000

*In early April, in an attempt to discredit me, Mrs. Teagle hired Gary Brown, an attorney, to interview students in an effort to turn up allegations of my misconduct. On April 11, Mr. Brown called Jinx Suhler at her home in Virginia and asked if I had ever invited her to participate in "informal therapy sessions." When I heard this, I retained counsel.*

• • •

In early 1980, Rhoda Teagle was getting more worked up than ever by what she thought she was learning about the school. She was getting little support from most of the Trustees. And when the school's outstanding loan increased above $500,000, the Vermont National Bank began to pressure her about its exposure, despite its 9.5% interest rate. On January 17, she provoked a crisis, writing a letter to the Trustees suggesting that the school should consider closing in June. The reaction was fractious. Two days of Trustee meetings, February 1 and 2, were inconclusive. So were two days of Trustee meetings February 22 and 23. No plans were adopted, but closing on June 30 kept coming up. Vermont National Bank strongly suggested closing at the end of winter term on March 15 and "not able to lend any additional money." At the March 18 executive committee meeting, four of the five members present voted (one abstained) to sell the whole school for $1.2 million, if a buyer could be found. This was at the low end of the school's valuations by several appraisals. The committee also decided to continue the search for a new headmaster and planned for contract contingencies in the event the school closed. Treasurer Steve Pollan "asked that school books be brought up to date… And be ready with no surprises for the next committee meeting."

During the winter and spring, the level of distrust and hostility among the Trustees continued to rise, mixed with fatalism and helplessness. At the April 12 board meeting, several Trustees objected to Rhoda's unilaterally visiting Vermont National Bank with attorney Gary Brown, who was her personal attorney, *not* the school's (presumably the board was unaware that, two days earlier, Brown had said of Robin, "I'm sure he's stealing the school blind," though there was no credible evidence presented then or later that it was true). At that same meeting, Trustee Steve Pollan, a corporate lawyer and board treasurer, took Rhoda to task for not finding buyers for the school property or carrying out other tasks the board assigned the executive committee. The board voted that

WCS would suspend operations as of June 30, 1980, and undertake an orderly sale of assets to meet its obligations. Only Pollan opposed the motion, but he agreed to serve on the "orderly closing task force" created after the vote.

According to the minutes, Robin left the April 12 meeting before it was over, affirming his commitment to WCS and promising to go on a fast until the board sold the school land and raised $500,000. Three days later, according to Robin, Rhoda and Trustee Georgina Williamson "came to my house and asked me to resign. I said I would be glad to do so if the board would meet four conditions. These, in summary, were: (1) a letter from the board "saying I had served the school well," (2) payment of back salary and interest already agreed to by auditors and executive committee (about $38,000) (3) permission to stay in Headmaster's house through August 31, or later if not paid, and (4) the board's promise to honor severance commitments already made to faculty members."

Robin understood that Rhoda would take these conditions to the board. Rhoda's own, somewhat sketchy notes on the meeting, apparently for a letter never sent, confirm Robin's four conditions. Rhoda also wrote: "When I came to see you, it was at the request of several board members – who asked me to clear the air. It didn't work that way." Rhoda had a long history of being unable to clear the air with people, including two husbands (and she once lost a lawsuit for high-handed actions she said she took for a humane society).

The orderly closing task force, formed April 12, still had not had its first meeting by May 1 when Rhoda wrote to inform them that they would meet May 30. Rhoda also reported that: (1) real estate ads were placed from Paris to San Francisco, with no real offers yet, (2) "I am working with the bank to see if there is any way we can keep going until graduation," (3) "We are going ahead with the summer program" (John Chater thinks he can break even), and (4) "We will suspend operations on June 30 – but will not give up all hope of trying to re-open in the fall." Also on May 1, Rhoda wrote the school's parents to tell them the school was closing. A few days later, on May 7, Rhoda wrote Robin, somewhat disjointedly, seeming to demand that either he resign or else she and two other trustees would resign.

### Rhoda Teagle letter to Robin Leaver, May 7, 1980

*It seems to me rather dreadful that you won't join me for lunch without the school lawyer present... I am frankly tired of making apologies for the School and excuses for its students, as I have for three years... With your many absences, the School has lost its direction... Several board members have suggested that you leave before the School comes down around your ears... Unless I have heard that you have taken positive steps by Monday, May 12, please tender my resignation to the Board, along with the resignations of Georgie [Williamson] and Marion [Taylor].*

• • •

On May 9, Rhoda wrote more calmly than she had two days earlier: "The majority of the Board of Trustees has agreed that it is best to make a formal request for your resignation at this time... no later than May 12, 1980, by 5 p.m." Rhoda acknowledged that, under his contract, the school owed Robin $37,583 through August 30. And she asserted that, unless Robin resigned, WCS could not find direction and leadership. Robin did not resign on May 12. Five days later, Buffy wrote Rhoda:

### Buffy Dunker letter to Rhoda Teagle, May 17, 1980

*I wish you had tried to reach me either early in the morning or after 11 p.m. as I would have been glad to cast my vote against asking Robin to resign. I consider it a bad move, both humanly and tactically. I also did not like the tone of your two letters at all. No matter what the provocation, I feel that courtesy and consideration are due anyone, especially anyone in difficulties.*

• • •

In the weeks leading up to the May 31 Trustees meeting, stories circulated on campus and in the newspapers that Robin resigned; that Robin was fired; that Robin was staying at WCS under a compromise. Rhoda's own, somewhat chaotic, notes on May 30 report fragmentarily, "School in chaos – no money etc., no classes etc. went to school community mtg – frank talk with all. Then with Robin." The May 31 Trustees meeting was billed as an open meeting, but when a reporter showed up, he was thrown out and the meeting closed. The board voted to accept Robin's conditions, as outlined in a letter from his attorney, Bruce Lawlor. Robin then read his letter of resignation, which the board accepted unanimously. The board then unanimously named John Chater as acting headmaster. The meeting had its prickly moments, but was not the contentious battle some, like the absent Russ Mead, had expected. After lunch, the meeting no longer had a quorum. In anticipation of greater conflict, Russ had submitted a strong formal statement that turned out to be something of an anti-climax to an anti-climax: "A headmaster's responsibility is to represent a school with dignity. I am ashamed to be a member of the same profession as Robin Leaver, who has cheapened it and this school by his behavior. Those of the public present at this meeting will, I hope, make an effort to become acquainted with the truly dedicated and professional educators who have been part of this school and not judge this school by this crisis or the behavior of this man."

### Robin Leaver, Burlington Free Press, June 1, 1980

*They didn't want to make it work... I can't work at a place where the board of trustees has run for the hills... The Country School has a national reputation as an elite progressive school.*

### NEASC's letter suggesting WCS withdraw without prejudice, June 4, 1980

*It would seem likely that a Progress Report and visit would reveal a deteriorated situation from the time of the evaluation.*

• • •

On June 21, Woodstock graduated 38 seniors, more than 40% of the student body. Woodstock's final summer term began July 7, with an enrollment of 16 and a faculty of five. It was something of an academic afterthought, but it served its purpose: allowing 13 "seniors" to complete their academic requirements and "graduate" from high school. For the final Country School commencement, on August 27, 1980, the seniors invited Robin Leaver to be their guest speaker.

"I intended to say something wise to you," Robin began, "but I'm not a wise man, so that would probably not be very wise. But then you are not a wise audience, so it would probably be wasted on you." Instead, he talked about himself and about a "SCHMUCK" bumper sticker he had seen recently: "We are all schmucks, we are all struggling as best we can." He talked about his struggle of the past several months, "because you care so much about me, you might learn something from it." He talked about the board's "vituperative criticism" when he "resigned in May, how that made him feel sad and angry and "a rage of impotence," so he went to a friend's house and drank two bottles of champagne: "I felt like I'd raised a child from adolescence only to have it die before it reached maturity." He talked about driving to see his old girlfriend, who gave him no sympathy, "she had drifted away from me and wanted to go her own way." He talked about going to the Coral Beach Club in Bermuda ("I've made a point of going to a lot of resorts") where he was alone and drank a lot and a man took pity on him and offered Robin his two daughters and a niece – "as I looked over at the table the three girls waved at me". He talked about the young woman he invited to join him for a "brief liaison" in Bermuda ("for the board's benefit, she has never been in any way involved with the school") but it was not a success, she was like any other girl he had known, "only her skin was a little bit squeakier." He talked about coming back to campus to find his house had been broken into. He talked about going away and coming back to find his house broken into again: "something in me snapped because they had taken a lot of personal things. I felt powerless, out of it. I sat in the dark in my living room with my rifle across my lap thinking it could protect me from the forces outside." He talked about help from his family and friends, about cutting back on smoking and drinking, about turning down a job as a company president: "I decided I would write a book because it would be therapeutic for me." He talked about developing "a strong preoccupation with women's breasts," so notable in public that one of his sons called it "gross" and told him to stop. He talked about how his fixation made him realize "I had made surrogate mothers out of all the women I had relationships with," so he was starting to become his own mother more. He talked about feeling sorry that the school would not continue, but "there are times when you should let go... Over the past four years there have been some magical things that have happened here between individuals... and those things are more important than the school" (Some of those "magical things" were in the four boxes of materials Robin took with him when he left the school, as he told those at the WCS 2000 reunion, where he read sample aloud.)

Before awarding the diplomas, acting headmaster John Chater acknowledged the school's recent failures as a community and the constant turmoil that resulted. He told the small gathering in the school's stone-terraced grassy amphitheatre, "this school has been mismanaged, exploited for personal gain and discredited." Perhaps it was a long time past worrying about the appropriateness of a school official trashing his own (about to close) school that way, especially after Robin's bizarre guest performance. Insofar as the acting headmaster was blaming Robin alone for the school's failings, Chater was inaccurate if not dishonest. Mismanagement of the school went back decades. Exploitation for personal gain was a potential slander (echoing attorney Gary Brown), without any clear meaning. (The school made no claim against Robin, the final audit (no longer extant) caused no scandal, and as it would turn out, Rhoda Teagle ended up with the most undeserved personal gain). And "discredited" was a philosophical libel, since it was not the school, or its abidingly humane philosophy that had been discredited, but so many of its would-be leaders who had failed to support or even understand the essence of the school with honesty and clarity.

When the ceremony ended, the Woodstock Country School was over, just a few days short of the 45th anniversary of its first opening day. David Bailey once said if he were to write a book about WCS, he would call it "Felicity Awhile," a reference to *Hamlet*, Act V, scene ii:

> If thou didst ever hold me in thy heart
> Absent thee from felicity a while,
> And in this harsh world draw thy breath in pain
> To tell my story.

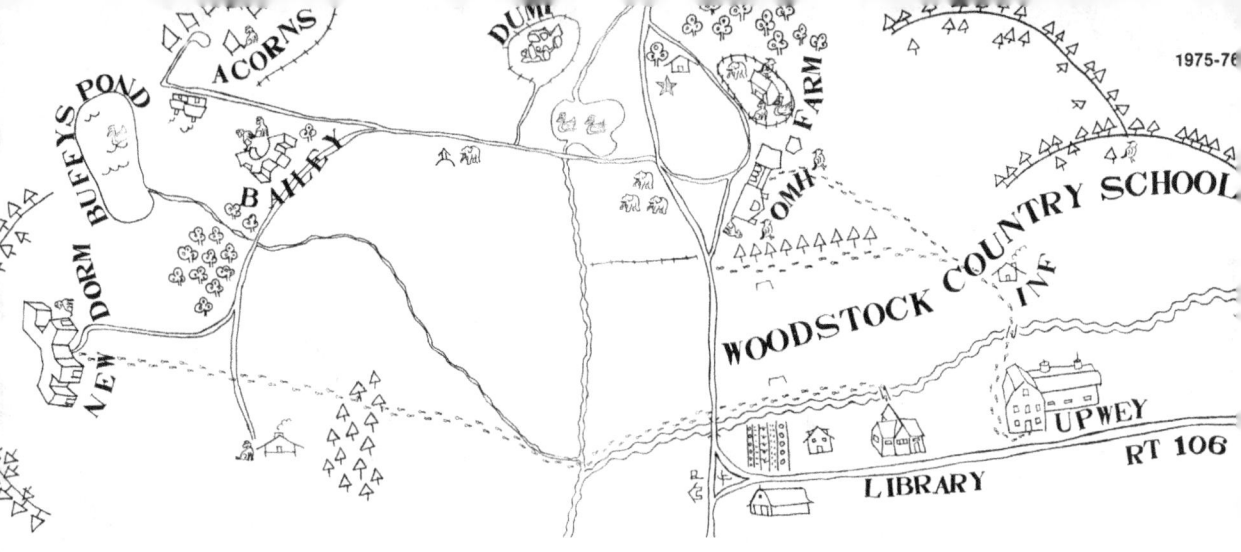

WCS campus map by Marianne Clemens for cover of WCS catalogue

Sheila Doherty '79

Leslie Parke '70

Chris Bacher '74

Martha Markham '73

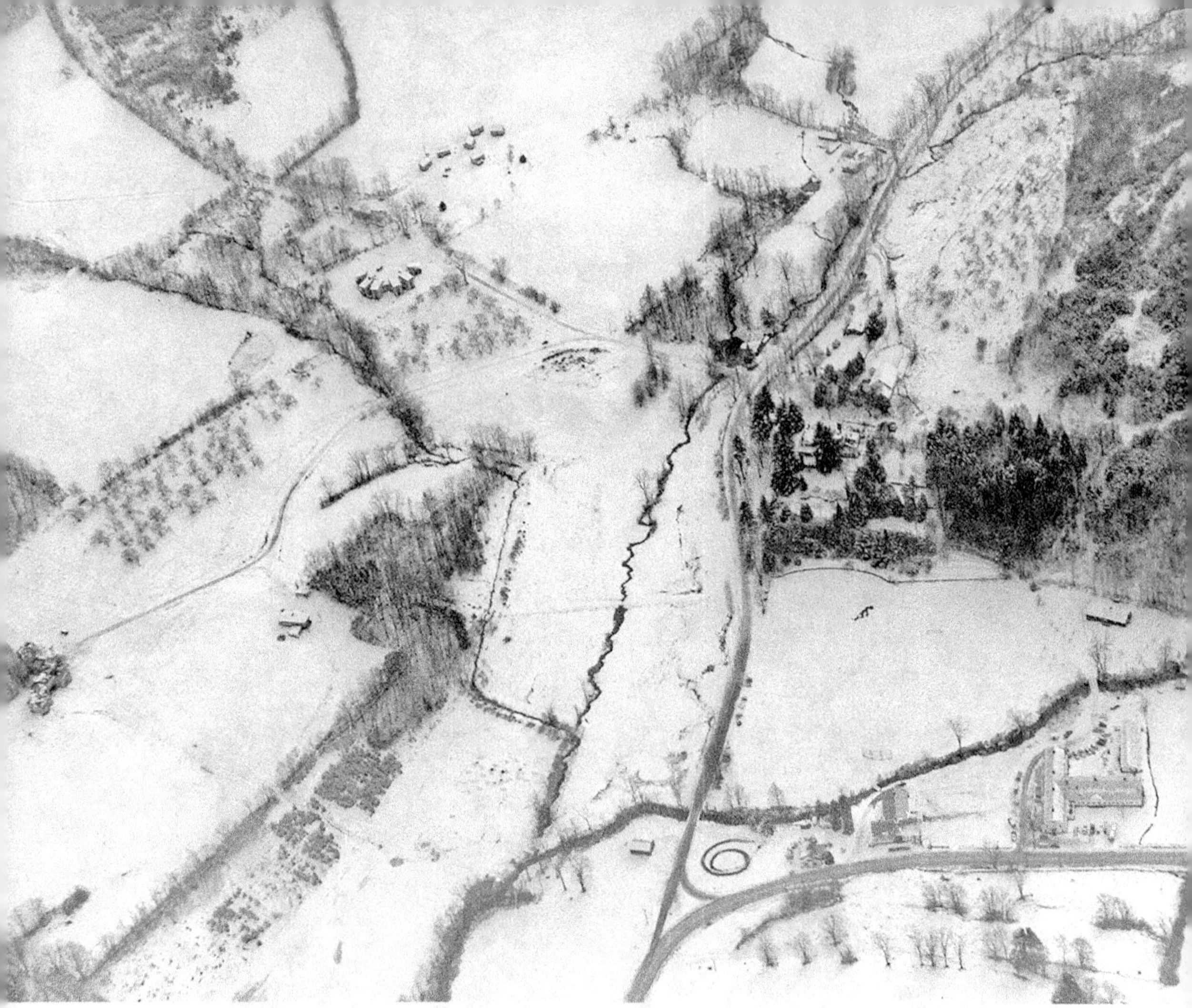

WCS campus aerial shot was a Pat Lee science project

Wini Ray '79

Scott Brownwood '78
& Chris Benson '79

# End Note #1

**HOW THE SCHOOL GOT SOLD...**
*"Oh! what a tangled web we weave...."* – Sir Walter Scott, *"Marmion"*

The Country School Trustees put the school property on the market some time in the early spring of 1980, before the board had decided to close the school or to have a summer term. The property comprised about 325 acres, with 20 buildings, playing fields, swimming pond, amphitheatre, and other amenities.

Conservatively, the property was worth more than $1.5 million. In July 1979 it was appraised at $1.54 million. In August 1980 it was appraised at $1.68 million. In 1975, the school had insured itself for a replacement value of $1.9 million, up from $1.3 million in 1973.

**March 18, 1980:** the executive committee of the Trustees met at Logan Airport in Boston moved to offer the property at $1.2 million, advertised as "Priced Below M.A.I. [Member of the Appraisal Institute] Appraisal" of 1979. Committee members Rhoda Teagle, Robin Leaver, Georgie Williamson, Steve Pollan, and John Roberts voted for for the motion without objection (with one unidentified abstention). The record does not explain why the asking price was more than $300,000 lower than the appraisal, or whether that choice met the Trustees' fiduciary duty to the school. Ads would run nationally and locally over the next several weeks.

**April 2:** the Baltimore Braille Association inquired about the school to real estate broker Clayton Adams, a friend and neighbor of Rhoda Teagle. After hearing from Adams, the Braille Association wrote on April 15 that its "plan for the facility would be continued operation of the WOODSTOCK COUNTRY SCHOOL, with present staff." (emphasis in original) On April 13, Adams, referring only to Rhoda Teagle, wrote back that "the Trustees insist on having the information requested earlier, namely "a profile of your Association(s), their purpose, history and planned use for the new facility, and also bank and professional references," before releasing operation and financial information." There is no further record.

**April 24:** Adams's partner Douglass Symmes wrote Rhoda Teagle about visiting the school in session under acting headmaster John Chater: "I know that I don't need to remind you of the deplorable conditions in both the classroom buildings and dormitories, however, it is our opinion that showing prospective purchasers around under these conditions can only hurt out chances for a sale!" He suggested the Trustees spend money on a "thorough cleaning" once the term was over in June.

**May 1:** Trustee Georgie Williamson wrote the rest of the board to report meetings with interested local people "about forming a group to purchase the school." Williamson, a Woodstock real estate agent for Sotheby, participated in the sale only as a WCS Trustee.

**May 2**: Tom Wright, the school's attorney, wrote the Trustees' task force about the same group of interested people by John Dunne, an attorney representing the Ottauquechee Land Trust, which was part of the group of potential buyers. Attorney Dunne asked the school to grant a right of first refusal, in order to give his clients time to conduct what Wright called "a feasibility study" that would cost $8,000 and be "available to the school or its brokers."

**May 5:** realtor Roger Maher inquired about the sale, adding by the way that "our younger daughter, Connie, went there when David Bailey was head and got a lot out of the school – she loved it and got a damn good secondary education which enabled her to go on and do well in college."

**June 16**: the WCS Trustees granted a right of first refusal to the Ottauquechee Land Trust in exchange for $1 and the benefit of the Trust's proposed study. There is no record of any objection to Rhoda Teagle being both a WCS Trustee and a Land Trust Trustee.

**In early July**, attorney Gary Brown drew up a purchase and sale agreement for his client, Sandell Development Corporation to buy the school property for $950,000. This agreement was not signed.

**July 29:** attorney Tom Wright, representing the Country School, notified the Ottauquechee Land Trust that the school had received an offer from the Sandell Development Corporation of $950,000 for the all the school's real estate and personal property, with a closing tentatively set for September 30. The Land Trust had 30 days to exercise its right of first refusal.

**July 31:** attorney Gary Brown wrote Rhoda Teagle as Woodstock Trustee, notifying her that his client, Sandell Development Corporation had secured financing

## END NOTE #1

for the purchase "and is now anxious to close as soon as possible. I have been very impressed by Mr. Wasserman's continued expression of his intent to preserve the unique rural qualities of South Woodstock. He plans to work with people from the community as well as with the finest available professional environmental planners to achieve that goal." (Max Wasserman was a graduate of M.I.T., 1935, with a long list of completed development projects, mostly around Cambridge, Massachusetts. He held 28 patents and during World War II had developed the heavy plastic bubble the protected bombardiers in planes like the B-17.)

**August 2:** attorney John Dunne drew up an offer to purchase under which his clients, Woodstock Education Associates and John Byrne, Jr., would buy the school for $540,000 plus unpaid unemployment compensation for the school's staff up to $104,000. The offer expired, unaccepted, on August 5. (A similar agreement appears to have been offered and expired in July.) Attorney Dunne was also general counsel for the Ottauquechee Land Trust. On the same day, attorney Dunne appears to have informally increased his clients' offer to $810,000 plus the unemployment payment capped at $104,000. John J. Byrne was a prominent insurance executive then highly regarded for having saved Geico from bankruptcy.

**August 11:** Peter Wasserman of the Sandell Development Corporation wrote to the WCS Trustees to reassure them of the corporation's plans: "We propose a planned unit development which would be environmentally sensitive to the existing landscape by preserving open space and maintaining woodland areas.... We plan to preserve existing barns and... to renovate dormitory buildings with particular emphasis on exterior restoration using natural materials and landscape design..." and other reassurances. On the same date, attorney Gary Brown proffered a purchase and sale agreement for his client, the Sandell Development Corporation to buy the school for $1,065,000.

**August 18:** the Country School Trustees met with only four board members present (Rhoda Teagle, Peter Sauer, John Roberts, and Anita McClellan), as well as two student and faculty representative. Rhoda had nine proxies. There is no record that the board considered whether this constituted a legitimate quorum. The board voted unanimously to accept the Sandell Development Corporation offer, only the faculty representative opposed it. The agreement (from August 11) included Sandell's obligation to give the Ottauquechee Land Trust roughly 15 acres of low-lying pasture lane across the road from Giles House (by then owned by John Byrne, whose purchase had been brokered by WCS Trustee Georgina Williamson).

**August 19:** in a letter to WCS attorney Tom Wright, attorney Gary Brown confirmed that his client, the Sandell Development Corporation had accepted modifications to the purchase and sale proposed by attorney Wright for his client, the Country School. Attorney Brown anticipated a closing within 60 days "of notice from the Ottauquechee Land Trust of *their non-exercise* of their right of first refusal." (emphasis added) According to attorney Brown, Max Wasserman "wants to make money, but do it right," using solar collectors, greenhouses, and other environmentally friendly tools.

**August 20:** attorney John Dunne prepared an agreement under which his clients, the Ottauquechee Land Trust, Woodstock Education Associates, and John Byrne would exercise the Trust's right of first refusal and pay the selling price of $1,065,000. The record is not clear as to when attorney Dunne shared his clients' decision with attorneys Brown or Wright.

**August 21**: the local Woodstock weekly, the Vermont Standard reported with unfortunate zero accuracy: "**Country School Is Sold; Aug. 31 Is Closing Date.**" The paper also reported that the buyer was Sandell Development Corporation. The same wrong story ran in the Rutland Herald, the Valley News of Lebanon, N.H., and in the Washington Post.

**August 25**: the school received a 90-page appraisal report from the James G. Thetford Company of Montpelier, Vermont, valuing the 46.75 acre campus & twenty buildings at $1,210,000 and 276.85 acres of development land at $470,000, for a total evaluation of $1,680,000, more than $600,000 over the agreed-upon purchase price.

**August 27**; the Ottauquechee Land Trust notified its board members of its plans to buy the Country School: "The support the Trust is receiving from the community of South Woodstock to proceed with the exercising of our right of first refusal is truly incredible. Almost 60 people, representing a complete cross-section of South Woodstock, have already pledges an amazing 1.2 million dollars in credit and cash contribution to allow for the purchase and follow-up work that will need to be done once we have purchased the property.... The Trust is fully protected in terms of covering all costs related to this project." There's no record of the Land Trust ever making any study.

## END NOTE #1

**August 28**: the Vermont Standard reported the Trust's plan to exercise its right of first refusal, as did the Valley News the next day. On September 4, the Rutland Herald reported: **"Millionaires May Buy School"** and went on to say that "The moneyed interests in Woodstock, however, were obviously alarmed by the prospects of condominiums spoiling their views, despite Wasserman's plans." The story added that "Sources said prominent Woodstock resident Laurance Rockefeller contributed $150,000 to the fund, while one unnamed Woodstock resident alone kicked in $500,000.... [And] talk surfaced in Woodstock that a legal battle would be waged against Wasserman in an effort to preserve the nature of the property and to fight development."

**September 4:** reacting to the Herald story, attorney Gary Brown commented: "God damned WASPs stole it from the Indians, then think they should keep it forever."

**September 5**: the Ottauquechee Land Trust held a press conference at which the director corrected the record in various ways, including: "Laurance Rockefeller has not contributed $150,000,... he has not contributed anything." He wasn't asked because he wasn't a South Woodstock resident (he's a New York resident). The director denied that anyone had contributed $500,000. Attorney John Dunne said more than 50 people had pledged, including the four (probably including John Byrne) that make up the Woodstock Education Associates, which "has nothing to do with education except that its buying school buildings." Dunne said he expected the Trust would sell off the property in pieces. Dunne said he encouraged Byrne to buy the entire school, "he ultimately agreed to do that." The Trust director said, "I guarantee you there won't be any condos." (But there were.)

**September 6**: the Rutland Herald published a long summary report on the Land Trust meeting and the status of the pending purchase, which needed loan approval for $565,000 from the Vermont National Bank to enable the Land Trust to exercise its right of first refusal. Realtor Robert McClaughery emerged as the only named principal of Woodstock Education Associates, although John Byrne's participation was tacitly acknowledged by the Land Trust. Although the Ladn Trust planned to study the property for a year after acquiring it, attorney John Dunne sais "he couldn't guarantee there wouldn't be some condominiums in the residences some day."

**September 10:** Rhoda Teagle talked to a reporter about her frustration, since her personal preference was to sell the school to the Sandell Development Corporation, represented by attorney Gary Brown, also her personal attorney. Rhoda complained bitterly that the Land Trust people had refused to meet with the Sandell people. As a Land Trust board member, Rhoda had attended the Land Trust meeting to discuss the purchase. She had asked WCS attorney Tom Wright to attend, but he did not (she said he hadn't called for three weeks). Rhoda complained that Land Trust attorney talked at such length "so nobody gets a chance to talk." Rhoda complained that "they don't want anyone to know who's in it for how much." She added that she had not voted at the Land Trust meeting, that there had been no call for nays or abstentions. Rhoda said that attorney John Dunn had told her the closing on the property would probably be in about sixty days.

**September 11**: the Rutland Herald published the news that the Ottauquechee Land Trust, having received loan approval, would buy the Woodstock Country School for $1,065,000. As a tax-exempt organization, the school had not paid property taxes (but it was the second largest employer in town, after the Woodstock Inn). The Land Trust planned to ask for a one year waiver of the estimated $47,000 annual tax on the property. The Land Trust estimated that, once it sold off pieces of the property with development restrictions, the whole would be worth about $2 million, generating about $95,000 in property taxes. The Sandell Development Corporation estimated that its plans would make the whole property worth as much as $7.5 million, generating about $325,000 in annual poroperty taxes for Woodstock (South Woodstock is a hamlet within the Town of Woodstock). The Herald quoted the Land Trust director saying: "We feel that this represents a unique approach to community land use planning that really has never been tried before – this has national significance.... [It's unique in Vermont] that a non-profit organization has been this aggressive in a community.... What we're doing is totally within the private sector, other than perhaps our request to the town to hold off on taxes." He also acknowledged that the Land Trust's non-profit status enabled supporters to benefit from "federal tax law which allows gifts to the Land Trust to be tax deductible, which is more beneficial to wealthier people." No closing date was announced.

**September 12**: former WCS teacher Isabel Stephens, who still lived in South Woodstock, said of the pending sale that she was "so far happy with it,… it seems to me on the whole the best solution… to try to keep Vermont rural." She said that she and Steve had subscribed for one share in the Land Trust fundraising effort, which she thought was a $6,000 (or $18,000) commitment. She said the general plan was to sell off the campus buildings in three or four lots, then protect the open land and woodlands. Isabel said that John Byrne "sounds like a very sensible man."

## END NOTE #1

**September 15**: Country School attorney Tom Wright wrote to brokers Clayton Adams and Doug Symmes to advise them that the Ottauquechee Land Trust had exercised its right of first refusal and "fully complied with the provisions of notifying the school.... I will begin working with the Land Trust in preparation for a smooth closing...."

**October 2**: by registered letter to the Ottauquechee Land Trust, attorney Sidney Gorovitz wrote, on behalf of his client, the Sandell Development Corporation, requesting a meeting, which had not yet happened. Gorovitz explained that "due to the total lack of cooperation and communication between your organization and myself over the past three (3) weeks, so that we have yet to sit down and hold a discussion of any type between appropriate members, I have authorized and taken necessary action **to place appropriate notices of pending litigation on the register record** of the Woodstock Country School, and shall file a **litigation within the next several days whose sole purpose is to restrain the transfer** by the Woodstock Country School to the Ottauquechee Land Trust, and air the manner in which the right of first refusal by the Ottauquechee Land Trust was exercised.... We would prefer, if [a release or waiver by Sandell] were a mandatory condition of your negotiation position, to litigate this matter publicly so that all could see the manner in which the land trust has conducted this negotiation." (emphasis added)

**October 3**: late on that Friday afternoon, the Vermont National Bank hosted the three-hour closing of the sale of the Woodstock Country School to the Ottauquechee Land Trust. The Town Clerk recorded the deed at about 6:30 p.m. According to the next day's Rutland Herald: "About 15 people attended the hastily organized closing in an effort to complete the property transfer before it could be blocked by court action. Those taking part included representatives of the school, the land trust, a development group known as Woodstock Education Associates, and the South Woodstock community, as well as six attorneys, including two from the high-powered New York law firm of Cravath, Swaine, and Moore (representing John Byrne). Sandell Development Corporation attorney Sidney Gorovitz said his client would fight the issue: "If we prevail in litigation, the land comes back. We're taking the school to court. Our contract is with the school, it's not with the Land Trust, so we have sued the school for wrongful transfer of the land." Land Trust attorney John Dunne said that "there's absolutely no basis for any lawsuit of any kind, against either the Woodstock Country School or the Ottauquechee Land Trust."

**October 5**: Vermont National Bank officer Greg Kennedy told a reporter that "they bludgeoned us into a closing on Friday," without saying who "they" was. Rhoda Teagle said that Greg Kennedy told her he was under political pressure. Rhoda did not want to go through with the October 3 closing. Her roles included being president of the WCS Trustees, a member of the Land Trust board, and a proponent of the Sandell Corporation (which has asked her to put off signing till the sixtieth day). Rhoda said that Greg Kennedy told her that if she did not sign off on the sale, then the bank would foreclose (on the school's roughly $560,000 debt) right away, even though the school had met its payments.

**October 6**: the Ottauquechee Land Trust issued a lengthy, misleading press release announcing the purchase of the Country School. The Land Trust repeated the explanation that it got its right of first refusal in exchange for an $8-10,000 planning process (even though that never happened). The Land Trust said it "felt it had a responsibility to the Woodstock Country School... to move forward rapidly so that the Country Schoolcould retire its debts and not face any additional carrying costs (which was a patent falsehood, since the school requested a much later closing). The Land Trust acknowledged in murky text that its haste was also prompted by the pending litigation by the Sandell Development Corporation. And with no apparent sense of irony, the Land Trust said that "now... a comprehensive planning process will begin to decide the ultimate use of the property."

**October 6**: WCS attorney filed closing papers with the Vermont National Bank, accounting for the $1,065,000 received for the sale and for various charges and payments and concluding: "Thus, as of October 6, 1980 there should be the sum of $355,733.74 in the School's account at the Vermont National Bank."

**October 8**: the Valley News reported that the Ottauquechee Land Trust "is prepared to assist the trustees of the Woodstock Country School in any lawsuit that may be brought against them." No lawsuit had been filed. The Land Trust director justified not meeting with the Sandell Development Corp oration "under threats of legal action," turning reality on its head: the legal action was threatened because the Land Trust refused to meet.

**October 18**: the Woodstock Country School Trustees held its annual meeting, perhaps with a quorum (eight Trustees present included Rhoda Teagle, Buffy Dunker, Gerry Freund, and Peter Sauer). No official minutes exist, only Rhoda's personal notes. Mounir Sa'adah suggested that the school turn itself into a foundation. The

END NOTE #1

board formed a committee on the Future of the School. Gerry Freund expressed his desire for a book, a full history of the school. (After the meeting, Peter Sauer visited William Boardman, who said he would be willing to contract to write a book.)

**Almost a year later, on July 2, 1981**, the Sandell Development Corporation's suit against the Woodstock Country School was dismissed in the Windsor County Superior Court.

**October 1, 1981**: Rhoda Teagle wrote to her fellow Trustees: "As you may remember, if you attended the last board meeting [October 18, 1980] of the Woodstock Country School, the ultimate disposal of the corporation was not completed. Since that time we have continued to pay unemployment and extended unemployment to almost all people connected with the school. It is now time to plan for a final board meeting, to close the office, settle the files in a permanent abode, and dispose of the assets."

**December 5, 1981**: nine remaining Trustees of the Woodstock Country School met and voted to dissolve Woodstock Country School, Inc. Rhoda Teagle's one-page, hand-written financial report indicated that the school had spent $43,022 on unemployment benefits and $58,360 on the Baileys' retirement benefits (time frame unspecified). The report also indicated monthly office expenses of $1,500. Current assets and expected income came to something more than $190,000.

**Sometime in 1983**, the Ulrich Franzen designed Bailey House, that was once a boys dorm, came on the market as Upwey Meadow Condominiums, four units marketed in a pleasant brochure complete with an out-of-date picture of the school.

**July 31, 1985**: in response to a query from the author about the restrictions placed on the Country School property, chairman John Wiggin of the Ottauquechee Land Trust wrote: "You will see in the deed that certain development is allowed. The purchase had to make some sense to the Byrnes and limited development was a part of it. Tax benefits were others.

"As you recall, the Woodstock Country School was in a financial bind and was on the verge of selling its assets to a party more intent on development. Considerable eleventh hour maneuvering by the school, the Trust and prospective buyers and by the lawyers, bank, and the community worked out this agreement. We feel that while encouraging some development, it served to protect the land for rural uses more than if the school had simply been sold and had the three hundred acres of land been done to it as zoning would have allowed. I am not sure how it all worked out for the new buyer; perhaps he now wishes that he was not so public spirited. I see his house is now for sale....

"Speaking for myself, I have most always enjoyed your writing and have appreciated the questions that you raise. If any possible piece done on us causes soul searching on our part, we would all the more benefit from it."

**August 5, 1985**: on "Upwey Farms" stationery, Tom Debevoise wrote the author. This Tom Debevoise is the son of the Tom Debevoise who was Woodstock's Trustee president and who was the prime mover in, among other things, seeing that the school built the Acorns and the New Dorm; and it was the New Dorm, built with no plan to pay for it, that tipped the school into what became unrecoverable debt.

The younger Tom Debevoise wrote following the WCS reunion of 1985: "Thank you for your note. I'm glad the reunion went well. I had very few complaints from people on this end, and appreciate the respect that was shown what is now private property.

"I hope your chance to look around changed your impression of what has happened to the property from that expressed in your article in the summer *Woodstock Common*. Nothing could be less fair to John Byrne, the new owner and my employer, that your comment about rich-out-of-staters with no plans to adopt Vermont's traditional values. He paid a huge price for the school property precisely so that it would not become the site of umpteen condominiums, which was the offer the trustees were originally prepared to accept. He then placed restrictions on his own deed so that no more than thirteen new houses could be built on the entire 300 acres; he may well restrict it even further. Yes he has subdivided – he really had no use for six houses and two dormitories – but he has restricted all those deeds so that no further subdivision of those lots is allowed (accepting a lower sales price as a result) and so that the bulk of the subdivided land can be used for the farming operation he has set up to revitalize the land the school had let deteriorate. Some people would say that by tearing down the New Dorm and most of the Acorns, he has shown more sensitivity to Vermont's traditional values than did the school; certainly no one who has taken the trouble to become familiar with what has happened to the school property since its sale would be so caustic as you were in your article.

"If people can laugh without bitterness at the financial blunders of the Woodstock Country School, it is only because John Byrne was willing to spend huge sums to keep the property from becoming Quechee South."

# End Note #1A

**ALL THE SIT-DOWN INTERVIEWS WERE TAPED, EXCEPT....**

October 6, 1986, about 10 a.m. at Tom Debevoise's law office in Woodstock.
I start to plug in my tape recorder.
Then this exchange, reconstructed immediately after the meeting, took place.

**TOM**: I don't want to be taped.
**ME**: I'm sure I mentioned it in our original conversation.
**TOM**: I don't want to be in any oral history.
**ME**: I can turn it off at sensitive parts.
**TOM**: There are no sensitive parts. I just don't want
to leave anything behind when I go.
**ME**: We could arrange to have the tapes go with you.
**TOM**: I plan to be cremated, tapes would pollute my ashes.
**ME**: We could arrange to burn them separately.
**TOM**: I just don't want to be taped.

So the three hour interview with Tom Debevoise was not taped.
I took 25 pages of notes.
His 12-year written record was extensive, if not always illuminating.

WCS community meeting in Upwey common room 1976 – all unidentified except for Marc Williams '77 & Sarah Winnett '78 (both left foreground) and Chip Kendall '77 (far right) & Mary Gafford '77 (head on table)

Commencement 1979: headmaster Robin Leaver with Lee McClure '79

# End Note #2

**HOW THE WCS FOUNDATION HONORED ITS CONTRACT....**

*"The Author shall have the sole editorial supervision and discretion over the final manuscript...."* – WCS Foundation contract with William Boardman, signed June 16, 1982

When Woodstock closed in August 1980, I was working as a reporter for the Rutland Herald. I had written several stories about the school's last few years. On October 18, the Trustees sent Peter Sauer as an emissary to sound me out about writing a history of the school. Peter was David Bailey's choice to write the school's history, but Peter was unavailable, none of which I knew when he came to sound me out. I said I'd be happy to write the history, but I needed a contract. Peter made no commitment. There was no prompt follow-up after that and I guessed that nothing would happen at least until David Bailey had died. I guessed right. He died in September 1981, as the school was in the process of legally dissolving itself and going out of existence.

During the same period that the school was turning into the foundation, my role as the possible author of this book was on hold. There were a few other possibilities, including Peter Sauer, Anita McClellan, and Mounir Sa'adah (the Arabic teacher of long tenure, opposed by David). After Peter's 1980 visit, I was pretty much outside of a process that, I suspect, wasn't particularly procedural. So I waited, more or less neutral about the prospect, which seems to have left me to be the default choice. It was all strange.

**August 19, 1981.** Rhoda, in a phone call, treated me as the presumptive choice and told me I could have money any time to write the book, that she'd be happy to give me money to get started. This was when we were still on good terms, before I even thought about confronting her about her failure to prevent her son from abusing the younger children in her household. Mainly I didn't accept any money because I wanted first to have as clear and formal an agreement as possible in place. That turned out to be what Gary Brown wanted as well.

**December 5, 1981.** Special Meeting of WCS Trustees held with five attending: Rhoda Teagle and four WCS "old guard" (Buffy Dunker, Gerry Freund, Anita McClellan, and Peter Sauer). The school bookkeeper was also present. The question of a quorum does not appear in the minutes (on October 18, 1980, eight Trustees had not appeared to be a quorum, which was ignored then, too). The board unanimously adopted five resolutions: the first three dealt with dissolving the corporation and distributing its assets. A fourth resolution set the priorities for distributing the assets:

(A) discharge all liabilities and obligations;

(B) establish a charitable trust to "support the publication of a history and philosophy of the Woodstock Country School," preserve student records, scholarship aid or "direct assistance to needy students;"

(C) financial support for Peggy Bailey;

(D) "education in the Town of Woodstock;" and

(E) transfer all remaining assets of the school to the charitable trust.

The fifth and last resolution directed Rhoda Teagle to formulate plans for the charitable trust, with the proviso: "The trust plans shall be presented to the Trustees for further discussion at a duly warned meeting for that purpose." There is no record that the school's Trustees ever met again. In January 1982, Gary Brown contradicted the plain meaning of the proviso above, writing to Rhoda: "The minutes are specific describing in some detail the complete authority given you to go ahead with establishing a trust and all other matters for the dissolution."

**December 7, 1981.** Rhoda, in a phone call, told me about the December 5 board meeting. She had particularly harsh words for Buffy. By then Rhoda had openly despised Buffy for more than two decades, at least since Buffy had become a significant parent-figure for me around 1953. By 1981, Buffy had come out as a lesbian, in a Boston Globe article, much to Rhoda's horror. When Buffy came to the board meeting with her girl friend, according to Rhoda, and "they giggled their way through on the couch... disgusting old creature." As for the book, Rhoda said there was "plenty of money" – about $200,000 – and that the project would be all mine. A few days later, Gary Brown called to talk about various contractual details, including preliminary money and a five-year timeframe.

**December 1981/January 1982.** At some time not too long after the December 1981 meeting, Rhoda Teagle, by way of her attorney Gary Brown, sent a memorandum to the four "old guard" members of the board announcing, metaphorically, that she had "formulated plans for a non-profit foundation" as resolved by the board. The attached, incomplete articles of association for the foundation reiterated the purposes voted by the board in December. The articles did not mention a board. Rhoda's memo discussed a board of three-to-five members, but not how they would be chosen. The memo suggested incorporating the foundation immediately and asked the other trustees to sign and return the memo if they agreed to this plan. There is no surviving record of any response to this sketchy plan, which was promptly implemented by Rhoda Teagle and Gary Brown, apparently in consultation with Gerry Freund.

**Winter 1982.** A later draft of the articles of association provided for three board members, which Rhoda changed to five. Rhoda, Gary Brown, and Gerry Freund were the first three. Rhoda added in her own hand two others who had no known relationship to the Country School but were local people socially important to her personally. At about the same time, Gary Brown's draft of the WCS Foundation by-laws provided for a board of three-to-five members, but never fewer than three. The by-laws offer no guidance as to how the original members would be chosen.

**February 4, 1982.** Gary Brown wrote me a memo outlining elements for "our literary Agreement." These elements included gathering a large oral history, drawing on the oral history to write a book-length narrative history, all of which I would complete within five years and for which I would be paid. Most importantly, Gary proposed that I would have "sole discretion" over the content of the book, without which I would not have proceeded. I responded with an expanded, more detailed proposal and a proposed budget, and the negotiation continued amicably with additional input from Gerry Freund.

Most of my focus that winter and spring was divided between the birth of my son Benjamin on January 19 and co-producing a show in New York with director Paul Lazarus. Benjamin, now in his thirties, has been a long-running hit. The N.Y. show was a satirical, musical revue titled "Rearranging Deck Chairs," for which I wrote the book. "Deck Chairs" played six scheduled performances at Playwrights Horizons in early June (five packed houses) but was not picked up for further production.

**May 20, 1982.** In a letter to Gerry Freund, Gary Brown wrote: "Rhoda asked that you and I act with her as the initial Board of Trustees for the Woodstock Country School Foundation, Inc. If we wish, we can add two additional Trustees at a later date." Those three would be the only board members the foundation ever had in its eight-year existence. Of the three, Gerry Freund was the only one who had any real love for the school. Rhoda had spent a couple of decades privately saying spiteful things about David Bailey personally and about the school in general; publicly she seemed the innocent flower but was the serpent under it. Gary Brown had no personal connection to the school, other than that he worked for Rhoda. As the last president of the school's Trustees, Rhoda carried herself over as the new president of the foundation. She had no apparent authority to do so, and apparently no one objected. Still acting without authority in the foundation's by-laws, Rhoda Teagle appointed the other two members of the foundation board (the by-laws provided for a 3-5 member board to be elected by the members – yes, the by-laws were sloppy and inherently contradictory, but there was no one left to care by this time). No other Trustees were ever added, even though the by-laws stated: "Each Trustee shall hold office for a 3 year term and until his successor shall have been elected and qualified." Rhoda, Gary, and Gerry simply ignored any provision they cared to till they dissolved the foundation in 1990.

**June 1, 1982.** The Woodstock Country School Foundation, Inc., registers with the Vermont Secretary of State. As its primary goal, the foundation's Article of Association say that it "shall support the publication of a history and philosophy of the Woodstock Country School."

**June 16, 1982.** I signed the final agreement to write a book-length history of the school including such material "as the Author deems appropriate" and "in the sole discretion of the author." The agreement included this section:

> *The Author agrees to present a draft, book-length manuscript to the School no less that sixty (60) days prior to the submission of the final manuscript. The School shall note its comments or corrections on the draft manuscript, which it will return to the Author. The Author shall have the sole editorial supervision and discretion over the final manuscript but may adopt School comments on the draft in the final manuscript.*

## END NOTE #2

The agreement also included this provision:

> *If any controversy arises between the Parties hereto, or from any person claiming under either of them, which controversy relates to this Agreement or to the performance or a breach thereof, such controversy shall be settled by arbitration....*

**June 1982 – July 1987.** I wrote the book. First I created a 400-page annotated chronology of the school's 35 years, based on the surviving official files and whatever additional documentation I could find. Ken Webb allowed me free access to his very personal diaries. I had extensive faculty meeting minutes by Buffy Dunker and Larry Roberts, as well as my own. I travelled the country to talk to hundreds of Country School people, and I corresponded with more. And I wrote a long book that still feels to me like too much is left out, even though what's in the book is what I thought was the best material. And one of the consistent, mixed responses from both Gerry and Gary was that it was too long and that too much was omitted, perspectives that neither tried to reconcile.

**October 14, 1986.** Rhoda Teagle wrote this encouraging note, in its entirety: "Congratulations on the first draft. What an opus. The whole Phil Hansen must have been dreadful to go through. U came in later, thank goodness. I'm amazed the W.C.S. lasted as long as it did. What a horrible period – after all the other horrible periods. And it started so well. Good job."

**July 1987.** I turned in the revised manuscript, incorporating notes from Gerry and Gary, pretty much on time. Even before that there were signs of trouble with the foundation's troika with regard to publishing the book. Rhoda had long since stopped speaking to me (and had disinherited me) because she was in denial about our family issues. Gerry Freund had stopped talking to me because he was in denial about David Bailey being in denial about his emphysema (even though two of Gerry's friends and fellow WCS Trustees, Roger Phillips and Barbara Sproul, both told me that he was wrong and they agreed with me). Gary Brown, who was only there to take orders anyway, was still talking to me for a little while longer.

**October 1987.** Gary and I talked. At that point, and for the next 30 years, no one gave me any greater specific idea of what they thought was wrong with the book, other than what I've already described. None of the three offered a fix, none of them seriously annotated the manuscript as contemplated in our contract. Gary and I discussed arbitration, but made no decision. He said he had met in August with Rhoda and Gerry. "They want to have it published," Gary told me, but they wanted changes – of which he specified none. The last substantive discussion of the manuscript between Gary Brown and me was on October 14: we discussed details of the last five chapters, he said it's not in publishable form (*ex cathedra*, unexplained), and offered no way forward.

**November 1987.** At Gary's request, I provided a clean copy of my manuscript for him to copy and return (which he did). He talked vaguely about having some "confidential committee" review the book. He assured me the confidential committee would not be confidential from me. I suggested 27 names of people familiar with the school who might be on such a committee. In my letter with those names, I wrote: "Indeed, I'd like to have evaluations from outside professionals most of all. I look forward to working with a professional editor, if and when that day ever comes." That day never came. Gary never responded to that letter.

Although they had paid me in full, $35,000, none of the foundation board members had ever met their obligation to assess the manuscript in anything like its wholeness. Gerry and Gary had had conversations with me about a few particulars. For Gerry, I had even deleted a long exchange of letters between him and Tawny Kilbourne, in which Gerry appeared to be courting Tawny very insistently to become the Country School's headmaster. Since Tawny turned out to be a big mistake for the school, as Barbara Sproul had warned the Trustees he would, Gerry apparently wanted to avoid retrospective blame. His letters didn't present very blameworthy behavior, Gerry was not solely responsible for the board's bad choice, and the evidence in the letters was largely circumstantial – so for the sake of peace in the family, I acquiesced to that singular act of censorship. David Bailey's denial of his emphysema, and its terrible impact on him and his school, was documented and supported by most witness (it's all in the book) and to give in to Gerry on this was to give up integrity. Presumably Gerry realized this and also knew at some level that he could not win the argument. That left him with few options, one of which was to suppress the book, which he tried to do with the help of Rhoda and Gary, who did nothing to stop him.

**December 1988.** I wrote a letter to the foundation board, reviewing the mostly non-events since July 1987 regarding the book, then I decided not to send it:

# END NOTE #2

*I have allowed this much time to pass without comment for a number of reasons. Among them, my desire to devote my energies to other projects and my willingness to give the board time to make such assessment as it saw fit.*

*However the passage of more than 18 months of almost uninterrupted silence makes it seem that the board is handling the history of the school in much the same way it handled the school itself.*

*Lacking any other explanation, I assume that the problem is as I outlined it in my memo to the board in February 1987. In that memo I discussed my central thesis, that David's denial of the importance of his illness evolved into an institutional denial that contributed, perhaps crucially, to the school's demise.*

*As you know, Gerry – alone among those with whom I've talked who knew the school at the time – rejects the denial argument out of hand. He does not refute it. He does not offer an alternative explanation that is more compelling. It is my belief that he is still in denial.*

**July 1989.** In a brief memo to the foundation board, I inquired about the progress of the "confidential committee" and said, without elaboration, "I'm close to finishing a new introduction. No one responded. There was no further substantive, direct communication between me and any foundation board member. The "confidential committee," if it ever existed, remained confidential.

**October 13, 1989.** Out of the blue, attorney Gary Brown wrote on behalf of the foundation to say that: "The Harvard Graduate School of Education has agreed to preserve the history of the Woodstock Country School." He demanded the surrender of "all material," much of which was already in the foundation's possession. He added that the movers would arrive November 14 "if this is convenient for you."

**October 14, 1989.** In response, I allowed that November 14 would not be convenient, that I disputed his assertions about our contract (I remained an owner of the copyright), I inquired about the "confidential committee," I lamented the two years' silence of the foundation, I noted that I was waiving none of my rights, and I expressed hope "for bringing it [the history project] to the fruition I had thought we all wanted, a published work."

**November 22, 1989.** Attorney John R. Hughes ("I represent the Woodstock Country School Foundation") sent a certified letter falsely asserting that I knew the foundation had decided ` not to publish the book. Hughes offered several broad criticisms of the book, none of which were supported by any specifics, and all of which I considered wholly or partly false. None of these issues had been discussed in good faith or in contractually provided arbitration.

**December 8, 1989.** I responded to attorney Hughes within his deadline to say that "the archival materials are available for pick-up after the holidays." I also wrote that "what I wanted then, and still want now, is an intellectually honest and detailed response to the 700 page plus manuscript [double-spaced] I have provided.... 'The Foundation' owes me better than this crabbed, squalid response, the shield of lawyers, and endless silence. If 'the Foundation' has good cause to suppress the manuscript, let them say so. Otherwise let them re-establish their good faith and make a sincere effort to make a publishable, truthful history of the school." Neither attorney Hughes not the members of the foundation made any substantive response.

**January 10, 1990.** Hanover Moving and Storage picked up 20 cartons of Woodstock Country School archival material for delivery to Harvard. I retained what I thought I might need someday to publish a truthful history of the school.

**December 7, 1990 and after.** The Woodstock Country School Foundation, Inc., officially dissolved itself with the Vermont Secretary of State's office, paying the proper fee. The Secretary of State has no record of any of the biennial filings required of domestic non-profit corporations. Nor is there any record of any accounting for the last $355,000 or so of the Woodstock Country School's assets. Gerry Freund died at 66 in 1997. Rhoda Teagle died at 91 in 2001. Peggy Bailey died at 98 in 2008. At some point, Gary Brown closed his law office and moved away from Woodstock. WCS alumni, with no institution left to support them, kept having reunions on the former school property, with the gracious blessings of the several new owners.

# End Note #3

## AFTERTHOUGHTS ON ONCE AND FUTURE WOODSTOCKS....

Somewhat incongruously, the principal of Phillips Exeter Academy, Richard W. Day, was a Trustee of the Woodstock Country School when David Bailey retired and the Trustees had to figure out how to preserve and perpetuate the school. As part of the search committee looking for a new headmaster, Dick Day wrote to committee chair Gerry Freund in July 1967 commenting dubiously on the early results:

> *I have reviewed the folders which you very thoughtfully sent to me on five men [including Tawny Kilborne]. I can't say I have been overwhelmed by these men, and I imagine that means that we must continue to keep looking. I am hopeful that John and Anne Holden will be able to help us some this fall.*
>
> *I had the pleasure of visiting Woodstock School this weekend [during David's last term, the first summer of the four-term plan]. I am tremendously impressed with the facilities that the school has; its physical resources are excellent. All that the place really needs is some vigorous leadership. I had a chance to talk with David and he seemed terribly tired, almost completely without energy. The Woodstock School is a wonderful opportunity for a man and woman who possess any vision at all....*

Well, that didn't happen. And it didn't happen because the Trustees chose people who didn't get Woodstock – suggesting that the Trustees themselves didn't get Woodstock at its most fundamental level. What was to get?

In the fall of 1978, Mounir Sa'adah wrote a report on WCS, at the request of David Bailey and Robin Leaver. Despite the changes in the world and in the school since 1964, Mounir "found the school vibrant and full of vitality. What made it persist? What kept it in the world of the living when all logic and common sense pointed that it should perish? What function does it render to American society, to the human endeavor, that makes it imperative... for it to survive?" His answer was, in part and somewhat grandiosely, that "The supreme significance of the Woodstock Country School is that it is a human society structured to deal with the unique [individual]... who had enough vigor and vim to endure and to seek authenticity and life.... Look at your transfigured children. There is not as magnificent a spectacle in the whole country."

Those transfigured children spanned all the years of a school that could and should have survived, if only those who led it has also understood it.

**Jim Barter '48:**
At age fifteen, I was a ward of the New England Home for Little Wanderers in Boston. I had failed in a placement at the Arnold School and the Home was looking for an alternative for me. Dr. Florence Clothier, the psychiatrist at the Home was taking her son Louis Wislocki to Woodstock. She thought it might be good for me to go there also. I was reluctant but eventually agreed to go along with her and look at the school. I knew little about it, except that it was starting its first year....

Woodstock was a life changing experience for me. Before being there I had no idea of what I wanted in the future. In my small fishing town the choices were limited. Fisherman, shop keeper, cobbler, barber, laborer and cook were the usual choices other than being on welfare. A college education was beyond my expectations. We were poor, no-one in my family had finished high school. The chores of day to day living didn't allow much time for dreaming of the future, you took what came along.

The three years I spent at Woodstock were a continuous revelation. I was exposed to literature, classical music, fine arts, languages, history, theater, science and politics. I gained an appreciation of the advantages of an education. This experience started me in a direction that led to college, graduate school in anthropology, medical school and a career as a psychiatrist. It didn't happen all at once. There was no blinding flash of insight. Rather it was a gradual process of being able to take advantage of what was being offered to me.

**Barbara Moss '72:**
At the age of 14, I was a public school student in Connecticut, getting along horribly with my mother, absorbing my father's unspoken-about descent into drug-and-booze-induced vapor. During heated bouts with my mom, she often chased me around the house, threatening me with: "I'm going to send you to Reform School!" (Oh, horrors!) A good friend of mine told me that a friend of hers had started going to an upstate NY boarding school (Barlow) and that I should look into it. Boarding School! Sounded pretty close to Reform School!

Maybe my mother would bite. They sent me to a shrink at Yale to find out if I was "running away" and it was lucky for me that he agreed I should run as fast as I could, since I was falling in with a bad (read: dark, skanky, heavily druggy) crowd at public high school. Barlow had no room for me, but the kind admissions woman there gave us a list of about 6 or 7 "kindred" schools. That icy winter, Mom and I skidded throughout the New England roadway system, visiting these tucked-away escape hatches of learning.

Though it was my second choice (luckily I wasn't accepted at my first), I arrived at Woodstock raring to go. I recall it as vividly as if it were yesterday: My parents and I signed in with the colorful Buffy Dunker at Upwey, who studied her clipboard, heralding: "Oh! You'll be rooming with the Bloustein girl in Acorn Number One...."

I cherish the good fortune I had to wind up the Woodstock Country School. On one of the Saturday trips into town I found a book at the Yankee Bookshop titled *An Anthology of New York Poets*, illustrated by Joe Brainard. This book introduced me to a whole world that awaited me in New York. It would just take another year or 2 for me to get there, where I studied with and became dear friends with (the sadly departed) Joe Brainard, a brilliant artist + poet, and an exquisite man. May the circle be unbroken.

**Renee Rebache '80:**
I have frequently found it difficult to explain the Woodstock experience to people who didn't attend. Personally, I have always been on a slight offset from the rest of human life, and feel certain that I ended up at Woodstock as a result. However I believe my experiences there, especially those of taking responsibility in great part for my education (intellectual or otherwise), my actions (well-intentioned or otherwise), and my choices (questionable or otherwise) has set me apart still further from the majority of individuals that I encounter even today.

I feel WCS did me a real service in creating a foundation of autonomy that arises from a true inner knowledge, assimilated from real experience, of myself, of my limits, and how limits are created from within.

**Arthur Keggereis '80:**
I attended WCS because I was different, but it was like coming out of Plato's cave. I didn't even know how different I was, despite living public school life as an outsider. Then suddenly I realized I wasn't the only different person and there were others like me and we could survive in this world and maybe even do it well.

# End Note #4

**Severn Darden '48,
performing as Prof. Walther von der Vogelweide
giving his "Metaphysics Lecture"
with the SECOND CITY company in Chicago in the early 1950s,
in response to the audience question,
"Do fish think?"**

*Well, that's a very good question, but it's not in the realm of metaphysics.*

*Now I had a fish once – her name was Louise, as a matter of fact. Small, fat fish. And every day at the same time I would go to the edge of the pond – a little iron tank in my house – and throw it a bunch of grapes, you know, every day at the same time that fish would be there. After a few days, she knew, at 1:45, grapes, bam! Fish!*

*However I began making it 15 minutes later every day, you see. And then when I was there at 2 o'clock, she'd be there at 1:45. She was 15 minutes behind. After awhile she was hours and days behind! And she starved to death.*

*Yes, fish think – but not fast enough.*

*Could I have another question, please?*

# End Note #5

The only reason for yet another end note is the opportunity provided by printing this revised version of the book that corrects many, perhaps most of the first version's typos and other minor errors. So far, no major errors have been identified. In 20 months since the first version appeared, respondents raised no serious disputes to the book's contents, much to my surprise. Well, there were ample years for anyone who wanted to speak up to say whatever they wanted, as hundreds did. Progressive draft manuscripts circulated from 1987 on. They're still out there.

The lengthiest and most detailed reader response has come from Nini Petrullo Rikoski '65 who (like others) asked for a more student-centric book than the institutional history that I wrote:

### Nini Rikoski '65, letter to William Boardman, February 2, 2017

*I am so glad you got this book out. Reading it brought back many memories, almost all of them very good. You have done an excellent job of chronicling the evolution of the school's administration and its dysfunction. But here is my chief thought: there is more that remains to be written. As it stands your book is interesting to those of us who knew the school through personal experience. For anyone else, I think the book would be puzzling. They would not understand what was lost when the school failed, or why so many of us who passed through it are still attached to what it and what we believed it could be....*

*Most people have never had any experience with a boarding school, so they neither know what a traditional boarding school might have been like in the WCS era or what WCS might have been like. Most people I have known in my adult life have believed that sending a child away to a boarding school is tantamount to child abuse because sending a child away to school before s/he reaches college age is itself cruel and neglectful and/or because they think boarding schools are Dickensian houses of horror. If I have known them well enough to tell them that I chose to attend a boarding school, the reaction has always been shock ....*

> During my years, the school offered courses in acting, directing, history of the theater, lighting, and set design. For a tiny school, that is huge.... Shakespeare's plays permeated the school [each English class read Shakespeare every year, including Twelfth Night, Merchant of Venice, Macbeth, or King Lear with all seniors reading Hamlet]....
>
> My senior year I was one of the ringleaders in the great dorm swap. The old barn that had been the boys' dorm [French House] was still standing then and we got the boys out of there and the girls out of [Owen] Moon House in the middle of the night and swapped dorms. We were careful to keep track of everyone, because we knew we would be in trouble if we didn't. The following morning, the boys had to do some outside work as punishment and the girls were sequestered in the drama loft at Upwey, where they had to compose poetry about their adventure, either a limerick or five lines in iambic pentameter....
>
> There are two questions I have thought about for years. One is whether it would have been possible to create enough institutional structure for the school to survive without fundamentally changing the character of the school. The other is what the school would have been like with fewer very troubled kids. (I remember students discussing that among themselves in my years there.) The two questions are linked because I suspect a more structured administration would have had a more structured admission process that would have resulted in a different mix of students. It is hard to judge how many of the so-called troubled kids were acting out in response to their life situations and how many had actual mental illnesses. I think most fit into the first category and David's willingness to take a chance on them turned out well for many of them. However, there were others that needed intervention beyond the latitude to figure out who they were in a supportive environment with caring adults.

From beginning to end, this was how Woodstock worked at its best. The testimonies of early alumni James Barter '48, Gerry Freund '48, and Roger Phillips '49 represent a paradigm that remained true for some till 1980: In essence, "the school saved my life," literally or figuratively. Clearly this was not always the case for any particular student, but it was always a possibility, even when the school structure was floundering – that was what made the place so inexplicably magical.

Another element of the magic lay in the possibility of close, informal relationships with teachers who saw their students as individuals, as in this example, complete with a surprise appearance by Leonard Cohen (yes, *that* Leonard Cohen):

END NOTE #5

## Ed Shiller '60, remarks at George Dickerson's memorial in New York City, March 2015

I first met George in January 1958 when I was a $10^{th}$ grader at the Woodstock Country School...and I took an immediate dislike for him. I don't recall why I felt that way – only that the feeling was intense.

George came to the school mid-year to teach algebra, and I, of course, manifested my dislike by being unruly and obnoxious in class. But instead of punishing me, George hit upon an extraordinarily simple, and for me, an extraordinarily profound, solution. My memory of what transpired has dimmed over the past 57 years, but the effect has stayed with me to this day. If George were here with us today, I'm sure he would correct any inaccuracies. Though, my guess is that George is with us here today, and that he will.

So now back to that algebra class in the winter of 1958.

"Eddie," George said in his soft baritone after one of my outbursts, "it's obvious you don't want to be in this class, which isn't doing any of us any good. And I don't want to make you stay against your will. So you have my permission to leave."

"You mean I can just go?"

"Yes."

"Are you going to tell David?" He was the headmaster.

"No. This is between you and me."

"What if I change my mind and want to come back?"

"Then you're free to do so."

I was stunned as I walked out of the classroom and into the common room, where I stood alone in silent confusion. George himself could at times be indignant, concerned, even despondent, but he always seemed so self-assured in his ability to see things clearly, to be decidedly unconfused no matter how threatening the circumstances – except once, many years later, when he confessed his inability to grasp the concept of the small and big blinds in Texas Hold'em.

But back in the Woodstock Country School common room, I was the one in a fog, though it didn't last long. Somehow, I felt, George had validated me in a way that no one had ever done before – and few since.

Surely, I said to myself, there's got to be a lot more to this guy than whatever it was I had chosen to dislike. So I resolved to banish *my ill-will and seek to embrace his friendship. I walked back into the classroom.*

*This decision paid off almost immediately. George lived in an apartment adjacent to the boys' dorm, and on many nights before lights out, a few of the students would congregate in his living room. One day, he told me to be sure to drop in that evening to meet a good friend of his – who he described as a budding poet – who was visiting from Montreal.*

*Leonard Cohen struck me as shy, even timid, but with an impish sense of humor – and he and George fed off each other, to the point where they – and us, the students – were alternately doubled over with laughter or seized by fits of giggling. What brought this on was the irresistible impulse to read a play, with each of us speaking a different part. But we needed more than one copy, with the subsequent search of George's library yielding three editions of Rostand's* Cyrano de Bergerac *– all in different translations.*

*The* non sequiturs *and unintended puns that flowed from the reading started us going. But the climax was the death scene, which we all took turns performing, with each of us vying to out-do the others with our sword flourishes as we shouted out Cyrano's final words.*

*"There is one crown I bear away with me....One thing without stain, unspotted from the world....And that is...my white plume!"*

Ed Shiller and George Dickerson had a lifelong friendship that started as a student-teacher relationship. At Woodstock, while teachers and students weren't actual equals, they often treated each other as equals. And it worked. Several of my teachers became friends, several of my students remain friends. This was structural from the beginning, with teachers being called by their first names: David, Ken, Buffy, Mou, Curt, Larry, Bus, Prill, Jo, Peggy, Tawny, JDI, Bonnie, Tek, teachers all. The school hierarchy remained in place, but it was not dominant, much less rigid. Rather both teachers and students had to earn whatever real respect they received, it was not just a matter of rank.

### Kathy Cronkite '69, phone call, June 3, 1984

*[Tawny Kilborne]* "was not the school's finest hour as far as I was concerned....I was a strike ringleader [November 1968, see Chapter Nine]....

## END NOTE #5

*Bruce Fairweather [school farmer/teacher] was the one in the school who really knew what was going on at any given moment....He was kind of outside it all....*

*Robin [Leaver] is weird....I don't like Robin....Severn [Darden] and I hosted a gathering [in Hollywood for fundraising]. Robin basically put the make on me in a way I didn't like – and was real weird when I turned him down....He turned a lot of students off by forcing Bruce out.*

### Jonathan Freund letter to William Boardman, April 10, 1990

*Finally, forgive me if I note an intriguing and telling irony, something you taught so well: My feelings of devotion and admiration, following hard on by a crushing sense of betrayal, in my relationship with Robin [Leaver], seem to mirror your description, and what I know from varied sources, of David's final years. Robin isn't half the teacher, or even man, that David was, but I think the point is still valid, if only in microcosm.*

*After his initial positive year or two (which students and faculty and staff deserve the real credit for), the school was overcome by a cult of personality and misguided missionary zeal: "Send me your expelled, your drugged, your walking wounded yearning to be indulged...." would have been a good plaque for the entryway. I knew the school was in trouble the day I heard Robin justify firing Bruce and Emily because they didn't understand "what we're trying to do here." That, for me, was truly the beginning of the endgame, the point at which the life force was gone.*

Robin didn't fire Bruce *and* Emily. He was much more inept than that. He fired Bruce, but invited Emily to stay on and continue running the riding program. That didn't happen. Bruce and Emily had been part of the school since 1960 or so, and they were an important part of the fabric of the institution, along with others including the kitchen staff – Ula Agar, Agnes Bar, and Rosie Guertler – and the maintenance staff – Earl Barr, Floyd Cowdrey, and Alan Bass, a relative newcomer. They all interacted with students on a daily basis, rarely with any difficulty. They were a source of continuity, tradition, reassurance, even comfort – vital to the institution's long-term stability, but not always appreciated.

The office staff often served the same institutional functions, but there the turnover rate was much higher. More stability was needed after Buffy Dunker left the school, having managed the school's finances for two decades, almost always bringing the budget in in the black. Before Tawny resigned, he had hired Dan Richardson as the school's business manager, starting in the summer of 1970 (see Chapter Ten, section II). With the increasing demands and complexities of the Four-Term Plan, Dan needed a new bookkeeper. He found Pat Heffernan (who makes a brief appearance in Chapter Eleven, section I). More should have been said about Pat, one of those people whom a sensible institution treasures if possible.

By 1972, Pat Heffernan was roughly 10 years out of college, having been a high school teacher for five years. During 1969-72 she was the manager of the Wobbly Barn, then New England's largest night club in Killington, Vermont. "I wanted to go back into education," she recalled, "and Dan and I hit it off instantly." She was overqualified to be just a part-time bookkeeper and soon became Dan's fulltime assistant business manager, proposing all sorts of orderly processes for running the school according to its own rules. This brought her into direct contact with Phil, who wanted the financial rules to apply only selectively. Despite her conflicts with Phil, Pat was devoted to Woodstock from the start, "excited by what the school represented, everything my prep school hadn't."

### Pat Heffernan interview, September 29, 1986

*I really liked the whole sense of community and participative governments by faculty and students and administration, the lack of formality,...calling everyone by their first name,...everybody having a work detail – that really impressed me as good preparation for citizenship. The courses – about half the courses in the catalog I wanted to take – and I was jealous, actually jealous of those students, that they got to take so many of those things....The idea of the working farm appealed to me, VINS (the Vermont Institute of Natural Science] was just getting started....The photography courses – the whole art thing – the way they tried to integrate those into what we would call substantive courses – I mean, I just really liked the concept of it all. So that's why I went there, and I thought they needed me, because it seemed they were having some difficulties from what Dan described in their systems....*

*We were in financial trouble, which Dan was aware of but I highlighted....It's real easy to explain although it took me nearly a year to convince the board. The trouble was that we had four terms, and the rules were that you paid for tuition at the beginning of the term in*

## END NOTE #5

*advance [of the term] for which you were coming. So, if you're following me, if your child was coming for summer session your tuition was due for summer session by the beginning of spring term. They has been spending more than they had, so the financials were showing a deficit. But there was always cash in the bank because they were spending next semester's money – in advance. And because there was cash in the bank, nobody believed [there was a deficit]....*

*There was a reluctance to look at it, address it, until it was very critical – until about a year after I started...that first full summer [1973] at which point I could see that we were going to run out of cash that summer, because enrollment was going down, and we had emergency board meetings....*

Summer of 1973 was a critical moment for the Country School and no one was really in charge. Dan Richardson had left for Costa Rica, his replacement had not been hired, and Pat Heffernan had no independent authority. She was the obvious, competent, in-place choice to succeed Dan. She said she would have taken the job if it had been offered, but it wasn't. Headmaster Phil Hansen had submitted his resignation two years hence and was on sabbatical. He later claimed he had offered Pat the job, but there's no evidence. Acting headmaster Marc Hurlbut played a lot of tennis that summer. The executive committee of the board acted quickly to solve the wrong problem, making $17,000 in budget cuts and advertising for more students. When this produced 53 new students for the fall, everyone went back to thinking all was well and continued spending next term's income on this term, just as before – denial in action (see Chapter Ten, sections VIII-IX).

Pat Heffernan continued to present fiscal reality to a hostile in-house audience. Phil continued to be incapable of dealing with her professionally. The new business manager, Mort Rosenstein gave her no meaningful support (Walter Hill later fired him). Mort never really engaged with the life of the school, even though his daughter was thriving as a student. After that, Pat said, "I just felt leaderless....I left the following spring [1974], confident the school was going under, because I saw no commitment to making the changes that would be necessary to insure its survival."

Pat "was very much in love with the school" and not thinking of leaving in the spring of 1974. But when Dan Richardson returned from Costa Rica to work for Tom Debevoise as the Vermont Law School business manager, he immediately moved to hire Pat away from Woodstock. Unable to appreciate Pat's institutional value, Phil made little or no effort to keep her at the school. The

Woodstock people who knew enough to value her hired her away to the Law School, where she flourished as Associate Dean for eight years.

Pat remembers that in the summer of 1976, in the wake of Walter Hill's sudden departure, Marc Hurlbut called to see whether she wanted to be the next headmaster. She did not.

Pat was not the only one sending warning signals for the trustees to ignore in 1974. In December 1973, longtime alumni trustee Anita McClellan sent a cheery report that acknowledged the departure of Liz Stevens, without noting that she was another person with institutional value that the institution had failed to appreciate sufficiently. Liz was the Assistant Director of Development and that position was never filled again. Four months later, in a letter primarily about recent Alumni Association mechanics, I also responded to Anita's rearranging deck chairs missive from December. At the time, Phil was still headmaster and Walter Hill's arrival was eight months in the future. Anita's letter was a fundamentally misleading exercise in denial, sent out as an official school document.

## William Boardman, letter to Anita McClellan '64, April 23, 1974

*Now, as to your recent public communications. I'm not at all as sanguine about the school's firm sense of self nor about a new headmaster not ruffling its feathers. My feeling is that the situation is extremely volatile, that the turnover of people is already rather high, and that a new headmaster will have to go to considerable lengths to keep the place from flying apart in his face (and Tawny, remember, deliberately set about to make changes and it flew apart in his face). We shall see.*

*As for the instructional facilities and the staff not being overtaxed [as Anita had written], that simply is not true. The majority of faculty are overtaxed and tired, in part because there is a minority that cuts corners ferociously. But I doubt that any clear, point-by-point recitation of that sort of thing ever reaches you (or would unless you made a point of seeking it out).*

*Mort Rosenstein's discussion of the school's finances last fall [that Anita spun as positive] ran well over its allotted twenty minutes largely because the figures presented were vague to the point of meaninglessness and a few of us were not satisfied with that (though we were unable to improve on it much by our questions).*

# END NOTE #5

Anita never responded to this letter. Two years later the school flew apart in Walter Hill's face (see Chapter Eleven).

OK, enough of the head-shaking bad stuff. Here's another illumination of how the school worked well for some students. This one more properly belongs in End Note #3. It comes from another transfigured child, posted on Upwey Online, a website created by Arthur Keggereis '80 that is no longer extant.

### Jonathan Freund '77, Upwey Online post, June 27, 2000

*I have learned, I hope, how to make practical applications of what I experimented with at Woodstock.*

*How to manage the eternal tension between freedom and responsibility, realizing that both need each other.*

*How to integrate experimentation and spontaneity in a life filled with deadlines, marriage, children, a mortgage, taxes, etc.*

*That walking in the woods and reclining in a field are more than good, they are regularly necessary.*

*Sex is wasted on the young – yet I'm glad I had my crazy fun early in life.*

*Most drugs and drinking, for me, are a waste period – yet I'm glad I had my crazy fun early in life, and even more glad I survived.*

*That life is long and a lot happens.*

*That personal style is a paint job.*

*That if we don't do the work, the work doesn't get done.*

*That I still love getting up before the sun, even though I'm no longer living in a Vermont valley.*

*That all people, and young people especially, need a free and open space where they can play and learn. And that free and open space needs a safety fence, a code of conduct, and referees and paramedics who aren't playing.*

By 2018, Jonathan Freund had followed a somewhat circuitous path though Oberlin and show biz to become the vice president of the Board of Rabbis of Southern California. Jonathan's father, Gerald Freund '48, who played a critical role in the life of WCS, died of lung cancer on May 4, 1997, without ever sharing his opinion on the WCS history manuscript he had effectively commissioned. There was no mention of Woodstock in his New York Times obituary, despite the school's seminal role in his family's life. The Times duly recounted Gerry's very real accomplishments at Haverford College, Oxford, Yale, and numerous foundations including Rockefeller and MacArthur. The Times did not mention his given name, Gerhard, and only fleetingly mentioned that his "family had fled Hitler's Germany." The Times did not mention that, with Jonathan's encouragement, on April 17, 1996, Gerald Freund had recorded Interview #14,298 for Survivors of the Shoah Visual History Foundation. In 2000, Jonathan sent me a copy of the Shah tape as well as a copy of Gerry's May 21, 1997 memorial service.

### Jonathan Freund '77 at the memorial service of Gerald Freund '48

*Like my brothers Matthew and Andrew, I have been searching for a defining image of our father. Something that will both explain him and do him justice. I keep coming back to a moment no one in this room witnessed. My father is eight years old [on November 10, 1938], holding tight to his governess' hand as he walks through the streets of Berlin the morning after Kristallnacht, surrounded by the stench of fire and a sea of broken glass, He was terrified, but he didn't know of what or why.*

*In many ways, that sensation remained with him for the rest of his years. He was perpetually anxious, and was always reaching for a hand to guide him through what he saw as the brittle shards of daily life. Yet even in the grip of that, he somehow managed to dedicate his life to improving that disordered world. Try as he might, he knew he could never make it safe. What he could do was provide seed and water for artists, writers and teachers, so that through them, knowledge and beauty might one day flower.*

In this broader context, Gerry Freund's effort to suppress this book remains an abiding mystery to me. Gerry and I were never close, we were essentially professional friends who seemed to me to trust each other, but his position was always superior in some sense. When I was a student, Gerry was the star alumnus. When I was a teacher, Gerry was a board member or president. When I was an aspiring theatrical satirist, Gerry was the inaccessible foundation officer. When I was writing the Country School history, he was, for five years, the engaged reader. And then, with no word of clarification, he wasn't. He made no serious intellectual effort to explore whatever he found troubling in my work here, he simply backed away and tried to kill it. As someone who had also suffered childhood trauma (in very different ways), I found – I still find – his abandonment of me and the book inexplicable. This absolute censorship, carried out by third parties, backed by the threat of lawsuit still seems antithetical to what had seemed to be Gerry's character. He only made it worse by allying himself with Rhoda Teagle, a woman who, in 1970, on hearing about the National Guard shooting students at Kent State University, expressed open satisfaction about their deaths. [The Country School Foundation at that point consisted of only Gerry, Rhoda, and an attorney. Their effort to suppress this book is described in detail in End Note #2. People who purported to want to see the school "die with dignity" instead finished it off with a breath-taking lack of intellectual integrity, a fundamental absence of accountability, and a final disdain for their lawful responsibilities.]

But that's really the heart of the WCS story, isn't it? Some of the school's most fervent supporters again and again ally themselves with people wildly inappropriate to the school's core values of humane tolerance and an honest respect for the varieties of truth. That's also the story of our country, steeped in denial from the beginning, evolving on a much broader canvas to the failed state superpower of 2018. The first is the fall of a sparrow, the latter has yet to play out.

Or as Hamlet put it (Act V, scene II) just before that play's happy ending:

*We defy augury. There's a special providence in the fall of a sparrow. If it be now, 'tis not to come. If it be not to come, it will be now. If it be not now, yet it will come. The readiness is all. Since man, of aught he leaves, knows aught, what is't to leave betimes? Let be.*

WCS Foundation sold off the Acorns in 1980-81. The Tipis were long gone.

# Acknowledgements

So many people over so many years (call it 35) have made so many contributions large and small to getting this book made that I can't possibly thank them all individually, but I'm grateful to everyone who helped get it done. To put it in perspective, the first draft was on an Epson (operating system CPM)

Thanks to the more than two hundred former students, teachers, and staff who agreed to talk to me on the record (and off the record) about the school – without their insights and perspectives there wouldn't be much of a book. Thanks especially to those who also provided food and shelter in the course of my travels around the country.

The remaining six Woodstock Country School Trustees approved the concept of my writing this history. The Woodstock Country School Foundation, the successor to the Trustees, signed me to a contract for the book. The Foundation's three members (Gerry Freund '48, Rhoda Teagle, and Gary Brown) and I all had lengthy and intricate relationships that no one called a conflict of interest (until about a decade later).

The most useful resources for this book were the school's records, as preserved by the Woodstock Country School Foundation after the school's closing. These records were incomplete for a variety of reasons: the Barn fire of 1954 destroyed most of the early records; more records vanished during the chaos of the school's closing in 1980; and the Foundation carelessly discarded a number of records after the closing. The inevitable gaps were covered in good part by the personal files of Gerry Freund '48. Additionally, Buffy Dunker and Larry Roberts shared their extensive personal notes on faculty meetings and other aspects of the school. And Ken Webb shared his personal diary.

Particular thanks to Dartmouth College for early issues of *Symposium*, the student literary magazine; to the Baldwin School for Elizabeth Forrest Johnson biographical material; and to Harvard College for biographical material on the Bailey brothers.

Nancy Cooper and Charlotte Cleveland each provided invaluable research and clerical support during the 1980s.

The ultimate award for service above and beyond goes to Kate Sandberg, whose only connection to the school was through me by way of performing Panther sketches over the years. After she moved to New York City and went to work in a law office during the 1990s, Kate re-typed the entire manuscript from its dot-matrix form, creating the manuscript that forms the basis of this book.

Over the decades, a number of WCS alumni kept asking me about the book, which was circulating in draft form after 1990. In 2015, two in particular, Nan Bourne '52 and Sarah Lorenz Mitchell '55, offered to proof the draft if I would move forward with it. Sarah especially kept me going with devoted counsel and support.

At the WCS reunion in the summer of 2015, more alumni inquired about the phantom book. Ed Shiller '60, Ira Chaplain '72, and Arthur Keggereis '80 volunteered to become the publishing team. Each of them has contributed greatly to the final book. With Ed's Yorkland Publishing came the excellent editing assistance of Margaret McAulay and John Cosway and the wonderful design skills of Iryna Spica.

During the year or so of re-writing, Robin Leaver engaged in an active and very helpful dialogue about his time at the school, as did Elizabeth Livingston '73 about hers.

Nancy Serrell provided miraculous last minute editing help, truly.

For all that others have done, and they have done much for which I am deeply grateful, no one did more, in more ways, over a longer period of time, to support me in this project and the rest of my life than Rebecca Silliman Boardman.

## PHOTOGRAPHS AND DRAWINGS

The cover is by Ira Chaplain '72, who went on to a career as a photographer. For the cover shot (which it was not at the time), he gathered as many of the school's community as possible on the soccer field at the end of the classroom wing of Upwey. He set his camera on the second floor landing by the art loft. As the timer ran, Ira went down the stairs to join the group. That's him sitting cross-legged, hands together, on the left edge of what seems to be the only all-school photo ever taken.

Of the other photographs in the book, many are Ira's, and Ira also spent days scanning images into usable format. Arthur Keggereis '80 supplied a slew of pictures, as did Jim Barter '48, including many taken by Bob Lake. Lowell Naeve left a substantial photo record of his art classes. Other contributors included Bill Dwight '74, Pat Lee, and many anonymous others (including me).

The art is all student work, including the drawings that are mostly signed.

Regrettably, not knowing attributions has meant that lots of people don't get the credit they deserve. But isn't that just like the school? And life?

Bob Demuth '73

Molly White '74

Mark Shapiro '73

Barbara Moss '72
& Lori Bloustein '72

# About the Author

William Boardman first went to the Woodstock Country School in 1952 as a tenth grader. As an eleventh grader he was expelled for drinking and being in a girls dorm (Greenhithe). He repeated eleventh grade, he graduated with honors in 1956. He was the first WCS graduate to go to Yale, where he earned his B.A. in 1960 and his M.F.A. from the Yale Drama School in 1964.

His credits include "That Was The Week That Was" (group Emmy nomination), "Captain Kangaroo," ABC News researcher (another group Emmy), and "Treasure Isle" (special material for John Bartholomew Tucker).

He taught English, US History, fiction, and drama at WCS 1971-1976.

He created "The Panther Program" for Vermont Public Radio and limited national syndication (supported by grants from the Corporation for Publication and the National Endowment for the Arts). Panthers won awards from the Writers Guild of America, Vermont Life Magazine, and the Corporation for Public Broadcasting (three times). In 1992 the Panthers were blacklisted by Vermont Public Radio.

From 1991 to 2011, the Hon. William Boardman was an Assistant Judge in the Vermont Judiciary.

He currently writes regular political pieces for Reader Supported news – online: rsn.org – that have led to appearances on RT and other media outlets.

William Boardman is a widower with three children (Michael, Benjamin, and Diantha) and four grandchildren (Samantha, Nicholas, Walker, and Carter). He lives alone in Vermont in the same house he moved to in 1971.

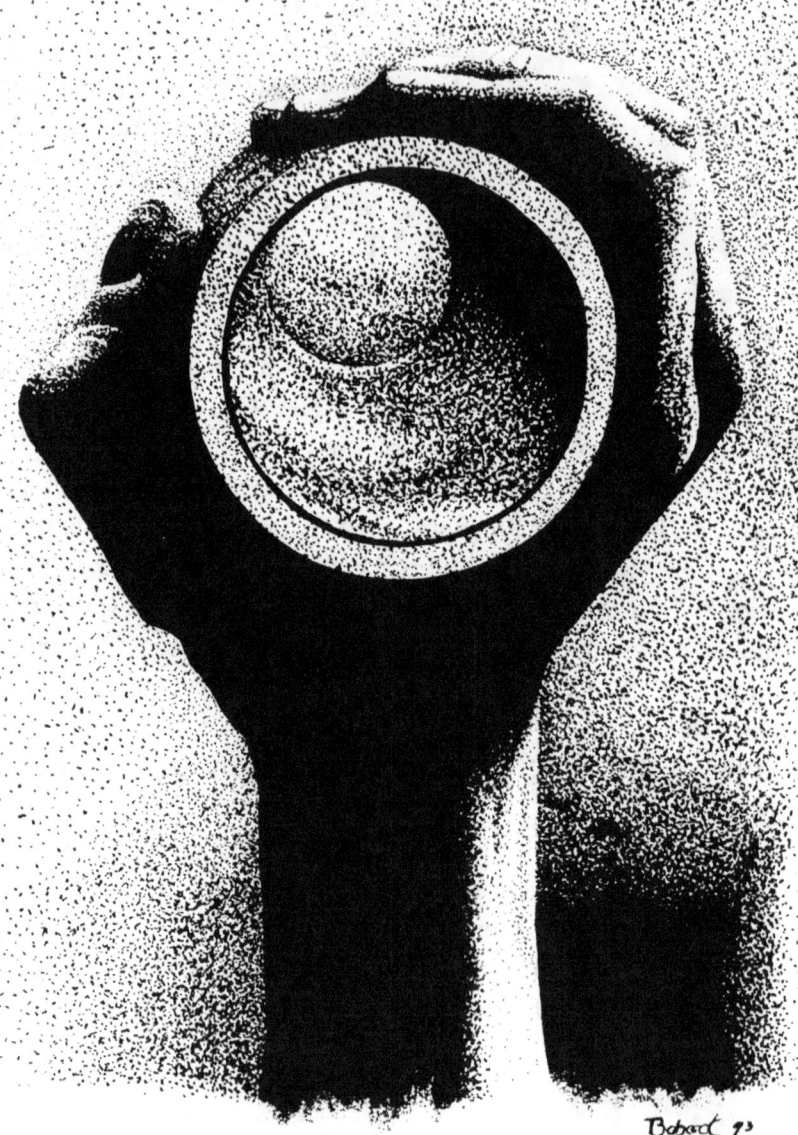

www.ingramcontent.com/pod-product-compliance
Lightning Source LLC
Chambersburg PA
CBHW081352290426
44110CB00018B/2349